STUDIES IN MIDRASH AND RELATED LITERATURE

Photograph courtesy of Grace Goldin

דור דור JPS
ודורשיו SCHOLAR
OF DISTINCTION
SERIES

JUDAH GOLDIN

STUDIES IN MIDRASH AND RELATED LITERATURE

edited by BARRY L. EICHLER
and JEFFREY H. TIGAY

The Jewish Publication Society
Philadelphia · New York · Jerusalem   5748–1988

The publication of this book was supported by
a generous gift from Arleen B. Rifkind
in memory of her parents,
Michael and Regina Brenner

Copyright © 1988 by The Jewish Publication Society
First edition   All rights reserved
Manufactured in the United States of America
Library of Congress Cataloging in Publication Data
Goldin, Judah, 1914–
    Studies in Midrash and related literature.
    (JPS scholar of distinction series)
    Bibliography: p.
    Includes indexes.
    1. Midrash—History and criticism. 2. Aggada—
History and criticism.   I. Eichler, Barry L.   II. Tigay,
Jeffrey H.   III. Title.   IV. Series.
BM514.G65 1987 296.1'4 86–31136
ISBN 0–8276–0277–4

Designed by Adrianne Onderdonk Dudden

דּוֹר לְדוֹר יְשַׁבַּח מַעֲשֶׂיךָ . . .
Psalms 145:4

Contents

THEMATIC STUDIES

Acknowledgments

The articles in the present volume are published essentially as they originally appeared, apart from a small number of minor editorial revisions and corrections by the author. The spelling, capitalization, and punctuation used in each original article have generally been retained in order to preserve the distinctive style of each article. The page numbers of the original sources as listed in the *Acknowledgments* appear in brackets within each article. In the footnotes, cross references to these articles refer to the original pagination.

We are grateful to the following publishers for their kind permission to reprint the articles included here.

The American Academy for Jewish Research, for "The Three Pillars of Simeon the Righteous," "Reflections on Translation and Midrash," "'This Song,'" and "Notes on The Fathers According to Rabbi Nathan."

The Journal of the American Oriental Society, for "Toward a Profile of the Tanna, Aqiba ben Joseph," volume 96, pages 38–56, 1976.

The Association for Jewish Studies Review, for "The First Pair (Yose ben Yoezer and Yose ben Yohanan) or the Home of a Pharisee" and "About Shalom Spiegel."

Harvard University Press, for "The End of Ecclesiastes: Literal Exegesis and Its Transformation," reprinted by permission of the publishers from *Biblical Motifs: Origins and Transformations*, Alexander Altmann, editor (Philip W. Lown Institute Studies and Texts, III), Cambridge, MA: Harvard University Press, Copyright © 1966 by the President and Fellows of Harvard College.

Harvard Theological Review, for "The Third Chapter of *'Abot de-Rabbi Natan*" and "On Honi the Circle-Maker: A Demanding Prayer." Copyright 1963 by the President and Fellows of Harvard College. Reprinted by permission.

Hebrew Union College Annual, for "The Two Versions of *'Abot de-Rabbi Nathan*," reprinted with the permission of the editors of the *Hebrew Union College Annual*.

The *Journal of Biblical Literature*, for "The Youngest Son, or Where Does Genesis 38 Belong?" reprinted with permission from the *Journal of Biblical Literature* 96 (1977).

Quest, published by The New London Synagogue, for "Reflections on a Mishnah," *Quest* 2 (London, 1967).

E.J. Brill Publishers (Leiden, The Netherlands), for "'Not By Means of an Angel and Not By Means of a Messenger'" and "Several Sidelights of a Torah Education in Tannaite and Early Amoraic Times."

History of Religions, for "Of Change and Adaptation in Judaism," reprinted with permission from the editor, Mircea Eliade, and The University of Chicago Press.

Yale University Press, for "The Freedom and Restraint of Haggadah," from *The Midrash and Literature*, edited by G. Hartmann and Sanford Budick.

Prooftexts, for "From Text to Interpretation and From Experience to the Interpreted Text," *Prooftexts* 3 (2): 157–168 (1983), reprinted by permission of The Johns Hopkins University Press.

Four Quarters Press, for "The Death of Moses: An Exercise in Midrashic Transposition," from *Love and Death in the Ancient Near East. Studies Presented to Marvin H. Pope on the Occasion of His Sixty-Fifth Birthday*. Ed. John Marks and Robert Good. Guilford, Conn.: Four Quarters Press, 1987.

Ancient Studies in Memory of Elias Bickerman, edited by Shaye J.D. Cohen, Edward L. Greenstein, and David Marcus: *Journal of the Ancient Near Eastern Society*, volumes 16–17 (1984–1985; published 1986), for "On the Account of the Banning of R. Eliezer ben Hyrqanus: An Analysis and Proposal."

The University of Pennsylvania Press, for "A Short Note on the Archangel Gabriel," from *Law, Church, and Society, Essays in Honor of Stephen Kuttner*, edited by K. Pennington and R. Somerville (Philadelphia, 1977).

University of Notre Dame Press, for "The Magic of Magic and Superstition," from *Aspects of Religious Propaganda in Judaism and Early Christianity*, edited by E. S. Fiorenza. Copyright 1976 by the University of Notre Dame Press. Reprinted with permission.

The Jewish Publication Society, for "Foreword to *Hebrew Ethical Wills*," edited by I. Abrahams. Copyright 1978 by The Jewish Publication Society of America.

Tradition, for "A Philosophical Session in a Tannaite Academy."

Full bibliographic information about the original publications will be found in the bibliography at the end of this volume.

We are also grateful to Professor Sid Z. Leiman for thoughtful advice at several stages in the preparation of this volume.

B.L.E.
J.H.T.

Preface

Judah Goldin is known to laymen and scholars alike for his learned and elegant expositions of classical Jewish literature and for his graceful translations of early rabbinic texts. His studies, focusing primarily on tannaitic texts (dating to the first two centuries of the Common Era), illuminate a major, formative period of Judaism to which all later periods react. These studies cover a wide range of themes, including biblical exegesis, the art of translation, philosophy, prayer, education, love, messianism, angelology, history, biography, magic and superstition, and the dynamics of change and adaptation in Judaism.

The present volume includes most of Goldin's scholarly articles, many of which appeared originally in periodicals and anniversary volumes that are not widely circulated or accessible. The purpose of the present collection, however, goes beyond the convenience of easy accessibility. Together these articles show Goldin's unique approach to classical Jewish literature much more clearly than they could separately. This whole is truly greater than the sum of its parts. Goldin forces students and readers to re-examine well-known texts they never doubted they understood. His own—often surprising—interpretations of these texts are characterized by a unique combination of qualities. Building on the textual erudition and technical skill that he learned from his teachers, who included some of the great modern philologists of talmudic literature, he applies to rabbinic literature his own unparalleled literary sensitivity, honed on the classics of Western literary tradition. As a humanist, he reads rabbinic texts not only as a legal and exegetical resource but also—as literature! He views the texts not only within the context of Judaism and not only against the cultural background of the ancient Mediterranean world, but also within the intellectual context of the universal human issues they address. No scholar has done more than he to clarify what is happening in the non-legal parts of rabbinic literature, or to place that literature squarely within the realm of humanistic studies. All of this is expressed with grace and elegant simplicity, in a style designed for clarity rather than for decoration but one that makes the articles works of art in themselves.

Goldin's essays offer a taste of the electrifying atmosphere in his classroom. It would take a consummate artist to render a full picture of that atmosphere: to describe the warmth, the affection, the wit, the wisdom, the pedagogic skill, the irreverence, and the sometimes outrageous statements by which students are shaken out of complacency. Several generations of students—at Duke, the University of Iowa, the Jewish Theological Seminary, Yale, and the University of Pennsylvania—have been nurtured in that atmosphere.

Many of the qualities that Judah Goldin brings to his teaching characterize him as a colleague as well. His wisdom and friendship have been part of our daily lives since his arrival at the University of Pennsylvania in 1973. It is a privilege for us to present some of the fruits of his scholarship to the reading public.

Barry L. Eichler
Jeffrey H. Tigay

Abbreviation List

AAJR	American Academy for Jewish Research
AB	Anchor Bible
ANET	J.B. Pritchard, ed., *Ancient Near Eastern Texts Relating to the Old Testament* (Princeton, 1969)
Ant. or Antiq.	*Antiquities*, by Josephus
ARN or Abot R. Nat.	Abot de Rabbi Natan (various spellings)
ARNA	Abot de Rabbi Natan, version A
ARNB	Abot de Rabbi Natan, version B
B. Bat.	Bava Batra
BT	Babylonian Talmud
BASOR	*Bulletin of the American Schools of Oriental Reserach*
BDB	F. Brown, S.R. Driver, and C.A. Briggs, *Hebrew and English Lexicon of the Old Testament*
BhM	*Bet ha-Midrasch*, ed. Jellinek
CAD	*The Assyrian Dictionary of the Oriental Institute of the University of Chicago*
CBQ	*Catholic Biblical Quarterly*
CCL	Corpus Christianorum Series latina
DS	R. Rabinowitz, *Diqduqei Soferim* (repr. New York, 1976)
HJP	S. Lieberman, *Hellenism in Jewish Palestine*
LXX	Septuagint
HTR	*Harvard Theological Review*

HUCA	*Hebrew Union College Annual*
ICC	*International Critical Commentary on the Holy Scriptures of the Old and New Testaments*
IEJ	*Israel Exploration Journal*
J.	Jerusalem Talmud
JAOS	*Journal of the American Oriental Society*
JBL	*Journal of Biblical Literature*
JPS	Jewish Publication Society
JPSV	Jewish Publication Society Version
JQR	*Jewish Quarterly Review*
JTS	Jewish Theological Seminary
Jub.	*Jubilees*
KAT	Kommentar zum Alten Testament
LC	Loeb Classics
LCL	Loeb Classical Library
Legends	*Legends of the Jews*, by Louis Ginzberg (Philadelphia, 1909–1938)
M.	Mishnah (or Mishna)
Mabo	L. Finkelstein, *Mabo le-Massektot Abot ve-Abot d'Rabbi Natan*
Mekilta, Mekilta Ishmael	*Mekilta de-Rabbi Ishmael*
M.G.W.J.	*Monatsschrift für Geschichte und Wissenschaft des Judentums*
MhG	Midrash ha-Gadol
Mid. Tan.	Midrash Tannaim
MRS, Mekilta Simeon	*Mekilta de-Rabbi Simeon b. Jochai*
MT	Masoretic Text
OED	*Oxford English Dictionary*
OhG	*Ozar ha-Geonim*
P. or PT	Palestinian Talmud
PA or P.A.	Pirkei Avot (various spellings)
PAAJR	Proceedings of the American Academy for Jewish Research
PGM	K. Presisendanz et al., *Papyri Graecae Magicae*, Leipzig-Berlin, 1928
PK	*Pesikta de Rav Kahana*
R.	Rabbi

R. or Rab.	Rabba or Rabbati (in name of midrash collection)
Razim	*Sepher ha-Razim*
RB	*Revue biblique*
REJ	*Revue des études juives*
RSV	Revised Standard Version
Strack-Billerbeck	H.L. Strack and P. Billerbeck, *Kommentar zum Neuen Testament*, Munich, 1922
T. or t.	Tosefta
T plus number (e.g., T 20)	Bodleian Pirkei Avot MSS in numbering of Charles Taylor, *Sayings of the Jewish Fathers* (New York, 1969 [two volumes in one])
Tg or Tg.	Targum
TK	S. Lieberman, *Tosefta Ki-Fshutah*
TS	Manuscripts in the Taylor-Schechter Collection, Cambridge University Library
VT	*Vetus Testamentum*
Yalqut	*Yalqut Shimeoni*

Editions Cited

Frequently cited rabbinic texts and related works are cited from the following editions:

Abot	Ed. C. Taylor (*Sayings of the Jewish Fathers*). Repr. New York, 1969 (2 vols. in 1).
Abot de Rabbi Natan	Ed. S. Schechter. Vienna, 1887; repr. New York, 1945, 1967; trans. J. Goldin. New Haven, 1955.
Ben Sira	Ed. M.H. Segal. Jerusalem, 1953.
Bet ha-Midrasch	Ed. A. Jellinek. Jerusalem, 1938.
Debarim Rabba	Ed. S. Lieberman. Jerusalem, 1964.
Ecclesiasticus	See Ben Sira.
Genesis Rabba	Ed. J. Theodor-H. Albeck. 3 vols. Repr. Jerusalem, 1965.
Kallah Rabbati	Ed. M. Higger. New York, 1936.
Lekah Tob	Ed. S. Buber – M. Katzenellenbogen. Vilna, 1884.
Leviticus Rabba	Ed. M. Margulies. 5 vols. Jerusalem, 1953–1960.
Mekilta de-Rabbi Ishmael	Ed. J.Z. Lauterbach. 3 vols. Philadelphia, 1933–1935.
Mekilta de-Rabbi Simeon	Ed. J.N. Epstein – E.Z. Melamed. Jerusalem, 1955.
Midrash ha-Gadol	
Genesis	Ed. M. Margulies. Jerusalem, 1947.
Exodus	Ed. M. Margulies. Jerusalem, 1956.
Leviticus	(1) Ed. E. N. Rabinovitz. New York, 1932 (2) Ed. A. Steinsaltz. Jerusalem, 1975.
Numbers	Ed. S. Fisch. 2 vols. London, 1957–1963.
Deuteronomy	Ed. S. Fisch. Jerusalem, 1975.

Midrash Tannaim	Ed. D.Z. Hoffmann. 2 vols. Berlin, 1908–1909.
Midrash Tehillim	Ed. S. Buber. Vilna, 1891.
Mishna	Ed. H. Albeck. 6 vols. Jerusalem–Tel Aviv, 1952–1959.
Pesikta de-Rav Kahana	(1) Ed. B. Mandelbaum. 2 vols. New York, 1962. (2) Ed. S. Buber. Lyck, 1868.
Pesikta Rabbati	Ed. M. Friedmann. Vienna, 1880.
Sepher ha-Razim	Ed. M. Margulies. Jerusalem, 1966.
Sekel Tob	Ed. S. Buber. 2 vols. Repr. New York, 5719.
Sifre Deuteronomy	Ed. L. Finkelstein. Berlin, 1939.
Sifre Numbers	Ed. H.S. Horovitz. Jerusalem, 1966.
Sifre Zutta	Ed. H.S. Horovitz. Jerusalem, 1966.
Tosefta	(1) Ed. M.S. Zuckermandel. Repr. Jerusalem, 1963. (2) Ed. S. Lieberman, 4 vols. New York, 1955–1973. Orders Zeraim, Moed, and Nashim cited from the latter.
Yalqut Shimeoni	Salonika, 1521 and 1526–27.

Other frequently cited works:

Baer, S.I. *Seder Abodat Yisrael*. Germany, 5697.

Charles, R.H., ed. *The Apocrypha and Pseudepigrapha of the Old Testament*. 2 vols. Oxford, 1913.

Finkelstein, L. *Mabo le-Massektot Abot ve-Abot d'Rabbi Natan*. New York, 1950.

Gaster, M. *Exempla of the Rabbis*. London–Leipzig, 1924.

Ginsberg, H.L. *Koheleth*. Tel Aviv–Jerusalem, 1961.

Ginzberg, L. *Legends of the Jews*. 7 vols. Philadelphia, 1909–1938.

Kasher, M.M. *Torah Shelemah*. 39 volumes to date. New York and Jerusalem, 1949–

Lieberman, S. *Tosefta ki-Fshutah*. 8 vols. New York, 1955–1973.

———. *Greek in Jewish Palestine*. New York, 1942.

———. *Hellenism in Jewish Palestine*. New York, 1950; 2d ed., 1962.

TEXTUAL AND LITERARY STUDIES

On *The Ethics of the Fathers* and
The Fathers According to Rabbi Nathan

In memory of Judith Marcia Lewittes (1934–1957)

The End of Ecclesiastes: Literal Exegesis and Its Transformation°

[135] The very fact that we have so much difficulty recovering the original meaning and objective of the sayings preserved in *Pirke Abot* is of itself a tribute to the achievement of the redactors of this treatise, who apparently regarded all the sentences in the work as maxims of the widest, most elastic application: the idiom of these sayings, you might say, lent itself to multiple, various, beautiful, ever new interpretations, and each generation, indeed every commentator, could discover in the vocabulary of the *Abot* sayings anticipations, observations, striking confirmations of what the commentator and his generation discovered in their own society and times. "Be of the disciples of Aaron, loving peace and pursuing peace, loving mankind and drawing them to the Torah."[1] Was there ever a century to which this exhortation could be irrelevant? Obviously, therefore, Hillel's words were not of an age only but for all time. Hence, more than a millennium later, reflecting on these words, a distinguished scholar could say,

> The Sages have said [*Genesis Rabba* 38:6]: "Even when Israel worship idols, so long as there is peace in their midst, no people or nation can have dominion over them.

° While in no way whatsoever do I seek to shift responsibility for any of the views I express in this paper, I cannot neglect to say that I am deeply indebted to four erudite, original, and dear friends—Professors Elias Bickerman, H. L. Ginsberg, Saul Lieberman, and Shalom Spiegel—who allowed me to discuss my ideas with them, and doubtless by their acute questions and reactions in the course of give-and-take, helped me to bring greater clarity and precision to my thoughts. I want also to thank Dean William C. DeVane and Provost Kingman Brewster, Jr., through whose interest I received a Yale University Grant to return to Cambridge to examine Genizah manuscripts. To the staff at the Cambridge University Library I am grateful for many courtesies; as for the staff of the Yale University Library, it is kindness itself.

1. *Abot* 1:12.

... Controversy is a terrible thing, for even if Israel carry out all the commandments of the Torah, if there is controversy in their midst, anybody may do with them what he pleases."[2]

And yet, despite the persuasiveness of great exegetes, and despite the surprising iridescences of polished sentences, every statement—every maxim, even—must originally have come into being because of a specific provocation; every statement must originally have been a specific, pointed [136] response to some event or challenge, verbal or otherwise. Consider, for example, the very saying of Hillel which we just cited. Geiger[3] and, later, Louis Ginzberg observed that originally Hillel's saying was directed to priests, and contentious ones at that; in effect Hillel was saying to them, For a priest it is not enough to be merely a descendant of Aaron; the *kohen* ought to strive to emulate his ancestor, he ought to be not just a son but a disciple[4] of Aaron, bringing peace into the world rather than stirring up controversy, drawing men to the Torah, rather than alienating them from it. Or, as Hillel's teachers retorted when a high priest said to them insultingly, "Come in peace, descendants of gentiles": "May descendants of gentiles who act as Aaron acted come in peace indeed; and may there be no peace for a descendant of Aaron who does not act as Aaron acted."[5]

Abot de-Rabbi Natan, the earliest commentary on *Pirke Abot*,[6] seems, however, to have no inkling of this literal meaning of Hillel's saying. Both Version A and Version B[7] have lovely explanations of Aaron's devotion to peace and homilies on its high value, but all in general terms, as though this were a maxim altogether independent of time and place from the very beginning.

Or consider the well-known Aramaic saying, also attributed to Hillel: "Moreover he saw a skull floating on the surface of the water. He said to it: 'For drowning others thou wast drowned; and in the end they that drowned thee shall be drowned.'"[8] The commentators (ad loc.) have a number of edifying

---

2. *Machsor Vitry*, ed. S. Hurwitz (Nuremberg, 1923), p. 473.

3. In *Ḳebuzzat Maamarim* (Berlin, 1877), p. 161; see also L. Ginzberg, *The Legends of the Jews* (Philadelphia, 1909–38), VI, 113, n. 643 (I have been unable to locate the reference in *Legends* to Ginzberg's remarks in Geiger, *Ḳebuzzat Maamarim*, p. 160). And see also L. Finkelstein, *Mabo le-Massektot Abot we-Abot d'Rabbi Natan* (New York, 1950), p. 238, n. 33; A. Kaminka, *Meḥḳarim be-Miḳra we-Talmud u-ba-Sifrut ha-Rabbanit*, 2nd ed. (Tel Aviv, 5711), II, 76f.

4. See also E. E. Urbach in *Tarbiz*, 25:276 (1955–56), on the expression "disciples of Abraham."

5. BT *Yoma* 71b. On the tradition of the ancestry of these sages, see also Ginzberg, *Legends*, VI, 195. On how people often felt about certain leading priestly families, see BT *Pesaḥim* 57a. Or, for that matter, see BT *Makkot* 10a for an interpretation of Hos. 6:9. Cf. Josephus, *Antiquitates judaicae*, XX, 8:8, 9:2.

6. Or, more accurately, on an early form of that tractate.

7. Ed. S. Schechter (Vienna, 1887), pp. 48ff., 163.

8. *Abot* 2:6 and Version A of *Abot de-Rabbi Natan*, chap. 12, p. 55; note, however, that Version B. p. 56, attributes the saying to R. Joshua! One more point: the sentence beginning with אף (אף הוא ראה) also seems to be a stylistic mannerism, suggesting that this was one of a

observations,[9] and they take full advantage of the homiletical [137] possibilities of the saying. Let me quote one which is not typical but passing strange; it is by the grandson of Maimonides, and one cannot help wondering what the rationalist grandfather would have said if he had heard it:

> Hillel, may he rest in peace, saw Pharaoh's skull floating on the water. It was Pharaoh who used to take one hundred and fifty young children of Israel every morning, and another one hundred and fifty every evening, and [after extreme torture] . . . cast them into the sea. That is why the Lord slew him and drowned him. And the ancients tell us that the Hillel referred to in the Mishna is really Moses our master, may he rest in peace . . . . And he said to the skull, "Because you slew human beings and threw them into the water, the Lord has slain you and cast you into the water" . . . . This is the hidden [mystic] meaning of this statement.[10]

Whatever else the different comments achieve, one thing is clear: the commentators hardly recognize that there is anything noteworthy about the literary style of this saying reminiscent of a particular genre, although of course they do recognize that the saying is in Aramaic. For them it is enough that *Pirke Abot* has preserved Hillel's words, which, to be sure, may very well have been prompted by his seeing a skull floating on some body of water. But in this connection the following must surely be of some interest:

> Seeing a fly settle on his table, he said, "Even Diogenes feeds parasites!" Seeing a woman learning her letters [= receiving an education], he said, "Now, there's a sword getting sharpened!" Seeing one woman giving advice to another, he said, "The asp is buying poison from the viper." Seeing a Negro chewing white bread, [he said], "Look at the night choking [= swallowing] the day!" Seeing a Negro defecating, he said, "Hullo, a split cauldron!"[11]

series of sayings in somewhat the same spirit; for a such a style, see, e.g., Mishna *Ma'aser Sheni* 5:15 (on which see S. Lieberman, *Hellenism in Jewish Palestine*, 2nd ed. [New York, 1962], pp. 140–143), Mishna *Ḥallah* 4:11, Mishna *Yoma* 3:10, Mishna *Beẓah* 2:7. And note also the reading in *Abot de-Rabbi Natan*, chap. 12, p. 55.

9. Cf. *Machsor Vitry*, p. 497, and also Maimonides, *Abot Commentary*, ed. M. D. Rabinowitz (Jerusalem, 1961), p. 47, who informs us that "this is something borne out by experience at all times and in all places: whoever does evil and introduces violence and corruption is himself the victim of the harms caused by those very evils he introduced; for he himself has taught an occupation which can only bring harm to him and to others. So too, he who teaches virtue and introduces some good activity will be rewarded by the results of that very activity; for he teaches something which will do good to him and to others. And the words of the verse are very apt in this connection, namely, *For the work of a man will He requite unto him, and cause every man to find according to his ways*" (Job 34:11).

10. Midrash David of R. David Ha-Nagid, trans. B. Z. Krynfiss (Jerusalem, 5704), p. 34, and cf. Lieberman, *Hellenism*, p. 137, n. 87, paragraph 2.

11. Ἰδὼν μυῖαν ἐπάνω τῆς τραπέζης αὐτοῦ εἶπεν. καὶ Διογένης παρασίτους τρέφει. Ἰδὼν γυναῖκα διδασκομένην γράμματα εἶπεν. οἷον ξίφος ἀκονᾶται. Ἰδὼν γυναῖκα γυναικὶ συμβουλεύουσαν εἶπεν. ἀσπὶς παρ' ἐχίδνης φάρμακον πορίζεται. Ἰδὼν Αἰθίοπα καθαρὸν τρώγοντα. ἰδού ἡ νὺξ τὴν ἡμέραν πνίγει. Ἰδὼν Αἰθίοπα δὲ χέζοντα εἶπεν. οἷος λέβης τέτρηται. P. Jaguet and P. Perdrizet in C. Wessely, *Studien zur Palaeographie und Papyruskunde* [Leipzig, 1906], pp. 157–158) I have used the translation (of sentences 1, 3, and 5; 2 and 4 are my own) as it is

In other words, our *Abot* maxim is one of those typical [138] χρεῖαι employed in the instruction of children. Is it too farfetched to suggest that just as in the primary education of the Hellenistic world, aphorisms of Diogenes were recalled and employed, so in the primary schools of Jewish Palestine Hillel aphorisms were similarly used? I do not think so, and this theory may further explain the neatly drawn contrasts in a number of stories about Hillel and Shammai:[12] these were delightful and effective *exempla* for young students.

At all events, even each of the maxims of *Pirke Abot* once rose in a specific setting, although it is difficult to recover it, and I am unable to resist the temptation of stating a general proposition, to wit: When do homiletical and even symbolic interpretations appear? When an original meaning is forgotten. Naturally, I do not mean to imply that in no other way can symbolic interpretation arise; but it certainly helps not to know the *peshat*, the immediate, literal meaning. And this can be demonstrated especially clearly by study of what overtook an exceptionally well-known Abot saying, the very first one in the treatise and attributed to the Men of the Great Assembly.[13] They said, as everyone knows, three things: הוו מתונים בדין והעמידו תלמידים הרבה ועשו סייג לתורה and, for a change, I suggest that we begin with the third, rather than the first part of their saying.[14]

עשו סייג לתורה, "Make a hedge about the Torah." What does this mean? As

---

given in H. I. Marrou, *A History of Education in Antiquity*, trans G. Lamb (New York, 1956), p. 156; see indeed Marrou's discussion, pp. 155–157, and his references; on the question of propriety see also Lieberman, *Hellenism*, pp. 33–34. For a number of anecdotes which include pointed comments made by Diogenes, see Diogenes Laertius, VI, 22ff. (trans. R. D. Hicks, Loeb Classical Library, II, 25ff.)—these have the flavor (but not the same stereotypical stylistic structure) of the sentences we have cited. On the first sentence cited above see Diogenes Laertius, VI, 40.

12. For example, in *Abot de-Rabbi Natan*, both versions, pp. 60ff., BT *Shabbat* 31a. And on *exempla* in education, see also Marrou, *Education in Antiquity*, pp. 169, 235.

13. Abot 1:1, *Abot de-Rabbi Natan*, both versions, p. 2 (see also p. 150, where the reading היו נתונים [!] is plainly a printer's error, for note immediately thereafter הוו מתונין בדין כיצד); cf. *Mekilta Ishmael*, Pisha VI, ed. H. S. Horovitz and I. A. Rabin (Frankfurt, 1931), p. 19 (ed. J. Z. Lauterbach [Philadelphia, 1933–35], I, 46), *Sifre Deut.* 16, ed. L. Finkelstein (Berlin, 1939), p. 25; note also BT *Sanhedrin* 7b.

14. Much as I have learned from his meticulous and thoroughgoing studies, as is evident from the course of my entire discussion, I am unable to accept the view of my teacher Professor L. Finkelstein of the so-called original reading of the *Anshe Keneset Ha-Gedolah* saying, already formulated by him in 1940 in "The Maxim of the *Anshe Keneset ha-Gedolah*," *Journal of Biblical Literature* 59:455ff. (1940); see also his *Ha-Perushim we-Anshe Keneset ha-Gedolah* (New York, 1950), pp. 54f., n. 151 (see also his *Mabo*, p. 28, p. 234, n. 18; and most recently in the third edition of his *The Pharisees, The Sociological Background of Their Faith* [Philadelphia, 1962], II, 580, and 881, n. 12). In addition to what emerges from the body of this paper, I might add one point: the reason the exposition of the third clause of the saying is treated in *Abot de-Rabbi Natan* before the exposition of the second clause is simply this: once הוו מתונים בדין was interpreted as "a man should be patient in his speech [בדבריו] it was natural to associate with this "make a hedge about thy words [לדבריך]"; indeed observe how *Machsor Vitry*, commenting on the third clause, introduces the *Abot de-Rabbi Natan* citation: ובמשנת ר' נתן אמרי' בן עזאי אום' הוי זהיר בדבריך מבטלתן ועשה סייג לדבריך כדרך שעשה וכו'! Yet in *Abot de-Rabbi Natan* the Ben Azzai statement is given at the end of the comment on "Be deliberate in judgment"!

usual, when one asks about the meaning of an *Abot* sentence, the first place to which to turn is *Abot de-Rabbi Natan*, and what does one find [139] here? Version B[15] first makes a sensible observation of a general character, that "a vineyard surrounded by a fence is not like a vineyard without a fence; but no man ought to make more of the fence than of the thing fenced in—for if then the fence falls, even what was planted will be ruined, as we find in connection with Adam": He made an excessive fence, and when the fence fell, even what was planted was ruined; that is, God had forbidden only eating of the fruit of the tree of the knowledge of good and evil, but Adam instructed Eve not only not to eat of that fruit, but also to beware of touching it.[16] After this comment, Version B continues in essentials the way Version A reads, to this effect:

> And make a hedge about the Torah. [This means:] And make a hedge about thy words the way the Holy One, blessed be He, made a hedge about His words, and Adam made a hedge about his words. The Torah made a hedge about its words. Moses made a hedge about his words. So too Job, and also the Prophets, the Holy Writings, and the Sages—all of them made a hedge about their words.[17]

A hedge about the Torah has manifestly become a hedge about one's words; and the whole discussion of *Abot de-Rabbi Natan*—and it is not a short one!—is built on that understanding, that by a hedge about the Torah is meant a hedge about one's words. Unlike what we frequently find in our classical texts, that along with the homiletical interpretation a more literal explanation is offered as an alternative (as a דבר אחר), often even as the first of alternatives, in the present instance only that one interpretation is presented, hedge about the Torah equals hedge about one's words.

That the interpretation offered by *Abot de-Rabbi Natan* is more *derush* than *peshat* was already felt by the earliest commentators. Maimonides, for example, ignores it altogether and says simply that the clause

> refers to the decrees and enactments (*gezerot* and *takkanot*] of the Sages which keep a man far from transgression; as the Blessed One said, *Therefore shall ye keep what I have given you to keep* [Lev. 18:30, ושמרתם את משמרתי], which the Talmud [*Yebamot* 21a] interprets to mean: "Add protection to what I have already given you as a protection."[18]

And although the commentator in *Machsor Vitry* does refer to the *Abot de-Rabbi Natan* explanation (but really in the most abbreviated fashion!),[19] note that first he gives substantially the interpretation which we meet with in

15. P. 3; cf. the idiom in Tosefta *Ḳiddushin* 1:11.
16. Cf. Gen. 2:17 and 3:3.
17. P. 3; note also pp. 151ff.
18. Maimonides on *Abot* 1:1, p. 1.
19. Pp. 464f.

Maimonides. And you may surely put this down as a general rule: Whenever the *Rishonim* either ignore an explanation plainly provided [140] by a classical source or give priority to an explanation not immediately given by the classical source, the *Rishonim* are having difficulty with that source.

In the present instance there is still another detail worth attending to. Even as the illustration of "the hedge which the Sages made," *Machsor Vitry* cites neither the reading of *Abot de-Rabbi Natan* nor the reading of the Mishna *Berakot* 1:1, but rather the text of the Mekilta:[20]

> All sacrifices that are to be eaten within one day's duration may indeed be eaten until the dawn of the following day. Why then did the Sages say, "Up to midnight"? To keep a man far from transgression, to make a hedge about the Torah, and to fulfill the words of the Men of the Great Assembly who had said three things[21]: "Be deliberate in judgment,[22] and raise many disciples, and make a hedge about the Torah."

Why cite the Mekilta? But, of course, while the Mishna *Berakot* does speak of "keeping a man far from sin," it says nothing about making a hedge—that is actually the Mekilta's interpretation of the earlier statement recorded in the Mishna.

The more one contemplates these facts, the more inescapable becomes the conclusion that the Men of the Great Assembly were not talking of such things as *sheniyyot le-arayot*,[23] or of adding *gezerot* and *takkanot*, as Maimonides puts it. Please note, by the way, that the very midrash of עשו משמרת למשמרתי although it occurs earlier in the Sifra[24]—as ושמרתם . . . שמרו לי משמרת—is cited in the Talmud in the names of Babylonian Amoraim[25] and if *Abot de-Rabbi Natan* makes no mention of such a notion—which by constant iteration and reiteration has become so plausible to us[26]—we are forced to conclude that *Abot de-Rabbi Natan* knew nothing of it, although it is evident that *Abot de-Rabbi Natan* likewise did not know any longer the real meaning of this exhortation.

But as late as the first three and a half decades of the second century at least

20. See above, note 13, for the reference. By the way, this passage does not occur in *Mekilta Simeon*. And note that Aknin (*Sepher Musar*, ed. W. Bacher [Berlin, 1910], p. 3) cites neither *Abot de-Rabbi Natan* nor the Mekilta nor the *baraita* in BT *Berakot* 4b—cf. below, page 154—but the Mishna, *Berakot* 1:1. And on this Mekilta passage, see further below note 107, paragraph 2.

21. Cf. J. Goldin, *Proceedings of the American Academy for Jewish Research*, 27:56, n. 51 (1958) [below, p. 12.—Ed.]

22. See further below, pages 146ff.

23. Cf. *Machsor Vitry*, p. 464.

24. End of *Aḥare Mot*, ed. I. H. Weiss (Vienna, 1862), 86d. Cf. below, note 111.

25. Cf. below, page 284. BT *Moʿed Katan* 5a (R. Ashi), BT *Yebamot* 21a (R. Kahana). By the way, in the Munich manuscript of *Moʿed Katan* 5a the reading is עשו משמרת למשמרת.

26. See C. Taylor, *Sayings of the Jewish Fathers*, 2nd ed. (Cambridge, 1897), p. 11, n. 1; R. T. Herford, *Pirke Aboth* (New York, 1945), p. 21.

one man knew what it meant, namely Rabbi Akiba, the very sage who urged his disciple Rabbi Simeon ben Yoḥai to teach his son from a [141] ספר מוגה.[27] Akiba said, "*Masoret* is a hedge about the Torah."[28] And what *masoret* means, *Machsor Vitry*[29] tells us plainly: "This is a reference to those Masoretic comments which are added to the margins of Biblical books, and these are known as *Masorah magna*."[30]

Let us therefore translate all of this into our own idiom. What the Men of the Great Assembly are talking about in their third clause is the proper protection and preservation of the *text* of the Torah (almost certainly the Five Books of Moses) lest it be corrupted by false or inferior readings. In the words of Rabbi David Kimḥi: "It seems that these words [that is, of the category of *ḳeri* and *kethib*] came into existence because the books were lost or dispersed during the first exile, and the Sages who were skilled in Scripture were dead. Thereupon *the Men of the Great Assembly*, who restored the Torah to its former state, finding divergent readings in the books, adopted those which were supported by the majority of copies and seemed genuine to them."[31] What the *Anshe Keneset Ha-Gedolah* are urging for the text of the Torah is just the sort of attention and scholarship that by the middle of the third century B.C.E. Hellenistic scholars, especially in Alexandria but elsewhere, too, were already devoting to and doing with their own classical texts, above all Homer.[32] When the philosopher Timon, the son of Timarchus (ca. 320–230 B.C.E.), was once asked by Aratus how he, Aratus, could obtain a trustworthy text of

27. See BT *Pesaḥim* 112a.

28. *Abot* 3:13 [Prof. S. Leiman calls my attention to J. Megillah 1: הכל בכתב זו המסרת].

29. P. 513. Maimonides says nothing on this sentence (and note therefore the interpretation Aknin—who is so deeply influenced by Maimonides' commentary—cites and then the one he offers as his own!); but cf. R. Jonah Gerondi in his commentary ad loc. and Taylor, *Sayings of the Jewish Fathers*, I, 55, n. 33, end.

30. Note also the ʿ*Aruk*, s.v. סג, VI, 14b: מסורת סייג לתורה פי' הן סימנין שעשו חכמים לסדר התורה בפיהם. Observe in ʿ*Aruk* the following reading: מעשרות סייג לתורה וכו'—obviously reflecting someone having difficulty with understanding Akiba's saying! I have deliberately made no reference to the expression יש אם למסורת (BT *Ḳiddushin* 18b and parallels; cf. Sifra *ad* Lev. 12:5, 58d), for there are several problems with it which I hope to discuss in a subsequent study, and therefore also I refrain from discussion of the literature cited, for example, in B. Gerhardsson, *Memory and Manuscript* (Uppsala, 1961), p. 49 and n. 2. For the time being, cf. ʿ*Aruk*, s.v. אם 2, I, 109 and 110, n. 1. At all events, it is noteworthy that one of the Sages concerned with this theme—and he maintains יש אם למקרא—is none other than Rabbi Akiba. (I am grateful to Professor I. Twersky for urging me to add this brief notation, despite my decision to postpone full discussion to another time.)

31. Cited by Lieberman, *Hellenism*, p. 21, but the italics are mine. Note also Tanhuma *Beshallah* 16, שהוא תיקון סופרים אנשי כנסת הגדולה . . ., and cf. Lieberman, *Hellenism*, pp. 30f. And see especially M. Zucker in *Tarbiz*, 27:68 (1958).

32. See J. E. Sandys, *A History of Classical Scholarship*, 3rd ed. (Cambridge, 1921), I, 105–144, but especially Lieberman, *Hellenism*, pp. 20–82, not only for a host of illuminating details but for the picture as it emerges as a whole; this study is indispensable. [Inexcusably, I completely forgot until now (21 February 1966) the important study by Moshe Greenberg, "The Stabilization of the Text of the Hebrew Bible," *JAOS* 76:157–167 (1956), which is extremely illuminating in this connection. Had I remembered this paper in time, I would most certainly have quoted from it, not merely referred to it.]

Homer, Timon replied, "You can, if you get hold of the ancient copies, and not the corrected copies [142] of our day [. . . εἰ τοῖς ἀρχαίοις ἀντιγράφοις ἐντυγχάνοι καί μή τοῖς ἤδη διωρθωμένοις].[33]

Note well: In the third century B.C.E. even a Timon speaks of the ancient, untampered-with texts as the best texts; even in Homeric scholarship what is most highly recommended is the ancient, the carefully preserved text. In Jewish Palestine such preservation was—and how apt is the expression—the hedge. And the carefully preserved and transmitted text was—again, how apt the term—Masorah.

Obviously the text of the Torah had to be carefully kept,[34] at least with no less a diligence than that lavished on the work of Homer, [35] "the prophet of All,"[36] for on the Torah text so much depended,[37]

אין לך בתורה אפלו אות אפלו תיבה ואין צריך לומר פיסוק שאין לו כמה טעמים.[38]

So important an assignment was it to take extreme care of the biblical text, that there is little wonder when we hear of a "special college of book readers," to use Professor Lieberman's phrase,[39] checking on the text kept in the Temple.

Now, to the second clause in the saying of the *Anshe Keneset Ha-Gedolah,* והעמידו תלמידים הרבה, "raise many disciples." And on this occasion too, let us first examine what the earliest source, *Abot de-Rabbi Natan,* and the earliest commentators have to say. To *Abot de-Rabbi Natan,*[40] apparently what the *Anshe Keneset Ha-Gedolah* are pleading for is what the Hillelites in their time—let us say early in the second half of the first century—are affirming: "For the School of Shammai says: One ought to [143] teach only him who is talented[41] and meek and of distinguished ancestry and rich. But the School of

33. Diogenes Laertius IX, 113 (Loeb Classical Library, II, 523). Cf. E. Bickerman in *Journal of Biblical Literature,* 63:342 (1944): "The earliest commentators of Hippocrates in Alexandria collected the oldest available manuscripts of the author because the current text was supposed to be corrupt through long transmission." See also Bickerman's notes on that page.

34. Cf. Mishna *Moʿed Ḳatan* 3:4 (note the reading adopted by H. Albeck in the Albeck-Yallon *Mishna,* and cf. Albeck's comment, p. 508), and see Lieberman, *Hellenism,* p. 22, n. 18.

35. See Lieberman, *Hellenism,* p. 46., and note how he takes the statement of BT *Baba Batra* 116a, top line.

36. Cf. Lieberman, *Hellenism,* pp. 20 and 108.

37. Cf. *Gen. Rabba* 1:14, ed. J. Theodor and H. Albeck (Berlin, 1912), p. 12, and on the possibility of Akiba being the author of the famous interpretation of Deut. 32:47a, see Theodor's note to line 6, *Gen. Rabba,* p. 12.

38. *Midrash Tannaim,* p. 205. Cf. E. Bickerman, "Some Notes on the Transmission of the Septuagint," *Alexander Marx Jubilee Volume* (New York, 1950), pp. 167f.; note especially: "To state it briefly: in Oriental philology, the principle for establishing a text was fidelity to the transmitted readings" [cf. Jellinek, *Bet ha-Midrash,* I, 65].

39. *Hellenism,* p. 22. See also the additional note by Taylor, *Sayings of the Jewish Fathers,* p. 135. The comments of D. Daube in *Hebrew Union College Annual,* 22:242f. and n. 10 (1949–50) are unsupported by the sources. See further below, pages 152–154.

40. Chap. 3, pp. 14f.; note, too, Version B.

41. Cf. J. Goldin, *The Fathers According to Rabbi Nathan* (New Haven, 1955), p. 181, n.2.

Hillel says: One ought to teach every man, for there were many sinners in Israel who were drawn to the study of Torah, and from them descended righteous, pious, and worthy folk."[42]

This thought, by association,[43] even leads to the recalling of how Rabbi Akiba explained Ecclesiastes 11:6; to wit, that even if one has in one's youth already raised disciples, one ought not to neglect raising disciples in one's old age.

These ideas, apparently, struck Maimonides as so self-evident—or perhaps we should say, as so typical of the whole classical tradition—that he did not bother to say anything about the clause in our mishna.[44] No less significant is the way *Machsor Vitry* explains the clause[45] —to the *Abot de-Rabbi Natan* comments it does not refer at all! It tells us to increase the wisdom (= learning) of disciples and cites, "The more the company of scholars, the more wisdom";[46] it reminds us of that famous remark, "Much have I learned from my masters, more from my colleagues, but from my disciples most of all,"[47] and finally refers to that midrash on Jabez, who prayed for many disciples.[48]

One cannot help wondering, why such turning of the back on the *Abot de-Rabbi Natan* comment? Again observe: the commentary of *Abot de-Rabbi Natan* alludes to a rather early give-and-take, one by Bet Shammai and Bet Hillel. Certainly as talmudic interpretations go, especially haggadic ones, this interpretation of "raise many disciples," namely, that one ought to attract as many disciples as possible, is hardly farfetched.

Whether or not the early commentators ignored it because they considered it farfetched, I would like to suggest that indeed by the time *Abot de-Rabbi Natan* was "composed," the original meaning had already been forgotten. And what the *Anshe Keneset Ha-Gedolah* had in mind was something else.

In pre-Exilic classical biblical Hebrew, how would you ordinarily say "many disciples?"[49] Surely תלמידים רבים! Note, for example, the frequently recurring ימים רבים, or expressions like עמים רבים, בתים רבים, and so on and [144] on.[50] Why is it, then, that the *Anshe Keneset Ha-Gedolah* speak of תלמידים הרבה? The literature of the Dead Sea Scrolls, for example, still does not resort to

42. Ibid., n. 3; Finkelstein, *Mabo*, p. 29.

43. Cf. *Abot de-Rabbi Natan*, both versions, pp.15f. Observe, incidentally, that Aknin, p. 2, cites only this part of *Abot de-Rabbi Natan* for his comment on raising many disciples and cf. his reading with that of *Abot de-Rabbi Natan*.

44. See preceding note and also above, note 29.

45. P. 464.

46. *Abot* 2:7

47. BT *Makkot* 10a and parallels.

48. BT *Temurah* 16a; cf. *Abot de-Rabbi Natan*, chap. 35, p. 105, and parallels.

49. On *talmid* spoken of in I Chron. 25:8 see E. Bickerman, "La chaine de la tradition pharisienne," *Revue Biblique*, 59:53 (1952).

50. E.g., Amos 3:15, Isa. 5:9, 2:3, Mic. 4:3; cf. indeed S Mandelkern, *Hekhal ha-Kodesh* (Tel Aviv, 1959), pp. 1065ff., s.v. רב, רבים. In no way, of course, is this meant to ignore the behavior of the biblical הרבה מאד.

that adjectival use of *harbeh*; why then do not the Men of the Great Assembly speak of raising[51] *talmidim rabbim*?

That I am not the first to raise this question is evident from a comment preserved in *Midrash Shemuel*:[52]

ואמר הרבה ולא אמר רבים, הכוונה שזמן הרבה יספיקו להם מזונותיהם, ואינו כינוי אל רבוי התלמידים רק אל רבוי הזמן.

So then our clause supposedly means, "Furnish students with support for a long time!"—a charming anticipation of our contemporary grants to graduate students and Ph.D. candidates.

Doubtless this is *derush*, but this should not prevent us from appreciating that someone has been struck by a *fact*, the fact of the textual reading. And he is not the only one to have observed that reading. In the Taylor-Schechter Genizah collection in the Cambridge University Library there is a one-leaf manuscript,[53] which, as the compiler of the hand list has already noted, is a kind of talmud to *Pirḳe Abot*, at least to the first mishna of the treatise. A number of lines on the obverse side are legible, but not enough to warrant detailed analysis in our present discussion. On the reverse side, however, occur only two lines, quite pertinent to us. Here they are:

תלמודייהו דיקא נמי דקתני [תלמידים הרבה]
ולא קתני הרבה תלמידים

And that is all. I am not a paleographer and therefore, alas, cannot even conjecture the place or date of that manuscript. Whether earlier than Samuel of Uçeda or later—and in my unprofessional opinion, it is earlier—one thing is clear: the author has noted that *talmidim harbeh* is a reading not to be taken for granted and that it requires some kind of explanation. I think so, too.

Not long after about 250 B.C.E.,[54] an attentive reader of the Book of [145] Ecclesiastes, who was deeply disturbed by its contents, appended to the book a kind of caveat, part of which cautioned against עשות ספרים הרבה אין קץ:[55] that is, he warned against the composition of many books, for there is no limit to such activity. The words עשות ספרים הרבה in that clause deserve some attention.

In his brilliant commentary on Ecclesiastes, Professor H. L. Ginsberg

---

51. Am I right in thinking that the *hiphil* of עמד in biblical Hebrew does not yet occur in the *general* sense of "raise" (train, develop, attract) (disciples)?

52. Of Samuel ben Isaac of Uçeda. In the edition of New York, 5705, the comment occurs on p. 8—I am unable to decide whether Samuel is giving his own views or is citing someone else's.

53. TS 20.56.

54. On the following, including dates, see H. L. Ginsberg's commentary, *Koheleth* (Tel Aviv–Jerusalem, 1961). On the date see also Ginsberg's *Studies in Koheleth* (New York, 1950), pp. 40–45.

55. Eccles. 12:12. See Ginsberg's commentary, pp. 134f.

interprets the clause as follows: כתיבת הספרים רבה לאין שיעור,[56] "the composition of books is an endless undertaking."[57] I do not necessarily or at all disagree with his grammatical explication of the clause, but in addition to establishing strict syntactical requirements in this connection, we should, I feel, attend also to the way some of the earliest readers we know of understood that clause. Observe that in Tannaitic Hebrew the biblical adverb הרבה is used very often in an adjectival sense,[58] and therefore in many (not all!) instances is located after the noun it modifies: in other words, treated like a regular adjective.[59] This explains, of course, the Septuagint reading, υἱέ μου, φύλαξαι ποιῆσαι βιβλία πολλά.[60] The character and probable date of the Septuagint translation of Ecclesiastes being what they are,[61] the translation naturally cannot constitute either independent or additional evidence. At least, however, it does demonstrate that in the second quarter of the second century, in Akiba's time, עשות ספרים הרבה was already rather widely taken as "the making of many books." But Professor Ginsberg too, who says [62] that in Ecclesiastes *harbeh* is to be taken as a term accompanying (מלווה) the verb, nevertheless calls attention to the fact that when *harbeh* has some association with the noun (מסונף לשם עצם), *harbeh* follows the noun. Even if one does no more than check a concordance, one will find how [146] prominent and recurrent is this feature of *harbeh* after the noun in Ecclesiastes above all.[63]

I would like to call this use of הרבה the adjectival *harbeh*. And if we now recall what the *Anshe Keneset Ha-Gedolah* said—namely, והעמידו תלמידים הרבה—I do not see how we can escape the conclusion that this clause is an echo of or comment on or response to עשות ספרים הרבה. What the *Anshe Keneset Ha-Gedolah* are saying is, "It is not the composition of many books we should strive for, but the raising of many disciples!" As a medieval scholar might have put it: מפי סופרים ולא מפי ספרים. Or more precisely: We are listening to one of the

---

56. Ginsberg, *Koheleth*, p. 135; but see also his comment on 1:16 (p. 64) and check all the passages he cites.

57. Note, too, his addendum on the unnumbered page at the end, which follows p. 137.

58. Or מרובים, etc.; see, e.g., the *Oẓar Leshon ha-Mishna* of Rabbi Chayim Yehoshua Kasovsky on the relevant forms, s.v. רבב, pp. 1644f. For the expression ימים רבים which seems to appear only once in the Mishna (*Menaḥot* 11:8), see Kasovsky, p. 1643; but the Mishna, as edited by Loewe, and the Kaufmann codex do not read רבים! The Naples edition does. Even with ימים the Mishna will say ימים הרבה; see, e.g., Mishna *Niddah* 1:1 (the time of Shammai and Hillel!).

59. In the literature of the Dead Sea Scrolls (thus far published), which strives so hard to emulate and imitate the classical biblical style, apparently הרבה is not used "adjectivally."

60. Hence also the Vulgate: *Faciendi plures libros nullus est finis.* By the way, although it proves nothing, cf. the *teamim* in this verse with the *teamim* at the end of MT Eccles. 9:18.

61. See the discussion in G. A. Barton, *The Book of Ecclesiastes*, International Critical Commentary (New York, 1908), pp. 8–11. On the association of Eccles. 12:12 with Akiba's view in Mishna *Sanhedrin* 10:1, see the passages cited and discussed by Lieberman, *Hellenism*, pp. 108ff.

62. Ginsberg, *Koheleth*, p. 64.

63. And it is not as though Ecclesiastes is no longer familiar with the adjective רבים; cf., e.g., 7:29.

earliest exhortations to develop the system and discipline and tradition of an Oral Torah. There is a Written Torah; it is all the Writing, the Scripture, we require; that is why it is absolutely imperative that its text be properly preserved. And to advance its teachings what is called for is not additional books, *many books*, but the raising of *many disciples!*[64]

We come now to the first clause of the saying by the Men of the Great Assembly, הוו מתונים בדין, and as with the other two clauses, we will look first to the classical sources and then examine the comments of the *Rishonim*. This time, however, we shall start not with *Abot de-Rabbi Natan*, but with a passage in a Tannaitic midrash, the Sifre on Deuteronomy,[65] commenting on Deuteronomy 1:16:

> *And I charged your judges at that time, saying: Hear the causes between your brethren, and judge righteously.* [That is,] I said to them "Be מתונים בדין": to wit, if some case has come before you once or twice or thrice, do not say, Such a case has already come before me again and again [and therefore it is unnecessary for me to deliberate and I can pass sentence at once]. Instead, "be deliberate in judgment"; and so indeed did the Men of the Great Assembly say: "Be מתונים בדין, and raise many disciples, and make a hedge about the Torah."[66]

As is manifest, we are dealing with an interpretation of the saying of the *Anshe Keneset Ha-Gedolah*, and as we read this interpretation, how eminently sensible it seems: certainly just the kind of counsel that should be directed [147] to judges, "And I charged your judges . . . judge righteously." Maimonides, for one, appreciated this; this is how he explains הוו מתונים בדין: "Proceed slowly in sentencing, and do not be hasty with the handing down of decision, [wait] until the matter is thoroughly understood; for it is possible that certain details will be revealed which at first thoughts were not manifest.[67]

And before Maimonides, *Machsor Vitry*,[68] even more explicitly, refers to our Sifre passage. But one look into *Abot de-Rabbi Natan* discloses immediately not only why we have a problem on our hands but also why *Machsor Vitry* reads as it does. Here is a paraphrase of the Vitry commentary: The word מתונים is to be understood as in the expression at the end of the treatise *Horayot*,

---

64. Cf. W. Jaeger, *Paideia* (New York, 1960), III, 194ff. And see Saadya's commentary on Eccles. 12:12, *Hamesh Megillot*, ed J. Kapaḥ (Jerusalem, 5722), p. 295: ואפשר עוד לומר בו שהוא זירז על הלמוד מפי הרבנים וקבלת הלמודים מפיהם כי זה יגיעתו קלה ותועלתו קרובה ולמודו מהיר, ולהתרחק מללמוד [רק] מן הספרים ולשקוד בקריאתם [בלבד] לפי שהם מטרידים וצורכים זמן רב, והלמוד בדרך זה קשה ומיגע את הגוף.
I fear, from his addition of the words רק and בלבד in the translation, that the editor has missed Saadya's point.
65. Ed. Finkelstein, p. 25; cf. *Midrash Tannaim*, p. 9.
66. And see, too, the manuscript, TS C2, fragment 181, in the Cambridge University Library.
67. On *Abot* 1:1, ed. Rabinowitz, p. 1: שיאחרו לחתך הדין ולא יפסקוהו מהרה עד שיבינוהו שאפשר שיתגלו להם הענינים שלא היו נגלים בתחלת המחשבה.
69. Cf. the note in *Machsor Vitry* ad loc.

דמתין מסיק,[69] "taking his time he arrives at a conclusion"; that is to say, they take their time to get to the very bottom of the law, of the case (עומק הדין). Then follows the substance of our Sifre passage. Only then comes the following from *Abot de-Rabbi Natan*:[70]

> And in the *baraita* of Rabbi Natan occurs this interpretation: "For thus we find concerning the Anshe Keneset Ha-Gedolah,[71] that they were מתונין בדין, as it is said, *'These also are the proverbs of Solomon which the men of Hezekiah king of Judah copied out'* [Prov. 25:1]: it is not that they copied, but that they took their time."[72]

Machsor Vitry does not stop with this, but concludes with a reference to Bar Kappara's midrash in the treatise *Sanhedrin*.[73]

Is the author of the *Machsor Vitry* commentary, perhaps, not entirely happy with *Abot de-Rabbi Natan*? It would seem so.

For two most striking facts are revealed by the *Abot de-Rabbi Natan* commentary. First, neither in Version A nor in Version B is there a word of that interpretation of the Sifre which we found to be so reasonable. Second, when we examine what *Abot de-Rabbi Natan* does do with הוו מתונים בדין, at first we are hardly enlightened and then we discover that we have been diverted to some other theme. Here is the *Abot de-Rabbi Natan* passage: Be מתונים בדין "teaches that a person should take his time in judgment [148] (שיהא אדם ממתין בדין),[74] for whoever takes his time in judgment is unruffled in judgment (מיושב בדין)." Then the verse in Proverbs is cited and explained as we observed it in *Machsor Vitry*. Seriously now, how much clarity has one gained from the remark שכל הממתין בדין מיושב בדין? And how apt after all is that Proverbs prooftext? Then מיושב seems to have been forgotten, and we are informed, ולא שהעתיקו אלא שהמתינו.[75]

Next we are off to a statement by Abba Saul on what was almost the fate of Proverbs, Song of Songs, and Ecclesiastes, which illustrates לא שהמתינו אלא שפירשו.[76] And then to our amazement we learn that "Be מתונים בדין" may also

---

69. Cf. the note in *Machsor Vitry* ad loc.

70. Cf. *Abot de-Rabbi Natan*, pp. 2 (both versions) and 150.

71. See next note.

72. The *Abot de-Rabbi Natan* text is somewhat difficult; note Schechter's n. 22, p. 2, and Goldin, *Fathers According to Rabbi Nathan*, p. 176, n. 22. I have begun to doubt the validity of the correction, for everywhere the reading *Anshe Keneset Ha-Gedolah* keeps recurring (note also the reading in the Schechter edition, p. 150), and I am now inclined to accept that reading, even though the sense of the *Abot de-Rabbi Natan* citing Prov. 25:1 is not too smooth. See also Finkelstein, *Ha-Perushim*, p. 74, n. 223.

73. BT *Sanhedrin* 7b, and see further below, page 151. Bar Kappara is a fifth-generation *Tanna* (cf. H. L. Strack, *Introduction to the Talmud and Midrash*, 5th ed. [Philadelphia, 1931], pp. 119, 316); in other words, he lived at the end of the second century or the beginning of the third century, at least 450 years after the Men of the Great Assembly!

74. Cf. Finkelstein, *Mabo*, p. 172.

75. The difficulties I have mentioned are not the only ones encountered; see above, note 72, and also Finkelstein, *Mabo*, pp. 234f., n. 18.

76. Cf. also Version B of *Abot de-Rabbi Natan*, p. 3, and see Finkelstein, *Mabo*, pp. 126f.

(דבר אחר) "teach that a man should be even-tempered, patient in his speech (שיהא אדם ממתין בדבריו) and not be short-tempered in his speech (ואל יהי מקפיד על דבריו), for whoever is short-tempered in his speech forgets what he has to say." And this is proved by what happened once to Moses; and if it could happen to Moses, can you imagine what it would be with the likes of us![77]

So *din* has become דברים, and we are not speaking of conduct in rendering judgment, but of controlling one's temper in general![78]

Is there any wonder Maimonides does not refer to this at all, and that *Machsor Vitry* refers to so little of this, and even that neither as the first nor the last explanation? Above all, let us repeat, why with so sensible a comment as the Sifre's available did not *Abot de-Rabbi Natan* at least allude to it, too, even if *Abot de-Rabbi Natan* wanted to suggest more homiletical ideas?

That we are not getting literal exegesis in *Abot de-Rabbi Natan* is evident; that the *Rishonim* are, to say the least, perplexed by the *Abot de-Rabbi Natan* exegesis is likewise evident; that the Sifre comment should be absent from *Abot de-Rabbi Natan* is again, to say the least, most puzzling.

Here, therefore, once again I am forced to the conclusion that if *Abot de-Rabbi Natan*—the earliest commentary we have on the sayings of *Pirke Abot*, and an early draft of that Mishna, by the way—if *Abot de-Rabbi Natan* shows no awareness of any explanation more or less plain, it must be because it no longer knew the real meaning of the text it was interpreting. *Abot de-Rabbi Natan* was guessing; the guesses were charming but had nothing to do with what the *Anshe Keneset Ha-Gedolah* were talking about, and I believe I can [149] show that even the Sifre, reasonable as is its comment, is not furnishing us with the original meaning of that first clause in the saying of the Men of the Great Assembly. To recover that, let us return to the verse in Ecclesiastes which has already opened one door for us.[79]

That verse begins: ויתר, and what is more, מהמה בני הזהר, "Take it easy, my son, take warning." Even those who would like to quibble with H. L. Ginsberg's extraordinarily brilliant reading מֵהֵמָּה surely cannot overlook the word הזהר and the fact that it is followed by the clause עשות ספרים הרבה אין קץ. The verse evidently opens with an exhortation to "my son": "Take care, my son, take warning, it is an endless and profitless exhaustion to compose more and more books."[80] And I submit that the saying of the *Anshe Keneset Ha-Gedolah*

---

77. On the word מתונים see also *Sifre Deut.* 323, p. 374 (cf *Midrash Tannaim*, p. 200); on the word מתון cf. *Midrash Tannaim*, p. 201, but in *Sifre Deut.* 325, p. 377, line 8, the reading is אלא ממתין.

78. To try to interpret דין as though it were part of the expression דין ודברים is no longer *peshat* but *derush*!

79. Once again, for what follows one must consult the *Koheleth* commentary, ad loc., by H. L. Ginsberg and see also the unnumbered page of his supplementary comments.

80. On the meaning of the word מתונים see H. L. Ginsberg in his commentary, *ad* 7:7, p. 98, and S. Lieberman, *Tosefta ki-Fshutah* (New York, 1955), Long Commentary on *Berakot* III, p. 47, s.v. ראש קלות and *Tosefta ki-Fshutah* (New York, 1962), Long Commentary, p. 1339. But this does not preclude, in my opinion, the use of the word in the meaning of "go slowly, take

originally also opened in this fashion: הוו מתונין בנין, "Careful, careful, children, instead of composing more literary works, raise many disciples;[81] for there is only one text we need, the Torah; and because without that Writing in a proper state there can be disastrous consequences, preserve the carefully edited readings furnished by the Masorah." The whole sentiment of this saying is like the first signs of the dawn of that intellectual day which is familiar to us as the talmudic period; here are the first explicit signals of the development of תורה בעל פה as a conscious undertaking. And note, quite independently of all this, Professor Ginsberg says of the peroration of Ecclesiastes, our verse and the two that [150] follow, that it summons up the traces of the religio-intellectual climate of the Mishnaic Sages rather than those of the biblical climate.[82]

In the saying of the Men of the Great Assembly, then, I suggest we have preserved a kind of commentary on or response to Ecclesiastes 12:12. But at an early time the original meaning was forgotten; maybe it was this that caused the mistaken change from בנין to בדין;[83] maybe the text was accidentally corrupted from בנין to בדין, and since as a result הוו מתונים בדין was puzzling, *Abot de-Rabbi Natan* had only its own resources—hence guesses—to draw upon, and could not really grasp what the clause meant. I would rather not try to add guesses of my own and am especially uneasy with the fact that I have to suggest an emendation of a text at all, and of a text at that which has had so long and well established a history. No one is more reluctant than I to engage in textual emendations or in speculations which cannot be controlled by something concrete, like a text or some preserved, hidden-away reading. But I have no

care"; see Targum on Cant. 5:12 (cf. *Midrash Shir Ha-Shirim*, ed. Grünhut, 40a–b) where, to be sure, the expression מתונין בדינא is based on what we may call the *Sifre–Abot de-Rabbi Natan* interpretation of מתונים בדין, but at the same time it reveals the potential meaning to which מתן could be extended. And on מתונים in the sense of "restrained," see Lieberman, *Tosefta Ki-Fshutah ad* Tosefta *Shabbat* 7:24, Long Commentary, p. 105.

81. The following communication (of March 10, 1961) to me from Professor Ginsberg will be of interest: "(1) First of all there is of course Ps. 34:12, לכו בנים שמעו לי. (2) Secondly, I wonder if בנין couldn't be an Aramaism for 'our sons.' The suffix for 'our' is still נא as a rule at that time, but the shorter ן may very well have been used even then in a familiar expression like 'our sons.'—The title רבן must be pretty old, yet it is רבן and not רַבָּנָא.—(The 5th century Elephantine papyri write ן nearly always, but they may have pronounced a short vowel at the end all the same.) (The syllable in question was unstressed.)"

Even at the risk of protesting too much, I should like to say that I well understand the foreseeable and likely strong reluctance to accept this "emendation," and (for four years) I have myself done everything I could to resist taking liberties with so long-established a text. But, as I say, I am left with no alternative. At all events, even if this "emendation" is found unacceptable, I hope that at least these two *facts* will not be overlooked; one, the real difficulty with ממתן בדין = מיושב בדין; two, the clear statement in Eccles., בני הזהר . . . .

82. ברור שהמפטיר שלנו, בעל פס' י"ב-י"ד, קרוב ברוחו לחכמים ההם [ז.א. לחכמים ראשונים כבעלי המקראות. תה' קי"א, י', משלי א', ז'; ט', י'. איוב כ"ח, כ"ח] יותר מקוהלת; אבל עושה הוא רושם פחות "מקראי" מהם, ויותר "יהודי", באשר אינו מבליט כל כך את החוכמה (אינו נוקב את שמה, ו"סוף דבר" הוא אומר תחת "ראשית חכמה") אלא מדגיש מצוות ודין, ושכר ועונש . . . מזכירים דבריו את שני מאמרות רבי חנינא בן דוסא (משנה, אבות ג', ט): כל שיראת חטאו קודמת לחכמתו חכמתו מתקיימת; וכל שחכמתו קודמת ליראת חטאו, אין חכמתו מתקיימת . . . כל שמעשיו מרובין מחכמתו חכמתו מתקיימת; וכל שחכמתו מרובה ממעשיו, אין חכמתו מתקיימת.

83. Because people no longer understood what that could mean.

alternative—the data force me to conclude that the literal meaning of the saying of the Men of the Great Assembly can be understood only in the context of the sentences appended by that pious soul to the book of Ecclesiastes.

Once the literal meaning was forgotten, it was inevitable that the intent of the words of the *Anshe Keneset Ha-Gedolah* should be transformed. First, each of the clauses in the saying came to be treated as a unit by itself;[84] and then in each unit, even as early as Tannaitic times, each generation discerned what was congenial to its own spirit or needs. A fifth-generation Tanna, for instance, already undertakes to support the first clause with a midrash of Pentateuch verses. Note the idiom carefully:[85]

[151] דרש בר קפרא, מנא הא מילתא דאמרי רבנן [!Rabbanan, no less] הוו מתונין בדין
דכרוב לא רסלח במסלדר. דקמון לוח דאלח חמדעיקט.

Perhaps in the latter half of the second century,[86] when discussion of the right behavior of judges was being described in midrashic moralizing terms, "Be deliberate in judgment" naturally suggested of itself a directive to judges to ponder carefully before arriving at a decision, regardless of how familiar the case seemed to be.

When in the latter part of the first century the original intention of "Raise many disciples" was no longer recalled, it seemed indeed that the *Anshe Keneset Ha-Gedolah* must have had in mind what was obviously preoccupying the sages of that age: Is everyone to be admitted as a student to the rabbinic academy, or only a select group? As is evident, the Shammaites did seek to limit admissions;[87] let us not forget that Hillel (according to the story)[88] was on one occasion unable to scrape together enough funds for the admission fees; Rabban Gamaliel the Elder did not look with the same eye on rich and poor students.[89] Rabban Gamaliel II would have certain students kept from

---

84. In a future study I hope to show that the three-clause structure of almost all the early sayings preserved in *Abot* (say, at least down through the disciples of Johanan ben Zakkai) is not intended to suggest individual and independent clauses, but clauses directed to a single thought. For the time being, this should certainly be clear in the following: 1:2, 3, 8, 9, 11, 12 (cf. above, pages 135–136), 18; 2:8a (Johanan ben Zakkai's saying), 11, 14 (cf. the Hebrew paper on the academy of Johanan ben Zakkai in the forthcoming *Wolfson Jubilee Volume*); 3:1. Moreover, cf. *Proceedings*, AAJR, 27:53 (1958).

After the present paper was read (March 20, 1963), Professor A. Altmann raised a question regarding the specific statement of the Mishna, "they said *three things*" (*sheloshah debarim*), which would by itself certainly not suggest that the sentence is directed to a *single* thought. The answer of course is that "they said three (different) things" is the editor's interpretation of those clauses both in 1:1 and 2:10—on which see further the paper in the *Wolfson Jubilee Volume* referred to.

85. See above, note 73.

86. Note, for example, the names of the authorities cited in *Abot de-Rabbi Natan*, chap. 10, p. 43. I hope to discuss this more fully in a future study.

87. *Abot de-Rabbi Natan*, both versions, pp. 14f., 154.

88. BT *Yoma* 35b.

89. *Abot de-Rabbi Natan*, chap. 40, p. 127; see Goldin, *Fathers According to Rabbi Nathan*, p. 218, nn. 15–17, and particularly the study by G. Allon to which I refer there.

entering the academy.[90] *Abot de-Rabbi Natan*, which I seem to be belaboring for forgetting so much, certainly recalls the possibility of a student paying fees!

> Another interpretation of "Let thy fellow's property be as dear to thee as thine own": . . . When a scholar comes to thee saying, "Teach me," if it is in thy power to teach, teach him. Otherwise, send him away at once and *do not take his money from him*, as it is said, *Say not unto thy neighbor, 'Go, and come again, and tomorrow I will give,' when thou hast it by thee* (Proverbs 3:28).[91]

And when as a result of the impetus created by Johanan ben Zakkai and his leading disciples in Jabneh, study of Torah came to be elevated as a primary obligation on the part of every member of Jewish society,[92] what was more natural than to see in the formulation of the *Anshe Keneset Ha-Gedolah* the urgent duty which, for example, Rabbi Akiba felt: "If thou hast raised many disciples in thy youth, do not sit back and say, It is enough for me. On the contrary, raise them in thine old age [too] and increase the [152] study of the Torah";[93] or Rabbi Ishmael: "If thou hast studied Torah in thy youth, say not, I shall not study in my old age. Instead study Torah [at all times]";[94] or Rabbi Meir: "If thou hast studied with one master, say not, Enough for me. On the contrary, go to another sage and study Torah."[95] Thus by association one thought on this theme stirs up another thought; and just as one urges the master at all times to raise many disciples, so one then goes on urging the disciples at all times and in many ways to keep studying.

As to the *seyag*—here, too, all is not of one piece; here, too, we are not dealing with a static concept. When Taylor in his splendid edition and commentary writes,[96] "The סייג (III:20; VI:6) lies at the root of the rabbinic system," or when Moore says[97] that making "a barrier about the law" (to use his translation) refers to "a body of legislation supplementary to the written law in the Pentateuch . . . [and] enactments meant to guard against any possible infringement of the divine statute,"[98] he is not unjust to the rabbinic attitude or zeal. The question is, however: did the expression *seyag la-Torah* always and uniformly mean, as the *Rishonim* and modern scholars assume, extending obligation or prohibition even into provinces not specifically demanded by the Torah? Let us see.

---

90. BT *Berakot* 28a. See also the statement by R. Simeon ben Yohai in *Mekilta Ishmael*, Beshallah I, ed. Lauterbach, I, 171.

91. *Abot de-Rabbi Natan*, chap. 17, p. 65 (and cf. chap. 6, p. 27). Is there a similar thought behind the statement in chap. 16, p. 63?

92. Cf. *Proceedings, AAJR*, 27:51–56 (1958).

93. Version B of *Abot de-Rabbi Natan*, chap. 4, p. 15; cf. Goldin, *Fathers According to Rabbi Nathan*, p. 28, and n. 15, p. 181.

94. *Abot de-Rabbi Natan*, chap. 3, p. 16.

95. Ibid; cf., however, the view attributed to R. Meir, chap. 8, p. 36.

96. *Sayings of the Jewish Fathers*, I, p. 11, n. 1; see also pp. 134f. (the numbering of the *Abot* paragraphs is Taylor's).

97. *Judaism in the First Centuries of the Christian Era*, I (Cambridge, Mass., 1927), 33.

98. Cf. also J. Bonsirven, *Le Judaïsme palestinien* (Paris, 1934), I, 265ff.

A *baraita* cited by the Talmud (not once but twice, by the way)[99] reports the following:

> *Tanya*—Rabbi Eliezer ben Jacob[100] says: I heard that the *bet din* [court] may impose flagellation and corporal punishments even in [cases where] the Torah does not do so, not thereby transgressing the view of the Torah, but in order to make a hedge about the Torah. Thus, it happened in the time of the Greeks that someone rode on a horse on the Sabbath. He was brought to the *bet din* and sentenced to be stoned— not because that was the proper [legal] penalty, but because שהשעה צריכה לכך, the times demanded it.[101]

Here then is a Tannaitic source expressly declaring that something was imposed כדי לעשות סייג לתורה. If a Tannaitic source so plainly uses *seyag* [153] *la-Torah*, how dare we, you may ask, depart from the generally accepted explanation of עשו סייג לתורה in the saying of the *Anshe Keneset Ha-Gedolah*?

But note attentively how the *baraita* itself describes its examples: שהשעה צריכה לכך, in unembroidered current English usage, means: "It was an emergency measure"; that is, at a particular, critical time, Rabbi Eliezer ben Jacob reports, apparently a *bet din* imposed an exceptionally severe penalty, and it never entered anyone's mind to say that as a result of that emergency, whenever in the future a Jew was found riding an animal on the Sabbath, he was to be sentenced to be stoned.[102] But when we speak of the prohibition of שניות לעריות or of שבת, that is a permanently binding regulation. Evidently, then, the expression לעשות סייג לתורה can be used to express a thought that is not strictly speaking what the commentators say "making a hedge about the Torah" means.

And now we can understand something which would otherwise be utterly eccentric. Not one of the classical commentators, neither *Abot de-Rabbi Natan* nor *Machsor Vitry* nor Maimonides nor any of the *Rishonim* before Duran (1361–1444)[103] —at least of the published *Rishonim*—not one, in commenting on the last clause of the *Anshe Keneset ha-Gedolah* saying, refers to that talmudic *baraita*, though as I have already remarked, that *baraita* appears not once but twice in well-known talmudic treatises: there is nothing recherché about that *baraita*. But of course the early *Rishonim* shy away from that *baraita*, although the very terms לעשות סייג לתורה occur in it, because they know

99. BT *Yebamot* 90b and BT *Sanhedrin* 46a. By the way, the reading of the Munich manuscript in BT *Yebamot* is simply לעשות סייג (no לתורה)!

100. On the problem of his identity see A. Hyman, *Toledot Tannaim we-Amoraim* (London, 1910), I, 183, col. b.

101. Cf. the second story in the Talmud, BT *Yebamot* 90b and *Sanhedrin* 46a, also illustrating "that the times demanded it."

102. Cf. indeed the commentary of R. Hananel in B. M. Lewin, *Ozar Ha-Geonim*, VII (Jerusalem, 5696), p. 322: התם דוקא משום מיגדר מילתא לעשות סייג ותקנה כי התם שהשיבן ע'י כך מעבודה זרה, וכן לקמן מפני שהיו פרוצים בעריות או שהיו מזלזלין בשביתת שבת, אבל בעלמא לא.

103. *Magen Abot* (Leipzig, 1855), p. 4a.

it is not speaking of what they are speaking of. And even Duran, note carefully, refers to it in connection with still another idea, which is at still another remove from what we generally apply to *seyag la-Torah*. Here is how Duran speaks:

וכן בכלל זה (של עשו סייג לתורה) הוא מה שאמרו בסנהדרין פ' נגמר הדין וביבמות פ' האשה, בית
דין מכין ועונשין שלא מן הדין ולא לעבור על דברי תורה אלא כדי לעשות סייג לתורה וחכמי
ישראל לא היו רוצים לגלות לכל אדם טעמי אלו התקנות לפי שהם סתרי תורה כמו טעמי המצות
כמו שנזכר במדרש חזית!

So we are already off to the world of "esoteric" teachings and their restriction to the qualified few![104]

[154] So much, therefore, for that *baraita*. There is, however, another *baraita (ke-de-tanya)*[105] which is not irrelevant to our discussion. This *baraita* instructs us that in the evening when a man returns from his work, before he sits down to his meal he should recite the evening *Shemaʿ*; otherwise he might discover that he has eaten and fallen asleep, and the time for the recitation of the *Shemaʿ* will have passed, and thus he will have been guilty of transgressing the injunction of the Sages. And this is the reason why the Sages made a hedge about their words. Note well, חכמים עשו סייג לדבריהם: the Sages made a hedge about *their words*. This *baraita*, then, is the same[106] as the one in *Abot de-Rabbi Natan*, either drawn from that treatise, or perhaps both the Talmud and *Abot de-Rabbi Natan* have drawn on the same source. At all events, this source is illustrating not עשו סייג לתורה but חכמים עשו סייג לדבריהם, the homiletical extension of the original saying, "Make a hedge about the Torah," as we observed earlier in our analysis, the homiletical extension which can hardly represent the meaning of what the *Anshe Keneset Ha-Gedolah* had in mind, as we have already seen.[107]

104. Cf., e.g., *Cant. Rabba* on 1:2b, 5c. On this last point made by Duran, see also Lieberman, *Hellenism*, pp. 139ff. I have put the word "esoteric" in quotes deliberately, for explanations were often withheld not only in esoteric lore, strictly speaking, but in legal matters, too, as the Lieberman reference shows. Note the interesting conjunction in the text of *Mekilta R. Simeon*, ed. J. N. Epstein and E. Z. Melamed (Jerusalem, 1955), p. 158.
105. BT *Berakot* 4b.
106. On the readings of the two versions of *Abot de-Rabbi Natan*, see Finkelstein, *Mabo*, pp. 24f., and *HUCA*, 19: pp. 102–104 (1945/46). The two *Abot de-Rabbi Natan* versions (cf. also *Abot de-Rabbi Natan*, p. 154) and the reading of BT *Berakot* 4b, if set side by side and compared, would reveal some interesting variants; but this is not the place for such discussion.
107. See above, pages 139ff. Note also the *baraita* in BT *Niddah* 4b (cf. PT *Niddah* 1, 48d) where we are told that Hillel would not accept Shammai's view because he, Shammai, would not make a hedge to his words, שלא עשה סייג לדבריו. As for the give-and-take between Shammai and Hillel in BT *Niddah* 3b, where Hillel is reported as criticizing Shammai ומיהו עשה סייג—לדבריך דמאי שנא מכל התורה דעבדינן סייג, עשה סייג לדבריך, but—not only do we meet here too with עשה סייג לדבריך, but more important: I do not believe that the Talmud BT *Niddah* 3b (compare, indeed, the whole *sugya*) is saying that the words דמאי שנא מכל התורה דעבדינן סייג are the *ipsissima verba* of Hillel; rather this is what the Amoraim conceive to be part of the exchange which lay behind the different views of Hillel and Shammai reported in the Mishna. Observe the very style of this sentence! Cf. below, note 110.

Something there is in Talmud that does love a wall, because it knows quite well what it is walling in and walling out, and what is likely to give [155] offense.[108] As we noted above,[109] the way talmudic sources express the idea of extending obligation or prohibition even into provinces not specifically demanded by the Torah is שמרו לי משמרת (Sifra) or עשו משמרת למשמרתי.[110] Is it not noteworthy that when this formulation is cited, no one in the primary sources bothers even to make use of the expression לעשות סייג לתורה?[111]

In other words, there is absolutely no need to assume that the notion of a hedge about the law, as we speak of it familiarly, appears late in the talmudic tradition.[112] All I am trying to demonstrate is that this notion is *not in the beginning* suggested by the third clause in the saying of the *Anshe Keneset Ha-Gedolah*, for indeed originally no one thought of עשו סייג לתורה in that sense. In my opinion, the equation of עשו סייג לתורה with עשו משמרת למשמרתי was first made in Geonic times,[113] and perhaps the *Geonim* were led to that equation because they remembered that the one who spoke of רמז לשניות מן התורה[114] was the same Amora—namely, Raba—who interpreted Ecclesiastes 12:12[115] as

And in the light of our analysis the *Mekilta Ishmael*, Pisha VI, passage cited above, page 140, should now be clear at a glance: that passage is really discussing a hedge the Sages made about *their words*, that though strictly speaking the sacrifices supposed to be eaten within one day's duration might indeed be eaten until the dawn of the following day, once again the Sages set a time limit in the night. And by citing the saying of the Men of the Great Assembly and calling this limitation a hedge about the Torah, the Mekilta is adopting the approach of *Abot de-Rabbi Natan* that "hedge about the Torah" equals "the Sages made a hedge about their words." Note the idiom carefully: עד . . . בקר לא תותירו ממנו עד הלילה, ת'ל לא תותירו ממנו עד בקר, שומע אני כל הלילה, בלילה הזה, בוקר למה נאמר, לא בא הכתוב אלא ליתן תחום לבוקרו של בוקר, ואיזה זה עמוד השחר, מכאן אמרו אכילת פסחים וכו' . . . עד שיעלה עמוד השחר, ולמה אמרו חכמים עד חצות להרחיק וכו'.

108. Note not only *Abot de-Rabbi Natan*, chaps. 1 and 2, but Tosefta *Ḳiddushin*, cited above, note 15; see too *Oẓar Ha-Geonim*, *Yebamot*, VII, p. 24 and Lewin's note 1 (but observe that this is wanting in *Mekilta Simeon*, ed. Epstein-Melamed). Of course the Rabbis objected to excessive hedges; see above, page 139. On the figure of hedge and vineyard see also *Mekilta Ishmael*, Pisha I, ed. Lauterbach, I, 15.

109. Page 140.

110. But apparently in Amoraic times, the thought of extending prohibition could be expressed sometimes by "make a hedge"; see the clause מאי שנא מכל התורה דעבדינן סייג in note 107 above: note that we still do not get דעבדינן סייג לתורה! In other words, that has still not yet become the commonplace formula for what we mean by "a hedge about the law."

111. Nor does R. Hillel in his commentary on Sifra, end of *Aḥare Mot*, say anything about making a hedge. Rabad, ad loc., says nothing.

112. See some fine remarks by A. Goldberg, "The Place of *Shevut* . . . in the Pattern of Sabbath Observance," in *Conservative Judaism*, (Winter-Spring 1962), pp. 71–78 (an expanded version appeared in *Sinai*, 46:181–189 [5720]).

113. Cf. *Oẓar Ha-Geonim*, *Yebamot*, VII, 24 אילו שאסר הקב'ה בתורה ובאו חכמים ועשו סיג . . . לתורה ואסרו עוד שמונה וכו'. See also note 110 above.

114. Bt *Yebamot* 21a; but cf. marginal reading in the Talmud ad loc. and *Diḳduḳe Soferim* ad loc.

115. BT *Erubin* 21b.

בני, הזהר בדברי סופרים יותר מדברי תורה, שדברי תורה יש בהן עשה ולא תעשה, ודברי סופרים
כל העובר על דברי סופרים חייב מיתה; שמא תאמר אם יש בהן ממש מפני מה לא נכתבו? עשות
ספרים הרבה אין קץ.

But of course this is only guesswork on my part, and I would hardly press it.

At all events, the *Rishonim* certainly took up the suggestion of this equation, and they have made the most of it. So let us return to the main point.

What, therefore, were the *Anshe Keneset Ha-Gedolah* saying? This: We [156] must be careful; the way to inculcate right teaching and piety is not through the multiplication of more and more books, but through the raising of many disciples to whom one will teach the Torah, that singular literary work which is at the root of all true wisdom and right conduct. And because that text is so fundamental, be sure to preserve it with greatest care. Or as that pious reader of Kohelet put it:

ויתר, מהמה בני, הזהר, עשות ספרים הרבה אין קץ ולהג הרבה יגעת בשר; סוף דבר הכל נשמע, את
האלהים ירא ואת מצותיו שמר, כי זה כל האדם.

This is what the closing verses of Kohelet speak of, and this is what the *Anshe Keneset Ha-Gedolah* are talking about. But all generations, even conservative ones, have their own problems. And great words are always hospitable. As new problems and new preoccupations arose, new thoughts were first inserted into these fine words and then in all innocence and great imaginativeness these very thoughts were re-extracted from those words, as though from the outset these words had had the new thoughts in mind. The active intellect will always reinterpret; but it is also said, אין מקרא יוצא מידי פשוטו.[116]

So much for the analysis and interpretation of the saying of the *Anshe Keneset Ha-Gedolah*, which is the only purpose of this study.[117] But one cannot study what these men said without at the same time being forced to consider again their identity and date. For my present purpose it is certainly unnecessary to review all the secondary literature on the subject of the Men of the Great Assembly. Those interested in that subject will find a comprehensive collection of all the early sources referring to the *Anshe Keneset Ha-Gedolah* and a bibliography of all the major secondary studies in Professor Louis Finkelstein's *Ha-Perushim ve-Anshe Keneset Ha-Gedolah*, pages 45–52. To

116. [Cf. also S. Gandz, "Oral Tradition in the Bible," in *Jewish Studies in Memory of George A. Kohut*, ed. S. W. Baron and A. Marx (New York: Alexander Kohut Memorial Foundation, 1935), pp. 264f.]

117. Obviously, with the interpretations, delightful as they are, in *Kohelet Rabba ad* Eccles. 12:12ff. (and parallels) this paper need not concern itself: once the haggadic homilist gets to work, the only limits are the richness or poverty of his wit (in the seventeenth-century sense of the word, no less than the modern). See also Lieberman, *Hellenism*, pp. 108ff., and especially p. 109, n. 58.

add to the mass of speculations seems to me unnecessary, or, perhaps more accurately, is beyond my powers. But several brief observations are inevitable as a result of the reflections thus far.

First, while all kinds of reports about the achievements of the *Anshe Keneset Ha-Gedolah* are made in midrashic-talmudic sources, note that the only saying of which they are presumably the authors is the saying in the first mishna of *Abot*. So that if we are to be on comparatively safe ground, [157] I think it best to come to conclusions, (if such are possible) on the basis of what these men themselves said and not on what later authorities credited them with.[118] The primary interest of the Tannaim and Amoraim was not historical study or research. As Bickerman pointed out with engaging lucidity and charm more than a decade ago,[119] neither the Synagogue Fathers nor their contemporaries among the pagan scholars—except for *quelques érudits moroses*—displayed strong historical interests, and of the past they knew accurately only some minor facts. Hence, methodologically I believe it would be wisest if scholarship, like urbane wit, aimed rather at understatement when reliable sources are so meager. It just will not do to project the *Anshe Keneset Ha-Gedolah* back to the age of Ezra and Nehemiah, and then in order to justify this and at the same time to try to make sense of the material at our disposal, to project hypotheses about successive generations of such an *institution*, the last of which functioned in the time of Simeon the Righteous, who was one of their last survivors.

Second, if we content ourselves with the so-called facts regarding the Men of the Great Assembly, we shall have to admit that we have only two: namely, one, that these Men were the authors of the saying we have been examining, and, two, that Simeon the Righteous was one of the last survivors (מששיירי) of that group.[120] The date of Simeon we know—about 200 B.C.E.[121] —and, remember, he was a high priest.[122]

Now, while the first part of the first chapter of *Abot* can hardly be set up as a paradigm for chronological fastidiousness, one thing is by and large clear: the Zugot are introduced in chronological sequence; if the first of these pairs took over from Antigonus of Soko (or from him and Simeon),[123] and he in turn took over from Simeon the Righteous, we are dealing in time spans of a generation more or less. Whatever the time span between the authorities quoted in each instance, it is certainly not one of centuries. *Abot* does not say that Simeon was

118. I hope to write on some future occasion on the historicity of the various attributions.

119. In his paper, *RB*, 59:44–47 (1952).

120. Note the reading משיירי כנסת הגדולה in Version B of *Abot de-Rabbi Natan*, chap. 6, p. 18; see also Taylor, *Sayings of the Jewish Fathers*, II, 70 (from the Loewe ed.), and Codex Kaufmann and the Naples ed.

121. See G. F. Moore, "Simeon the Righteous," in *Israel Abrahams Memorial Volume* (Vienna, 1927), pp. 348–364.

122. See the data in Moore, "Simeon the Righteous," pp. 348–364, and cf. below, page 158 and also my note 124.

123. Cf., e.g., *Machsor Vitry* and Rabbi Jonah Gerondi ad *Abot* 1:4.

a member or survivor of some so-to-speak "original" or "final" *Keneset Ha-Gedolah,* and it is certainly plainest of *peshat* to assume that he was the survivor of that *Keneset Ha-Gedolah* cited in the mishna preceding the one citing *him.*

[158] We are therefore less likely to exaggerate if we assume that the authors of the saying in *Abot* 1:1 began to function about fifty to thirty years before Simeon, who was משיירי that group of men. And that date fits most admirably with the date of Kohelet.[124] As the discussion above also suggested, the concern reflected by the statement of the *Anshe Keneset Ha-Gedolah* fits best what we know of the religio-intellectual climate and preoccupations of the mid–third century B.C.E. and is to be understood against the background of Kohelet's last words.

Whether there was a *Keneset Ha-Gedolah* before that, I cannot say, nor do I necessarily deny that some such body or some authoritative assembly could have existed in the days of Ezra and Nehemiah and after. But if such a body existed then, it was not the author of the saying in *Abot* 1:1. That saying belongs to the *Anshe Keneset Ha-Gedolah* of the latter half of the third century B.C.E., not too long (about a decade?) after 250 B.C.E.

But who were they? This is much more difficult to answer. Perhaps they were one of the synods the Ptolemies liked to convene from time to time.[125] "Les Ptolémés, on le sait," writes Bickerman, "avaient souvent convoqué des synodes du clergé égyptien."[126] Perhaps we have in *Pirke Abot* a record of a Jewish general council summoned by Ptolemy III (247–221 B.C.E.), who hoped in this way to strengthen Jewish allegiance to his cause. But here again we are on the border of conjecture, and "I cannot see what flowers are at my feet";[127] it is best therefore to stop right here.

---

124. See above, note 54.

125. See E. Bevan, *A History of Egypt under the Ptolemaic Dynasty* (London, 1927), p. 180, and esp. pp. 208ff., for the text of the decree passed by the synod at Canopus in March, 237 B.C.E.; see also A. Bouché-Leclercq, *Histoire des Lagides* (Paris, 1906), III, pp. 20–21; I, 265ff. Cf. *RB,* 59:48, n. 2. By the way, of synods in general, in C. V. Daremberg and E. Saglio, *Dictionnaire des antiquités grecques et romaines,* (Paris, 1877–1919), vol. IV, part 2, p. 1588b, s.v. "Synodos," it is said by G. Colin, "Les plus importantes sont les associations réligieuses vouées, au culte d'un dieu ou d'un prince divinisé."

126. E. Bickerman, "La chaîne de la tradition pharisienne," *RB* 59:48, n. 2 (1952).

127. J. L. Maimon's "Who Were the *Anshe Keneset Ha-Gedolah*" (Heb.), in *Mazkeret, Kobez Torani le-Zeker Rabbenu Geon Yisrael Maran Ha-Rav Yizhak Eisik Halevi Herzog* (Jerusalem, 5722), pp. 565–569, is of no help.

The Three Pillars of Simeon the Righteous

[43] So fundamental to the architecture of classical Judaism are the three pillars of Simeon the Righteous, that we take them for granted, for reassurance sake touch them every once in a while to see if they are still in place, and then pass on to our next chore or our next text without having taken a good look at them. But I think it will not be unprofitable to stop and look at them closely. Once again, therefore, what are the pillars? התורה, העבודה, וגמילות חסדים. Or better still, let Simeon the Righteous speak for himself: על שלשה דברים העולם עומד, על התורה, ועל העבודה, ועל גמילות חסדים.[1]

What do these terms mean?

At first blush, this sounds like a preposterous question. After all, *Abot de-Rabbi Natan* had already answered this question a long time ago. על התורה כיצד; על העבודה כיצד; על גמילות חסדים כיצד, Version A of *Abot de-Rabbi Natan* (chap. 4), had asked and then proceeded to answer; and with the answers Version B is in accord. עבודת בית המקדש=העבודה; תלמוד תורה=התורה; and גמילות חסדים? Why, *gemilut ḥasadim* is of course *gemilut ḥasadim*. This certainly requires no comment! The best commentary indeed is apparently to suggest how important *gemilut ḥasadim* is—העולם מתחלה לא נברא אלא בחסד (Version A, p. 21)—to tell how Rabban Joḥanan ben Zakkai once comforted Rabbi Joshua with the reassurance that though the Temple was in ruins, אל ירע לך, יש לנו כפרה אחת שהיא כמותה, ואיזה זה גמילות חסדים שנאמר כי חסד ... (ibid.), or, as Version B (p. 22) records it, אל תירא יש לנו כפרה אחת תחתיה ... כי חסד חפצתי ולא זבח. And yet, it is not impertinent, I hope to ask: what is *gemilut ḥasadim*?

---

1. M. Abot 1.2.

[44] There is of course the statement in the Tosefta[2] which almost defines, and certainly implies, what *gemilut ḥasadim* is: הצדקה בחיים, גמילות חסדים בחיים ובמתים; צדקה בעניים, גמילות חסדים בעניים ובעשירים; צדקה בממונו, גמילות חסדים בממונו ובגופו.[3] I submit, however, that this is a later characterization of *gemilut ḥasadim* and not its original meaning; or, to put it more precisely, the Tosefta characterization of *gemilut ḥasadim* came into being only after the destruction of the Temple, and most likely as a result of the influence of Rabban Joḥanan ben Zakkai. In the days of Simeon the Righteous *gemilut ḥasadim* was not yet "acts of lovingkindness, acts of love surpassing charity."

I shall present the evidence in a moment. First it will be helpful to recollect what is well known, the tannaite report on the term *abodah*, Simeon's second pillar. *Abot de-Rabbi Natan* (ibid.) had defined *abodah* as עבודת בית המקדש, and had even gone on with a homily emphasizing שאין עבודה שהיא חביבה לפני הקב"ה יותר מעבודת בית המקדש (p. 20). But we read in the Sifre (Deut. 41, ed. Finkelstein, pp. 87f): ולעבדו, זה תלמוד ... דבר אחר ולעבדו זו תפלה. אתה אומר זו תפלה או אינו אלא עבודה; תלמוד לומר בכל לבבכם ובכל נפשכם. וכי יש עבודה בלב, הא מה תלמוד לומר ולעבדו, זו תפלה ... וכשם שעבודת מזבח קרויה עבודה כך תפלה קרויה עבודה. We are manifestly dealing with a passage which reflects the reinterpretation of a basic Jewish concept after there was no longer a Temple and sacrificial ritual had become impossible. Contrary to those who would despair because there was no longer an opportunity for *abodah*, the spokesmen for the interpretations we have just reread demonstrate that there is *abodah* available. Some think it may be *talmud Torah*; others say—and they have prooftexts to bear them out (cf. Sifre, ibid.)—*abodah* is now *tefillah*, prayer.

Now let us look at *gemilut ḥasadim*. In Scripture, the verb גמל, in addition to meanings like "wean," "ripen," is used for "to pay, repay, do something to a person in return for something [45] he did" and such like actions.[4] We have the noun גמול for "recompense, return, reward or benefit," and so on. גמילות[5] we meet for the first time in Simeon the Righteous' saying.[6] In post-biblical Hebrew *gamal* continues to denote a paying back, a doing of something to someone in return.

The word *ḥesed*, as scholars[7] have been pointing out with increasing insistence, is not merely "love" or "mercy" or "lovingkindness"; it is instead a

2. T. Peah 4.19, ed. Lieberman, pp. 60f.; for the parallel passages see the references in Lieberman, ad loc.

3. Cf. Lieberman's comment in his short commentary ad loc., R. Joḥanan b. Maria's comment in the Yerushalmi, and the whole statement in *Eccl. R.*

4. Cf. Koehler-Baumgartner, *Lexicon*, p. 188.

5. For the spelling גמילת cf. T. Peah 1.1, ed. Zuckermandel; for the spelling גמלות, T. Peah 4.19, ed. Lieberman, p. 61, line 1, last word.

6. The reading in Sirach (M. Z. Segals, *Sefer Ben Sira Ha-Shalem*, Jerusalem, 1953, p. 231) either as תגמל חסד or as גמילות חסד is not to be accepted. The Greek of Ecclus, 37.11 is μετὰ βασκάνου περὶ εὐχαριστίας, and εὐχαριστία is not *gemilut ḥasadim*. On the Hebrew of Sirach which we have, cf. H. L. Ginsberg in *JBL*, LXXIV 1955, pp. 93ff.

7. See the large number of references given by H. H. Rowley in *The Biblical Doctrine of Election*, London, 1950, p. 22, n. 2. See also N. Glueck, *Das Wort hesed u. s. w.*, Jena, 1927.

word expressing the phenomenon of "loyalty," "devotion." It is, as A. Lods[8] put it, "a very comprehensive word, which, for want of an adequate equivalent, we are obliged to translate, now by piety, now by mercy, love or grace: it corresponds fairly closely to the Latin *pietas*. . . ."

Taken literally, the term גמילות חסדים[9] is an action that represents a doing something in return, which doing is expressive of a loyalty—or less clumsily, *gemilut ḥasadim* is an act by means of which one demonstrates his response to someone, in obedience to him or out of loyalty to him. In short, it is really an act of piety. And strictly speaking, any action—it need have nothing to do with charity, *ṣedakah*, at all—any action which an individual carried out as a fulfillment of a divine command, was an act of *gemilut ḥasadim*. What we frequently call doing a מצוה (but not only limited to the sense of ἐντολή[10] =charity, though it might include that too) was originally expressed by *gemilut ḥasadim*.

[46] Thus far word surgery. But is there anything in our sources to bear this out? Oddly enough, there is. We read in *Abot de-Rabbi Natan* (p. 21) that Daniel used to engage in *gemilut ḥasadim*.[11] The text continues: ומה הן גמילות
חסדים שהיה דניאל מתעסק בהם; אם תאמר עולות וזבחים מקריב (or) היה מקריב:
בבבל והלא כבר נאמר (Deut. 12:13–14) השמר לך פן תעלה (cf. Schechter's n. 36
עולותיך בכל מקום אשר תראה כי אם במקום אשר יבחר ה' באחד שבטיך שם תעלה עולותיך.
If *gemilut ḥasadim* from the very beginning meant simply "acts of loving-kindness," what kind of question is this? Who would ever dream of asking if the *gemilut ḥasadim* of Daniel were the sacrifices he offered?[12] Moreover, let us hear out *Abot de-Rabbi Natan* to the end. The *gemilut ḥasadim* of Daniel, we saw, could not be "burnt-offerings and sacrifices." אלא מה הן גמילות חסדים שהיה
מתעסק בהן, היה מתקן את הכלה ומשמחה ומלווה את המת ונותן פרוטה לעני[13] ומתפלל שלשה
פעמים בכל יום ותפלתו מתקבלת ברצון שנאמר ודניאל כדי ידע וגו' (Dan. 6:11) [!] So then,
in addition to outfitting and cheering a bride, accompanying the dead, giving a *perutah* to the poor man, prayer, too, is *gemilut ḥasadim*! We have here, therefore, a distinct recollection of a time when *gemilut ḥasadim* still included an act of worship, an act like prayer.

We are not in a position to appreciate, I feel, the opening of the Mishna Peah. אלו דברים, says the Mishna,[14] שאין להן שיעור הפיאה והביכורים והראיון וגמילות
חסדים ותלמוד תורה. Frankly, I don't know what to do with *talmud Torah* here,

---

8. Cited in Rowley, op. cit.
9. Or גמילות חסד—cf. the variant recorded by Lieberman in T. Peah 1.1.
10. On מצוה and ἐντολή, see S. Lieberman in his edition of *Debarim Rabba*, p. 36, n. 10. See also idem, *Hellenism in Jewish Palestine*, N. Y., 1950, p. 189, n. 73 and the reference there cited.
11. "All his days," as the version of the passage in the *Exempla*, ed. Gaster, 133 f. has it.
12. Indeed, note Schechter's difficulty with the passage ad loc.
13. Note that in the *Exempla* version, in addition to presenting some minor variants, the passage stops at this point! Fascinatingly enough, note how *Pirke de-R. Eliezer* (chap. 16) attaches Daniel's praying to *abodah*! Cf. the comment of Luria (no. 4) and *Hagahot*, ibid.
14. Cf. the Tosefta 1.1.

though I don't dare touch it, because I find no authority to omit it. I will only say that in addition to the fact that it strikes me as suspicious in this place—probably due to the influence of the statement in the latter half of the Mishna;[15] that in addition to the fact that [47] in one group of Mishna manuscripts[16] "*talmud Torah*" is wanting; in addition to these facts, apparently Maimonides in his *Code* did not see fit to say of *talmud Torah* what he is prepared to say on the basis of the Mishna, of *peah, bikkurim, reayon* and *gemilut ḥasadim*[17] — and that group of manuscripts I have referred to is a group with Maimonides' Mishna commentary. I must say, had four, rather than five, items in the Mishna been listed, the sentence would have seemed to me more in keeping with certain habitual stylistic features of the Mishna.[18] But I am really afraid to say more about this; and I *need* say no more, for this is not the central issue. The central issue is: What kind of combination is הפיאה והביכורים והראיון and גמילות חסדים? But that does make excellent sense if we recognize that this old sentence of the Mishna still preserves the original signification of *gemilut ḥasadim*, namely, acts of piety, and they may well have been of cultic character, or of social character. They were simply מצוות.

Originally, therefore, *abodah* meant Temple ritual; *gemilut ḥasadim* meant acts of piety.[19] Which brings me to the first pillar, the Torah. What is it? כיצד, as *Abot de-Rabbi Natan* likes to say.

[48] Both versions of *Abot de-Rabbi Natan* explain it, as we have seen, in terms of תלמוד תורה. That is to say, according to *Abot de-Rabbi Natan*, Simeon the Righteous declares that one of the pillars of העולם is the study of Torah. But is that in fact what Simeon the Righteous had in mind?

It is important, I feel, to take note of the exact idiom of Simeon the Righteous. He speaks of *ha-Torah*, not of *Torah* without the definite article. Everyone has observed that in our sources sometimes we come upon the form *ha-Torah*, sometimes *Torah*; and generally it is explained as follows: Once

---

15. Cf. M. Peah 1.1b.

16. Cf. *The Mishna* prepared by the Fellows of the Harry Fischel Institute, Jerusalem, 1945, Peah, p. 6.

17. See *The Mishna*, ibid., comment no. 3 at bottom of page.

18. See indeed M. Peah 1.1b and cf. ARN, chap. 40, p. 119. Note also the number of items listed in T. Peah 1.2.

19. It is worth noting that both in the early and the Palestinian versions of the first benediction of the Amidah, the clause גומל חסדים טובים is wanting; see L. Finkelstein, "The Development of the Amidah," *JQR*, N. S. XVI, p. 143 (on the reading of the benediction in Vitry, cf. the variant recorded there on p. 142). The clause למגמדל חסד עם הדין אכסניא in the story about Hillel the Elder (*Lev. R.* 34.3) is of no help to us. Truth to say, the more that story is analyzed the more its difficulty becomes apparent. For exactly what is the *gemilut ḥesed* Hillel intends for his soul which is ξένος in the body? The story about bathing, which precedes the anecdote about the soul, is clear enough. Obviously the story about the soul has been brought because (a) it is a "counterpart" to the story about the body, and (b) it serves as a homily on the very vocabulary of Prov. 11.17a. But the question, exactly what was it Hillel would do for his soul, still remains. Note too the rather interesting reading preserved by the Meiri in S. Lieberman, *J. N. Epstein Jubilee Volume*, Jerusalem, 1950, p. 114. This story about Hillel, by the way is *not* given in ARNB chap. 30, p. 66, though the story of bathing the body is told there.

Torah was personified, reference could be made to it without a definite article, as we refer to people when we speak of them by name.[20] But in essence there is nothing to distinguish *ha-Torah* from *Torah*. I wonder.

The Mishna *Abot* begins: משה קבל תורה מסיני. So far as I know[21] not one manuscript or edition ever read *ha-Torah*. *Abot de-Rabbi Natan* in both versions (pp. 1–2) preserves the same form: משה נתקדש בענן וקבל תורה מסיני; על ידי משה נתנה תורה בסיני; משה קבל תורה מסיני (twice in Version B). The commentators[22] who insist that the phrase is intended to underscore that Moses received the Oral Torah too, are undoubtedly right and reveal a very delicate sensitivity. I am tempted to put it even more strongly: In the time of Simeon the Righteous, *Torah* without the article was intended to express what we express by "Oral Tradition," תורה שבעל פה. The first Mishna in the first chapter of *Abot* has come to validate the authority of the sages, to demonstrate that what they teach and say is not of their own invention but can be traced back through successive links to Moses.[23] That the written Torah was authoritative nobody questioned. The question was: Have the teachings of the sages authority? What is it that the [49] Sadducees challenged? "The Pharisees," writes Josephus in a very well known passage,[24]

had passed on to the people certain regulations handed down by former generations and not recorded in the Laws of Moses, for which reason they are rejected by the Sadducean group, who hold that only those regulations should be considered valid which were written down (in Scripture), and that those which had been handed down by former generations (i.e., by the fathers, $\tau\hat{\omega}\nu$ $\pi\alpha\tau\acute{\epsilon}\rho\omega\nu$) need not be observed. And concerning these matters the two parties came to have controversies and serious differences. . . .

An early Mishnaic statement[25] —which really tries to establish what from the Pharisaic point of view would be regarded as heretical, and reflects the three theological points at issue with the Sadducees[26]—reads: ואלו שאין להם חלק לעוה"ב האומר אין תחיית המתים[27] ואין תורה מן השמים ואפיקורס. Here again, the reading,

20. Cf. L. Ginzberg in M. Kadushin, "Aspects of the Rabbinic Concept of Israel," *HUCA*, XIX, 1946, p. 64, n. 30; see also Ginzberg's comments in idem, *Organic Thinking*, New York, 1938, p. 272, n. 68.

21. See the Hebrew text in C. Taylor, *Sayings of the Jewish Fathers*, Cambridge, 1897–1900.

22. Cf. Vitry, etc.

23. See E. Bickerman's essay "La Chaîne de la Tradition Pharisienne" in *RB*, LIX, 1952, pp. 44ff.

24. *Antiq.* XIII, 10.6, Loeb Classics, VII, pp. 376–377.

25. M. Sanhedrin 10.1. On the way this Mishna begins, see the readings in MS Kaufmann and Loewe, *The Mishnah*, Cambridge, 1883, p. 128a. MS Parma and the Munich MS of the Talmud do have the introductory formula "All Israel" etc. See further the discussion in the reference cited below, n. 27.

26. Cf. Bickerman, op. cit., p. 47, n. 4.

27. On the words מן התורה cf. L. Finkelstein, *Mabo le-Massektot Abot ve-Abot d'Rabbi Natan*, New York, 1950, p. 229, n.

apparently everywhere,[28] is not *ha-Torah*, but *Torah*. The Sadducees did *not* deny that Scripture was מן השמים; what they denied was that תורה שבעל פה, the Oral Tradition, was מן השמים. They denied that משה קבל תורה מסיני; they never would have denied that משה קבל את התורה מסיני.

I should like to go on calling attention to the fact that in our sources we always read of תלמוד תורה and not התלמוד התורה;[29] that [50] on the other hand apparently one is עוסק בתורה.[30] I admit I cannot yet explain to my own full satisfaction why we say ספר תורה and not ספר התורה. But I do not want to get too far afield, particularly before I have gathered all the data I need. The point I wish to make is that in the time of Simeon the Righteous the expression *ha-Torah* did not yet take on the rich color of the concept *talmud Torah*. For the large canvas which included oral traditions enlarging upon the Written Torah, one used the expression *Torah*, without the definite article. *Ha-Torah* referred more narrowly to the books of the Written Torah which were recognized as authoritative, perhaps the Torah of Moses. When Simeon the Righteous said that one of the pillars was *ha-Torah* he meant the books of the Torah.[31]

What he gives us therefore, one might say, is three purely [51] religious

---

28. So in the regular editions of the Mishna and in the Naples edition as well as in the Kaufmann and Parma MSS and in Loewe, *The Mishnah*. And despite a peculiar dittography, the Munich MS of the Talmud has the same reading.

29. So far as I know the only occurrence of Torah in an inflected form when connected with Talmud is in the אהבה רבה prayer (I do not know how to account for the expression תלמוד תורתך in ARNB, p. 32, ll. 2–3 from the bottom. There really are many difficulties with that version of the story about R. Eliezer, as an examination of the text will reveal. Interestingly enough, the version of this story in *Pirke de-R. Eliezer*—Warsaw, 1852, 4b—which is so close to that of ARNB, does *not* have ושמחתי בתלמוד תורתך. It would not surprise me if the reading in ARNB were really a "later" expansion, by way of explanation, of ועתה שבאתי לראותך וראיתי כל (השבח הזה); see Baer, *Seder Abodat Yisrael*, p. 80—ולקים את כל דברי תלמוד תורתך—and the phrase seems to me "inflated." [See now also *Leshonenu* XXVII–XXVIII, p. 216, photostat of prayer.] Needless to say, I am not suggesting that it be emended in any way, for that reading occurs in R. Amram's order (cf. D. Hedegård, *Seder R. Amram Gaon*, Motala, 1951, Hebrew section, p. 20), in Saadia Gaon's *Siddur* (ed. Davidson, Assaf, Joel; Jerusalem, 1941, p. 14) and in a number of *siddurim* and *mahzorim* MSS I have examined in the library of the Jewish Theological Seminary of America (and I want to thank the librarians, G. Cohen and N. Sarna, for their kindness). Interestingly enough, however, in two Yemenite MSS (MS, JTS, EMC 414/241, folio 144b and MS, JTS, S.A. 07, ENA 456) of the *Code* of Maimonides, the reading is ונשמח ונעלוז בדברי תורתך. A very queer reading is preserved in the Louis M. Rabinowitz MS of the code: ולקיים את כל תלמוד דברי קרשיך את דברי תלמוד תורתיך באהבה. Professor Shalom Spiegel, whom I consulted on the reading of that clause (כל דברי תלמוד תורתך) in the prayer, suggests tentatively that if the phrase is inflated, it might reflect the anti-Karaite polemical emphasis R. Amram Gaon was eager to make, particularly in a blessing where Torah is so central a theme.

Apparently with the verb עשה (which sometimes refers to study and sometimes to practice; cf. S. Abramson in *Leshonénu*, vol. 5714, pp. 61–65) one may say either *Torah* or *ha-Torah* (or *Torah* in an inflected form).

30. On the expression עוסקי תורתך in Berakot 11b cf. *Dikduke Soferim*, ad loc., that it is wanting in the MSS.

31. I would like to underscore that I am speaking of the time of Simeon the Righteous and that this distinction between *Torah* and *ha-Torah* which is suggested is intended only for early statements, say, up to the time of Johanan ben Zakkai. What the distinction is between *Torah* and *ha-Torah*, if any, in later statements, is another matter entirely.

pillars. The *olam* rests on the books of the Torah, the Temple cult, and acts of *pietas*.

And now, I believe, we are able truly to appreciate the grandeur of Rabban Johanan ben Zakkai's achievement. We read in *Abot de-Rabbi Natan*[32] that when Rabban Johanan was finally received by Vespasian and the conqueror allowed the sage to make a request, Rabban Johanan said: "I ask of you only Jabneh where I might go ואשנה בה לתלמידי ואקבע בה תפלה ואעשה בה כל מצות." Here are the three pillars of Simeon the Righteous brought to reinforcement at a moment when for almost every other Jew the end had come. Johanan ben Zakkai made of *ha-Torah*, the pillar of studying and teaching Torah (note, Version A reads ואשנה בה לתלמידי; Version B reads ואלמוד בה תורה).[33] Out of Temple worship what was to be done? The ancient cult dramatizing man's service to God, he now redefined in terms of prayer (ואקבע בה תפלה) or other acts like prayer.[34] Out of *gemilut ḥasadim*, acts of *pietas*, which he wanted to carry out—ואעשה בה כל מצות, or as Version B reads ואעשה בה שאר כל המצות—he would underscore those acts which man carries out in an exemplary relation with his fellow man. And *gemilut ḥasadim* thus become the acts of loving-kindness so typical of those who are known as רחמנים בני רחמנים. Is it any wonder that at least three of the five famous disciples Rabban Johanan ben Zakkai had were so impressed by the new emphasis their master gave to *gemilut ḥasa-dim*—after all, he had comforted Rabbi Joshua with the daring words: Don't fear, or, (no less!) אל ירע לך, יש לנו כפרה אחת שהיא כמותה-ז. א. כמו בית המקדש-ואיזה הוא גמילות חסדים שנאמר כי חסד חפצתי ולא זבח. Is it any wonder that disciples of such a teacher should be eager to emphasize in their turn [52] יהי כבוד חברך חביב עליך כשלך; עין הרע ויצר הרע ושנאת הבריות מוציאין את האדם מן העולם; יהי ממון חברך חביב עליך כשלך?"

And what do these statements mean? שכשם שרואה את כבודו כך יהא אדם רואה את כבוד חברו. וכשם שאין אדם רוצה שיצא שם רע על כבודו, כך יהא אדם רוצה שלא להוציא שם רע על כבודו של חברו (ARN, p. 60). יהי כבוד חבירך חביב עליך כשלך-הוי חס על כבוד בניו ובנותיו. אם רוצה את שלא יטול אדם את שלך, אף את לא תיטול את של חבירך. אם רוצה את שלא יאמר אחריך דבר, אף אתה לא תאמר אחריו דבר (ARNB, p. 60). שכשם שאדם רואה את ביתו, כך יהא רואה ביתו של חברו. וכשם שאדם רוצה שלא להוציא שם רע על אשתו ובניו, כך יהא אדם רוצה שלא להוציא שם רע על אשת חברו ועל בניו של חברו (ARN, p. 62). שלא תהא עינו של אדם רעה בממונו של חברו, לא בבניו ולא בבנותיו ולא בצאנו ולא בבקרו ולא בכל מה שיש בידו (ARNB, p. 63). כשם שאדם רואה את ממונו, כך יהא רואה את ממון חברו; וכשם שאדם רוצה שלא יצא שם רע על ממון שלו, כך יהיה רוצה שלא יצא שם רע על ממון חברו

---

32. Version A, chap. 4, p. 23; note the reading in Version B, chap. 6, p. 19. This "request" is not recorded in the version of the story as preserved in B. Gittin 56a–b or *Lam. R.* 1.31.

33. That Shammai's famous saying עשה תורתך קבע need not apply to the "large" concept of *talmud Torah* is evident from the comments of *Abot de-Rabbi Natan* (in both versions!); cf. ARN, pp. 46 and 56. That Hillel's ומקרבן לתורה similarly does not apply to *talmud Torah* is evident from ARN (both versions), p. 53. Note indeed an interesting "slip" in ARNB, ibid.

34. Note Version B ואעשה בה ציצית; but cf. Schechter's note ad loc.

35. M. Abot 2.10, 11, 12.

הוי חס על ממון חברך כשלך ועל ממון בניו ובנותיו; ואם רוצה אתה שלא .(ARNB, p. 65)
יטול אדם את שלך, אף אתה אל תיטול את שלו (ARNB, p. 65).

Note well how *Abot de-Rabbi Natan* in both versions has captured the preoccupations—I can't resist saying, the fixation—of Rabbi Eliezer and Rabbi Joshua and Rabbi Yose. They certainly understood how revolutionary was Rabban Joḥanan ben Zakkai's reinterpretation.

Of course you will have observed that I have consistently avoided translating העולם in Simeon the Righteous' saying. For I must confess I am no longer sure that Simeon is speaking about the universe, the world. Here I do not want to speak categorically at all; I wish merely to raise questions.

Everyone knows that in Scripture the word עולם is used in a temporal sense. And even that so-called one exception in Ecclesiastes 3:11, as H. L. Ginsberg has shown,[36] can at best mean something like "eternity," if it is not in the last analysis to be emended to העמל. Since in rabbinic literature *olam* appears as world, for example, העולם מתחלה לא נברא אלא בחסד, we have gotten into the habit of saying that the first one to use *olam* in the new sense is Simeon the Righteous. But really, why? Is not the burden of proof on those who *say* he is the first to use it in [53] the sense of "world"? Would it not be more logical to assume that Simeon is still using the old term in the old way, in its temporal sense, and what he is saying in effect is, The Age—that is to say, your whole *future*[37] —is supported by three pillars?

For the more we study the age Simeon lived in—about 200 B.C.E.[38] —the more we read Maccabees and Jubilees, the more distinctly we feel the force of his declaration—it is not just a bon mot, it is not merely a felicitous epigram. It is really a program.[39] At a time when there were those who

> persuaded many, saying: "Let us go and make a covenant with the nations that are round about us; for since we separated ourselves from them many evils have come upon us." And the saying appeared good in their eyes; and as certain of the people were eager to carry this out, they went to the king, and he gave them authority to introduce the customs of the Gentiles. And they built a gymnasium in Jerusalem according to the manner of the Gentiles. They also submitted themselves to uncircumcision, and repudiated the holy covenant; yea, they joined themselves to the Gentiles, and sold themselves to do evil (I Macc. 1:11ff.);

at a time when basic biblical commandments seemed to many apparently so only of parochial and transient importance, that the author of Jubilees had to keep insisting that one commandment after another had been observed by angels of the presence in heaven from the beginning of time, had been

---

36. *Proceedings, AAJR*, XXI, 1952, p. 39.
37. Cf. the parallel terms לעולם הבא and לעתיד לבא. See also L. Finkelstein, *Mabo*, pp. 220–221 for speculations on *olam* still being used in a temporal sense in early rabbinic literature.
38. Cf. G. F. Moore in *Israel Abrahams Memorial Volume*, New York, 1927, pp. 348–364.
39. I hope to amplify on this point in a forthcoming monograph.

observed by the patriarchs long before Sinai and Moses—at a time, in other words (for I really am going on too long), when there was a spreading temptation to feel that the books of the Torah were, to be sure, important in a sense, but there are other books one ought to read too;[40] when everyone appreciated that the Temple service, to be sure, was important, but a civilized man ought not cut himself off from all other forms of worship, and so if there is [54] a spectacular celebration of Tyre, a cultivated high priest could do no less than send envoys (best that they be polished Antiochene citizens rather than the typical Jerusalemite with no knowledge of savoir faire)[41] to represent Jerusalem with a h .ndsome gift for the sacrifice of Heracles (II Macc. 4:18f.); at a time when a number of native acts of piety had become either no more than quaint or downright embarrassing; at a time, in short, when there were many who felt that the future of Jerusalem society rested on more cosmopolitan, less parochial, commitments;—at a time like this Simeon the Righteous rose in defense of the *tradition*, in defense of the *old* values, rose to declare that *these* books of the Torah, *this* particular Temple service, *these* acts and works of piety were the pillars that would sustain them all. Their future would rest on *these* three old, established pillars. These were pillars, like the famous pillars of Wisdom (Prov. 9:1). And Wisdom, as everyone knew, indeed as Sirach made clear again and again,[42] was really the Torah.

Let me repeat, I am not sure that *olam* is to be taken in a temporal sense in Simeon's saying, particularly since pillars most naturally would support a structure, something occupying space, rather than something abstract like time.[43] But I cannot help thinking *olam* received the sense of world, in reinterpretation by Rabban Joḥanan ben Zakkai. It is to him, or at least to his school, that I would attribute עולם חסד יבנה as meaning העולם מתחלה לא נברא אלא בחסד. I do this in the light of what we saw him do to *gemilut ḥasadim:* He took an old concept and gave it a new direction! The times he lived in and the catastrophes he witnessed really seemed to put an end to Jewish existence. Brutalization was increasing;[44] the Zealots and *Sicarii* were destroying provisions on which the besieged population [55] depended; they would not be restrained even though it was becoming clear (to him at least) that the Temple would be reduced to ashes.[45] This extraordinary sage recognized that unless a

40. Note the well-known protest in Ecclesiastes 12.12, and on the dating of Koheleth, cf. H. L. Ginsberg, *Studies in Koheleth* (New York, 1950), pp. 42, 44.

41. On these "Antiochenes" see E. Bickermann, *Der Gott der Makkabäer*, Berlin, 1937, pp. 59ff. (comp. A. Tcherikower in *Epstein Jubilee Volume*, pp. 61ff. and F.-M. Abel, *Les Livres des Maccabées*, Paris, 1949, pp. 331f., nn. on II Mac. 4.9 and 4.18ff.

42. See also H. A. Wolfson, *Philo*, Cambridge, Mass., 1947, pp. 21ff.

43. And when you stop to think of it, Simeon after all does not use the noun "pillars" (as Professor H. L. Ginsberg says to me); he speaks of three *debarim*. That he has pillars in mind *as an image*, is borne out by the verb he uses, *omed*.

44. משרבו המנאפים, משרבו הרצחנין; see M. Sotah 9.9 and T. Sotah 14.1

45. Cf. ARN, pp. 19–20, 22f., 31, 32f., J. Goldin, *The Fathers According to Rabbi Nathan*, New Haven, 1955, pp. 184f. and nn. 32–37.

new vitality were put into the old concepts, the destruction of the Temple and the state might well mean the destruction of the people: and not just the people, but the life this people was chosen to exemplify. And so he now declared—I don't mean merely for pragmatic reasons; I am sure he felt it was so!—*gemilut ḥasadim* are the acts of piety, the מצות, which apply to the relations of men to each other—and these are one of the chief pillars of the *universe*.[46] Indeed, "from the very first, the world was created only with mercy, as it is said, *For I have said, The world is built with mercy; in the very heavens Thou dost establish Thy faithfulness*" (Ps. 89:3). The future had to be based on such a pillar, for the world from its beginning was brought into being on this very basis. Mercy was not only a quality for the ages; it was a property in the nature of the world—an ingredient, an element of God's universe. Note indeed what was his conception of the pillar of Torah: אם עשית תורתך הרבה אל תחזיק טובה לעצמך כי לכך נו צ ר ת, לפי שלא נוצרו הבריות אלא על מנת שיתעסקו בתורה.[47] Study of the Torah was not merely a meritorious act for which man would be rewarded. It was an act which constituted the very purpose for which man was *created*!

And note, too, that it is beginning with Rabban Joḥanan ben Zakkai's disciples that sages receive the *title* "Rabbi," a title unquestionably reflecting an *authority* they are being invested with. Apparently this was part of the large, new program of *talmud Torah. Everyone* must study Torah—this is the new pillar—and henceforth the man of authority—not just of influence[48] [56] but of authority—is the rabbi, the sage who goes through the discipline of a תלמיד חכמים[49] and becomes a master of Torah. Little wonder then that Rabban Joḥanan ben Zakkai could be hailed as אב לחכמה אב לדורות.[50]

But we began with Simeon the Righteous; let us therefore conclude with him. He is the author of the following statement:[51] On three things the age (or

---

46. Is there an echo of this in the exclamation at the time of Rabban Joḥanan ben Zakkai's death? ע מ ו ד הגבוה נר ה ע ו ל ם, פטיש החזק—ARN, chap. 25, p. 79; cf. the reading in B. Berakot 28b, and on פטיש החזק see *Dikduke Soferim*, ad loc. On the expression נר ישראל see G. Allon, *Mehkarim be-Toledot Yisrael*, I, Tel Aviv, 1957, p. 187. On "pillars of the world," cf. the expression in Ps. 75.4 and Job 9.6; on "pillars of the heavens (skies)," cf. Job 26.11.

47. ARN, p. 58; cf. ARNB, p. 66. On the reading of R. Joḥanan's saying as preserved in Abot 2.8, see also Taylor, op. cit., ad loc.

48. That teachers had influence was of course true even before the time of Joḥanan ben Zakkai; see the story in Josephus on the "two doctors with a reputation as profound experts in the laws of their country, who consequently enjoyed the highest esteem of the whole nation. . . . Their lectures on the laws were attended by a large youthful audience, and day after day they drew together quite an army of men in their prime" (*War*, I, 33.1).

49. See L. Ginzberg, *Students, Scholars and Saints*, Philadelphia, 1928, p. 267, n. 5.

50. ARNB, chap. 28, p. 57; cf. J. Nedarim, chap. 5, end.

51. That is the meaning of הוא היה אומר. The clause does not mean, "he used to say," (cf. the commentary of Meiri and Duran on 1.2). Note that throughout Pirke Abot the only time we get the expression היה אומר is with a pronoun. Not once does it occur as ר' פלוני היה אומר. The form היה אומר occurs only with a pronoun and either (a) after one statement has already been cited in the name of a sage and then still another saying by him is cited—in which event הוא היה אומר seems to mean something like "he was also the author of" the following; or (b) after something has been reported about the sage, and *then* he is cited—for example, "Antigonus of Soko took over from Simeon the Righteous. הוא היה אומר וכו': in which event the clause seems to mean, In

the world, if you insist) stands—on the Torah, on the Temple Service, and on Acts of Piety.[52]

Postscript

[57] Despite the number of legends preserved in talmudic literature,[53] and despite the eulogy by Sirach (50), it has never really been explained satisfactorily[54] why Simeon is the only one of the sages to be called הצדיק. Granted that he deserved the title δίκαιος; but were *none* of the later sages entitled to such a characterization? Why only Simeon?

I would like to suggest that the explanation of the term as attached to Simeon's name, merited though it was no doubt,[55] does not lie in any contrast intended between the character of Simeon and other, later sages, or in any emphasis over against the term *ḥasid*,[56] but in "literary usage."

The one human being in Scripture called צדיק is Noah (Gen. 6:9). Neither Abraham, nor Moses, nor Elijah, nor any other biblical hero is so called, *in Scripture itself*.[57] Now, Noah is the first biblical personality (after Adam) about whom we have a more than casual account, more than a verse or two report; he might indeed be described as the first distinct character whose history is the

---

addition to what was reported of So-and-so, he was also the author of the following saying. In 1.1 where we read of the Men of the Great Assembly הם אמרו, the meaning seems also to be, "They were the authors of," for in ARNB, p. 2 the form is (twice!) היו אומרים (though once ואנשי כה״ג היו אומרים). In 4.5, when R. Zadok *quotes* Hillel the reading is not הלל היה אומר but וכך היה הלל אומר. It may be worth noting that one of the Geniza fragments, TS, E3, no. 61, has the reading וכך הלל אומר.

52. Cf. J. Goldin, *The Living Talmud, the Wisdom of the Fathers*, New York, 1957, p. 46. On the other hand, *olam* in the saying of R. Simeon ben Gamaliel (Abot 1.18) is of course "world." That the reading קים is to be preferred (despite J. Taanit 4.2, 68a), cf. Taylor, op cit., II, p. 139; see also R. Jonah and Meiri on Abot 1.2. In this connection perhaps it is worth observing that in a number of Pirke Abot sayings by "later" sages, there is a kind of commentary on (or echo of) sayings and parts of sayings by "earlier" sages: for example, comp. 1.2 and 1.18, 1.6 and 1.16, 2.1 (last part) and 3.1; note also 4.5 (R. Zadok). But I hope to discuss this phenomenon at length in a subsequent study. [On עלם cf. also H. L. Ginsberg, קהלת on Eccl. 1:10, Tel Aviv–Jerusalem, 1961, לעלמים.]

53. Cf. the references in Taylor, *Sayings of the Jewish Fathers*, I, p. 12, and see A. Büchler, *Studies in Jewish History*, Oxford, 1956, pp. 32ff.

54. Z. Frankel (*Darke Ha-Mishnah*, Warsaw, 1923, p. 30), who, however, identifies our Simeon with Simeon I, cites Josephus (*Antiq.* XII, 2:5) by way of explanation: "Simeon, who was surnamed the Just because of both his piety toward God and his benevolence to his countrymen." According to Smend (cited in Charles, *Apocrypha and Pseudepigrapha*, I, p. 507), Simeon (II) received this title "because he was the last of the house of Zadok to observe the Law."

55. Not only because Sirach sings such high praises of him; why otherwise should rabbinic tradition remember him by name and so favorably?

56. On the terms צדיק and חסיד, see S. Lieberman, *Greek in Jewish Palestine*, N. Y., 1942, pp. 69ff.

57. In post-biblical literature, the term is of course applied to other biblical personalities, especially Joseph; cf. ARN, chap. 16, p. 63, ARNB, p. 36, n. 8; see also *Wisdom of Solomon*, 10:13—in 10:10 Jacob is also referred to as *dikaios*—and comp. Testament of Benjamin 5:5; cf. Ginzberg, *Legends*, V, 324–325. For a non-biblical person so called see ARN, chap. 3, p. 17.

subject of detailed narrative. And what was he [58] according to that history? The one righteous person in a generation of the wicked, indeed the only one of that generation who deserved to survive.[58] Recalling him, Sirach says, in fact, that there was κατάλειμμα τῆ γῆ[59] (Ecclus. 44:17).

If we stop to think of it, Simeon is the *first* of the individual sages in the development of the Oral Torah whom we know of by name. Further, if we recall what his emphasis was in an age when Hellenism was aggressively ascendant, if we recall that to Hasideans and their later descendants, Hellenists were nothing less than מרשיעי ברית[60] it is hardly surprising that the chief antagonist of a hellenizing generation should later come to be called by that title the first righteous man had, הצדיק.

One more minor point worth paying some attention to. When he spoke of Noah, Sirach had referred to being κατάλειμμα, שארית.[61] Is there some echo of this in the Pirke Abot (and ARN) statement that Simeon was משירי the Great Assembly?[62] Note that Pirke Abot always reads משירי כנסת הגדולה, and the same reading recurs in ARNB (ARNA—p. 18—reads משירי אנשי כנסת הגדולה). Is the intention of the report that Simeon was משירי כנסת הגדולה, *in part* to underscore that he was of the few worthy to survive the *age*, the *generation*, of the Keneset Ha-gedolah?

I do wish to press this last point; but it seems to me worth noting that in connection with the biblical צדיק, a later author uses the term κατάλειμμα, and that Abot speaks of its צדיק as "of the *survivors*."

In short, to understand the term הצדיק as applied to Simeon, I suggest we look for the cue in the similar application of the term in Scripture.

58. Cf. Ginzberg, *Legends*, V. p. 179.
59. Cf. the critical note in Charles, *Apocrypha and Pseudepigrapha*, ad loc.
60. Dan. 11:32.
61. Cf. M. Z. Segal, *Sefer Ben-Sira Ha-Shalem*, p. 306.
62. Cf. Taylor, *Sayings*, II, p. 133.

The First Pair (Yose Ben Yoezer and Yose Ben Yohanan) or the Home of a Pharisee[*]

I

[41] No student of *Pirqei 'Avot* or *'Avot de-Rabbi Natan* can have failed to observe that the sayings of the Sages in the first chapter of PA and the sayings of the disciples of Yohanan ben Zakkai[1] inside the second [42] chapter are transmitted in a style distinguished by threeness. Occasional seeming departures from this style have been plausibly explained by reference to the readings of ARN or to variant manuscript readings.[2] We may safely say, therefore, that the triadic character of all these sayings reflects stylization,[3] resort to a particular

[*] I am grateful to the American Council of Learned Societies for the grant which made possible my study of the *Pirqei 'Avot* manuscripts at the Bodleian, and thus the preparation of the present paper.

Whether the pairs are historical or historicizations has no bearing on this paper; what is attributed to these teachers is what we are analyzing.

1. And perhaps also of Yohanan ben Zakkai himself, if we adopt the reading of his saying in Version A of ARN (p. 58), thus: "(a) If thou hast wrought much in thy study of Torah, take no credit for thyself, (b) for to this end wast thou created: (c) for men were created only on condition that they study Torah." Contrast the reading in PA 2:8, beginning. Note also Version B, pp. 58, 66. On ʿasah torah, cf. Shraga Abramson, "Mi-leshon hakhamim," *Leshonénu* 19 (5714): 61ff.

2. Cf. David Hoffmann, *Die erste Mischna* (Berline, 1881–82), pp. 26f. (Hebrew version, Berlin, 1913, p. 33); Louis Finkelstein, *Mavo lemassekhtot Avot ve-Avot d'Rabbi Natan* (New York, 1950), 42; Judah Goldin, "Mashehu ʿal beit midrasho shel Rabban Yohanan ben Zakkai," in *Harry A. Wolfson Jubilee Volume*, 3 vols. (Jerusalem, 1965), Hebrew vol., pp. 72ff.

3. Cf. Chanoch Albeck, *Mishnah, Nashim* (Jerusalem, 1954), p. 342, top. Perhaps under the influence of Isa. 6:3 or Ezek. 21:32. See now a suggestion for an interesting new example, Yaakov Sussman, "The Boundaries of 'Eretz Israel'" (Hebrew), *Tarbiz* 45 (1976): 250, n. 258. On the subject of stylization, cf. also H. A. Fischel, *Rabbinic Literature and Greco-Roman Philosophy* (Leiden, 1973).

rhetorical form for statements from the earliest spokesmen of the Oral Torah (the *'Anshei Keneset ha-Gedolah*, approximately 250 B.C.E.) down through Yoḥanan ben Zakkai's best known disciples (at the end of the first and beginning of the second century C.E.), before and after the destruction of the Temple. (Even that catastrophe could not block the advance of the uninterrupted continuity of the oral tradition.) And if each of the sayings exhibits three clauses or phrases or items or other kinds of threefold, it may very well be that not three separate, independent, unrelated things, but one principal concern, formulated in the stylized manner, is being underscored.

Not always, of course. The Mishnah is perfectly capable of taking "three things" strictly and literally, as can be seen, for example, in M. Beiṣah 2:8/ʿEduyot 3:12, or ʿEduyot 2:5 or 2:7–8 or Shabbat 2:7 or in that long list of threes and classifications compiled in the twenty-fourth chapter of M. Kelim. But this does not eliminate the possibility that there are three things with a single law or objective in mind: note M. ʿEduyot 2:6. "Three things," in other words, in halakhic contexts, are likely to mean three things literally; but the expression can also refer to three cases governed by one law, or to the thought that "the world is established by three things" (PA 1:18)—three terms whose aim is to emphasize one basic idea. Antigonus of Soko said (PA 1:3): "(a) Be not like slaves who serve their master for the sake [43] of an allowance;[4] (b) be rather like slaves who serve their master with no thoughts of an allowance; (c) and let the fear of Heaven be upon you." The last clause is what the first two were headed toward. "On three things the age [or, the world] stands" (PA 1:2): It is on three pillars that the particular age or the whole world rests. Judah ben Tabbai said (PA 1:8): "(a) Do not play the part of chief justice;[5] (b) and when there are litigants standing before thee, look upon them as likely to be guilty; (c) but when they depart from thy presence, look upon them as likely to be innocent, as soon as they have accepted the sentence." Three clauses with one intention, to remind judges on the bench how to behave.

II

It should be noted that in the block of PA sayings to which we have referred, there occurs a change that deserves some attention. In the first three *mishnayot* of the first chapter of PA the exhortation or observation is either in the second person plural or in impersonal, general terms. Thus, the *'Anshei Keneset ha-Gedolah* say, *Hevu* (be), plural, *haʿamidu* (raise), *ʿasu* (make); Antigonus says,

---

4. Cf. E. J. Bickerman, "The Maxim of Antigonus of Socho," *Harvard Theological Review* 44 (1951): 153–65.

5. For this translation, cf. Julius Theodor's note in Gen. R. 50:3, p. 519, to line 5; Charles Taylor, *Sayings of the Jewish Fathers* (New York, 1969), "Notes on the Text," p. 137; E. Y. Kutscher, *Words and Their History* (Hebrew, Jerusalem, 1961), pp. 90–91. With "accepting the sentence," contrast Adam's behavior, in Pesiqta Rabbati (ed. Meir Friedmann, Vienna, 1880), p. 26b (Resh Laqish), after sentence was passed. On what is expected of relatives of convicted persons, cf. M. Sanhedrin 6:6.

'*Al tihyu* (Be not), plural, '*ella hevu* (but be), and let the fear of Heaven be upon you (plural, '*aleikhem*). Simeon the Righteous spoke of the age or world (*ha-'olam*):[6] a general statement, an observation (doubtless with homiletical overtones). However, from the moment we come upon the sayings of t! ɔ first Pair, everything is exhortation in second person singular (on 1:11, see below; I am unable to explain the exception in R. Joshua's "generalized" saying in 2:11). A shift from plural and general to second person singular, and a well-nigh consistent singular at that, must reflect something happening in the culture of a society, and I would like to put it this way: the first three PA sayings are addressed to (Jewish) society at [44] large, so to speak. The sayings may indeed be directed to a particular audience at the outset, but that audience is regarded as representative of the whole community regardless of differentiations or affiliations. You, plural, do this or that. The fundamental pillars of this age or of the world are the following—a general statement addressed to all who might care to listen. But beginning with the first Pair, it is consistently "thou," "thee," "thine," "thy," as though one were talking not just to an audience at large but to members of one's own circle or profession or party, almost with an intimacy, with directness, with a message especially appropriate to those who share the speaker's convictions. This is how a master addresses his disciples or colleagues. Thus, the plural of PA 1:11 is no exception. It is a direct warning to the *ḥakhamim*, the scholars: Beware of what you say, lest you and your disciples meet with disaster (and the name of Heaven be profaned).

(Obviously we are not commenting here on the additional sayings of Hillel in chapter 1 or on the closing sayings of this chapter or on the "interruption" in the first part of chapter 2 before 2:8).

In other words, if this is true, Yose ben Yoezer and Yose ben Yoḥanan may be the first (or be remembered or imagined as the first) leaders of the pharisaic party, quoted in this eminently pharisaic-rabbinic document, PA.[7] It has been observed by other scholars also that in *Antiquities* 13.171ff., when Josephus introduces the three famous *haireseis*, he is in the midst of his account of affairs under Jonathan the high priest.[8] The description of the sects follows immediately upon the report of the renewed treaties with Rome and Sparta (13.163–70) in 143 B.C.E. Why Josephus should have inserted the passage on the sects at this point is not clear.[9] Nevertheless, this does not allow us to say that the Pharisees came into being at that moment. But it does allow us to say that

6. Cf. Judah Goldin, "The Three Pillars of Simeon the Righteous," in *Proceedings of the American Academy for Jewish Research* 27 (1958): 43ff.

7. Note the very beginning of PA 1:1 on the transmission of the oral plus the written Torah, as recognized by the commentators.

8. Cf. Emil Schürer, *Geschichte des jüdischen Volkes*, 3rd ed., 2 vols. (Leipzig, 1898–1902), 2: 388; Louis Ginzberg, "Meqomah shel ha-halakhah," in '*Al halakhah ve-'aggadah* (Tel Aviv, 1960), p. 22; Louis Finkelstein, *The Pharisees* (Philadelphia, 1962) 606ff.; idem, *Haperushim* (New York, 1950), n. 119 (pp. 33f.). But see also idem, *Pharisaism in the Making* (New York, 1972), pp. 175–86.

9. Cf. J. A. Goldstein, *I Maccabees* (New York, 1967): pp. 65–66, 170.

though inchoately groups were forming for about two or three decades before that, from about 170 B.C.E. on—when attitudes began to harden more and more because of the deteriorating behavior of hellenizers, the Syrian offensive against the Jewish religion, and the reverses and successes of the Maccabean wars—by the time of Jonathan, [45] and certainly by the time of John Hyrcanus, there were distinct parties, crystallized and organized; their main beliefs on certain issues standing out clearly as platforms, and in debate with each other.[10] Inevitably, however, there was debate also within each party:[11] Argumentativeness was always to be true of the rabbinic academies, as of all academies.

At some time between approximately 165 and 130 B.C.E., the two Yoses served as leaders of the pharisaic *hairesis.* Thanks to PA and ARN we can recover, I believe, what these teachers-leaders were concerned with and urged upon their disciples-followers.[12] Let us for the present consider the statements of the first Pair.

III

Yose ben Yoezer said: "(a) Let thy home be (*yehi beitkha*; Codex Kaufmann: *beitakh*) a meeting-place (*beit va'ad*) for the Sages, (b) and be thou covered with the dust [stirred up] by their feet, (c) and thirstily do thou drink their words" (cf. Isa. 55:1).[13] Three clauses to one end.

What is the theme? The kind of home a Pharisee ought to make, according to Yose ben Yoezer, for, as we shall see shortly, there is another view of the matter. The home of a Pharisee ought to be a *beit va'ad* for the men of *ḥokhmah,* the men of learning, the scholars, the teachers. Indeed, the host ought to regard himself as subservient to them, humbly thirsting for their words as they hold forth.

A *beit va'ad* is an indoor locale where people are in the habit of assembling or meeting for some purpose. In our own age and circle we might say, "Let's meet at the Faculty Club," and a *beit va'ad* would be just that: People met at a spot which had been selected or had become known as a favorite meeting-place.[14] And truly that is all, as we can tell from the comment in Mekhilta, Kaspa 4 (ed. J. Z. Lauterbach, 3 vols. [Philadelphia, 1933–35], 3:180), on the verse (Exod. 23:13), "Make no mention of the names of [46] other gods."[15] . . .

10. Cf. S. W. Baron, *Social and Religious History of the Jews* 2 (Philadelphia and New York, 1952): 38ff. and notes ad loc.

11. Cf. Louis Ginzberg, "Meqomah shel ha-halakhah," 22ff.

12. Cf. *Encyclopaedia Judaica* (Jerusalem, 1972), s.v. "Avot."

13. PA 1:4. The translation "home" is deliberate, to state that our concern is not with real estate property, but with *chez toi.*

In Bodleian MS Opp. Add. 4to, 62 (Neubauer 1065), fol. 107v, Yose ben Yoḥanan is quoted first and then Yose ben Yoezer (momentary scribal lapse?).

14. Cf. Abba Bendavid, "'Al sifrei 'atiqot: Beit She'arim," *Leshonénu la-'am* 23 (5732): 248.

15. Equals the "gods of others," i.e., of gentiles; cf. Saul Lieberman, *Tosefta Ki-Fshuṭah, Shabbat* (New York, 1962), p. 294 and n. 35.

[This teaches] that you are not to make it [i.e., the place where the god is housed] into a *beit va ʿad*," a place that serves as a [familiar] meeting-place.

Scholars, however, have a favorite meeting-place of their own, the *beit midrash* or *ha-midrash* (a term possibly in existence as early as the time of Sirach: Ecclus., ed. Segal, p. 358), the academy. Since for the Sages no getting together for any purpose is as significant as a gathering together for the study of Torah, when they want to refer to *their* meeting-place, they speak of it as *the* meeting-place, *beit ha-va ʿad*; and this reading (for scholars' meeting-place) is consistent in our sources despite the reading that appears on occasion in our printed texts as well as in the Kaufmann Codex of the Mishnah (Soṭah 9:15/23). The evidence is presented in the note at this point.[16] It is even possible that the more frequent *beit ha-va ʿad* derives ultimately from Yose ben Yoezer's having spoken of a *beit va ʿad* for the *ḥakhamim*—*beit va ʿad*, not yet *beit ha-va ʿad*. Besides, "*beit ha-va ʿad* for the *ḥakhamim*" might almost seem redundant.

What kind of home should a disciple of Pharisees create? According to Yose ben Yoezer it should be a place where as a rule scholars congregate; or, as ARN says, "A person's home ought to be ready to receive the Sages and [47] disciples and the disciples of disciples, as it is when a man says to another, 'I shall await thee at such and such a place.'"[17] The home Yose ben Yoezer is advocating is a place where sages, disciples, and disciples of disciples congregate; in other words, a well-known "salon" for the intellectual élite. They all (=of all grades, but all identified as the intellectuals) know where to go.

16. The biblical expression (Job 30:23) is *beit mo ʿed*; the same occurs in *The War of the Sons of Light Against Sons of Darkness*, ed. Yigael Yadin (Hebrew, Jerusalem 1955), p. 272 (3:4).

The reading *beit ha-va ʿad* as reference to scholars' meeting-place: B. Sanhedrin 97a, and so too *Haggadoth hatalmud* (Jerusalem, 1961, photocopy of ed. Constantinople, 1511), p. 112b (citing R. Judah ben Batyra).

The reading of M. Soṭah 9:15 = B. T. Soṭah 49b, *beit va ʿad*, should be *beit ha-va ʿad* as in *Haggodoth hatalmud*, p. 80a; note also Massekhet Derekh ʾEreṣ, ed. Michael Higger (New York, 1935), p. 244. Soṭah 9:131 and Sanhedrin 11:165 of Jacob ibn Ḥabib, *ʿEin Yaʿaqov* (New York, 1955) also read *beit ha-va ʿad*.

T. Megillah 3(4):5, ed. Saul Lieberman, p. 354, similarly, *beit ha-va ʿad* (and note also Lieberman, *Tosefta Ki-Fshuṭah*, pp. 1168–69).

On the reading *meqom ha-va ʿad* in B.T. Sanhedrin 13b, cf. ᴅs ad loc. (that the MS reading is *le-veit ha-va ʿad*). The reading *meqom ha-va ʿad* in M. Rosh ha-Shanah 4:4 occurs also in Codex Kaufmann, MSS Parma and Paris, and ed. W. H. Lowe (Cambridge, 1883); in ed. Naples the whole statement of R. Joshua ben Qorhah is omitted, but is quoted immediately (*li-meqom ha-va ʿad*) in the commentary which follows. See further J. N. Epstein, *Mavo le-nusaḥ ha-Mishnah* (Jerusalem, 5708), pp. 488–89.

On *beit ha-va ʿad* and *beit ha-midrash*, cf. Louis Ginzberg, *Commentary on the Palestinian Talmud* (Hebrew), 3(New York, 1941–61):175. Cf. Gedalia Allon, *Studies in Jewish History* (Hebrew), 2 (Tel Aviv, 1957–58):299–300.

On Immanuel of Rome's use of the saying "Let thy home be a meeting-place for the Sages," cf. his *Maḥbarot*, ed. Dov Jarden, 2 (Jerusalem, 1957):394, line 214.

17. Version ᴀ, p. 27; Version ʙ, p. 28.

IV

If it were not for the statement of his colleague, Yose ben Yoḥanan, perhaps this would not stand out so clearly. The latter, Yose ben Yoḥanan, is also describing an ideal home to his disciples-followers, *yehi beitkha* (Codex Kaufmann: *beitakh*), "Let thy home be," but something else is uppermost in his mind. Once again there will be three clauses to one end, in second person singular. "(a) Let thy home be wide open, (b) and let the poor (*'aniyyim*) be members of thy household, (c) and talk not overmuch with *ha-'ishah*."[18] And that is all.

This is how ARN, p. 33, reads and how PA read originally; but before we analyze this saying, we must note that PA 1:5, as it already reads in the Kaufmann Codex, continues after "*ha-'ishah*" as follows:

> "[One is not to talk overmuch] with his own wife, they [the Sages] said,[19] all the more then with another's wife.[20] Hence the Sages said: So long as a man talks overmuch with *ha-'ishah*,[21] he brings evil upon himself, neglects the study of Torah, and in the end what he inherits is Gehenna."

The very style of this addition—first, commentary on *ha-'ishah*, that it [48] refers to one's own wife (note the third person!), that one is not to talk overmuch with her, and then further commentary on the preceding comment, why such conversation is fatal[22]—is already a departure from the recurring manner of speaking of the PA sayings of the early Sages. This is strikingly preserved in ARN version A (p. 35) where the whole passage "even with one's own wife, all the more . . . another's wife" and so on to "what he inherits is Gehenna," is actually presented as *commentary*[23] on Yose ben Yoḥanan's third clause, not as part of the Mishnah text.

---

18. Cf. Xenophon *Oeconomicus* 3.12.

19. Cf. Albeck, *Mishnah, Neziqin* (1953), p. 493 (on 1:5).

20. For similar construction, cf. M. Bava Batra 9:7.

21. The addition in Codex Kaufmann of "when his wife is *niddah*, menstruant," although followed by several authorities, is not to be adopted (cf. S. Schechter in his Introduction to ARN, pp. xvii–xx, and Appendix 4). That reading is itself an attempt to make sense out of the third clause of ben Yoḥanan's saying.

(The reading *be-'ishto niddah* is reported as a Rashi or French version. Is it possible that this reading, an attempt at softening the impact and brusqueness of the accepted reading, is due partly to fears of heresy? Avoiding overmuch talk with one's wife even when she is not *niddah* might well lead to more and more withdrawal from his wife. In the first half of the eleventh century in Christian France and then again in the twelfth century, attacks on traditional marriage—Bogomilism, Catharism—were a real danger to the established Church; and perhaps beyond the Church, too, a threat or influence was felt. This suggestion is tentative of course, for the subject requires thorough investigation by a medievalist.)

22. Note threeness in the rhetoric here too: "(a) he brings evil upon himself, (b) neglects the study of Torah, and (c) in the end what he inherits is Gehenna."

23. Note the way Version A, p. 35, puts it: "'And talk not overmuch with *ha-'ishah*': even with his own wife, and needless to say with his fellow's wife! For so long as a man talks overmuch with *ha-'ishah*, he brings evil . . . ," etc. No word of "they [the Sages] said," or, "hence the Sages said." Note the reading in Version B, p. 35, end paragraph of chap. 15.

The commentary itself requires examination before we return to Yose's own saying, "Talk not *overmuch* with *ha-'ishah*." If this were a reference to women in general, what is the meaning of "overmuch"? What business has a man holding conversations at all with women other than his wife? In late tannaite times, the Babylonian R. Aha(i) ben R. Josiah was to say that anyone who keeps staring at women will in the end fall into the transgression (of adultery).[24] According to the Sages, to stare at a woman's heel is to bring on a calamitous decree—defective children.[25] Conversations with women lead to whoring.[26] True, these statements do not come from as early a period as that of the first Pair. Nor are they always Palestinian. But the view they reflect is as early as Sirach (ca. 200–180 B.C.E.):

Do not look upon anyone[27] for beauty,
And do not sit in the midst of women;
[49] for from garments comes the moth,
and from a woman comes woman's wickedness.
Better is the wickedness of a man than a woman who does good;
and it is a woman who brings shame and disgrace.[28]

Do not look intently at a virgin,[29]
lest you stumble and incur penalties for her . . . .
Do not look around in the streets of a city,
nor wander about in its deserted sections.
Turn away your eyes from a shapely woman,
and do not look intently at beauty belonging to another;
many have been misled by a woman's beauty,
and by it passion is kindled like a fire.
Never dine alone with another man's wife,
nor revel with her at wine;
lest your heart turn aside to her,
and . . . you be plunged into destruction.[30]

24. B. T. Nedarim 20a; Kallah, ed. Michael Higger (New York, 1936), p. 193; Derekh 'Ereṣ, ed. Higger, p. 276. What caused the downfall of fallen angels: Kallah, p. 230.

25. Derekh 'Ereṣ, ibid.; B. T. Nedarim, ibid. Is there any connection between this view and that in Version A of ARN, chap. 31, p. 92, which associates man's heels with the angel of death? Cf. L. Ginzberg in J. Goldin, *The Fathers According to Rabbi Nathan* (New Haven, 1955), p. 204, n. 30. Professor Saul Lieberman once called my attention to this interpretation in R. Joseph Rosen, *Zaphnath Paneaḥ*: see ed. M. M. Kasher (Jerusalem, 1961), pp. 116ff. ad ARN, and cf. notes ibid.

26. Derekh 'Ereṣ, ibid.; cf. the reading in Israel Al-Nakawa, *Menorat ha-ma'or*, ed. H. G. Enelow, 4 (New York, 1932):56. And note the warning to a scholar (*talmid ḥakham*) in B.T. Berakhot 43b, toward bottom (cf. ps ad loc.).

27. But cf. the Hebrew (*Sefer Ben Sira ha-Shalem*, ed. M. Z. Segal [Jerusalem, 1953], pp. 284, 287).

28. Ecclus. 42:12–14. Segal, *Sefer Ben Sira ha-Shalem*, p. 287, calls attention to Josephus, *Contra Apionem* 2.201 (see LCL ed. 1:372, n. 4).

29. Act as Job acted? Version A of ARN, pp. 12–13; Version B, pp. 8–9.

30. Ecclus. 9:5, 7–9.

The first interpretation of "talk not overmuch with *ha-'ishah*" is consequently correct, that it is a reference to one's own wife[31] (all the more, then, to someone else's wife). And therefore Yose ben Yoḥanan deliberately says, "Talk not *overmuch* with *ha-'ishah*, the wife," and not, "Talk not with thy wife"— that would be preposterous, not virtuous.

Once this early pharisaic teaching becomes a popular saying, it may cease to be restricted to its original intention and will be generalized—if one wishes to be witty or sarcastic. Thus,[32] when R. Yose the Galilean (but cf. DS and note ad locum) asked R. Meir's wife for directions to Lydda and used too many words, she could reprimand him, One must not talk overmuch with *ha-'ishah*, with a woman; it's enough to say, "How to Lydda?" But more pointed is that comment upon the first comment now included in the PA mishnah, that he who talks overmuch with *ha-'ishah* is his own enemy, for he will be neglecting study of Torah and in the end Gehenna will be his [50] inheritance. Here a new motif has been introduced: neglecting the study of Torah and its terrible consequences.[33] But the single thought of Yose ben Yoḥanan, as we shall see, is of something else.

Why this ambiguity, however, whether one should avoid long conversations with one's wife or with women, that is, why should it even be necessary to spell out that *ha-'ishah* in our mishnah equals "his own wife"? The answer is, the ambiguity is not in what Yose ben Yoḥanan said; it is in the word *'ishah*, which means "woman" but also "wife," and only context discloses the precise meaning (and sometimes does not). It would be going too far away from the evidence to say that only *ha-'ishah* is used when "wife" is intended. A few examples: In M. Yoma 1:1 R. Judah says that a week before Atonement Day, among other arrangements made for the high priest, another wife, *'ishah* (woman?—but *ha-'ishah ha-'aḥeret* would be clumsy and misleading) is prepared lest his wife (*'ishto*) die. Better: M. Giṭṭin 3:1: a bill of divorcement not written specifically in name of the wife (*'ishah*). Or, M. Yevamot 6:6—If a man was married to a woman (*'ishah* = wife) for ten years and she bore no children. M. Nedarim 10:6, a wife (*'ishah*) he himself acquired, a wife (*'ishah*) whom Heaven has led him to acquire. There are other examples (e.g., PA 5:5, "No *'ishah* ever miscarried . . ."), a number possibly even more striking than these.

On the other hand, *ha-'ishah*, "the" *'ishah*, is again and again favored as the expression for "wife." *Ha-'ishah* can be interpreted as "woman" (cf., e.g., M. Rosh ha-Shanah 1:8, M. Sanhedrin 6:4, "The Sages say, You hang a man, not a woman [*ha-'ishah*]," even as *'ishah* can refer to a wife, as we just observed). But at least in the Mishnah many of the *ha-'ishah* instances seem to refer to

31. Cf. Samuel ben Isaac Uceda, *Midrash Shemuel* (New York, 5708), p. 18, line 8, quoting Abarbanel (for this spelling, cf. S. Z. Leiman, "Abarbanel and the Censor," *Journal of Jewish Studies* 19 [1968]: 49, n. 1); but Abarbanel also relates the statement to giving of charity.

32. B. T. 'Eruvin 53b (bottom).

33. Cf. above, n. 23.

women in marriage. For example (to choose from well-known mishnayot): M. Yevamot 15:1, "husband and wife who went overseas" (lit., *ha-'ishah*, wife ... and her husband); Qiddushin 1:1, "a wife is acquired (*ha-'ishah niqneit*");[34] 2:1, "the *'ishah* is betrothed"; 'Eduyot 8:5, "R. Aqiba reported ... that *ha- 'ishah* may be remarried on the testimony of one witness [that the husband has died]."

This is not intended as a statistical summary of word frequency, or anything like that—which cannot even be arrived at by means of a concordance alone (useful, of course, as that is!): Note, for example, when C. Y. Kasovsky in the Mishnah concordance vocalizes *be-'ishah* and H. Yalon (in the [51] Mishnah, ed. Albeck-Yalon) vocalizes *ba-'ishah* (Ketubbot 8:1, bis; Ḥullin 4:7; Parah 5:4; Miqva'ot 9:2; Niddah 2:5, 6; 5:7; Nega'im 6:7; Zavim 2:1; Bekhorot 3:1). There are similar disagreements between them in connection with *le- 'ishah* and *la-'ishah*.[35]

Ha-'ishah, then, that is, *'ishah* with the definite article, does often refer to "wife"; and in our particular mishnah, PA 1:5, that meaning is insisted on, made explicit, rightly as we have seen, by the first part of that early comment.

V

"*Yeḥi beitkha*, let thy home be," Yose ben Yoḥanan also, like his colleague, had begun his sentence. He too, in other words, seeks to teach his disciples what one's home ought to be like. Unlike his colleague, however, he underscores that a home ought to be inviting not only to the élite, to the scholars; on the contrary, let thy home be *wide* open, in other words, open to all. Hospitality is extended even to nonscholars,[36] to any who seek to enter, even to the poor, but not exclusively to them. We will return to the poor shortly.

Probably everyone devoted to improvement of human conduct has at one time or another beseeched his audience to practice charity.[37] Yose ben [52]

---

34. Cf. D. H. Weiss, "The Use of קנה in Connection with Marriage," *Harvard Theological Review*, 57 (1964): 244ff.

35. Yevamot 14:1; Ketubbot 5:2; Soṭah 3:8—note Codex Kaufmann; Giṭṭin 8:8, bis; Qiddushin 2:1, 3:1, 2, 5, 6, 10; Bava Batra 3:3 (context supports Yalon); 10:1 (ditto); 10:7 (ditto); Horayot 1:7, bis; 'Arakhin 6:2, Keritot 2:4. In these Yalon reads *la-'ishah*, while Kasovsky reads *le-'ishah*. On calling attention to the significance of the definite article in "related" nouns, cf. Tosefot Yom Tov ad M. Ketubbot 1:1, s.v. "betulah." And in the commentary of R. Joseph ibn Shoshan—fourteenth cent.; cf. *Jewish Encyclopaedia*, s.v. "Ibn Shushan"—Bodleian MS Mich. 265, [Neubauer 385], fol. 44v) there is explicit emphasis that *ha-'ishah*, because of the definite article, refers to wife, "for if reference is to other women, what sense does *overmuch* make?"

36. Note the high praise for "entertaining guests" by a number of Amoraim in B. T. Shabbat 127a (and in name of R. Yoḥanan, enlargement of M. Pe'ah 1:1; cf. Seligmann Baer, *Seder 'Avodat Yisra'el* [Redelheim, 1868], pp. 38–39. [On "open door" cf. W. S. Heckscher, "Petites perceptions," *Journal of Medieval and Renaissance Studies* 4/1 (1974): 113, n. 23].

37. Even cynics and Bernard Shaw do not advocate cruelty, though they may quarrel with the popular notion of what constitutes charity. Plutarch *Moralia* 235E ("Sayings of Spartans," 56), quotes the following: "A beggar (*epaitēs*) asked alms of a Spartan, who said, 'If I should give to you, you will be the more a beggar (*mallon ptōcheuseis*); and for this unseemly conduct of yours he who first gave to you is responsible, for he thus made you lazy.'" (See also

Yoḥanan is no exception (cf. Isa. 58:7), but he has something more inclusive in mind, particularly since in his time (the same is doubtless true of other times) there were those who might take exception to his point of view. Sirach (Ecclus. 11:29, 34) says:

"Do not bring every man into your home, for many are the wiles of the crafty.[38] . . . Receive a stranger (*allotrion*) into your home and he will upset (*diastrepsei*) you with commotion (*tarachais*), and will estrange you from your family (*tōn idiōn sou*)."

Yose ben Yoḥanan on the contrary says, "Let thy home be wide open," rather than open only to a favorite group, or rather than shut to strangers.

In its commentary on the clause "Let thy home be wide open," ARN (in both versions, p. 33) applies the teaching to treatment of the poor.

This teaches that a man's house should be wide open to the north, south, east and west, like Job's, who made four doorways to his house.[39] And why did Job make four doorways to his house? So that the poor would not be troubled to go all around the house [seeking the entrance]: one coming from the north could enter in his stride, one coming from the south could enter in his stride, and so in all directions. For that reason Job made four doorways to his house.[40]

Though picturesque, this is not an unreasonable interpretation, that is, that Yose ben Yoḥanan is eager to emphasize that a person's home should in every way welcome the poor.[41] That ben Yoḥanan has the poor in mind, one might argue, can be seen in his second clause, "and let the poor be members of thy household (*ve-yihyu ʿaniyyim benei beitekha*)."

Artemidorus *Oneirocritica* 3:53 [trans. R. S. White, (Park Ridge, New Jersey, 1975), pp. 171–72].) And yet (235F, 60), "Only in Sparta does it pay to grow old"! Respect or reverence for the old has nothing to do with charity, of course. But at least it reveals the possibility of civilized attention to others existing without the presence of compassion for the unfortunate.

38. Cf. B. T. Yevamot 63b and B. T. Sanhedrin 100b (see *Sefer Ben Sira ha-Shalem*, ed. Segal, p. 75, on what he numbers 11:36), and note that in Sanhedrin this view is said to be the view of Rabbi (Judah the Prince) also! In *The New Yorker*, July 23, 1979, p. 37, Ved Mehta reports his father quoting the following Punjabi saying to his mother:
Those who have not been born of your blood
Come into your house
And separate the real blood brothers.

39. The prooftext is provided by Version B of ARN (p. 33), Job 31:32, "My doors [*dlty*, i.e., *delatai*] I opened to the wayfarer." My former student, Mary Rose D'Angelo, once observed that there was also a play on words here, *dlt* (*dalet*) = 4 and *dlt* (*delet*) = door. In several MSS at the Bodleian (Mich. 507 [ol. 665], fol. 4r; see also T 25 [5b] and T 26) the commentary adds that the poor may be enabled to enter in one door and go out another, so that those standing by the entrance may not see him leave, to his embarrassment. See also ARN, p. 138, line 14 from bottom.

40. Cf. L. Ginzberg, *Legends of the Jews* (Philadelphia, 1909–38), 5:248, n. 223.

41. Note also Tobit 2:2 (or 4:7ff), dated fourth century B.C.E. by E. J. Bickerman, *Studies in Jewish and Christian History* 1 (Leiden, 1976):55.

[53] Nevertheless, the way the two versions of ARN proceed to interpret the latter clause suggests that something like a retreat from such understanding of that second clause is being recommended by them.

For on the second clause of that saying which speaks of the ʿaniyyim becoming part of one's ménage, both versions immediately enter their respective reservations. Version A declares that the ʿaniyyim, the poor, are not actually to be "members of thy household," and Version B declares that the term ʿaniyyim in that sentence is not a reference to the "poor," but to the duty of the members of the household to be humble and soft-spoken, ʿanavim,[42] "let the members of thy household be humble."

If, therefore, the second clause refers in some fashion to ʿaniyyim, it is not simply repeating what the first clause urged. Both versions of ARN are at one in this. The first clause may well have the poor in mind in some sense—if a home is to be open to all without distinction, a word about the poor (the world's most uninvited generally) is certainly not out of place. If the poor are not to be members of my household actually, let them be so treated as to keep them talking of the generosity of my hospitality; if the members of my household are not actually to be poor but humble, then the poor arriving at my door must and will be received decently.

But nothing compels us to assume that the second clause is no more than a repetition of the thought of the first clause: Even ARN, in its understanding, tries to distinguish somehow between the two, as we have just noted. On the contrary, the first is a plea to open one's door to all ("Let thy home be wide open"), without distinctions; that is all it says. And the second is a special [54] appeal on behalf of the poor when they come my way, or a plea to us, householder and family, to behave without arrogance toward the poor: then even our dogs won't harm a soul![43]

---

42. See BDB on ʿnw and ʿny (pp. 776–77). On Version A of ARN also undertaking interpretation of ʿnw, cf. ibid., p. 34. Of course, I am not denying that bny bytk (bnei beitekha, on which cf. E. Y. Kutscher, *Hebrew and Aramaic Studies* [Jerusalem, 1977], p. 92 [of Hebrew part] has the meaning of "servants, stewards," as both PA commentators (e.g., Vitry, Maimonides, etc.) and modern scholars say (e.g., E. Z. Melamed, "Li-leshonah shel massekhet 'Avot," *Leshonenu* 20 [5716]: 110–11; H. L. Ginsberg, *Koheleth* [Hebrew, Tel Aviv-Jerusalem, 1961], p. 68; W. F. Albright, "Abram the Hebrew: A New Archaeological Interpretation," *Bulletin of the American Schools of Oriental Research*, no. 163 [October 1961], p. 47 and nn. 54–56). Note how the Amora Raba quotes the saying in B. T. Bava Meṣiʿa 60b. But that need not always be the case: note the expression in the context of Version A of ARN, pp. 34–35 (top). On benei beito = his wife, cf. S. Lieberman, *Tosefta Ki-Fshuṭah*, Pesaḥim, p. 627, lines 48–49. In his *Commentary to the Mishna Shabbat* (Jerusalem, 1976, p. 384), Abraham Goldberg notes the meaning "guests." For the expression brbyy, see Lev. R. 25:8, p. 584, line 5 and note, ad loc. and cf. S. Lieberman, ad loc., pp. 877–78. See further, E. Y. Kutscher in Franz Rosenthal, ed., *An Aramaic Handbook*, 2 vols. (Weisbaden, 1967), vol. 1, pt. 2, p. 55b, and again Kutscher, *Hebrew and Aramaic Studies*, p. 66. For Persian title vispuhr = Aramaic, bar baita, ibid., p. 16 of Hebrew part.

43. Version B of ARN, p. 33. Like master like dog! (Beasts belonging to saints, saintly like their masters: Version A of ARN, p. 38.) On opening the doors to rich and poor alike, cf. Samuel ben Isaac Uceda, *Midrash Shemuel*, p. 17, nine lines from bottom.

This finally brings us back to the third clause, "and talk not overmuch with [thy] wife." Conversation with one's wife reflects what is going on inside the home.[44] The question is, What specifically does Yose ben Yohanan have in mind when he adds this statement to the preceding two? One answer we have already met above, that talking and talking with a wife interfere with the study of Torah (and Gehenna is inherited as a result). But such interference is surmountable: Let a man escape to where he cannot be disturbed or distracted (cf. ARN, chap. 21, p. 74, "the conversation of children," and the reading in Schechter's note 10), and not come home till his studies exhaust him (cf. B. T. Sanhedrin 26b, R. Hanan/Yohanan: DS ad locum; Maimonides, *Code*, "Nashim, 'Ishut" 14:1). And maybe this is implied by the Sages of the exhortation closing PA 1:5, but they do not say it. In any event, this warning against long conversation because it interferes with Torah study—although it occurs in our printed and manuscript Mishnah texts—is not, however, what Yose ben Yohanan said, but what Version A (not Version B!) of ARN says. There is no mention of sages or disciples or study or academy or Torah in Yose ben Yohanan's own saying. What is more, the explanatory reflection on neglecting to study Torah may even have come into being from an effort to harmonize the teaching of the latter Yose with the teaching of the former Yose.[45]

Trying to make sense out of that saying, *Mahzor Vitry* (ed. Simeon Hurwitz [Nürnberg, 1923], p. 468), rightly rejecting the reading *be-'ishto niddah*, [55] says that talking overmuch with one's wife, "idle chatter," leads to frivolity and sexual desire. Maimonides proceeds along similar lines: "It is well known that for the most part conversation with women has to do with sexual matters."

But if these had been Yose ben Yohanan's concerns, it is difficult to see a connection between the first two clauses and the third. Open thy house to all, let the poor enjoy thy hospitality (or, let the members of thy household be modest toward the poor); and don't converse at length with thy wife. This sounds dissonant. If one begins with thoughts about hospitality to others, does that lead him to talk about making or not making love to his wife?

Little wonder that Samuel ben Isaac Uceda (*Midrash Shemuel*, p. 18) is led to the "possible" suggestion (*ve-'efshar li lomar*) that a man might refrain from inviting guests to his house because (a) he wishes to spend as much time as

---

44. Note also the expression in M. Yoma 1:1, *beito zo 'ishto* (his house-home = his wife). See also R. Yose in B. T. Shabbat 118b (toward bottom). A scholar (*talmid hakham*) should not be conversing with any women (even his wife, his daughter, his sister) out of doors: B. T. Berakhot 43b, bottom; and cf. DS ad loc. (This does not appear in Derekh 'Eres, ed. Higger, p. 116.) "Scholaris, qui loquitur cum puella, non praesumitur dicere Pater Noster" (Adriaan Beverland, 1654?–1712, *The Law Concerning Draped Virginity* [Paris, 1905], pp. 132–33, quoting Baldo).

45. That such attempts at harmonization occur can be seen in ARNB, second paragraph, p. 28, on "Let thy home be a meeting-place for the Sages," compared with ARNA, p. 33, lines 2 and 3 of the comment on "And let the poor be members of thy household." Note a scribal lapse in MS Bodleian Opp. 245 (ol. 422) (Neubauer 390), fol. 21v, "Let thy home be wide open, a meeting-place for the Sages!"

possible with his wife alone, or (b) he suspects that the guest might be attracted by his wife! Rabbi Samuel's hunch is right. There should be a connection between the three clauses. But surely there is still another possible thought, less farfetched in my opinion, accompanying the theme of the hospitable home, to demonstrate that the three clauses belong together.

The classical host of Scripture—and in their discussion of Yose ben Yohanan's saying, both versions of ARN refer to him—is Abraham.[46] He is eager to entertain the three men who appear in the heat of the day. A little water, a morsel of bread, he says to them. But he hurries (*va-yemaher*) into the tent and says to his wife, "Quick now (*mahari*), three measures of choice flour!" (One measure per guest?) "Knead and make cakes!" Not another word. Then he runs to see to it that more is prepared, and the attending servant also hurried (*va-yemaher*). Swiftness is of the essence. When it comes to [56] entertaining strangers, the command to Sarah is brief, even peremptory, and he hastens to provide the rest.[47]

This, it seems to me, is what Yose ben Yohanan has in mind: as in the case of that model host, Abraham, let all who come thy way be welcome; as for the poor, entertain them properly, well; and with the lady of the house, let thy speech be brief and to the point: Quick, prepare the food. That is what *beitkha*, thy home, should be like.

VI

From the sayings of the two Yoses, the first of the five Pairs, we learn what the early pharisaic masters in the first half of the second century B.C.E. were concerned with: *yehi beitkha*, let thy home be of a certain character. For Yose ben Yoezer it should be a place where the savants are in the habit of assembling. That the wife might have a role in the home, he does not even

---

46. ARN speaks of Abraham's hospitality to all, and of how he surpassed Job in hospitality: how he ran forth looking for guests; how he served them with dishes they never before tasted (could not afford)! The midrash on Abraham's entertaining the three wayfarers (Gen. 18:1ff.) is in Mekhilta, ʿAmaleq 3 (ed. Lauterbach, 2:178 and parallels).

The indefatigable emphasis on charity and hospitality in Judaism (and later, Christianity too) in Greco-Roman centuries, is not just relief of the poor for reasons of policy or politics, or quid pro quo beneficence. (The phenomenon of public gifts to the state, or polis, or even some collegia to establish funds and foundations, etc., is an entirely different subject; see A. R. Hands, *Charities and Social Aid in Greece and Rome* [London, 1968]. See especially his chapter 5 on the poor.) Emphasis obviously reflects the need to emphasize, that people may not be responding spontaneously as they should. Nevertheless, the tireless rhetoric reveals what has become a fixed value within a moral "system." In this, even a scholar may have to be taught a lesson or two: Lev. R. 9:3, pp. 176ff. Cf. n. 54 below.

47. This view is perhaps in the back of the mind of Joseph ibn Shoshan (n. 35 above): *u-vi-qesarah* (the husband is to speak briefly). In Version B of ARN, p. 126, one view has it that women are lazy (dawdlers) and the prooftext offered is that of Abraham ordering Sarah, "Quick now, three measures" (etc.). Note how in B. T. Bava Meṣiʿa 87a the Abraham-order to Sarah of Gen. 18 is interpreted as support for the view that women are less generous than men (cf. Sifrei Num. 110, p. 115), and this is referred to by Samuel ben Isaac Uceda, *Midrash Shemuel*, p. 18, lines 12ff. But this is not what I am driving at.

mention—because that is irrelevant to his chief preoccupation. What his attitude was regarding hospitality to the poor, we do not know, for he has not told us. But evidently he did feel strongly about instructing his students and followers that the proper home is a place which the intellectual élite frequent. The voice is the voice of the aristocracy of learning. Let hoi polloi keep out. (And in his commentary ad locum, R. Jonah Gerondi [thirteenth century] insists that scholars would assemble only in the house of the distinguished, not just any house!)

As to Yose ben Yoḥanan, he seems to be protesting against this view. But even if he is ignoring it, or is unaware (?) of it, his attitude is, Thy home is to be open to all, even to the poor of course—but whoever the guest, from far or near, poor or otherwise, receive him as Father Abraham received the three travelers (who in his eyes were no more than wandering Bedouins, idol worshippers).[48] The proper household welcomes everyone, not only the scholars. The poor, the not-poor too, should be treated hospitably; and be [57] brief (rather than long-winded) in instructing the lady of the house to serve the company.

Once the original meaning was forgotten,[49] other explanations were bound to appear. A favorite one for PA (so preoccupied with study of Torah in many of its sayings: 2:2, 7, 8a [beginning], 12, 16; 3:2b, 3, 6, 7b, 8, 9, 17, 18; 4:5, 10, 13, 14, 20; 5:12, 15 [and practically the whole of the supplementary sixth chapter]) would almost certainly be in terms of admonishment against behavior that might lead to neglect or slackening of Torah study. Therefore, one should not talk overmuch with his wife; it diverts from study. But as ARN reveals in both versions (pp. 34–35), still other interpretations are possible (although some readings remain unclear). Note well: no longer mention of neglecting Torah study and inheriting Gehenna! Version A suggests that if at the academy one has fallen out with a colleague, or has not been shown proper respect, he is not to go and tell his wife; the end of such tale-telling is a disgrace to all concerned and leads to his being held in contempt by his wife. Version B warns a man not to brag to his wife of the honors he has enjoyed at the academy; it comes to no good (he ceases to make the effort to improve, grows self-satisfied?). Or, not to tell his wife of quarrels he has had with someone else; before you know it, everyone is involved in insults and mutual recriminations, even passersby. Or (apparently—the text is euphemistic and mutilated), to beware lest his wife become a hussy and the man be disgraced.[50] Or, to learn a lesson from Samson,

48. Cf. the Mekhilta reference in n. 46, above.
49. Cf. J. Goldin, "Of Change and Adaptation in Judaism," *History of Religions* 4 (1965): 282–83, 285–86 [below, pp. 215–237—Ed.].
50. The following is a tentative translation and interpretation of the passage:
"Another interpretation of 'Do not talk overmuch with the wife': [for] he brings disgrace on himself. How so? In the first week [of their married life?], she comes to where he is. [Subsequently,?] when she hears him coming into the courtyard, she goes into a room [and] from the room into the *triclinium* [i.e., a room with the couches for dining, in the interior: cf. the imagery—PA 4:16]. He follows after her, and in his presence she 'uncovers' her head and he

who [58] met with disaster because he talked too much to his wife. All these explanations have this in common: they are no longer aware of the original meaning of Yose ben Yoḥanan's saying and are groping for an answer to the question, Why should not a man talk at length with his own wife?

VII

I am unable to locate anything in Hellenistic literature that corresponds to this "Let thy home be," although it may be hiding somewhere,[51] and although even if it did or does exist, it would in no way diminish the significance of the teachings of our two Sages. Xenophon's *Oeconomicus* is not only of an earlier period, but is concerned with an altogether different theme: How to break the old (young) girl in! He also is not prepared to hold long conversations with his wife, the general rule with Athenians at least in the Classical Period.[52] The attitude of the pharisaic Sages and later of most Tannaim and Amoraim is very likely not radically different. (The second person singular in PA is masculine; it is the man one addresses. But this is probably merely stylistic, even as it is in our speech. Until one gets accustomed to it, "chairperson" sounds prim, and Hebrew has no neuter). Like Thales or Socrates who could be grateful to

enters into long conversation with her. What caused him to disgrace himself? His having entered into long conversation with her." Cf. also the translation and interpretation by Anthony Saldarini, *The Fathers According to Rabbi Nathan, Version B* (Leiden, 1975), p. 110.

Something like a man's losing face seems to be involved here—at first the husband plays the dominant role, but by prolonging conversation with his wife, the text implies (or seems to imply), that she gets the upper hand and he has to beg for her favors. A woman, of course, is not to "uncover" (cf. *The Torah* [Philadelphia, 1962], Lev. 10:6, note) her head in public (cf. M. Ketubbot 7:6; M. Bava Qamma 8:6; see also Samuel Krauss, *Talmudische Archäologie*, 1 [Leipzig, 1910]:651, n. 874, and *Qadmoniyyot ha-Talmud*, 2 [Tel-Aviv, 1945], pt. 2:274–78); but the expression here seems to suggest that she is brazen in her demands on her husband (not waiting for him to make the proper overtures or forcing him to sue at length). Unfortunately, several specific points are still unclear to me. Going from room to room and the husband following after her may also be part of the humiliation he is subjected to, and long conversation may refer to the husband's entreating.

51. And yet, cf. Semonides (seventh cent. B.C.E. as translated by M. Arthur in S. B. Pomeroy, *Goddesses, Whores, Wives, Slaves* (New York, 1975), p. 52, lines 3–4: "For whosever wife she is, she won't receive graciously//Into the house a friend who comes to visit." (In the *Oxford Book of Greek Verse*, chosen by Gilbert Murray et al. [Oxford, 1954], pp. 161ff., these lines are not included.)

52. Cf. above, n. 18; and cf. C. Taylor, *Sayings*, 1:140, top. Note also W. K. Lacey, *The Family in Classical Greece* (Ithaca, 1968), pp. 158 (bottom)ff., 167ff. See also Pomeroy, *Goddesses*, p. 74. Though he speaks of the Roman woman ("The Silent Women of Rome"), Sir M. I. Finley's essay in his *Aspects of Antiquity* (London, 1977), pp. 124ff., is instructive also for our subject. In *The New Yorker*, loc. cit., (n. 38 above), Ved Mehta quotes a Punjabi quatrain his father recited to his mother:

Yours is a life without help,
The same is your story:
Milk under your veil,
Always water in your eyes.

A suggestion has been made to me orally that entertaining in the ordinary Greek home was unlikely because Greek houses were small. But surely ordinary houses in Judea and Jewish Palestine were hardly more spacious than their Greek counterparts.

Fortune for being born a man [59] and not a woman (Diogenes Laertius 1:33), a Jew could thank God that He had not made him a woman.[53] But this is not the immediate concern of Yose ben Yoḥanan.

In her studies of women in classical antiquity, S. B. Pomeroy has pointed out that in Hellenistic times, "The legal and economic responsibilities of [wealthy and aristocratic women] increased, but political gains were more illusory" (p. 125). She goes on (p. 130): "Not only in Egypt but in other areas of the Greek world respectable women were participating more actively in economic affairs." (Not so in Athens.)[54] Nevertheless, peripatetic philosophers "theorized that more education would turn women into rather lazy, talkative busybodies [cf. R. Eliezer in M. Soṭah 3:4 and Albeck, *Mishnah Nashim*, p. 383]. Even the upper class, to which one would naturally look for an endorsement of schooling for women, did not educate its daughters" (p. 131). And in a Neopythagorean text quoted by Professor Pomeroy (p. 135), we read, "A woman must live for her husband . . . thinking no private thoughts of her own . . . must bear all that her husband bears. . . ." and more of the same. There are sentences in this short treatise that do reflect husband-wife relations in the home, but basically it is the woman's conduct that author is ordering (the injunctions are addressed to her), not formulating what a *home* should be.

There is, needless to say, such a thing as entertaining friends, and when possible, many friends, even lavishly when the occasion calls for it. There is furthermore benefaction, setting up funds for the benefit of fellow citizens and for the acquisition of a reputation as a generous and public-spirited person, as a philanthropist. But this subject is different from ours.[55]

Rostovtzev[56] is right to insist that even in Hellenistic times the Greek continued to be a *homo politicus* ("especially in the mother country"); he too, however, acknowledges the growing emphasis on individualism, especially [60] by the "dogmatic philosophies of conduct." These could provide the individual with guidance for family life[57] among other necessary relations. But a specific prescription for the ideal character of the individual home is still wanting.

What was there in Judea of the first half of the second century B.C.E. which

53. T. Berakhot 6(7):18, ed. Saul Lieberman, p. 38; see also Lieberman, *Tosefta Ki-Fshuṭah*, p. 120, and now also Naphtali Wieder, "'Al ha-berakhot 'goy, 'eved, 'ishah,' 'behemah,' 'u-vur,'" *Sinai* 85 (1979):97–118.

54. On economic emancipation of Jewish women already almost at the beginning of the Maccabean period, cf. E. Bickerman, *Studies in Jewish and Christian History* 2 (Leiden, 1980): 170.

55. As we said above, n. 46, second paragraph (see also n. 55, end). See especially A. R. Hands, *Charities*, chaps. 3–6. Here may well lie the crucial difference between pharisaic charity and Hellenistic (-Roman): in the former, all sorts of persons are to be invited in; cf. Version B of ARN, p. 34.

56. M. I. Rostovtzev, *Social and Economic History of the Hellenistic World*, 2 vols. (Oxford, 1964), 2:1118–21 (I owe this reference to Professor J. Frank Gilliam). For a picture of domestic felicity by a first century C.E. Stoic, cf. C. E. Lutz, "Musonius Rufus," in *Yale Classical Studies* 10 (1947):96–101; but still no word about inviting others to share with family. We are not talking of inviting *friends*, but of others = strangers, anyone in need.

57. See also Plutarch *Moralia* 769 ("A Dialogue on Love," pp. 23–24).

prompted leading pharisaic sages to encourage their disciples to create a particular kind of home life which included entertainment of others as well, scholars, or scholars and nonscholars too? To my knowledge, nothing relevant appears thus far in the literature of the Dead Sea Scrolls (and that includes the Temple Scroll).[58] I have only guesses, and none of them satisfactory, because they are no more than guesses. Perhaps this concern with the Jewish home is a by-product of the diffused individualism of the Hellenistic world at large. Perhaps it is a reaction against the spreading hellenization of upper social classes among the Jews in pre-Maccabean and Hasmonean times: not from such is the pharisaic Jew to choose his example of the proper home (note also Version A of ARN, p. 26; Josephus *Antiquities* 18.12). Perhaps it is anti-Sadducean— welcome *ḥakhamim*, the scholars devoted to the Oral Torah; or, all men (unlike Sadducees who "even among themselves [are] rather boorish in their behavior, and in their intercourse with their peers are as rude as to aliens").[59] Perhaps it is meant to discourage too active participation in public life and instead to encourage one to cultivate his private, moral life[60] where he can or might accomplish what he undertakes to do.

Be the reason or the combination of reasons what they may, the sayings of the two Yoses reveal what early pharisaic leaders have set their minds on, the home the Pharisee is to make for himself; and already at the outset we can detect what was to be true later too of the successors of the Pharisees, the Rabbis, that is, agreement on the fundamental but different interpretations thereof. Both Yoses insist that the private home is of great importance, [61] but one believes that it is to be a center for scholars, the new and emerging intellectual aristocracy; while to the other such exclusiveness is unsatisfactory, for to him hospitality—the unrestricted reaching out to the members of society —is what will make for the proper kind of host and modesty, uniting rich and poor, scholar and nonscholar (Pharisees and affiliates of other sects too?), family, and those knocking on the door. Two independent courses are here drawn up, that of Torah study and that of acts of lovingkindness (as *gemilut ḥasadim* was to be redefined later). What is paramount for one sage is not paramount for the other.[61]

58. Nevertheless, see *Damascus Covenant* 6:21, but see also Louis Ginzberg, *An Unknown Jewish Sect* (New York, 1976), p. 202. Reference to pagans giving alms in late antiquity, in anecdote, in *The Wisdom of the Desert Fathers*, trans. Benedicta Ward (Oxford, 1975), p. 38, no. 131.

59. Josephus, *War* 2.166 (LCL 2:387; and on "peers," cf. Thackeray's note *b* ibid). As for early emphasis on oral Torah, cf. J. Goldin in Alexander Altmann, ed., *Biblical Motifs* (Cambridge, Mass., 1966), pp. 138–46, 149–56.

60. Note later Shemaiah in PA 1:10, Version B of ARN, p. 46, first part of second paragraph. And note the variety of explanations of why one should "love work," in Version A, pp. 44–45.

61. Miss Rhoda Grady suggests to me that in his saying Yose ben Yoezer speaks of the home in terms of receiving, whereas Yose ben Yoḥanan talks of the home as a place of giving. As to *gemilut ḥasadim*, cf. the reference in n. 6, above.

VIII

However, it was Rabbi Simeon ben Yoḥai in the second century C.E.—perhaps even some earlier sage—who noted that the two courses have to intersect, possibly to overlap.[62]

> Rabbi Yoḥanan said in the name of Rabbi Simeon ben Yoḥai: What is the meaning of the verse (Isa. 32:20), "Happy shall you be who *sow* by all *waters*, who send out cattle and asses to pasture"? [This:] Whoever engages in study of Torah and acts of lovingkindness is worthy of the inheritance of two tribes [Joseph and Issachar] . . . For *sowing* is a reference to naught but charity (*ṣedaqah*)—here equated with "acts of lovingkindness": note the Hosea verse now to be quoted in full—"as it is said (Hosea 10:12), 'Sow charity (*ṣedaqah*) for yourselves; [reap in accordance with lovingkindness (*ḥesed*)].' And *water* is a reference to naught but Torah, as it is said [Isa. 55:1], 'Ho, all who are thirsty, come for water.'"[63]

---

62. I am not referring back to the saying of Simeon the Righteous in PA 1:2, for he is not speaking of Torah and *gemilut ḥasadim* in their later sense (cf. again the reference in n. 6, above). As for Shammai's saying (PA 1:15), note the meaning of *qeva'* in both versions of ARN (pp. 47 and 56)—hence, despite the third clause, which may or can be an aspect of *gemilut ḥasadim* (ARN, pp. 48, 57), the first clause is not speaking of *study* of Torah.

63. B. T. Bava Qamma 17a, end of chap. 1 (see ibid, on the two tribes). Al-Nakawa, *Menorat ha-ma'or*, first chapter (on *ṣedaqah*, charity), opens with this passage.

For further thought: Though the name Yose is not uncommon both in literary texts and inscriptions, is it coincidence or is it significant that both leaders are called Yose (or, Yosef)? that the one who wants the home to be a meeting-place for scholars is from Ṣeredah, while the one who wants the home to be wide open is from Jerusalem? Is there some remote, however slight connection between the popular name Yose and that soubriquet formula (M. Sanhedrin 7:5), "Yose [God] damn Yose?" (Cf. J. N. Epstein, "Li-leshon nezirut," *Sefer Magnes* [Jerusalem, 1938], p. 11.) Was Yose(f) ben Yoezer known as *ḥasid she-bi-khehunah* (*the* pious one of the priesthood, M. Ḥagigah 2:7), because, though a priest, he esteemed the Sages? But see Zacharias Frankel, *Darkhei ha-Mishnah* (Warsaw, 1923), pp. 33–34 and Albeck, *Mishnah, Neziqin*, p. 485. Rabban Yoḥanan ben Zakkai called his disciple, R. Yose the priest, *ḥasid* (PA 2:8). Coincidence? Note the second clause in his saying, PA 2:12. What of R. Yose Qatunta, whoever he was (M. Soṭah 9:15, cf. Aaron Hyman, *Toldoth Tannaim Ve'Amoraim*, 3 vols. [London, 1910], 2: 741–42)?

A Philosophical Session in
a Tannaite Academy°

[1] Commenting on the verse[1] which reports the devastation of Jerusalem by Nabuzaradan, that "he burnt the house of the Lord, and the king's house; and all the houses of Jerusalem, even every great man's house," ואת כל בית גדול,[2] the Midrash[3] makes the following remark:

> And to what does the clause "every great man's house" refer? That's the academy (*bet midrash*) of Rabban Johanan ben Zakkai. And why is it called *bet gadol* [literally, "the house of the great one"]? Because there the *shebaḥ* (*shevaḥ*) of the Holy one, blessed be He, was rehearsed, related, recited.

The verb is *teni*, which means not only "to recite" but "to study" and "to teach." To translate *shebaḥ* by the neutral word "praise" is to miss the real intent of the statement. *Shebaḥ* in the present sentence, as in a great many others in talmudic-midrashic literature, is clearly δόξα; and one of the traditional commentators on our midrashic passage has already correctly explained it: in Johanan ben Zakkai's academy they were engaged in the Creation and

° A slightly longer and more fully documented version of this paper, written in Hebrew, appears in the *Harry A. Wolfson Jubilee Volume*, recently published by the American Academy for Jewish Research. Several notes in the present English version, as well as a brief amplification at the conclusion of the discussion, do not appear in the Hebrew.

1. 2 Ki. 25:8f.; cf. Jer. 52:13. While the Vulgate of Jer. *ibid.* does read *omnem domum magnam* (LXX: πᾶσαν οἰχίαν μεγάλην), in 2 Ki. 25:9 it reads simply *omnemque domum* (see also LXX ad loc. ed. Rahlfs I, 750), though in the Hebrew (MT) in both the reading is *bet gadol* (in Jer. *bet ha-gadol*).

2. This translation is, of course, in accordance with MT; cf. the translation of the Jewish Publication Society.

3. *Lamentations Rabba, Petihta 12*, ed. Buber, 12.

Merkabah (Chariot) speculations.[4] The parallel passage in the Palestinian Talmud[5] bears him out. Here we do not read *shebaḥ*, but *gedulot*, the Magnificence, and the citation of 2 Ki. 8.4 as prooftext (Vulgate: *narra mihi omnia* magnalia [2] etc.; LXX: πάντα τὰ μεγάλα)[6] makes the meaning perfectly clear. As G. Scholem wrote long ago in another connection,[7]

> The term employed: *shivḥo shel haqadosh barukh hu*, signifies not only praise of God—in this context that would be without any meaning—but glory, δόξα, *shevaḥ* being the equivalent of the Aramaic word for glory, *shuvḥa*. The reference, in short, is not to God's praise but to the vision of His glory.

Our Midrash, in other words, testifies that in the academy of Johanan ben Zakkai there were sessions devoted to speculations on the theme of visions of God's glory. And in fact this should not surprise us, for it is in keeping with what talmudic literature tells us elsewhere[8] about an exchange between the great sage and his favorite[9] disciple, Eleazar ben ʿArak—how on one occasion, when Eleazar discoursed brilliantly on the Merkabah theme, Johanan could not resist praising him in most superlative terms. "He rose and kissed him on his head and exclaimed: Blessed be the Lord, God of Israel, who gave such a descendant to our father Abraham," and so on and so forth.[10]

We shall shortly examine more closely this well-known encounter of Johanan and Eleazar ben ʿArak. I have referred to it at this point, however, because along with our midrashic passage it may serve to suggest something about the nature of the curriculum (if I may be permitted such a term) in Johanan's academy. That is to say: it is already evident that in this famous academy not only were there sessions devoted to the study and development of Halakah, Law, as talmudic literature abundantly demonstrates, but there were

4. The commentary is *Yefeh ʿAnaf* by Samuel ben Isaac Ashkenazi Jaffe of the second half of the sixteenth century (see *Lam. Rab.*, Vilna edition, 3b). Cf. *Encyclopaedia Judaica*, 8:744f. And on *shebaḥ* = *doxa*, cf. also S. Lieberman in G. G. Scholem, *Jewish Gnosticism, Merkabah Mysticism, and Talmudic Tradition* (New York, 1960), 123.

5. *J. Megillah* 3:1. And note the combination of *gedulah* and *shebaḥ* in *Pesikta de-Rav Kahana*, ed. Buber 41b (but ed. Mandelbaum 76 reads only *gedulato*, and even in the variant readings does not give the Buber reading). *Pesikta Rabbati*, ed. Friedman 65b reads simply *gedulato*, and the same is true of *Tanhuma Numbers*, ed. Buber 60b.

6. Is this perhaps what lies behind *magnalia Dei* of Acts 2:11 also, at least in part? Cf. the commentary by K. Lake and H. J. Cadbury in F. Jackson and K. Lake, *Beginnings of Christianity* 4 (London, 1933), 20.

7. *Major Trends in Jewish Mysticism* (Jerusalem, 1941), 65 (paperback ed. New York 1961, p. 66). Note also *The Scroll of the War of the Sons of Light Against the Sons of Darkness*, ed. Y. Yadin, trans., B. and C. Rabin (Oxford, 1962), 274f., ". . . GDL 'EL, TŠBWHT 'EL, KBWD 'EL."

8. *T. Hagigah* 2.1 (on which see now S. Lieberman, *Tosefta Ki-Fshutah*, New York 1962, part V, Order Moʿed, pp. 1287ff.); *B. Hagigah* 14b; *J. Hagigah* 2.1; *Mekilta Simeon*, ed. Epstein-Melamed, 159.

9. See further n. 16 *infra*.

10. For a similar exclamation and enthusiasm in connection with another of his disciples, see version B of *'Abot de-Rabbi Natan*, ed. S. Schechter, p. 32.

also sessions devoted to esoteric lore, the kind of speculation that one customarily associates only with mystics and gnostics, and supposedly shunned by the talmudic rabbis. As Scholem proved in some of his most recent publications,[11] so-called gnostic themes can be traced back to the "normative" rabbinic thought of the second century C.E., and even late first century. I hope in the near future to prove that already *early* in the first half of the first [3] century, Pharisaic teachers were aware of theurgic practices, of which at least one sage did not approve, outspokenly.[12] The point is, talmudic sources evidently reveal that in the academy of Johanan ben Zakkai there was more than preoccupation with the Law. This there is no need to belabor. But I would like to suggest that in addition to halakic studies, in addition to general haggadic (non-legal) sessions, in addition to concerns with esoteric lore, there were also sessions devoted to the consideration of philosophical questions.

Needless to say, it is not always easy to draw a sharp line between esoteric statements that involve one in metaphysics, and philosophical expositions. But when I speak of philosophical questions in the present study, I have in mind the exploration of ethical problems in the idiom which had become characteristic of Hellenistic philosophical circles, particularly after the period of classical Greek philosophy. As scholars have universally observed, in the Hellenistic period, more and more, ethics came to be central in the preoccupation of philosophers.[13] This does not mean that there was no interest in the other branches of philosophy—physics, or rhetoric, or metaphysics. But as A. D. Nock put it,[14] to quote one historian out of many, " . . . in the Hellenistic age the philosophic centre of interest became primarily ethical."

It is with this, therefore, that we are here concerned when we speak of philosophical questions. But one more preliminary observation before we proceed to analysis of the talmudic texts: I do not seek to blur distinctions, to make of the vineyard of Jamnia an Epicurean garden with Hebrew Florilegia, to equate a talmudic epigram lifted out of context with some Greek sentence also uprooted from its natural habitat. The rabbis were not Platos in Hebrew disguise, nor were they students (much less disciples) of Plato. On the other hand, however, especially after the detailed researches of E. Bickerman, Hans Lewy, and S. Lieberman,[15] it is impossible to deny that in the tents of Shem

11. See especially the work referred to in n. 4 *supra*, and cf. the review by M. Smith in *Journal of Biblical Literature* 80 (1961): 190f.

12. For the present, see ARN, 56. I hope to show that the exegesis occurring there is indeed *literal* exegesis.

13. See, for example, E. Zeller, *Outlines of the History of Greek Philosophy* (New York, 1911), 208: " . . . in the systems of Hellenistic philosophy ethics and social theory occupy the most prominent positions. . . ."

14. *Conversion* (London, 1933), 114.

15. Merely by way of example (for very many details are scattered throughout the rich and numerous studies of these men) the following may be listed: by E. J. Bickerman, *Der Gott der Makkabäer* (Berlin, 1937); *The Maccabees* (New York, 1947); "La chaîne de la tradition pharisienne," *Revue biblique* 59 (1952): 44ff.; "The Maxim of Antigonus of Socho," *Harvard Theological Review* 44 (1951):153ff.; by Hans Lewy, the collection of essays in ʿ*Olamot*

quite a number of Japhet (Hellenistic) influences took up residence. That being the case, one may not a priori dismiss the possibility that in a [4] tannaite academy there should be sessions devoted to philosophical problems. Some texts at least suggest otherwise; let us look at them without more ado. And we shall begin with Johanan ben Zakkai's *favorite* disciple, Eleazar ben ʿArak.[16]

To him, chapter 2 of *Pirqe ʾAbot*[17] attributes the following saying: "Be diligent in the study of Torah, and know how to answer an Epicurean. Know in whose presence thou art toiling; and faithful is thy taskmaster to pay thee the reward of thy labor." A typical rabbinic view, one is tempted to say: There is emphasis on the study of Torah, there is opposition to epicureanism, there is affirmation of the doctrine of reward. No doubt. The difficulty is this, however: What *exactly* did Eleazar ben ʿArak say? Already in *ʾAbot de-Rabbi Natan*,[18] when Eleazar is quoted, the last clause, "to pay thee the reward of thy labor," is omitted, and there is good reason to believe that this clause came to be attached to Eleazar's maxim as a result of its similarity to part of Rabbi Tarfon's maxim cited immediately thereafter in the same chapter of *Pirqe ʾAbot*.[19] Not only that, but in *Pirqe ʾAbot* Eleazar's term for God appears as "thy taskmaster," *baʿal melakteka*, whereas in ARN the term used is "author of the covenant with thee, thy confederate," *baʿal beritka*.[20] Perhaps these are small matters. But more serious is the following: An examination of each of the maxims by Johanan ben Zakkai's disciples cited in the second chapter of *Pirqe ʾAbot* reveals that each is made up of three sentences[21]—this is their basic design and stylistic character. On the other hand, if you analyze Eleazar's saying, you discover not three, but four sentences, even if the clause about reward is omitted; thus: (1) Be diligent in the study of Torah; (2) Know how to answer an Epicurean; (3) Know in whose presence thou art toiling; (4) Faithful is thy taskmaster. ARN is of no help in this regard; actually it complicates matters all the more, for in addition to these sentences it adds still another, to wit, "Let not one word of the Torah escape thee."[22]

[5] Textual difficulties of this sort can prevent us from ever getting at the

---

Nifgashim [Heb.] (Jerusalem, 1960); by S. Lieberman, *Greek in Jewish Palestine* (New York, 1942) and *Hellenism in Jewish Palestine* (New York, 1962).

16. See *Pirqe ʾAbot* 2:8–9; ARN, 58f.; and cf. J. Goldin, *Fathers According to Rabbi Nathan* (New Haven, 1955), 74 and n. 13 ad loc. And note in particular *Mekilta Simeon*, 159.

17. PA 2:14.

18. P. 66.

19. 2:15–16; cf. ARN (both versions), 84. See also C. Taylor, *Sayings of the Jewish Fathers* (Cambridge, 1897–1900)1:12 (Heb. Text), and 2:45.

20. Cf. Taylor 2 ibid. and A. Marmorstein, *Old Rabbinic Doctrine of God* (Oxford, 1927), 78. [Cf. *Midrash ha-Gadol*, Leviticus, ed. Rabinowitz, p. 243.]

21. And this applies no less to Rabbi Eliezer ben Hyrqanos' saying in 2:10, as D. Hoffmann, *Ha-Mishnah ha-Rishonah* (Berlin, 1913), 33, showed. See also n. 84 in J. Goldin, "The End of Ecclesiastes" in *Studies and Texts* 3, ed. A. Altmann.

22. This statement does not occur in Version B of ARN ibid.; on that version's reading, see the idiom in the citation from Rabbi Ephraim bar Samson in G. Scholem, *Reshit ha-Qabbalah* (Jerusalem–Tel Aviv, 1948), 40.

substance of an author's statement. But in the present instance we are rather fortunate in having a reading preserved by a large number of Genizah manuscripts in the Cambridge University Library. Here we find the following version of Eleazar's saying—and note that it is indeed composed of three, rather than four, sentences: "Be diligent to learn how to answer an Epicurean, know in whose presence thou art toiling, and faithful is thy *ba'al berit*."[23] Not a word, in short, about the study of Torah. And this is unquestionably the correct reading. The expression *lilmod Torah*, to learn to study Torah, is so fixed a stereotype and cliché in rabbinic literature, that one can easily see how Eleazar's saying came to be garbled. Be diligent to study? Surely, said some later transmitter or copyist, Eleazar had in mind studying Torah.[24] No wonder the editor of ARN decided to improve even on this, and added, "Let not one word of the Torah escape thee."[25]

Since, however, we are interested in what Eleazar said, and not in what later teachers thought he said, we had best focus on his own words, which are, to repeat: "Be diligent to learn how to answer an Epicurean, know in whose presence thou art toiling, and faithful is thy taskmaster (or, thy *ba'al berit*)." If we focus on these words we cannot, I believe, fail to recognize that a kind of anti-Epicurean polemic is before us, some as-it-were Stoic (I emphasize "as-it-were") remark. I insist: this is not to say that Eleazar is a formal member of a Stoic school. All that is intended thus far is to call attention to the fact that if we hear what Eleazar is saying, we shall discern that he is *urging* us to learn how to refute an Epicurean (note his idiom: "be diligent to learn to refute," *hewe shaqud lilmod le-hashib*), that he exhorts us to remember that our toils in this world do not go unattended, and that there is one to whom we are subject and He is trustworthy, dependable.

One notion we had best dispose of at the outset, and that is, that talmudic sources use the term *epiqurus* indiscriminately to suggest any kind of heretic or unbeliever.[26] Despite widespread impression to the contrary, the term occurs in the Mishnah only in the *Pirqe 'Abot* passage we have cited and [6] once more, also in an old Mishnah,[27] which incidentally describes the points of difference on dogmatic issues between Pharisees and Sadducees. "The following have no

23. This reading, "Be diligent to learn how to answer an Epicurean," sometimes indeed with the *'et* accusative sign rather than the prefix *lamed*, occurs *at least* in the following MSS and MS fragments: TS, E 3, 40, 55, 63, 74, 82, 93, 103, 111, 124, 128, 141. Note in fragment no. 40 the interesting reading *she-toṣi'* (rather than *she-tashib*).

24. One example may be instructive. In Codex Kaufmann of the Mishnah the reading is, "Be diligent to study (learn) how to answer an Epicurean"; and on the margin of the MS someone has noted that the word "Torah" should be inserted after "learn"!

25. Perhaps it is this editor in fact who is responsible for that word "Torah" getting into the text.

26. Cf. R. Marcus in his note d ad Josephus, *Antiquities* 10.281 (Loeb Classics; Josephus VI, 313).

27. *Sanhedrin* 10:1, and for the correct reading and the implications thereof cf. J. Goldin in *Proceedings, American Academy for Jewish Research* 27 (1958):49, and notes ad loc. [above, p. 60–Ed].

share in the '*olam ha-ba*', the world to come (or, age to come): He who says, there will be no resurrection, Torah was not revealed, and Epicurus" i.e., an Epicurean—note especially that the text reads, [*an*] Epiqurus, not *the* Epicurean; note further, that in all the best manuscripts and editions, the transliteration of the word is excellent—אפיקורוס, not אפיקורס[28] as in many later indifferent appearances of the term. Except for these two places the word does not appear anywhere else in the Mishnah—all other appearances of the term in the Mishnah, as one may learn even by consulting Kasovsky's *Concordance*,[29] are untrustworthy. In the Mishnah, then, the word has not yet been worn thin by frequent usage. All of which is simply meant to underscore that it is wisest not to water down Eleazar's remark, and if he said an Epicurean, he meant just that. Very likely he had not non-Jewish, but Jewish Epicureans in mind. But he very likely did have in mind such Jews as had become Epicurean more or less in outlook, not just any heretic at all.

To be sure, by the latter half of the second century, as would appear from Lucian's "Alexander the False Prophet," the term "Epicurean" seems to have become a dirty word; one can frighten audiences with it[30] although they might not know what the term meant really, somewhat like the word "communist" in some circles today. But that Eleazar was using Epicurean in a slovenly, name-calling manner is most unlikely. Observe, he does not say, Beware (*hewe zahir*) of an Epiqurus—an idiom so congenial to *Pirqe 'Abot*.[31] What he says is, Be *shaqud*, diligent, *lilmod*, to study, to learn, *le-hashib*, to reply, to refute. He is speaking of serious refutation of the Epicurean, and like a Stoic insists that there is a trustworthy God before whom we engage in our toiling.[32]

We are now in a position, I believe, to understand part of the story of Rabban Johanan's enthusiasm over his disciple's brilliant Merkabah discourse. [7] The talmudic sources relate that when Eleazar finished speaking, his master not only kissed him and exclaimed "Blessed be the Lord, God of Israel, who gave such a descendant to our father Abraham," but went on as follows:

> There are some who teach, interpret (*doresh*) becomingly, but do not practice, do not carry out, becomingly; there are some who practice what is becoming, but do not teach becomingly. But Eleazar ben 'Arak teaches becomingly and practices becomingly. How fortunate you are, O Father Abraham. . . .

---

28. And though the copyist of the Version B manuscript for S. Schechter's edition of ARN, 66 recorded אפיקורס, I personally checked Vatican MS heb. 303, and found the reading to be definitely אפיקורוס.

29. C. Y. Kasovsky, *Thesaurus Mishnae* [Heb.] 1 (Jerusalem, 1956) 261. And note its *single* appearance in the *Tosefta, Sanhedrin* 13:5.

30. Cf. ed. M. Harmon (in Loeb Classics, IV, 175ff).

31. See for example PA 1:9, 11; 2:1, 3, 10, 13; 4:13.

32. Cf. R. D. Hicks, *Stoic and Epicurean* (New York, 1910), 304: "The Epicureans were never tired of arguing against the conception of God as either Creator or Providence. . . . On these points their chief antagonists were the Stoics. . . ."

"Practices what he preaches," *na'eh doresh we-na'eh meqayyem*, has become so familiar an expression in Hebrew, that occasionally one imagines that it occurs frequently in the classical sources. That fact is, it occurs only in one other context. When, it is reported, the bachelor Ben 'Azzai held forth on one occasion, on the importance of the first biblical commandment, to be fruitful and to multiply, his colleague Eleazar ben 'Azariah rejoined stingingly:

> Things are well said when they come from the mouths of those who put them to practice, *na'im debarim ke-she-hen yoṣ'in mi-pi 'oṣehen*. There are some who teach becomingly and practice becomingly. Ben 'Azzai teaches becomingly but does not practice becomingly.[33]

Or as we might put it, he *talks* a good line. Now, in this context Eleazar's rejoinder is perfectly intelligible. But what can that remark mean in the story of Eleazar ben 'Arak's Merkabah discourse in the presence of Johanan ben Zakkai? What practice, ill or otherwise, would be at issue? That when Johanan warned him that esoteric subjects are not discussed in public, Eleazar assented? As the texts read, it is no wonder commentators (e.g. the *Maharsha*)[34] have had difficulty with that sentence. What meaning can *na'eh meqayyem* have here, even if *na'eh doresh* does apply to a brilliant discourse?

It is a Hellenistic source which furnishes the answer to this question. Diogenes Laertius says that when the Athenians honored Zeno, the founder of the Stoic school, among other things this is what they said of him.[35]

> . . . Zeno of Citium . . . has for many years been . . . exhorting to virtue and temperance those of the youth who come to him to be taught, directing them to what is best, affording to all in his own conduct a pattern for imitation in perfect consistency with his teaching (παράδειγμα τὸν ἴδιον βίον ἐκθεὶς ἅπασιν ἀχόλουθον ὄντα τοῖς λόγοις οἷς διελέγετο).[36]

And so, "practices what he preaches" is a *topos*, a way of complimenting, pure and simple. And since I wrote the paragraph above, S. Lieberman has [8] graciously sent me in private communication two or three additional examples, one of them by the way from Plutarch (*Moralia* 1033a seq.), in which *Stoics* are criticized for not living, conducting themselves, as they themselves teach. One cannot help therefore recalling what Lucian writes of the philosophers in his *Mennippus*:[37] τοὺς γὰρ αὐτοὺς τούτους εὕρισκον ἐπιτηρῶν ἐναντιώτατα τοῖς αὑτῶν λόγοις ἐπιτηδεύοντας.

---

33. *T. Yebamot* 8.4 (and see S. Lieberman, *Tosefeth Rishonim* [Jerusalem, 1938] II:22); cf. *B. Yebamot* 63b and *Genesis Rabba* 34, ed. Theodor-Albeck, 326f.

34. I.e., Rabbi Samuel Edels (1555–1631), the author of impressive talmudic *novellae*. His comment occurs ad *B. Ḥagigah* 14b.

35. Diog. Laert. 7.10–11 (ed. Hicks in Loeb Classics, II, 121, whose translation I am using).

36. On the genuineness of the decree see Hicks' reference loc. cit., 120.

37. *Men.* 5 (in Loeb Classics, IV, 82).

It may be no more than a coincidence that Eleazar ben ʿArak should be praised by his teacher as the founder of the Stoics was praised. And I certainly do not intend to press this too hard. Let us therefore get on with our sources. We read:[38] When Johanan ben Zakkai's son died, his five famous disciples came to comfort him. Each one made the earnest effort—Eliezer ben Hyrqanos, Joshua ben Hananiah, Jose the Priest, Simeon ben Nathanel, and Eleazar ben ʿArak. But all of them, except the last failed. As Johanan put it to each one in turn as each finished his little homily, "Is it not enough that I grieve over my own, that you remind me of the grief of others?" But when Eleazar appeared, the outcome was different. As soon as he appeared, Johanan knew he would be comforted, and in fact he was. And here is what Eleazar had said and what proved to be the genuine consolation:

> I shall tell thee a parable: To what may this be likened? To a man with whom the king deposited some object. Every single day the man would weep and cry out, saying: "Woe unto me! When shall I be quit of this trust in peace?" Thou too, master, thou hadst a son: he studied the Torah, the Prophets, the Holy Writings,[39] he studied Mishnah, Halakah, and Haggadah, and he departed from the world without sin. And thou shouldst be comforted when thou hast returned thy trust unimpaired.

Now, this notion of the soul of one's beloved held in trust is not unknown in rabbinic sources; it is especially familiar in the anecdote of the death of Rabbi Meʾir's sons.[40] It occurs also in non-rabbinic sources,[41] and I would like to cite a relevant passage from Philo (*de Abrahamo* 44),[42] who in praising Abraham says:

> . . . I will speak of one [merit] which concerns the death of his wife, in which his conduct should not be passed over in silence. When he had lost his life-long partner, . . . when sorrow was making itself ready to wrestle with his soul, he grappled with it, as in the arena, and prevailed. He gave strength and high courage to the natural antagonist of passion, reason, [9] which he had taken as his counsellor throughout his life and now particularly was determined to obey. . . . The advice was that he should not grieve over-bitterly as at an utterly new and unheard-of misfortune, nor yet assume an indifference as though nothing painful had occurred, but choose the mean rather than the extremes and aim at moderation of feeling, not resent that nature should be paid the debt which is its due, but quietly and gently lighten the blow.
>
> The testimonies for this are to be found in the holy books. . . . They show that after weeping for a little over the corpse he quickly rose up from it, holding further

---

38. ARN, 58f.

39. The correct reading of the text is preserved in Israel ibn Al-Nakawa, *Menorat Ha-Maor*, ed. H. G. Enelow 3 (New York, 1929–32), 523.

40. *Midrash Mishle*, ed. Buber, 108–109.

41. See for example Sapientia 15.8, 16, and especially Josephus, *Wars* 3.8.5.

42. I am using Colson's translation (Loeb Classics, VI, 125ff.).

mourning to be out of keeping with wisdom, which taught him that death is not the extinction of the soul but its separation and detachment from the body and its return to the place whence it came; and it came, as was shown in the story of creation, from God. *And, as no reasonable person would chafe at repaying a debt or deposit (χρέος ἤ παρακαταθήκην) to him who had proffered it, so too he must not fret when nature took back her own, but accept the inevitable with equanimity.*

The passage, as is clear, reverberates with Stoic echoes.[43] "Never say about anything," Epictetus tells us,[44] "'I have lost it,' but only 'I have given it back.' Is your child dead? It has been given back (ἀπεδόθη). Is your wife dead? She has been given back." Interesting enough, when Tarn comes to summarize Stoic teaching, even he chooses as one of its distinctive emphases, "the Stoic will not grieve for his son's death."[45]

Once again, perhaps it may be wise to repeat the note of caution already struck. It does not *necessarily* follow from all we have thus far explored, that without the Stoics the talmudic Fathers could not have arrived at the idea of the soul as a deposit—though I must say, even Ps. 30:6 (MT 31:6), *In manus tuas commendo spiritum meum*, does not *altogether* suggest the idea to the tannaite midrash, the *Mekilta*,[46] which cites the verse as prooftext for the statement that "all souls are in the hand of Him by whose utterance the world came into being." In the companion midrash, *Mekilta of R. Simeon*,[47] the idea is not even given the benefit of this prooftext; the verse isn't cited at all! Be that as it may, even a novice knows that it is fake scholarship to declare that there is necessary dependence simply because one finds [10] similarity of ideas. But, firstly, similarity should be recognized if it exists, even if there may be no dependence. Secondly, however, there is a detail that must be introduced in this connection.

Josephus cannot be depended on either when he protests *pro vita sua* or— and it is this which concerns us here—when he describes sects in Jewish Palestine as though they were Greek schools of thought. This has been underscored so frequently by so many scholars that it would be childish to ignore their remarks. And yet, even if we grant that it is grotesque to look upon Pharisees, Sadducees, and Essenes as though they were imitation Greek schools, perhaps we may learn something from the particular form of absurdity of

43. See also Colson's note, loc. cit. 598f. Cf. Philo's *Quaestiones*, ed. R. Marcus (in Loeb Classics, I, 350–52).

44. *Encheiridion* 11, ed. W. A. Oldfather (in Loeb Classics, II, 491).

45. W. W. Tarn, *Hellenistic Civilization* (London, 1936), 299. In *Republic* 10, 603, Plato also says that the good man will not mourn excessively over the loss of his son; but though he gives several reasons for this, he does not speak of the soul as a deposit or trust.

46. Ed. J. Z. Lauterbach, 2:67. St. Augustine on that verse does not speak of this either. Note that primarily the verse recalls to him its use in Luke 23:46, and hence he underscores 'Audiamus vocem Domini,' cf. *Enarrationes in Psalmos*, ad loc. (ed. Dekkers and Fraipont, CCL 38 [1956], 199). Cf. St. Jerome on Ps. 145:4 (MT 146:4) (ed. Morin, CCL 78:324).

47. *Mekilta Simeon*, ed. Epstein-Melamed, 95.

which the author is guilty. It is instructive that, when Josephus describes the Pharisees, of all schools he chooses the Stoics to compare them with: "the Pharisees, a sect having points of resemblance to that which the Greeks call the Stoic school."[48] The statement is not to be dismissed cavalierly; observe how carefully he has expressed himself, "a sect having points of resemblance," ἡ παραπλήσιός ἐστι. That Josephus is capable of giving an accurate characterization of a Greek school, we know from his observations on the Epicureans:[49]

It therefore seems to me, in view of the things foretold by Daniel, that they are very far from holding a true opinion who declare that God takes no thought for human affairs. For if it were the case that *the world goes by some automatism* (εἰ συνέβαινεν αὐτοματισμῷ τινι τὸν κόσμον διάγειν),[50] we should not have seen all these things happen in accordance with his prophecy.

Josephus may be stretching a point, and more than a point, when he feels he has to. But he is undoubtedly registering something real about the Pharisees—they *were* affected by a Stoic climate; and as Tarn has written:[51] "The philosophy of the Hellenistic world was the Stoic; all else was secondary." Jewish Palestine was not immune to this.

Such at least is the climate of notions around Eleazar ben ʿArak, Johanan ben Zakkai's favorite disciple of whom the text says: "Happy the disciple whose master praises him and testifies to his gifts!"[52] And if we keep this climate in mind we shall understand a famous block of passages in *Pirqe ʾAbot*, often cited but perhaps not sufficiently appreciated.

[11] When the second chapter of PA resumes the chain of tradition which is the basic scheme of the first chapter, it quite properly introduces Johanan ben Zakkai with the customary formula, "Rabban Johanan ben Zakkai took over from Hillel and Shammai."[53] Then, as is the practice of PA, it quotes his saying. Since the editor is eager to show that that chain of tradition, whose first link was forged with Moses at Sinai,[54] was not broken even after Johanan ben Zakkai—though in his day the Temple had been destroyed[55]—he proceeds to introduce the five famous disciples of Johanan, and to quote *their* sayings. But as everyone knows, this introduction is not quite like all the previous introductions. Before the editor quotes these men, he first informs us how Johanan used

48. *Vita* 2, end, ed. Thackeray, 7.

49. *Antiquities* 10, end, ed. R. Marcus (in Loeb Classics, VI, 313).

50. See also S. Lieberman, "How Much Greek in Jewish Palestine," in *Studies and Texts* 1, ed. A. Altmann (Cambridge, Mass., 1963), 130. By the way, rabbinic sources reflect also an awareness of the fact that as regards Providence and belief in God, there are varieties of views; cf. *Sifre* Deut. 329, ed. Finkelstein 379 and *Midrash Tannaim* 202.

51. Op. cit., 290. And regarding semitic influences on Stoic thought, cf. M. Rostovtzeff, *Social and Economic History of the Hellenistic World* (Oxford, 1941), 1426, n. 232.

52. Cf. Goldin, *Fathers . . . Nathan*, p. 74, and note ad loc.

53. PA 2:8; cf. the idiom in 1:3, 4, 6, 8, 10, 12.

54. PA 1:1.

55. See the story in Goldin, *Fathers . . . Nathan*, 35ff.

to describe them.[56] Even after that he does not quote the disciples; before the editor gets down to their sentences he introduces a long conversation piece, a section recording an exchange between Johanan and his disciples.[57] Only after all this does he transmit their sayings. Nothing like this, description[58] or conversation, occurs anywhere else in PA.

The insertion of a description of the disciples is easily explainable. Since the editor is eager to assert that despite the national, the political and institutional, disaster, the destruction of the Jerusalem Temple, the Pharisaic chain of tradition remained unbroken, we can appreciate why he feels he ought to report the master's own testimony regarding the stature of his disciples. These were no ordinary disciples, no run-of-the-mill sages. Eliezer ben Hyrqanos was "a plastered cistern which loses not a drop. Joshua—happy is she who gave birth to him. Jose—a saint. Simeon ben Nathanel—fears sin. Eleazar ben ʿArak—ever-flowing stream." I wish I could understand specifically each of these compliments—they are obviously intended to suggest something extra-ordinary; and perhaps to have called Eliezer ben Hyrqanos "a plastered cistern which loses not a drop," was more or less what Zeno meant when he compared his successor Cleanthes "to hard waxen tablets which are difficult to write upon, but retain the characters written upon them."[59] But, as I say, while it is not the practice of PA otherwise to include such data regarding the other sages, in the case of the five disciples of Johanan the motive is understandable. But why, after he has introduced them so handsomely, does not the editor begin to quote them, as he does with all other sages? Why before quoting their sayings does he insert the long conversation, especially in a treatise where no other give-and-take is presented, [12] halakic *or* haggadic? And since this is not the only question raised by the long passage, perhaps it would be wise to quote it, so that we may see vividly what the problems are:[60]

Rabban Johanan said to them: Go forth and see which is the right way to which a man should cleave.
Rabbi Eliezer replied: A liberal eye.
Rabbi Joshua replied: A good companion.
Rabbi Jose replied: A good neighbor.
Rabbi Simeon replied: Foresight.
Rabbi Eleazar replied: Goodheartedness.
Said Rabban Johanan ben Zakkai to them: I prefer the answer of Eleazar ben ʿArak, for in his words your words are included.

56. PA 2:8.
57. 2:9.
58. On the other hand, see how the compiler of Version A of ARN (chap. 18) pp. 66–69 was led by this to draw up additional material (but not of a master describing *disciples*, but of a sage describing his teachers and predecessors, and a sage describing other sages).
59. Diogenes Laertius 7.37 (II, 149).
60. PA 2:9; for the translation of cf. J. Goldin, *Living Talmud: The Wisdom of the Fathers* (Chicago, 1958), 99.

Rabban Johanan said to them: Go forth and see which is the evil way which a man should shun.

Rabbi Eliezer replied: A grudging eye.

Rabbi Joshua replied: An evil companion.

Rabbi Jose replied: An evil neighbor.

Rabbi Simeon replied: Borrowing and not repaying; for he that borrows from man is as one who borrows from God, blessed be He, as it is said, "The wicked man borrows and does not repay, but the just man shows mercy and gives" (Ps. 37:21; MT 37:21).[61]

Rabbi Eleazar replied: Meanheartedness.

Said Rabban Johanan to them: I prefer the answer of Eleazar ben ʿArak, for in his words your words are included.

There it is, a conversation (as I said) unlike anything else in PA, and only after it has been reported, are we offered the sayings of these sages. As one reads it, not only must he ask, what in the world is it doing here, but he cannot escape at least two other questions. First, what are these men talking about? True, their master had asked them about the right way, or course, to which a person ought to cling, and they had offered their replies. But is it not fantastic that these men, the best disciples Johanan ben Zakkai had—Johanan ben Zakkai who had been quoted a paragraph or so before[62] as the author of the saying, "If thou hast wrought much in the study of Torah take no credit to thyself, for to this end wast thou created," and as ARN added,[63] "for men (*haberiyot*) were created only on condition that they study Torah"—is it not fantastic that, when the best disciples of such a master, leading sages in Israel, are asked about the right course to which a man should cleave, not even one of them suggests in his answer something connected with Torah? [13] Jewish sages without a word about the Torah? Second, what is the meaning of asking first about the right way and then about the evil way, and then the answers which are simply the negation of the former affirmations? What have I learned from the second conversation that I did not already learn from the first one?

That the ancients already found the passage something of a serious problem is evident from the way it is preserved in ARN.[64] To give only a couple of examples: In PA Johanan had asked, which is the right way to which a man should cleave. In ARN, his question appears as, "Which is the good way to which a man should cleave, *so that through it he might enter the world to come?* . . . Which is the evil way which a man should shun, *so that he might enter the world to come?*" In other words, "the world to come" has suddenly made an entrance. Or again: In PA, to the first question Rabbi Jose had replied,

61. With St. Augustine's comment on this verse *Quid si pauper est* etc. (CCL 38.355f.), cf. ARN, 48 and 57, and Maimonides' Code, *Mishneh Torah*, Sefer Zeraʿim, Hilkot Matnot ʿAniyyim X (and note X,4).

62. PA 2:8.

63. P. 58; and see also Version B of ARN, 66.

64. P. 58.

"A good neighbor," and to the second question, "An evil neighbor." In ARN on the other hand, he seems to have grown a little more garrulous in his answers. To the first question he replies, "A good neighbor, a good impulse (*yeṣer ṭob*), and a good wife"; to the second, "An evil neighbor, an evil impulse, and an evil wife."[65] These are not the only variants; study of the parallel passages will reveal interesting variants in Eleazar ben ʿArak's answer, too.

The answers of the disciples are far from clear, but if we wish to capture something of the meaning of this exchange between Johanan and his disciples, it is terribly important to listen to his question with utmost attention. Johanan did not ask a trivial question, nor did he express himself carelessly. He asked about the way to which a man should cleave, *dabaq*. Properly to feel the force of this verb *dabaq*, one might compare Johanan's question with the almost identical—*almost* but not entirely so—question later raised by Judah the Prince, the redactor of the Mishnah, also quoted in the second chapter of PA— indeed he is the first sage cited there.[66] Judah asks: "Which is the right course that a man ought to *choose* (*she-yabor*) for himself?" But Johanan speaks not just of choice, but of *cleaving*. That the Hebrew sources take the verb *dabaq*, cleave, very seriously, can be demonstrated by a number of texts. The biblical verse (Deut. 11:22) exhorts, "to love the Lord your God, to walk in all His ways, and to cleave (προσκολλᾶσθαι) unto him (*adhaerentes ei*)." At which the tannaite midrash, the *Sifre*, exclaims:[67] "But how is it possible for a human being to ascend on high and cleave to the Fire?" Even in Scripture the verb *dabaq* has a fervor to it; here is Jeremiah (13:11) expressing himself: "For as the girdle cleaveth (*yidbaq ha-ʾ ezor*, κολλᾶται) to the [14] loins of a man, so have I caused to cleave unto Me (*hidbaqti ʾ elai*, ἐκόλλησα) the whole house of Israel and the whole house of Judah, saith the Lord." (*Sicut enim adhaeret lumbare ad lumbos viri, sic agglutinavi mihi omnem domum Juda, dicit Dominus.*) That the Midrash is fully sensitive to this verse can be seen in the *Tanhuma* comment on Lev. 19:2:[68] "Be ye holy! Why? For I am holy, for it is said, 'As the girdle cleaveth to the loins of a man,' etc." "Let him kiss me with the kisses of his mouth" (*Osculetur me osculo oris sui*), says the poet of Canticles (Cant. 1:1, MT 1:2); and the midrash in its homiletical pun explains, "*Let Him kiss me*, let Him cause me to cleave to Him (*yishaqeni, yadbqeni*).[69]

65. And note the reading of Version B, 59.
66. PA 2:1, beginning; cf. Version B of ARN, 70.
67. Ad Deut. 49, ed. Finkelstein, 114.
68. Ed. Buber, III, 37b.
69. *Canticles Rabba* 1:2, 6. For the pun on the verb *nashaq* ad loc. see the commentators. On the intensity of the expression in Cant. see also Origen's commentary (Origen, *The Song of Songs, Commentary and Homilies*, trans. R. P. Lawson [Ancient Christian Writers 26; London, 1957], 60): "But, since the age is almost ended and His own presence is not granted me, and I see only His ministers ascending and descending upon me, because of this I pour out my petition to Thee, the Father of my Spouse, beseeching Thee to have compassion at last upon my love, and to send Him, that He may now no longer speak to me only by His servants the angels and the prophets, but may come Himself, directly, and kiss me with the kisses of His mouth— that is to say, may pour the words of His mouth into mine, that I may hear Him speak Himself,

So long as we are lingering over the word *dabaq*, "cleave," I hope it is not out of place to call attention to one more point, especially for the benefit of Hebraists. According to our sources, both PA and ARN, the question Johanan asked was: What is the way (or course) to which a man should cleave (איזוהי דרך ‏‎... שידבק בה האדם)? In other words, he is speaking of *cleaving to a way*. But though *dabaq* is not a rare word in Scripture, nowhere does such an expression occur—and not only in Scripture, but at least for the time being, in none of the documents from the Dead Sea. A man cleaves to his wife,[70] the tongue cleaves to the roof of the mouth,[71] one cleaves to the truth and good deeds and the testimonies of the Lord,[72] curses cleave to a man,[73] and Ps. 62:9 (MT 63:9) offers even "My soul cleaveth unto Thee" (*Adhaesit anima mea post te*), literally, "after thee," דבקה נפשי אחריך (cf. LXX 62:9, ἐκολλήθη ἡ ψυχή μου ὀπίσω σου); as we have seen, there are those who cleave [15] to the Lord (cf. Deut. 4:4; LXX, Ὑμεῖς δὲ οἱ προσκείμενοι [!] κυρίῳ, *Vos Autem qui adhaeretis Domino Deo vestri*). But nowhere else will one find this combination דבק בדרך — nowhere else, that is, except in a statement of old exegetes whom the tannaite sources call *doreshe reshumot* or *doreshe haggadot*. Lauterbach once called *them* "the Allegorical Interpreters."[74] Be that as it may, the exegesis of these anonymous teachers is of a figurative-speculative kind. And it is in one of their comments, preserved in the tannaite *Sifre*[75] that the following occurs: "If it is your wish to recognize [acknowledge?] Him at whose utterance the world came into being,[76] study haggadah—for thus you come to recognize God and cleave to His ways" ומדבק בדרכיו.

The term *dabaq*, then, is no ordinary term, and it was no ordinary question Johanan asked, and the give-and-take with his disciples was no ordinary conversation. The idiom reveals a certain intensiveness, a certain *fervor*, and this is the telling thing. It is the idiom which suddenly summons up remem-

and see Him teaching. The kisses are Christ's, which He bestows on His Church when at His coming, being present in the flesh, He in His own person spoke to her the words of faith and love and peace, according to the promise of Isaias who, when sent beforehand to the Bride, had said (cf. Isa. 33:22): *Not a messenger, nor an angel, but the Lord Himself shall save us.*" Cf. also S. Lieberman, *Yemenite Midrashim* (Jerusalem, 1940), 14.

70. Cf. Gen. 2:24.
71. Ps. 136:6 (MT 137:6).
72. *Dead Sea Scrolls* II, 2: *Manual of Discipline*, ed. M. Burrows (New Haven, 1951) Plate I, line 5; *Thanksgiving Scroll*, ed. J. Licht (Jerusalem, 1957), 202; Ps. 118:31 (MT 119:31).
73. *Dead Sea Scrolls* II, Plate II, lines 15f.; *Zadokite Documents*, ed. C. Rabin (Oxford, 1958), 5.
74. See. J. Z. Lauterbach, "The Ancient Jewish Allegorists in Talmud and Midrash" in *Jewish Quarterly Review* n.s. 1 (1910–11): 291–333, 503–31.
75. Ad Deut. loc. cit., and note ibid. the variant readings in the critical apparatus.
76. Literally, "Him who spake and the world (*ha-ʿolam*) came to be." I would like to call special attention to the variants "The Holy One, blessed be He" and "thy Creator" recorded by Finkelstein, ad loc. (I neglected to do this in the Hebrew version of this study), for if these *doreshe haggadot* are pre-70 c.e., they did not use *ha-ʿolam* for 'world'. See my note 39 in "Of Change and Adaptation in Judaism" in *History of Religions* 4 (Chicago, 1965), 283 [below, p. 227.—Ed.].

brances of a mood and a tone of voice which were current in Hellenist circles. As Nock wrote three decades ago:[77]

> ... this idea [that devotion to philosophy would make a difference in a man's life] was not thought of as a matter of purely intellectual conviction. The philosopher commonly said *not* "Follow my arguments one by one, check and control them to the best of your ability; truth should be dearer than Plato to you," *but* "Look at this picture which I paint, and can you resist its attractions? Can you refuse a hearing to the legitimate rhetoric which I address to you in the name of virtue?" Even Epicurus says in an argument, "Do not be deceived, men, or led astray: do not fall. There is no natural fellowship between reasonable beings. *Believe me*, those who express the other view deceive you and argue you out of what is right. Epictetus, II, 19, 34 also employs the same appeal, *Believe me*, and counters opponents by arguments which appeal to the heart and not to the head. Inside the schools, at least inside the academic school, there was an atmosphere of hard thinking, of which something survives in the various commentaries on Aristotle. Yet even in the schools this was overcast by tradition and loyalty. . . . The philosophy which addressed itself to the world at large was a dogmatic philosophy seeking to save souls.

[16] This is the mood of our PA passage, and this is the mood of Johanan's question, which I believe can almost be rendered in the words from Diogenes Laertius, τί πράττων ἄριστα βιώσεται.[78] It was then a philosophical question Johanan asked; and first he asked which is the right way, and then which is the evil way. In other words, what is he doing? He formulates his question first in the positive, then in the negative, one way and its opposite. And when his disciples replied, as we saw, they did the same thing (to Simeon's answer we shall get shortly), one way and its opposite: liberal eye, grudging eye (עין טובה, עין רעה); good companion, evil companion; good neighbor, evil neighbor; goodheartedness, meanheartedness (*leb tob, leb ra ʿ*).

It will now be instructive to review the summary of Stoic teaching drawn up by Diogenes Laertius[79] (of which Hicks says,[80] by the way, "the summary of Stoic doctrine in Book VII (39–160) is comprehensive and trustworthy"):

> Amongst *the virtues* (τῶν δ' ἀρετῶν) some are primary, some are subordinate to these. The following are the primary: wisdom, courage, justice, temperance. Particular virtues are magnanimity, continence, endurance, presence of mind, good counsel.
>
> Similarly *of vices* (τῶν κακιῶν) some are primary, other subordinate: *e.g.*, folly, cowardice, injustice, profligacy are accounted primary; but incontinence, stupidity,

---

77. *Conversion*, 181. And see also H. I. Marrou, *History of Education in Antiquity* (New York, 1956), 206.

78. 7.2 (Loeb Classics II, 110). And cf. Marrou, op. cit., 209: "The more the Graeco-Roman period advances, the more important the moral aspect becomes, until it is the essential if not the only object of the philosopher's speculation and activity and whole life."

79. 7.92ff. (II, 199ff., Hicks' translation).

80. In his introduction, p. xx.

ill-advisedness subordinate. Further, many hold that *the vices* are forms of ignorance of those things whereof the *corresponding virtues* are the knowledge....

Another particular definition *of good* which they give is "the natural perfection of a rational being *qua* rational." To this answers virtue and, as being partakes in virtue, virtuous acts and good men; also its supervening accessories, joy and gladness and the like. So *with evils*: either they are vices, folly, cowardice, injustice, and the like; or things which partake of vice, including vicious acts and wicked persons as well as their accompaniments, despair, moroseness, and the like.

Again, *some goods* (τῶν ἀγαθῶν) are goods of the mind, and others external, while some are neither mental nor external. The former include the virtues and virtuous acts; external goods are such as having a good country or a good friend, and the prosperity of such. Whereas to be good and happy oneself is of the class of goods neither mental nor external. Similarly of *things evil* (των κακῶν) some are mental evils, namely, vices and vicious actions; others are outward evils, as to have a foolish country or a foolish friend and the unhappiness of such; other evils again are neither mental nor outward, *e.g.*, to be yourself bad and unhappy.

Again, *goods* (τῶν ἀγαθῶν) are either of the nature of ends or they are the means to these ends, or they are at the same time ends and means. [17] A friend and the advantages derived from him are means to good, whereas confidence, highspirit, liberty, delight, gladness, freedom from pain, and every virtuous act are of the nature of ends.

The virtues (they say) are goods of the nature at once of ends and of means. On the one hand, insofar as they cause happiness they are means, and on the other hand, insofar as they make it complete, and so are themselves part of it, they are ends. Similarly *of evils* (τῶν κακῶν) some are of the nature of ends and some of means, while others are at once both means and ends. Your enemy and the harm he does you are means; consternation, abasement, slavery, gloom, despair, excess of grief, and every vicious action are of the nature of ends. Vices are evil both as ends and as means, since insofar as they cause misery they are means, but insofar as they make it complete, so that they become part of it, they are ends....

Of the beautiful (τοῦ καλοῦ) there are (they say) four species, namely, what is just, courageous, orderly and wise.... Similarly there are four species *of the base or ugly* (τοῦ αἰσχροῦ), namely, what is unjust, cowardly, disorderly, and unwise....

Goods ('Αγαθά) comprise the virtues of prudence, justice, courage, temperance, and the rest; while the opposites of these are *evils* (κακά), namely, folly, injustice, and the rest.[81] ... *To benefit* (ὠφελεῖν) is to set in motion or sustain in accordance with virtue; whereas *to harm* (βλάπτειν) is to set in motion or sustain in accordance with vice....

Things of the *preferred class* (προηγμένα) are those which have positive value, *e.g.*, amongst mental qualities, natural ability, skill, moral improvement, and the like; among bodily qualities, life, health, strength, good condition, soundness of organs, beauty, and so forth; and in the sphere of external things, wealth, fame, noble birth, and the like. To the class of *things "rejected"* (ἀποπροηγμένα) belong, of mental qualities, lack of ability, want of skill, and the like; among bodily

---

81. Since at this point Diogenes presents also the view of those who believe that in addition to the good and evil, there is also the neutral, he adds that neutral (neither good nor evil) "are all those things which neither benefit nor harm a man: such as life, health ... and the like. This Hecato affirms in his *De fine* book vii," etc. Cf. Diogenes on Plato in 3.102 (II, 365–66).

qualities, death, disease, weakness, being out of condition, mutilation, ugliness, and the like; in the sphere of external things, poverty, ignominy, low birth, and so forth....[82]

Again, *of things preferred* some are preferred for their own sake, some for the sake of something else, and others again both for their own sake and for the sake of something else. . . . And similarly with the class of *things rejected* under the contrary heads....

Befitting acts (καθήκοντα)[83] are all those which reason prevails with us to do; and this is the case with honoring one's parents, brothers and country, and intercourse with friends. *Unbefitting, or contrary to duty* (παρὰ τὸ καθῆκον) are all acts that reason deprecates, *e.g.*, to neglect one's [18] parents, to be indifferent to one's brothers, not to agree with friends, to disregard the interests of one's country, and so forth...[84]

Surely this is enough, more than enough. The summary of Stoic ethics has manifestly been drawn up along a certain line, first the positive, then the negative, first in terms of the good and then immediately thereafter in terms of the evil. I am in no position to say whether this pattern or idiom is unique to the Stoics, especially when I recall some sections in the *Republic*, for example;[85] and I would indeed be grateful to classicists if they could inform me whether such a style is characteristic of study and discussion in Hellenistic schools generally. But it is impressive, is it not, that only in Diogenes' summary of *Stoic* teaching, and in no other summary of his (including the long presentation of Epicurean teaching),[86] is this style so distinct. Whatever else one may wish to conclude, this at least seems to me legitimate—that in Stoic circles defining and discussing were carried on in this style, first the one term, and then its opposite.

And this is precisely the form of the give-and-take between Johanan and his disciples, first the good course, and then the evil course. It is a philosophical *façon de parler* Johanan is using. And since it was a philosophical question he had asked, as we saw earlier in our analysis of the idiom of his question, his disciples answered him in the philosophical way, first the positive, then the negative. Since it was a philosophical question, his disciples answered in characteristic philosophical terms—and that is why not one of them even bothered to refer to Torah. And since it was an important session, though nothing like it occurs elsewhere in the treatise, the editor of PA preserved the record of it, put it down right after he had recounted the praises of the disciples—but before he cites their sayings. It is as though the editor were

82. Here, too, Diogenes adds: "But again there are things belonging to neither class; such are not preferred, neither are they rejected." Cf. preceding note.

83. Cf. Diogenes 7.108: "Zeno was the first to use this term καθῆκον of conduct"; and see Hicks' note ad loc.

84. Cf. notes 81–82 *supra*.

85. Cf. 3.400; 4.442–43; and compare especially 8–9 with the earlier books. See also Diogenes on Plato, 3.103ff. (II, 367f.).

86. ". . . Book X is made up largely of extracts from the writings of Epicurus, by far the most precious thing preserved in this collection of odds and ends" (Hicks in his introduction, p. xx).

asserting: You see, not only did their master Johanan testify to the greatness of these men, but here is a transcript of a very significant session conducted in their academy. Only after all this does the editor begin to cite them—and significantly enough, these sayings are introduced by the very formula he had used in introducing the Men of the Great Assembly, the first spokesmen of the Oral Torah: "and they said three things."[87]

One more point, and then we shall arrive at the conclusion. We noted that the disciples had replied to Johanan's questions first positively, and [19] then negatively: "Liberal eye, grudging eye; good companion, evil companion; good neighbor, evil neighbor; goodheartedness, meanheartedness." So the answers of four of the disciples. But what of the reply by Simeon ben Nathanel? To the first question, what is the good course, he had replied, "Foresight"; to the second question, what is the evil course, he had replied, "Borrowing and not repaying." Many a commentator has insisted, and probably correctly, that since the other four replies were in the fixed form of Johanan's question, of positive and negative, the same must no doubt be true of Simeon's reply. This stands to reason. But one thing we surely cannot fail to recognize:

> But speaking of this very thing, justice, are we to affirm thus without qualification that it is truth-telling and *paying back what one has received* from anyone . . . ? I mean, for example, . . . if one took over weapons from a friend who was in his right mind and then the lender should go mad and demand them back, that we ought not to return them in that case and that he who did so return them would not be acting justly. . . . Then this is not the definition of justice: to tell the truth and return what one has received.
>
> "Nay, but it is, Socrates," said Polemarchus breaking in, "if indeed we are to put any faith in Simonides". . . .
>
> "Tell me, then, . . . what is it that you affirm that Simonides says, and rightly says about justice." "That it is just," he replied, "to render to each his due (ὅτι . . . τὸ τὰ ὀφειλόμενα ἑκάστῳ ἀποδιδόναι δίκαιόν ἐστι). In saying this I think he speaks well."
>
> "I must admit," said I, "that it is not easy to disbelieve Simonides. For he is a wise and inspired man. . . ."[88]

To be sure, Socrates is being ironic, but Simonides' definition was, as we know, the current and generally accepted one. As Shorey remarks in his note: "Owing to the rarity of banks, *reddere depositum* was throughout antiquity the typical instance of just conduct." And see also what Shorey cites as regards Stoic terminology.[89]

---

87. Cf. PA 1:1 and 2:10, ARN, 59, and see C. Taylor, *Sayings of the Jewish Fathers* 2:144 (and the duplication is *not* to be preferred).

88. Plato, *Republic* 1, 331D–E, ed. P. Shorey (in Loeb Classics I, 20f.); cf. Diogenes Laertius 3.83 (I, 351).

89. P. 22, note a. And cf. the citation from Stobaeus (ἀπονεμητικὴ τῆς ἀξίας ἑκάστῳ) and the note in A. C. Pearson, *The Fragments of Zeno and Cleanthes* (London, 1891), 175.

At least, therefore, in one of his answers, Simeon is echoing the kind of opinion that one overheard in the schools of the larger world outside the rabbinic academy. And perhaps "foresight" is, as some commentators suggest, the opposite of *reddere depositum*.[90]

[20] What does all this add up to? In a sense, not very much. We certainly have no evidence that the Palestinian Jewish sages read Plato or Zeno, much less studied them. But one result seems to me inescapable: Living in the Hellenistic-Roman world, the Tannaim could not remain unaffected by that world. It is not simply a matter of loan words; it is something much more profound. Not only did the Palestinian sages appropriate the terminology for some hermeneutic rules from the Hellenistic rhetors,[91] but inside the *bet ha-midrash*, the rabbinic academy, apparently one did take up from time to time philosophical questions, and one did attempt to answer these questions in the current philosophical idiom. Study of the Law of course remained paramount. But along with such activity went an awareness, at least in the school of Johanan ben Zakkai, of the subject and style popular in intellectual circles generally.

One thing should not mislead us. The fact that in a number of stories the *philosophos* is bested in his encounter with the rabbi[92] indicates nothing more than a typically recurring popular attitude: Anything they can do, we can do better. This is not anti-philosophy as such; indeed, there is in such stories a distinct acknowledgment that among the Gentiles the wisest are the philosophers; but of course the *hakam* is superior since he is a master of the Torah.[93]

90. See. e.g., *Midrash Shemuel* of Samuel ben Isaac of Uçeda (16th cent.) (New York, 5705 [1935], 71f. Interestingly enough, in B. Tamid 32a "foresight" is the answer given by the elders (sages) of the south to Alexander the Great!

91. See on this the important researches of S. Lieberman, *Hellenism in Jewish Palestine*, 28–114.

92. E.g., *Genesis Rabba* 1:9, ed. Theodor-Albeck, 8. Note indeed the subject of their discussion: was Creation *ex nihilo* or not?

93. See the real note of respect in the story told in *Derek 'Ereṣ, Pirqe Ben 'Azzai*, chap. 3, 3, ed. Higger, 183 ff. (and note the literature he cites on 184f.).

The statement by Rabbi Abba bar Kahana (*Gen. R.* 65:19, ed. Theodor-Albeck, p. 734, and parallels) that the greatest philosophers among the nations of the world were Balaam and Oenomaus of Gadara cannot seriously illuminate what was or was not known by first-century Tannaim, particularly before the destruction of the Temple in 70 C.E. (see below n. 95): Abba bar Kahana is a third generation Amora (in other words, late 3rd cent. and early 4th cent. C.E.)! Certainly Rabbi Me'ir (the second-century Tanna) in his relationships with Oenomaus is downright warm (see briefly on this *Jewish Encyclopedia*, 9:386). But much, much more to the point (and perhaps, therefore, I would do well not to sound so condescending towards Abba bar Kahana and his information): In the second century to have regarded Oenomaus as nothing less than outstanding is the very reverse of being philosophically not knowledgeable; see for example the discussion on the Cynics—their influence and their intellectual-spiritual role—in S. Dill, *Roman Society from Nero to Marcus Aurelius* (London, 1904), 359ff., and particularly the references in his notes. As for some early Christians (cf. Dill, 361), for Jewish sages, too, much in what Cynics preached would be a joy indeed. Observe, for example, Dill (and his references!), 363: "[The Cynics] were probably the purest monotheists that classical antiquity produced. . . . The most fearless and trenchant assailant of the popular theology among the

Such stories are in spirit and intent like those [21] anecdotes in the first chapter of the Midrash on Lamentations where an Athenian, in other words, one universally reputed to be particularly clever, is outwitted by Jerusalemites, and even by youngsters of Jerusalem.[94] In no way do such stories demonstrate that philosophy, and the current manner of discussing what was generally regarded as philosophical questions, were repugnant to the talmudic sages and therefore were excluded from the rabbinic academy. Whether professional philosophers would have been impressed by the level or range of philosophical discussion inside the rabbinic academy is beside the point: It would be like asking what a Kant would think of various courses offered by many collegiate departments of philosophy. No one is suggesting that the talmudic sages were technical philosophers. But the popular terms and ethical themes of dominant Hellenistic philosophical speculations were not alien at least to the circle around Johanan ben Zakkai. He and his disciples did not shun either the subject or the style.[95] Their place of meeting was of course the *bet ha-midrash*, but inside it they found the spaciousness for the study of Scripture and the study of Mishnah, the dialectic of Law and the contemplation of mystic lore, the engagement with the dogmas of Revelation and the deliberations of philosophy.

Cynics was Oenomaus of Gadara, in the reign of Hadrian. Oenomaus rejected, with the frankest scorn, the anthropomorphic fables of heathenism. In particular, he directed his fiercest attacks against the revival of that faith in oracles and divination which was a marked characteristic of the Antonine age." And more to the same effect on p. 364 (let alone p. 361, "With rare exceptions, such as *Oenomaus of Gadara* [my italics] they seldom committed their ideas to writing"). So then, R. Me'ir—of the Antonine age!—is really up to what this effective philosopher is deeply concerned with; the Tanna need not at all be presumed to be ignorant of the ideas of the popular philosopher. Questions like, Is Oenomaus of the stature of a Plato or Aristotle in the history of philosophy? have nothing to do with the case; cf. above, p. 3 and notes ad loc. and pp. 19. Surely Seneca was no philosophical illiterate; and what does he say of Demetrius? 'Vir meo judicio *magnus etiamsi maximis comparetur*' (quoted by Dill, 362)! (Quintilian's stricture, 10.1.128, Loeb Classics IV, 73 that "Seneca had many excellent qualities, a quick and fertile intelligence with great industry and wide knowledge, though as regards the last quality he was often led into error by those whom he had entrusted with the task of investigating certain subjects on his behalf," is hardly a disqualification in our present context. One: apparently Seneca was prepared to accept his assistants' judgments. Two: at least we can discover what his assistants regarded as intellectually respectable. And this is surely relevant to our immediate study.)

Finally, to speak of Balaam as a philosopher clearly reflects not a discrediting of philosophy, but a more than average respect for it—for not only is Balaam the recipient of divine revelations recorded in Scripture, but he is likened to Moses for the Gentiles: cf. *Sifre Deut.* 357 on Deut. 34:10, ed. Finkelstein 430, *Midrash Tannaim* 227. There is even a tradition that, like other eminent personages, Balaam was born circumcised, ARN, 12. [On the esteem people had for philosophers cf. *J. Berakot* 9:1].

94. *Lamentations Rabba* on Lam. 1:1; cf. ed. Buber, 23b ff.

95. That the give-and-take recorded in PA 2:9 took place before Johanan withdrew to Jamnia is clear from an analysis of the sources; see also G. Allon, *Studies in Jewish History* [Heb.] I (Tel Aviv, 1957), 261f. (and the text, ibid, when it speaks of Eleazar ben Azariah, should be corrected to Eleazar ben 'Arak).

תוך כדי עיונים במסכת אבות דר' נתן

I

[59] שנינו במשנה סוכה ד', ח': "ההלל והשמחה שמונה, כיצד?¹ מלמד שחייב אדם בהלל ובשמחה" וכו'. וכן בכ"י קופמן ובכ"י פריז ופרמא וכן בדפוס נאפולי ובמתניתא דתלמודא דבני מערבא הוצ' לו. לפנינו משנה מקוצרת, מעיד הרי"ן אפשטיין. מעניין, אע"פ שישנן עוד משניות שלמות, מקוצרות, וקטועות,² אין "כיצד – מלמד ש . . ." חוזר בהן. "כיצד", "שהוא משמש כרגיל לפרש הלכה שקדמה לו",³ מופיע בלבדו בכל הספרות המדרשית – התלמודית; אף "מלמד" בלבד ובלי "כיצד" וכהתחלת תשובה,⁴ שכיח. ברם זיווג זה של "כיצד" ו"מלמד ש . . ." מיד אחריו, כמעט ואינו מצוי במקורות הקלסיים. בדקתי עניין זה בעזרת הקונקורדנציות של ר' ח. י. קאסאווסקי ז"ל ושל ר' בנימין בנו יבלח"א, ואף אם יתכן שנעלמו ממני דוגמאות אחדות, המסקנה שהגעתי אליה בעינה עומדת, והיא, שכרגיל אין חז"ל מעדיפים מטבע זה, של "כיצד מלמד ש . . ." על ניסוחים אחרים הרווחים בספרות.

מאידך גיסא, נוסח זה של שאלה ופתיחה לתשובה שבצדה מופיע באבות דר' נתן נוסחא א', לא פעם ולא שתים אלא פעמים רבות, במספר רב של סעיפים הבאים לפרש מימרא מהמשנה אבות (וג' פעמים אף מימרא לא מפרקי אבות, דף י"ג עמוד א', והשוויה את הנוסח בתוספתא סנהדרין ח', ו' ובירושלמי סוף פרק אחד דיני ממונות ובבבלי ל"ח, א'). המדובר כאן הוא בנוסחא א', ולא בנוסחא ב' (אלא שכאן תמצא "מלמד" לבדו, למשל: ג' עמ' ב', י"א עמ' ב', כ"ד עמ' א', כ"ה עמ' א'), שכן בנוסחא ב' חסר הצרוף הזה לגמרי. הוה אומר ששתי הנוסחאות לא מבית מדרש אחד או מעריכה אחת יצאו; לא זה שעיבד [60] את א' עיבד את ב' – וזה מסייע לטענתו ולהוכחותיו של הפרופ' אליעזר אריה פינקלשטין עוד לפני כארבעים שנה במאמרו על שתי

1. על "כיצד – מלמד ש . . ." במשנה זו, עיין הרי"ן אפשטיין, מבוא לנוסח המשנה, (ירושלים, תש"ח), 1038, וד"ח אלבק, משנה סוכה, (ירושלים–תל־אביב, תשי"ט), 477.
2. על משניות קטועות ומקוצרות עיין הרי"ן אפשטיין, 38–1037.
3. הרי"ן אפשטיין, 1032. ועיין עוד ר"א הפרופ' גולדברג, פירוש למשנה מסכת שבת (ירושלים, תשל"ו), 219.
4. על "מלמד", ראה גם ר'בנימין זאב בכר, ערכי מדרש (תל־אביב, תרפ"ג), 66, 214.
5. *Journal of Biblical Literature*, 57, (1938) 16f., 39ff.

הנוסחאות של אדר"ן.' והפעם אולי מותר להוסיף, שבבית המדרש בו נוצרה נוסחא א' שמש "כיצד
מלמד ש..." שיגרה אקדמית טכנית. כשם שבמדרשי ר' ישמעאל מובאים, למשל, פעמים רבות
פירושים בנוסח "למה נאמר? לפי ש...", כן באדר"ן נוסחא א' משמש "כיצד – מלמד ש..." סגנון
קבוע ומקובל בתורת הפרשנות וההסבר של בית מדרש מיוחד. ולא נוסחה זאת בלבד מופיעה כאן,
להוציא את כל האחרות. יש ויש שמופיע גם "כיצד" לחוד, וכן גם "מלמד ש..." בלי "כיצד", לריבות
צורות אחרות של פתיחה לפירוש, הידועות לנו מהמקורות בכלל. אולם "כיצד – מלמד ש..."
תופס באדר"ן חלק חשוב מהפתיחות לפירושי הטקסט, מה שאינו מצוי בטקסטים אחרים.

כהוכחה לדברי הנני מצרף כאן את הרשימה דלהלן המבליטה מה חביב היה הסגנון של
"כיצד–מלמד ש..." לעורכים או לעורך של אדר"ן נוסחא א' (הכל ע"פ הוצאת רש"ז שכטר ז"ל):

א' (עמוד) ב' – "הוו מתונין בדין, כיצד, מלמד שיהא ...

שם, למטה – "ד"א הוו מתונים בדין, כיצד, מלמד שיהא ...

י"ג, א' – "בקול, כיצד, מלמד ששינה הקב"ה...

שם – "בנעימה, כיצד, מלמד ששינה הקב"ה...

שם – "במראה, כיצד, מלמד ששינה הקב"ה...

י"ד, א' – "ביתך בית ועד לחכמים, כיצד, מלמד שיהיה ביתו ...

י"ז, א' – "פתוח לרווחה, כיצד, מלמד שיהא ביתו ...

י"ח, א' – "עשה לך רב, כיצד, מלמד שיעשה לו את רבו ...

י"ח, ב' – "וקנה לך חבר, כיצד, מלמד שיקנה אדם ...

כ"א, ב' – "מן הפורענות, כיצד, מלמד שיהא לבו של אדם ...

כ"ב, א' – "כעורכי הדיינין, כיצד, מלמד שאם באת לבית המדרש ...

כ"ב, ב' – "אהוב את המלאכה, כיצד, מלמד שיהא אדם ...

כ"ג, ב' – "ושנא את הרבנות, כיצד, מלמד שלא יניח אדם ...

שם – "ואל תתודע לרשות, כיצד, מלמד שלא יצא לו לאדם שם ...

כ"ד, א' – "ד"א (השני) אל תתודע לרשות, כיצד, מלמד שלא יכוין אדם ...

כ"ד, ב' – "אוהב שלום, כיצד, מלמד שיהא אדם ...

כ"ו, א' – "דורף שלום, כיצד, מלמד שיהא אדם ...

כ"ו, ב' – "אוהב את הבריות, כיצד, מלמד שיהא אדם ...

כ"ז, א' – "ומקרבן לתורה, כיצד, מלמד שיהא אדם ...

[61] כ"ח, ב' – "נגד שמא ואבד שמיה, כיצד, מלמד שלא יוציא (!) לו לאדם ...

שם – "ודלא מוסיף פסיד, כיצד, מלמד שאם שנה אדם ...

שם – "עשה תורתך קבע, כיצד, מלמד שאם שמע אדם ...

כ"ט, א' – "אמור מעט ועשה הרבה, כיצד, מלמד שהצדיקים אומרים ...

שם – "בסבר פנים יפות, כיצד, מלמד שאם נתן אדם ...

ל', ב' – "כבוד חברך חביב עליך כשלך, כיצד, מלמד שכשם שרואה ...

שם – "ואל תהא נוח לכעוס, כיצד, מלמד שיהא עניו ...

ל"א, ב' – "עין הרע, כיצד, מלמד שכשם שאדם ...

ל"ב, ב' – "ושנאת הבריות, כיצד, מלמד שלא יכוין אדם ...

ל"ג, א' – "כיצד, מלמד כשם שאדם ...
(האם טעות הדפוס כאן, ועלינו לקרא "מלמד שכשם שאדם' וכו'?)

ל"ז, א' – "שינה של שחרית, כיצד, מלמד שלא יתכוין אדם ...

שם – "יין של צהרים, כיצד, מלמד שלא יתכוין אדם ...

ל"ז, ב' – "ושיחת הילדים, כיצד, מלמד שלא יתכוין אדם ...

שם – "בתי כנסיות של עמי הארץ, כיצד, מלמד שלא יתכוין אדם ...".

בסך הכל שלש ושלושים פעם. גם ה"הוספה ב' לנוסחא א'" בהוצאת רש"ז שכטר, 166–150,
על אף השינויים וההוספות שחלו בה, יסודה בנוסחא א'. בהוספה זו מופיע "כיצד – מלמד ש...".

מספר פעמים, למשל, בעמ' 131, 157, 163, ו־166 (חמש פעמים בעמוד האחרון בלבד). ואם כן,
שימוש זה לא ארעי הוא אלא בבחינת מטבע לשון אקדמית שנוצרה בכוונה בבית מדרש מסוים
משום איזה שהוא טעם פדגוגי.

II

יוסף בן יוחנן אומר: "ויהיו עניים בני ביתך". מה זאת אומרת? לפי נוסחא א' של אדר"ן "ויהיו עניים
בני ביתך" פירושו "ולא בני ביתך ממש, אלא שיהיו עניים משיחין מה שאוכלים ושותים בתוך ביתך
כדרך שהיו עניים משיחין מה שאוכלין ושותין בתוך ביתו של איוב" וכו'. לפי נוסחא ב' של אדר"ן
פירוש הדברים "ויהיו עניים בני ביתך" הוא "לא עני ממש, אלא מי שהוא ענו ואשתו ענוה ובניו ובני
ביתו ענוים, אף הכלבים שלו אינן מזיקין" וכו'.

שני הפירושים אינם זהים. נוסחא א' באה להסביר שבני ביתך אינם בני אדם ממש, והמדובר
הוא בעניים דעלמא. נוסחא ב' מדגישה שעני במאמר זה, משמעו ענו. מכל מקום, לא רב הוא
המרחק בין שתי הנוסחאות. נוסחא א' (בפרק השלם) מגישה לפנינו בעצם שני הסברים: א) "בני
ביתך", לאו דווקא בני ביתך הם, אלא אזהרה לקבל את העניים בעין טובה, כעין קבלתך את בני
[62] ביתך במאכל ובמשתה. ונוסחא זו ממשיכה בתיאור הנהגתם המעולה של איוב ושל אברהם
כלפי עניים ואורחים. (ב) אחרי זה מוסיף הפרק ללמדנו שחייבים אנחנו ללמד את בני ביתנו ענוה.
גם לנוסחא ב' שני פירושים: (א) שעל בני ביתנו להיות ענוים, ו־(ב) שלפנינו מספר רעיונות ואמרות
על עניים מרודים. סוף דבר, מה שנראה היה ברגע ראשון כפירושים שונים מפני שאינם זהים לגמרי,
נראה לבסוף כשתי נוסחאות שיצאו מתוך השקפה מוסרית כללית אחת. שתיהן עוסקות גם
בעניות וגם בענוה.[6]

אולם, מהו הגורם לפירושים שונים אלו בכלל, שהאחד מדגיש לא בני ביתך ממש והאחד לא
עני ממש?

דומה אני שגם נוסחא א' וגם נוסחא ב' באות להעיר שהמשפט "ויהיו עניים בני ביתך" לא
קללה הוא. אחרת אולי אפשר להבין את המשפט כאילו רצה יוסף בן יוחנן לקלל את בעל הבית,
כדברי הצועק מתוך רוגז, מי יתן והיו בני ביתך עניים! [אמנם אפשר הוא (אע"פ שאין זה נראה בעיני
כלל וכלל), שיוסף בן יוחנן התנגד לגמרי להכנסת אורחים ולעזרת עניים, כאילו הוא מזהיר, אם
יהיה ביתך פתוח לרווחה אזי בעתיד ישארו כל בני ביתך (כולל אנשי משפחתך – עיין, למשל,
נוסחא א', דף י"ז, ב') עניים מרודים.[7] ואדר"ן הופך את כל המאמר לטובה ולחסד. ולא על הסבר –
בדוחק זה רצוני להתעכב כאן, אלא להדגיש שאכן, דברי יוסף בן יוחנן דו־משמעיים הם]. על כן
מורה נוסחא א' שלא על בני ביתך ממש נאמר שיהיו עניים, ונוסחא ב' מסבירה, שכאשר נאמר
"ויהיו עניים בני ביתך" לא לעניות מתכוון בעל המאמר במשנה, אלא לענווות, שענוים יהיו בני
ביתך.

III

קרוב לוודאי שאין לך תרבות, עתיקה או בת ימינו, שאינה עושה שימוש מיוחד במספרים מסוימים.
יתכן שתופעה זו נעוצה במשהו פסיכולוגי או מיסטי, או בשניהם יחד. לא כאן המקום להפך ולהפך
בנושא הזה כמו שדרוש, אבל ברור ש(בפרקי אבות ו)באדר"ן נמסרים מאמרים שבהם מספר מסוים

---

6. שיטה אחרת לרא"א פינקלשטין, מבוא למסכתות אבות ואבות דר' נתן (ניו־יורק, תשי"א), עמ' ל"א ול"ב.
ועל "בני ביתך" עיין רע"צ הפרופסור מלמד בלשוננו, כ', תשט"ז, עמ' 110–11; והשווה דעתו של W. F. Albright,
על "מטיבים לבן ביתו של בשר ודם", עיין ספרי בהעלתך BASOR 163 (October, 1961):47 and nn. 54–56.
ע"ח, עמ' 67. ועל בני ביתו = אשתו, עיין הגר"ש הפרופסור ליברמן, תוספתא כפשוטה, פסחים, (ניו־יורק,
תשכ"ו), 627, שורות 49–48. ועתה עיין עוד מ. סוקולוף, Maarav 1 (1978):82.
7. על "עניים מרודים", ראה את דבריו של רא"ש הפרופסור רוזנטל ב־ Israel Exploration Journal, 23
(1973):75.

[63] – למשל, עשרה או שבעה או ארבעה או שלשה ועוד – מקיף ענינים שיש קשר ביניהם,
ולפעמים ענינים שהקשר ביניהם רופף. כך למשל, פותחת שורה של מאמרים ב"שבעה בריות זו
למעלה מזו"... ומכאן והלאה יסופר על שבעה פרושים, שבעה דברים שרובן קשה ומיעוטן יפה,
שבעה דברים שבהם ברא הקב"ה את עולמו... שבעה מדות שדרש הלל לפני בני בתירה, ועוד.
(ועל מספר שלש, עיין הרע"ב למשנה שקלים ג', ג', ד"ה שלש פעמים). ומכיון שהעיקר במאמרים
אלה הוא הצהרת המספר, אין תימה שלפעמים מתוספים או נגרעים פרטים מעצם הענין (עיין
למשל באדר"ן נוסחא א', נ"א עמ' א', הסעיף "אחת עשרה היא כתיב ביו"ד בתורה; עמ' ב', "עשר
מעלות נסתלקה שכינה"; נ"ב עמ' א' "עשרה נסים נעשו לאבותינו בירושלים"). ואין הכרח להחליט
תמיד שהטקסט טעון תיקון. אף כשהטקסט בסדר, ברי שיש לפנינו מספר עגול, שהעורכים
הקדמונים אספו את החומר שירשו וסידרו אותו ע"פ המספרים העגולים שהיו קיימים בזמנם. ואין מן
הנמנע אפילו שגם מלכתחילה בא המאמר צמוד למספר.

נוסף על המספרים שכבר הזכרנו לעיל, וגם אחרים, מופיע באדר"ן (נוסחא א', ג' עמ' א')
המספר כ"ב. על בנימין הצדיק שקים אלמנה ושבעה (!) בנים, מסופר שמלאכי השרת בקשו רחמים
עליו לפני הקב"ה. תפילתם נענתה ולבנימין נוסף כ"ב שנה על שנותיו. בן עשרים ושתים שנה (בן
כ"ח על פי נוסחא ב' ופרקי דר' אליעזר) היה ר' אליעזר בן הורקנוס עת שהתחיל ללמוד תורה.
קודם שששרפו קנאים את כל מה שצבר כלבא שבוע (נוסחא א', ט"ז, ב') מצא שיש לו מזון עשרים
ושתים שנה סעודה לכל אחד ואחד בירושלים (בנוסחא ב', "מזון ג' שנים לכל אחד ואחד
שבירושלים"). אולי ראו הקדמונים הקבלה בין המספר כ"ב ומספר אותיות האלף-בית.[8] אף יהא
מקור המספר מה שיהא, הרוצה בדוגמאות נוספות לשימוש במספר כ"ב כמספר עגול, יעיין בכרך
המפתחות (שהכין המנוח פרופ' בועז כהן ז"ל) לאוצר היקר של הגר"ל הפרופ' גינצבורג ז"ל,
Legends of the Jews, VII, 483f.

עוד מספר שכדאי לעמוד עליו הוא המספר ארבע מאות. באדר"ן נוסחא א' הוא מופיע פעמיים:
"מעשה בשני בני אדם... (ש)המרו זה את זה וזה את זה בארבע מאות זוז' וכו' (ל' עמ' ב') (ובנוסחא
ב' ל"א עמ' א', הסיפור מסתיים: "מוטב לך שתפסיד ארבע מאות דינר על ארבע מאות דינר" וכו').
אולם לפני זה, בפרק ג', ח' עמ' א', מובא בנוסחא א' "מעשה בר' עקיבא שחייב לאדם אחד לשלם
ארבע מאות זוז לאשה שביזה אותה. סיפור המעשה ידוע כבר ממשנת בבא קמא ח', ו'. והמספר
ארבע מאות נראה בעיני כמספר עגול שפרושו סכום עצום, כאילו בחר המספר בלשון גוזמא
והפלגה. אין [64] זאת אומרת שהמשמעות של ארבע מאות היא תמיד רק מליצית. כך, למשל, אם
המשנה (כתובות א', ה') מעידה שב"ד שלכהנים היו גובין לבתולה ארבע מאות זוז, ולא מחו בידם
חכמים, אין טעם מספיק להכחיש עדות זו – ומה גם שרב יהודה אמר בשמו של שמואל (בבלי י"ב,
ב') שלא בית דין של כהנים בלבד נהגו כך, אלא אף משפחות המיוחסות בישראל, אם רצו, עושות
כן. ואולי איפכא, אפשר שמה שמעיד רב יהודה בשמו של שמואל מוכיח להפך, שסכום קצוב לאו
דווקא, אלא "ארבע מאות" מובנו כמות גדולה עד מאד אצל העשירים והמיוחסים.

והוא הדין אף בסיפור על ר' עקיבא. נכון שקודם שמוסרת המשנה את המעשה על ר' עקיבא,
היא פוסקת "פרע ראש האשה בשוק, נותן ארבע מאות זוז". אולם זהו המבנה של משניות, שמראש
מזכירות את ההלכה ואחר כך מביאות את ספור המעשה שממנו מתפתחת ההלכה. לכל הפחות
באדר"ן ניכרת חשיבותו הגדולה של ר' עקיבא. כאן אנו קוראים "מעשה באדם אחד שעבר על
דברי רבי עקיבא" (ח' עמ' א'). הוא הוא שהוציא את המשפט על אותו אדם גס. יש לומר שהכונה
היא כי קנס עצום קנס ר' עקיבא את המבַזה אשה (ואפילו "בזויה" – ראה אדר"ן) ללמדו גם דרך
ארץ וגם חומרת ההלכה ביחסים שבין אדם לחברו.[9]

---

8. [ועתה ראיתי את הערת הגר"ל גינצבורג באוצרו, V, 107, הערה 98. (ועיין גם בראשית רבא, א', י"ז, 12 ,1.) על ד'
מאות עי' שם, VI ,326, הערה 53.]

9. ואע"פ שבתלמוד נושאים ונותנים בשאלת נתינת זמן, וגם (למשל ברמב"ם, פירוש המשנה, בבא קמא ח' י') גומרין

ברור איפוא שאין כוונתנו לומר שלעולם אין מובן מדויק למספר "ארבע מאות". אך ראוי גם
לציין שבחכמה מאמרים ומסורות ואגדות אנו נתקלים במספר זה כמליצה בלבד. נציין רק שתיים:
"ארבע מאות בתי כנסיות היו בכרך ביתר ובכל אחת ואחת היו בה ארבע מאות מלמדי תינוקות,
וכל אחד ואחד היו לפניו ארבע מאות תינוקות של בית רבן" (גיטין נ"ח, א'). כמו כן מה שמסופר על
אותה כמין חוה נאה ומפורסמת שהיתה נוטלת ארבע מאות זהובים בשכרה וכו' (ספרי שלח,
פיסקא קט"ו, 29–128). ועוד דוגמאות ב־ *Legends of the Jews*, VII, 169.

השימוש התכוף במס' ארבע מאות ידוע לכל הולכי לבית המדרש, אולם, מה סיבתו? מדוע
נתייחד מס' זה כביטוי של הגזמה? לדעתי, הסיבה לכך היא שמספר זה מופיע פעמים בספר
בראשית (חוץ מ"ארבע מאות שנה" בט"ו, י"ג. ושמא אף כאן רמז לתקופה ארוכה מאד): "ארבע
מאות שקל כסף" [65] שֶשָּׁקַל אברהם לעפרון (בראשית כ"ג, ט', ט"ז), "וארבע מאות איש" שהיו
במחנה של עשו (ל"ב, ז'). כפי שהעירו רבים על המשא והמתן בין אברהם ועפרון, קיחת מערת
המכפלה עלתה לאברהם ביוקר; אל עשו נלוו אנשי זרוע לא מעטים.

סח לי פעם עמיתי לשעבר Professor Frederick A. Pottle שאולי ארבע מאות כגוזמא
משקף את ערכה המספרי של האות "ת", האות האחרונה באלף־בית: כשם שהיא האות שאין
למעלה הימנה, כך 400 הוא הסכום הגדול ביותר. לכאורה פתרון נאה, אך קשה, כי לדעת המומחים
לא השתמשו באותיות הא"ב לשם מספרים קודם לתקופת ההלניזמוס,[10] ואם כן אין לפרש את
המספרים במקרא על פי שיטה זו. מאידך, מי יערוב לנו שבתקופת חז"ל, כאשר בדקו ומנו כל ביטוי
ותיבה שבמקרא, לא רחפו לנגד עיניהם גם ערכי המספר של אותיות האלף־בית השונות?[11]

ש"אין הלכה כר' עקיבא בהשוותו כל אדם" (בתרגומו של הרב יוסף קאפח), אין חולק כנראה על עצם סכום הקנס
שחייב ר' עקיבא לאותו אדם לשלם. ועניין קרוב לעניננו ראה באוצה"ג על מסכת בבא קמא, תשובות, עמ' 67. עיין גם
בדבריו של ג. אלון ז"ל, תולדות היהודים בא"י בתקופת המשנה והתלמוד (ישראל, תשי"ט), I,135 ואילך.
אגב, אך פריעת הראש ע"י האשה בפני בעלה נראית כפריצות (?), עיין אדר"ן, נוסחא ב', י"ח עמ' א'.
10. עיין עמ' 32 והערה 21 בספרו של הפרופ' ח.א. גינזברג, (Studies in Koheleth, New York, 1950). וכן בספרו
של הגר"ש ליברמן, Hellenism in Jewish Palestine (New York, 1962), 73, n. 11.
11. [לאחר ששלחתי דפים אלה לעורך, העיר לי ר"ד הפרופסור הלבני שמ"א שאצקעס, ספר המפתח (ניו־יורק,
1929), ח' ע"ב ט' ע"א, כבר עמד על המס' 400 כגוזמא ואף רמז ללקיחת שדה עפרון. אך הפרוש שונה מפירושי;
ושמשלם פישל בעהר, דברי משלם (פרנקפורט ענ"מ, תרפ"ו), עמ' מ"ה-מ"ז, פירש את מס' עשרים ושנים כ"דק
גוזמא בעלמא"; והוא מונה שם ט"ז מקומות שבהם מופיע השימוש המוגזם הזה.]

The Two Versions of
Abot de Rabbi Nathan[*]

[97] Ever since Solomon Schechter published his edition of *Abot de Rabbi Nathan* (1887), it has been customary to refer to the two forms of this midrash on *Abot* as two versions of one treatise.[1] The idiom, in fact, was employed by Schechter and he has been followed by all subsequent students. This is not to say that differences between the versions were overlooked. Schechter himself called attention to variants, despite his conclusion that basically "both are one book (not like the *Tanna d'be Eliahu Rabbah* and *Zuta* or *Derek Erez Rabbah* and *Zuta*).[2] And although after repeated study that conclusion has been modified by some scholars,[3] the view still is current that substantially both versions—regardless of the fact that each contains material which does not occur in the other; that even when both express the same general thought, hardly if ever do the readings strictly coincide—present the same ideological commentary on *Abot*. The relationship between the two versions is reduced in effect to this: Sometimes the one, sometimes the other retains the better reading; sometimes one supplements the other; sometimes one preserves a more original order.

The fact is, however, that a careful examination of the two versions of *Abot de Rabbi Nathan* reveals a relationship of more than *textual* nature. There is

---

[*] I wish to express my thanks to Professors Louis Ginzberg and Alexander Marx, who were kind enough to read this paper and make several suggestions. Responsibility for the views here expressed, however, rests with me.

1. It should be recalled that as early as 1872 Solomon Taussig published a substantial portion of the second version in נוה שלום.

2. *Abot de Rabbi Nathan*, ed. Schechter, Vienna 1887, introduction, p.xx.

3. Cf. Kaufmann, in *M.G.W.J.*, vol. 36, 1887, pp. 382–83; Finkelstein, *J.B.L.*, vol. 57, 1938, part 1, pp. 39ff.

nothing wrong in regarding these treatises as versions, so long as we are not led to overlook [98] a very interesting *thematic* difference between them. Indeed, had Schechter recognized the theme of his texts, he would have been spared a number of difficulties with several passages.

Now, "theme" may possibly strike many as a strange word where a text like *Abot de Rabbi Nathan* is concerned. Is it a story, or an essay, or a logical treatise of any sort? Does not *Abot de Rabbi Nathan*, like *Abot*, contain material on a multitude of subjects? Does it not read like a collection of various epigrams with commentary thereon, rather than like a dissertation on some one specific proposition? All this is true. Nevertheless, a recurring note in the treatises as they read today is hardly accidental, and the feeling is inescapable that *Abot de Rabbi Nathan* has more than various reflections on numerous subjects; it is more than a catalogue of maxims with illustrations.

It is almost tempting to suggest that in the difference of theme may lie an explanation for the existence of two separate versions of one treatise. Louis Finkelstein is essentially correct, I feel, when he says that "the two versions of ARN are independent from one another."[4] The question is, Why should two versions have developed from one tradition? Did the respective compilers perhaps wish to deduce different emphases or make prominent different concepts? Be that as it may—since it is very difficult to discover just how collections of oral traditions were undertaken—the treatises today do present a significant divergence in thought.

One word more, before stating this theme and presenting the evidence. By the word "theme" I mean in effect something like "emphasis," or perhaps what Max Kadushin would call "point of reference."[5] The theme, in other words, is that idea which is repeatedly emphasized, and/or that idea in relation to which other ideas are studied. When an idea becomes so central in treatment, it is entitled to be a theme.

The theme or empahsis of version I of *Abot de Rabbi Nathan* is the study of Torah. Again and again throughout the text our version goes out of its way to underscore the importance of Torah [99] study. And this emphasis is so strong as to leave the impression that version I is primarily concerned with the study of Torah, while version II would underline "good works" or "good deeds." In any event, this strong insistence upon Torah study is characteristic of version I only.

To the evidence we shall turn in a moment; and naturally the only evidence that may be introduced is evidence derived from passages which occur in *both* versions. Unless a paragraph or a maxim is presented in both versions, there is little opportunity for comparison. Here, however, something must be said lest the hypothesis be misunderstood.

4. Finkelstein, op cit.
5. Cf. his *Theology of Seder Eliahu*, 1932, pp. 33–34, and *Organic Thinking*, New York, 1938, *passim*.

It would be preposterous to say that version I only is interested in the study of Torah. Was not the editor or were not the editors of version II anxious for תלמוד תורה? Could a Jew, with any sensitivity toward his tradition, be indifferent to that "crown" which above all others raised his people from commonness? Or, on the other hand, was there ever a devoted Jew who regarded מעשים טובים as inconsequentials? Was the editor, or were the editors, of version I contemptuous of practical virtues? Patently, no! And if this categorical reply needs proof, both versions of *Abot de Rabbi Nathan* stand ready to demonstrate that the study of Torah *and* good works must be part of every Jew's equipment. Nevertheless, even in unanimity there are differences of inflection. Version I and version II would agree on what makes the perfect Jew. But version I presents an emphasis which is lacking in II. Version I, with a certain emphasis in mind, is always—or almost always—referring whatever it discusses to this central idea. And this central idea, as I have said, is the study of Torah.[6]

a) Perhaps the most striking passage—indeed, it was the first to catch my attention—in all the evidence is the comment of version I on Rabbi Jose's saying, "Let all thy deeds be for the sake of Heaven."[7] This is the comment:[8] "And let all thy deeds be for the sake of Heaven: for the sake of Torah; as it is said, 'In [100] all thy ways acknowledge Him (דעהו) and He will direct thy paths' (Prov. 3:6)." "For the sake of Torah" is certainly not "for the sake of Heaven" unless one's regard for Torah is extraordinary. Indeed, if we look to the parallel passage in version II we meet no such extravagant interpretation. "And let all thy deeds be for the sake of Heaven," reads version II,[9] "like Hillel.

> When Hillel used to go forth to [some] place, [people] would say to him, "Whither art thou going?" [He would reply,] "I go to perform a commandment." "Which commandment, Hillel?" [they would ask.] [He would reply,] "I am going to the privy." "Is this, then, a commandment?" He would say to them, "Indeed! so that the body not deteriorate."
>
> ["Moreover," men would say to Hillel,] "Where art thou going, Hillel?" [He would reply,] "I go to perform a commandment." "Which commandment, Hillel?" "I am going to the bath house." "Is this, then, a commandment?" He would say to them, "Indeed! To clean the body. Know thou that it is so: if he, that is appointed to polish and clean the statues which stand in the palaces of kings, receives a stipend each and every year; moreover, he is magnified together with the magnates of the kingdom—how much more so we that have been created in the image and likeness [of God]; as it is said, 'For in the image of God made He man' (Gen. 9:6)."

---

6. Professor Ginzberg notes, "I = דרכן של תלמידי חכמים; II = דרכן של כל בני אדם!"
7. Version I, chap. 17, p. 65; version II, chap. 30, p. 65. Cf. *Abot* 2:12.
8. I, 17, p. 66.
9. II, 30, p. 66.

The comment of version II is not only a lesson on the proximity of cleanliness to godliness, but certainly less forced than the one offered by our version. Only on the basis of the assumption that version I is emphasizing the study of Torah can we understand what has happened.[10] [101] b) On the statement of Nittai the Arbelite.[11] "Consort not with the wicked,"[12] version I gives us two interpretations.[13] The [102] first is an exhortation, with illustrations from biblical history, not to associate with evil or wicked persons. The second

10. Schechter was apparently bewildered by this passage; cf. his note 19, p. 66.

A note is perhaps in place at this point. Some may feel that the text is very likely corrupt. לשם שמים, it may be said, is definitely not לשם תורה, and the reading is, to say the least, suspicious.

Now, Dr. Schechter in his note (19) observes that the Oxford MS reads וכל מעשיך יהיו לשם תורה. Furthermore, Editio Princeps (so, too, the Zolkiev edition) of *Abot de Rabbi Nathan* has לשם שמים שנא' בכל דרכיך דעהו והוא ישר אורחותיך. Is this not further evidence that our text does not read properly?

Before explaining why I consider the text correct, I think it profitable to point out that even if the reading had been otherwise, the theory offered here serves to explain how such a "corruption" could occur. If scholars recognized that version I of *Abot de Rabbi Nathan* was stressing Torah study, a late editor would without embarrassment interpret לשם שמים as לשם תורה.

However, I do not believe that our text ever read otherwise. In the first place, the Oxford MS is obviously wrong since we have no statement from R. Jose וכל מעשיך יהיו לשם תורה. True, the phrase וכל מעשיך יהיו לשם שמים, at the beginning of the chapter, has been added to our edition by Schechter, on the basis of the Mishnah reading. Nevertheless, where is there a statement by R. Jose which reads like the epigram recorded in the Oxford MS? Version II can at least serve us as an aid in establishing the general maxim! Version II reads clearly וכל מעשיך יהיו לשם שמים.

The form in Editio Princeps is absolutely unwarranted. It may be urged that the verse from Proverbs proves that not Torah study is involved. I am not sure about that. Perhaps the emphasis is on דעהו—*know* Him! It is worth noticing, for example, that version II (ibid.) gives the same verse at the end of the next paragraph, which reads: "Rabbi Eleazar (not Eliezer) says, Be diligent in the study of Torah, and know how to reply to an unbeliever (אפיקורס) in words of Torah, so that they be not destroyed (reading יסתרו—cf. Bacher, *Agada der Tannaiten*, I, p. 72, n. 5; see also Felix Perles in *Jewish Studies in Memory of Israel Abrahams*, p. 382). And know before whom thou toilest and who is author of the covenant with thee; as it is said, 'In all thy ways acknowledge Him (דעהו)' (Prov. 3:6)."

My reluctance to yield on this point—though the hypothesis is in no way weakened, as I observed—is due to the fact that the term לשם שמים *is* used in association with an activity centering around the study of Torah. For thus we read (I, 40, p. 129; cf. *Abot* 5:17; see also II, 46, p. 128): כל מחלוקת שהיא לשם שמים סופה להתקיים . . . אי זו מחלוקת שהיא לשם שמים, זו מחלוקת הלל ושמאי. If the controversies of Hillel and Shammai might be described—as they unquestionably deserve to be—as controversies לשם שמים, it is not, I feel, impossible to associate deeds לשם שמים with the concept לשם תורה.

Professor Ginzberg adds the following note: "As to the interchange between שמים and תורה, comp. the use of רחמנא, 'the All Merciful,' one of the names of God in Palestinian sources, while in Babli it stands-hundreds of times!—for אוריתא, Torah. A very interesting discussion on the identity of שם שמים-שם תורה is found in נפש החיים, chap. 4 by R. Hayyim Volozhin, the famous pupil of the Gaon. There are many places in rabbinic literature where תורה and הקב"ה are used interchangeably; the idea is that the will of God is expressed in the Torah. It is quite possible that לשם תורה was used for לשם שמים for another reason, to avoid the two almost identical syllables שֵׁם and שָׁם."

11. II, 16, p. 35 attributes it to Rabbi (!) Joshua ben Perahiah.

12. I, 9, p. 38; cf. *Abot* 1:7.

13. I, 9, p. 42.

reads tersely as follows: "Another interpretation: Consort not with the wicked, even for Torah!"[14] A glance at the comments—and there are several—of version II on אל תתחבר לרשע reveals some interesting thoughts, but nothing even remotely resembling our treatise at this point.[15] Version I, indeed, I feel, has a significant variant from the statement in *Mekilta*[16] and *Yalkut*,[17] which resembles ours. These latter read אפילו לקרבו לתורה, which conceivably might mean: "Consort not with the wicked, even to bring him close to those things for which Torah stands, those lessons which Torah teaches."[18] That לקרבו לתורה does not necessarily refer to Torah study is evident from the comment on ומקרבן לתורה of Hillel's saying.[19] The reading, however, of version I indicates that again and again Torah study is the author's point of reference. The full meaning of the passage seems to be, Although Torah is so very, very important, nonetheless consorting with the wicked is hazardous—certain men cannot be taught Torah.[20]

c) A very subtle distinction between the reading of our two versions in one of the early chapters throws into sharp focus the motives of the different editors. Like God, like Adam, like Torah and others, we are told, the Sages too made a hedge about their words. Now, asks version I,[21]

What is the hedge which the Sages made about their words? For the Sages say, The recitation of the evening *shema* [may take place] until midnight. Rabban Gamaliel says, Until the cock crows. How is that?[22] When a man returns [103] from his work, let him not say, I will eat a bit, and drink a bit, and nap a while, and afterwards I shall recite the *shema*—for thus he will sleep through the night and not recite the *shema*. Rather, when a man returns from his work in the evening, let him go to the synagogue or to the house of study. If he is accustomed to study Scripture, let him study Scripture; and if he is accustomed to study Mishnah, let him study Mishnah; and if not, let him recite the *shema* and pray.

And now let us look at version II.[23]

Whence do we learn that the Sages made a hedge about their words? For the Sages said that the [evening] *shema* may be recited until midnight. Rabban Gamliel says,

14. In a translation that is to appear shortly I have rendered the phrase, "even for [the study of] Torah."
15. Cf. II, 16, p. 36.
16. *Mekilta*, מסכתא דעמלק, 3, ed. Lauterbach, II, p. 166.
17. *Yalkut Joshua*, I, par. 3.
18. On the other hand, the reading in Aknin's ספר מוסר, ed. Bacher, Berlin, 1910, p. 14, is ואפילו לקרבו לתורה. Is this perhaps a case of אשגרא דלישנא?
19. Cf. I, 12, p. 53. But see II, 26, p. 53. This passage is to be discussed below in the appendix.
20. Cf., on the other hand, the attitude of the school of Hillel, I, 3, pp. 14–15, and II, 4, ibid.
21. I, 2, p. 14.
22. That is, What is the hedge which the Sages made?
23. II, 3, p. 14.

Until the cock crows. [And why do the Sages say, Until midnight?] For a man should not say, Since I am permitted to recite the [evening] *shema* all night, I shall go to sleep; whenever I please, I will recite the *shema*: [because] sleep will overtake him, and he will not have recited it. Lo, such a one is guilty against his own soul! Hence the Sages said, When a man mounts his couch let him recite [the *shema*]; if he is a scholar, let him first recite the *shema*, and then if he wishes to study, let him study.

Version II certainly makes more sense than does our version. The hedge, let us remember, is a hedge connected with the reading of the *shema*. The first thing, therefore, one should do in the evening is recite the *shema*. What is the meaning, then, of "If he is accustomed to study, let him study"; "and if not, let him recite the *Shema* and pray?" Is study perhaps more important than prayer? Is prayer only for those who cannot study?[24]

Moreover, what fears pursue version II, that it should declare pointedly— after stating what all men must do—"if he is a scholar, let him first recite the *shema*, and *then* if he wishes to study, let him study"? Is this version afraid lest scholarship reduce prayer to secondary significance? The variant reading in Dr. Schechter's note[25] makes all the more emphatic the duty to recite the *shema* first: a scholar must first recite the *shema* and *afterwards* (ואח״כ) if he wished to study he might do so.

[104] Can this variant between the two versions be described as a mere accident?[26]

d) Many are the sayings attributed by *Abot de Rabbi Nathan* to Hillel. The form of one of these will be of immediate interest. In Babylonian he said, according to version I,[27] "And he that does not attend the Sages is worthy of death." In order to amplify this brief remark, our text, shortly thereafter, tells a story of a priest whose efforts at piety were of no avail, since he had neglected to attend the Sages, that is, to study under them.[28] Version II,[29] on the other hand, adds one further saying to Hillel's credit: "And he that does not attend the Sages is worthy of death; and he that attends the sages but does not practice (ולא מקיים) is worthy of the death of deaths." Like the previous version, version II tells the story of the priest who did not attend the Sages.[30] The story, in other

---

24. Notice how the commentators have called attention to the fact that the parallel reading of this passage (*Berakot* 4b) does not record ואם לאו.

25. II, 3, p. 14, n. 24.

26. Moreover, I feel that Aknin (op. cit., p. 3) sensed the difficulty created by the reading of version I: although he quotes *Abot de Rabbi Nathan* to illustrate the various hedges, for the hedge of the Sages he gives the reading from *Berakot* 1.1! Did Aknin too recognize that the reading of version I did not quite apply to the saying of the Men of the Great Assembly? One could of course say that Aknin preferred to refer to the Mishnah directly; but that would be forced. If he is quoting A. R. N. throughout and substantially the same illustration in this instance too occurs in A. R. N., why suddenly express a preference for the Mishnah reading?

27. I, 12, p. 55.

28. Cf. I, 12, p. 56.

29. Cf. II, 27, p. 56.

30. Cf. II, 27, pp. 56–57. Incidentally, the very conclusion of the chapter, [מכאן אמרו חכמים(!), needs examination.

words, is the same in both instances; but the final moral deduced differs in each version. Our version is anxious to demonstrate that he that fails to study with the Sages is mortally guilty, while version II leaves the whole subject with the words, "he that attends [the Sages] but does not practice is worthy of the death of deaths!" Do not the two versions appear to be underscoring different themes?

e) Not very far from Hillel's maxim, in our version, is recorded a saying of Shammai.[31] "Make thy [study of] Torah," [105] Shammai used to say, "a fixed habit." And this is the comment:

"Make thy [study of] Torah a fixed habit": how is that? This teaches us that if a man has heard something from a sage in the house of study, let him not treat it casually (אל יעשה אותו עראי),[32] but let him treat it attentively (קבע); and what a man learns let him practice himself, and then teach others that they may practice it; as it is said, "That ye may learn them and observe to do them." (Deut. 5:1). And so too in Ezra it says, "For he had set his heart to seek the law of the Lord, and to do it." And afterwards, "And to teach in Israel statutes and ordinances" (Ezra 7:10).[33]

Now, version II,[34] on the same phrase, has this to say:

Make thy [study of] Torah a fixed habit: Be thou not lenient with thyself and severe with others, or lenient with others and severe with thyself. Instead, even as thou art lenient with thyself, so shalt thou be lenient with others; and even as thou art severe with thyself, so shalt thou be severe with others. As it is said. "For Ezra had set his heart to seek the law of the Lord and to do it." And afterwards, "And to teach in Israel statutes and ordinances" (Ezra 7:10).

In the first place, it is interesting to notice that the verse from Ezra applies more smoothly to version I than it does to version II—although, even in the latter instance, the Ezra passage is not altogether irrelevant. Secondly, however, version II has but one understanding of Shammai's teaching. Version II sees in Shammai's words an exhortation to consistent practice only. Version I would have no quarrel with such an attitude; but it relates Shammai's counsel to study as well as to practice. First our version, at Shammai's suggestion, recommends what a man is to do when he hears something from a sage in a school; then, it prescribes what he is to do if he hopes to teach others.

f) Another slight yet significant variant in the light of the present hypothesis is reflected in the statement of Rabbi Ishmael. According to version I[35] Rabbi

---

31. I, 13, p. 56; cf. *Abot* 1:15. On the significance of the order in versions I and II in which Hillel and Shammai are quoted, see Schechter's introduction to his edition, pp. xx–xxi.

32. That this is the proper meaning is, I feel, clearly brought out by the continuation of the paragraph. In the latter half, practice is spoken of.

33. I shall have additional comments on this passage in the forthcoming translation, ad loc.

34. II, 23, p. 47.

35. I, 27, p. 84; cf. *Abot* 4:5.

Ishmael said, "He that [106] studies in order to teach, it is granted him to study and teach; and he that studies in order to practice, it is granted him to study and to teach and to practice." Version II,[36] on the other hand, quotes Rabbi Ishmael to this effect: "He that studies in order to teach, it is not granted him to study and to teach. But he that studies in order to practice, it is granted him to study and to teach, to observe and to practice." Again it is clear that both versions I and II agree that practice is the culmination of study. But version I insists that study for the purpose of teaching will bear fruit; to this version II objects.

g) After all these examples—and before proceeding with others—one may introduce as evidence a passage which has all the earmarks of later interpolation. The point is, of course, that we now have an explanation for such an interpolation. Only he who recognized the emphasis of version I would have felt no compunctions in inserting such a thought.

Early in our text,[37] where Moses' independent decisions are described, and they are said to have had God's unqualified approval, we read as follows:

He broke the tables [of the Commandments]. How is that? It was said, When Moses went up to heaven to receive the tables [of the Commandments], which had been inscribed and put away since the six days of Creation—as it is said, "And the tables were the work of God, and the writing was the writing of God, graven upon the tables" (Ex. 32:15): read not *ḥarut* [graven], but *ḥerut* [freedom], for whosoever studies Torah is a free man—at that time, the ministering angels conspired against Moses [and so forth].

None of this interpolation, אל תקרי חרות אלא חירות שכל מי שעוסק בתורה הרי הוא בן חורין לעצמו, is in the parallel passage of the second version[38] —and as a result, indeed, it reads more fluently. Merely to dismiss the passage as a later addition to our text is to overlook, I feel, the theme which the later editor detected in the treatise. With such a theme easily recognizable to him, why should he have felt any scruples in adding more material? This [107] was very likely his sentiment; and even when we recognize his intrusion, we ought to understand his motives.

h) One interpolation leads to another; and so it may not be unprofitable to compare the account in the two versions of Ben Zoma's saying, "Who is wise?" we read in version I:[39]

He that learns from all men; as it is said, "From all my teachers have I got understanding"[40] (Ps. 119:99). Who is most humble? He that is as humble as Moses our master; as it is said, "Now the man Moses was very meek" (Num. 12:3). Who is

36. II, 32, p. 68.
37. I, 2, p. 10.
38. II, 2, pp. 10–11.
39. I, 23, p. 75; cf. *Abot* 4:1.
40. See, on the other hand, the regular translation in the J.P.S. Bible.

most rich? He that rejoices in his portion; as it is said, "When thou eatest the labour of thy hands, happy shalt thou be, and it shall be well with thee" (Ps. 128:2). Who is most mighty? He that subdues his evil *yezer*; as it is said, "He that is slow to anger is better than the mighty; and he that ruleth his spirit than he that taketh a city" (Prov. 16:32). And whoever subdues his evil *yezer* is accounted as though he had subdued a city full of mighty men; as it is said, "A wise man scaleth the city of the mighty, and bringeth down the stronghold wherein it trusteth" (Prov. 21:22). And the mighty are none but the mighty of Torah; as it is said, "Ye mighty in strength that fulfill His word, hearkening unto the voice of His word" (Ps. 103:20).

The passage gives two other possible interpretations of גבורים but these need not concern us especially at this point. What is immediately interesting is the expansion of the term "mighty." The mighty, in short, are not only those who subdue their passions, but the "Torah-braves." An examination of version II is now appropriate. Here[41] we read:

Ben Zoma says, Who is wise? He that learns from all men; as it is said, "From all my teachers have I got understanding" (Ps. 119:99). Who is honored? He that honors mankind; as it is said, "For them that honor Me I will honor and they that despise Me shall be lightly esteemed" (I Sam. 2:30).[42] Who is mighty? He that subdues his evil *yezer*; as it is [108] said, "He that is slow to anger is better than the mighty" (Prov. 16:32). Who is rich? He that rejoices in his portion; as it is said, "When thou eatest the labour of thy hands, happy shalt thou be, and it shall be well with thee" (Ps. 128:2): Happy shalt thou be in this world, and it shall be well with thee in the world to come.

Not only does version II read more like *Abot*, but it reads better than does our version. What happened to version I can be explained, I believe, by the hypothesis which each of these examples is intended to substantiate.

i) Very instructive, I feel, will be an analysis of what the two versions of *Abot de Rabbi Nathan* do with a saying by Elisha ben Abuyah. This time we quote first from version II. It reads:[43]

Elisha ben Abuyah says, "He that studies Torah in his youth, to what may he be likened? To lime which is spread on stones: even if all the rains come down, they do not injure it. But he that studies Torah in his old age, to what may he be likened? To lime which is spread over bricks: as soon as one drop of water falls on it, it disintegrates and is washed away [והולך לו—literally, "disappears"].

A parable is told: to what may this be likened? To a king who said to his servant, "Protect [this] bird for my son." The king said to his servant, "If thou dost protect the bird, thou dost protect thine own life; but if thou dost destroy the bird, thou dost

---

41. II, 33, p. 72.
42. On the proof offered by this verse, cf. the commentary of R. Obadiah of Bertinoro to *Abot* 4:1. See also the commentary ad loc. in *Mahzor Vitry*, Rabbenu Jonah, ps. Rashi, etc.
43. II, 35, p. 77.

destroy thine own life." [The servant] protected the bird. . . . Thus says the Holy One blessed be He to Israel: "My children, if you keep[44] the Torah, you keep your own lives; but if you destroy the Torah, you destroy your own lives." So too, whoever keeps one word of the Torah, keeps his own life; but whoever destroys one word of the Torah, destroys his own life; as it is said, "Only take heed to thyself, and keep thy soul diligently, [lest thou forget the things which thine eyes saw]" (Deut. 4:9).

Does this parable have anything to do with Elisha's statement? The editor, in fact, seems to have had a very strange conception of analogies.[45] Both the tale and the conclusion [109] emphasize "observance" of Torah—in other words, the practical implication of Torah—while the statement of Elisha had as its theme study. Is the same, perhaps, true of version I? Let us see.

Version I has no single passage which runs completely parallel to the Elisha passage of II. For example, the metaphor of lime on stones, our version employs in the description of men with Torah and with or without good deeds.[46] The parable of the king with the bird, our version attaches to a statement concerning those who stimulate others to good works. This is, however, what version I does have on the subject of studying in youth and in old age:[47]

He that studies Torah as a child, the words of Torah are absorbed in his blood[48] and they come forth from his mouth distinctly. But he that studies Torah in his old age, the words of Torah are not absorbed in his blood and do not come forth from his mouth distinctly. And thus the maxim goes [אומר—literally, "says"]: If in thy youth thou didst not desire them, how shalt thou acquire them in thine old age?

The reading of our text is obviously better, more logical. And I believe that once more we have an instance of version I clinging to its point of reference—study; version II, on the other hand, takes the theme of study and turns it into a sermon on the importance of observing Torah.

Here we have an opportunity to repeat the caution recommended at the very outset of this paper. There is a danger that in focusing evidence on a theory, the picture as a whole may be blurred. To say that version I of *Abot de Rabbi Nathan* is emphasizing Torah study is not to imply that this treatise prescribes a neglect of practice. The chapter in which Elisha's views are recorded is an excellent case in point. Most of the paragraphs in it emphasize the incompleteness of study alone. The man without [110] מעשים טובים, Elisha

44. The word is משמר—the same as the word translated "protect."
45. Schechter (II, 35, pp. 77–78, note 2) also observed the difficulty. Taking a hint from the Gaon, he suggests that possibly the parable illustrates the saying of Rabbi Dostai (*Abot* 3:8) which should come into our text. I do not agree at all. Notice, incidentally, the difficulty with this parable in I, 24, p. 78, and there too no word is heard of R. Dostai. For a more detailed discussion see note 51, below.
46. Cf. I, 24, p. 77.
47. I, 24, pp. 77–78.
48. Bacher, op. cit., I, p. 432, n. 5, alludes to the Roman proverb, *in succum et sanguinem*. As for the maxim, see Ecclus. 25:3.

tells us again and again—and who knew it better than he—is like a stone structure atop brick foundations, or like lime poured on bricks, or like a cup without a flat base, or like the rider of an unbridled horse. None of these would one choose to be. The point is that our version, while admitting all this, seeks to underline the concept of study of Torah; as a result it stresses that theme, or relates other ideas to it, or refrains from turning it into other directions.

The thesis is here restated because version I affords us the occasion in this instance to examine how it applies the parable which II had attached to a statement on study. In our version, too,[49] truth be told, the parable is not without its problems.[50] Nevertheless, here the parable is said to illustrate not *study*, but the statement, "Whoever makes his fellow perform some command-ment, the verse accounts it to him as though he has performed it himself."[51]

j) After having observed the two versions in their treatment of Elisha's statement, it is interesting to notice the variants in their description of them that frequent the house of study. "There are four types" we read in our version,[52]

among them that frequent the house of study: [there is one] that draws near [111] [the sage] and sits down, [and] has a portion [of reward]; [there is one] that draws near and sits down, [and] has no portion [of reward]; [there is one] that keeps at a distance and sits down, [and] has a portion [of reward]; [there is one] that keeps at a distance and sits down, [and] has no portion [of reward]. [There is one] that asks and replies, [and] has a portion [of reward]; [there is one] that asks and replies, [and] has no portion [of reward]; [there is one] that sits and keeps quiet, [and] has a portion [of reward]; [there is one] that sits and keeps quiet, [and] has no portion [of reward].

The text then proceeds to explain what distinguishes one man from the next. The individuals to be rewarded are those who approach the sage in order the better to hear his lesson, or keep at a distance out of sincere humility, or ask questions the better to understand, or do not interrupt the lecture with ques-tions, the better to hear. Those who go without reward are the ones who come up front out of arrogance, or keep at a distance out of false modesty, or ask

---

49. I, 24, p. 78.

50. See ibid., Schechter's note 24; see also my note in the forthcoming translation ad loc.

51. Is not the following a possible explanation of what happened in version II? The state-ment of Elisha unquestionably discussed "study." The editor of version II, however, being prin-cipally concerned with good works, determined to read his theme into the words of Elisha. Consequently he attached the parable and the concluding sentences to Elisha's dictum. For there was a particularly good reason to do so in this case! The author of the saying was none other than *Aher*. Was he not a splendid example of those who do not "keep the Torah"? Moreover, Elisha's own career seemed to belie his words: הלמד תורה בנערותו למה הוא דומה, לסיד שהוא שח על גבי אבנים אפילו כל הגשמים יורדין אין מזיקין אותו. But Elisha had studied in his youth! Not study at too late a date was the stumbling block of this man; probably he failed to supplement his many studies with good deeds. That was the cause for his failure.

In light of this, perhaps we can understand too why version II quotes so little from Elisha, while version I gives a goodly number of his statements.

52. I, 40, p. 126.

questions to leave the impression that they are wise, or keep quiet to indicate their independence of the sage.

The "catalogue" and description, in brief, are devoted to an analysis of various types of behavior at study. Some students belong to one category, some to another, but the categories are descriptive of conduct at study.

The "four types among them that frequent the house of study" presented by version II,[53] are entirely different. They are, significantly enough, as follows: "He that goes[54] and practices, is a saintly man. He that neither goes nor practices, is a wicked man. He that goes but does not practice, has the reward for going. He that practices and does not go, has the reward for practice." The word עושה has changed the complexion of the passage. We are dealing with something else entirely; we are dealing with a different perspective. The הולכי בית המדרש are examined for different qualities by the two versions.[55]

[112] k) The theme of version I of *Abot de Rabbi Nathan* will perhaps serve us in understanding a passage in the text which has baffled many scholars. We read toward the end of the treatise:[56] "The sword comes upon the world because of the delaying of justice and the perverting of justice; and because of them המורין בתורה שלא כהלכה." Before translating this last clause as it is understood by version I, it is necessary to examine the story which follows our sentence. We are told that when Rabbi Simeon ben Gamaliel and Rabbi Ishmael[57] were being led to their execution, Rabbi Simeon wept. He could not understand why it was destined for him to be treated like a criminal. Yet God could not be unjust! Therefore Rabbi Ishmael advised him to think of certain sins in his lifetime which conceivably warranted the present punishment. The conversation deserves more than a paraphrase.

> "Perhaps," said Rabbi Ishmael to him, "when thou didst settle down to dinner, poor men came and stood at thy door, and thou didst not permit them to enter and eat?" [Rabbi Simeon] said to him, "By Heaven, I did not do thus! Rather, I had guards sitting at the door. When the poor would come, they would be brought in to me, and they would eat and drink with me and recite a blessing in the name of Heaven."[58] [Rabbi Ishmael] said to him, "Perhaps when thou didst sit expounding on the Temple Mount, and all the hosts of Israel sat before thee, thou didst grow proud?" He said to him, "Ishmael, my brother, Man is destined to receive the punishment [he deserves]."[59]

---

53. II, 45, p. 126.
54. I.e., to school.
55. See, incidentally, II, 46, p. 129, where different types of "frequenters" are described.
56. I, 38, p. 114; cf. *Abot* 5:8.
57. Cf. Finkelstein, "The Ten Martyrs," in *Essays and Studies in Memory of Linda R. Miller*, New York, 1938, pp. 29–55.
58. I.e., recite the Grace.
59. The text reads מוכן אדם שיקבל את פגעו. The phrase is not without its difficulties. Nonetheless, it does not affect what is here involved. There will be a note in the translation ad loc.

The narrative then goes on with the execution proper; finally it brings the verses from Zechariah (3:17) and from Exodus (22:33) which speak of slaughter by the sword.

The question is, What is this story intended to illustrate? Its connection with the introductory statement of the paragraph is far from clear. The commentators have gone to no end of [113] trouble to relate the statement about the sword and the story to each other.[60] Their suggestions, though fine, fail to explain what has happened to our text.

As usual, when the text gives one trouble, he turns to the parallel passage of the second version. The reading here[61] is of great assistance.

"The sword comes upon the world because of the perversion of justice and the delaying of justice."[62] Immediately thereafter comes the story of the execution of Rabbi Simeon ben Gamaliel and Rabbi Ishmael, with the details of which we are already familiar. Nevertheless, it will be instructive to eavesdrop on their conversation.

> "Shall I not weep," said Rabbi Simeon, "when I am being led forth to be killed like them that worship idols, and like them that commit incest, and like them that shed [innocent] blood, and like them that profane the Sabbath?" Rabbi Ishmael said to him, "Is it, [then,] for naught? Did never a woman come to ask thee concerning her menstruation, or a man concerning his vow, and thou wast asleep, or at dinner, or perhaps thy time was not free, or perhaps the servant did not permit him to enter?"[63] [Rabbi Simeon] said to him, "Whether I was asleep or at dinner, the servant was commanded that no man be prevented from entering. Yet,[64] it is not for naught! Once, as I was sitting down, men stood before me[65] and my heart swelled within me." Rabbi Ishmael said to him, "We deserve to be led forth to be killed."

From version II, in other words, we learn that the story of the execution of the two sages is an illustration of the consequences of עינוי הדין—particularly is this clear from the reading in the *Menorat Ha-Maor*. Is it not significant that the second version, [114] substantially, does so read, while version I reads כשהיית יושב ודורש בהר הבית? Moreover, the form in version I is all the more impressive when we inspect other sources in which the story occurs. Most of them[66] say nothing of "expounding on the Temple Mount." Only one manuscript[67]

60. See Schechter's note 7, ibid. See also what the Gaon recommends.

61. II, 41, p. 114.

62. See also II, 41, p. 116.

63. See the reading at this point in Al-Nakawa, *Menorat Ha-Maor*, ed. Enclow, vol. 4, p. 189–90, which makes the connection to the introductory statement sufficiently obvious.

64. I am following the reading of *Menorat Ha-Maor*, ibid., which omits א״ל here and the very next one. My feeling is that Rabbi Simeon is saying all this.

65. At this point *Menorat Ha-Maor*, ibid., pointedly adds לדין.

66. Cf. *Mekilta, Mishpatim*, מסכתא דנזיקן, 18, III, p. 142; *Semahot*, ed. Higger, ch. 8, p. 153; *Tanna d'be Eliahu*, ed. Friedmann, ch. 30, p. 153; *Yalkut Exodus*, 349 (these references are given by Schechter, I, 38, p. 115, n. 7). For other references see Higger, op. cit., pp. 36–38.

67. סדר חיבור ברכות, p. 266—quoted by Higger, op. cit., p. 38.

resembles the idiom in our treatise: שמא כשהיית דורש ברבים היה לבך שמח והנאה (לכך) [לבך] אמ' לו (ניוומתי) [ניחמתני]. Another source[68] has this interesting expression: שמא כשהיית יושב בדין ודורש וכל אכלוסי ישראל יושבין לפניך שמא זהת דעתך עליך. Apparently there were two forms in which the conversation between Rabbi Simeon and Rabbi Ishmael was handed down, and our last source represents an effort to combine them both.[69]

In any event—and particularly if the last assumption is true—the story in version I reflects the emphasis which it is constantly making. Either the phrase was deliberately changed to כשהיית יושב ודורש בהר הבית or that form was selected by version I because Torah study—and hence an activity, "expounding," related to it—was its point of reference.[70]

If the interpretation offered thus far is plausible, we may return to the clause המורין בתורה שלא כהלכה. The words, in this instance, are extremely difficult, particularly since I believe that the story about the execution of the Sages (in version I) is [115] meant as an illustration not of ענוי הדין but of המורין בתורה וכו'. Although Professor Ginzberg informs me that in rabbinic literature מורין is always "decide"—not merely "teach"—perhaps *Abot de Rabbi Nathan*, for purposes of *derush*,[71] amplifies the meaning of the word in this connection to instruction in general. Moreover, שלא כהלכה here means "improperly" and has nothing to do with the *halakah* as such.[72] The clause would then mean, The sword comes upon the world because of them that teach Torah with improper conduct. The teacher who is proud is not behaving well, for humility must characterize him at all times.

I am thoroughly aware of the serious objections to such an interpretation.[73] Nevertheless, the crux of the evidence resides not in the validity of my understanding of המורין בתורה וכו', nor in the hypothesis that the story illustrates that principle; the important factor is the variant between the readings in version I and version II of the cause of Rabbi Simeon's punishment.

l) Every example introduced thus far has been taken from such passages as both versions of *Abot de Rabbi Nathan* discuss. This was deliberately done, for,

---

68. *Exempla of the Rabbis*, ed. M. Gaster, passage 76, p. 51. See incidentally, Büchler, *Studies in Sin and Atonement*, p. 199, n. 1.

69. I must confess that this is indeed my feeling about the passage in the *Exempla*. There seems to have been one tradition which regarded the tragic end of R. Simeon as a punishment not for ענוי הדין, but as a punishment for lack of humility. Witness the account in סדר חיבור ברכות (I quote in full so that the context be clear): כשיצאו רשב"ג ור' ישמעאל כהן גדול ליהרג אמ' לו רשב"ג לר' ישמעאל, אחי אוי לי שאיני יודע למה אני יוצא ליהרג, אמ' לו שמא כשהיית דורש ברבים היה לבך שמח והנאה (לכך) [לבך] אמ' לו (ניוומתי) [ניחמתני], על כן כשעושה אדם מעשים טובים יעשם בצניעות, ואל יהנה בפני העולם שנוטל שכרו בזה העולם.

70. The difficulty felt by Schechter (note 7, pp. 114–15) thus becomes clear, and his suggested reading is altogether unnecessary.

71. See, for example, what the text does to Jose ben Johanan's statement in I, 7, p. 34 and II, 14, p. 33.

72. See, for example, II, 40, p. 111 and also p. 112 where the phrase (in describing the clod) שואל כענין ומשיב כהלכה occurs as a contrast to שאל שלא כראוי ומשיב שלא כענין.

73. Incidentally, neither is the passage in II, 41, p. 116 בעון בטול תורה ועוות הדין חרב בא לעולם וכו' of much assistance. For, is pride an instance of בטול תורה?

as was early observed, some comparative standard is necessary. The next, and last illustration, however, represents material in two separate paragraphs which occur in version I only. Nevertheless, more than passing significance, I believe, is theirs.

At the very beginning of version I,[74] immediately after the controversy between Rabbi Jose the Galilean and Rabbi Akiba, Rabbi Nathan—allegedly the author-editor of this treatise[75]—is quoted. Rabbi Nathan offers a reason why Moses was detained six days before the word of God came to him. With that view, apparently, Rabbi Mattiah ben Heresh cannot agree; [116] consequently, he explains otherwise what happened with Moses. This done, the paragraph concludes as follows:

> It once happened that Rabbi Josiah and Rabbi Mattiah ben Heresh sat together engaged in the study of Torah. Rabbi Josiah withdrew to attend to his occupation. Said Rabbi Mattiah to him, "Master, why dost thou leave the words of the living God to pursue an occupation? Now, although thou art my master and I am thy pupil, [I declare] it is not good to leave the words of the living God and pursue an occupation." It was said [of them], So long as they sat studying Torah, they acted as though they were jealous of each other: but when they departed, they were like friends from childhood on.

On this note the first paragraph in our treatise ends. The theme calls attention to itself quite adequately and needs no amplification on my part. The connection, likewise, of this brief story with the preceding material is far-fetched.

Nothing like this story is to be found at the beginning of version II.[76]

And now we turn to the very last paragraph of our work.[77]

> Rabbi Hananiah ben Akashya said, It pleased the Holy One blessed be He to grant merit to Israel; therefore, He gave them Torah and commandments in abundance; as it is said, "The Lord was pleased for his[78] righteousness' sake, to make Torah great and glorious" (Is. 42:21).

Certainly the theme here is clear enough, and the verse from Isaiah is as felicitous for our hypothesis as it is for a peroration of the volume.

The sentiment expressed at the conclusion of version II[79] is unquestionably noble; moreover it is a tribute to scholars, those "philosophers-kings" of Israel. But an emphasis on Torah it is not.

74. I, 1, p. 1.
75. See my note in the translation, ad loc.
76. Cf. II, 1, p. 1.
77. I, 41, p. 134.
78. I.e., Israel's. Cf. translation, ad loc.
79. Cf. II, 48, p. 134.

Now, Dr. Schechter[80] is very likely correct in assuming that the saying of Rabbi Hananiah ben Akashya is a late conclusion attached to our treatise. Nevertheless, "And there is no doubt that these words were added here either by the copyists [117] or by the printers in order to conclude on a happy note" is not enough of an answer. There are many "happy endings" in the literature of Israel. The conclusion of version II, for example, leaves nothing to be desired. The question is, Why was this particular passage with this particular theme employed?[81] The question is not petulant; for my feeling is that both the opening and closing paragraphs of a treatise are often strategic. There the author or compiler can make a deeper impression than almost anywhere else in his work. The fact that version I strikes the note of Torah both at its start and its finish indicates (when all the other facts are added to this one) that at one time students recognized what this text was emphasizing throughout; in other words, the closing paragraph of the book became the closing paragraph of the book because its appropriateness was evident to the later editors. And when Torah is the keynote, the beginning and the end are becoming unto the treatise (to use the idiom of the prayer) even as it is becoming unto them.[82]

---

80. I, 41, p. 134, n. 27.

81. It is of course with this passage, as is well known, that each chapter of *Abot* is concluded in the synagogue service. But the centrality of Torah to *Abot* has likewise been observed. See especially R. T. Herford, *Pirke Aboth*, New York, 1925, pp. 15–16 and Mordecai M. Kaplan in *Jewish Education*, vol. 14, no. 2, pp. 72–73.

82. The passages discussed in this section do not exhaust all the evidence. Of course, I have selected the most impressive (or what I thought to be the most impressive) examples, so that the hypothesis would be most clearly presented. Nevertheless, it is not unprofitable to examine every passage in the text very carefully. Some "minor" variants between the readings of the two versions are, I feel, extremely illuminating. To give just one more example: I, 26, p. 82 reads אין עם הארץ חסיד, while II, 33, p. 72 reads (פירוש) [פירוש] ולא עם הארץ חסיד. Why this qualification in version II? Why is version II almost all alone amongst sources (cf. *Mekilta de R. Simeon*, p. 169; the reading in *Mekilta de R. Ishmael* מסכתא דעמלק, 1, vol. II, pp. 139–140, is very interesting!) to read ג' חזרו למקומן, ישראל והתורה (ו) וכו' (II, 47, p. 130; cf. I, 41, p. 133)? These and other passages might be analyzed, but the point is well enough taken. Again I must state that in both I and II there are certain passages on Torah which cannot serve our immediate purpose since these occur in only one of the treatises. I have not referred to any of these (except for the last example in the body of the paper). I has many which II does not have; II, on the other hand, has many which I does not have. Only comments which occur on passages common to both texts can help us at this stage. And in addition to all the examples in the paper, and the two hinted at earlier in this note, one would do well to inspect the following: II, 3, p. 12 (though scholars are talked of, prayer is emphasized); I, 3, p. 14f. and II, 4, p. 14; I, 4, p. 18 and II, 5, p. 18 (see also II, 8, p. 22); II, 12, p. 28 and I, 6, p. 27; II, 13, p. 30 and I, 16, p. 64; II, 15, p. 34f. (but see Schechter's note); I, 10, p. 43; I, 11, p. 47 and II, 22, p. 47 (see also I, 11, p. 48—מים הרעים כמשמעו—and Schechter's note); I, 12, p. 55; I, 12, p. 56 and II, 27, p. 56; I, 14, p. 58 and II, 29, p. 58 and II, 31, p. 56; I, 16, p. 62 (ד"א עין הרע); I, 16, p. 64 (but see II, 13, p. 30); I, 17, p. 65 (notice the difficulty in the passage ד"א יהי ממון; incidentally, the Zolkiev edition gives this as the only [!] interpretation of R. Jose's saying); I, 17, p. 66 and II, 30 p. 66; II, 31, p. 67 and I, 22, p. 74f. (notice here the emphasis on מעשים in II); II, 31, p. 68 and I, 28, p. 85; II, 31, p. 68 and I, 24, p. 78; II, 32, p. 68 and I, 20, p. 70f. (see too I, 29, p. 87, כל השוקד על ד"ת); II, 32, p. 68 and I, 27, p. 83; II, 32, p. 69 and I, 22, p. 74 (notice the length to which II goes to emphasize מעשים טובים); II, 32, p. 70 and I, 22, p. 75; II, 32, p. 70 and I, 22, p. 75 (שמעון בנו); II, 33, p. 71 and I, 26, p. 82; II, 33, p. 73 (see I, 29, p. 87; notice, incidentally, how II adds to *Abot* 4.10); I, 21, p. 73f. and II, 34, p. 73 (II simply gives R. Dosa's statement); I, 22, p. 75 and II, 34,

APPENDIX

[118] The discussion of any hypothesis is never complete unless all available evidence, favorable and unfavorable, has been examined. Perhaps where there is no contradictory material, a hypothesis is almost superfluous. In any event, there are two passages in version II which must be referred to at this point, because they raise embarrassing questions. Unlike many other passages which occur in this version only, there is no material in version I to cancel them out of existence.

The first of these passages occurs in the commentary of version II upon a saying of Hillel. Hillel had said, "Be of the disciples of Aaron, loving peace and pursuing peace, loving mankind and bringing them nigh to Torah."[83] Each of the versions records this beautiful epigram and each comments on its separate clauses. [119] However, version II, in its comment on the last clause,[84] reads as follows: "And bringing them nigh to the study [!] of Torah."

This is certainly strange, particularly in the second version. Moreover, a glance at the reading of the comments on the same thought in version I,[85] reveals that it—the version which is so preoccupied with Torah study, according to the theory—has simply, "And bringing them nigh to Torah." What follows resembles essentially the ideas expressed in version II.[86] What shall we say, therefore?

My feeling is that the text of version II is corrupt. This is usually the easiest and most unoriginal way out of a difficulty; but there are indices in the treatise to make what I say plausible.

In the first place, nowhere do we find attributed to Hillel the phrase ומקרבן לתלמוד תורה. The reading in Tosefta *Horayot*[87] to which Schechter refers[88] contains the idea expressed in our passage, but no mention is made of Hillel. Thus the Tosefta: מנין שכל המשנה לחבירו מעלין עליו כאילו יצרו וריקמו והביאו לעולם שנ' אם תוציא יקר מזולל כפי תהיה באותו הפרק שזרק בו נשמה באדם, כך כל המכניס בריא אחת תחת כנפי השמים מעלין עליו כאילו יצרו וריקמו והביאו לעולם, יקר זו תורה שנ' יקרה היא מפנינים וכל חפצים לא ישוו בה וא' יש זהב ורב פנינים וכלי יקר שפתי דע'.

In the second place, at the beginning of chapter 24, where the complete

---

p. 75; II, 34, p. 75 (R. Hananiah) and I, 29, p. 87 (see also II, 35, p. 79); II, 34, p. 76 and I, 24, p. 77; II, 35, p. 81 and I, 26, p. 82 and I, 29, p. 88; II, 35, p. 82 and I, 30, p. 89; II, 35, p. 82f. (see I, 24, p. 78); I, 26, p. 82 and II, 35, p. 87; I, 27, p. 84 and II, 35, p. 84 (see, too, I, 27, p. 84); I, 28, p. 85 and II, 48, p. 132; I, 28, p. 86 and II, 35, p. 87 (the statements are not really parallel, yet they are interesting; above all see Schechter's note 22, p. 86. One of the things always to keep in mind is: Is it Torah study which is emphasized, or the efficacy of Torah? For an excellent analysis of these terms see Kadushin's *Organic Thinking*, pp. 68–79. (Even in this list I have often omitted passages which occur in only one version.)

83. II, 24, p. 48; cf. I, 12, p. 48 and *Abot* 1.12.
84. II, 26, p. 53.
85. I, 12, p. 53.
86. Cf. II, 26, p. 53 and II, 26, p. 54 (the last paragraph of the chapter).
87. II:7.
88. II, 26, p. 53, n. 12.

saying of Hillel is first quoted by our version, the reading is explicitly ומקרבן
לתורה—not ומקרבן לתלמוד תורה.

In the third place, the text in version II already reveals some tampering
with. As we have it, the phrase goes ומקרב לתלמוד תורה. Schechter is quite right
when he corrects ומקרב to ומקרבן—the word may easily have been an abbre-
viation of ומקרבן. Nevertheless, since on other accounts the reading is suspect,
the additional problem must be reckoned with.

How, however, did the expression enter the text?[89] This question cannot be
answered with certainty. Perhaps originally the reading was ומקרבן לתורה כל
המכניס בריה וכו'. A later scholar, [120] reading this passage, suddenly remembered the Tosefta idiom כל המשנה לחבירו. In order to make the phrase of Hillel
all the more clear, he inserted the word תלמוד.[90] Nevertheless, the wording at
the beginning of the chapter, where Hillel is quoted directly, he did not touch.

Regardless of how convincing this explanation is, the fact that the text
should read ומקרבן לתורה is, I feel, indubitable.

The second of the difficult passages is likewise connected with Hillel. We
read in version II:[91]

> He (i.e., Hillel[92]) used to say, The more wives, the more witchcraft; the more
> bondswomen, the more lewdness; the more bondsmen, the more theft; the more
> witchcraft, the more evils; the more possessions, the more toil;[93] the more flesh, the
> more worms; the more Torah, the more life; he that acquires a good name, has
> acquired it for himself, he that acquires the words of Torah for himself, has
> acquired for himself the life of the world to come.

After such a passage, the reading in version I is a disappointment. Here[94] we
have, "He used to say, The more one eats, the more one eliminates; and the
more flesh, the more worms and maggots; and the more one performs good
works, the more he brings peace upon himself."[95] Is there no word about
Torah?

It is significant that the reading of the Rome manuscript[96] is as follows: הוא
היה אומר כל המרבה מעשים טובים משים שלום בגופו וכל המרבה תורה מרבה חכמה.

I do not know how to explain what has happened.

Despite the difficulties created by these two passages, my feeling still is that
the hypothesis presented in the body of this paper is correct: namely, that the
theme of version I of *Abot de Rabbi Nathan* as it reads today is the study of
Torah, while the theme of version II is "piety" and good works.

---

89. I.e., if it is not a mere slip of the pen, since *talmud Torah* is so common a combination.
90. He may also have inserted, therefore, the story which follows: II, 26, p. 54.
91. II, 31, p. 67; cf. *Abot* 2:7.
92. Notice, incidentally, that he is here called Rabbi (!) Hillel.
93. Our text reads יגיעה. I wonder whether the reading might not have been originally ראגה.
94. I, 28, p. 86.
95. The last phrase is משים שלום בגופו. The phrase is peculiar; see my note in the translation,
ad loc.
96. See appendix 2 in Schechter's edition of *Abot de Rabbi Nathan*, p. 157.

The Third Chapter
of 'Abot de-Rabbi Natan[1]

I

[365] It was Solomon Schechter who (in accordance also with the emendation of many commentators) first[2] (1887) suggested in his important edition that the third chapter of Version A of 'Abot de-Rabbi Natan begins with the quotation of the second clause in the saying of the *'Anshe Keneset ha-Gedolah,* "and raise many disciples,"[3] and with the comments of the Shammaites and Hillelites which follow:

> For the School of Shammai says: One ought to teach only him who is talented and meek and of distinguished ancestry and rich. But the School of Hillel says: One ought to teach every man, for there were many in Israel who had been sinners and were drawn to the study of Torah, and from them descended[4] righteous (*ṣaddiqim*), pious (*hasidim*), and worthy folk.[5]

1. In order to avoid overcluttering this paper with footnotes, I would like to list here the principal texts and studies on which so much of the discussion is based, and subsequent reference to these will therefore be kept at a minimum: S. Schechter, *'Abot de-Rabbi Natan* (Vienna, 1887). J. Goldin, *The Fathers According to Rabbi Nathan* (New Haven, 1955). L. Finkelstein, "Introductory Study to *Pirke Abot*," *JBL* 57 (1938), 13–50. Idem, "The Maxim of the *Anshe Keneset Ha-Gedolah*," *JBL* 59 (1940), 455–69. Idem, *Mabo le-Massektot Abot ve-Abot d'Rabbi Natan* (N.Y., 1950). The following abbreviations will be employed: ARN = 'Abot de-Rabbi Natan, ARN^A = Version A of ARN, ARN^B = Version B of ARN, *Mabo* = L. Finkelstein's *Mabo*, see above.
 Unless there is some special reason for doing so, I shall not refer to any of the notes I have already written in *The Fathers According to Rabbi Nathan* (see above). Therefore, for the translations which appear in the body of this paper, that volume may be consulted directly.
2. Note, however, Schechter's n. 4, p. 15.
3. 'Abot 1:1.
4. See further n. 34 below.
5. An echo in actuality of the tensions already encountered in the "Hellenistic" world. See

[366] Since 1940 Louis Finkelstein has correctly kept insisting that one ought not neglect the fact that this is not the way the ARN manuscripts and the first edition read. Moreover, Finkelstein has consistently refused to pretend that the closing sentence of the second chapter is something better than clumsy and problematic. Generally it is understood as, "The Sages arose and [=thereupon] made a tall hedge about their words." "Made a tall hedge" or "made many a hedge" is surely a faute de mieux rendering of והרבו ועשו סייג. What is more, as Finkelstein with good reason suggests, the reading הרבה of two manuscripts, rather than והרבו is doubtless the correct reading. At first glance, then, that sentence can be taken to say, "Many sages arose and [=thereupon] made a hedge about their words." But what would be the point of such a remark? It certainly does not hang together comfortably with the material immediately before, on the evening *Shema* recitation and the view of Rabban Gamaliel (or perhaps Rabban Simeon ben Gamaliel).[6]

To be sure, this is not decisive. One could say that the last sentence is intended as an embracing recapitulation of the theme of the whole last section (paragraph) of the second chapter. That section is a demonstration of the proposition that the "Sages made a hedge about their words." After having illustrated this with the evening *Shema* theme, and after citing the view that sometimes it is possible to recite the *Shema* twice in one night, a general statement is added to the effect that many sages made a hedge about their words, not only the one or the ones cited in connection with the *Shema*.

This is not a happy solution, however, for, as Finkelstein rightly emphasizes, the reading שבית שמאי at the beginning of the present chapter three clearly must refer back to what precedes: some connection surely exists between the last sentence of chapter two and the following "*For* the School of Shammai says." It is infinitely more reasonable to detect in the last sentence of the second chapter something of the idiom of the second clause of the saying of the Men of the Great Assembly, and the views of the Shammaites and Hillelites which follow are brought as reflection and commentary on that clause.

[367] For this reason Finkelstein retains the older division of the chapters. Instead of "many sages arose," he recommends reading עמדו in the *pi'el*, imperative, for which he proposes a meaning like that of the *ha'amidu* (raise); *hakamim harbeh* (many sages) he takes as accusative, rather than nominative; and—here he is not entirely clear: Is he suggesting that *w'św* be read as imperative plural (*wa-'aśu*); or is the word to be read *we-'aśu*, third person plural perfect *qal*, "and they made," and referred to an independent statement that other sages made a hedge about their words?[7] If the latter, I cannot accept this at all, and a clumsier structure is hard for me to imagine—the citation of

H. I. Marrou, *History of Education in Antiquity* (N.Y., 1956), pp. 39f., and cf. his reference to Jaeger, *Paideia*, on p. 368.

6. Cf. further, *Mabo*, p. 178.

7. See *Mabo*, p. 28.

the Shammaites and Hillelites he views as part of the discussion of making a hedge; i.e., unlike what the Men of the Great Assembly recommended, the Shammaites made a hedge[8] about such an exhortation and declared that one is to teach only the talented, the meek, the offspring of distinguished ancestors, and the rich. The third chapter then begins, as in the manuscripts and in the first edition, with the statements by Rabbi ʿAqiba (to which we shall refer shortly).

That ʿ*mdw* is to be read as a *piʿel* imperative and to be understood in the sense of the *hiphʿil haʿamidu* is not impossible to me at all; and perhaps even the consonants ʿ*mdw* were once read as ʿ*amidu*[9] =*haʿamidu*, "raise." Beyond that, however, I am unable to follow this acute scholar, who properly and always scrupulously calls attention to the early readings of texts. Let alone the difficulties with *wʿśw* to which I have already referred, how are we to explain the presumptive, correct beginning of the third chapter? I assume (correctly, I believe)[10] that Finkelstein also sees in the third chapter a commentary and discussion of the second clause in the saying of the Men of the Great Assembly. If the citation of the Shammaites and Hillelites is essentially a commentary on hedge-making, what has happened to "raise many disciples" (or, "sages," as Finkelstein insists)? Is it likely that the second clause in that famous saying is brushed [368] aside, merely alluded to in passing and obliquely, while the focus is on the hedge-making? And the very substance of the Shammaite and Hillelite statements—is it not in all plainness devoted to the theme of whom one ought to teach, in other words, to the theme of raising disciples?

Although Schechter may not have been sufficiently restrained in his editing of the end of chapter two and the beginning of chapter three, his instinct did not mislead him, I believe, the division of the manuscripts and the first edition notwithstanding. The third chapter is indeed, all of it, built around the second clause of the *'Anshe Keneset ha-Gedolah* saying. The text of Version B manifestly bears this out. So too will an analysis of Version A; and such an analysis will also give us an insight into the organizational joints of a talmudic text.

II

First, then, let us return to the conclusion of chapter two. Its last section deals with "the hedge the Sages made about their words." And note indeed that the comment on that rubric also begins with שחכמים אומרים, "*For* the Sages say."[11] That section illustrates the hedge-teaching by reporting what is proper conduct for recitation of the evening *Shema*, although strictly speaking the

8. So he already proposed in his 1938 JBL study.

9. On possible omissions of *yod*, cf. J. N. Epstein, *Mabo le-Nusah ha-Mishnah* (Jerusalem, 5708), pp. 1237ff.

10. Cf. Finkelstein's 1938 JBL paper.

11. And perhaps this accounts for the attaching of the beginning of chapter three to the end of chapter two in the MSS.

evening *Shema* may be recited late into the night, long after midnight. In fact, according to one sage it could happen—and be valid—that a person would recite the *Shema* just before the morning star rises and again just after it rises, and thus fulfill two obligations. And here properly, I suggest as did Schechter, is the end of the second chapter.

The third chapter then takes up the one clause in the saying of the *'Anshe Keneset ha-Gedolah* which had not yet been commented on. That clause, in the original, is "raise many disciples." Finkelstein has been insisting since 1940 that the original formulation by the *'Anshe Keneset ha-Gedolah* was "raise many *sages*," and only Rabbi Judah the Prince changed "sages" into "disciples." This is most unlikely in my view, not only because [369] such a reading of 'Abot 1:1 is nowhere preserved, but wherever the saying of the *'Anshe Keneset ha-Gedolah* is quoted—and in the Mekilta[12] and in the Sifre ad Deut., too[13]—the reading is uniformly *talmidim* (disciples), and not *hakamim*. If we adopt Finkelstein's reading of `mdw* as `amdu (pi`el)* or as `amidu* with the sense of *ha`amidu*, "raise," why does ARN change *talmidim* to *hakamim*? And what is the meaning of the following phrase, "*w`św* a hedge to their words?"

No student of ARN can have failed to observe one prominent feature in the opening chapters (and often in later ones too, but this is not the moment to digress) of the treatise, namely, that the clauses in the saying of the *'Anshe Keneset ha-Gedolah* are not given a literal, but a homiletical, midrashic interpretation. "Be deliberate *bdyn*" becomes very rapidly a teaching that "one should be patient in his speech (*debarim*) and not be short-tempered in his speech." "Make a hedge about the Torah" becomes

> Make a hedge about thy words (*debarim*) the way the Holy One, blessed be He, made a hedge about His *words*, and Adam made a hedge about his *words*. The Torah made a hedge about its *words*. Moses made a hedge about his *words*. So too Job, and also the Prophets, the Holy Writings, and the Sages—all of them made a hedge about their *words*.

Moreover, although the original order of the last two clauses in the saying of the *'Anshe Keneset ha-Gedolah* was—and this order is preserved not only in all editions (and manuscripts, too, apparently) of 'Abot, and in both[14] versions of ARN, p. 2, top, but in the Mekilta and in the Sifre cited above—"raise many disciples and make a hedge about the Torah," the commentary in ARN is first devoted to "make a hedge" and only after that to "raise many disciples." As I have shown elsewhere,[15] this rearrangement of order in ARN is not at all

---

12. Ed. J. Z. Lauterbach, I, 46.

13. 1:16, section 16, ed. L. Finkelstein, p. 25; cf. ARN[A], p. 2; ARN[B], p. 2 (top).

14. While Finkelstein (in JBL [1938], p. 30, end of n. 31) is correct in calling attention to the reading of ARN[B], p. 2, bottom, he seems to have ignored the reading on p. 2, top.

15. In the essay "The End of Ecclesiastes," in *Studies and Texts*, III, ed. A. Altmann [see above, p. 7.—Ed.].

baffling, and certainly no record of some alternative reading of the famous saying, but an almost inevitable result of ARN's midrashic approach: once "be deliberate [370] *bdyn*" came to be interpreted as "be deliberate in thy *debarim*," and a hedge about the Torah was to be equated with a hedge about *debarim*, what more natural than to carry on discussion of the proper attitude toward one's *debarim*? Hence Ben 'Azzai's caution in regard to one's *debarim* is cited;[16] hence too, if hedge about the Torah equals a hedge about one's *debarim*, one carries on with this theme.

It is this midrashic approach which may easily have brought about some confusion in the last sentence of ARN^A, chapter two. One had just been speaking of a hedge of the Sages (*hakamim*); the Shammaites were soon to be quoted on the importance of teaching (the Oral Law, *yashneh*!) only to the talented (the *hakam*). The term *hakamim* slipped in, with no one ever dreaming of changing the original text. And once that slip, the clause "*w' św* (= *wa-'aśu*) a hedge about their words"—which certainly does not belong here, for with that subject we are already done—was inevitable as a kind of *shitfa*, the frequent tendency in midrashic-talmudic sources to finish a sentence you have begun to quote, though the extra clauses are superfluous.[17] Indeed, *shitfa* was practically inescapable here, for not only has "hedge about the Torah" been equated just a moment before with "the Sages made a hedge about their words," but the two clauses "raise" and "make a hedge" are thus reproduced in their proper order.

III

The whole third chapter of ARN^A (chapter four in ARN^B) is thus a talmud on the saying "and raise many disciples." First the view of the Shammaites was quoted; then, however, the Hillelite view was quoted to the effect that a person ought to teach (*yashneh*) everyone, for there were many sinners who were drawn to Torah study and these had impressive descendants.

Here (p. 15) ARN^A quotes a block of six sayings by Rabbi 'Aqiba—not one of these has anything to do with the study of [371] Torah. It is terribly tempting to regard all this as an interpolation, and perhaps meaningless, too, at this juncture. But that we are not dealing with foreign matter is evident from the fact that a good deal of this (though not necessarily in 'Aqiba's name) is incorporated in Version B (p. 16) also. Here are the sayings:

Rabbi 'Aqiba says: Whoever takes a *perutah* from charity when he does not need it shall not depart from this world before he falls in need of his fellow men.

16. ARN^A and ARN^B, p. 3.
17. That words and phrases get themselves into our talmudic texts for a variety of reasons (not only *shitfa*) is a recognized phenomenon; see for example J. N. Epstein, *Introduction to Amoraitic Literature* (Heb.) (Jerusalem, 1962), p. 176 (on B. Pesahim 30a—correct misprint in Epstein accordingly).

He used to say:[18] He that binds rags on his eyes or his loins and cries, "Help the blind, help the afflicted," shall in the end be speaking the truth.

He used to say: He that tramples his bread in the dust or in frenzy scatters his coin shall not depart from the world before he falls in need of his fellow men.

He used to say: He that in frenzy tears his clothes, or in frenzy smashes his furniture, will in the end worship idols. For such is the art of the evil *yeṣer*: today it says to him, "Tear thy clothes," and on the morrow it says to him, "Worship idols."

And he goes and worships idols—being unable to resist the goadings of the evil *yeṣer* in grave matters, after never having learned to resist in what might seem minor matters.

He used to say: He who has his eye on his wife in the hope that she die so that he may get the inheritance, or that she die so that he may wed her sister; and whoever has his eye on his brother in the hope that he die so that he may wed his wife, will in the end be buried in their lifetime. Of him the verse says (Eccl. 10:8), "He that diggeth a pit shall fall into it; and whoso breaketh through a fence, a serpent shall bite him."

At this point Version A of ARN introduces a story (*ma'aseh*) familiar to us from the Mishnah, Baba Qamma 8:6, with one significant deviation from the Mishnah text. This is the story, and the significant deviation[19] I shall put in italics:

There was once a certain man *who transgressed the words of* [372] *Rabbi 'Aqiba*[20] *and* uncovered a woman's head in the market place. So she came before Rabbi 'Aqiba, and he sentenced him to pay her four hundred *zuz*.[21] Said the man to him, "Master, let me have some time." 'Aqiba granted it.

When the man came out, his friend said to him: "I shall give thee advice and thou shalt not have to give her even as much as a *perutah*."

"Let me have it," he said to his friend.

"Go," said the friend to him, "take about an *issar's* worth of oil and break the jar at the woman's door," [This the man did.][22]

What did the woman do? She came out of her house, uncovered her head in the

18. I so translate for convenience sake or out of habit. It is clear that *hu' hayah 'omer* in these passages does not mean anything like "he was in the habit of saying," but something like "he was also the author of the following statement." Cf *Proceedings, American Academy for Jewish Research* 27 (1958), 56, n. 51 [above p. 100.—Ed.].

19. There are some minor ones, too. And note also the text in M. Gaster *Exempla* (London-Leipzig, 1924), pp. 68f.

20. Note 'Aqiba's statement in the Mishnah, ibid., just before the story.

21. This round figure means "very much, a very great amount." For instances of this use cf. ARN^A, p. 60; the story in Sifre Numbers 115, ed. Horovitz, p. 128; M. Ketubot 1:5 (on the priestly *bet dīn*); B. Bekorot 31a; and frequently. Ultimately this goes back to the story in Gen. 23:1–20; and this, too, will explain Gen. 32:7.

22. Note the Mishnah Baba Qamma, ibid.

market place, and began scooping up the oil in her hand and putting it on her head.[23]

Now, the man had stationed witnesses to observe her. So he came before Rabbi ʿAqiba and said to him: "To this slut I am to give four hundred *zuz*! Why, over an *issar's* worth of oil she did not spare her self-respect, but went out of her house and uncovered her head in the market place and began scooping up the oil in her hand and putting it on her head!"

"Thou hast said naught," Rabbi ʿAqiba answered him; "for he that injures himself, albeit he is not permitted to do so, is not culpable; but if others injure him, they are culpable. She who abused herself is not culpable; but thou who didst abuse her, go and give her four hundred *zuz*!"

This story does not appear in Version B; it does not appear in that version of the Vatican manuscript which Schechter published as Appendix 2 (pp. 150ff.); it is not included apparently in the manuscript which Schechter cites in his supplementary notes, page 137. Above all, of course, it hasn't the slightest relation to the theme of raising disciples.

Interpolation? Very well. But, surely, whoever inserted this [373] story could not have been so obtuse as not to recognize that admirable or precious as the anecdote may be, the story as such is out of its element in this place. Why then did he drag it in?

Let us return to that significant deviation: There was a certain man *who transgressed the words of Rabbi* ʿAqiba. In other words, for the redactor of ARN[A] this anecdote is an illustration of misconduct in connection with Rabbi ʿAqiba's teaching. But the previous paragraph had quoted a source containing six teachings by Rabbi ʿAqiba! Rabbi ʿAqiba, then, is occupying the center of the stage, and the redactor has introduced the story (to provide as it were a seventh—fine round number?—saying by ʿAqiba?) because we are taking lessons from ʿAqiba now.

IV

But this is too facile and incomplete a solution. It is of course a fact that often in midrashic-talmudic sources, once an authority is introduced, strings of sayings by him and about him will then be presented though little logic is perceptible in the connections. Such and similar artificial devices of organization are preserved for us in some of the oldest strata of the Mishnah, for example.[24] The fifth chapter of ʿAbot is clearly constructed in large part on the number principle, that is, statement after statement, each with the introductory formula, for instance, "There are four things" or "four qualities." Have

23. Literally: She wet (her hand with the oil) and laid her hand on her head (i.e., she rubbed into her hair the oil in her hand).
24. See L. Ginzberg, "Zur Entstehungsgeschichte der Mischnah," Festschrift zum 70. Geburtstage D. Hoffmann's (Berlin, 1914), pp. 311–45.

Rabbi Helbo quote something in the name of Rab Huna, or Rabbi Yohanan in the name of Rabbi Yose, [25] and the Talmud will furnish a number of sayings by Rabbi Helbo in Rab Huna's name or Rabbi Yohanan in Rabbi Yose's name. There is nothing surprising, therefore, in ARN^A's quoting Rabbi ʿAqiba extensively.

And yet the question continues to nag: Why should Rabbi ʿAqiba have been invoked in the first place?

The commentators have naturally not overlooked this question, and have found the answer in the section of the text which follows the anecdote about the man who insulted the woman. This section [374] is devoted to an interpretation of Ecclesiastes 11:6, whose relevance to our theme of raising disciples emerges as a result of an exercise in midrashic exegesis. And as often in midrashic-talmudic sources, first a more (and sometimes less) literal explanation of the verse is presented—or, first an interpretation not immediately germane to the theme is presented—and then, later, we get to the heart of the matter. And so ARN^A proceeds:

> Rabbi Dostai, son of Rabbi Yannai, says: If thou wast early and didst sow in the first rainfall, go again and sow in the second rainfall; for if a hail comes down on the world and the former sowing is blighted, the latter will survive. "For thou knowest not which will prosper, the one or the other": or perhaps both shall survive in thy hand and they "shall both" alike "turn out well" (cf. Eccl. 11:6b). As it is said, "In the morning sow thy seed, and in the evening withhold not thy hand" (Eccl. 11:6a). If thou wast early and didst sow in the first and second rainfall, go again and sow in the third rainfall; for if a blast comes upon the world and the first sowings are blasted, the last will survive. "For thou knowest not which will prosper, the one or the other"; or perhaps "both shall alike turn out well." As it is said, "In the morning sow thy seed," etc.

Here, then, is a literal explanation, put first, exactly as in Version B too, which reads:

> Rabbi Eliezer says: "In the morning sow thy seed" etc.—literally: that is, if thou wast early and didst sow, do not [now] sit back and say, "Enough for me." Instead, sow [again] in the later season. Perchance no rains will fall and the first sowings will perish, or perchance the blast will come and the latter ones will perish. Or perhaps both will prosper. "Thou knowest not which will prosper, the one or the other."

But let us return to the first version. After Rabbi Dostai's comment, Rabbi Ishmael is quoted; four applications of that verse by him are offered.

> Rabbi Ishmael says: If thou hast studied Torah in thy youth, say not, "I shall not study in my old age." Instead, study Torah [at all times, "for thou knowest not which

25. See, for example, B. Berakot 6b–7a.

[study] will prosper," If thou hast studied Torah in riches, do not sit idle in poverty. If thou hast studied Torah on a full stomach, do not sit idle when hungry. If thou hast studied Torah in times of comfort, do not sit [375] idle when hardpressed—for better for man is one thing in the midst of distress than a hundred in comfort—as it is said, "In the morning sow thy seed, and in the evening withhold not thy hand."

None of this is in Version B, but we are getting warm; at least study of the Torah is being discussed, and that cannot be too remote from raising disciples. Our text in ARN^A continues:

Rabbi ʿAqiba says: If thou hast studied Torah in thy youth, study Torah in thine old age. Say not, "I shall not study Torah in my old age," "For thou knowest not which [study] will prosper," if both will survive in thy hand or "both shall" alike "turn out well," [If thou hast raised disciples in thy youth, raise disciples in thine old age (also),] as it is said, "In the morning sow thy seed" etc.

Here we are at last. Perhaps it is even unnecessary to add the bracketed sentence as I have done, and the first statement by ʿAqiba should be translated "If thou hast *taught* Torah in thy youth" and so on, rather than "If thou hast *studied* Torah" and so on, that is, taking the verb as a *piʿel* rather than as a *qal* formation.[26] Under either alternative, however, we can see at last what the destination of all those comments really was. Version B makes this entirely clear, for immediately after quoting Rabbi Eliezer (see above), it proceeds: "Rabbi ʿAqiba says: If thou hast raised many disciples in thy youth, do not sit back and say 'Enough for me.' Instead raise [disciples] in thine old age, and increase (*we-harbeh*) Torah study, 'for thou knowest not' (etc.)."[27]

Our text has still more to tell us about that Ecclesiastes verse, and we shall not ignore it. But we seem to have arrived finally at an answer to the question, Why were so many ʿAqiba statements assembled here? We *seem* to, but not really, I believe.

V

Whenever one deals with interpolated material, it is methodologically hardly satisfactory to assume that the interpolator must be simple-minded, is less sensitive to the problems which disturb a later student. True, there are copyists and redactors whose craftsmanship leaves much to be desired. But to *begin* with the [376] assumption that he who put a text into more or less final form was deficient in intelligence is not exactly the height of literary criticism or perception. That the editor of ARN^A, once he quoted ʿAqiba, would be inspired to quote some more from that sage, is to be expected. But if so, why did not the editor first quote ʿAqiba on the Ecclesiastes verse, and then go on to the other ʿAqiba teachings? The question is not, Why did not the editor first

26. And see also above, n. 9.
27. Neither p. 137 nor p. 154 in ed. Schechter is of any help here.

quote ʿAqiba on the Ecclesiastes verse, and then Rabbi Ishmael and Rabbi Dostai (or the other way around—this makes no material difference)? As we have already observed, in many *midrashim*, when there is real interest in only one interpretation of a verse, but more than one interpretation of the verse is available, the nonrelevant interpretations will be furnished first, and the relevant interpretation will be presented at the end, climactically as it were.[28] Our question then (to repeat) is not why ʿAqiba's interpretation of the Ecclesiastes verse wasn't put at the head of all the interpretations. Our question is: Granted that once you cite ʿAqiba when he is relevant, you may go on and cite him on other subjects too, why was ʿAqiba first cited on the other subjects—taking charity when not in need, pretending to be a pauper, failing to control one's fits of rage, casting eyes on one's relations so as to get the better of them, defending the principle that I may not injure my fellowman regardless of what he does to himself—and only after all this getting to the point? Note well: Even ʿAqiba's interpretation of the Ecclesiastes verse, as we shall see shortly, is not the last interpretation of that verse ARN^A supplies. Even more: A glance at Version B reveals that the editor or compiler of that text truly followed a sensible arrangement. The theme of the chapter being raising disciples, he quoted first the views of the Shammaites and Hillelites. Then he quoted Rabbi Eliezer's literal interpretation of Eccl. 11:6. This he followed at once with Rabbi ʿAqiba's interpretation. Only then did he continue with another statement which he attributes to ʿAqiba.[29] [377] Thereafter come other sayings which occur also in ARN^A, though Version B does not apparently attribute them to ʿAqiba. Why should the editor of ARN^A have chosen another and seemingly less plausible course?

The answer must be that he had his reasons, and fortunately these are not

---

28. Note, for example, the beginning of Leviticus Rabba, ed. Margulies, pp. 1–6 (top).

29. "He used to say: If a poor man came to thee in the morning and after thou gavest him an *issar* he went on; and then another came in the afternoon [for alms]; do not say, 'I've already given to the first one.' On the contrary, better that thou give to the latter [also], 'for thou knowest not' [etc.]. Rabbi Joshua ben Qorḥah says: If thou didst wed a wife in thy youth and she bore three children, and then died—it is not [right] for thee to sit back and say 'Enough for me.' On the contrary, in thine old age [too] add (*harbeh*) fruitfulness and increase, 'for thou knowest not' [etc.]. He used to say: . . ." Now come the statements, familiar to us from ARN^A, about casting one's eye on the wife to inherit her or to marry another [and the woman acting the same way], scattering coin and being destructive in a rage. One additional statement occurs, but the text is garbled.

Incidentally, the clause in ARN^B, "He who casts his eye on his wife . . . in the hope that she die so that he might take to himself another wife," is probably *not* just a *façon de parler*. Note the statement attributed to Rabbi Judah ben Batyra in ARN^B, p. 9: "Job kept deliberating with himself: 'For what would be the portion of God from above, and the heritage of the Almighty from on high' (Job 31:2)—had it been fitting that Adam be given ten wives, He would have given [them] to him. But it was not fitting that any more than one wife be given to him. So too for me: sufficient unto me is my wife, sufficient unto me my portion." Comp. C. Rabin, *The Zadokite Documents* (Oxford, 1958), pp. 16ff.

What is more, while the statement in ARN^A obviously reflects the possibility of marrying one's widowed sister-in-law, the wife's sister or the brother's wife, nothing like this is even alluded to in ARN^B.

beyond recovery. In providing commentary on the clause "raise many disciples," ARN had reported the different outlooks of the Shammaites and Hillelites, and the latter had insisted that no previously established credentials be required of students, but that "one ought to teach every man, for there were many in Israel who had been sinners (*she-harbeh poshe'im hayu bahem beyisra'el*) and were drawn to Torah study, and from them descended righteous, pious, and worthy folk." Would you like exhibit A, as it were, of this truth? None will serve better than 'Aqiba. That he had not even begun to study until he was forty was a popular story, and later in the text ARN will tell it (Version A, ch. 6; Version B, ch. 12). What 'Aqiba was like as a young man he himself reports: "When I was an *'am ha-'areṣ* I used to exclaim: Would that I could get hold of a scholar! Like a donkey I'd bite him" ["and break his bones"].[30] Little wonder that years later, as he once

sat teaching his disciples and remembered what he had done in his youth, he exclaimed: "I give thanks unto Thee, O Lord [378] my God, that Thou hast set my portion amongst those that sit in the study house, and didst not set my portion amongst those that loiter at street corners in the market place."[31]

Talk about raising disciples, forsooth—after he became expert in Torah, twelve thousand pairs[32] of disciples from Antipatris inland he had sitting and studying in the synagogues and study houses.[33] What was the end of this 'Aqiba? He continued assembling students and teaching them, in other words, raising disciples, even at the risk of his life, and died cheerfully sanctifying the Name and absolute uniqueness of God.

What kind of man was he, once he became a scholar; what kind of views did he hold? Those six (seven?) teachings display the man. Can there be any doubt then of the legitimacy of the Hillelite confidence? What would 'Aqiba have been if the Shammaite view had been adopted? Raise many disciples, ARN[A] asserts boldly, for you never can tell; look at 'Aqiba. Indeed, how much bolder is ARN[A] than ARN[B]! ARN[A] declares that there were many who had been sinners, but once drawn to Torah study, from their midst came (*we-yaṣe'u mehem*)[34] some of the finest people. For ARN[B] this is perhaps a bit overenthusiastic, and the statement had best appear with some moderation: "A parable is told; to what may this [Hillelite policy] be likened? To a woman who

30. B. Pesahim 49b.

31. ARN[A], p. 74. Cf. L. Ginzberg, *Commentary on the Palestinian Talmud* (N. Y., 1941), III, 223.

32. Corresponding to twice the twelve tribes of Israel and to the twenty-four books of Holy Scripture? "Pairs"—Grace Goldin suggests: because a student ought to have a companion, *haber*? Cf. 'Abot 1:6 and ARN, pp. 36 and 40.

33. ARN[B], p. 29. Note indeed Gen. R. 61:3, ed. Theodor-Albeck, p. 66c.

34. I believe this is indeed the literal translation. Up to this point I have translated "descended" because the verb is a bit ambiguous. Note the use of *yaṣa'* as "born" in ARN[A], p. 12.

sets a hen on eggs; out of many [eggs] she produces a few [chicks], but out of a small number, she produces nothing." In other words, it's simply statistical prudence: obey the law of averages. In that mood it's pointless playing up ʿAqiba.

VI

For the editor of ARN^A, therefore, ʿAqiba is not only an articulate advocate of the proposition that one should raise many [379] disciples, that late and soon one dare not lay waste his powers of raising disciples; ʿAqiba is in addition himself a splendid example of the consequences of the Hillelite policy in practice. Strictly speaking, then, by now the point has been made; yet the editor of ARN^A does not let go of the discussion. Immediately after citing Rabbi ʿAqiba he continues with a statement by Rabbi Meʾir:

> Rabbi Meʾir says: If thou hast studied[35] with one master, say not, "Enough for me." On the contrary, go to another sage and study Torah. Yet go not to anyone, but first to him that is nigh to thee, as it is said (Prov. 5:15), "Drink waters out of thine own cistern, and running waters out of thine well."[36]

This statement by Rabbi Meʾir appears also in ARN^B, but not at this point. In Version B it appears later (ch. 18, pp. 39f.) as part of the comment on the saying "Get thee a master for wisdom,"[37] and seems even to be attributed to Rabbi ʿAqiba.[38] But in ARN^B it is not part of the interpretations of Eccl. 11:6. On the other hand, apparently, for the editor of ARN^A, this statement and what we shall now proceed to quote—and which ARN^B also substantially reproduces later, on "Get thee a master for wisdom"—does belong to the Eccl. 11:6 exegesis:

> A man is duty bound to attend upon [four][39] scholars, such as Rabbi Eliezer, Rabbi Joshua, Rabbi ʿAqiba, and Rabbi Ṭarfon,[40] as it is said (Prov. 8:34), "Happy is the man that hearkeneth to me, watching daily at my gates, waiting at the posts of my doors": read not "my gates" (*daltotai*) but "my four gates" (*dalet daltotai*). "For thou knowest not" if both will survive in thy hand, "if both shall alike turn out well," as it is said, "In the morning sow thy seed [etc.]."

When a man has studied with one teacher, he is not to be content with that, but should go on to study with others. As interpretations of Eccl. 11:6 go, this is

---

35. See Schechter's note ad loc., and see also the interesting reading in appendix 2, p. 154. With this cf. ARN^B, p. 39, *Mabo*, p. 118, and N. Tur-Sinai in *Mordecai M. Kaplan Jubilee Volume* (Heb.) (N. Y., 1953), p. 84.

36. Note Rabbi Meʾir, however, in ARN^A, p. 36; observe this *anonymously* in ARN^B, p. 39.

37. Cf. this reading with 'Abot 1:6, and note also ARN^B's attribution.

38. Cf. Schechter's n. 5 ad loc.

39. So ed. Schechter; but cf. below in body of paper.

40. But see Schechter's note, p. 137, for which I see no sufficient justification. Note the order in the quotation from the Passover Haggadah, below.

certainly not extreme. [380] Indeed we may say that the editor was attracted by this statement because it makes a nice counterpart to that interpretation of the verse which elucidates "raise many disciples": as the teacher is encouraged to teach many students, so the student is encouraged to learn from many teachers. But those four scholars who are named as models—are they a random selection for the editor of ARN^A? They recur, as we can see, in ARN^B (p. 39) in another connection,[41] and so evidently serve as a stock example. Yet, if the editor of ARN^A introduced them into the chapter on raising many disciples, is it likely that he had nothing but the stock example in mind? Moreover, these four sages are listed together in still another famous source, the Passover Haggadah. Obviously therefore they *are* a stock example; why seek additional explanations? Note, however, that in the Passover Haggadah when they are named, still another sage is named: "Once as (*ma'aseh*) Rabbi Eliezer and Rabbi Joshua and *Rabbi Eleazar ben Azariah* and Rabbi 'Aqiba and Rabbi Ṭarfon were dining in Bene Beraq" and so on.[42] Why is Rabbi Eleazar ben Azariah omitted in the ARN passage? Granted that the midrash on Proverbs 8:34 requires *four*, not five, sages. But why omit Eleazar ben Azariah? Of course one might ask this about any sage whose name had been omitted. Yet this is not a petulant question, for who knows if the statement "A man is duty bound to serve [a number of] scholars" rather than only one, did say "four" originally? Observe the lack of certainty of the reading in our text here, in the eighteenth chapter of ARN^B, in the patent version of the Vatican manuscript (p. 154), ". . . a man is duty bound to attend upon *three* such *talmidim* (scholars) as Rabbi Eliezer and Rabbi Joshua and Rabbi 'Aqiba"![43]

The midrash on "my gates equals my four gates" (*dalet daltotai*) is doubtless legitimate, and doubtless responsible for ARN^A's reference to *four* scholars. But the four are no accident. They are present here at the deliberate invitation of the ARN^A editor, who may even be the one responsible for the midrash *dalet daltotai*, but who certainly believes that each of these particular [381] four great sages serves his, the editor's, exegetical needs.[44] For in furnishing commentary on the saying "raise many disciples," the editor had quoted not only the Hillelites—the victorious school—but also the Shammaites, who had insisted that one ought to teach only persons that are talented (*hakam*) and meek ('*anaw*) and of distinguished ancestry and rich. If each of the four sages named be looked at carefully, we shall not fail to observe that each is, so to speak, an exemplar of one of the four qualities or requirements listed by the Shammaites. Rabbi Eliezer? The rich one. Rabbi Joshua? The '*anaw*. Rabbi

41. See note 38 above.

42. *Haggadah shel Pesah*, ed. E. D. Goldschmidt (Jerusalem, 1960), p. 118, and see ibid., pp. 19f. On these sages, see also Mekilta, ed. Lauterbach, II, 280f.

43. [Cf. S. Lieberman, *Siphre Zutta* (New York, 1968), pp. 89f.]

44. And perhaps our explanation will serve to account for their becoming a stock example. In essentials, as we have said, this midrash appears also in ARN^B, p. 39; however, observe not only the textual difficulties ibid., but the point at which it is introduced.

'Aqiba? The talented one, the one who became the *hakam* par excellence, though to begin with he had been poor, an *'am ha-'areṣ* (and therefore certainly not *'anaw*), of no distinguished ancestry.[45] Rabbi Ṭarfon? He was certainly rich; I suppose his conduct toward his mother might, homiletically, be the equipment of the *'anaw*, but otherwise that would not be the epithet one would immediately associate with him; he was a scholar (*hakam*), to be sure, but above all, he was of distinguished ancestry—already while he was still young he could apparently take a station so close to the High Priest as to hear that eminent personage pronounce the ineffable Name. Eleazar ben Azariah? It would defeat the whole purpose of Rabbi Me'ir's statement to refer to Eleazar! For Eleazar ben Azariah in himself combined all four of these qualities: a scholar, rich, of distinguished ancestry, and so great an *'anaw* (endowed with what Vaughan might call "high humility"), when high office came his way, how he hesitated and feared. Luckily his hair turned white in time! What point is there to his being mentioned?[46] After all, Rabbi Me'ir is urging the disciple to attend upon more than one master, to attend upon *many* masters.

VII

[382] Say what one will about the editor of the third chapter of ARN[A], it is evident that he introduces material, interpolates too, with one purpose always uppermost in mind: to explain and by amplification make vivid the basic substance of the 'Abot de-Rabbi Natan chapter devoted to "raise many disciples." This editor is a *commentator* in his editorial activity. And this emerges no less effectively from the closing portions of the chapter than from material up to this point.

For, as Version B demonstrates (though it assigns the statements to two other authorities), the citation of Eccl. 11:6 encouraged introduction not only of interpretations of that verse immediately affiliated with the theme of raising disciples, but of other meaningful interpretations too. In ARN[A], immediately after Rabbi Me'ir's comment and the remark about the four sages, Rabbi Joshua is quoted, as follows:

> Rabbi Joshua says: Wed a wife in thy youth and wed a wife in thine old age. Beget children in thy youth and beget children in thine old age. Say not, "I shall not wed a wife." On the contrary, wed a wife and beget sons and daughters, and add (*we-*

45. And see also B. Berakot 27b. On 'Aqiba being extraordinarily talented, cf. ARN[A] (R. Ṭarfon's testimony) and ARN[B] (the same testimony in R. Eliezer's name), p. 29. Note also ibid. the statement by R. Simeon (ARN[A], ben Eleazar; ARN[B], ben Menassiah), and cf. Mark 11:23.

46. See the biographical sketches on each of these sages in the *Jewish Encyclopaedia*, under the respective headings. In an oral communication, Professor A. S. Rosenthal suggested to me that perhaps the four sages selected by ARN[A] might signify respective representatives of both Shammaite and Hillelite points of view; thus, R. Eliezer and R. Ṭarfon would represent Shammaites, and R. Joshua and R. 'Aqiba, Hillelites.

harbeh) fruitfulness and increase to the world. "For thou knowest not" if both will survive in thy hand, if "both alike shall turn out well." As it is said, "In the morning sow thy seed," etc.[47]

He used to say: If thou hast given a *perutah* to a poor man in the morning and another poor man came and stood before thee in the evening, give him [too]; "for thou knowest not" if both acts will survive in thy hand, if "both shall alike turn out well." As it is said, "In the morning sow thy seed," etc.

That this has led us far away from the principal theme of raising disciples needs no pressing; it has come here because of Eccl. 11:6; but obviously these statements on marrying as a young man [383] and as an old man and bringing children into the world, and on giving again and again to the poor, must have been part of ARN, for essentially the same statements recur in ARN[B] (though, as I said, in the name of other authorities). Yet once again, how different were the editors of ARN[A] and ARN[B]! In ARN[B] only the statements occur. In ARN[A], however, these statements are followed by three (!—an ideal way to create emphasis in this literature) anecdotes. And the stories are carefully told.

The first is a story (*ma ʿaśeh*) of "a certain *hasid* who once gave a *denar* to a poor man during a famine." His wife was apparently profoundly irritated with him for this extravagance, and as a result he left and spent the night in a cemetery—presumably to escape her nagging and get some quiet. Here, however, he overheard female[48] spirits of the dead in conversation and thus learned of calamities in store for the world. For example, he learned that first sowings would be destroyed. He thereupon sowed in the second rainfall. Consequently, he was the only one to escape disaster that year. Having discovered how useful that cemetery could be, he returned there the following year on his own,[49] and overheard the prediction of the spirits again, that this time the second sowings would be destroyed. He therefore sowed during the first rainfall, and thus again was the only one to escape disaster.

The ARN[A] editor finishes the story, but we need not, for we have other business on hand. What is the point of the story?

This is not a difficult question. Since the previous section had closed on the theme of charity-giving, and had used for its formulation the language of Ecclesiastes on sowing early and late, the editor introduces a tale on this theme

47. I would like to suggest that in this statement we can overhear echoes of Rabbi Joshua's "response" to the contemporary reactions to the destruction of the Temple and defeat by the Romans; see for example T. Soṭah 15:11f. (cf. S. Lieberman, *Tosefeth Rishonim* [Jerusalem, 1938], II, 67), and cf. also the mood reflected in B. Baba Batra 60b (end of chapter 3). Note also *Mabo*, pp. 129f.

48. I am not sure, of course, but I cannot help feeling that there is an element of irony at play here, suggesting that even in their death women won't shut up. And that *hasid* too in the end, because he could not keep his mouth shut, lost the advantage he had enjoyed.

49. Neither in the ARN[A] version, nor in the version of B. Berakot 18b, nor in the version of Midrash ha-Gadol, Genesis, ed. Margulies, p. 804, nor in Gaster's *Exempla*, p. 73, is there any suggestion that this time he was driven to leave home.

and in this language, and suggests even the lesson of reward—that *hasid* gave charity during a famine, and behold how he was rewarded.

This anecdote, however, is followed by a second, also a *ma'aseh* [384] of a certain *hasid*, but he is described as one "who was in the habit of giving charity" (*she-hayah ragil bi-ṣedaqah*); in other words, we are dealing not merely with a person who once gave charity but with a person who was habitually charitable. Here the events are even more sensational—and interestingly enough, one of the dramatis personae this time is Rabbi 'Aqiba. Charity saved this *hasid* from drowning, though his ship went down (*we-ṭaba'*[!][50] *sefinato ba-yam*); the very waves rushed to his assistance, "for he practised charity all his days."[51] That the reward is more extraordinary in the second than in the first anecdote is only fair; the virtue of the second *hasid* excels the virtue of the first one.

Finally the third anecdote (*ma'aseh*) with which the chapter also comes to an end. There was a Benjamin the Righteous (*ha-ṣaddiq*) "who was in charge of the community charity chest." Not just a *hasid*, but a *ṣaddiq*;[52] and not just a man who makes it a [385] regular practice to give charity, but one who carries the constant responsibility of providing for the poor who are always with us, not only the poor who chance to cross our path. And what is more: On one occasion, after all the funds of that chest had been exhausted, a widow and her seven[53] sons appeared before him and clamored for help: "If thou dost not take

50. Perhaps only a printer's error; note the clearly feminine form of the verb, for example, in ed. Schechter, p. 155, and in *Exempla*, p. 69.

51. Cf. *Mabo*, pp. 145f. For the clause "hath chosen . . . the words of the Sages" in Rabbi 'Aqiba's exclamation, see the version of the story in B. Yebamot 121a. Observe indeed that in the Yebamot version there is no talk of one who gave charity! The *Exempla* version, loc. cit., is essentially like that of ARN[A] (note the end of the *Exempla* version, however.) As for the version of the story in Eccl. R. 11:1, cf. Schechter's note 56 on p. 17 of ARN.

52. On the terms *hasid* and *ṣaddiq*, see S. Lieberman, *Greek in Jewish Palestine* (N. Y., 1942), pp. 69–71. Note well "that the Jews in Palestine were not too eager to confer this title (*ṣaddiq*) even on a deceased person, that in practical life this epithet was not abused in the first centuries c.e., despite its frequent appearance in rabbinic literature." Except for this Benjamin and the famous Simeon the Righteous of the beginning of 'Abot (and, of course, except for biblical worthies like Joseph who in legend are called *ṣaddiq*—in Scripture only Noah is, Gen. 6:9, except for God), I cannot recall one talmudic person so called. I would therefore like to suggest the following: *ṣaddiq* is indeed a very high compliment, and whenever it is used, it is intended to convey that the individual in question is one who in the *agon* of life has overcome some great trial or temptation—as in the case of Joseph and Potiphar's wife; cf. ARN[A], p. 63— and is therefore worthy of being crowned with a kind of *stephanos*, *'aṭarah* (see for example LXX on Cant. 3:11)—note ARN[A], p. 5, bottom, on the *ṣaddiqim*, and parallels—or, as we might put it, is deserving of the highest rewards. I hope to discuss this more fully in a future study. On the *ṣaddiq* see also R. Mach, *Der Zaddik in Talmud und Midrasch* (Leiden, 1957). Professor S. Lieberman once called my attention to the Sifra on Lev. 25:10, ed. Weiss, 106d, that in the Jubilee year, according to Rabbi Yohanan ben Baroqah (and cf. B. Rosh ha-Shanah 8b), the emancipated slaves are also crowned with an *'aṭarah*. Now cf. Weiss' note ad loc., and see also Rashi in B. Rosh ha-Shanah, ibid. In Wisdom of Solomon 5:16, the righteous will receive a *diadem of beauty*.

53. See *Mabo*, p. 147; but the widow and her seven sons is a *dramatic* stereotype. See also G. D. Cohen in *Mordecai M. Kaplan Jubilee Volume* (Heb.), pp. 109ff.

care of me thou wilt be the death of a widow and her seven sons." And Benjamin supported them out of his own pocket! The reward must fit the virtue. Some time thereafter, though he lay mortally sick, the death decree was annulled, and twenty-two years were added to his life. Why twenty-two? It is one of the midrashic-talmudic round numbers.[54] But what is so noteworthy about twenty-two? Twenty-two are the letters of the Hebrew alphabet. How would we describe Benjamin's reward? A reward from A to Z—a reward in the full sense of the word. For he who saves a single soul is regarded as though he has saved a whole world.[55] "How much more so Benjamin the Righteous who saved a widow and her seven sons!"

Not one of these stories is provided by ARN[B]. All three the editor of ARN[A] has introduced, declaring as it were: Note well the crescendo—a man once gave charity, another made it a practice to give charity, but the third took on the permanent burden of providing for the poor and acted even beyond the demands of his responsibility. Here are gradations of charitableness, and here too are their rewards; morning and evening withhold not thy hand.

VIII

In 1955 I wrote the following about the third chapter of 'Abot de-Rabbi Natan, Version A:[56] "The whole of the . . . chapter, [386] except for the opening paragraph, is out of place and properly should form part of the discussion in the next chapter on 'acts of loving kindness.'" I was obviously tone-deaf. For his literary and pedagogic art the editor of ARN[A] III deserves a public apology.

---

54. Cf. for example ARN[A], p. 30 (but see ARN[B], chap. 13, p. 30, and Pirqe R. Eliezer, chap. 1!) and p. 32; and see the index volume (by B. Cohen) to L. Ginzberg, *Legends of the Jews*, vol. VII, s.v. "twenty-two."

55. See Ginzberg, *Legends*, vol. V, 67; Schechter's note 59 (end) on the MS reading and appendix 2, p. 155, Cf. *Mabo*, pp. 84f., n. 138.

56. *The Fathers According to Rabbi Nathan*, p. 182, n. 28.

TEXTUAL AND LITERARY STUDIES

Other Texts

The Youngest Son, or Where Does Genesis 38 Belong?

[27] Not only modern scholars[1] but also medieval commentators like Rashi (1040–1105) and Ibn Ezra (1092–1167) have almost been stopped short by the insertion of the thirty-eighth chapter of Genesis between the thirty-seventh and thirty-ninth, i.e., by the insertion of the Judah and Tamar story into the carefully wrought and arranged narrative of Joseph. As Rashi put it,[2] Why was the thirty-eighth chapter placed here to interrupt the account about Joseph? Even Obadiah Sforno (ca. 1475–1550), who doesn't ask the question outright, feels that an explanation is called for:[3] The Judah story is placed here because it was by Judah's counsel that Joseph was sold and thus Jacob lost a son; hence we are now to be informed how Judah lost two of his own sons.

As we would expect, however, neither renaissance nor medieval commentators are the first to be sensitive to the literary-editorial difficulty. It disturbed the author of *Jubilees*, as far back as approximately the middle of the second

1. See, e.g., A. Bentzen, *Introduction to the Old Testament* (Copenhagen: Gadd, 1949), 2.12: "Gen. 38 in the context of the Joseph-story has the effect of a dog among ninepins. . . ."
  Essentially the same is said by G. von Rad, *Genesis* (Philadelphia: Westminster, 1972), 356–57: "Every attentive reader can see that the story of Judah and Tamar has no connection at all with the strictly organized Joseph story at whose beginning it is now inserted. This compact narrative requires for its interpretation none of the other patriarchal narratives."
  H. Gunkel's view (*Genesis* [KAT; Göttingen: Vandenhoeck & Ruprecht, 1901], 371) is different: "Die Erzählung gehört nicht zum Hauptfaden des J. . . . ist erst von RJ hier eingesetzt worden. . . . Die Einstellung der Geschichte an dieser Stelle der Josephsage ist indess nicht ungeschickt: in der Josephsage liegt nach cap. 37 eine Zeit, wo wir nichts von den Brüdern . . .hören: in dieser Zwischenzeit wird — so dachte der Einsetzer — die Geschichte c. 38 geschehen sein."
2. *Commentary* (ed. A. Berliner, Jerusalem: Kiryah Neemanah, 5722), ad Gen. 38:1.
3. *Commentary, Miqra'ot Gedolot* (Berlin: Schocken, 5697), ad Gen. 38:1.

century B.C.E., if not earlier. Since chapter 37 closes with the statement that Joseph was sold to Potiphar, and chapter 39 proceeds from that point (after a repetition with a minor variant, possibly for editorial transition),[4] to interrupt them with the account of Judah and Tamar seemed poor composition. *Jubilees*, therefore, first presents the Joseph narrative through Joseph's elevation in Pharaoh's court, his marriage, and the gathering of food [28] in preparation for the years of famine. Only then[5] is the Judah-Tamar affair reported. Perhaps this is a kind of Sforno in reverse, to suggest that if Judah was forgiven for a very grave sin (sleeping with his daughter-in-law),[6] he would be forgiven for the sale of Joseph, who by now, after all, had arrived at a high station, as his dreams had promised.

Philo appears to say nothing about the order of the chapters, though he interprets the Judah-Tamar story allegorically on several occasions.[7] Again a conjecture: Perhaps the extreme allegorization — Judah the "chief captain," "the investigator, the lover of learning, who refuses to leave aught of the things that are veiled, unexamined and unexplored," and Tamar "the art or science that is studied," seizing and taking hold of the learner and persuading him to be her lover[8]—*perhaps* such rarefied interpretation reflects Philo's reaction to the

4. [In a lecture on "The Structure of Biblical Books," presented at Yale University in March 1971, S. Talmon cited Gen. 40:1 as a case of "resumptive repetition" (*Wiederaufnahme*), a technique whereby an author or an editor following a digression or an interpolation resumes the interrupted narrative by repeating, more or less verbatim, the last sentence before the interruption. See S. Talmon and M. Fishbane, "Aspects of the Literary Structure of the Book of Ezekiel," *Tarbiz* 42 (1972–73):35–38; cf. J. H. Tigay, *JBL* 94 (1975):338 n. 28. In Talmon's view, Gen. 40:1 is one of the cases in which this technique is used to indicate that what follows is simultaneous with the digression/interpolation J.T.] [See n. 84. — Ed.]

5. Chap. 41. [Such variations in the location of biblical episodes are common in late literature. E.g., *Jubilees* itself reports Isaac's death after the sale of Joseph (chap. 36), while the Torah reports it before the sale (Gen. 35:28–29). 1 Chron. 13–14 reverses the order of events following David's occupation of Jerusalem in 2 Sam. 5:11–6:12. Josephus (*Ant.* 5.2.8–12 § 136–174) reports the outrage at Gibeah before the episodes of the chieftains, whereas the Bible reports it afterwards (Judg. 19–21). Such "displacements" may reflect differing exegetical and literary purposes, or at times a variant *Vorlage* (as in the case of Jeremiah in the LXX and a similar Hebrew recension found at Qumran). J.T.]

On the Gibeah outrage, see also the suggestion of R. Marcus in *Josephus* LCL, 5. 62–63, note b. For a Tannaitic principle that location in the biblical text is not final determinant of sequence, see *Mekilta, Shirta* 7 (ed. J. Z. Lauterbach; Philadelphia: Jewish Publication Society, 1933–35), 2. 54–55.

6. *Jub.* 41:23–28.

7. See *On the Virtues* 221–22 (LCL, 8. 299–301); cf. F. H. Colson, *Philo* LCL, 10. 427–28. On Tamar as proselyte, see b. *Sota* 10a; and L. Ginzberg, *Legends of the Jews* (7 vols.; Philadelphia: Jewish Publication Society, 1909–38), 5. 334.

Pseudo-Philo refers in brief paraphrase to the Tamar (*mater nostra!*) story, in connection with the beginning of Exodus (Amram addressing the elders), not in the midst of the Genesis Joseph story: "Thamar, quia non fuit consilium eius in fornicatione . . . dixit: Melius mihi est socero meo commixte mori, quam gentibus commisceri (*Liber antiquitatum biblicarum*, 9. 5 [ed. G. Kisch; Notre Dame, IN: Notre Dame University, 1949], 137–38; [ed. M. R. James; New York: Ktav, 1971], 101).

8. *Preliminary Studies* § 125–126 (LCL, 4. 521–23).

peculiar position of the chapter,[9] as though to say, The literal sense and arrangement must mean more than meets the eye.[10]

When we get to some of the midrashic-talmudic rabbis, reaction is more direct. Thus in *Genesis Rabba* 85:2 we read:

> What was the text saying a moment ago? "And the Midianites sold him to the Egyptians." Should it not have continued with, "And Joseph was brought down to Egypt?" What is this chapter [about Judah] doing here? R. Lazar answered, "[It is deliberate juxtaposition] in order to connect the one 'descent' (38:1) with the other [29] 'descent'" (39:1).[11] R. Yohanan said, "In order to connect the one 'recognition' statement (37:33) with the other 'recognition' statement" (38:25).[12] R. Samuel bar Nahman said, "In order to associate the Tamar incident (chap. 38) with the incident of Potiphar's wife" (chap. 39).[13]

What these third-century teachers are doing — whether or not we are persuaded by their specific explanations — suggests an approach: Whoever put the story as we have it in its present position must have been guided by what seemed to him a sound literary principle: Either a thematic or idiomatic connection or association must be present between the story of the sale of Joseph into bondage and the account of Judah's encounter with Tamar.

It seems to me that the approach has merit. In no way do I mean to imply that the Judah-Tamar unit could not have been originally an independent tale for purposes completely of its own.[14] Nor need we either reject or adopt any of the documentary-source theories recommended by different Bible critics.[15] One day, however, the Judah-Tamar story as we have it was united with our present Joseph story. That union, like discrimination of hypothetically independent sources, also deserves attention.

The chapter begins *wyhy b'-t hhw' (hhy')*, "And it came to pass at that time," but unfortunately that tells us almost nothing. As A. B. Ehrlich demon-

---

9. I make this conjecture because though Philo comments on the Judah-Tamar story in several treatises and once even (*On Dreams,* 2. 44 [LCL, 5. 463]) contrasts Judah's pledges to Tamar with the gold "collar" and "royal ring" which Pharaoh gave to Joseph, in the treatise *On Joseph* there is no reference to the story of Genesis 38.

10. Cf. Maimonides's moral interpretation in *Guide of the Perplexed,* 3. 49 (Pines trans.; Chicago: University of Chicago, 1963), 603–4.

11. Cf. Rashi, *Commentary* ad Gen. 39:1.

12. See also U. Cassuto, "Ma'aseh Tamar Wi-Yehudah," in *Biblical and Canaanite Literatures* (Jerusalem: Magnes, 1972), 109.

13. In the last interpretation (cf. *Gen. Rab.*: 88:2) a contrast is emphasized (see J. Theodor-Ch. Albeck, *Genesis Rabba* [2 vols.; Berlin: Itzkovski-Poppelauer-Akademie, 1912–36]). Note also Ibn Ezra, *Commentary, Miqra'ot Gedolot,* ad 38:1.

14. See E. A. Speiser *Genesis* (A B 1; Garden City: Doubleday, 1964), 299–300.

15. Ibid.; cf. R. Pfeiffer, *Introduction to the Old Testament* (New York: Harper, 1941), 159–67: "Gen. 38 should precede Gen. 36" (p. 165); H. Gunkel's view in n. 1 above; U. Cassuto, "Ma'aseh," 109 n. 4.

strates,[16] the chronological data supplied by the Joseph chapters make the time required for the events in chapter 38 impossible. Ibn Ezra had already been embarrassed by this.[17] "It came to pass at that time," however, never tells us much, for this expression, which occurs three times in Scripture,[18] may well refer to time approximate rather than exact, as though the author, unable to fix the precise moment but aware that what he had to report belonged to the framework of his narrative, stated limply, It was about this time, without committing himself to the exact instant or duration. "It came to pass at that time" in this chapter speaks neither of before nor after,[19] though something in its theme has much to do with before and after.

If the beginning of a story is of no help, let us turn to the end. At the end of [30] this chapter we read that when the time came for Tamar to give birth,

> there were twins in her womb! While she was in labor, one of them put out his hand, and the midwife tied a crimson thread on that hand to signify: This one came out first. But just then he drew back his hand, and out came his brother; and she said, "What a breach (*perez*) you have made for yourself!" So he was named Perez. Afterwards his brother came out, on whom was the crimson thread; he was named Zerah.

An attractive symmetry has been achieved. Judah, who had lost two sons, Er and Onan, now begets twins — a sign certainly that Judah has been forgiven. But even more interesting is the behavior of the twins. There is one who is to be the older one, and to make no mistake about it, the midwife ties a crimson thread on his hand. "Rot," Ehrlich quotes, "ist von allen Farben die schreiendste and auffallendste,"[20] and cites striking evidence beyond this story. But the second, the younger, twin breaks through ahead of his older brother. One of the major themes of Genesis, and beyond Genesis, has suddenly overtaken us.

It is a theme, the triumph of the younger son over the older, with which everyone is familiar, and not only with the theme at large but with the examples that add up to make a theme. It deserves notice, by the way, that despite stories like "Cinderella,"[21] or tales in which a lowly boy becomes king, or a youngest son is abused by elder brothers, or a young son with only a cat far

16. *Mikra ki-Pheshuto* (3 vols.; New York: Ktav, 1969), 1. 103; cf. S. D. Luzzatto, *Commentary on the Pentateuch* (Tel Aviv: Debir, 1965), 157–58.

17. *Commentary* ad Gen. 38:1.

18. Here; Gen. 21:22; 1 Kings 11:29. There is, of course, in addition the expression *baʿēt ha-hîʾ* without *way-yĕhî.*

19. I agree with E. A. Speiser's comment on 38:1 (*Genesis*, 297) that the "phrase is formulaic," but do not agree that literally in this context it would amount to "at the precise time that Joseph was being sold to Potiphar." However, see U. Cassuto, "Maʿaśeh," 116.

20. *Mikra*, 1: 105–6.

21. In which the miraculous is essential. None of this is in the biblical account where the naturalistic leaves practically no room for anything else. Unlike the youngest brother in "Puss in Boots," the biblical youngest brother is not presented as at a disadvantage at first.

surpasses older brothers with mill and donkey, to which Stith Thompson refers, the theme of the younger son triumphing over the older is not found with anything like the frequency it has in the Hebrew Bible.[22] My colleague, Professor Kirshenblatt-Gimblett, reassures me that outside the Hebrew Bible and Jewish sources dependent on it, while the theme is distributed cross-culturally, tales like the Joseph story are not reported often. It is not super-fluous, then, to review the biblical situation although it is familiar to us.

In dealing with an inheritance problem which might arise as a result of a particular domestic complication, the author of Deut. 21:15–17 declares:

> If a man has two wives, one loved and the other unloved, and both the loved and the unloved have borne him sons, but the first-born is the son of the unloved one — when he wills his property to his sons, he may not treat as first-born the son of the loved one in disregard of the son of the unloved one who is older. Instead, he must accept the first-born, the son of the unloved one, and allot to [31] him a double portion[23] of all he possesses; since he is the first fruit of his vigor, his birthright is his due.

Some of the terms in this formulation (a man with two wives, one loved and one unloved, the first-born the son of the unloved one) are like echoes of a story we shall look at. At any event, note that the Deuteronomist has not even taken the trouble to tell us first of the general law on which his particular case is based, viz., that when a man wills his property to his sons, the first-born is to receive a double portion. That general rule is apparently in no need of publication. What the Deuteronomist feels he must underscore is that the rule applies even under the special condition of the first-born of an unloved wife. Even then, he says, the double-portion birthright belongs to the son born first.[24]

Except for the legal technicalities in the meaning of double portion,[25] the law is plainspoken and categorical. Nor is such a law unique in the ancient Near East. In the Middle Assyrian Laws (which may go back to the 15th century B.C.E.) we read:[26]

---

22. [However, the theme of the younger son eclipsing the older is not unknown in ancient Near Eastern literature. Kings Idrimi of Alalakh (late 16th century) and Esarhaddon of Assyria (680–669) tell in their own inscriptions how they rather than their older brothers attained the throne (*ANET*[3], 289 and 557). Some omens predict the same phenomenon (examples are cited in the *CAD*, 16. 181–82). The phenomenon of younger sons attaining superiority over older ones is discussed in wisdom literature (*ANET*[3], 603–4, par. XXIII and XXIV). J. T.]

23. Lit., "two-thirds" (see note in the new *JPSV* [Philadelphia: Jewish Publication Society, 1973], 363).

24. Note Ishmael, according to R. Simeon ben Yohai, in *t. Sota* 6:6. See how M. Weinfeld (*Deuteronomy and the Deuteronomic School* [Oxford: Clarendon, 1972], 291) characterizes the deuteronomic law. [In *Tanhuma* Genesis, ed. Buber p. 77a, association of Leah and Rachel with the Deuteronomy passage is already made.]

25. See *B. B. Bat.* 122b.

26. *ANET* 185. ["Additional" and "double" shares for the oldest sons are attested even earlier in Sumerian and Old Babylonian texts; see G. R. Driver and J. C. Miles, *The Babylonian Laws* (Oxford: Clarendon, 1960), 1. 331; I. Mendelsohn, "On the Preferential Status of the

[If brothers divide the estate of their father . . . the orchards and wells on] the land, [the eldest son] shall choose (and) take two portions [as his share] and then his brothers one after the other shall choose [and] take [theirs]. The youngest son shall divide up any *cultivated* land along with all the [produce of their] labors; the oldest son shall choose [and] take one portion and then cast lots with his brothers for his second portion.

Commenting on this passage G. R. Driver and J. C. Miles say:[27]

The preferential right of the eldest son which is found in this section, occurs also in Babylonia but only in the southern part of the country, for which it is attested in various Sumerian documents, although it is probably not found in the Babylonian code. In these documents he generally receives something in addition to his proper share, but not, as here, a double share. But this right to a double share in his father's property which the Assyrian law concedes to the eldest son is amply attested in the approximately contemporary tablets from Arrapha. The same custom is found amongst the Hebrews, for whom the Deuteronomic law prescribes that the first-born son, even if the child of the hated wife, is entitled to a double portion of his father's estate.

The fundamental biblical law therefore is not exceptional; and one might hazard a justification for the deuteronomic provision. The *bkr*, the "first- [32] born," is he who is *peṭer reḥem*, the first issue of the womb,[28] who is con-secrated, who possesses a special dignity.[29] It is possible that this notion may be related to still another: Since the *bkr* is the first-fruit of that bond where man and wife become one flesh,[30] he represents the full confirmation of the blessing and the first commandment to be fruitful and to multiply. And maybe, later, the reason a man is to divorce his wife if he has lived with her ten years and they have had no children[31] is that there is an incomplete union here. The first-born may enjoy singular status because he not only validates the union but brings promise of future fruitfulness.

Needless to say, this is speculation which may or may not throw some light on the privileged rank of the first-born in the law. The fact of that rank in the deuteronomic law is unmistakable, however, and it is even supported, as Joseph

Elder Son," *BASOR* 156 (1959) 38–40. For examples of the former, see *CAD, E* (vol. 4), 78; for the latter see *ANET*[3], 545, § 13 (from Mari, ca 1800 B.C.E.); for a later case of the double share from Nuzi, see *ANET*[3], 220. J. T.]

27. *The Assyrian Laws* (Oxford: Clarendon, 1935), 296–97, also n. 2 on Hindu law. Cf. R. de Vaux, *Ancient Israel* (New York: McGraw-Hill, 1965 [paperback]), 1. 53.

28. Exod. 13:2; cf. *Enṣiqlopedya Miqra'it* (6 vols.; Jerusalem: Bialik, 1955–71), 2. 122 (reference to Tur Sinai).

29. Cf. N. Sarna, *Understanding Genesis* (New York: McGraw-Hill, 1966), 184–85.

30. Cf. *Gen. Rab.* 18:5, 167; and Rashi, *Commentary* ad Gen. 2:24, who may or may not be hinting at this. Ibn Ezra and Naḥmanides (ed. C. B. Chavel; Jerusalem: Mossad Harav Kook, 1962), 1. 39–40, offer different explanations.

31. Cf. *Gen. Rab.* 45:3, 449 (and parallels listed there).

Jacobs observed already in the nineteenth century,[32] by several of the stories we must review, where the very preference of the youngest son is explained as something irregular.

We meet with this preference in the family and descendants of Abraham; but intimations are present even earlier, in the very first set of children. Details do not stand out boldly as yet. Cain brings an offering of the fruits of the earth, and Abel brings of the choicest of the firstlings of his flock; and God finds only the latter gift acceptable. We are not told why Cain's gift was unacceptable, or why it could not have been he who brought the acceptable gift. When we find later explanations, like the one presented by Josephus,[33] or others as in the Midrash[34] (and those dependent on it), that Abel's offerings "found more favour with God, who is honoured by things that grow spontaneously and in accordance with natural laws, and not by the products forced from nature by the ingenuity of grasping man," we know that here is one more Bible student stumped by what the text reports and striving desperately to discover its underlying common sense. As a matter of fact, everyone, even a king, is dependent on produce of the field, the Midrash states;[35] what objection can there be to Cain's gift as it is described by Scripture?[36]

32. *Studies in Biblical Archaeology* (New York: Macmillan, 1894), 53–54, 62–63.

33. *Ant.* 1.2.1 § 53–54 (LCL, 6. 25–27). Cf. *Gen. Rab.* 22:3, 206.

34. Cf. *Leqaḥ Ṭob* (ed. S. Buber; Wilno: Rom, 1884) on Gen. 4:3–4. Note also Ibn Ezra on 4:3, (I am indebted to H. L. Ginsberg for removing the ambiguities of this statement and clarifying it for me.) Cf. Joseph Bonfils, *Ṣophnath Paneʿaḥ* (ed. D. Herzog; Heidelberg: C. Winter, 1911), 1. 65. With Ibn Ezra's view, cf. *Saadia's Polemic against Ḥiwi Al-Balkhi* (ed. I. Davidson; New York: Jewish Theological Seminary of America, 1915), 40. See further n. 36, below.

35. *Midrash ha-Gadol, Genesis* (Jerusalem: Mosad Haraw [*sic*] Kook, 1947), 113 and see M. Margulies's notes. See also Kimḥi's observation (see next note for complete reference) on Gen. 4:2.

36. Ibn Ezra's interpretation (see n. 34 above) — that since only in connection with Abel's offering is it said *bĕkōrōt* (firstling or choice), evidently Cain's offering was not of prime fruits — has appealed to many. E.g., Speiser (*Genesis*, 30) also says to the same effect: "The manifest contrast. . . . is between the unstinted offering on the part of Abel and the minimal contribution of Cain."

This view is not universally shared, but has a long history. Essentially, it appears already in Philo (*Sacrifices of Abel and Cain*, 13 § 52–53 [LCL, 2. 132–5] and 20 § 72 [LCL, 2. 148–49]) as the *second* of two charges against Cain, who "offered of the fruits and not of the earliest fruits, or in a single word the first fruits." (Nevertheless, see *Questions and Answers on Genesis*, 1. 62 [LCL Sup. 1. 38.) Similar sentiments are expressed by some Midrashim: cf. M. M. Kasher, *Torah Shelemah* (New York: American Biblical Encyclopedia Society, 1944), 2:309 § 31; 311, § 34, § 39; 312, § 40, also § 46.

I find myself reluctant to accept it. *Tg. Ps.-Jonathan* (ed. D. Rieder; Jerusalem: Salomon's Printing Press, 1974) 6 does not hesitate to say of Cain's gift *qrbn bykwry'*, though it too, like a number of Midrashim (and Rashi), describes the offerings as of flaxseed, an inferior gift to bring to God. Judah ha-Levi in *Cuzari*, 1. 95 and 2. 14 (ed. Y. Even Shmuel [Tel Aviv: Bialik, 1972], 32 and 54) talks of Cain's hostility to Abel in terms of succeeding Adam, without any reference to offerings. See also *'Abot R. Nat.*, 133, on Cain's "hankering for greatness." (*Exod. Rab.* 31:17, 59b and parallels had also spoken of Cain's being greedy and overreaching without a word about the offerings.) Kimḥi's allegorical commentary (in L. Finkelstein, *The Commentary of David Kimḥi on Isaiah* [New York: Columbia University, 1926], LXX–LXXI) contrasts

[33] There is no objection visible to the human eye, and we are not privy to the reasons for God's refusal of the gift of the elder brother. God, we are told, preferred the offering of Abel the younger son, and thereby we have been put on the alert. For in the anecdotes that follow there is more than once the striking element of seeming arbitrariness. And it may be added: Though Scripture speaks of Shem, Ham, and Japhet, in that order, there is a view in the Midrash that Shem is really the youngest.[37] Is this an innuendo that, in this instance too, to be preferred one must be the youngest?

But it is with the story of Abraham, who himself may have been the youngest of the Terahides,[38] and his descendants, that the displacement of the older by the younger becomes a pattern. The stories are thoroughly familiar: Isaac supersedes Ishmael, and Jacob, Esau. For the moment we shall skip the [34] Joseph story; but even in a dry list mention may be made of Joseph's being loved by his father more than all the other sons. "For he was the child of his old age,"[39] the narrator adds. Is this an alibi because he feels an alibi is called for? In the next case we mention, viz., Ephraim given precedence over Manasseh, Jacob takes the initiative. (Joseph's irritation is a masterly stroke.) This time no alibi is presented. Jacob simply says stubbornly, I know, I know, but the

---

philosophical-spiritual personalities, not the contents of the gifts. Naḥmanides refers to "a profound mystery" in regard to the inherent "rightness" of sacrifices (see ed. Chavel, I. 43 and the long comment on Lev. 1:9, II. 11–14) and *may* be implying that Cain should have brought an animal sacrifice.

The attempts to discover an inferior quality in Cain's offering seem to me an exercise in providing a rational defense of God's conduct. Of both Cain and Abel it is said, "he brought of," and there is nothing necessarily stingy or shabby about "of the fruit of the soil." See also B. Uffenheimer, "Cain and Abel," *Essays in Jewish History and Philosophy: In Memory of Gedaliahu Alon* (Israel: Hakibbutz Hameuchad, 1970), 58. Had Cain's gift been grudging, why did not God say so when he rebuked him? The words *hlw' 'm tytyb š't* hardly convey immediately pointed criticism. The words could just as well mean, Do not be sullen because you do not understand my preferences. Why invest a story with Cain's as the rejected gift?

Ehrlich's suggestion (*Mikra*, 14) that God does not approve of farming because it keeps a man rooted to his spot, whereas shepherds travel and thus come into contact with the world and civilization, is pure romanticization of the shepherd's opportunities.

On the lore about Cain and Abel, see V. Aptowitzer, *Kain und Abel in der Agada, den Apokryphen, der christlichen und muhammedanischen Literatur* (Wien/Leipzig: R. Löwit, 1922); cf. also B. Uffenheimer, "Cain and Abel," who discussed the Sumerian background, aggadic, and gnostic speculation. On what Cain and Abel are said variously to symbolize, see E. Levine, "The Syriac Version of Genesis IV 1–16," *VT* 26 (1976) 70 n. 2.

37. *Gen. Rab.* 26:3, 245–46; 37:7, 349. Cf. L. Ginzberg, *Legends*, 5. 179–80 n. 30. As for Ham being called *hqṭn* in Gen. 9:24, see *Legends*, 5. 192.

38. J. Jacobs, *Studies*, 50 and n. 1. He points out that the principle "the younger is favorite," appears also in connection with the matriarchs.

39. Gen. 37:3. Note how *Tg. Onqelos (Targum Onkelos*, ed. A. Berliner [Berlin: Gorzelanczk & Co. 1884], 41) on 37:3 interprets this. Joseph as wise courtier belongs to still another theme (see W. Lee Humphreys, "A Life-Style for the Diaspora: A Study of the Tales of Esther and Daniel," *JBL* 92 [1973], 216 n. 17; cf. E. J. Bickerman, *Four Strange Books of the Bible* [New York: Schocken, 1967] 97). In his dissertation, *The Motif of the Wise Courtier in the Old Testament* (New York: Union Theological Seminary, 1970), 191, Humphreys also writes, "Gen. 38, which deals with the encounter of Judah and Tamar, is here excluded. . . ."

younger brother shall be greater than the older.[40] He does not tell Joseph how he knows what he knows. (Jacob is capable of prophesying: Gen. 49:1.)

This is not the complete list. Moses is the youngest. Gideon, if we could take him literally (Judg. 6:15), is the youngest (*hṣʿyr*) in his father's household. But Saul later (1 Sam. 9:21) uses a similar idiom. So perhaps this is only a manner of speaking modestly.[41] Jotham, who alone escaped and composed a glorious fable, was the youngest in an enormous family. But this, like literary gifts in general, may be a freak coincidence. However, David is the youngest of seven, and Solomon is clearly not the oldest of David's surviving sons.

It is impossible to continue our discussion at this point without a brief aside on methodology, only very lightly alluded to earlier. Nothing in our analysis is intended to obscure the plausible suggestion that in the patriarchal narratives we have eponymous myths in dramatized and personalized form, preserving ancient traditions of the adventures and experiences of tribal groups. If — to offer only one example — Jacob can be portrayed as foretelling that Manasseh "too shall become a people,[42] he too shall be great. Yet his younger brother shall be greater than he, and his offspring shall be plentiful enough for nations," it is not extravagant to follow Speiser who writes,[43] "Thus the story anticipates history: Manasseh, originally the more prominent of the two tribes in question (cf. the order in Num. XXVI 29, 36), was eventually outstripped by Ephraim, the ultimate leader of the Israelite group." Whether J or E is credited as the ultimate literary source, the Northern Kingdom was not likely to quarrel with the anecdote.

Nor is this all. These Genesis stories of the younger son preferred to the elder appeared to Ehrlich[44] as the biblical protest against sanctification or consecration of the first-born — "to drive out of people's minds the thought that the first-born were holy; for in ancient times, even after they began [35] worshipping the Lord, they sacrificed these sons. And God rejected the first-born to make plain that such practice was loathsome to Him."[45]

That there was a practice of human sacrifice in historical times, and even echoes of the sacrifice of the first-born (cf. Mic. 6:7b),[46] might well encourage writers and storytellers who, like prophets and law-givers, abominated this practice, to speak of the first-born in disparaging terms. Biblical tales are

40. Gen. 48:19. Note the approach of E. C. Kingsbury, "He set Ephraim before Manasseh," *HUCA* 38 (1967), 129–36.

41. See G. F. Moore, *Judges* (ICC; 2d ed.; Edinburgh: Clark, 1894) 186 (on Judg. 6:15) and note on 187.

42. But cf. E. A. Speiser, *Genesis*, 357 (on Gen. 48:19).

43. Ibid., 360.

44. *Mikra*, 16, 105.

45. Perhaps in a remote way this may be connected with the plague of the Egyptian first-born (Exod. 12:29). On the other hand, Exod. 4:22 ("Israel is my first-born son") seems to be an entirely favorable signal.

46. Cf. *Enṣiqlopedyah Miqra'it*, 2. 123–26; 4. 1113–18.

essentially didactic, and the story of Lot and his daughters, for instance, was certainly not publicized as a compliment to Moab and Ammon, Israel's close neighbors.[47] On the other hand, Aaron the first-born could become high priest, for priests and first-born are not strangers to each other.[48]

Almost a century ago Joseph Jacobs offered still another attractive approach to the several stories of the youngest-son theme, and this time his approach influenced J. G. Frazer as well.[49] These Genesis stories, J. Jacobs has suggested, reflect "a system of succession corresponding to 'Borough English,' by which the youngest son succeeded to his father's flocks and property, the elder ones having probably provided for themselves before their father's decease."[50] Since by the time of the Israelite theocracy the rule was "the eldest son had preferential rights" and this rule had the support of "the priesthood, who depended for their maintenance on the sanctity of the first-born," Pentateuch writers adopted a number of narratives to explain how the so-to-speak ancient irregularity came about. In other words, in the beginning ("in the pastoral stage") was the system of junior rights; later came primogeniture. It was in this period that the youngest-son stories were given currency in order to reconcile present established practice with the memory of an ancient system.

Nowadays it has become customary to explain the displacement of the older by the younger, by reference to "documents from various parts of the ancient Near East" which reflect the setting aside of the rules of primogeniture.[51] The tables are turned, in other words. It is not altogether exceptional or unheard of, we are informed, for oldest sons to be pushed into the background. The Genesis stories, therefore, are not erratic. But if displacement is not deviation, one wonders why Esau raised such a howl. What happened was unpleasant but not unprecedented!

[36] Behind the Genesis stories, in short, lurk many remote historical migrations, institutions and conceptions of right, social norms, feuds and victories, tribal units and larger compounds of peoples, and perhaps individuals too. And stories about these were surely told, sometimes briefly, sometimes elaborately, and one's heroes got the best of it in the telling. From the various hypotheses about what lies behind the stories occasional glimmerings are acquired. Maybe through these an otherwise overlooked detail of the narrative will be caught sight of. Yet whatever the circumstances behind the story or cleverly camouflaged by it, a day did come when the stories as we have them now were given

---

47. I am unable to follow Speiser (*Genesis*, 145–46) fully in this instance, though I, too, take a positive attitude toward the conduct of the daughters. The biblical narrator has real irony in mind; see Lot's "generous" offer of the girls in Gen. 19:8 and what it finally comes to! At all events, "All this adds up to praise . . ." is inaudible in the text. On the expression "come upon" in Gen. 19:31 (rather than the customary "come to"), see S. Abramson, *Sinai* 76 (1975); 193–97.

48. J. Jacobs, *Studies*, 53. Cf. *Exod. Rab.* 31:8, 57d.

49. *Folk-Lore in the Old Testament* (London: Macmillan, 1918), 1. 429–566, esp. p. 431.

50. *Studies*, 62 (Summary).

51. Cf. N. Sarna, *Understanding Genesis*, 185–88, 190. See also n. 22 above.

shape and then arranged in a sequence. The question, What is *that* composition trying to tell us? also calls for an answer (and maybe, since it was in that shape and that sequence that the stories were to play an extraordinary role in Near Eastern and Western thinking, the question may be granted some rights of its own).

As we have seen, there is no overlooking the presence of the theme of the younger son chosen over the older in the Book of Genesis. But a student of Scripture knows the law of Deuteronomy too, and, what is more, in some of the Genesis stories, too, detects an element of embarrassment. Abraham does not want to drive out Ishmael; he consents only after God tells him to obey his wife. If Esau had not been famished,[52] or if Rebecca had not prevailed on Jacob to cheat, the birthright theoretically would have remained with Esau. So the biblical narrators imply,[53] and thus the law would have been obeyed. But this is precisely the moment when the ancient reader or auditor of the Pentateuch stories and laws must have been brought up with a start. What then, Ishmael have the birthright? Esau succeed Isaac? Merely because they were born first? That is out of the question. What are Ishmael and Esau to us, or we to them? Enemies! Are the fathers of our folk archers and hunters, who do not even marry girls, from the proper stock (Gen. 21:21; 26:34–35; 28:8–9)? It is doubtless disquieting that Ishmael and Esau should have been first-born of God-fearing parents, but their careers demonstrate that they did not deserve *bkrh*. God's ways are indeed puzzling, but time vindicated His judgment. The behavior of Ishmael and Esau proves that they did not deserve to be treated like first-born.

If the Book of Genesis had ended here, or at the wedding party of Jacob and Rachel, what a neat and comfortable theology could have been constructed. There are times when God acts mysteriously (e.g., makes Esau the first-born), but if you suspend judgment and observe what is taking place (e.g., Esau's despising the birthright), you discover that God is just (how ridiculous, Esau our patriarch). YHWH knew all along.

Genesis does not stop here; Jacob, the man with the birthright, marries two wives, one of whom, the older, he does not love, and one, the younger, he does. (Deuteronomy is no figment.) God, who keeps an eye out for the rejected (Gen. 29:31), makes Leah fertile, and four sons come: Reuben the first-born, [37] then Simeon, Levi, and the last pro tem, Judah. It takes a while for Rachel, the favored wife, to give birth, but she has suffered so much shame because of her barrenness that God finally remembers her too, and she gives birth to Joseph (Gen. 30:22). Incidentally, only now, finally, does Jacob give thought to leaving Laban's house and setting up for himself (Gen. 30:25).[54]

52. So E. A. Speiser, *Genesis*, 194, and new Jewish Publication Society Version.
53. That the narrator himself may no longer have understood a very ancient tradition is irrelevant. As he tells the story, he speaks of something irregular.
54. See the reason offered by *Tg. Ps.-Jonathan* on the verse (ed. D. Rieder, 46).

On the face of it, this time there should be no complications with succession. There is a proper first-born, Reuben, and while he may not be the smartest person in the world,[55] he is basically one of the most decent characters in Genesis. When he finds mandrakes in the field, he brings them to his mother. This was obviously no small gift, for Rachel wanted it! And she was prepared to make a sacrifice to get it (Gen. 30:14–16).[56] Reuben is no Ishmael, no Esau, not an unworthy successor to Jacob the Patriarch.

But once again, the natural law is ignored. Jacob loves Joseph, at the moment the youngest. This is rather important to underline, for in the stories (regardless of what tribal realities condensed in Benjamin's name), Benjamin is either the cause of Rachel's death or simply the passive member of the cast in the dramatic meeting of Joseph with his brothers.[57]

When in chapter 37 we are told that Jacob loved Joseph above all his other sons because Joseph was born in his old age, we are being informed of a seventeen-year relationship. The brothers did not begin to hate him overnight. It is not said that Jacob loved Joseph because he was Rachel's son, but there is something of a hint of that when he remembers Rachel's death and burial, as he resolved to "adopt" Ephraim and Manasseh (Gen. 48:7).[58]

Jacob prefers Joseph though this is an injustice to Reuben, the rightful, even upright, hence legitimate, first-born. We are informed of Benjamin's birth and the consequent death of Rachel. But then we come upon a half sentence, as it were, which reveals and tries to obscure. Reuben went and slept with his father's concubine Bilhah (Rachel's handmaid!) and his father heard about it. No more.[59]

This is not a story of a man overcome by sexual passion, e.g., like David and Bathsheba or Amnon and (another) Tamar. When a man goes after his father's concubines, he is declaring publicly, I am now the master, I have now succeeded. One of the first things Absalom did when he drove David from his throne was to take over his father's concubines "in the sight of all Israel," on [38] the counsel of Ahitophel (2 Sam. 16:21–22). When Adonijah asked for the Shunamite Abishag, Solomon was quick to snap back at his mother who was

---

55. See Gen. 42:37; cf. S. Schechter, *Abot de-Rabbi Natan* (New York: Feldheim, 1945), 112.

56. On mandrakes, see T. H. Gaster, *Myth, Legend, and Custom in the Old Testament* (New York: Harper & Row, 1969), 200.

57. On Benjamin, see n. 76 below.

58. See Ehrlich, *Mikra*, on the verse. Note (in v. 5) that he refers to them as (first) Ephraim and (then) Manasseh, even before his blessing them. See also Gen. 33:2.

59. In this connection E. A. Speiser (*Genesis*, 274) wrote: "In terms of history, these scattered hints suggest that the tribe of Reuben once enjoyed a pre-eminent position, only to fall upon evil days. In the Song of Deborah, Reuben is reproached and taunted for his failure to respond to the national emergency (Judg. 5:15f). Together with Simeon and Levi (cf. [Gen.] 34), the two descendants next in order of seniority, Reuben became politically insignificant. But tangible evidence about the events in question is unfortunately lacking." True, and we are left, in other words, with the "story" itself.

presenting the request[60] (Adonijah knew better than to dare to make the request vis à vis!), "Ask for him the kingdom also; for he is my elder brother . . ." (1 Kings 2:22, see also 2 Sam. 3:7–11).[61]

In the light of the continuation of the Joseph story, I see no other way to explain the Reuben-Bilhah incident than this: Reuben was the first-born and in his own conduct could see no justification for his father passing him over. He knew, of course, that his mother was not the favorite wife, but he, or at least the narrator, also knew the law which declared that (in the matter of inheritance = succession) favorite or non-favorite was not the determining factor. Yet it was clear that Joseph was father's pet, and every sign, the *ktnt psym* — whatever that was — pointed to Joseph as Jacob's successor. The old man did not really discourage the boy from his dreams of ruling over all of them (Gen. 37:11). And so when they settled down after Rachel's burial, Reuben decided to take matters in his own hands in a spirit of now or never.

Seizing authority which is not yet yours must be quick, must be complete, and must scorn all regrets of conscience. Perhaps other conditions are also required. One thing is certain: If the one who attempts such revolt fails, for any one of a number of hesitations, one is ever after ruined. That one will not succeed. The MT reads simply, "And Israel (i.e., Jacob) heard of it."[62] The LXX tries to help us out by adding *kai ponēron ephanē enantion autou*, "and the thing appeared grievous before him" — an understatement brought to the zero line of description. If there ever was a Hebrew *Vorlage* of that clause, it has mercifully disappeared. More likely Jacob's reaction must have been so violent that, as the MT felt, the less said, the better. "And Israel found out," with the following Masoretic pause or blank equals, What happened can't be put in words. We are not told what Jacob did, but we have no difficulty guessing. Maybe the genealogical list which follows immediately after the statement about Israel's hearing, presumably from P, is some redactor's or narrator's deliberate didactic addition, as the Midrash, medieval commentators, and Ehrlich also are prepared to believe; to preserve or juxtapose a record of the original family sequence over against the changes that will now occur.[63] Be that as it may, Reuben's expectations and ambitions are wrecked. He will not give up trying to recover his loss, as we shall see; but it is useless. He [39] too, like all

---

60. Did she dislike Abishag because the young woman had shared David's bed in his last days?

61. [The subject of this paragraph has been discussed by S. Gevirtz, "A Father's Curse," in *Mosaic (Univ. of Manitoba Journal of Comp. Literature)*, Spring, 1969, pp. 56–61. J. T.]

62. On the subject of a break or hiatus in the middle of the verse (*psq' b' mṣ' hpswq*), see the detailed discussion (reviewing also earlier views from the 19th century on) by P. Sandler in *Sefer Neiger: Pirsume ha-ḥevrah le-ḥeqer ha-miqra be-yiśra'el* (ed. A. Biram et al.; Jerusalem: Kiryat Sepher, 1959), 7. 222–49; S. Talmon, *Textus* 5 (Jerusalem: Magnes, 1966):14–21.

63. See *Midrash ha-Gadol, Genesis*, 605; Rashi, *Commentary*, ad Gen. 35:22b; A. B. Ehrlich, *Mikra*, 99. Cf. S. D. Luzzatto, *Commentary on the Pentateuch*, 143, which strikes me as much more plausible. See 1 Chron. 5:1–2.

of us, will discover that while there is such a thing as forgiveness, it is very rare; but even then, a first choice is not expelled by a first-born.[64]

The brothers hate Joseph, obviously — he's a tattler, he enjoys a special coat, which he does not remove even when he goes off to locate his brothers in the wilderness (Gen. 37:22), he not only dreams outrageous dreams of power, he delights in telling them to his family. It is no wonder the brothers decide to kill him — this is not exaggeration: A younger son was once upon a time murdered; Joseph's father too — himself a younger brother — was almost killed. Bloodshed is never far away from this complicated reversal of the natural order. How Jacob could have sent off Joseph alone — and why wasn't he with the boys in the first place? (of course, this is needed for the dramatic turn of the narrative) — remains common, human thoughtlessness. Like sons, fathers are stupid. Someone ought really to write an essay on the stupid Jacob. He is always described as cunning, and, like his mother and her brother, his father-in-law, cunning he has. But he is the most stupid of the patriarchs. He knows that passions rage in this family: Witness the conduct of Simeon and Levi; witness what Reuben has done. He knows what Esau is capable of doing to him. And so on, with a constant streak of timidity. Yet he sends Joseph to learn of the welfare of the boys and the flocks; and Joseph does not even know the way; he gets lost in the fields.

Obviously all this is told by the storyteller, and we have no way of knowing whether actual or imagined events are being reported. But the imaginings and account of the storyteller are themselves a statement of something, imagined or recalled, imperfectly, producing a more or less consistent story. A story, like a document, may not be historical, though it may eventually become part of history. Meanwhile it reveals glimpses of what the narrator had in mind.

Of course, they will kill that *b'l hhlmwt*, "the one given to dreams," and will put an end to his dreams of glory. At this moment Reuben intervenes.

We are told by one scholar[65] that verses 21–24 of chapter 37 come from the E source; other critics would emend verse 21 to read "Judah" and thus attribute the verses to J. That there are difficulties with the chapter, especially with the Midianites-Ishmaelites,[66] is not to be glossed over under any circumstances. Schematized attributions at this point, however, may obscure what the narrative is designed to display. To repeat, Ishmaelites-Midianites remain something of a puzzle, as does the course of the actual sale and who finally sold Joseph to the Egyptian Potiphar (Gen. 37:36, 39:1); the silence about Reuben's temporary withdrawal is surely disconcerting. But whoever combined the materials from verse 21 on with the rest of the chapter knew that both Reuben and Judah were essential to the story. And what does the story tell us?

---

64. Cf. Augustine, *City of God*, 15:5 (LCL, 4.428): "Cain's envy was . . . of that diabolical sort that the wicked feel for the good just because they are good, not wicked like themselves."

65. E. A. Speiser, *Genesis*, 288, 293–94.

66. Cf. Bonfils, *Ṣophnath*, 100 (on Ibn Ezra ad Gen. 16:12).

[40] When Reuben heard what they planned to do, he said to them, Do not kill him; throw him into the pit if you like, but do not take his life. And the narrator tells us — one is eternally grateful to him for this, for who knows what wild conjectures he left stillborn thereby—that Reuben advised what he did "intending to save him from them and restore him to his father." Rashbam, following his grandfather, who takes a cue from the Midrash,[67] says it well: *hpswq m'yd 'l R' wbn ky lhṣylw ntkwwn kmw šmwkyh swpw.* Reuben would restore him, the youngest son who was the real cause of Reuben's rejection.[68] Reuben would bring him back safely to the father so he could doubtless say: See now who acts with the responsibility required of the first-born. If not for me, you would now be without your favorite! Or as the *Tg. Ps.-Jonathan* (vs. 29) says: Reuben returned to the pit *l'sqwtyh l'bwy, m'ym ysb lyh 'pyn,* "to bring him back to his father, perchance he might recover favor."

Little wonder that when he later returned[69] to the pit and found it empty a terrifying outcry broke from him: The lad is gone and now, *w'ny 'nh 'ny b',* "what now is left me." *Midrash Leqaḥ Ṭob* understood well: "Reuben said, I thought I had found a remedy for the Bilhah affair; and now what is left to me!"[70] Reuben had even less reason than the other brothers to pity that spoiled and insufferable brat. But the way these idiots have now acted, they've destroyed what he regarded as his great opportunity. Moreover, the father might well blame him for the disaster: You are the oldest, why did you not stop them?[71] And maybe this is what Rashi means when he says "Where shall I flee from father's grief?"

No reader of Genesis can have failed to notice that thereafter only twice do we hear a sound out of Reuben, and each time so pathetic. When the brothers come down to Egypt to buy provisions and run into difficulty with that Egyptian grandee, they all suspect instinctively that there is a connection between what they are being subjected to and their crime against Joseph, more

---

67. Cf. *'Abot R. Nat.*, version B, 125.

68. That there is some connection with Reuben's rejection is already recognized in *Gen. Rab.* 84:15, 1018–19.

In Gen. 44:27 Judah quotes his father saying, "As you know, my wife [singular!] bore me two sons," and so forth. Whether Jacob ever put it just that way or the narrator imagined Jacob putting it that way, it is impossible to know (contrast 42:36). But it is revealing that one of Jacob's sons by Leah (Judah especially) should so interpret his father's attitude, and so quote him!

69. Although Genesis 37 does not say in so many words that Reuben *withdrew* (that he *returned* is, of course, said), the problem is not as serious as it is sometimes made out to be. Naturally, from midrashic days on explanations have been offered as to where Reuben went. It might even be conjectured that possibly Reuben went to look for assistance for he was outnumbered (and found none). See the *Leqaḥ Ṭob* quotation of an unknown midrash, and note repetition of *nšlkhw, hšlykw, wyšlkw,* and also *wymškw wy'lw* in 37:28: to get him up, you would need a rope. Cf. Josephus, *Ant.* 2.3.2 § 31 (LCL, 4. 180–81). In any event, from v. 23 on, after Joseph's arrival, the narrator is focusing on the behavior of the *brothers*, and only after the sale (v. 28) does he consider Reuben again.

70. Cf. the reference to Abarbanel in Luzzatto, *Commentary on the Pentateuch*, 152.

71. Ibid.

than thirteen years ago! And Reuben says, "I told you, do not harm the lad; [41] but you paid no attention."[72] "I told you" — the perennial complaint of the defeated man.

The second occasion is even more heartbreaking. The brothers know they must bring along Benjamin on their next visit,[73] and Jacob will not consent under any circumstances. Whereupon Reuben speaks up hysterically, "Kill my two sons if I do not bring back Benjamin." Of course, only a man in desperation uses such language. Jacob brushes him off. One can see how embarrassed *Tg. Ps.-Jonathan* is by Reuben if one pays attention to the word *bšmt'*, "with a curse," which the *targum* has added. Rabbi Abba in the Midrash[74] is even more disgusted: "When Jacob heard Reuben speaking in this fashion, he said, 'The first-born is out of his mind (*šwṭh*)! What benefit is it to me to slay his sons? Does he not realize that his sons are like my own?'"

Never again will we hear from Reuben, though in the final "blessing" of his sons, Jacob will refer to him too, and as a first-born; but the only event the father will see fit to recall is that Reuben got into his father's bed. So much for that nice boy who brought his mother mandrakes. He was displaced and nothing could restore him.

On the other hand, when the famine got worse and they were growing hungry, Jacob asked again, "Go down to Egypt and get a bit of food" (*mʿṭ 'kl* (Gen. 43:2). This time Judah spoke up (rationally, of course: "I will be surety for the boy, hold me responsible"). Jacob yielded, reluctantly and with fear, to Judah's appeal. The smoothest tongue in Genesis is Judah's. We have not said very much about Judah up to now, because it would have been premature to do so. For who was he to begin with in the Jacobite family? Manifestly not the first-born. That, however, was not decisive. But it would not be long before everyone would recognize that the father, himself the youngest son, was favoring a youngest son, Joseph, himself the child of the youngest daughter whom the father loved (Gen. 29:18). To be sure, Judah enjoyed a quasi-youngest-son status — he was the last of Leah's sons in the first period of fruitfulness. But not too long later she continued to bring children into the world, at first with the collaboration of her handmaid (these would not prove a major interference) but then by her own reproductive gifts, even a daughter (whose existence would prove helpful).[75] Judah, in short, could have no prospects, and with election there's no plotting.

At the beginning, then, there was nothing for Judah to do but be. Neverthe-

---

72. Gen. 42:22; for the reaction of the brothers, see v. 21.

73. Simeon (the second son!) is already being held hostage. How overly cautious Joseph is. He knows that Reuben is no threat and takes no chances with the second son.

74. Cf. *Midrash ha-Gadol*, Genesis, 729, and parallels listed. For a tentative suggestion of a Babylonian view reflected by Reuben's offer, cf. R. Yaron in *P'raqim [sic]* (Jerusalem: Schocken Institute, 1969–74), 2:231 n. 11.

75. Gen. 34. Helpful, that is, in terms of the dénouement of the full Jacob-Joseph story. Cf. H. Gunkel and G. von Rad in n. 1 above.

less, events took an unpredictable turn. Dinah was raped, Simeon and Levi took horrendous vengeance of the Shechemites, and Jacob turned on them with, "You made me odious among the inhabitants of the land." On his deathbed he still could not forget their violence. They would certainly not be [42] favored. Then poor Reuben went and did what he did, and failed. Joseph alone, and still, remained the favored one. It was most unlikely that the latest youngest, Benjamin, would displace Joseph.[76] The baby was the death of Rachel: she might call him *Ben 'ni*, "son of my suffering" or "son of my strength"; but the father preferred the name *Ben Yamin*, "son of the right hand" or "son of the south." The exact significance of the names is not clear;[77] but the very ambiguity of the mother's choosing one name and the father another may be symptomatic of the shadowy part he plays in the story.

There was no mistaking who was the favorite: You could tell it by the father's display of his love, by the boy's outfit, by the dreams he would not keep to himself. And suddenly the brothers had him to themselves and made up their minds to kill him: "We shall see what comes of his dreams!" (Gen. 37:20). But, as we saw, Reuben tried to save him, to bring him back to his father. Maybe that would recover the birthright for him, wronged Reuben.

And who knows, maybe it would.

That Simeon and Levi, the sons immediately after Reuben, were in no way in line of succession, the Dinah experience underscored. If Joseph could be got rid of once and for all and Reuben remain in disfavor, who stood to gain?

Is it surprising that the one who speaks up now is Judah? "Let us get rid of that boy, sell him. There's nothing to be gained from killing him — that leaves a stain on the soul: we are not Cains." The objective is attained by selling him or letting those passing Ishmaelites-Midianites sell him. Joseph is finally removed, and there are no traces.

Henceforth Judah is never out of sight. In anticipation we have already met him successfully prevailing on his father to send Benjamin along with them to Egypt. And when the cup is found in Benjamin's sack, who comes back before Joseph? Judah and his brothers, the verse says, not just "they."[78] And who pleads, "What can we say and how can we prove our innocence?" Still Judah. And who makes the irresistible appeal (one of the highest achievements of biblical eloquence), which finally breaks Joseph down? Judah. And whom does *Jacob* send ahead to inform Joseph of their coming? Judah (Gen. 46:28). (The very man responsible for the sale of Joseph.)

In short, from the moment Judah speaks up in chapter 37, with the advice of how to get rid of Joseph (and simultaneously contriving [?] to make impos-

---

76. See also S. D. Luzzatto, *Commentary on the Pentateuch*, 150–51. And note that in all of Genesis we do not hear a word out of Benjamin.

77. Cf. E. A. Speiser, *Genesis*, 273–74. Solomon also received two names (2 Sam. 12:24–25), but it was not one from his father and another from his mother.

78. Gen. 44:14. All this is, of course, in keeping with Judah's having said that he would be surety for the lad.

sible Reuben's rehabilitation), it is Judah who is the chief spokesman, and hopefully the successor.

Where do we stand at the end of chapter 37? Joseph has presumably vanished; Reuben is not only scorned as first-born but has lost even the faint possibility of coming back to good grace. Simeon and Levi are unquestionably disqualified. Who is next in line? Judah, and it is inevitable that he now speak up and speak up as he did. And as we listen to or read the [43] story, we cannot help asking impatiently — for the question of succession is a pressing one — Will it really be Judah? That must be answered promptly in order to try to discover God's intention and to put an end to suspense. With Joseph gone (seemingly for good), Reuben, Simeon, and Levi out of favor, who but Judah is left? Forthwith the editor inserts chapter 38 to inform us of events in Judah's life. Here the *vita* of the chosen one belongs. And what do we learn? Twins are born, and the younger gets ahead of the older. The pattern survives. Having been informed of this, we can return to the Joseph story and learn that God's designs are never destroyed.

That behind these stories lies recollections (or maybe even records) or invented memories of complex tribal and political movements, of clan struggles for ascendancy and compromise, of conflicts with neighboring Canaanite peoples, is almost a truism. But we are faced in the end with stories put in a particular form and sequence, and must ask: What is the motive of these? And if these heroes, as heroes will, come to us as personalities, as individual figures, we must try to understand how the narrator conceived of his *dramatis personae*.

If he, or many narrators, or perhaps better, the final editor, reverted to the theme of the youngest triumphant, he must have been eager to make an emphasis. And the baffling chapter 38, recounting the story of Judah and Tamar in its present setting, makes that emphasis plain. Nothing about Judah's conduct (until he confesses that he is the father) is complimentary to him. He marries a Canaanite woman. His older sons displease the Lord. Judah sleeps with his daughter-in-law: Yes, he did not know it was Tamar, but it is not flattering to be described as going to a prostitute and leaving with her some of his most personal belongings as a pledge:[79] Judah, the father of a leading tribe in Israel. There is no rational explanation for Perez pushing Zerah out of the way. This is God's will and His decision,[80] and Perez will therefore be the ancestor of David. Or, the other way around, when the genealogy of David is drawn up,[81] Perez the son of Judah, the forward pusher son of the self-pusher,

79. The *Tgs. Ps-Jonathan and Yerušalmi* II and *Neofiti* (on 38:25) are certainly embarrassed by this. Tamar is suddenly unable to find the pledges; she implores the Lord who sends the angel Michael to her assistance, so that she has the evidence to place boldly before the judges. Cf. L. Ginzberg, *Legends*, 5. 335 n. 89.

80. R. de Vaux, *Ancient Israel*, 42: ". . . these stories stress the fact that God's choice is absolutely unmerited and quite gratuitous. . . ." Cf. above, n. 36.

81. See end of the Book of Ruth.

grandson of him who was pushed into the blessing of succession, will be named first.[82]

But how are we to account for such stories alongside the law in Deuteronomy? Let me attempt an answer, briefly for the time being.

The stability of society depends on law and the efficiency of the establishment. When law is defied and continuity is disrupted, all hell breaks [44] loose. The ancients appreciated this no less than we. That the first-born should succeed the father and inherit the great share was the orderly and hence right way, and not only for Israel, as we have seen. But law and established order — any law and any order — not only stabilize but tend also to become arbitrary and presumptuous; precedent is on their side. The oldest son begins to lord it over his brothers and sisters and demands an obedience which is second only (perhaps equal) to the father's. He becomes, in short, something of a bully.[83]

The law of God may not be abolished, and besides, for the most part, the society assents to its terms because without these there would be chaos. But the resentments are nonetheless real! How are these to find an outlet? By folktales and folklore. Here no frontal attack is made on the divine law. That is the policy of rebellion. But in stories and fables one turns the order of the world upside down, without giving up the establishment that provides protection. This is the revenge of the weak against the strong. The king becomes the pauper, and the girl who picked her miserable food from the cinders will marry the prince.

The election of the younger is God's inscrutable device of choosing whom He will, the last-born in place of the first. This is his built-in correction of the possible abuse growing out of the law which is meant to establish justice and sometimes does not. The folk love such stories because they are a weapon against the powerful, complacent and learned authorities. God, the stories tell us, chose the patriarchs as He pleased, i.e., the folk who created these stories said that God passed over the oldest and chose the youngest.[84]

---

82. Note the general absence of the first-born principle of succession in the kings of Judah. However, see 2 Chron. 21:3. (Was Josiah's son Jehoahaz the oldest? Cf. 2 Kings 23:30, 34. The text says nothing of older and younger; but cf. 1 Chron. 3:15.) On a non-first-born appointed head, see 1 Chron. 26:10.

83. See 1 Sam. 17:28.

84. My colleague Professor Jeffrey Tigay has kindly given me several notes which I have included above in brackets and indicated with the initials J. T.

Since writing this paper, I have come upon the study of J. A. Emerton, "Some Problems in Genesis XXXVIII," *VT* 25 (1975) 338–60. With an entirely different analysis from that presented here, he concludes (p. 360) that chap. 38 "never stood anywhere but between the accounts of the selling of Joseph into slavery and the doings of Joseph in Egypt in that source." In *VT* 26 (1976) 79–98, Emerton offers a critique of E. R. Leach's "structuralist interpretation of Gen. 38" and promises to return to the Judah-Tamar story in another issue.

Reflections on a Mishnah

[44] Not only the regularly printed editions of the Mishnah, but the Kaufmann Codex, the Naples edition (the first edition), and the edition of "the Mishnah on which the Palestinian Talmud rests," published at the Cambridge University Press in 1883 by W. H. Lowe, all conclude the Mishnah treatise *Yoma* with the following statement attributed to Rabbi Akiba:

> How fortunate you are, O Israel! Before whom are you made clean? Who is it that makes you clean? Your Father that is in heaven! As it is said (Ezek. 36:25), "And *I* will sprinkle clean water upon you, and ye shall be clean"; it says also (Jer. 17:13), "The *mikweh* of Israel is the Lord—even as a *mikweh* makes clean those who are unclean, so the Holy One, blessed be He, makes Israel clean."

The temptation to paraphrase Rabbi Yose, at the end of another and very long mishnaic treatise (*Kelim*), is irresistible: How fortunate you are, O *Yoma*! You began with preparations for the high priest's cleanness and ended with the cleanness of all Israel.

That it takes a kind of pun to establish the biblical base for the charming thought that God is Israel's *mikweh*—both Israel's *hope* and *ritual cleansing pool*—rabbinic literature can take in its stride. Wordplays come naturally to the biblical authors, to the midrashic masters, to Plato, to all language lovers, and produce no embarrassment or trivialization. "That one talent which is death to hide lodged with me useless" in no way diminishes the agony nor the kingly state. And on further thought, the double entendre of the verse may owe something to Jeremiah himself, who called the Lord Israel's *mikweh*, for this very verse, in its parallel member, describes the Lord as "the fountain of living waters," which to forsake is to die of thirst; or, as the prophet puts it in an earlier chapter and verse (14:8), "O *Mikweh* of Israel, his savior in time of trouble!"

To Akiba one is always grateful, for he knows the outside and the inside of human nature so thoroughly, and reveals its currents and cravings with such candor, he compels our lively attention.

> "If in a rage," Akiba said, "one tears his clothing, or in a rage smashes his furniture, he will practice idolatry in the end. For such is the art of the Evil Impulse: Today it says to a man, Tear your clothing, and on the morrow it says to him, Go, practice idolatry—and he goes and worships idols."

The course and destination of human rage, from ordinary decline to uncommon fall, Akiba knew, even as he knew why man was so precious a creature, why Israel, and what specifically made Israel so dear a creation. If Akiba says that God is Israel's *mikweh*, he must have his reasons.

However, just as the wordplay on *mikweh* may not be Akiba's invention, so also perhaps the entire midrashic teaching derived therefrom may not be his to begin with, despite the reading of our Mishnah text. For in the *Pesikta de-Rab Kahana*,[1] the statement is transmitted in the name of Rabbi Eliezer, though here the Ezekiel verse is not quoted—nor is it quoted in still another source which preserves the statement, the *Midrash Tehillim*,[2] which also records the statement in a Rabbi Eliezer's name. But which Rabbi Eliezer? Shall we assume that it is Rabbi Eliezer ben Jacob, as *Midrash Tehillim* reads, as well as the *Yalkut Shimeoni* on Psalms (§627)? And if Rabbi Eliezer ben Jacob, which one? Is it the Rabbi Eliezer ben Jacob whose Mishnah was small but spotless, or the Rabbi Eliezer ben Jacob who was Akiba's disciple?—and in that event, Akiba may after all be the original author of the statement, and his disciple is simply passing on what he learned from his master.

I can, of course, engage in guessing as well as the next man. In the first place, it is even possible that at least once the reference to the Eliezer ben Jacob whose mishnah is characterized as small but spotless may be to the second Rabbi Eliezer ben Jacob, seeing that chapter 18 of *Abot de-Rabbi Natan* includes him, and this characterization of him, in a list of post-Akiba sages. Needless to say, maybe the aptitude for brevity and cleanliness ran in the family, assuming the two Eliezers were related, and it might be said of both Eliezer I and Eliezer II that his mishnah was *kab we-naki*, small and unsullied. But this gets us nowhere. Nor, in the second place, is there any genuine progress in following my purely subjective impression that the Eliezer ben Jacob to whom *Midrash Tehillim* assigns the statement is most likely to be the first Eliezer ben Jacob, because he lived before the destruction of the Temple; and a man who had the opportunity to know intimately of the goings-on in the

1. Ed. Mandelbaum, p. 350; ed. Buber 147b.
2. IV. 9, ed. Buber 23b.

Temple, and whose uncle was even capable of falling asleep during a temple-watch, was bound to have thoughts of ritual purity on his brain and would be expressing himself in terms of ritual cleanness. And since Rabbi Eliezer ben Jacob I is the redactor of the treatise *Middot*, there is something of stylistic congruence in attaching to the end of the treatise *Yoma* an appropriate statement by that sage, for *Yoma* has material akin to *Middot*. Finally, is there anything irretrievably [45] to preclude the possibility that Rabbi Akiba could have heard that teaching from the first Eliezer ben Jacob?

Undeniably it would be comforting if we could dismiss the words "ben Jacob" altogether. That would leave us with Rabbi Eliezer of the *Pesikta de-Rab Kahana*, and a Rabbi Eliezer without patronymic would encourage us to think of Rabbi Eliezer ben Hyrcanus who *was* Rabbi Akiba's teacher. That Rabbi Eliezer ben Hyrcanus would be concerned with cleanness and uncleanness goes without saying. Concerned, did I say? He could be downright stiff-necked and intransigent about it. If he first said what the Mishnah *Yoma* quotes in Akiba's name, we can be sure that Akiba would not forget those words, because they were bound to be as heated as glowing coals. And it is becoming for a student to quote his teacher.

But if Eliezer ben Hyrcanus had indeed been the author, why should someone attribute the thought and the words to Eliezer ben Jacob who was not as famous as his first namesake? No, the likelihood is that the *Pesikta* editor or copyist failed to give the full name. For the same reason, we had best assume that the editor of the Mishnah which was later copied by the scribe of the Kaufmann Codex, the typesetter of the Naples edition, the compiler of the Mishnah for the Palestinian Talmud which Lowe published, the printers of the regular editions, all of whom generously fastened the beautiful saying to Akiba's name, and Akiba's name only, meant no more than that Akiba found that saying an admirable statement of his own sentiments: He, too, said that even as a *mikweh* makes the unclean clean, so the Holy One, blessed be He, makes Israel clean. Akiba must have found that view especially congenial, for when all is said, even the poorest in Israel are of noble stock, offspring of none other than Abraham, Isaac, and Jacob.

Does it matter who said it? Even those who quote accurately have not yet brought redemption to the world. Yet it isn't altogether a matter of pedantry or millennial hankerings. It's plain civility to give credit where credit is due. And I notice distressingly that the contemporary idea-lifter who snarls with impatience at the demands of scholarship and its prim insistence on thorough research, on "the minute and accurate study," its compulsive addiction to ever more exacting searching-out, is the first to howl when a subsequent popularizer helps himself without due acknowledgments to one of *his* petty thefts. Yes, it makes a difference, maybe not to Akiba, maybe not to Eliezer ben Jacob I or II, maybe not to Eliezer ben Hyrcanus, but to me. I would like to know who first said "Even as a *mikweh* makes the unclean clean" and so on, because I'm curious, because it unsettles me in my mind and in my moods and in my method to have driftwood of opinions and sayings washed this way and that endlessly, restlessly. How fortunate indeed were those righteous scholars who could persist and persist and still persist in their investigations until finally their faces would light up with success at recovery of what they had almost lost.

Who first said that the Holy One, blessed be He, makes Israel clean as a ritual pool makes the unclean clean can still not be established. Whether first or not, however, Akiba *said* it, so the Mishnah redactor reports.

Nevertheless, does the Mishnah redactor report it, really? To be sure, there's the Kaufmann Codex, and the Naples edition, and the Mishnah edited by Lowe in Cambridge which is so beautiful, it deserved to have the Genizah manuscripts as permanent companions. Any printed edition would be proud to have such supporting witnesses. But there are respectable witnesses with conflicting testimony, as the student who consults that indispensable guide, the *Variae Lectiones . . . auctore* Raphaelo Rabbinovicz (when I see his name on the title page in this form I imagine him at once as a Chopin virtuoso), speedily discovers. There are signs in this manuscript, and that commentator, and the other textual reading of a Palestinian talmudic treatise, suggesting that the "Akiba statement," and the eminently civilizing midrash by Rabbi Eleazar ben Azariah which precedes it, did not once upon a time form the conclusion of the treatise *Yoma*. How, one wonders, could the readers of that version of *Yoma* have managed without it? They surely did not object to the sentiment; they surely did not *remove* it from their edition if it was in. Why would they not add it?

Obviously because they were honest scholars, because beautiful as is Akiba's exclamation, noble as a peroration though it be, since the text they inherited did not include the passage, they refused to doctor it merely to satisfy their homiletical need. They probably trusted their piety to get along without additional propaganda. Presumably their Mishnah text stopped in what is today the middle of chapter 8, mishnah 9, with the fine observation,

> Sins of a man against God—that's what the Day of Atonement atones for; sins of a man against his fellow man—that the Day of Atonement does not atone for, until the guilty one has made his peace with his fellow.

Even if no more were to follow, here is a note every bit adequate to close a treatise devoted to the service of the Atonement Day. If the treatise ever did come to its end that way, there's no justice to any murmuring against the editor or editors who chose such a closing line.

And those who chose the other, the more familiar ending? Were they less strict in their scholarship? Were they uncertain of their piety's firmness and taking unwarranted liberties with the text? The scribe of the Kaufmann Codex, for example, was he treating his sources cavalierly? Few hypotheses could be more grotesque, particularly regarding the transcriber of that [46] manuscript—for time and again he surprises us by preserving expressions, clauses, formulations which forsake the run-of-the-mill and pet ways of saying things, and restores to us the authentic, antique, the unquestionably original idiom of a saying. The man who would take pains to put down "Be diligent to learn how to refute an Epicurean," though reader after reader—and that includes one of the early readers of the Kaufmann Codex itself, as can still be seen by the naked eye on the margin of the *Abot* folio in question—read by force of habit, "Be diligent to learn Torah," and so on—the man who was so painstaking in his transcription, and is vindicated by one Genizah fragment after another, let alone citations of medieval authors; the man who was so dedicated to copying down with precision what the source he copied contained, did not either willfully or whimsically or as a result of an onrushing appetite for moralizing add to his source. Akiba's statement was already in the Mishnah long before the Kaufmann Codex scribe began his work. Long, long ago a Mishnah editor added it, even as to the whole Mishnah of Rabbi Judah the Prince passages were added by scholars after Rabbi Judah. And when *they* added, this, too, was understood not as invasion of foreign matter but as proper editorial activity— for the editing of the Mishnah was no one-time enterprise. Editing a Mishnah had gone on generations before Rabbi Judah, and continued for quite some time after Rabbi Judah.

Editing, we call it, and the tone of voice almost implies pedestrian activity, as though what it takes to edit is either scissors and paste or dullness of wit which wins respectability by protuberant learning (perhaps the better word would be "informativeness") and ponderous industry. You'd think that by this time A. E. Housman would have taught us better.

> To believe that wherever a best *ms* gives possible readings it gives true readings, and that only where it gives impossible readings does it give false readings, is to believe that an incompetent editor is the darling of Providence, which has given its angels charge over him lest at any time his sloth and folly should produce their natural results and incur their appropriate penalty.

Regardless of the tillers on the plantations of variorum editions, the ancient editors of the classical texts were *commentators*. They knew that by adroit location or arrangement of sentences and passages, new lights and shadows would emerge, lights and shadows the *editors* were eager to make visible. Sometimes doubtless these lights and shadows were implicit in the material, sometimes who knows if the author on his own at first did have in mind what his 'editor' discovered in it. The poet, Mr. T. S. Eliot reminded us, does not have the last word even on his own poem.

Take note indeed of what happens in the *Midrash Tehillim* to the statement that God makes Israel clean as a *mikweh* makes the unclean clean, the midrash to which, by the way, we are indebted for the information that the original author of the statement may have been Rabbi Eliezer ben Jacob. No sooner has the midrash quoted the statement, than it continues with the following:

> Who properly should come to whom? The pool to the unclean man or the unclean man to the pool? Surely it's the unclean man who has to go down into the pool and bathe there! So [it is with] the Holy One, blessed be He, making Israel clean. Said the Holy One, blessed be He, to Israel . . .

and so on and so forth. Was this the original intent of Eliezer ben Jacob's words? Was this the point Rabbi Akiba wished to emphasize, that the *mikweh* of Israel is the Lord; therefore don't just stand there and do nothing, but you, Israel, move forward toward Him?!

If this is principally what Akiba had in mind, let alone that there are *midrashim* which strike a different note, like that tender comment and parable on Hosea 14:2 in *Pesikta Rabbati*,[3] at the end of the Mishnah *Yoma* the statement is pathetically ineffective. First of all, it makes no mention at all of the problem and imagery of "who properly should come to whom" and so on. More than average fancy guesswork would be required to discover that this is the intention of Akiba's words. Second, the thing *Yoma* does not lack is plenitude of movement, seven-eighths of it at length describing how the high priest, and other activists, are kept constantly on the move; and in the last chapter which finally gets down to telling me what *now*, when there is no Temple, there is for me to do—or, more accurately, what there is for *me* to do who am no priest, Temple or no Temple—here, too, I am not standing still. For the mother who recently gave birth there are even sandals provided, and I presume if she had anywhere to go on that day after she got through nursing her infant, where would she go if not to "the synagogue in her town to pray"? To make peace with my fellow man whom I offended, I have to be up and going.

The editor of the Mishnah who felt that without Akiba's words *Yoma* would be incomplete had something else in mind, and I continue to gasp whenever I consider his daring. Let us recall again, and repeat Akiba's words—they're beautiful and worth repeating:

> How fortunate you are, O Israel! Before whom are you made clean? Who is it that makes you clean? Your Father that is in heaven! As it is said (Ezek. 36:25), "And *I* will sprinkle clean water upon you, and ye shall be clean"; it says also (Jer, 17:13), "The *mikweh* of Israel is the Lord!—even as a *mikweh* makes clean those who are unclean, so the Holy One, blessed be He, makes Israel clean."

3. Ed. Friedmann 184b–185a.

Imagery apart, what is it that Akiba is telling us? That God makes Israel clean? Do I need Akiba to tell me that? Who else could possibly remove Israel's sin, who else is there to forgive this people, who otherwise could wash away the dirt that falls on Israel through sin? There [47] wasn't a reader of Scripture who had any doubts about the matter. Must one wait for Akiba to be informed what Isaiah almost a millennium earlier had announced, "Therefore saith the Lord, the LORD of Hosts, the mighty one of Israel . . . , I will turn My hand upon thee and purge away thy dross as with lye, and will take away all thine alloy" (Isa. 2:24–25)? And did not Jeremiah report God's promise that if the backsliding ones would turn back to the Lord, He would heal them? What do I need Akiba for?

Perhaps, however, all Akiba undertook in this statement is to suggest the image of the *mikweh*. Very well, it is legitimate for an artist to delight in figures of speech. But in this respect as well, as Akiba's own midrash reveals, he has long been anticipated by Ezekiel and Jeremiah; they have already told us that God washes Israel clean, Ezekiel, at least, certainly did. Above all, listen to Akiba's opening exclamation, "How fortunate you are, O Israel!" Suddenly one recalls where that exclamation was first heard, and how effective it really was *ad locum*: at the conclusion of Moses' blessing, when the prince of prophets blessed the children of Israel before he took final leave of them:

How fortunate you are, O Israel! Who is like you,
A people by the Lord delivered,
A Shield your protector, your Sword triumphant!
Your enemies shall come cringing before you,
And you on their backs shall tread!

How fortunate indeed. But "How fortunate, because God makes you clean" is worse than anticlimax. And who, still thinking as Akiba thought, makes *anyone* clean, Israel or non-Israel, if not God? Did Akiba think that only Israel was made free of sin by God, but others were freed of sin by not-gods? Is there anywhere, even in his most passionately patriotic statements, so much as a hint that Akiba believed that those who were not Israel were washed clean by anyone less than God? What's all his excitement about anyway?

This that early anonymous editor—who was later to be copied by the copyist of the Kaufmann Codex, the printer of the Naples edition, the scribe of the Mishnah that was to appear in Cambridge, the publishers of the popular Mishnah texts—knew. So he put the words Akiba loved at the end of the Mishnah *Yoma* to share his, Akiba's and the editor's, secret with us.

No awake reader of *Yoma*—for that matter, no high priest or even spectator of the proceedings in the busy Temple on the Atonement Day—could fail to be impressed by the agenda of the day, *the* day, as the treatise, too, is called in Aramaic. A full week, seven days, before Yom Kippur they began putting the high priest in readiness, even trained an understudy if at the critical time the high priest were disqualified, alas. The necessary moves and acts and routines were rehearsed. There were the preliminary exhortations, the practical cautions. The day arrived and with it began immersions and lavings, lavings and immersions, undressing and dressing, this kind of garment and that kind; then the preparing of the several beasts for sacrifice, turn this way and that way, recite this and that, entrances into the inner sanctum and exits, blood sprinklings, incense offerings, keeping the right count and following the right sequences, electing a scapegoat and sending it off, passing the Scroll from one official to the next, reading the relevant scriptures, some from the text and some by heart, the requisite number of benedictions and remembering not to forget anyone or anything: the Torah, the Temple worship, the thanksgiving, the forgiving of sin, the Temple, Israel, very likely Jerusalem in particular too, the priests, and more still. What a busy-ness and pother. And how right. Decorum plainly demands this; elementary decency agreed that so momentous an occasion deserved no less a fussing. It was both touching and just that the high priest should celebrate his successful performances of that day with a gay rendezvous with his cronies. Imagine, to have gone in and out of the Holy of Holies more than once without mishap! Quite a day and quite a program; but all fitting and proper, for after all, much was at stake: in absolute literalness a matter of life and death. The wages of sin being what they are, the machinery of atonement had to be flawless. And if a person survived the following twelve-month period, he was right to feel deeply grateful to the high priest and his performance, his skill, and his intercession. Only a fool or churl would be remiss in his appreciation of what the holy prelate had done for him.

Least of all would the high priest be tempted to take himself lightly. If he had married a woman with independent means, at some point of his life he could very likely count on a gift of truly smashing vestments. It is even possible that during the rehearsal week before Atonement Day he was reduced to tears because of the suspicious and weeping nature of some people. What reading he did that week was little calculated to cheer him up: Job, and, O my God, those name lists in Chronicles! The food they served him would not harm him, but it would hardly fatten him up. They won't even let you take a nap!

And why all this trouble and pottering and bustle and passion and precision and solemnity, and do this, do that, do the other, go again, say again, and change your outfit and change once more? Because on the tenth day of the seventh month throughout your generations in all your dwellings as a statute for ever, from the evening of the ninth to the nightfall of the tenth was a sabbath of so solemn a rest, you had to afflict your soul and curb your impulses and the high priest had to make atonement "for the children of Israel because of all their sins"; "For on this day [48] atonement shall be made for you to cleanse you of all your sins; you shall be clean before the Lord."

What in the world would you do, could you do, if there were suddenly no high priest, if the Temple were to disappear? Granted such a thought is mad, but supposing, supposing. Do you remember Solomon's Temple, Miranda? Who can blame Rabbi Joshua, the gentle man, for bursting into sobs when after the year 70 he once beheld the Temple ruins, and moaning, "Woe is us because of this ruin, the place where Israel's sins were atoned!"

If it had not been for me, generals have been known to say, the battle would have been lost. They may be right. And if the high priest similarly were overcome by the feeling, If it had not been for me, this people would still be wallowing in their sin, who could gainsay him? He was probably not the only one to succumb to such an estimate of his indispensability. Ben Sira would have agreed with him, I'm sure. And there were certainly plenty of others, in Alexandria no less than in Jerusalem. It makes little sense to look condescendingly upon high-priest fans, because they had Leviticus and Numbers on their side, the Mishnah too—the Mishnah which we have inherited and in whose composition Akiba had so big a hand.

We reach here to the root of embarrassment that makes decorum ultimately insecure. The crude life is hardly bearable. And the graceful life? It tends fatally to assume that nice manners make good men. Priests are right to remind us that their prerogative to bless is established on long enduring, high, "marvellous and merited authority," and it's not any ragamuffin with holes in his hose or his station who can lift his hands over a whole congregation, even if it keeps its eyes averted. It was the Lord who instructed Moses, "Tell Aaron and his sons: thus shall *you bless* the people of Israel—say to them." But apparently Aaron and his sons, and all their cousins too, need the perennial reminder of the verse which comes shortly thereafter (Num. 6:27), "Thus they shall put My name upon the children of Israel, and it is *I* (*wa-ani*) who will bless them" with the accompanying admonition from the *Sifre:*

> "And it is *I* who will bless them," lest Israel say, Our blessings depend upon the priests. The verse teaches, "And it is *I* who bless them." Lest the priests say, It is we who bless (*anu nebarek*) Israel, the verse teaches, "And it is *I* who bless them": *I* bless My people Israel. And so too it says (Deut. 2:7), "For it is the Lord your God who blesses you in all your handiwork."

After going through seven-eighths of *Yoma*, and even part of the eighth-eighth, it is completely natural to assume that, Who is it that makes Israel clean? The high priest manifestly and his staff. "Said Rabbi Akiba: How fortunate you are, O Israel!" We had almost forgotten in whose presence we were recovering our cleanness, who it was that makes the unclean clean. "Your Father that is in heaven," Akiba reminded us. I almost mistook the bath attendant for the bath. Akiba also reminded us that he was not the first to say this. Centuries before, Ezekiel said so, before him Jeremiah had already made it clear who is Israel's "fountain of fresh waters." And that inspired editor who saw where these words belonged put them in the only place where the note they struck could be heard distinctly.

"This Song"

[539] On the phrase את השירה הזאת of Exodus 15:1, the *Mekilta*[1] comment as it has been preserved is almost frustratingly difficult, and, what is more, it has been so for a long, long time. Has *Mekilta de-Rabbi Simeon* (henceforth *MRS*) been of some help perhaps? Not a bit. With a few virtually trivial variants, it reads like the *Mekilta* (of R. Ishmael), and thus naturally compounds bewilderment: How come what makes no sense is simply repeated?

What is the *Mekilta* comment? It begins seemingly as follows: "This song. Now then, is there only one song? Are there not indeed ten songs?" את השירה הזאת, וכי שירה אחת היא, והלא עשר שירות הן. Even before proceeding with the remainder of the passage, one is certainly entitled to ask in turn: What can the *Mekilta* possibly mean? Supposing there are a number of other songs, so what? After all, the biblical verse is reporting that at the miracle at the Red Sea Moses and the children of Israel sang this particular song of Exodus 15. That on other occasions other worthies in Israel sang other songs is perfectly natural. What therefore is bothering the Tannaim when they come upon "This song" as they read Exodus 15:1? That this puzzled at least the author of *Midrash ha-Gadol* is clear from the way he remarks, "This song: evidently there are also others," מיכלל דאיכא אחריתי.[2] The late Mordecai [540] Margulies was quite right in his comment ad loc., that this sentence is wanting in the sources and is very likely the emphasis of the author of the *Midrash ha-Gadol*. But that author, too, is of

---

1. The text I use is the Lauterbach edition, though I keep consulting the Horovitz-Rabin edition as well; and the edition of *Mekilta de-Rabbi Simeon* is that by Epstein-Melamed.

2. *MhG*, Exod., ed. Margulies, p. 285. And note that in 'Efat Ṣedeq also there is no question, "Now then, is there only one song?"; however, cf. the commentary in Horovitz-Rabin, ad loc. According to M. M. Kasher, *Torah Shelemah*, XIV, 289, this "evidently there are also others" occurs also in the MS of מדרש הביאור.

no help, for he continues at once with, ‏תניא וכי שירה אחת היא, והלא עשר שירות הן.‏
Our difficulty therefore remains. Perhaps, however, as the *Mekilta* text
proceeds immediately after its initial question, some clarity emerges. Let us
see.

Are there not in fact ten songs? the *Mekilta* had asked presumably; whereupon to leave nothing hazy, it undertakes to tell us what the ten songs are. The
first is that referred to in Isaiah 30:29; the second is the one in our verse, Exodus
15:1; third is the one referred to in Numbers 21:17; for the fourth, see
Deuteronomy 31:24f.; the fifth, Joshua 10:12f., where, although the word
"song" does not appear, a poetic quotation is transmitted;[3] the sixth is found in
Judges 5; the seventh is spoken of in 2 Samuel 22:1ff.; the eighth in Psalm 30:1;[4]
the ninth in 2 Chronicles 20:21;[5] as for the tenth, which is the song for the Age
to Come,[6] we are referred to Isaiah 42:10 as well as Psalms 149:1.[7]

Very well, we now know what the ten songs are. Observe however, that our
primary difficulty has not disappeared: so what?[8] What's wrong with "This
song" in Exodus 15:1 even though for other occasions there were and are other
songs?

[541] Bewilderment only increases when we reach the concluding remarks
of the *Mekilta* comment. For immediately after quoting Psalm 149:1, the
Mekilta says:

> For all the songs[9] referring to past events the noun used is in the feminine, [because]
> even as a female brings to birth, so the triumphs in the past were succeeded by
> subjugation; but the triumph which is yet to be will not be succeeded by subju-
> gation. That is why the noun used for it is in the masculine, as it is said (Jer. 30:6),
> "Ask ye now, and see whether a man doth travail with child": [for] just as no male
> gives birth, so the triumph which is yet to come will not be succeeded by subju-
> gation, as it is said (Isa. 45:17), "O Israel, that art saved by the Lord with an
> everlasting salvation."[10]

That there should be reflection on the gender of the noun for song-in-the-
future, coming right after the statement on the tenth song, that it will be the

---

3. And there may even be a play on the word (*Sefer*) *ha-Yashar* (*hyšr*). Cf. *Peshitta.* By the
way, note how the verse is quoted in *Midrash ha-Gadol.*
4. For the long digression at this point, see further below.
5. Cf. preceding note.
6. In other words, presumably it has not yet been sung! Note indeed that the author of *We-
Hizhir* (20a-b) therefore introduces his quotation of the "ten songs" passage as follows: "Our
sages said, *Nine* songs were recited." Thus when he cites the tenth song, it is unambiguously
"for the Age to Come."
7. Note, however, that *Yalquṭ ha-Makiri* on Ps. 18:1 (52a) quotes Isa. 48:20 instead of this
psalm verse.
8. That I am not alone in asking this, is evident from the comment by Rabbi Abraham, the
author of *Be'er Abraham*, ad loc. See further below.
9. *MRS*, "triumphs," *teshu'ot*, may reflect some unease with the reading *shirot.*
10. Note that this whole conclusion is not supplied by *Yalquṭ Makiri*, loc. cit.

song for the Age to Come, is not out of the ordinary, certainly as midrashic texts are generally organized. Mention a theme, and by association a related thought will be introduced. And if the verses "speaking of" the song for the Age to Come used for the word "song" not *shirah*, in the feminine (as Exodus 15:1, for example, reads), but *shir*, in the masculine, then the concluding remarks are midrashically apt. The trouble is that among the ten songs listed by the *Mekilta*, there are a couple which their prooftexts call quite explicitly *shir*, in the masculine, not *shirah*. Note carefully the biblical text for the first song, Isaiah 30:29 (for the sixth song, Judges 5:1 is noncommittal and it would be pressing a little desperately to enlist the support of '*ashirah* of 5:3; if anything, 5:12 embarrassingly speaks of *shir*); Psalm 30:1, the prooftext for the eighth song, reads plainly *shir*.[11] What sense therefore does the *Mekilta*'s conclusion make?

One thing is fairly certain: the author or compiler of the Tanḥuma was already a victim of the confused and confusing text and [542] he is of no help to us. In pericope *Be-Shallaḥ*, although he has helped himself liberally[12] to *Mekilta* material, he omits the section quoted above on the masculine and feminine forms of the word for "song." My guess is, because he's utterly bewildered by it. The way he presents the ten songs (in *Be-Shallaḥ* 10) is interesting[13] but no remedy at all. He reports in commentary on Exodus 14:15 that at the sea ten miracles were performed for the benefit of the Israelites; correspondingly (!), he tells us, the Israelites recited ten songs. Thereupon he quotes the first eight songs of the list familiar to us, and then goes off on a tangent. When shortly thereafter he begins to comment on 15:1, he follows the *Mekilta* order once again, and thus arrives at '*et ha-shirah ha-zot*, where we read: "This song. Now then, is there only one song? Are there not indeed ten songs, as specified above?" (כדמפרש לעיל). He repeats song number eight, and goes on as the *Mekilta* does;[14] finally he specifies songs nine and ten. Date the final compilation of the *Tanḥuma* as you please;[15] the trouble is already there, and our initial problems are still with us.

That the author of the *Leqaḥ Ṭob* was ill at ease with the midrash is evident at a glance. "'*Et ha-shirah ha-zot*. There are ten songs," he informs us, and lists the ten we are familiar with. No question like "Now then, is there only one song," and so on; plain statement of fact, "There are ten songs." Despite this,

---

11. Nor does the alternative (ד"א) referred to by *MhG* get us out of the difficulty: "*shir*" *ha-shirim*.

12. See the reference in the following note.

13. See Zunz-Albeck, *Ha-Derashot be-Yisrael* (Jerusalem, 1974), pp. 366f., and 100 et seq.

14. Note, by the way, that apparently the Jehoshaphat song of 2 Chron. 20 he does not count as one of the ten songs, though he does refer to it. For him, the ninth song is Solomon's "Song of Songs;" and his tenth song, which is also of the future, is Ps. 98:1. The author of *We-Hizhir* does not refer at all to Jehoshaphat, and his ninth song is also Solomon's Song of Songs. As for the eighth, he, too, cites Ps. 30:1, but attributes it to no one!

15. See note 39 in Zunz-Albeck, p. 368. Cf. also *Deut. R.*, ed. S. Lieberman, introduction, p. xxiif.

however, he is still at the mercy of his source, as his very attempt to make sense of it reveals. For after he has quoted Isaiah 42:10[16] for his tenth [543] song (which is for the Age to Come), he continues:

> This song is different (משונה שיר זה), for the noun used for it is in the masculine, while for all the [other] songs (וכן השירות כולן) the noun used is in the feminine —for it is like a female who brings to birth (כשם שהנקבה יולדת) — because all the [past] triumphs were succeeded by subjugation. But in the Age to Come there will be a triumph which will not be succeeded by subjugation, as it is said (Isa. 45:17), "O Israel, that art saved by the Lord with an everlasting salvation." That is why [in Isaiah 42:10] it is written *shir ḥadash* [in the masculine], for it is like a male who does not give birth.

He even quotes Jeremiah 30:6 at this point. Clearly, therefore, he attaches this male-female remark to the verse of the tenth song. But surely the list he quoted explicitly had verses with *shir* in the masculine, as we observed; the problem he himself must have noted, as his very משונה שיר זה so lamely and hopelessly seeks to solve. *Hadara qushya le-dukta*, we are back where we started!

The author of *Sekel Ṭob* tries even harder, and from the way he presents his comments I fear I have to accuse him of double-talk. First (ed. Buber, p. 191) he says:

> 'et ha-shirah ha-zot. Why is this said? For nine other songs are spoken of לפי שנאמר תשע שירות אחרות; but this one they recited at the Sea. And why is the word for song (*shirah*) in the feminine form? To tell thee, that even as a female gives birth, so the triumphs in the past were succeeded by subjugation; but as for the triumphs [sic] in the future, the word used for their songs (שיריהן) is in the masculine, because they are not succeeded by subjugation, as it is said (Isa. 30:29), "Ye shall have a song (*shir*) as in the night when a feast is [the feast was? will be?] hallowed"; and it says (Ps. 98:1), "A Psalm. O sing unto the Lord a new song"; and it says (Isa. 45:17), "O Israel, that art saved by the Lord with an everlasting salvation."

This is not cricket, as one might say — hiding behind the unspelled-out "nine other songs" and relocating the Isaiah 30:29 verse without so much as an if-you-please. And what *does* he mean by triumphs, in the plural, in the future? Then, second (pp. 200f.), he quotes the commentary of the sages (ורבותינו דרשו), as we are already familiar with it, and here is how he concludes: "The [544] tenth [n.b. העשירי! and not העשירית] in the Age to Come. And once it [the song? the triumph?] begins it will never again be interrupted (וכיון שמתחלת אין לה הפסק), as it is said" — and he quotes first Psalm 149:1, then [I guess] Isaiah 42:10, and finally Isaiah 26:1, "In that day shall this song (*shir*) be sung." No help from this quarter.

Nor is there any from *Yalquṭ Shimeoni* (sec. 242); it reads almost word for

16. He does not quote Ps. 149:1 after it.

word like the *Mekilta*. There are some differences, it is true. For example, after song number three and its prooftext, no more numbers, ordinals, are supplied. Instead we read, "And [the one] that Moses recited" (Deut. 31:24f.), "and [the one] that Joshua recited" (Josh. 10:12), "and [the one] that Deborah and Barak recited" (Judg. 5), and so on until we get to the tenth song where once again we read, "the tenth" etc. Further, for the songs of David and Solomon the reading is as follows: "And [the one] that David recited, 'And David spoke unto the Lord' (II Sam. 22:1), 'A Psalm, a Song at the dedication of the House' (Ps. 30;1).[17] And [the one] that Solomon recited, as it is said (I Kings 8:12ff.), 'Then spoke Solomon.'" But the *Yalquṭ* concludes no differently from the *Mekilta*.[18]

That neither first aid nor any other kind is forthcoming from the *Midrash ha-Gadol* we have already seen. And that we are dealing with a long-established and accepted text is evident not only from these sources which we have reviewed but from the fact that *MRS*, as we said right at the outset, reads as does our *Mekilta*.

Let us consult the commentators. R. Moses of Frankfort[19] explains why among the ten songs Miriam's song is not listed; as for the question, what sense does the *Mekilta* conclusion make, [545] he says:[20]

> This is the answer to the question raised above, "Now then, is there only one song?" And the answer is, the reason it says *'et ha-shirah ha-zot* is not to imply that there aren't others. On the contrary, there are many [others]. But it is written (in Exod. 15:1) *ha-zot* [this, fem.] to indicate feminine gender, for it [the song, or, the triumph] was succeeded by subjugation; hence *ha-shirah ha-zot*. But for the Age to Come [the word for song] is in the masculine, as it is written, "Sing unto the Lord a new song (*shir ḥadash*)," for it will be in a new idiom (בלשון חדש, or, it will be in the masculine gender, *ḥadash*), in the masculine, hence, Sing unto the Lord *shir ḥadash*, and it is not written *shirah ḥadashah* [in the feminine].

But how does this answer *our* question? What about those songs among the ten that are called *shir*? And where does R. Moses get the idea that the Midrash in commenting on *'et ha-shirah ha-zot* of Exodus 15:1 principally intends to explain the reading *shir ḥadash* (and not *shirah ḥadashah*) of some other verse?

Like R. Moses of Frankfort, R. Judah Najar[21] also recognizes that the concluding reflection of the *Mekilta* on the masculine and feminine forms of the word for "song" is meant to serve as a reply to the initial question, But is there only one *shirah*, are there not indeed ten? He too, however, acknowl-

---

17. In this fashion the *Yalquṭ* apparently avoids the necessity to digress briefly as the *Mekilta* does, and in turn can comfortably ignore the long digression (cf. above, n. 4) present in the *Mekilta* as it continues.

18. The variants are trivial.

19. In his commentary זה ינחמנו. I am using the recent (date?) reprint of the Warsaw edition, 5687. And cf. the commentary עץ יוסף in the *Tanḥuma*, s.v., עשר שירות.

20. S.v., כל השירות כולן.

21. In his commentary שבות יהודה.

edges that among the ten songs cited by the *Mekilta*, some are called *shir*. He admits he has his problems and therefore is grateful (והנאני) to the author of the *Yefeh To'ar* (R. Samuel Yafeh Ashkenazi) for *his* explanation *Exodus Rabba* 23:11, that the midrashic exegesis is occasioned by the words *zot* and *ḥadash*. To put it mildly, the *Yefeh To'ar* (which is as a rule a splendid commentary on the Midrash) leaves us still almost where R. Moses left us, in the dark.

R. Isaac Elijah Landau[22] apparently recommends eliminating [546] the question, "Now then, is there only one song?"[23] and, under catchword '*et ha-shirah ha-zot* remarks, "The word *ha-zot* excludes others, for there are ten songs (*shirot*)." This is surely as flat a comment as can be made, and leaves our question unanswered. Later, under catchword "the tenth, etc." (*ha-'aśirit we-ku'*) he says, "And possibly this, too, qualifies (excludes, ממעט) the word *zot*, for in the Age to Come the song will not be in the feminine, for no subjugation will follow; there will be only a *shir ḥadash* (a new song, in the masculine)."[24]

R. David Moses Abraham[25] is no more enlightening. "In many places" [in Scripture], he says, "*zot* occurs for purposes of exclusion" (דזאת בכ"מ מיעוטא). As regards the theme of masculine and feminine forms for the word "song," he has some mystical thoughts, but he does not solve our problem.[26] As far as I can make out, the Malbim seems to have no comment to offer. R. Abraham of Slonim[27] also senses the real difficulties and is manifestly unable to resolve them.[28]

Is the matter hopeless? I do not think so. Is the Mekilta text corrupt? I do not think so, although I believe that it has been clumsily preserved, and I think this can be proved by the Mekilta text itself.

From the way the *Mekilta* commentary on '*et ha-shirah ha-zot* concludes, it is evident that some reflection on the masculine and feminine forms of the word for "song," *shir* and *shirah*, is in the Tanna's mind. And, truth to say, it is worth asking oneself — particularly if one approaches a biblical text midrash-ically—why [547] does the verse say '*et ha-shirah ha-zot* in Exodus 15:1 and not '*et ha-shir ha-zeh*? To be sure, *shirah* is not an uncommon word; on the other hand, *shir* is certainly the more frequent term. I regret that even with the help of the lexica I am unable to perceive any significant distinction in seman-tic range between *shir* and *shirah*.[29] Whether or not there is one, the Midrash,

---

22. In his edition (Wilna, 1844) and commentary בירורי המדות. On this edition, cf. J. N. Epstein's introduction to *MRS*, pp. 14f.

23. See also above, n. 2. And so too, apparently, R. David Moses Abraham; see below.

24. On his comment in מיצוי המדות, see n. 56.

25. In his מרכבת המשנה (Jerusalem, 5725).

26. Note, however, that in his commentary on the Isa. 30:29 prooftext he is fully aware of our problem.

27. In his באר אברהם (Warsaw, 5687).

28. I. H. Weiss in his edition of the *Mekilta* says almost nothing. Friedmann's faute de mieux explanation gets us nowhere: מוכרחין אנו לפרש דלאו קושיא היא, כיון דלא תירץ מידי, אלא סגנון לשון הוא דנקט בלשון תמיה, לחזק הענין.

29. However, cf. A. Ehrlich, *Miqra' ki-Pheshuṭo* on the Pentateuch (New York, 1969), p. 4. top.

however, would not let pass a phrase like 'et ha-shirah ha-zot if one could just as easily have said 'et ha-shir ha-zeh, particularly if the more common word for "song" is shir. So the Mekilta (or the source the compiler of this particular treatise drew on)[30] must have asked, "Why 'et ha-shirah ha-zot?"[31] And to this question came the retort: "But does ha-shirah ha-zot occur once only?" Is it a hapax; does it occur only here? Why, it occurs ten times in Scripture! — And the fact is, this observation is correct! The feminine absolute form ha-shirah, specifically ha-shirah ha-zot, occurs ten times in Scripture, as even a glance at Mandelkern's Concordance will reveal.[32] The words והלא עשר שירות הן do not mean "Are there not indeed ten songs?" but "Does not indeed the expression ha-shirah ha-zot occur ten times?"[33] In other words, if you ask why 'et ha-shirah ha-zot and not 'et ha-shir ha-zeh, best recall that 'et ha-shirah ha-zot occurs not only here, it's not a freakish use; it occurs ten times!

Nevertheless, the midrashic question is still a question: Whether ha-shirah ha-zot occurs once or ten times, one has a right to ask, Why was not ha-shir ha-zeh adopted by the verse? And the Mekilta answered: On all occasions when ha-shirah ha-zot was used, the triumph, the joyful occasion, was followed by a reversal of fortune, [548] by subjugation. But the song which will be sung in the Age to Come will celebrate a triumph that will not be succeeded by subjugation. For the song then, in that age, the word will be shir, in the masculine, for it will be as with a male, he does not give birth. In that day Israel will be "saved by the Lord with an everlasting salvation," as Isaiah said.

This was the original and complete Mekilta commentary on 'et ha-shirah ha-zot; and read this way, the beginning and end fit perfectly, like a lid on a kettle (if I may appropriate a midrashic expression). The midrashic question was a natural one, and its answer furnished a midrashically reasonable explanation for the particular biblical idiom. And, by the way, in that state of the text, no more than the other nine songs, the tenth, too, was thought of as a song not of the Age to Come. For the additional song for the Age to Come there was a verse or there were verses using the word shir, and those verses may very well have been Isaiah 42:10 and Psalm 149:1, exactly as the Mekilta reads to this very day.

But if this seemingly radical amputation of a whole in-between section is correct, how in the world did our preserved Mekilta get to read as it does? Only on the surface is this a hard question.

Already, at a very early stage — who can say how early? maybe already in

---

30. My reason for this parenthetical remark is that both the Mekilta and MRS read "alike," hence one source underlies both.

31. Perhaps thus: את השירה הזאת, למה נאמר.

32. Cf. also BDB, p. 1010 b. As for Ps. 42:9; it is not hšyrh hzʾt, and above all, note the qeri!

33. With this idiom of עשר שירות הן cf. ARNB: /(א', ג', נ' ; וראה נוסחא א' ;א', מ"ט) עשרה נקודות בתורה. עשר תולדות בתורה (מ"ט, ב', /'א ;י"א יודות שבתורה (נ"א, א) Cf. also such constructions as M. Negaʿim 13:1, which does not mean that here are ten houses, but there are ten different conditions regarding a בית המנוגע.

later tannaite times, possibly by amoraic times and absolutely certainly not too long after the time of Saadia Gaon,[34] perhaps even while he was yet alive[35] — the correct meaning of [549] והלא עשר שירות הן was forgotten, and woodenly, mechanically, the clause was interpreted as, "Are there not indeed ten songs?" And once that misunderstanding occurred, what happened was inevitable.

"Ten songs."[36] What *are* the ten songs? a student of the *Mekilta* wondered. This question indeed is not easy to answer. Take a look not only at the *Mekilta* and the sources dependent on it, but also at the beginning of the Targum to the Song of Songs,[37] at the geonic responsum referred to in a preceding note,[38] at Kasher's *Torah Shelemah* (XIV, 289–290), and at Louis Ginzberg's *Legends of the Jews* (VI, 11, note 59). In other words, while there was a general tradition to the effect that there were ten songs, there were, it seems, variant "lists" in circulation; and as a result, it is no wonder that "helpful readers" would undertake *on the margins* of their copies to spell out what the ten songs were. That such puzzlement is not necessarily post-talmudic can be seen, for example, by variant explanations of the Ten Utterances Abot 5:1 tells us the world was created with.[39]

But would correct meanings be so "quickly" forgotten and misunderstanding of והלא עשר שירות הן happen "early"? Yes, indeed. There are not a few traces of forgetting and misunderstanding and guessing in our classical sources (and it would be foolish to dismiss this as a possibility). "There are seven types of Pharisee," a *baraita* (תנו רבנן) reports,[40] and it is anybody's guess, in the Talmud too, not only what the terms mean but even how to pronounce (or even transcribe!) the names. Such being the dilemma, it is not surprising that a modern scholar can even come up with [550] sexy conjectures.[41] Once upon a time Antigonus of Soko admonished his contemporaries, ". . . and let the fear of Heaven be upon you."[42] If he could see how he is quoted by *Abot de-Rabbi Natan*, in both versions, he might shudder. "Three days before the festivals of

34. Cf. *Teshubot ha-Geonim*, ed. Harkavy, no. 66, pp. 30f. Saadia is dead by the time this responsum is written: note ע"נ. As to the problem of the Song of Abraham, cf. *Agadat Shir Ha-Shirim*, ed. Schechter, p. 10, and especially p. 29.

35. Note in Kasher, XIV, 289: וכן פי' להדיא רס"ג מובא בפי' לאחד מהקדמונים: והגאון רצה לדרוש עשר שירות מטעם השירה הזאת, כי אמר נראה מזה שיש שירות אחרות וכו'. And I would say that it is likely that Simon ben Isaac of Mainz (10th and 11th centuries) also got his idea of the ten songs (familiar to us) from exegesis of the *shirah*. See his poem (*Zulat*) אי פתרוס בעברך (*Maḥzor for the Seventh and Eighth Days of Passover* [Roedelheim, 1827] pp. 87b–90b). Note ibid. the slightly variant list (absence of our fourth song and for the eighth, 1 Kings 8:12).

36. Needless to say, we are dealing with a typical round number.

37. Cf. *Midrash Zutta* on Canticles (Wilna, 1925), p. 6f., and Buber's n. 32 ad loc.; *Agadat Shir Hashirim*, p. 10.

38. ויש שקיבצו שירות הרבה.

39. Cf. C. Taylor, *Sayings of the Jewish Fathers*, I, 78. See also *ARNB*, p. 90, and Schechter's note ad loc.; Ginzberg, *Legends*, V, 63, n. 1.

40. B. Soṭah 22b, and for parallels cf. *ARNA*, 109, and Schechter's note ad loc., and *Fathers According to Rabbi Natham*, pp. 153 and 213.

41. Cf. N. Tur-Sinai in *Mordecai M. Kaplan Jubilee Volume* (Hebrew part) (New York, 1953), p. 86 et. seq.

42. *P.A.* 1:3, and cf. E. J. Bickerman in *Harvard Theological Review*, XLIV (1951), 153ff.; *ARN*, pp. 25f.

the heathen," the Mishnah[43] lays down, "it is forbidden to transact business with them." But what *is* the word for heathen festivals, and what exactly does it mean?[44] Already Rab and Samuel can't agree in their explanations. There is no lack of other instances.[45] There is nothing reckless, then, in assuming (naturally only if the state of the sources gives reason for such assumption) that even by the third century misunderstanding could occur.

Let us return to the ten songs. Having misunderstood the statement והלא עשר שירות הן, a "learned" reader decided to spell out on *the margin* of his copy of the *Mekilta* text what the ten songs were (and he assumed that the tenth referred to by the Mekilta was the song for the Age to Come). And to begin with, that is all that list was, a marginal explanation of "ten songs." But before the *Mekilta of R. Ishmael* and the *Mekilta of R. Simeon* were drawn up in the form more or less as we have inherited them — for the texts of both *Mekiltas* on *'et ha-shirah ha-zot* incorporate that list — some copyist who failed to recognize that the list *was* only marginal, and *not* original to the *Mekilta* (at least here), embodied it in the *Mekilta* text itself. He thus sundered the beginning from its end and created our problem for us, and for our predecessors no less — as the *Tanḥuma* and *Leqaḥ Ṭob* and *Sekel Ṭob* and *Yalquṭ Shimeoni* and *Midrash ha-Gadol* demonstrate.

There is no need for me to argue at length that into our classical [551] texts have been interpolated passages which did not belong there originally, for since the early thirties of this century this has been convincingly demonstrated by Ch. Albeck, J. N. Epstein, S. Lieberman,[46] and especially L. Finkelstein in his fundamental studies of the texts of tannaite *midrashim*.[47] Our texts suffer often from lacunae; they suffer from improper additions as well: The itemizing of the ten songs in connection with *'et ha-shirah ha-zot* is merely a particularly vivid instance of such addition.

And concerning this addition of ours we may say one thing more: It was infectious. For within the framework of the ten songs that found their way into the *Mekilta* text, still another addition was made. It is easily recognizable; what is significant, however, is that it too cannot have been terribly late, for it too appears both in the *Mekilta* and MRS.

The eighth song, we are informed, "was the one Solomon recited." A song that Solomon sang, one would think, should not be hard to find.[48] But our

43. *'Abodah Zarah* 1:1.

44. Cf. W. A. L. Elmslie, *The Mishnah on Idolatry* (Cambridge, 1911), pp. 2f., 18f.

45. Cf. briefly *History of Religions* (Chicago, 1965), IV, 281–287 [Below, p. 290. —Ed.].

46. Who incidentally calls attention to the fact that כבר הלכה במדרשי תוספות של הדבר עצם על העיר הרש"ש בהערותיו לבבלי ע"ז ל"ח, א' לתוספ' ד"ה לעולם. Cf. the reference in the following note.

47. See, for example, his study in *JQR* XXXI (1940–41), particularly pp. 231ff., and the references he supplies to the works of the other scholars, as well as his own earlier researches. See also his *Sifra According to Codex Assemani* (1956), introduction, p. 9 et seq. I have read carefully the study by B. Z. Wacholder, "The Date of the Mekilta de-Rabbi Ishmael," *HUCA*, XXXIX, 117 et seq., and remain unconvinced.

48. Cf. the ninth song in Tg. to Cant. 1:1, and see also *Agadat Shir Ha-shirim*, 10. And note too the "alternative" suggestion in *MhG*. Cf. also *We-Hizhir*, 20b.

marginal annotator did not choose the easy way out. He had a tradition that Solomon's song was Psalm 30, and he refused to suppress it. But does not Psalm 30:1 belong to David? Only if we punctuate it, let us say, as do the Septuagint, the Vulgate,[49] the Jewish Publication Society Version (I would, too, I suppose). The translators of the King James Version, on the other hand, rendered the sentence, "A Psalm and Song at the dedication of the house of David." They may have gotten the idea from the view favored by Ibn Ezra above others reported by him. [552] Ultimately however, the *hint*[50] for that syntactical understanding derives from the *Mekilta:*

> "A Psalm; a song at the dedication of *ha-bayit le-Dawid.*" Was it then David who built it? On the contrary, was it not Solomon who built it . . . ? Why, then, does Scripture say, "A Psalm; a song at the dedication of the House of David?" Only because David gave over his life to it, to have it built; that is why it goes by this name.

For this fact, that David had the building of the Temple on his mind and in his plans, there are prooftexts; hence it is in a profound sense fitting that the House should be named after him even though in the strict and literal sense it was built by Solomon.[51] For, now the *Mekilta and MRS*[52] declare, "You will find the same true of every man, that whatever he gives over his life to, goes by his name." And the *Mekilta* (so too, *MRS*) does not merely declare this but goes on to demonstrate the truth of it by the case of Moses; and it's quite a while before we return to the subject at hand, namely, the listing of songs. Even an amateur can recognize that we are once again on a detour from the main course, despite the fact that the *Tanḥuma*, too, contains the "Moses passage."[53]

Who is responsible for *this* interpolation? Who indeed? Perhaps this too was a marginal annotation incorporated by that first copyist who could not resist leaving things where they were and [553] dragged in what was better left out. Perhaps it was another copyist. The notion is after all not alien to *Mekilta* thinking, as is evident from the *Mekilta* (and *MRS*!) comment on Exodus 15:20, "Aaron's sister."[54] However, congenial as this notion may be to *Mekilta* think-

49. Cf. Sabatier's note on the Versio Antiqua.

50. "Hint," for of course Ibn Ezra refers to David's house, and not to the Temple (as the *Mekilta* takes it). Rashi says, שיאמרוהו הלויים בחנוכת הבית בימי שלמה; Radaq: חברו דוד שיאמרוהו בחנכת בית המקדש.

51. Note the "clever" adaptation by *Tanḥuma* (followed in this respect by *We-Hizhir*): "Did then David *dedicate* it? Was it not Solomon who *dedicated* it?" But, of course, that avoids the whole issue and renders the question and answer almost otiose.

52. The *MRS* variants ad loc. are slight. *We-Hizhir*, too, has a brief digression at this point, but quoting only the passage about Miriam, "Aaron's sister," from the *Mekilta* on Exod. 15:20.

53. But not *Leqaḥ Ṭob*, not *Sekel Ṭob*, not *Yalquṭ Shimeoni*, not *Yalquṭ ha-Makiri* (on Ps. 18, 52a; not even on Ps. 30:1, 96b, does he exploit the opportunity to enlarge on Moses). On the "Moses passage" see *Midrash Tannaim*, p. 96 (and p. 212 briefly), and cf. Hoffmann's לקוטי בתר לקוטי, p. 13.

54. Note, however, that in *MRS* the example of Simeon and Levi, Dinah's brothers, does not occur. As for the Cambridge MS reading, it does not get that far; cf. *MRS*, ed. Epstein-

ing and teaching, in explanation of 'et ha-shirah ha-zot and in the list of ten songs it is marginal, and by having been brought *into* the text, it interrupts the principal discussion. And that interruption, too, is not modern: As we have said, it is already to be found in MRS as well, and, as we saw, in the *Tanḥuma*, too.[55]

Let us therefore return to what first occasioned our present study. As the *Mekilta* text on 'et ha-shirah ha-zot has been preserved, it is in a sorry state. The beginning and end of the original comment were separated from each other because of a misunderstanding and the consequent insertion of what did not belong. It all began with a misunderstanding. The misunderstanding was clearly early. Later (but not too much later) came interpolation, and this deepened misunderstanding. Remove *that*, and the original *Mekilta* shines with clarity.

'*Et ha-shirah ha-zot*: [Why is it said ('*et ha-shirah ha-zot*, rather than '*et ha-shir ha-zeh*)?]

But does (this term) *shirah* occur only once [here, in Exodus 15:1]? Does not indeed the word *shirah* occur ten times [in Scripture]? [Why then should its occurrence here call for comment?]

For all the songs referring to past events the noun used is in the feminine, [because] even as a female brings to birth, so the triumphs in the past were succeeded by subjugation; but the triumph which is yet to be will not be succeeded by subjugation. That is [554] why the noun used for it [for example, in Isaiah 42:10 and Ps. 149:1] is in the masculine, as it is said (Jer. 30:6), "Ask ye now, and see whether a man doth travail with child" [for] just as no man gives birth, so the triumph which is yet to come will not be succeeded by subjugation, as it is said (Isa. 45:17), "O Israel, that art saved by the Lord with an everlasting salvation."[56]

Melamed, p. 238. On the idea of giving over one's life to Israel, see also Pisḥa, 1 (1, 10f.) and *Sifre Deut*. 344, ed. Finkelstein, p. 400.

55. As for the brief enlargement on the ninth song, it is hard for me to decide (although my instinct tells me that here, too, we have something that was originally marginal) — because it occurs in MRS, *Tanḥuma*, *Sekel Ṭob* 201, *Yalquṭ Shimeoni*.

56. And by way of postscript (cf. above, note 24) perhaps this may be added: *maybe* the clause (שבחו חדשה) שירה חדשה of the Prayer Book does not mean "The redeemed (from Egyptian bondage) sang a new song" (see both עץ יוסף and עיון תפלה in סדור אוצר התפלות who recognize that the expression *shirah ḥadashah* calls for comment, but their explanation seems to me forced: why *new* only if the real emphasis is on *first*; cf. also the comment in *Abudraham*, Jerusalem, 5719, pp. 89f.; Baer, ad loc., senses that some thought expressed in the *Mekilta* is relevant here, but he is of no help in making it clear), but something akin to, "The redeemed (from Egyptian bondage) sang a Song of the New Age," to wit, ה' ימלוך לעולם ועד. In other words this would be an interpretation of *shirah* not like that of the *Mekilta*, that only *shir* in the masculine is to be associated with the song for a future age. Per contra, note that Yannai does not hesitate to use *shir* for the song of the redemption from Egypt: כאשר שוררנו שיר, עוד כן נשיר וכו' (*Piyyute Yannai*, ed. Zulay, p. 263).

I can't tell whether שירה חדשה does or does not occur in *Seder R. Amram Gaon* (cf. ed. Hedegård, Lund, 1951, p. 29, of the Hebrew text, trans., p. 68). Possibly it does. It does occur in *Maḥzor Vitry*, p. 66); it is not in Maimonides' Order of Service (cf. D. Goldschmidt in Alei Ayin *Studies*, Salman *Schocken*, VII [Jerusalem, 1958], 193).

Judah ha-Levi was certainly familiar with the expression; see the second line (and refrain) of his שירה חדשה גאולה לפסח (*Selected Poems*, ed. Brody [Phila., 1928], p. 139).

As for the so-called reading שירה חדשה in the Passover Haggadah, cf. D. Goldschmidt in his edition ad loc., p. 54, n. 17, and the critical apparatus in Kasher's *Haggadah Shelemah*, pp. 66f.

"Not By Means of an Angel and Not By Means of a Messenger"

I

[412] The verse being commented on by the Midrash (Sifre Deuteronomy 42, ed. L. Finkelstein, p. 88) is Deuteronomy 11:14, which reads, "[If ye hearken diligently to the commandments,] then I will give the rain of your land in its season," and so on; and the Midrash interprets the verb *we-natatti*, "then I will give," as follows, "'Then I will give': I—not by means of [by the hands of] an angel and not by means of a messenger."

How does the Midrash arrive at this interpretation? R. Hillel ben Eliakim, for example, explains the Sifre exegesis this way: Since Scripture does not use the expression "I will *send* the rain of your land," but rather "I will *give*," the emphasis is on God's personal and unmediated action. As the Sifre continues, there might almost seem to be justice in R. Hillel's view. For in the commentary on the phrase "the rain of your land," the Sifre declares that such direct action is reserved for the Land of Israel only;[1] and as prooftext quotes Job 5:10, "He *giveth* rain upon the Land, but *sendeth* waters upon the other lands."[2] In this Job verse we see clearly that onto other lands God sends, *sholeah*, i.e., acts by means of a *shaliah*, a messenger; whereas to *the* Land, the Land of Israel, He gives, *noten*, presumably without resorting to a *shaliah*, hence directly. And the same verb, *natan*, "to give," occurs in the verse we are engaged with, Deut. 11:14.

This interpretation is hardly satisfactory however, and it is not surprising

---

1. Cf. also Sifra 110d.
2. Naturally, I'm translating the biblical verses in accordance with the meaning given them by the Midrash.

that the *Neṣib*, that is, R. Naphtali Ṣebi Yehudah Berlin,[3] refuses to accept it. I'm not sure I understand how the *Neṣib* derives the Sifre interpretation, but he is certainly explicit in stating that the source of the interpretation cannot be in the verb *we-natatti*, "then I [413] will give." Truth to say, the Job verse is able to serve the Sifre authority in his desire to distinguish between the Land of Israel and the lands outside of Israel, because of the terms 'ereṣ and huṣot, not because of the verbs in the verse (at best these offer only auxiliary support): 'ereṣ is easily understood as 'ereṣ Yiśra'el, the Land of Israel; huṣot is easily equated with huṣ la-'areṣ, countries outside the Holy Land.[4] While in the Midrash it would be quite plausible to say of *sholeaḥ* that it is underscoring use of a messenger, and *therefore* if in the same verse in another clause *noten* is employed, *it* must wish to underscore action *not* by means of a *shaliaḥ*, hence direct on God's part, in Deut. 11:14 it would be stretching even homiletical Midrash too far to insist that *natan* is here declaring the same thing, viz., God's personal action. As the *Neṣib* rightly remarks, the verb *we-natatti* is in no way excessive, in no way at loose ends to be picked up for special exegesis. Just as, if *shalaḥ* were by itself, one could say that God personally sends,[5] so by the same token when *natan* appears by itself, one might press that God gives, makes a present, by means of an agent. Plenty are the gifts sent by messenger, and by itself the verb reveals neither mediated nor unmediated activity.

R. David Pardo is of no help on this point. He undertakes to reconcile the view here that it is possible for rain to be provided (to other lands) by means of an angel, with the talmudic statement (B. Taʿanit 2a) that the key to the treasure of rain is never out of God's hands. But this has nothing to do with our problem which is, to repeat, how from the expression "then I will give" does the Midrash derive, "I—not by means of an angel and not by means of a messenger"?

II

Whenever we have a problem with a text, the best thing to do is to consult other passages where a like statement or similar idiom is employed, and see whether those passages can be of assistance. Since we are dealing with a passage in the Sifre (on Deuteronomy), let us therefore first turn to another section in this treatise (325, p. 376)[6] where we meet our troublesome clause. This time the comment is on [414] Deut. 32:35, "*Mine* is vengeance, and recompense;"[7] and

---

3. In his ʿEmeq ha-Neṣib ad Sifre Deut., Jerusalem, 5721, p. 59.
4. On the other hand, cf. Sifre Deut. 37, p. 70.
5. Note, for example, that in connection with the plague of ʿarob (swarms of insects, or, wild beasts) Exod. 8:17 uses the verb *shalaḥ*, and in the *hiphʿil noch dazu*, and yet the Midrash, Exod. R. 12:4, does not hesitate to attribute this plague (along with *deber* and *bekorot*) to God directly.
6. Cf. Midrash Tannaim, p. 201. See LXX on Isa. 63:9.
7. I am deliberately preserving the order of the Hebrew.

the Sifre says, "I personally will exact retribution from them, not by means of an angel and not by means of a messenger."

Here there is no problem at all. The order of the biblical words virtually makes the Sifre interpretation self-explanatory: *Li naqam we-shillem, Mine* is vengeance and recompense. If the emphasis is on *Mine*, it is not farfetched to say that what is being taught is that the action is God's alone—He personally will reward or punish and not resort to agents to assist Him or act in His behalf. This Sifre comment is clear, but alas of no help to us in our passage.

III

Let us now follow the order of references Finkelstein furnishes in his notes. First, then, the Passover Haggadah,[8] where we read (p. 122), "And the Lord brought us forth out of Egypt with a mighty hand, and with an outstretched arm, and in a great manifestation,[9] and with signs, and with wonders" (Deut. 26:8). Thereupon the midrashic exegesis continues:

"And the Lord brought us forth out of Egypt," not by means of an angel, and not by means of a seraph, and not by means of a messenger. On the contrary, the Holy One, blessed be He, by His own glorious self [did it],[10] as it is said (Exod. 12:12), "For I will go through the land of Egypt in that night, and will smite all the firstborn in the land of Egypt, both man and beast; and against all the gods of Egypt I will execute judgments: I the Lord."[11]

"For I will go through the land of Egypt," I, and not an angel.
"And will smite all the firstborn," I, and not a seraph.
"And against all the gods of Egypt I will execute judgments," I, and not a messenger.
"I the Lord," it is I and none other.

All editions of the Haggadah apparently[12] carry this midrash which is not in the least difficult to follow: the emphasis attached to the [415] Deuteronomy verse is "substantiated" by the Exodus prooftext, whose meaning is established by the seemingly superfluous "I the Lord" clause at the end of the verse.[13] But this passage too is of no help to our attempt at understanding the Sifre on Deut. 11:14.

---

8. The edition I'm using, and to it the pagination refers, is that of E. D. Goldschmidt, Jerusalem, 1960.

9. So of course the midrash, and see also Goldschmidt's note 65 on p. 46.

10. Cf. Midrash Tannaim, p. 173.

11. Note how the midrash continues.

12. Cf. Goldschmidt, pp. 44f. and notes 60 and 61. See also M. Kasher, *Torah Shelemah*, 11, p. 117, note to no. 250.

13. The question whether more than verbal exegesis is here performed, need not detain us now; but I think Goldschmidt (p. 45) has disposed of the problem too cavalierly, *Shibbole ha-Leqet* notwithstanding; cf. Kasher, op. cit., 12, pp. 27f.

IV

The next reference supplied by Finkelstein is to the Mekilta on Exod. 12:12 (ed. J. Lauterbach, I, p. 53)[14] the details of whose terms in the Passover Haggadah we just confronted; but the Mekilta treatment differs from the one in the Haggadah. Observe:

> By "And I will smite [all the firstborn in the land of Egypt]" shall I understand [that He will do this] by means of an angel or by means of a messenger? The verse (Exod. 12:29) however teaches the following[15]: "Now it was the Lord who smote all the firstborn," [that is,] not by means of an angel and not by means of a messenger.[16]

Note that although Exodus 12:12 concludes with the so-called superfluous words "I the Lord" which proved so useful to the Passover Haggadah, the Mekilta has ignored this opportunity altogether; instead it has sought its proof-text in a subsequent verse. But this very prooftext calls for explanation: By what right does the Mekilta impose on verse 29 of that Exodus chapter the meaning of "Now it was the Lord who smote"? Why should we not read, as the regular translations do in fact read,[17] "[And it came to pass at midnight,] that the Lord smote all the firstborn," and so on?

But, midrashic as the approach of the Mekilta may be, this is not arbitrary · or carefree midrash. What is the ordinary sentence structure in the Hebrew Bible? As all the grammars will reveal,[18] the general order of a verbal Hebrew sentence is, first the verb, *then* the subject, and then the object. To be sure, when there are two coordinate clauses and the first one is introduced by the verb in the imperfect with the [416] *waw* conversive, the second clause will begin with the subject and its verb will take the perfect. *But this need not be the case.* It would make a perfectly good Hebrew sentence to read *wa-yehi ba-haṣi ha-lylah, wa-yak YHWH*. Compare, for example, *wayehi raʿab ba-ʾareṣ, wa-yered ʾAbram* (Gen. 12:10), "And there was a famine in the land, and Abram went down." There is nothing rare or extraordinary about this latter syntax. The Mekilta is therefore entirely within its legitimate ground rules when it decides that the order of the subject and predicate in the second clause of Exod. 12:29 may release a special meaning: *we-YHWH hikkah* may indeed suggest not just "And the Lord smote," but "Now it was the Lord who smote," that is to say, He personally, without recourse to any agency. And apparently

---

14. Notice that Mekilta R. Simeon (ed. Epstein-Melamed), p. 15 (ditto p. 227, ibid.) does not offer this interpretation.

15. Cf. Bacher, *ʿErke Midrash*, pp. 135f.

16. Contrast *Memar Marqah* (ed. J. Macdonald) I, 9, Text, p. 23 (translation, p. 36).

17. Cf. JPS; RSV ("At midnight the Lord smote," etc.); new JPS ("In the middle of the night the Lord struck down," etc.).

18. See for example, M. Greenberg, *Introduction to Hebrew*, Englewood Cliffs, N.J., 1965, pp. 129f.

the Mekilta preferred deriving its emphasis from this feature of Exodus 12:29 to the alternative proving from 12:12 itself, as the Passover Haggadah did.[19]

Here too, then, no special difficulty with the midrashic commentary exists. However, we are not yet done with this passage. For when we arrive at the Mekilta comment on Exod. 12:29 (ed. Lauterbach, I, p. 97), we discover to our amazement a virtual repetition of the passage we have just read through:

> By "Now [it was] the Lord [who] smote all the firstborn" (Exod. 12:29) shall I understand [that He did this] by means of an angel or by means of a messenger? The verse (Exod. 12:12) however teaches the following: "And I will smite all the firstborn," [that is,] not by means of an angel and not by means of a messenger.

This is plainly going in circles, for Exodus 12:12 could be given its particular interpretation only by virtue of Exodus 12:29—certainly not the other way around! What shall we say therefore to this last passage? Three possibilities present themselves:

(1) The present passage is simply a mistaken repetition by copyists and should be eliminated. But this is not only the easiest way out of the difficulty, it is patently nonsense. All copyists may be fools some of the time; some copyists may be fools all the time; but that all copyists are fools all of the time is not yet an axiom in literary criticism. At all events, despite the garbled readings recorded by Horovitz-Rabin in the critical apparatus of their Mekilta edition,[20] there is hardly justice [417] to the bland assumption that the whole passage is to be censored. See further below.

(2) It may well be that our Mekilta here, in citing Exod. 12:12 as prooftext, may be referring not merely—or not at all almost—to the three words of the verse which it quotes, but to the whole of that verse, and particularly to the closing words thereof, "I the Lord," the very words which the Passover Haggadah found so profitable. Every student of midrashic-talmudic texts knows that it is far from uncommon for a verse to be adduced and for the key terms that are required for the homily or exposition, the very words in fact which drive home the point, to be wanting in the text. So common indeed is this feature that it is pedantry to bring illustrations.[21] If this be so, then we would say that the Mekilta on Exod. 12:29 enlists 12:12 for support because of its concluding clause, "I the Lord." I am not persuaded that this is the case, but the possibility is a real one.

(3) Finally there is a likelihood that originally the Mekilta on Exod. 12:29

---

19. Of course I cannot say for sure why the Mekilta had this preference. Perhaps because the clause 'ani YHWH occurs in a number of contexts where the present interpretation would simply not apply. Note the formula in Leviticus 19, for example.

20. P. 43.

21. In order not to appear grudging, let me refer to one example, and since we're discussing a Sifre Deuteronomy passage principally, let me mention the Dan. 6:11 citation in Sifre Deut. 41, p. 88. Here of course the text reads "etc." Very well then, cf. the Isa. 63:11 citation ibid., p. 86.

may have simply given its interpretation of *we-YHWH hikkah* without the give-and-take that now encloses it, more or less in this fashion: "*we-YHWH hikkah*, not by means of an angel and not by means of a messenger"; and the present form of our Mekilta passage on 12:29 might have been adopted by someone eager to make it conform in appearance with the comment on 12:12. This is not as arbitrary or wishful a suggestion as may seem at first. In the first place, such a style would be in keeping with the style of our Sifre Deuteronomy 42 passage; it is not far off the style of the Sifre Deuteronomy 325 comment; as we shall see shortly, it would be like the reading in still another Mekilta passage. In the second place, however, and more significantly, it would be in keeping with the substance of the reading we have on Exod. 12:29 in Mekilta R. Simeon,[22] where we find in straightforward language, "'*We-YHWH hikkah* all the firstborn in the land of Egypt,' and not by means of a messenger." No question and answer, no entertaining of an alternative to be dismissed; direct interpretation which, as our analysis above has demonstrated, may be justified by the reading *we-YHWH hikkah*.

The net result of this investigation of the relevant Mekilta comments on the two verses of Exodus 12 is what? The way in which subject and [418] predicate of the second clause in verse 29 are placed allows the midrashic conclusion that the action was God's own, and not via some emissary. Can these Mekilta comments help us to arrive at an understanding of our Sifre statement? Perhaps. But before we explore that possibility, let us investigate one more Mekilta passage, and then still one last source.[23]

V

Commenting on the verses in Exod. 31:12–13, the Mekilta (III, p. 197) says: "'And the Lord spoke unto Moses, saying: "And thou,[24] speak unto the children of Israel," not by means of an emissary[25] and not by means of a messenger.'" Horovitz-Rabin seem to have recognized that the familiar formula was being applied this time not to God's action but to the action of Moses[26]—that is, since verse 13 says *emphatically*, "And thou, speak," the Mekilta is emphasizing that God instructed Moses himself to speak to Israel on this occasion, and not to pass on his message to them by means of some intermediary. The reading in Mekilta R. Simeon (p. 221) bears out the Horovitz-Rabin explanation,[27] for here we

22. P. 28. But note that this is wanting in MS Antonin (ibid., p. 231).
23. For other sources, based on the ones we are studying, see Kasher, op. cit., 11, pp. 117ff., nos. 250 and 251, and notes ad loc.
24. Cf. the reading in ed. Horovitz-Rabin, p. 340.
25. The word is *mal'ak* which we have been translating all along as "angel," but here such translation would be out of place. Cf. the dictionaries and Lev. R. 1:1.
26. See their commentary ad loc., and cf. S. Lieberman in *Kirjath Sepher*, 12, p. 65. See now also Kasher, op. cit., 21, p. 57.
27. Note the discussion in Kasher, however.

have, "'And the Lord said to Moses . . . :[28] "And thou, speak to the children of Israel," thou, not by means of an emissary[29] and not by means of a messenger.'"

The present passage therefore tells us little of God's behavior apparently;[30] yet it, too, is instructive for our purposes. As we saw in an earlier selection also, the exegesis here is determined by the special position of the subject: WE-'ATTAH dabber, And thou, speak. Indeed, in the present passage, emphasis is doubly underscored. For had one wanted merely to emphasize the *thou* element, it would have been quite sufficient to add the second person pronoun to the imperative and simply locate it, as Hebrew likes to locate its nominatives, after the verb. How, for example, does the verse (Exod. 20:19) put it when it reports [419] the demand of the Israelites that Moses and not another speak to them? *Dabber 'attah 'immanu . . . we-'al yedabber 'immanu 'Elohim*, "You speak to us . . . but let not God speak to us." What do we have, however, in Exodus 31:13? *We-'attah dabber*, the subject pronoun put first.[31] Midrash which, if it can help it, never lets a jot or tittle of the biblical text escape its notice, would be sure to capitalize on this order: You, Moses, speak to the Israelites, you personally; don't pass it on to someone else to deliver for you: yours is the task to instruct them in the right way, as the Midrash Leqah Tob (100b)[32] puts it.

VI

We come now to the statement in Version B of *Abot de-Rabbi Natan* (p. 2):

Moses received Torah from Sinai—not from the mouth of an angel and not from the mouth of a seraph,[33] but from the mouth of the King of kings over kings, the Holy One, blessed be He, as it is said (Lev. 26:46), "These are the statutes and ordinances and laws (which the Lord made between Him and the children of Israel in mount Sinai by the hand of Moses)."

Great indeed was Moses, as ARNB asserts at its very opening;[34] he received his communications from God alone, no *memra*,[35] no logos, no spirit, nothing intervening.

But how does the Leviticus prooftext bear this out? And why if ARNB

28. Note also the reading in ed. Lauterbach.
29. Note the reading *meliṣ* in ed. Hoffmann, p. 160, and cf. the *'Efat Ṣedeq* reading quoted by Kasher in his note no. 26.
30. And doubtless that is why in Sifre Deut. 42 Finkelstein did not bother to refer to this passage.
31. See also 2 Sam. 17:6 and cf. Driver ad loc.
32. See also Kasher's note.
33. Note that Duran on Abot 1:1 gives this as the reading of the *Mekilta!* Cf. above p. 418 n. 4 for the Lieberman reference.
34. P. 1.
35. See on the other hand the typical Targum Onkelos approach on Lev. 26:46 (cf. Tg. Jonathan too).

wants to underscore that it was directly from God's mouth that Moses heard his communications, does it not quote the explicit verses of Numbers 12:6–8, ". . . My servant Moses . . . is trusted in all My house; with him do I speak mouth to mouth, and not in dark speeches," and so forth?

The latter question is not difficult, for the fact is ARNB does quote it, at the very beginning of the treatise where it proclaims the true greatness of Moses.[36] On the other hand, the former question does demand some attention. How does the Leviticus prooftext establish that Moses received the statutes and so on directly from the mouth of [420] God? Note, for example, that Version A of *Abot de-Rabbi Natan* (p. 1) uses this verse to prove that Moses was found worthy of serving as God's agent to Israel. In other words, all the verse really declares is that the "Torah which the Holy One, blessed be He, gave to Israel was given by none save by the hand of Moses."[37] And so, too, the Sifra (ed. Weiss, 112c): "'Which the Lord made *between Him and the children of Israel*' [teaches that] Moses was found worthy of being made[38] the messenger between Israel[39] and their Father in heaven."

If, however, we will understand precisely what ARNA says, I believe we can grasp the reasoning of ARNB; and for the *precise* understanding of ARNA, a term (and reading) discovered by Louis Finkelstein sixteen years ago[40] is particularly helpful. From Lev. 26:46 ARNA derived that "Moses was found worthy of being the *bynyy*, the *middle*-man, between the children of Israel and God." Between Israel and God, then, there stood only one being, namely, Moses.[41] And if it was by the hands of Moses only that the statutes and the ordinances and the laws, and lots more, as the Sifra (ibid.) insists, were given to Israel, he could have received all these only from the One Being on the other end of the line of communication. For Moses was in the middle: '*Anoki ʿomed*[42] *ben YHWH u-benekem ba-ʿet ha-hi*', "It was I standing *between the Lord and you* at that time, to declare unto you the word of the Lord" (Deut. 5:5).[43] From none other than God, directly, did Moses receive Torah, as ARNB states. Prooftext? *Natan, YHWH beno u-ben bne Yiśra'el . . . be-yad Mosheh*, "the Lord gave by the hand of Moses who at Mount Sinai was in the middle between Him and the children of Israel."

36. As *Memar Marqah* (4, 12, trans., p. 186) exclaims, "Where is there a prophet like Moses whom God has addressed mouth to mouth?"

37. ARNA, ibid.

38. Midrash ha-Gadol, Lev., p. 680, like ARNA, reads *lihyot*, "to be."

39. ARNA reads, "children of Israel."

40. See *J. N. Epstein Jubilee Volume*, Jerusalem, 5710, p. 96, and cf. S. Lieberman, *Hellenism in Jewish Palestine*, N. Y., 1962, pp. 81f. and note 271 ad loc.

41. Cf. Philo, Quis . . . heres, 206 (Loeb Classics, IV, p. 384), though for a different purpose: μέσος τῶν ἄρκων, ἀμφοτέροις ὁμηρεύων.

42. Note the order of subject and predicate.

43. And maybe ARNB speaks of a seraph because of Deut. 5:19 (cf. 5:5). Besides, the emphasis as we now see of "Moses merited being the *shaliah*" equals "Moses merited being the *only shaliah*." Hence the reading *lo' ʿal yede shaliah* would be impossible.

VII

For all the instances of "neither angel nor messenger" there is an explanation. Can none of these be of assistance in the interpretation of [412] Sifre Deuteronomy 42? I must say, I have been tempted to take a cue from the Mekilta and to some extent also from ARNB. And with that in mind, as we reexamine Deuteronomy 11, beginning with verse 13, a solution suddenly does seem to spring up. For note: "And it shall be, if ye hearken diligently unto My[44] commandments which *'anoki meṣawweh, I* command you this day . . . then I will give the rain of your land in its season." In other words, once again the position of the subject may be the root cause of the emphasis. That this is no mean matter, or that it is something unlikely for the Midrash to pass over lightly, we have already observed. And regardless of the validity or invalidity of the midrashic interpretation, to take note of that construction is a sign of the fine sensibility of the Midrash toward the behavior of Hebrew speech. Does Scripture put the pronoun subject after a participle? In the concordance I have counted no less than fifteen examples of this with *'anoki;* if therefore *'anoki* precedes the participle, the Midrash would not necessarily be taking unwarranted liberties in attempting to make a stress. There are certainly times when, Midrash or no Midrash, subject before the participle plainly means, Read with italics. Look at Amos 7:16, for example, and then go on to the next verse. And I am virtually certain that passages like Jeremiah 1:11–12 mean something like this:

> THE LORD: What do *you* see, Jeremiah?
> JEREMIAH: What *I* see is an almond (*shaqed*) rod.
> THE LORD: You see excellently for I'm *shoqed*[45] to carry out My word.

And similarly with a number of other passages. "*'Anoki meṣawweh*" could bear this extra stress.

But "I command" is introduced by *'asher, which* I command. Can a clause introduced by *'asher* have the subject follow the verb? Any number of times, as even a glance in the concordance will disclose.

What the concordance will not disclose—or, rather, when it does, the instances are so rare, that *these* will demand explanation[46]—is a [422] clause

44. So JPS; new JPS, Pentateuch (p. 346), gets around it by translating "If, then, you obey the commandments that I enjoin upon you" etc. See however LXX, ed. Rahlfs, on the verse (p. 307).

45. I'm on the alert, ready to spring into action(?). At all events, in this sentence, this is the word receiving special attention, hence *shoqed 'ani* (and not *'ani shoqed*).

46. 2 Sam. 17:13 is clearly emphatic (cf. verse 12). On Deut. 16:22 perhaps Midrash Tannaim, p. 98, is making the right emphasis. If there is a special emphasis in Job 6:4, I don't get it. Is it really possible, as Szold seems to hint (tentatively?) that a pun on *hamas shoteh* of Prov. 26:6 may be intended, and therefore (this Szold does not say) in the Job verse *ruhi* is put after *shotah*? Seems fantastic to me.

introduced by *'asher* with the *participle* preceding the subject. What a dividend *'asher meṣawweh 'anoki* would bring! But *'asher 'anoki meṣawweh*, "which I command," is so typical a construction, I fear it cannot help us out in our present need. We are therefore back again to our problem; so I suggest we return to *we-natatti*, which we may have abandoned too hastily. The truth is the solution has been lying in this verb all along, and perhaps we have overlooked what we were looking for because of overfamiliarity with the passage—sometimes it's fatal for a biblical passage to be incorporated into daily prayer: Constant repetition creates the delusion that the text is intelligible, and then even the rudimentary steps of investigation are forgotten.[47]

[423] No one reading Deuteronomy 11:13 *et seq.* attentively can fail to be struck by the ambiguity of subject: If you obey the commandments which I command you, then I will give you rain, I will give the grass in your field. Beware lest you serve other gods, for then the anger of the Lord will be inflamed and He will hold back the rainfall, and you will perish from off the land which the Lord gives you. So keep my words carefully in order that your days may be multiplied on the land which the Lord swore to give to your fathers.

Before these verses in the same chapter when actions of the Lord are described, He is expressly referred to and the verb is given in the third person.

As for Eccl. 8:10, cf. H. L. Ginsberg's commentary (Tel Aviv-Jerusalem, 1961), p. 94, for the meaning of *'asher* here.

Is Lam. 1:12 meant to be even more emphatic than 1:5; or is (the second) *'asher* of verse 12 like *ki* of verse 5 and 1:5 is really the more emphatic; and is the point that when *YHWH* strikes it's more devastating than during any other catastrophe (note 12a)?

As 1 Chron. 13:6 stands it is confused (cf. 2 Sam. 6:2 in Kittel, *Biblia Hebraica*, 1950), but see further in a moment.

Is Sifre Numbers 78 (ed. Horovitz, p. 75) in any way reacting to the structure of the clause in Ezek. 47:23? Note that there's no reference to this Sifre Zuta (ibid., p. 264); see also Midrash ha-Gadol, Numbers, ed. Fisch, p. 231. Cf. Y. Kaufmann, *Religion of Israel*, trans. M. Greenberg, p. 445.

One expression however merits special attention, "called by . . . name," *niqra' shem*. . . . To the best of my knowledge and checking, the first time we come upon this idiom clearly (nevertheless cf. the 2 Sam. 6:2 reference given above), and it's in connection with Solomon's prayer after the Temple has been built, it reads *ki shimka niqra'*, "that (this house . . .) is called by Thy name" (1 Kings 8:43). Thereafter it's *'asher niqra' shmi* (*'alaw*; Jer. 7:10, 11, 14, 30; 32; 34; 34:15; cf. also the prayer in the Grace after Meals in Baer, *Seder Abodat Yisrael*, p. 556, but note also J. Heinemann, *Ha-Tefillah bi-Tequfat ha-Tannaim we-ha-Amoraim*, pp. 39f. and 48f.). Jeremiah however speaks also of the City (Jerusalem) *'asher niqra' shmi* (*'aleha*; Jer. 25:29; and note Dan. 9:18 too). Then in II Chron. 7:14 we hear of My People *'asher niqra' shmi* (*'alehem*). In these cases, it seems to me, some emphasis is certainly intended, something like an overtone suggesting that this House, this City, this People have "stamped" upon them His name—even in their destruction and desolation and dispersion. The same conception would apply to the Ark. If *niqra'* in Amos 9:12 is a participle, then perhaps Qimhi and Ehrlich are right in their interpretation (for Kaufmann's explanation see *Toledot*, 3, i, p. 91).

Needless to say, all I am doing in this long note is speculating and raising questions. The principal point however should not be lost sight of: *'asher* introducing a clause with a participle normally brings the subject first and then the participle.

47. Of course the Law provides a remedy which I suppose works for half-a-dozen times half-a-dozen saints.

So, too, with the content from verse 22 on. However, when we read verses 13–15, the subject seems now to be Moses, now to be God. "Which I command you" in verse 13 would seem to be referring to Moses. But then in verses 14 and 15 is Moses the subject? Is it Moses who brings rain and grass? Moses who rewards for obedience? In his commentary on Deuteronomy,[48] S. R. Driver explains the shift as "the discourse of Moses passing insensibly into that of God, as very often in the prophets: so," he continues in his comment on Deut. 7:4, "11:14f., 17:3, 28:20, 29:4f." This is obviously in accordance with what the traditional Jewish commentators feel, and Rashi, for instance, even refers to that nice observation at the end of Sifre Deuteronomy 41 (p. 88): "If ye have done what is up to you to do, then I will do what is up to Me to do, 'I will give the rain of your land in its season.'"

The interpretation may well be right, but no less a fact is the ambiguity of subject in we-natatti. And that this latter fact is noticeable not only to carping grammarians is borne out by this: The Samaritan version, the Septuagint, the Vulgate—and now we know still other versions too—read not "Then I will give," but, "Then *He* will give:"[49] "If ye hearken diligently to the commandments which I command you today, to love the Lord your God and to serve him with all your heart and with all your soul, then He will give the rain," and so forth.

We need not undertake to decide which is the correct original reading,[50] or if there was such a thing. One thing, however, is clear: the [424] reading we-natatti was not a universal reading. And if its legitimacy was to be insisted on, its use had to be defended, its form had to be justified by a particular interpretation. We-natatti, says the Sifre. Why we-natatti? To underline, *I* the Lord give the rain, and not by means of an angel and not by means of a messenger.

VIII

One final word. It may be of some significance that the emphasis of "not by an angel and not by a messenger" occurs in the following contexts: (1) God's redemption of Israel from Egyptian bondage; (2) God's punishment of Israel; (3) God's providing for Israel on its land; (4) God's revelation of the Law to Moses at Sinai; (5) Moses' communication to Israel of the Sabbath as covenant-sign—and see Rashi's comment on Exodus 31:12, catchword la-da'at, as well as the Mekilta (III, p. 199) on "That I am the Lord who sanctifies you." Let the theologians make what they can of that.[51]

48. ICC, pp. 99 and 130.
49. See M. Baillet, J. T. Milik, and R. de Vaux, *Discoveries in the Judaean Desert of Jordan*, 3, Oxford, 1962, p. 159, lines 33 and 34!
50. Cf. *Discoveries*, op. cit., p. 151! Also, P. Benoit, J. T. Milik, and R. de Vaux, *Discoveries in the Judaean Desert*, 2, Oxford, 1961, p. 84, lines 82 and 86! And see H. L. Ginsberg, "New Light on Tannaite Jewry and on the State of Israel of the Years 132–135 C.E.," In *Proceedings, Rabbinical Assembly of America*, 25, N.Y., 1961, pp. 132ff.
51. [See also Pesiqta R. (ed. Friedmann), p. 149b.]

For Marvin Pope

The Death of Moses: An Exercise in Midrashic Transposition

[219] How the contemporaries of Moses, or perhaps better, how the contemporaries of the author of the last chapter of Deuteronomy felt about Moses' death sentence, is not recorded. Scripture does say (Deut. 34:8), "And the Israelites bewailed Moses in the steppes of Moab for thirty days" — a detail to which we shall return. But this is not singular. Aaron's death too, earlier (Num. 20:29), was bewailed for thirty days by all the house of Israel. (See further, n. 39.)

On the other hand, what was superlative about Moses is explicitly announced. Though he lived 120 years, his eyes remained undimmed and his vigor unabated; the spirit of wisdom filled Joshua because Moses had laid his hands upon him. "Never again did there arise in Israel a prophet like Moses— whom the Lord singled out, face to face, for the various signs and portents that the Lord sent him to display" in Egypt and before all Israel. Nevertheless, Moses had to die and be buried (Deut. 34:5–6), in the land of Moab, just before the Israelites entered the Promised Land. Before dying he was allowed to gaze at the various regions of the land[1] from a distance, but under no circumstance was he permitted to cross over. אראה is granted but no אעברה נא.[2] As we have said, he had to die.

For the exclusion from the land and death penalty, Scripture offered two

---

1. See the nice observation of S. E. Loewenstamm in "Mot Moshe," *Tarbiz* 27 (1958): 147, n. 7. Note how in *Sifre Deut.* 357, ed. L. Finkelstein, pp. 425–27, geographical terms are given a historical interpretation, to emphasize Moses' prophetic powers. On the lore of death and mountains, see T. H. Gaster, *Myth, Legend, and Custom in the Old Testament* (New York, 1969): 234f. However, Moses was buried in the valley (Deut. 34:6).

2. Cf. Deut. 3:25, 34:4.

reasons,[3] probably derived from two distinct traditions or literary sources. According to one tradition or source, Num. 20:2–13 (alluded to also in Deut. 32:48–52; but see also Ps. 106:32), it was because instead of commanding the rock to produce water, "Moses raised his hand and struck the rock twice with his rod" (Num. 20:11). This was tantamount to not trusting God enough (Numbers) or to breaking faith with Him (Deuteronomy).[4] Still another explanation is offered in Deut. 1:37 (also in 3:26 and apparently 4:21, too): When the spies delivered their evil report of the land, God grew incensed with that whole ungrateful generation and swore that with the exception of Caleb and Joshua (and the younger generation) none would enter the land. "Because of you," Moses says, "the Lord was incensed with me, too"; or as he put it again, "Now the Lord was angry with me *on your account* and swore that I should not cross the Jordan and enter the good land that the Lord your God is giving you as a heritage" (Deut. 4:21). In other words, in this explanation Moses himself appears to be blameless; he is simply swept along by the penalty imposed on his contemporaries.[5]

Nothing in this summary is unknown to students of Scripture. Nor very likely the following: We must presume that the reasons given for Moses' death sentence must have appeared sufficient, more or less—or, more rather than less—to the biblical narrators. The reasons they offer are not challenged, and presumably the narrators are satisfied with the contents of their accounts. Only one appeal against that sentence is heard, the appeal by Moses—by the very victim, the interested party—and all he does is plead, "Let me, I pray, cross over and see the good land on the other side of the Jordan, that good hill country, and the Lebanon" (Deut. 3:25). The charges, if charges there be, are not denied or contradicted: either striking the rock, or, one must die along with one's own (sinful) generation; the appeal is a petition after the invocation of God's omnipotence (Deut. 3:24), as though one were asking for special favor. Hence we will have to say that in the framework of Scripture, the death sentence is legitimate, even to Moses.[6] God's decisions are just.

In the end, the same is true of the Midrash, but not without expression first of many protestations, all illustrating on the one hand how profoundly disturbing the [220] fate of Moses was to later generations,[7] and on the other hand

---

3. Nevertheless, see Loewenstamm (n. 1) 146.

4. On these and additonal verses regarding the waters of Meribah, cf. Loewenstamm (n. 1) 142ff. On the *ḥillul ha-Shem* "(as it were)," cf. *Midrash ha-Gadol*, Num., ed. S. Fisch, II, 125 and n. 32. Note also III Armenian account, 120 (thanks to Professor Michael E. Stone, I was able to get a copy of his "Three Armenian Accounts of the Death of Moses" [in G. W. E. Nickelsburg Jr., ed., *Studies on the Testament of Moses* (Cambridge, MA, 1973): 118–21]; all references to Armenian accounts are to the Stone paper).

5. Note the complaint made by Moses in *Tanḥuma wa-Etḥanan* 1 (ed. Buber 2, 4b–5a). See also *Midrash ha-Gadol*, Deut., ed. Fisch, 82 and n. to line 10; also 64, lines 18ff.

6. Note also Deut. 4:22. In Deuteronomy 34, there's not a word out of Moses. On proper presentation of petition, see *B. Berakot* 32a, bottom. Cf. also *Sifre Deut.*, 343, p. 394.

7. Cf. also *Memar Marqah* (J. Macdonald, ed. and trans.; Berlin, 1963): 5:1ff. (trans., 193ff.).

how God's sentence might be defended. The latter was not always successful but remains instructive nonetheless.

First, however, the view quoted in a tannaitic midrash[8] that Moses did not really die: יש אומרים לא מת משה אלא עומד ומשרת למעלה.[9] Although he does not accept this view, Josephus is already familiar with it: "But he (i.e., Moses) has written of himself in the sacred books that he died, for fear lest they should venture to say that by reason of his surpassing virtue he had gone back to the Deity."[10] Before him Philo, too, seems to have known of this.[11] The view, therefore, seems to have been current for some time (although I can't say how far back). And after all, why not? If Enoch[12] and Elijah (2 Kings 2:1, 11) could escape death, why not Moses?

It is not a serious problem that it is distinctly stated Moses died (Deut. 34:5; Josh. 1:2). On a number of occasions the Midrash does not hesitate to go its independent way, ignoring the biblical plainspoken statement. Let me give just one example. Forty years, Scripture tells us, the Israelites had to spend in the wilderness because they accepted the defeatist report of the scouts sent in advance to the Promised Land: "You shall bear your punishment for forty years, corresponding to the number of days—forty days—that you scouted[13] the land: a year for each day. Thus you shall know what it means to thwart Me" (Num 14:34). The forty years, therefore, are a punishment, measure for measure and then some.

Despite this, there is a view in the *Mekilta*[14] that at the very outset, at the exodus from Egypt, God had resolved not to lead the Israelites directly into their land because He feared that on their arrival they might rush immediately to the labors required by their newly acquired fields and thus neglect to study Torah. That is why He kept them going round and round in the wilderness for

---

Attempts at "explanation" never cease, even whimsical speculation. Here is I. B. Singer in an interview (*New York Times*, Magazine Section, 3 December 1978, pp. 40, 44), "from the point of view of religion. When Moses gave the Torah, he believed it was possible to create a nation of spiritual people. . . . This never became a reality. I would say that the reason why, according to legend, Moses wasn't allowed to cross the Jordan was because what he wanted to create and what followed in the years after the revelation on Mount Sinai were two different things altogether."

8. *Sifre Deut.* 357, p. 428; *Midrash Tannaim*, 224; see also Finkelstein's references (*Sifre Deut.* p. 428) to *B. Soṭah, Sefer Ḥasidim*, and *Yalqut ha-Makiri*. Cf. Philostratus, *Apollonius of Tyana*, VIII, 2, end (Loeb Classics, II, 277), that Socrates did not die "though the Athenians thought he did."

9. Or as *B. Soṭah* reads, עומד ומשמש (already noted by Freimann in *Sefer Ḥasidim*, p. 313) and without the word למעלה.

10. *Antiquities*, IV, 326 (Loeb Classics, IV, 633).

11. Philo, *Sacrifices of Abel and Cain*, 8 (LC, II, 99, bottom) and L. Ginzberg, *Legends of the Jews*, VI, 162, top.

12. See H. St. John Thackeray's note *d* in LC, Josephus, *Antiquities*, IV, 633. (Is Elijah in chariot and whirlwind an attempt to make up for the death of Moses?)

13. See R. Ishmael in *Sifre Zuta*, ed. H. S. Horovitz, p. 279; *Midrash ha-Gadol*, Num., ed. Fisch, vol. I, p. 224.

14. *Be-Shallaḥ* 1, ed. J. Z. Lauterbach, I, p. 171; *Mekilta R. Simeon*, ed. Epstein-Melamed, p. 45. Cf. Ginzberg, *Legends*, VI, 2, n. 8.

forty years: for here their needs were taken care of, they could study without distraction of livelihood worries, and the Torah would be thoroughly incorporated in themselves.

Regardless of the Book of Numbers, then, the forty years, according to this (and still another)[15] interpretation in the *Mekilta*, were no punishment for adopting the negative report of the land, but on the contrary an ideal opportunity provided in order to achieve mastery of the Torah. Similarly, the verse in Deuteronomy may say "So Moses the servant of the Lord died there," the verse at the beginning of Joshua (1:2) may quote God as saying "My servant Moses is dead," but that will not prevent some people from believing that Moses did not die, that in his role of "servant of the Lord" he still ministers on high (to the Lord). The reference to death may be no more than what Philo may have had in mind when he wrote,[16] ". . . the time came when he had to make his pilgrimage from earth to heaven, and leave this mortal life for immortality" and so forth.

It does not necessarily follow that this view is merely and from the first one more attempt to come to God's defense against what seems a spectacular unfairness, injustice. Ascensions are not unheard of.[17] Interestingly, however, the view that Moses did not die is not included in that lore assembled, for example, by the *Midrash* [221] *Petirat Moshe*,[18] where the exchanges between Moses and God are the direct result of the feelings that Moses is being treated

15. *Be-Shallaḥ*, ibid., p. 171f.; *Mekilta R. Simeon*, p. 45.

16. *II Moses*, 288 (LC, VI, 593). See I. Lévy, *La Légende de Pythagore* (Paris, 1927), 151f. On the resurrection of Moses as witness to the divinity of Christ, see III Armenian account, 121.

17. Cf. *Interpreter's Dictionary of the Bible*, s.v., "Ascension"; "Moses, Assumption of"; "Isaiah, Ascension of." E. Rohde, *Psyche* (New York, 1966), 2:538 and 568, n. 109. See now also L. Nemoy in *Essays on the Occasion of the Seventieth Anniversary of the Dropsie University* (Philadelphia, 1979), 361–64, and nn. 1–2. Perhaps this too should be noted: *Sifre Deut.* 338 and 357 (pp. 387, 425) emphasize that Moses was summoned to *ascend* (noun: *aliyyah*) the mountain; hence his death is not to be regarded as punishment. (Contrast this with *Gen. R.* 85:3, 1034, where *yeridah*, "descent," is spoken of.)

For *Gedullat Moshe*, cf. Ginzberg, *Legends*, V, 416ff., nn. 117, 118. See I. Lévy n. 16), pp. 154ff.

18. In *Bet ha-Midrasch*, ed. A. Jellinek, I, 115–29 (I *Petirat Moshe*); VI, 71–78 (II *Petirat Moshe*). See also *Batei Midrashot*, ed. Wertheimer (Jerusalem, 1950), 1:286–87. Additional material in J. D. Eisenstein, *Ozar Midrashim* (New York, 1915), 368ff. Also Z. M. Rabinowitz, *Ginzé Midrash* (Tel-Aviv, 1976), 222–24 (*Midrash Mishle* 14, ed. Buber, 39a–b); *Abot de-Rabbi Natan* (ed. S. Schechter), pp. 49ff., 156f. Cf. *Mekilta*, Amalek 2, II, 149ff. and parallels. See *Deut. R.* and the two *Tanḥumas* on *Wa-Ethanan* and *Zot ha-Berakah*. For poetry on the death of Moses theme, see L. J. Weinberger, in *HUCA* 37 (1966): 1–11 and additional references, 1f. (Hebrew); idem. on the theme of searching for Moses, in *Tarbiz*, 38 (1968–69): 285–93. On the theme of Moses' wealth and the significance of the criticism thereof, cf. M. Beer in *Tarbiz* 43 (1973–74): 70–87.

In I *Petirat Moshe* (121 and 122f.; cf. Eisenstein, *Ozar*, II, 377a, 378b) there are two poems: the first, 13 lines of essentially 3 words to a line (but not throughout), being God's promise to Moses of the splendor that awaits him; the second (a doxology recited by Joshua, *ha-midrash she-darash Yehoshua!*—as introduction to a homily?) approximately 33 lines of essentially 4 words to a line (not always). Cf. Zunz-Albeck, *Ha-Derashot*, 67 and 316, n. 116. Are these poems meant to be imitations of the style of Merkabah hymns? Cf. G. Scholem, *Jewish Gnosticism, Merkabah Mysticism, and Talmudic Tradition* (New York, 1960), 21ff.

unjustly, in that he had to *die* (see below n. 23, and p. 180): it is, we must remember, a midrash of *petirat* Moses, of Moses' *death*. It is in these exchanges primarily that complaint and efforts at clarification rise to the surface: Moses' complaint articulating what obviously human readers or auditors of the Moses story in midrashic-talmudic times feel, God's retort articulating what human readers of the story imagine to be God's self-justification. The dialogues are at the same time protest and theodicy.

There are times when God has no answer except repetition of a biblical verse. For example: Moses pleads, "After all the toils I endured, You tell me to die?" To which God replies in the words of Deut. 3:26b, "Enough! Never speak to Me of this matter again."[19] Hardly an answer; it is no surprise that Moses is not silenced.

Then there are what may be called belabored defenses. For example,[20] Moses says, "All Your other creatures You are prepared to forgive once, twice, and thrice; I have been guilty of only one iniquity, yet You refuse to forgive me." To which God replies, "Not of one but of six iniquities you were guilty, though I never before told you about them"—and He lists the biblical verses which contain traces of sin. This defense by inventory hardly does justice to God, for if our prophet indeed merits immortality, the punishment does not fit the crimes, even if there were those six instances.

One exchange of plea and denial must have grown out of academic experience. Moses pleads:[21] "Since my death is intended to make it possible for Joshua to succeed, let him begin at once to be the master and I will be his disciple." At that Moses starts to serve Joshua: "Moses began to do for Joshua what Joshua had previously done for him." But when he entered the Tent of Meeting and the cloud descended and separated Joshua from Moses, when Joshua was admitted into the (holy) interior and Moses was left outside, then Moses cried out, "Better a hundred deaths than one experience of envy." The master cannot endure being replaced by his disciple. Here it is Moses who begs to die; God does not deprive him of this!

Another exchange immediately relevant to midrashic-talmudic centuries is preserved in *Deut. R.* 2:8 (see also *Mid. Tan.*, 178; cf. 19): here the issue is entry into the land. "You allowed Joseph's bones to be carried into the land," Moses says to God, "why not mine?" And the Lord replies, "Joseph never denied his origins, in Egypt he admitted he was a Hebrew (Gen. 40:15; cf. 39:14): but when you were identified as an Egyptian by the daughters of the priest of

---

19. I *Petirat Moshe*, 116; see also line 2 from bottom of the page.

20. Ibid. 117. Note also 119, top, for the charge that Moses on his own, without permission, slew the Egyptian! Cf. *Assumption of Moses*, ed. R. H. Charles (London, 1897), 106. Contrast this with ARNA, chap. 20, p. 72. Or Moses "cornered" by God: I *Petirat Moshe*, 120, top. And on the retort by Moses, cf. *Gen. R.* 49:9, 511.

21. I *Petirat Moshe*, 116; see also 124, 127. This is contrary to the cliché quoted by *Leqaḥ Ṭob* on Deut. 34:9. The relationship between Moses and Joshua is conceived of as the relationship between a *ḥakam* and his *talmid*. For what a disciple does for his master, see I *Petirat Moshe*, 123. Cf. *Deut. R.* 9:9, 117c.

Midian (Exod. 2:19), you heard but held your peace." Moses became the model of Jews seeking to pass as non-Jews!—Jewish hellenizers and all their descendants down through the ages. The moral was clear to all—even Moses could not escape punishment for that. But what is noteworthy is this, that in his defense of God the homilist does not flinch from attributing such behavior to Moses.[22]

Nor should this be overlooked: When the *galgallim* and seraphim on high[23] observed that even toward Moses God would not show partiality, they exclaimed in praise of Him (ברוך כבוד ה' ממקומו) who is scrupulously fair and plays no favorites. Not God's injustice but His meticulous [222] justice is witnessed here. Let there be no more talk of injustice! God has to take into account the reactions of more than men.

There are, however, retorts where the human conception of justice is made secondary to a fundamental principle of monotheism. For example,[24] in one exchange God reassures Moses that he is in fact blameless, but that he must nevertheless die because he is a descendant of Adam, i.e., death is the fate of all human beings (no reference to Enoch and Elijah here!); or, put alternatively, "You have sipped from the cup of Adam"; or, even more acutely, "If you remain alive, people will be misled by you, they will make you into a god and will worship you."[25] There is danger of apotheosis here, in other words, that like the cult of emperor (?) or hero worship there will develop a cult of Moses

22. That in periods of persecution there was no objection to disguising oneself in order to escape identification as a Jew (see *Gen. R.* 82:5, 984ff., two disciples of R. Joshua), hardly affects our midrashic passage (yet, note the taunts of the apostate *stratiotes* in the *Gen. R.* anecdote!).

23. I *Petirat Moshe*, 121. In *Deut. R.* 11:8, 120a, "the *galgallim* of the Merkabah and the *seraphim* of flame (*lehabah*)." See also *Midrash ha-Gadol*, Deut., 65, lines 17–20. Cf. *Sifre Deut.* 29, p. 46.

24. ARNB, p. 51. Loewenstamm, 147, rightly underscores that in this passage not entry into the land is being discussed, but death. Indeed, death and exclusion from the land are referred to as two separate penalties (for the sin at Meribah, not entering into the land; but why *die*?). Note that in ARNA, 48–50, also, death is the subject and that Moses requests a death like his brother Aaron's. See also Ginzberg, *Legends*, VI, 148, n. 888. Cf. ARN, 156.

This, too, deserves to be noted, that (approximately) in I *Petirat Moshe* first appear Moses' appeals not to die (116f.), then (117, 120, top, 123ff.) specifically his appeals to be permitted to enter the land, one way or another. This arrangement seems to be deliberate: if Moses can't persuade God to let him live on, then perhaps he might get from Him the permission to enter the land; sometimes there is an overlapping of the appeals for continued life and for admission into the land (e.g., 120, 125f., 127)—possibly the result of the homilist's healthy instinct, that if Moses is admitted into the land, the transition to immortality would follow (consummation of all one has projected is the privilege of those who live forever). Nor is Moses indifferent to the fact that neither his own sons nor Aaron's will succeed him (121, bottom). Contrast Philo, *On the Virtues*, 66f. (LC, VIII, 203); *Sifre Num.* 141, p. 187, *Sifre Zuta*, 322, top.

Let no one imagine that the reason Moses wanted to enter the Holy Land was his desire to enjoy its delicious fruits. He wished to carry out the commands having to do with the land (II *Petirat Moshe*, VI, 74)!

25. I *Petirat Moshe*, 116, 118. On the cup of Adam, see also *Deut. R.*, ed. S. Lieberman, 125 (and n. 2). Drinking from the same cup = sharing same fate: *Sifre Deut.* 349, p. 407. Cf. Prov. 1:13.

worship.[26] The very remarkable achievements of Moses from Egypt on are themselves the cause of his undoing, to underscore that even Moses is not a divine being—though he spent time with angels on high (God "made him equal in glory to the holy ones": Ecclus. 45:2; cf. ARN, 157) and did not taste food or drink for forty days and nights.[27] Moses may outweigh all the works of creation;[28] though his days come to an end, his light never will.[29] But all men die; Moses is a man, although with extraordinary virtues; hence he must die.[30]

(Yet if Scripture says of Moses that at the age of 120 his eyes remained undimmed and his vigor unabated; if when God asks Moses, "Are you better than ancient worthies?" or "Did not your parents and all your ancestors die?" Moses rejects comparison between himself and them [I *Petirat Moshe* 118f.; II *Petirat Moshe* 71ff.]—evidently for the homilist there *is* something more than human to this *ish Elohim* who is superior to Adam, Noah, the Patriarchs.)

There are a number of still other exchanges,[31] assembled conveniently (with some repetition) in the *Midrash Petirat Moshe* I and II,[32] all emphasizing that in debate with God (for his own benefit), Moses cannot prevail. (This is not unexpected!) The protests put in the mouth of Moses reveal to us a moral disquietude of sensitive readers of the Moses stories in midrashic-talmudic times; God's various retorts reveal how in those days men tried to justify His ways, for His ways must be just. Protest and retort brought together create a complex religio-intellectual involvement with the ethical and theological (there's something Kierkegaardian about this): Is this how the righteous is rewarded, the one trusted throughout Your household? What *is* a just reward? Shall the righteous be rewarded even if that may undermine a principle without which the purity of the faith cannot survive? "How can a man be just before God? . . . Behold, He snatches away; who can hinder Him? Who will say to Him, 'What doest Thou?'"

And parenthetically I would like to add: Whether or [223] not so intended by the haggadic interpreters, the problem exemplified by the pleas of Moses

26. Cf. J. Goldin in *Mordecai M. Kaplan Jubilee Volume* (New York, 1953): 278ff. See also the quotation from Josephus, above (n. 10). And see also III Armenian account, 120, bottom paragraph! Cf. the Nilsson quotation, below, p. 184.

27. Exod. 34:28; Deut. 9:9. According to III Armenian account, 121, Moses fasted three forty-day periods, "corresponding to the number of his years."

28. II *Petirat Moshe*, VI, 71ff.

29. I *Petirat Moshe*, 121.

30. Cf. *Deut. R.*, ed. Lieberman, 130. As he gave up his ghost, according to II Armenian account, 119, he exclaimed, "Oh for the heavenly things that are sweeter than honeycomb." For the theme of the righteous refusing to die, see also, e.g., *The Testament of Abraham* (trans. M. E. Stone, Society of Biblical Literature, 1972). Cf. L. Ginzberg in *Jewish Encyclopedia* (New York, 1901), 1.93–96.

31. One even draws on the Osiris motif: I *Petirat Moshe*, 124, bottom. Cf. E. R. Goodenough, *Jewish Symbols in the Greco-Roman Period*, II (Bollingen, 1953) 197. For another excruciating appeal, cf. ARN, 156, and S. Lieberman in *Louis Ginzberg Jubilee Volume* (Hebrew; New York, 1945) 254; idem, *Shkiin* (Jerusalem, 1970) 39f., n. 4 and p. 101 (to p. 40).

32. See above, n. 18. Were the *Petirat Moshe* midrashim drawn up in order to put a stop to dangerous speculation, in order to demonstrate that Moses was given every opportunity to argue his case? However, see the last paragraph of this paper.

and their rejection recalls the outcry in other contexts of grief: זו תורה וזו שכרה, So this is the reward for devotion to the Torah! Here is how *Deut. R.* 11:10, 120a, puts it: "So this is the compensation for forty years of service (שילום עבודה של מ' שנה) in which I toiled to make them a holy and faithful nation?" And here is I *Petirat Moshe*, 121: "Where is my reward for the forty years (היכן שכרי של מ' שנה) I wore myself out for Your sons and in their behalf went to great pains," etc. It's almost as though the Moses story, unique as it surely is, is treated as a forecast of what to expect in the centuries to come: a lifetime of loyalty without commensurate reward in this world. The problem, growing out of Israel's experience, may have suggested to the midrashic-talmudic homilist how to interpret the biblical Moses story.

Since if the purity of the faith fails to survive, it is futile to ask about the justice of rewards or punishments—and Moses, after all, is pleading only for what he feels he deserves—something like a compromise must be attempted. Note incidentally that no Job-like, God-out-of-the-storm, answer is resorted to, i.e., the Lord is just but *we* can't understand His ways, just as we can't understand much else (though this may be implied occasionally): but no overwhelming theophany—though in the end God does appear to take his soul. Hence, after Moses finally realizes that there is no one in the whole universe, animate or inanimate, who can help him and that he cannot persuade God to revoke His sentence, and discovers that his intellectual strength has vanished, he asks to die—but he does not want to die as all men die, he wants to die at God's own hand, not at Samael's, the chief of the satans,[33] not by the hand of the angel of death. This is indeed granted to him: the angel of death is powerless in the presence of Moses. Finally God and the archangels Michael and Gabriel and the angel Zagzagel put him to his final rest.[34] The treatment of Moses at death would therefore seem to be exceptional. Moses has had at least and at last one wish of his granted in regard to his death; his uniqueness is thereby dramatically confirmed.[35]

But is it really? Has God then yielded to Moses' importunings? It is true that no one knows where he is buried (Deut. 34:6),[36] that his soul is reluctant to quit his clean and pure and holy body which was never subject to the affliction of flies or of leprosy,[37] that beneficent angels attend him at his death. Yet even in

33. I *Petirat Moshe*, 125. From the fire of gehenna he was created and to the the the fire of gehenna he will return (ibid., 128). Cf. Jude 9.

34. I *Petirat Moshe*, 128f. Zagzagel was Moses' teacher (ibid., 127). Cf. Ginzberg, *Legends*, V, 417. According to III Armenian account, 120, Michael buried him.

35. I *Petirat Moshe*, 119, line 5 from bottom. According to *Ps.-Philo* 19:16, p. 132 (M. R. James, ed. and trans.; New York, 1971, on the day Moses died the hymn of the angels was not recited. This never happened with any other human being, before or since.

36. Note also *Assumption of Moses* 11:8, and Charles' note, p. 46, s.v., "All the world . . . ." Cf. III Armenian account, 120.

37. I *Petirat Moshe*, 129, and Ginzberg, *Legends*, VI, 161, n. 948. Is the reference to flies associated with the thought in Abot 5:5? (Nevertheless, cf. S. Lieberman, *Hellenism in Jewish Palestine* [New York, 1962], 174ff.) Is the reference to leprosy reminiscent of what happened to his sister (Num. 12:9), that Moses never gossiped? On leprosy, see also *Eleh Ezkerah* in *Bet ha-Midrasch*, II, 66.

making concessions, the Midrash Masters feel that they must exercise restraint. The reason no one knows where Moses is buried, says *Leqaḥ Ṭob* on Deut. 34:6, is a precaution, lest his sepulcher become a shrine of idolatrous worship. Besides, Aaron's burial place also disappeared from sight.[38] For thirty days the children of Israel mourned for Moses, the same period of mourning as for Aaron (as we have noted)—but not so, for Moses only the males of Israel, בני ישראל, mourned, while for Aaron *all* the house of Israel, כל בית ישראל, mourned (because Aaron went about making peace, while Moses did not refrain from reproving them).[39] It was by God's kiss that Moses died.[40] But Aaron too, and Miriam, and the Patriarchs,[41] and all the righteous so met their deaths.[42] And maybe even that comment[43] on "Never again did there arise in Israel a prophet like Moses," that "one such did arise among the gentiles," is also partially intended to keep the praise of Moses within bounds.

What is the point? Along with reverence ("Moses our master, the greatest of great scholars, the father of the [224] prophets")[44] went a deep religio-intellectual fear of Moses—at least on the part of thoughtful students and teachers of Scripture—I don't think that is putting it too strongly, in the light of these and still other available references, for no other biblical personality so succeeded in shortening the distance between God and man as he did. For this reason his humanity must be repeatedly underlined, even (above all?) when he gets what he asked for. Even the manner of Moses' death does not release him from the limits of the human condition: the extraordinary honors paid him are paid to other outstanding personalities as well. The give-and-take between Moses and God is not suppressed: hear the response of the Lord! The death of Moses before Israel's entrance into the Promised Land did not—at least in midrashic-talmudic times and circles—entirely cease to be an embarrassment[45] or a perplexity, because of the gross unfairness it represented; on the other hand, considerations regarded as higher, or profounder, than the miscarriage of

---

38. *Midrash Petirat Aharon* in Jellinek, *Bet ha-Midrash*, I, 95, top. Lest Israel think he is alive and therefore a god: ibid.

39. ARNA, p. 49; see also ARNB, p. 51. At Aaron's death also, angels mourned, ARNB, p. 51; as for Moses, see also ARNB, p. 52, end of chap. 25. Cf. I *Petirat Moshe*, 128f. Further, as A. B. Ehrlich points out (*Mikra Ki-Pheshuto* [New York, 1969], 1:383), the captive woman was also given a month's time to lament her father and mother (Deut. 21: 10–14). On thirty-day mourning for Moses, cf. also III Armenian account, 121 top. On thirty-day mourning, see one view in P. Nazir 1:3 and Maimonides, *Code*, Book of Judges, Mourning 6:1 and Radbaz and *Leḥem Mishneh* ad loc.

40. I *Petirat Moshe*, 129. Cf. Ginzberg, *Legends*, VI, 161, n. 950.

41. Cf. Ginzberg, *Legends*, VI, 112, n. 639.

42. Cf. *Midrash Tannaim*, 225; M. Soṭah 1:9, end (cf. reading in ed. Lowe).

43. *Sifre Deut.* 357, p. 430. Balaam's wisdom superior to Moses': *Seder Eliyahu R.* (ed. Friedmann), 142. See also ARNA, p. 41, on the (relative) meekness of Moses! The soul of Moses is of course put in safekeeping under the Throne of Glory, but the same is true of the souls of all the righteous (ARNA, p. 50).

44. ARNA, p. 3 (and despite this he forgets what God commanded him to say when he lost his temper). Cf. S. Abramson in *Leshonénu* 41 (1977): 159.

45. Is this also why God weeps (and the angels too) when Moses finally dies (I *Petirat Moshe*, 129)? That even God can do nothing about it? See below, notes 53–54.

justice (by human standards) had to triumph particularly in a world where in the popular mind the nature and treatment of the gods were sometimes indistinguishable from that of men. "When . . . we think, says Epictetus,

> that the gods stand in the way of [our own interests], we revile even them, cast their statues to the ground, and burn their temples, as Alexander ordered the temples of Asclepius to be burned when his loved one [Hephaestion] died.[46]

On a more cultivated level possibly, but still flowing too easily from God to man and back again, we hear Apollonius of Tyana,[47] when the Emperor asks him, "Why is it that men call you a god?" reply, "Because every man that is thought to be good, is honored by the title of god," ὅτι πᾶς ἄνθρωπος ἀγαθὸς νομιζόμενος θεοῦ ἐπωνυμίᾳ τιμᾶται.

Of course this is not to say that the Midrash on the death of Moses is a direct counterattack on Apollonius or Epictetus. But the Midrash is aware of a world where, as Martin Nilsson once put it, a time came when "The ancient gods were tottering. . . . Men began to worship personages in authority." Even that ambiguous characterization, *ish ha-Elohim, anthrōpos tou theou* (or, *anthrōpos theou*), as the Greek Bible translates with admirable literalness, is evidently not without its risks, for the Targum insists that it means "prophet of the Lord," not just man of God or divine man, whatever that might mean.[48] It was a natural question: Should such a one die? At one point Moses defended himself thus, "Did You not put me to the test when the golden calf was made and I destroyed it? Why is it necessary for me to die?"[49] Moses doesn't seem to

---

46. Epictetus, II, 22:17 (LC, I, 397). Cf. R. Aqiba in *Mekilta, Ba-Ḥodesh* 10 (II, 277, lines 10–12). Cf. F. de Coulanges, *The Ancient City* (Garden City, NY, n.d.) 152.

47. 8:5, LC, II, 281; cf. 3:18 (LC, I, 269).

48. M. P. Nilsson, *A History of Greek Religion* (2nd ed.; New York, 1964), 285; and note how he goes on (286ff.) to review the historical development—which is almost a confirmation of what the late Harold Rosenberg once observed (*The New Yorker*, 14 April 1975, p. 77), "In the absence of a supernatural order, men are impelled to seek the aid of supernatural powers. If religion is the opium of the people, the fading of religion turns people toward opium."

In the second century, to describe someone as *theos* probably did not mean too much; on the other hand, neither was it altogether meaningless. And, as A. D. Nock said, "The words a man uses do in religion also use him" (*Essays on Religion and the Ancient World* [Oxford, 1972], 1.61). To one of an entirely different commitment—on the sidelines, as it were, of the official or popular religions—to witness the easygoing and loose use of terms or conduct that ought to express reverence but doesn't, was bound to serve as warning; beware of this happening in our own midst. I'm tempted to say that one reason Jews and Christians refused to take pagan worship seriously is that not infrequently they beheld pagans themselves adopting an indifferent or flippant attitude towards gods and sanctuaries (Nock, op. cit., 59).

On *ish ha-Elohim* (Deut. 33:1; cf. Josh. 14:6; Ps. 90:1, Ezra 3:2) cf. *Sifre Deut.* 342, p. 393 and ARNB, pp. 95f.; and the very listings may suggest (at least in part) that the Rabbis are eager to point out that even as regards this expression, Moses is not unique. Cf. Ginzberg, *Legends*, VI, 166, n. 965. As for the biblical *ish ha-Elohim*, see now J. A. Holstein in *HUCA* 48 (1977): 69–81, esp. 74f.

As to the recurring Greek and targumic renderings of *ish ha-Elohim*, cf. these versions of the biblical verses cited by *Sifre Deut.*, ibid., and all others listed in Mandelkern's *Concordance*.

49. I *Petirat Moshe*, 118.

understand that not *his* motives are suspect but the impulse and attitude of his people to him. Therefore he must die, with honors as all the righteous die, but not in a unique manner. Moses himself had proclaimed "that the Lord alone is God, there is none beside Him" (Deut. 4:35, II *Petirat Moshe*, VI, 78); consequently *His* sovereign will shall be done (though it might fill Him, too, with inexpressible grief!).[50]

Are we to say then that for the Midrash there is nothing unique about Moses? The conclusion of the *Midrash Petirat Moshe*[51] suggests otherwise, seems indeed prepared to have God adopt some of the appeals made earlier by Moses and at that time dismissed by Him.[52] Once Moses has made his peace with the death sentence and his soul is taken from him, God begins to weep, the [225] Midrash informs us; and not only God but heaven and earth and all the orders of Creation, all with appropriate biblical verses of lament. At this point Metatron[53] attempts to comfort God; he says to the Lord, "Master of the universe, while he was alive Moses was Yours, and now that he's dead he's still Yours," that is, he's still at Your service;[54] why weep then?

But God responds:

It's not for Moses only that I mourn[55] but for Moses and Israel. For [Israel] angered Me many times, and in their behalf he would offer up prayer and placate Me. He said of Me, "that the Lord alone is God in heaven above and on the earth below [there is no other, *'od*] (Deut. 4:39). I in turn therefore bear witness[56] that "never again (*'od*) did there arise in Israel a prophet like Moses whom the Lord singled out face to face" (Deut. 34:10).

For the Midrash even Metatron misses the point. Moses is indeed still in God's service. But what was unique in the life of Moses was his role as Israel's advocate on frequent critical occasions before a God given to anger, and his teaching Israel[57] that only the Lord is God, none else.[58] Now Israel's intercessor

50. See also, for example, *Midrash Eleh Ezkerah* in *Bet ha-Midrasch*, II, 67. On dualism reflected by the "original" *Assumption of Moses*, see Loewenstamm (n. 1), pp. 155–57.

51. I and II; they are not identical, but they are in agreement.

52. Cf., e.g., I *Petirat Moshe*, 117.

53. I *Petirat Moshe*, 129, and other midrashim (in *Ginzé Midrash*, 223: Michael). On Metatron, cf. G. Scholem, *Major Trends in Jewish Mysticism* (New York, 1961), 67–70; idem, *Gnosticism*, chap. 7; idem, *Kabbalah* (New York, 1974), 377–81. (Is Metatron deliberately introduced here to emphasize that no second deity exists?)

54. On the expression *shel-lak* "was/is Yours," cf. *Tg. Onqelos* for Num. 8:14b.

55. Text, *mitnaḥem* (and so, too, in *Deut. R.*, ed. Lieberman, 42), as euphemism. Should one understand: "for *God* and Israel?"

The exchange between Metatron and God does not occur in II *Petirat Moshe*. In the *Tanḥuma* midrashim, *wa-Ethanan* (also *Deut. R.*, ed. Lieberman, 41f.), it does appear along with an explanatory parable in God's reply.

56. II *Petirat Moshe*, 78 *meqalles* ("praise, hail"). Cf. *Deut. R.* 11:5, 119b.

57. Note how this thought is expressed (paraphrased?) in *Ginzé Midrash*, 224.

58. It may be that the play on the verses with the word *'od* is intended only as a peroration on an auspicious note. These verses do not follow the exchange between Metatron and God in *Tanḥuma* midrashim, etc. Is the emphasis, regardless of the appearance God adopts on

is gone, the great teacher, *safra rabba*, is taken away. The death of Moses is so great a loss (to God and Israel), even the Almighty, by whose decree the man Moses dies, cannot hold back His tears. Moses had to die, but not because he deserved to die: no longer any mention of "waters of Meribah," of belonging to a faithless generation.

The death is not punitive. It is even regrettable. This the divine regret,[59] is the specific midrashic addition to the biblical account. In Scripture the sentence on Moses is pronounced with majestic severity. "And die on the mountain that you are about to ascend" (Deut. 32:50). "Go up to the summit of Pisgah and gaze about . . . for you shall not go across yonder Jordan" (Deut. 3:27). In the Midrash, on the other hand, what is heard is not only God's verdict but God's grief. A transposition has taken place—as often in haggadic midrash, especially on tragic occasions—from the heavenly to the paternal. The petitions of Moses and their denial are still audible, but now there is also the mourning Voice of the Lord for His favorite:

בכה עליו הקב"ה והתחיל לקונן עליו ...
מי יקום לי עם מרעים
מי יתיצב לי עם פועלי און

The Holy One, blessed be He, wept over him and began to keen, "Who will rise up before Me[60] when men are evil, who will stand up before Me in behalf of wrong-doers? (Ps. 94:16).

We owe this insight of course (as we owe the earlier dialogues between Moses and God) to the homilist, who felt that, although Scripture said nothing about it, over the death of Moses God could not be less distressed than Israel. It is perhaps the only way that he, the homilist, and his audience could be persuaded anew that "The Rock! His deeds are perfect . . . all His ways are just; a faithful God, never false" (Deut. 32:4).[61]

different occasions (*Pesiqta Kahana*, ed. B. Mandelbaum, 223f.), it is always He and none but He? Or simply, only God is God, not Moses?

59. Plus the long give-and-take, of course. For examples of divine regret in Scripture, cf., e.g., Gen. 6:6f., or Amos 7 (several times). In our midrash, the notion of regret is not an outgrowth of disappointment with Moses, but the contrary: he deserves better!

60. Such is the midrashic interpretation. Who (in the future) will rise up before Me as advocate for those who have done wrong.

61. Dr. Judith S. Neaman has graciously called my attention to a woodcut from the Cologne Bible showing the burial of Moses, reproduced on p. 199 of Gustav Davidson, *A Dictionary of Angels* (New York, 1967), from James Strachan, *Pictures from a Mediaeval Bible* (Boston, 1961):63, fig. 49: on left, God in the act of interring Moses; in center and on right two assisting angels, presumably Michael and Gabriel (or "Zagzagel"). Moses' hands are crossed (but not across his chest: I *Petirat Moshe*, 129, line 5). Another illustration from the Leon Bible (12th century, Spain) in *Encyclopaedia Judaica* (Jerusalem, 1972) 5. 1426. And I am especially grateful to Professor Roland M. Frye for bringing to my attention the paper "Moses Shown the Promised Land," by A. Heimann, in the *Journal of the Warburg and Courtauld Institutes* 34 (1971), 321–24; plates 52–53.

There's no lineage like right conduct, no legacy like trustworthiness.

Foreword to *Hebrew Ethical Wills*, edited by Israel Abrahams

I

[1] The introduction of a beautiful Hebrew book, *Mesillat Yesharim (The Highway of the Upright)*, opens with the following words by the author, Moshe Hayyim Luzzatto (1707–47):

> Author to reader: I have not composed this work to teach people what they do not already know, but to remind them . . . of what is well known to them indeed. For most of what I say is nothing more than what most people do know and have absolutely no doubts about. But what is said in the following pages is constantly ignored, most often forgotten, *because* it is common knowledge and obvious. That is why no profit will be derived from a single reading of this book, for quite likely after such reading the intelligent reader will find little that is new. Only constant reading and rereading will prove beneficial. Then the reader will recall those things that naturally tend to be forgotten and take to heart the obligations he tends to ignore.

The frustration felt by Luzzatto accompanies or haunts every moralist: what he wishes to say has been said, he knows, hundreds of times before and is therefore hardly audible any longer. Virtue is [2] praised in literature of remote antiquity, as far back as the third millennium before our era, and even then is probably repetition. There is no lack of later parallels for Babylonian-Assyrian counsels of wisdom like

> Unto your opponent do no evil;
> Your evildoer recompense with good. . . .
> Do not slander, speak what is fine.
> Speak no evil, tell what is good.

Similarly at a later date in China:

> To the good I act with goodness;
> To the bad I also act with goodness:
> Thus goodness is attained.

Such counsel is hard to pay attention to even when it is delivered orally, when the words can be related to the emphasis created by the speaker's gestures and facial expression and voice-pitch. Read in printed text or written document, the response almost inevitably is *déjà entendu*.

All moralistic discourse is at a disadvantage, however, not only because it says nothing new. Novelty or lack of novelty as such is not ultimately the determining factor. We are capable of revisiting certain paintings, granted not endlessly but at least many times, or rereading certain poems or listening again to some musical compositions, with considerable (though not necessarily the same kind of) enjoyment. On the other hand, moral treatises fail to affect us this way because what they say is not only not new, but even when we listen with only half an ear we know that they are an invasion into the most private interiors of our nervous system. They not only impinge on our esthetic or intellectual [3] receptiveness. They attack us in the secret regions where the total personality has already settled down in the habits and tastes and excuses it prefers, and does not want to be disturbed. To change these is more than addition or variation of understanding. It is mutation, possibly forced reclamation, of human character. Since ethical warnings aim to upset what has become customary and comfortable, it takes more than one telling to get the painful message across. The necessary repetition, even if tolerated out of politeness, doesn't make listening easier.

And there is this, too, about repetition. Everyone repeats. Painters look at a landscape with eyes that have looked and look at earlier pictures ("looking alone [at nature] has never sufficed to teach an artist his trade"—E. H. Gombrich), and even as they compose, composers study earlier compositions and, wittingly or unwittingly, borrow—here the position of a tree or a hill, there a chord or motif. But principally the effect the artist is after is originality, or at least novelty; and that can emerge from the successful transformation of the loan-image or musical bar into individual statement: by free association, by subduing or salience, by disguising. The artist strives to become a creator.

Moralists likewise repeat. They likewise read earlier moralists and take over from them: vocabulary, illustrations, rhetoric of persuasion, the subject headings that require more than a single review. The moralist, too, seeks to convert what he has borrowed into personal declaration; but theoretically his principal ambition is not originality. Nor is it to increase our capacity for (spiritual) pleasure or the extension of our enlightenment. The moralist wants to rehabilitate the inner as well as the outer man. [4] He wishes to to be a *re*former. With little self-consciousness, therefore, he repeats—sometimes verbatim—what has been said before, for he feels that until man is remade, the inherited appeals are not outdated. (How often has one been advised to reread Psalms or *Pirqe Abot?*) His aim is almost exclusively didactic, practive, as they would have said in the sixteenth and seventeenth centuries. In his own name the moralist will say again what has been said, because to him that still sounds urgent. Maybe someone else will finally hear. How many times have you been told . . . , he likes to say, as though that helps. Sometimes he may not even trouble to transpose what he took over. It might almost take him by surprise to find out that he has said something not said before.

One word more about moralists: While in their formal treatises they exhibit different approaches to their theme—some are content simply to appropriate terms of the classical midrashic-talmudic homilies and anecdotes; others, a combination of the midrashic-talmudic teachings and philosophical argument; and still others, kabbalistic demonstrations and reinforcement—the tone of voice they adopt is, if not uniform, then predictable and seldom dispassionate. It is paternal, experienced (no one is better informed of the subtle devastations of sin than the saints: Isaiah seems to have known the names of every dangle and bangle of Jerusalem flirts), threatening, and beseeching. The very literature they create encourages those who take it seriously to address their own children similarly in both private and semiprivate communications.

Of course fathers have "always" exhorted their sons to choose the right course of life. The biblical [5] historian (1 Kings 2:1–4) reports that when David was close to death, he instructed his son and successor, Solomon, not only to settle some old scores but to mind the following:

> I am going the way of all the earth; be strong and show yourself a man. Keep the charge of the Lord your God, walking in His ways and following His laws, His commandments, His rules, and His admonitions as recorded in the Teaching of Moses, in order that you may succeed in whatever you undertake and wherever you turn. Then the Lord will fulfill the promise that He made concerning me: "If your descendants are scrupulous in their conduct, and walk before Me faithfully, with all their heart and soul, your line on the throne of Israel shall never end" (JPS new translation, with permission).

Back in the third-second century before our era there appeared a Jewish work that Byzantine scribes called "The Testaments of the Twelve Patriarchs" (E. J. Bickerman). In it each of the sons of Jacob (the Fathers of the twelve tribes of Israel) is represented as repenting of some transgression (when that is relevant) and proceeding at once to admonish his children to avoid sin, to beware of the spirit of deceit and envy, to keep the law of God, to fear the Lord and love their neighbor: "For he that feareth God and loveth his neighbor, cannot be smitten by the spirit of Beliar, being shielded by the fear of God." And much more along these lines.

The Talmud, too, preserves several brief obituary accounts of sages who in their last hours teach their students a lesson to remember all their lives. For example,

> "May you fear Heaven as much as you fear flesh and blood." "Only that much?" "Would it were that! Whenever a man commits a transgression, [6] what does he say? I hope nobody sees me!" (Babylonian Talmud, Berakot 28b).

In other words, it may well be that those who were reflective and articulate, and had responsibilities to hand on, always and everywhere spoke to their descendants and successors in hortatory words which they hoped would be heeded in the future. But it is a fair guess (not certainty) that the *writing down* of ethical testaments by individuals for the reading on the part of their immediate family and kin (though they might sometimes wish for a wider circle, too) became something of a "general" practice, a kind of adopted, personal ritual, only after moralistic *treatises* began to circulate. ("In the Geniza there are no ethical wills, a document so frequent in later centuries"— S. D. Goitein.) The formal, written treatises would have provided a model of themes that should be uppermost in a person's mind as he thinks about guiding principles for a righteous life. Not that multitudes of virtuous admonitions were unavailable in the classical sources, nor are quotations from these lacking in the written, informal testaments. But the written testaments suggest the development of a genre, a more or less distinctive form of composition, beyond the ad hoc address. Once moralistic treatises began to be read, a focus was provided and even, one might say, a table of contents, a concentrated assembly of directives that a human being required and could consult if he was not to disgrace his life in this world now and had hopes of the world to come.

Here finally were systematic works for inculcation of moral conduct: memorandums for immediate and future performances. The author of moralistic treatises gave to the writer of private testaments a [7] rhetorical example to imitate, to adapt to his particular condition, to invent variations on. The testaments gathered together by Israel Abrahams in this volume are thus a refraction of the whole tradition of Jewish moralistic expression, and at the same time completely personal admonitions to intimates. One may be a scholar but now he speaks chiefly as parent. One may be a simple man but he is not an illiterate parent; he has obviously read, if not a lot then a little.

II

Israel Abrahams called these testaments "Hebrew ethical wills" (he may actually have invented the expression "ethical wills"). In Hebrew, testaments that are drawn up in contemplation of death are called simply *ṣawwaot* (in the singular, *ṣawwaah*), "commands," "injunctions" (to the survivors), and of course may refer to material inventories as well as ethical instructions. The *Oxford English Dictionary*, relating the term to law, defines testaments as "a formal declaration, usually in writing, of a person's wishes as to the disposal of his property after his death; a will." *Hebrew Ethical Wills* is not an unattractive title for the collection of writings in the following pages. For here, too, is a declaration of wishes, if not as regards the disposal of property, then as regards the attempt to transfer magnanimity. To avoid possible misunderstanding, however, it's not so much the word "testament" or "will" that must detain us, as the word "ethical."

For us, perhaps not altogether justifiably, the [8] ethical is taken as the rubric for rules governing only the relations of human beings to one another. Regardless of philological or philosophical explorations of the terms "ethics" and "morality," for the post-Enlightenment man the ethical can be autonomously prescriptive of human conduct—as though, so to speak, the second half (or three-fifths or more) of the Ten Commandments would be acceptable and compelling without the first. There is the human domain, and it can be ordered without reference to any authority beyond human sanction. What relates to God is another, independent province of speculation and actions, although interhuman relationships interest Him too. At all events, according to this view, ethics and ritual piety draw on separate sources of imperatives.

The recognition that there are indeed different provinces of conduct is far from new in historic Judaism. Long ago the biblical prophets underscored the fact that ceremonial fasting, for example, could never serve as a substitute for feeding the hungry and letting the oppressed go free; and to this day Jews recite the passage, from which this example is taken, in their *ritual!* Prophetical illustrations are too familiar to need review. More immediately plainspoken is the talmudic formulation of the categories "man vis-à-vis God" and "man vis-à-vis his fellowman": *ben adam la-maqom, ben adam la-havero;* thus it is said toward the end of the Mishnah treatise Yoma:

> Sins of a man against God—that's what the Day of Atonement atones for; sins of a man against his fellowman—that the Day of Atonement does not atone for unless the guilty one has first made his peace with his fellow.

The [9] consciousness of the presence of this twofoldness never disappears.

Nevertheless, the ethical in Judaism, at least until modern times (and even then not always), is not an independent field of values. It is not a secular exercise with its own momentum and accomplishments. *Ben adam la-maqom* and *ben adam la-havero* are a description or classification, if you wish, of the contents of the whole Law, but both are regarded as equally the statement of one divine will. Both serve each other. Both are of religious origin and concern. There is one overarching expectation to which the obligations to God and to man belong. It follows, then, that the moralist sees nothing incongruous about including in one and the same treatise, or testament, exhortations about prayer at the proper hour, a married woman's monthly religious duties, the halakhic regulations of animal slaughter for meats, the appointment of a beadle to announce the hour for the beginning of the Sabbath, as well as self-evidently moral warnings: Be sure to visit the sick; honor your wife; set aside a tithe of your income for charity; abandon anger and do not lose your temper; remember that truth and righteousness (= honest dealing) are the ornaments of the soul, that controversy is an abomination, that whiskey will undo you, that when in a rage, husband and wife should not make love, that from the poor the physician is not to demand a fee. And more of the same. The mood may be summed up in the words of one father: My son, remember, "He brought you into this world, not you Him; for He has no need of you, but you need Him!" (See *Midrash Debarim Rabbah*, ed. Lieberman, 70).

[10] It is true that all the examples brought together above, the ritualistic along with the moralistic, do not come from the same testament but are lifted ad lib from many selections in the volumes. But the choosing and the choice are not unfair to them. Not one of the testators whom the reader will meet would have denied that both the ritual fastidiousness demanded by the Law and what we call moral conduct derive from One Sovereign. For them, the human is never separated from the divine inspection, even at its most human. A philosophical moralist (in a well-known passage in Bahya ibn Pakuda, *Hovot ha-Levavot*, of the eleventh century) may be upset by intellectuals who take pains with recherché and complicated religiolegalistic problems but neglect to explore fervently the duties that are the piety of heart and soul: "You ask about something where ignorance won't kill you; do you know what you have to know about those commands where ignorance is fatal?" This is natural impatience with those for whom only complex intellectual concerns are respectable. Is a milk spoon in a meat pot a weightier matter, protests a father who is trying to persuade his son to study philosophy, than questions about the existence or unity of God? He is not minimizing the seriousness of milk spoons in meat pots; he is pleading for what he considers a proper balance. No one within the framework of the classical Jewish tradition is tempted to propose a dualism of ritual obligations and ethical doctrine or of the strictly legal and the unlimited humane. All the statutes of God bear His imprint. Of course the unity is a biblical inheritance. And the writers of the testaments accept the legacy.

III

[11] They may be at one in the fundamental assumptions and in some modes of rhetoric, and I think it would not be unjust to say that taken all in all and scrambled together—particularly if they are (unwisely) all read in one sitting—an astonishing consensus could be achieved, to the point of monotony. Fear God, obey His commandments, live honestly and forgivingly, avoid the disgraceful and demoralizing, and remember what I taught you all my life. This may summarize a characteristic last will of a Jew to his children. Except that we may add one more detail that deserves notice: biblical verses are on the tips of their tongues and at their fingertips. And it is not as a literary "showing off," some flourish to add elegance to their own sentiments and speech, though

it is invoked as confirmation. They talk Bible. For when they express themselves in Hebrew, it is virtually their deepest reflex and at the same time their
most precise, indispensable, natural vocabulary: they have made it their own
voice, all of them. We have here a consequence of pedagogy from midrashic
centuries on. If you have something to say, get the Scriptures to help you out.

My son, cast your burden on the Lord [Ps. 55:23] and what you regard as very far off
from you, may be ready at hand. Know that your mouth is not yours nor is your
hand within your own reach. For everything that will be done is in *God's* hand.
Always take this to heart, "Unless the Lord builds the house, its builders labor on it
in vain" [Ps. 127:1]; but if the Lord builds it, those who would wreck it labor in vain.
Unless the Lord watches over the city, the watchman keeps vigil [12] in vain [ibid.];
but if the Lord watches over a city, the watchman goes to unnecessary troubles.

So one father, now a second:

And now, behold, I am going the way of all the earth [1 Kings 2:2]. Take care not to
be lured away and turn [Deut. 11:16] from the course in which I directed you, and
the Lord be wrathful with me [!] on your account [cf. Deut. 3:26]. But, if you will
obey me faithfully and keep my covenant [Exod. 19:5], know that reverence for the
Lord will be your treasure [cf. Isa. 33:6] and in the grave my lips will always whisper
[Babylonian Talmud, Yebamot 97a] in your behalf. My prayer will be set out in
order before the Lord for your sake at all times. He will slake your thirst in drought
and you shall be like a watered garden, like a spring whose waters do not fail [cf. Isa.
58:11].

There is an artfulness, a self-consciousness in the second selection that is
almost entirely absent from the first, in which one doesn't hop from one biblical
book to the next and figures of speech are minimal. But it would be a mistake to
treat the latter selection as only contrived and belabored prose. (The talmudic
phrase is no departure from the norm.) The testator is not posturing. These
men reach up for biblical speech (and talmudic expression) because it is within
easy reach of their own manners of speaking as a result of a lifetime of prayer.
Even when they are not scholars, by constant synagogue attendance they have
become thoroughly familiar with psalms that are recited daily, with the Scriptures that are read in recurring cycles, as well as with the interpretations of the
most popular commentators. The writers of the testaments are hardly "quoting," or if they are, there's nothing unexpected or [13] dramatic about it; they
are using the sacred dialect they were raised in from childhood on. This, plus
the constancy of the universal themes of moral instruction, gives to these
testaments a quality of sameness.

But they are not the same. I do not mean (what is true enough) that
sometimes we find touches of superstition in one, or more than one, that we do
not find in others—

It was my practice Friday afternoons to recite the afternoon prayer (*minḥah*) with a congregational quorum and after that, as an unbroken rule, to do my fingernails . . . , and in honor of the Sabbath, another unbroken rule, to go to the bathhouse. How fortunate is he who in the ritual bath can concentrate on some mystical meditations and confessions of what he did the past week.

Or again: "Don't spend the night alone in any house. For then Lilith is disposed to attack." Or:

My father, of blessed memory, wrote in his book: When the time comes for a man to die, Satan stands by his side and tempts him with, "Deny [forsake] the God of Israel." At that moment, God spare us, a man is not in control of his mind. Therefore, as of now, I stand up to declare before the Great and Blessed Name and His Shekhinah and the court on high and the court below, and I solemnly proclaim that if at that moment I say anything improper, Heaven forbid, what I then say is null and void . . . . Only what I am now saying is binding.

Superstition is revealing but not singular, and every age, rationalistic ones no less, has its favorite fears and hocus pocus, springing from the terrors of life and death. Especially from the terrors of death. What is noteworthy indeed is that although we are dealing with last testaments in this volume, there is not more of superstitious conceit in them than we [14] find. And some may have advanced beyond superstition regardless of what they were in origin. They have by now become a hand held out tremblingly for supererogative assistance: "With a rope drag my coffin to the grave, and after each four ells stop and wait a bit. Do this seven times up to the grave and may this be atonement for my sins." To break the habit of slander and taking the Lord's name in vain it helps to put up a tablet over the doors of rooms, with the inscription (Exod. 20:7), "Thou shalt not take the name of the Lord thy God in vain." In the movie *The Garden of the Finzi-Continis*, over the entrance to the dining room of Giorgio's family there was a plaque with the verse, "The Lord our God be with us" (1 Kings 8:57), in Hebrew.

But individuality breaks through notwithstanding a unanimity of assent to traditional values. Partly this is because of differences of personality and social background; partly, no doubt, because some forms of conduct appeal especially to one's temperament; partly, too, because one has been offended by particular exhibitions of misconduct. One father can't stop reminding his son that it is very important to write Arabic beautifully if he is to succeed in life (this was true enough in his time and place). His testament, which as a matter of fact he worked on for many years with an author's eye and polish, is a mirror of life in a well-to-do ménage where almost no tension is visible between piety and the graces (but appearances may be deceptive). The author is even something of a bore as he quotes endlessly from the poetry of Samuel ha-Nagid—lines that were doubtless fresh and sparkling once upon a time and now read like wilted middle-class practical advice. Needless to say, someday we too will sound [15] like that: Nothing goes out of date faster than the up-to-date.

Then there is the testament of a grandfather with almost no pretensions to outstanding accomplishments. He is not without learning, for what pious Jew would be without it unless he was the victim of some outrageous misfortunes or heartbreaking retardation. But there is nothing in what this man writes to hint at extraordinary scholarly attainments. An average Jew, Abrahams calls him, but the average is high. He urges his sons and daughters (note well!) to behave as befits a decent person, to be careful with Sabbath observances, not to overindulge in games of chance (would that my children gave it up alto-gether!), to be humble and forgiving but to resist false accusations against themselves, not to be extravagant in expenditures for food but to dress well (though eschewing gentile styles and buckles!), to engage in study, to keep away from slander and falsehood and envy. From all this it is difficult to distinguish the individual features of a person. But as he closes, something happens. For a moment the instructions still sound as though they might have come from any number of men like himself; suddenly a vibrato:

> Bury me to the right side of my saintly father, of blessed memory. And even if it's a bit crowded there, I can depend on my father's love that he will draw himself in to make room for me to be beside him. And if under no circumstance will it be possible to lie at the right side of my father, try his left side, or near my grandmother Mistress Yuta. And if that's impossible, bury me by the side of my daughter.

His immediate family apart, and even they not certainly, who without that last sentence in this last [16] will would have guessed the grief our gentle man carried with him to the grave? Or the love of his own father *he* still feels?

Another man wants his children always to keep in their homes a bench on which is to lie a volume of the Talmud or a talmudic composition, so that the first thing met with on entering the house will be a summons to study. So frequent is the reminder to study Torah in these testaments, by the way, that its occasional chance absence goes unnoticed at first. The Gaon of Vilna advises his womenfolk to keep away from the synagogue (and other public places obviously), because whenever women get together they gossip, and besides, envy is stirred up by the sight of other women in their elegant and modish dress. He pleads with his mother (whom he loves and who, he knows, is saintly) and his wife to live peacefully with each other. One man is grateful that he had a private room to himself for prayer and meditation and thanks God when his snuffbox falls out of his hands yet doesn't break. And still another, on the night before his execution, composes a long poem (it is not a testament, strictly speaking) to remind the zodiac of all he had studied in a very short lifetime.

All the moral testaments are a reaffirmation of what all moral writers and preachers have emphasized and defended in their treatises. But since in his "last" will a person chooses to talk about those moral injunctions that best correspond with his own fears and past experiences and ideas of right and wrong (what else is there to talk about at the irreversible transition?), his testament becomes a unique statement. He may even knowingly say what others have said, but because *he* says it and wants to say it, [17] and may say it with an accentuation of his own, his message is genuinely his.

IV

Even today a person frequently draws up his last will long before his last days and then in the course of time changes his original text in various ways. The same is true of course among authors of Hebrew ethical wills. A quarter of a century may sometimes elapse between a man's composition of his will and the day of his death. It seems fair to say, therefore, that the testament he finally leaves represents those ideals of his that he wants made explicit and memorable. His most cherished commitments are now on display and to be put on record: This is what I want of you, this is what I stand for, this is the counsel I transfer to you. "Reread this book at least once a week, and all the chapter headings at the beginning," the anonymous author of *The Ways of the Righteous (Orḥot Ṣaddiqim)* recommends ("end of the 15th to early 16th century . . . either in the Italian or mideast region"—H. Z. Dimitrovsky). In the same spirit fathers are prompted to ask their sons and other members of the family to "read this communication once a day" or once a week, "along with two other testaments which I reproduce below"! One man hoped that his testament might be printed as a preface to the prayer book, for all to contemplate. "My son," one father will say—and in a sense this is implied by all of them—

> remember me at all times. Let the image of me be before your eyes and may it never be withdrawn from before your eyes. Don't develop a taste for doing what you [18] know I abhor. Be with me at all times. Keep my commandments and you will live. May the following verse of Scripture be on your lips, "I am only a sojourner in the land; do not hide Your commandments from me" [Ps. 119:19]. Then the good and gracious God will increase your tranquillity and prolong your life in pleasantness. Then will your honor and good repute thrive as you wish and as is the wish of your father who begot you.

From the monitions and pleas to the son emerges the outline of the father's self-portrait, including a measure of self-approval, even when he does not spare himself in self-criticism. A last will and testament thus attempts to preserve for descendants and disciples the image one wishes to leave of himself. The ways of the fathers are urged in part because they are the fathers' ways, and because the fathers want to be remembered as having always practiced what they now preach. In dreams our vices catch up with us; in fantasy our virtues grow to more than life-size. In exhorting or reprimanding others, there is a little of both. By definition sons fall short:

Why don't you walk in the way of your fathers, and why isn't fear of the Lord before your eyes always? Why don't you study His Torah day and night? Why don't you get to the synagogue early morning and evening?

Another father has still other complaints: "Thank God that you are God-fearing in all your ways, as I know, except in the matter of honoring your father!" He continues peevishly:

When you wrote your letters or composed poems to send to another country, you never showed me a thing. . . . And when I used to say to you, "Show me," you used to say to me, "Why do you want to see it?" . . . Why, R. Zerahiah of blessed memory, who was sui generis in [19] his day, and was more gifted than I, from the time he knew me never wrote a letter or composed a poem to send to anyone without showing it to me first.

Typical parental talk that sons will later adopt with their sons, spontaneously too, and it will not be confined to the contents of testaments. But this forward projection of self, natural enough at any time and well-nigh inescapable in closest relationships ("Let the boy discover the truth for himself" is either humbug or callousness), is especially likely to take place as thoughts of death come to mind.

For although there may be varieties of terror crowding in as one tries to imagine extinction, it is intolerable (so long as there is life) to acquiesce to being silenced—not to being silent, but to being silenced. There is still something left unsaid, still something to tell one's flesh of his own flesh or mind of his mind. And within those to whom right attitude and action and loyalty to the faith of the fathers are the supreme government of life, there is a compulsive wish to speak from beyond the grave. They know how close lies chaos to the disorders of the living, and they want the volume of their warning not to be reduced. They want to be heard across the deadening silence. Read me once a week or once a month, the fathers plead. Maybe this will save the descendants, and maybe this will protect the one who leaves the world from becoming zero.

The Hebrew ethical will is not mere valediction but an audacious attempt at continuing speech from fathers in the grave to children in a reckless world. The teacher's absence is not the end of instruction. It was said a long time ago, When the dead are quoted, their lips move.

THEMATIC STUDIES

Several Sidelights of a Torah Education in Tannaite and Early Amoraic Times

[176] In his magisterial way, as he summarizes the laws of *talmud Torah*, of Torah study, Maimonides writes:

> Every Jew (*kl 'yš myśr'l*) is obliged to study Torah, be he poor or rich, enjoying good health or in pain, young or so old as to be failing in strength—even if he is so poor as to be dependent on charity and [in his begging] must make the rounds from one house to another; and even if he is a family man with wife and children [to support], he must set aside fixed times for study of the Torah, day and night. . . . Until when must one study? Until the day he dies. . . .[1]

Of course Maimonides is not inventing, much as this view is doubtless congenial to his temperament. He is stating in concentrated form (that's why it sounds so apodictic) what is either stated explicitly or implied in several places of the Talmud. As the commentators observe, what Maimonides has in mind here is very likely such passages as the *baraita* (*tnw rbnn*, the tannaite statement) in B. Yoma 35b, that on the Day of Judgment neither the poor man nor the rich man nor the philanderer will have a real alibi for having neglected to study—the poor man was no poorer than Hillel was, when he first settled in the Holy Land; the rich one did not own as much real estate and other properties to take up all his time and thoughts, as Rabbi Eleazar ben Ḥarsom owned; and the

---

1. Maimonides, Code, Book of Knowledge, Hilkot Talmud Torah, 1:8, 10. See also ,the reaffirmation in Joseph Karo's Code, Yoreh De'ah, 246:1, 3. And note how Rabban Yoḥanan ben Zakkai is quoted in Midrash Tannaim, 58. Is the last clause really R. Yoḥanan's, or is it the addition of the compiler of Midrash ha-Gadol? Even if it should be the latter, the compiler of the Midrash ha-Gadol has caught Yoḥanan's emphasis correctly. See ARNA, 58, top.

philanderer[2] had no more lusty an appetite or better opportunities than Joseph had in Potiphar's house.

[177] That many talmudic scholars were poor and supported themselves by menial occupations, Maimonides also asserts[3]—of course, again, on the basis of talmudic records. So too, he manages to persuade us that until the day of death one must study, by a neat exercise of biblical exegesis; for it is said in Deuteronomy 4:9, "Take utmost care and watch yourselves scrupulously" lest the [divine] "'*dbrym* fade from your mind as long as you live'; and so long as one does not engage in study, he *does* forget." Hence, to call a halt to study before one dies is to transgress.[4]

Needless to say, what such statements reflect is an ideal, perhaps in truth so lofty an ideal, that even most of those who would assent to it cheerfully would be unable to fulfill it. The significant thing, however, is that so extreme or hyperbolic a demand is not a priori dismissed as a manifest impossibility and therefore not to be taken seriously, or therefore to be excluded from codified programs for human conduct. A man's reach must exceed his grasp, or what's the Talmud for? In other words, the significant thing about the talmudic views which Maimonides adopts and organizes is that they do serve as ideals, that they are regarded as *feasible*.

And it's not as though talmudic Sages are ignorant of what's really going on in the world. "Here's the way it is (*bnwhg šb'wlm*)," they tell us; "of the thousand who start out with an education in Scripture, only a hundred go on further; of the hundred studying Mishnah, only ten go on further; of the ten studying Talmud, only one comes forth [to become an authority]."[5] One in a thousand therefore makes it—if that, we may add, not because we are cynical, but because *we* are not called upon to interpret the verse in Ecclesiastes (7:28), "I found only one human being in a thousand, and the one I found among so many was never a woman."[6]

What really takes place, then, is much less spectacular than what one might be tempted to derive from Maimonides' imperatives or some rococo haggadot. Nevertheless, only such imperatives make [178] comprehensible a number of halakic and haggadic passages in the midrashic-talmudic sources. For example: The Mishnah[7] declares that if one goes to recover something his father had lost and something his teacher had lost, he is first to recover what the teacher lost; only thereafter does he go to recover what his father lost: "for his father

2. That's what *rš'* means in that passage.
3. Op. cit., 1:9.
4. Cf. Haggahot Maimoniyyot on Hilkot Talmud Torah 1:10; Naḥmanides on Deut. 4:9. See also the statement by R. Jonathan in B. Shabbat 83b, on "never" staying away from the *bet midrash*, even in the hour of death. On the moving story of R. Akiba continuing to teach as *his son* was dying, see Śemaḥot VIII (ed. Zlotnick), 63.
5. Lev. R. 2:1, ed Margulies, p. 35; cf. Eccl. R. 7:28, and *here* we read, "(only) one of them comes forth to become an authority (*lhwr'h*)."
6. See *Five Megilloth and Jonah* (introductions by H. L. Ginsberg [Philadelphia, 1969]), 69.
7. Baba Meṣi'a 2:11. [Cf. M. Keritot, end.]

brought him [only] into this world; his teacher on the other hand brings him to the life of the world to come."[8] Again, if one's father and one's teacher were taken captive, first to be ransomed is the teacher; only after that is the father ransomed.

Talmudists will be quick to remind us that this is far from the last word on the subject,[9] and that already the Mishnah itself, on the spot, introduces a qualification or two. True enough. But the basic principle here involved—that my first responsibility is to him that teaches me Torah—is unmistakable. Does not the Mishnah in still another treatise[10] admonish me that *mwr' rbk kmwr' šmym*, that towards my teacher I must feel the same awe as I feel toward Heaven?

Or, an even bolder example: "Do thou toil away over the words of Torah," says a well-known treatise,[11] "and do not engage in idle matters." Then by way of explaining this proposal, the treatise continues as follows:

Once as Rabbi Simeon Ben Yoḥai went about visiting the sick, he came upon a man laid up with an affliction of bowel sickness, uttering blasphemies against the Holy One, blessed be He.

"*Racca* (wretch)!" Rabbi Simeon cried, "you should be beseeching mercy for yourself; yet you utter blasphemies!"

Said the man, "May the Holy One, blessed be He, remove the sickness from me and lay it on you!"

[Thereupon] Rabbi Simeon exclaimed: "Well has the Holy One, blessed be He, done with me, for I neglected the words of Torah and engaged in idle matters."

Even Solomon Schechter was baffled by this anecdote.[12] Who in the world of the talmudic Sages would call an act of lovingkindness [179] like visiting the sick[13] "idle matters"? Schechter therefore emended the text, and unwittingly almost made a barbarian out of Simeon ben Yoḥai. Simeon ben Yoḥai is often enough hard to take even without conjectured textual emendations. He is the man who felt (not altogether mistakenly) that Torah was for manna-eaters or those with guaranteed private incomes[14] who didn't have to work for a living. This reminds one of Breasted who, I'm told, when asked by a student, How does one become an Egyptologist? replied, "First, he must marry a rich woman." The correct reading of our talmudic story is fortunately preserved in

8. [Cf. Diogenes Laertius, V, 19.]
9. See Maimonides, Hilkot Talmud Torah, 5:1, and Kesef Mishneh and Leḥem Mishneh ad loc.
10. Pirqe 'Abot 4:12; cf. C. Taylor's commentary (*Sayings of the Jewish Fathers*) ad loc.
11. '*Abot de-Rabbi Natan*, ed. Schechter, Version A, 130.
12. Cf. J. Goldin, *The Fathers According to Rabbi Nathan* (New Haven, 1955), 219.
13. "Whose fruits one eats in this world, while the stock is laid up for him in the world to come"; cf. Baer, *Seder 'Abodat Yiśrael* (Schocken, 5697), 38f.
14. Mekilta, Wa-Yassa', III (ed. Lauterbach, II, 104). On Simeon ben Yoḥai discouraging scholars from physical labors, cf. Sifre Deut., 42, ed. Finkelstein, 90. [See also F. Rosenthal, *Knowledge Triumphant* (Leiden: Brill, 1970), 296.]

the Oxford manuscript and first edition of *'Abot de-Rabbi Natan*. And what the story tells us is that Simeon ben Yoḥai once had an experience which emphasized for him that so important is Torah study that, compared to it, even as meritorious an act as visiting the sick may be regarded as an "idle matter." Which is exactly what I would expect from Simeon ben Yoḥai.[15] So also, a father was not wrong when he complained to his son, "Look here, I sent you away to college to study, and not to spend your days piling up virtues. For that, we have plenty of corpses to bury in our own town!"[16] At all events, the value judgment [180] expressed by our story about Simeon ben Yoḥai, even if one were to take exception to it, is comprehensible only in terms of the injunction, Every Jew must study Torah till the day he dies. No wonder an ancient commentary on the saying, "Let all your deeds be for the sake of Heaven" has it that "for the sake of Heaven" equals "for the sake of Torah."[17] More radical still is God Himself. "Would they had forsaken Me," He says, "but kept My Torah."[18]

So much for the rhetoric in praise of Torah and Torah study, although on this theme one can go on seemingly endlessly; see, for example, the long chapter of talmudic and midrashic passages (174 pages) devoted to the theme of *talmud Torah* in volume 3 of H. G. Enelow's edition of *Menorat ha-Ma'or* (New York, 1931) by the fourteenth-century martyr Israel ibn Al-Nakawa.

---

15. Even in amoraic times, and in Babylonia, note what Raba said about R. Hamnuna taking a long time at *prayer!* B. Shabbat 10a. See also the perfectly intelligent question raised in B. Berakot 32b about the reported conduct of the "early saints."

16. Literally, "R. Abbahu sent his son R. Ḥanina to study Torah" (*yzky*, cf. Qorban ha-'Edah ad loc.) "in Tiberias. [Some people] came and reported to him that (R. Ḥanina) was occupying himself with acts of lovingkindness. [R. Abbahu thereupon] sent the following message to his son: 'Is it for lack of burial places in Caesarea that I sent you to Tiberias?'" P. Pesaḥim 3:7. The parallel passage occurs in P. Ḥagigah 1:7. See further S. Lieberman, *Hayerushalmi Kiphshuto* (Jerusalem, 1934), 425f.

I am unable to suppress the following (which is not entirely irrelevant even to our theme; cf. G. F. Moore, *Judaism*, II, 247), especially since I must acknowledge indebtedness in any event. The anecdote about R. Abbahu and his son I knew from some earlier studies, though I did not remember that it had to do with Abbahu. However, when I came to draw up the present footnotes, I could not recall where the story occurred, though I rummaged high and low. After four days of futile efforts, I finally telephoned Professor Lieberman long distance, and had only begun the anecdote when he interrupted with, "It's in Yerushalmi Pesaḥim 3:7, 30b; the parallel is in Yerushalmi Ḥagigah 1:7. Be sure to consult Ibn Shuaib's *Derashot* which has an interesting reading. See my *Yerushalmi Kiphshuto*." Now cf. George Foot Moore again. And on the importance of reviewing in order to remember, see also *ARNA*, 78. How terrible it is to forget, cf. R. Gamaliel, ibid., 76.

17. *ARNA*, 66.

18. Lam. R., Petiḥta 2, ed. Buber, 1b–2a, and cf. Buber's n. 12 (the correct reading is *hś'wr*).

Of course I do not mean to leave the impression that acts of lovingkindness were uniformly treated as of inferior status to the obligation to study Torah. Contrast, for example, the conduct of R. Judah bar 'Il'ai when a bridal procession passed by as he was teaching: *ARNA*, 19; *ARNB*, 22. Significantly, however, it seems that R. Judah feels called upon to explain his decision to his disciples (will they otherwise not understand?), and that his model was nothing less than God's conduct! (Lovingkindness, however, one always learns from God: B. Soṭah 14a, and cf. S. Schechter, *Some Aspects of Rabbinic Theology* (N.Y., 1936), 202f.).

If we move on now to passages *descriptive* of learning, primary and higher, as it was actually carried on, only sidelights are granted us. That is to say, no systematic account or even outline of the course of higher learning is preserved. Nor are we too much better off in regard to primary schooling. Our sources are much too often quiet where we wish they'd been more talkative, and maybe the reverse is also true. The kind of questions asked by S. D. Goitein,[19] for example, in connection with learning and education in late geonic and early post-geonic centuries, as reflected by the Genizah documents, is valid also for the tannaite and early amoraic times in Jewish Palestine: What was the curriculum? How was instruction carried on? How were students tested? Where and in what ways were so-called secular subjects taught?—mathematics, astronomy, zoology, aspects of human physiology—subjects which had to be studied if only to understand, or to determine, the halakah in pressing, practical [181] problems of living: the calendar, for example;[20] permitted and forbidden foods; conditions of likely impurity when husbands and wives must keep apart from each other; bodily blemishes which disqualified a marriage;[21] and so forth.

For some of these questions there are some and partial answers. In the elementary school, for instance the *bet ha-sefer*, the first things taught apparently were the recitation of the *Shema* and the *Tefillah*, and the Grace blessings—the *birkat ha-mazon*.[22] One also learned to write there, and presumably practised writing the alphabet forwards and backwards on a pinax[23]—which is somewhat reminiscent of primary Hellenistic education in Roman times, when "it was not enough to know the alphabet from alpha to omega. It had to be learned backwards, from omega to alpha and then both ways at once, $A\Omega, B\psi, \Gamma X, \ldots MN$."[24]

In his *History of Education in Antiquity* from which I have just now quoted, H. I. Marrou describes[25] how after learning the alphabet,

> the pupil went on to syllables; and, with the same passion for system, he was taught a complete list of them, in their proper order. No words were attempted until all the syllables had been combined in every possible way. The simplest came first: $\beta a, \beta \epsilon$, $\beta \eta, \beta \iota, \beta o, \beta \upsilon, \beta \omega \ldots$; $\gamma a, \gamma \epsilon, \gamma \eta \ldots$ up to $\psi a, \psi \epsilon, \psi \eta, \psi \iota, \psi o, \psi \upsilon, \psi \omega$; and these apparently were not simply pronounced according to their sound but by the name of each individual letter first and then as joined together—thus: *beta-alpha-ba; beta-ei-be; beta-eta-be* . . . .

19. *Sidre Ḥinuk* (Jerusalem, 1962), 143ff.; cf. 46f.
20. Note M. Rosh ha-Shanah 2:8 for the visual aids Rabban Gamaliel II had in his attic.
21. See, for example, M. Ketubot 7:7–10.
22. Note the question put by Yoḥanan ben Zakkai to Eliezer ben Hyrcanus when the latter appeared in Yoḥanan's school, *ARNB*, 30.
23. See *ARNA*, 29.
24. H. I. Marrou, *History of Education in Antiquity* (N. Y., 1956), 151.
25. Ibid.

Even today, there are men who surely had such first lessons in learning to read Hebrew from a textbook called *Reshit Da'at* and the opening pages of an edition of the traditional Jewish Prayerbook:[1] אָ, בְּ, בָּ, גְּ, גָ, דְּ, דָ, הְ, הָ, וְ, וָ and so on. Perhaps such instruction is still going on; my wife tells me that this is how she was taught to read English, close to fifty years ago in Tulsa, Oklahoma. There is even a Yiddish folk song nostalgically referring to this method of learning,[27] and I [182] think the mood it wishes to create is, Ah, those were the days! The method was doubtless common in the ancient Palestinian elementary school.[28]

For the child—the boy, that is[29]—formal elementary education began when he was about five[30] or six or seven;[31] and it was an immediately relevant, functional education: that is, the child learned the principal prayers he had to recite every day of his life; he learned Scripture, which taught him his history, not for the sake of learning history in the abstract, but to teach him whose descendant he was and what were the values and goals to be pursued in life, what was expected of him;[32] by the Pentateuch especially, but not exclusively, he was informed of the mandatory, the permitted, the forbidden. It was clearly the practice for children to memorize: "Tell me the verse you've learned by heart,"[33] an adult might say to a child. This was also excellent practice for the memorizing he would later do when and if he progressed to study of the Oral Law. It is possible that the boy spent as much as five years on biblical studies, till the age of ten,[34] when *ideally* he began the study of Mishnah. Until then, however, and with the preliminaries out of the way, he learned his Bible thoroughly. The scroll he learned from probably was not a copy of the best editions;[35] nevertheless, as we've said, he learned his Bible thoroughly. Even in St. Jerome's time (fourth century) one could not help being impressed by the

---

26. *Siddur Śefat 'Emet he-Ḥadash*, ed. A. Hyman (N.Y., 1936).

27. I don't know the title of the song, but the relevant lines go, *"kometz aleph aw, kometz bes baw, kometz gimmel gaw."*

28. Cf. also what is reflected by the halakic problem in M. Shabbat 12:3ff.

29. On the education of girls, see T. Perlow, *L'Éducation et l'enseignement chez les Juifs à l'époque talmudique* (Paris, 1931), 98–101. In sixteenth century Safed we hear of special teachers for women (and children) to teach them the liturgy and the prescribed benedictions: cf. S. Schechter, "Safed in the Sixteenth Century," *Studies in Judaism*, Second Series (Phila., 1908), 242 and n. 98 ad loc. S. D. Goitein, op. cit., 70, tells of a woman who knows part of Scripture by heart. On European (Ashkenazi) practice, see I. Twersky in *'Enṣiqlopedia Ḥinukit*, IV (the volume on the history of education), 260f.: a woman lectures even on Talmud. (For something similar in 12th century Baghdad, cf. S. Asaf, *Tequfat ha-Geonim* [Jerusalem, 1955], 116 and 129.)

30. PA 5:21, but the figures in that Mishnah may be schematized.

31. B. Baba Batra 21a.

32. Note what are the first things to teach the child when he begins to speak: note 52, p. 209 below. In Sifre Zuṭa, 288, it is said that in addition a father must teach his son Hebrew, lešon ha-qodeš.

33. Cf. B. Ḥagigah 15a–b. See also the interesting example of this in Esther R. 7:13, 13a.

34. PA 5:21.

35. Cf. S. Lieberman, *Hellenism in Jewish Palestine* [hereafter HJP] (N.Y., 1962), 22f.

stunt of some Jews "to recite all the [183] generations from Adam to Zerubbabel with such accuracy and facility, as if they were simply giving their names."[36]

One began as a rule with the Book of Leviticus;[37] what order was followed thereafter is nowhere indicated, I think. Yet a bright boy was evidently at home in all parts of the Bible; what is more, he knew how to turn a biblical verse or clause into gracious response. When,[38] on a visit to Rome, Rabbi Joshua ben Ḥananiah was told of a good-looking Jewish boy who had been taken captive, from Jerusalem possibly, he approached the lad and called out in the words of Isaiah (42:24), "Who gave up Jacob to the spoiler, and Israel to the robbers?" The lad replied promptly with the latter half of the verse, "Was it not the Lord, against whom we have sinned, in whose ways they would not walk, and whose Torah they would not obey?" To round out the story let me add that Joshua ransomed the boy and brought him home; and, according to some, the boy is supposed to be none other than Ishmael ben Elisha, a leading Tanna of the first half of the second century.

The thorough mastery of Scripture which was aimed at will explain in part a fact to which Professor S. Lieberman has called attention [184] in connection with some of his researches,[39] namely, that we find the talmudic rabbis quoting from all books of the Scriptures with complete familiarity, we find them noting with punctilio various peculiarities of the biblical texts; but nowhere is there so much as a suggestion that they had dictionaries or concordances to consult or to help them out. They knew their Bible inside out, and could put its sentences to halakic use and aggadic exhortation whenever the need arose. For a student of Midrash this remains a perpetual source of wonder.

36. Cf. S. Krauss cited in L. Finkelstein, *The Jews*[3], 171 and 212, n. 23, and see also *HJP*, 52.

37. Lev. R. 7:3, p. 156. E. Ebner (*Elementary Education in Israel* [N.Y., 1956], 78f.) writes: "In the opinion of this author [i.e. Ebner] the practice to begin the study of the Bible with Leviticus is based upon nationalistic-religious sentiments that crystallized in the era following the destruction of Temple and state. The leaders of Jewish life were anxious to lead the people away from despair and resignation by holding out to them the promise of future glory. The Temple would be rebuilt and the priestly service reinstituted. In the meantime the attachment to Israel's past eminence had to be kept alive. To that end they introduced several customs designed to impress the memory of the Temple upon the people, like R. Johanan ben Zakkai's ordinance to repeat the service of the Lulab for seven days, as it was done in the Temple, or the custom to eat on the Seder night unleavened bread together with herbs 'in memory of Hillel at the time of the Temple.' One other such custom was the practice to let the school boys begin the study of the Pentateuch with Leviticus, the Priestly Code. And since this was meant merely as an expression of faith, it was not necessary to study the book of Leviticus till its end and thus unduly tax the learning capacity of the student. The purpose was well served by studying only the first part. Hence R. Judah's permission to edit special children's scrolls containing only the first eight chapters of Leviticus. Thereafter the boy would return to Genesis and study the Torah in the proper order. Many years later, after the people had long made its adjustment to existing conditions, this custom had lost its original urgency. But because it was so well established it was continued and R. Assi advanced another reason to justify its perpetuation."

38. Lam. R. 4:2, ed. Buber, 72a, and cf. Buber's notes ad loc. [cf. also Diogenes Laertius, IV, 29.]

39. HJP, 52.

I am personally convinced that like their counterparts in the general Hellenistic schools, Jewish boys were taught aphorisms (χρεῖαι).[40] While the Greek boy learned and memorized aphorisms commonly attributed to Diogenes, the Jewish boy learned and quoted Hillel, for instance, "Moreover he saw a skull floating on the face of the water. He said to it: 'For drowning others wast thou drowned; and in the end they that drowned thee shall be drowned.'" In the Jewish primary and secondary schools—and not necessarily in the advanced schools—they heard *exempla* which were a delight and a lesson in good conduct—like the story of Hillel who refused to lose his temper, or the story of the irascible Shammai and the patient and witty Hillel: a model for all good boys who hoped someday to win over strangers to the study and love of Torah; or the stories of how the poor Akiba became a great scholar or how the rich Eliezer ben Hyrcanus acquired his great learning.[41]

Although there are still other bits and pieces of information regarding primary education—for example, on the proper size of a class;[42] on children's responsive recitations with a *pasoqa*,[43] a person who simply starts the children off with the first words of a verse and they continue merrily on their own; on the proper ways to punish a child ("Smack him down at once or hold your peace and say nothing")[44]—everywhere in the ancient world discipline was brutal, and even Aristotle was persuaded that "amusement does not go with learning—[185] μετὰ λύπης γὰρ ἡ μάθησις (for learning is a painful process)."[45] Although, as I say, more can be said about elementary education, in the little space that remains let us examine a few of the sidelights of secondary and advanced Torah education. It is not always easy, by the way, to draw a hard and fast line between them, despite the mishnaic "At ten, the study of Mishnah.... At fifteen, the study of Talmud."[46]

Even among those who studied as children, not all were able to go on to advanced learning (as we were told above by the Midrash on the verse in Ecclesiastes), and even among those who did go on, not all were the teacher's comfort. Rabban Gamaliel the Elder had a habit of classifying disciples, students, in terms of fish, and was not overly fond of the poor fish (nor, by the way, like Mark Twain, did he think much of the Jordan, or, to be precise, of fish from the Jordan).[47] There were (according to some old lists) four kinds of

---

40. Cf. J. Goldin, "The End of Ecclesiastes: Literal Exegesis and Its Transformation," in A. Altmann (ed.), *Biblical Motifs* (Cambridge, Mass., 1966), 136–138 [above, p. 6.—Ed]. See now, too, H. A. Fischel in *Religions in Antiquity* (Leiden, 1968), 372ff.

41. On Hillel and Shammai, *ARN*, 60–62; on R. Akiba and R. Eliezer, ibid., 28–33.

42. See B. Baba Batra, loc. cit.

43. See S. Lieberman, *Tosefta Ki-Fshuṭah on Shabbat*, 10f.

44. Cf. Semaḥot (ed. Zlotnick), 232.

45. Politics, VIII, 1339a, 28 (Loeb Classics, 1932, 651)—I owe this reference to Marrou, 159.

46. PA 5:21, and see Taylor's *Sayings of the Jewish Fathers*, 97f.

47. *ARNA*, 127: "On the subject of disciples Rabban Gamaliel the Elder spoke of four kinds: an unclean fish, a clean fish, a fish from the Jordan, a fish from the Great Sea.

"An unclean fish: who is that? A poor youth who studies Scripture and Mishnah, Halakah and Aggadah, and is without understanding.

disciple, four kinds of those frequenting the *bet midrash*, four kinds of those in attendance when the recognized Sages lectured (*ywšbym lpny ḥkmym*);[48] in each instance, the fourth kind is not to be envied. Like the debate in Hellenistic circles over whom one ought to admit to higher education, in Jewish circles, too, there were opponents of the Hillelite policy which encouraged teaching even the poor and those of humble origin.[49] Despite idealistic protestations that Torah was intended for all, that the crown of Torah was to be had for the toiling, there very definitely were favorites, like the *bny ḥkmym*, scholars' sons, whose privileged position the late Gedaliah Allon analyzed so finely.[50] [186] I would not call their schools democratic; but then there are very few schools I would call democratic; and I would say for those in ancient Jewish Palestine that they did what they could to make education widespread,[51] because learning was commanded by Him who is the Commander of all.[52] And yet, and yet . . . bastards, for instance, had a tough time of it.[53] For until the devastations of the Great War (66–73), the leading schools were in Jerusalem; and what appears to be an old homily admonishes men against illicit relations by warning that the boy born as a result of such an *affaire de coeur* will not be able to accompany his school mates beyond Ashdod, as they proceed to Jerusalem, for "a bastard may not enter Jerusalem under any circumstance."[54] Maybe such expostulations did discourage infidelity. In any event, though a bastard *tlmyd ḥkm* takes precedence or is superior to an ignoramus high priest,[55] he still can't get into the top schools. (Incidentally, Ashdod must have been quite a town, located by the sea south of Jabneh [of all places!]. At least it had a synagogue with a nice inscription, ἀγαθὸν καὶ εὐλογίαν, שלום.[56])

In the secondary and advanced schools the curriculum revolved around the

---

"A clean fish: who is that? That's a rich youth who studies Scripture and Mishnah, Halakah and Aggadah, and has understanding.

"A fish from the Jordan: who is that? That's a scholar who studies Scripture and Mishnah, Midrash, Halakah, and Aggadah, and is without the talent for give and take.

"A fish from the Great Sea: who is that? That's a scholar who studies Scripture and Mishnah, Midrash, Halakah, and Aggadah, and has the talent for give and take."

48. Cf. *ARN*, 126f.

49. Cf. J. Goldin in *Harvard Theological Review*, 58 (1965), 365, n. 5 [below, p. 210.—Ed.].

50. *Meḥqarim*, 2 (Tel Aviv, 1958), 58–73. Cf. Mid. Tan., 212f.

51. Contrast this with the conception of culture as a privilege of the governing classes spoken of by C. J. Gadd, *Teachers and Students in the Oldest Schools* (London, 1956), 23–25—but this was of course of much much earlier times—and by Marrou, 295f.

52. The first "words" to be taught a child when he begins to speak are "Moses charged us with the Torah, the heritage of the congregation of Jacob" (Deut. 33:4) and "Hear, O Israel! The Lord is our God, the Lord alone" (ibid. 6:4). Cf. Maimonides, Code, Talmud Torah, 1:6. The reason Deut. 33:4 says "*Moses* charged us with, commanded us, the Torah," when the Commander is really God, is that Moses gave his life for the Torah (Mid. Tan., 212, and cf. Mekilta, Ed. Lauterbach, II, 3f.).

53. *ARNA*, 53, and see also *ARNB*, 54 (though this latter text is poorly preserved).

54. There are difficulties with the meaning of this statement. See S. Bialoblotzki in *Alei Ayin: Salman Schocken Jubilee Volume* (Jerusalem, 5708–5712), 40.

55. M. Horayot 3:8.

56. *Sefer ha-Yishuv*, I (Jerusalem, 1939), s.v. Ashdod.

Oral Law, what one might (and did) call Mishnah. That study is to be *oral*, that learning is to be from the teacher's word of mouth rather than from books, was already emphasized by the middle of the third century B.C.E..[57] The Oral Law in turn seems to have been composed of three parts, Midrash, Halakot, and Aggadot.[58] As a matter of fact, those who advocated that a man find himself one teacher to study with and not run from teacher to teacher, saw in their [187] counsel this distinct advantage:[59] If by chance the master had failed to make something clear in the course of Midrash lessons, he could take care of that during the subsequent study of Halakot; if something were left unclear in the course of Halakot study, it could be cleared up during the Aggadah sessions. In some respects, Rabbi Meir felt that one teacher rather than several was best for a man;[60] but if we can depend on our sources, there were occasions when Rabbi Meir also felt as did others, that a man ought to study under more than one teacher.[61] An ideal faculty for an advanced student was made up of three scholars the like of Eliezer ben Hyrcanus, Joshua ben Ḥananiah, and Ṭarfon (or, possibly, Akiba).[62]

A word about the tripartite division of the Oral Torah. Midrash seems to refer to more complex forms of interpretation of Scripture than were undertaken in the elementary schools (where emphasis for the most part may have been on memorizing), perhaps with emphasis on the employment of hermeneutic rules, such as the seven rules of Hillel[63] or the thirteen rules of Rabbi Ishmael, or perhaps the principles favored by Naḥum of Gimzo and his disciple, Akiba.[64] There are several chapters devoted to "rabbinic interpretation of Scripture" in Professor S. Lieberman's *Hellenism in Jewish Palestine*[65] which will reward any student of biblical exegesis, regardless of how many times he rereads them.

"Halakot" is a term that is used for collections or statements of laws, [188]

57. Cf. "End of Ecclesiastes" (above, n. 40), 142 ff.

58. See, for example, *ARNA*, 34f., 127, and cf. above, n. 47.

59. *ARNA*, 35f., but the text is not completely clear; even more garbled is the reading in *ARNB*, 39.

60. *ARNA*, 36.

61. *ARNA*, 16.

62. *ARNA*, ibid.; *ARNB*, 39; cf. *Harvard Theological Review*, 58 (1965), 379ff. [above, p. 209.—Ed.]. And now see also S. Lieberman, *Siphre Zutta* (N.Y., 1968), 89f. (in n. 54).

63. *ARNA*, 110 (and cf. Schechter's n. 12 ibid. for parallels). I would like to take this occasion to remark that while quite rightly it is nowhere even suggested that Hillel was the inventor of these rules, it seems to me significant that they are quoted as the rules Hillel used in his exegesis in the presence of the Ben Bathyra. To me this means that Hillel was known not as the author of these rules, but as a vigorous advocate of the use of these rules, as a well-known *practitioner* of these rules. His resorting to them was neither a one-time affair, nor merely one more thing that characterized him. Hillel was *noted* as a constant advocate of their application.

64. On what characterized the exegetical methods of the two principal schools, see the indispensable chapter in J. N. Epstein, *Mebo'ot le-Sifrut ha-Tannaim* (Jerusalem-Tel Aviv, 1957), 521–536.

65. Pp. 20–82.

the kind of material we generally associate with the Mishnah.[66] Probably this included learning the laws and the reasons for them, as well as their logical and extended consequences. Or a session might be devoted to a student's questions and the master's answers. Thus, even on his deathbed,[67] for example (recall Maimonides' statement!), Eliezer ben Hyrcanus was asked halakic questions, and he answered them and continued teaching—at least so it was later reported; his disciples, according to one of them, responded with greater enthusiasm to what they then learned from their teacher than to what they had learned from him in his lifetime. They asked him: If a round cushion, a ball, a shoe last, an amulet, or a phylactery which was torn contracted uncleanness, what was the status of the substance or stuff inside them? He replied: "It's unclean; be careful with such objects and immerse them in an immersion pool as they are—for these are established laws (*hlkwt qbw'wt*)[68] which were transmitted to Moses at Sinai." As his close disciples kept putting questions to him, he answered "Unclean" for the unclean and "Clean" for the clean—and he breathed his last breath with the word "Clean" on his lips.

This then is an illustration—admittedly on the dramatic side—of a session of Halakot study. We can get an idea of the frame of mind accompanying such study in a remark once made by Rabbi Joshua when he heard that a number of partly metallic wood objects were declared to be susceptible to uncleanness:[69] ועל כלן אמר ר' יהושע דבר חדוש חדשו סופרים ואין לי מה אשיב, "With regard to all these objects which the Sages had declared susceptible to uncleanness, Rabbi Joshua said, 'The Scribes have invented something novel, but I can think of no adequate arguments against their view.'"

Or even more vividly: When[70] Rabbi Eliezer ben Hycranus was once asked concerning a particular case of ceremonial impurity, he declared that that particular plague was one of those whose victim had to be shut up (*ysgyr*) by the priest. Why? the Sages asked him. [189] What is more, they showed that they had good reason to reject Eliezer's view. When they cornered him with their arguments, he admitted he had no valid proofs for the correctness of his decision, but the decision was nevertheless the one that had been handed down to him, and he had no intentions of being an innovator.[71] Whereupon Judah ben Bathyra spoke up: "Master, may I say something that I have learned in my studies?" "You may," Eliezer replied, "but only on condition that it is in support

66. Cf. Ch. Albeck, *Mabo la-Mishnah* (Jerusalem-Tel Aviv, 1959), 2.
67. Cf. *ARNA*, 70 and 80f.
68. In *ARNA*, 80, *hlkwt gdwlwt*.
69. M. Kelim 13:7, M. Ṭebul Yom 4:6. Note the reading in Codex Kaufmann for both these sources. Cf. Albeck at Ṭebul Yom 4:6, who points out that Joshua has this feeling about quite a number of additional laws where teachers arrived at a more lenient ruling than he was comfortable with; and cf. Mishnah, ibid., pp. 458 and 602.
70. M. Nega'im 9:3; cf. 11:7. And in M. 'Ahilot 16:1 (ed. A. Goldberg, 117) we come upon Akiba also eager to confirm the view of the early Sages. See also the statement by R. Meir (or, Rabbi) in K. Kil'aim 2:11 and the comment by Albeck ad loc.
71. Cf. in another connection his exclamation in M. Yadayim 4:3.

of the view of the earlier Sages from whom I got my view." With that permission granted, Rabbi Judah explained and defended the old view, presumably to everyone's satisfaction. When he finished, Rabbi Eliezer declared, חכם גדול אתה שקימת דברי חכמים, "You are a great scholar because you confirmed the view of the [early] Sages."

In other words, in the study of Halakot, the inherited views are the preferred views. Who is a great scholar (*ḥkm gdwl*)? He who knows how to justify the views of earlier Sages. Note that it is not only Rabbi Eliezer who leans in that direction—from Eliezer ben Hyrcanus we would expect it; Rabbi Joshua, too, is uncomfortable with *debar ḥiddush*, and regrets he is unable to think of a refutation. Even a bold spirit like Akiba undertakes to confirm "the view of the Sages," chafe at it as Rabbi Ṭarfon might. Allow me to quote Marrou again,[72] this time in his description of secondary Hellenistic education, because his remarks are apt also for much of the study of the Oral Law, and the Halakot in particular: "Classical culture did not know any romantic need to make all things new, to forget the past and be original; it was proud of its inherited wealth, proud of its pedantry, proud of being what our modern pedantry—whose only sign of progress seems to be that it has replaced literary scholarship by technical science—would call the victim of a culture complex."

The third component of the Oral Torah was Aggadot. Intellectuals were often tempted to slight it (although in tannaite centuries especially, the leading halakists were among the leading aggadists)—and not only in geonic or medieval times.[73] We can tell that this is so from the remark in the Sifre on Deuteronomy:[74] Beware lest you [190] say, I've studied Halakah and that's quite enough for me; on the contrary, one must go on and study Midrash and Aggadah too. In truth, this is the field in which the Creator of the universe is caught sight of and man adopts and cleaves to His ways.[75] The extent of the Aggadah was almost limitless; here individual speculation had if not complete freedom then at least ample space to try out ideas and the imagination's capabilities.

Lots more should be said about advanced study of the Oral Law: of the existence of various study circles—there were clubs (*ḥbwrwt*)[76] for Scripture study, clubs for Mishnah study, clubs for Talmud study, and Moses held an honorary appointment in all of them. Lots too can be said of the rabbinic objection to certain kinds of water sports,[77] particularly in centuries when

72. Op. cit., 170.
73. Cf. ʾOṣar ha-Geonim, IV, Ḥagigah, 59f., and cf. the quotations from Rišonim (early medieval authorities) in S. Lieberman, *Shekiin* (Jerusalem, 1939), 82f.
74. Sifre Deut., 48, p. 113; cf. Mid. Tan., 43, 205, 262; Midrash ʿAśeret ha-Dibrot (*Bet ha-Midrasch*, ed. Jellinek, I, 65).
75. Sifre Deut., 49, p. 115. Such characterization itself testifies to the vigorous recommendations Aggadah required.
76. Sifre Deut., 355, p. 418.
77. Cf. M. Makširin 5:1 and S. Lieberman in *Sinai*, IV, 54ff. On the significance of athletics even after the decline of gymnastics set in in the Hellenistic world, cf. Marrou, op. cit., 130ff.

athletics still formed part, even if only a relatively small one, of the education of the cultivated man. This strong objection did not apply of course to swimming,[78] or to bathing in order to keep the body clean—*that* could actually be called a *miṣwah*, a religious act.[79] I wish there were room to say a little at least about the importance of *šmwš tlmydy ḥkmym*, attendance upon and close observing of the Master Scholar by his disciples as he went about his various tasks. Without this attendance and observing, one's education was bound to be deficient, and led at times to disastrous results.[80] In the classical world, *paideia* was not held to be a book enterprise principally. It is instructive, too, to learn of the way men specialized, some hoping to get a reputation as experts in Halakah (רעותיה מתקרי בר הלכן) or experts in Midrash (רעותיה מתקרי בר מכאלא) or as Talmud experts, רעותיה מתקרי בר אולפן.[81] And more besides: Of those of them who studied Greek, for example, who were their teachers? And what exactly did they study:[82] Homer?[83] Anything [191] else? Let me conclude, however, with a quotation that can serve at the same time as one answer to the question that inevitably must rise at some point: What did Torah study achieve? Of what use was it? There are several eloquent answers, and they keep being referred to by every Talmud anthologist. But there is one which is a favorite of mine, although it too is probably well-known.[84]

ג' נתמעטו משריבה ת"ת. Three began to diminish when Torah study increased: נתמעטו המזיקים, demons went on the decrease, נתמעטה מהומה,[85] pandemonium declined, נתמעטו עושי רע, [and the number of] evil-doers diminished. And some say: The same applies to the planting of cucumbers.

This is no mean achievement, in any age. I should explain, of course, that planting of cucumbers was a form of magic, and Rabbi Eliezer ben Hyrcanus was singularly expert in it. He could fill a whole field with them by saying one word; so, too, by one word he could empty a field.[86] What a pity that the word has not come down to us!

---

78. A *baraita* in B. Kiddushin 29a; cf. T. Kiddushin 1:11 and Mekilta (Pisḥa XVIII), I, 166.
79. *ARNB*, 66.
80. See *ARNA*, 56, Ṣemaḥot, 225.
81. Lev. R. 3:1, pp. 54f.
82. Cf. HJP, 105, 113.
83. Cf. M. Yadayim 4:6.
84. *ARNB*, 130.
85. I think the reading in ed. Schechter requires a minor correction (not *ntm'ṭ hmhwmh* but *ntm'ṭh mhwmh*): it's probably a typographical mistake.
86. *ARNA*, 81, B. Sanhedrin 68a.

Of Change and Adaptation in Judaism[*]

[269] To change we are all subject, perhaps most profoundly when we offer greatest resistance; adaptation, on the other hand, requires genius. We may insulate or fortify ourselves as much as we please, but we may still be invaded by Hyksos,[1] or the Temple may be destroyed, or the trade routes may change and pass us by.[2] Thereafter the world is never quite the same. Of course it is possible to pretend that nothing is altered and that the old order is still quite adequate as it was. But if we do this, we run the risk of mummification, like that which overtook Egyptian religion and [270] society when they sealed themselves off from Hellenism completely.[3]

Having said this, however, I suspect I am expressing no more than that staple belief of modern man to whom change is both an articulate and unarticulated category of existence: perhaps for him it is even more than that, perhaps he even regards it as a value worth cherishing. I am not entirely sure of

[*] This paper was read April 25 at the 1964 meeting of the American Society for the Study of Religion. The meeting was devoted to the general theme of "Adaptation of Tradition to New Conditions—a Discussion of Change in Religion."

1. On the Hyksos invasion and its effect on Egyptian history, see G. Steindorff and K. C. Seele, *When Egypt Ruled the East* (Chicago, 1971), pp. 24–33, and J. A. Wilson, pp. 158–59: *The Burden of Egypt* (Chicago, 1951), pp. 158–65, 167–70. Note esp. Wilson, pp. 158–59: "If [the Hyksos] conquest were as critical to the course of Egyptian culture as we claim, how could Egyptian writings have blanketed it with silence? The answer lies in the nature and purpose of Egyptian texts, which asserted the eternal and not the ephemeral and which presented for eternity those aspects of life which were felt to represent most truly the gods' purposes for Egypt" (see also, by the way, the reference in n. 9 below). "In that psychology, there was no impulse for writing down the record of a great national humiliation; that record would come when and as the Hyksos were successfully expelled" (see also H. Frankfort, *Ancient Egyptian Religion* [New York: Harper & Bros., 1961], pp. 50–51).

2. Cf. M. Rostovtzeff, *Caravan Cities* (Oxford, 1932), pp. 70–71, 208.

3. Cf. E. Bickerman, *The Maccabees* (New York, 1947), pp. 113–14, especially p. 114.

what the present mood is.[4] As to what constitutes adaptation: Although future speculators or historians enjoy a perspective and presumably a knowledge of consequences of the particular transformation that the immediate experiencer is deprived of, even they may disagree with each other. What is adaptation to one is surrender to another or trivial modification to a third.

When we study a complex tradition like classical Judaism, it might not be amiss to start by asking the question: Is there in Judaism a conscious, expressed recognition of the naturalness of change and the corresponding function of adaptation? Consider, for example, the following statement by Maimonides:[5]

> It . . . will not be possible that the laws be dependent on changes in the cir-
> cumstances of the individuals, and of the times, as is the case with regard to medical
> treatment, which is particularized for every individual in conformity with his
> present temperament. On the contrary, governance of the Law ought to be absolute
> and universal, including everyone, even if it is suitable only for certain individuals
> and not suitable for others; for if it were made to fit individuals, the whole would be
> corrupted and *you would make out of it something that varies.*[6] For this reason,
> matters that are primarily intended in the Law ought not to be dependent on time
> or place; but the decrees ought to be absolute and universal, according to what He,
> may He be exalted, says· As for the congregation: *there shall be one statute
> (ḥuqqah) for you.*[7]

Especially if you consult the whole chapter from which I have lifted this excerpt, you will observe that Maimonides is not discussing the problem of historical changes. He is here formulating a juristic principle, that when you enact a law, although there may certainly exist exceptional instances where that particular law will not lead to the perfection you are striving to attain, the law must be "directed only toward the things that occur in the [271] majority of cases." Combine, however, what Maimonides says here with the talmudic view he summarizes correctly in his great *Code*,[8] that the words of the Torah are permanently fixed, subject neither to change nor to subtraction or addition, and the preference of the tradition is, I believe, unmistakable. Put succinctly, for classical Judaism change is not an *ideal*, it is not even something inevitable, something inherent in the nature of things. How Judaism tries to face up to the reality of change and the accompanying need of adaptation, we shall proceed to explore shortly. But especially since some modern students have been tempted to say things of the so-called progressive character of Judaism which, I

---

4. See, e.g., the last chapter (particularly pp. 200–209) of E. H. Carr, *What is History?* (New York, 1962).

5. *Guide of the Perplexed*, III, 34. trans. S. Pines (Chicago, 1963), pp. 534–35.

6. A talmudic formula; cf. Pines' n. 3, p. 535, for the references.

7. Num. 15:15. See also the comment of Crescas on this passage of the *Guide* (in the Hebrew edition [Warsaw, 5690]).

8. *Sefer ha-Mada'*, *Yesode ha-Torah* 9:1ff. Cf. also Maimonides, *Commentary* on M. Sanhedrin X, in *Sefer ha-Ma'or*, ed. M. D. Rabinowitz (Tel Aviv, 1948), I, 142.

think, reflect more our own preferences or unexpressed dogmas, I feel it is not out of place to restate plainly what seems to me to be the fact: Change, for classical Judaism, is not presumed to be a congenital property of law or institutions or history;[9] and certainly, as I said, it is not an ideal devoutly to be pursued.[10]

One or two familiar examples, often invoked to illustrate the readiness with which Judaism supposedly welcomes change, may help make my contention vivid. We read in I Maccabees (2:40) that after "many who were seeking righteousness and judgment" (*ṣedaqah u-mishpat*, 2:29) had been slain because they would not defend themselves from attack on the Sabbath, Mattathias and his associates resolved, "Whosoever attacketh us on the Sabbath day, let us fight against him, that we may not in any case all die as our brothers died." We even hear immediately thereafter that "Hasidim, mighty men of Israel who willingly offered themselves for the Law," joined Mattathias' band. Strict pietists, in other words, are prepared to come to terms with an important revision of the Law. But as the text itself makes clear, this was change into which circumstances *forced* them. Naturally, this is what change always does: it is only automobile manufacturers and couturiers who cannot let well enough alone. My point is that there is nothing in the Maccabees account to suggest that the change adopted was regarded lightly or without regret by the men who had to make the decision. They speak one to another, καὶ εἶπεν ἀνὴρ τῷ πλησίον αὐτοῦ (2:40)—in other words, there is a real heart-to-heart [272] exploration of what to do in this emergency, after many had "died, they and their wives, and their children, and their cattle, about a thousand souls" (2:38).[11]

Again, it is either Pharisaic or tannaite teaching[12] that declares that the biblical (cf. Exod. 21:24, etc.) "eye for an eye" means "monetary compensation for the injured eye." Regardless of how we look upon this postbiblical injunction, nothing in the sources suggests that, for the Sages of the Oral Law, *new* teaching was involved, or that change and adaptation are reflected. Observe indeed that Eliezer ben Hyrqanus disagrees[13]—but not because it entered his

9. On whether some concept of history is possible without an acknowledgment of the role of change, see the fine study of J. J. Finkelstein, "Mesopotamian Historiography," in *Proceedings of the American Philosophical Society*, 107 (1963), pp. 461–72.

10. See some apt observations by L. Finkelstein in the "Introductory Note to the Third Edition," *The Pharisees* (Philadelphia, 1962), I, li et seq.

11. On this incident see also Josephus, *Antiquities*, XII, 6:2 and note (a) by R. Marcus in the Loeb Edition, VII, pp. 142–43; cf. F.-M. Abel, *Les livres des Maccabées* (Paris, 1949), pp. 42–43.

12. Megillat Taʿanit 4, ed. Lichtenstein, *HUCA*, 8–9, p. 331, and B. Baba Qamma 83b–84a; and cf. Finkelstein, op. cit., p. 815. See also nn. 13 and 14 below.

13. B. Baba Qamma 84a, and cf. Mekilta Ishmael, Neziqin, 8, ed. Lauterbach, III, pp. 68–69 (the difficulties with this latter source—cf. ed. Horovitz-Rabin, p. 277—persist despite all the explanations I have been able to consult; and see on this subject the long discussions in M. M. Kasher, *Torah Shelemah* [New York, 1956], 17, pp. 126–28, and esp. pp. 258 et seq. Note also L. Finkelstein's discussion, op. cit., pp. 721ff. and cf. the discussion in Kasher, p. 262). See also n. 14 below.

mind that there may have been a time when *talio* was literally exacted. He protests that this verse cannot serve as the prooftext for what to him, too, is an ancient institution, and that if you impose on that verse the interpretation of the other Sages, you are misinterpreting it.[14]

14. On R. Eliezer's view see also Z. Frankel, *Darke ha-Mishnah* (Warsaw, 1928), p. 81. The view I am following is (with some modifications) along the lines of L. Ginzberg in his notes to A. Geiger's *Qebuṣat Ma'amarim*, ed. Poznanski (Warsaw, 1910), pp. 390–92, whose overall view is the only one that makes sense to me (see also Kasher, p. 263). I *do* believe that the Talmud (B. Baba Qamma 84a) is asking a real and not academic-harmonizing question when it exclaims, "Is R. Eliezer in disagreement with all these other Tannaim?" [cited in the text]. J. Wellhausen, *Die Pharisäer und die Sadducäer* (1874), p. 62, is absolutely right when he says, "Die Talio kann unmöglich in der Zeit, um die es sich handelt, noch seit Alters her zu Recht bestanden haben, und wiedereinführen liess sie sich noch unmöglicher." And note also Herdlitczka in *Pauly-Wissowa*, s.v., "talio" (col. 2073): "Die T. überlebte die Republik, der sie ihre gesetzliche Regelung verdankte, nicht. Wahrscheinlich schon weit vor der Lex Aebutia war sie abgekommen." On the date of Lex Aebutia, cf. A. Berger, *Encyclopedic Dictionary of Roman Law* (Philadelphia, 1953), p. 547, and see also ibid., p. 730, on "talio."

On the primary context of the language of talio, eye for an eye and so on, see the extremely important observations of S. Spiegel, "Me-'Agadot ha-'Aqedah" in *Jubilee Volume in Honor of Alexander Marx* (New York, 1950), pp. 498–99 (Heb. vol.), and especially the quotation in ibid., n. 12, which can help throw light on our problem.

Now, Frankel believes that R. Ashi's reply in the Talmud (ibid.) is not forced; and, I must say, although at first sight Ashi's "casuistry" may strike one as farfetched and purely theoretical, in the light of what we learn from Spiegel, R. Ashi's remark is not in the least fanciful. If the language of "eye for an eye," etc., is indeed rooted in cultic conceptions and expression, *mammash* may mean in fact and originally, it is the value of the *injurer's* eye you pay, not the value of the eye of the injured one! Note how Finkelstein, op. cit., pp. lxxvi–lxxvii and 724ff., explains what is involved. That even as early as the second millennium B.C.E. compensation rather than actual retribution may be exacted can be seen from [273] the commentary by A. Goetze, *The Laws of Eshnunna* (New Haven, Conn., 1956), pp. 117–23; compare the discussion in G. R. Driver and J. C. Miles, *The Babylonian Laws*, I (Oxford, 1952), p. 408 [see also their *The Assyrian Laws* (Oxford, 1935), pp. 106ff.]; cf. A. S. Diamond, "An Eye for an Eye," in *Iraq*, 19 (1957), pp. 151–55. (I owe this last reference to the kindness of my colleague, Professor W. W. Hallo.) In connection with the related Hittite law, see also E. A. Speiser in *JBL*, 82 (1963), pp. 303. (I would like to thank my distinguished colleague, Professor A. Goetze, for the opportunity to discuss the problem with him in terms of ancient Mesopotamian civilization.)

As I said in the body of the paper, Eliezer protests that Exod. 21:24–25—had it stood alone—could never serve as a prooftext that talio is *not* literally exacted. But since we have the texts of Lev. 24:19–20, we know that one who injures his fellow is subject to payment of an indemnity. This, I believe, underlies the very difficult text of Mekilta Ishmael; cf. n. 13 above.

The following seems to me to be the sense of the Mekilta: "R. Eliezer says: From the (Exod. 21:24–25 [or should this really be Lev. 24:20?]) 'eye for an eye' I might conclude that whether one intends injury or does not intend it, he is subject only to payment of indemnity. But does not Scripture exclude the one intending to inflict an injury from payment, [insisting] on the contrary that he literally [suffer a like—retaliatory—injury]!—for it is said (Lev. 24:19) 'And if a man maim his neighbor, as he hath done so shall it be done to him'? [However:] This is a generalizing statement. 'An eye for an eye' (etc., which follows ibid., v. 20)—specifics. Now when there is a generalizing statement followed by specifics, the generalizing statement includes no more than there is in the specifics statement. But when that verse (ibid.) goes on to say, 'As he hath maimed a man [so shall it be rendered unto him],' Scripture returns once more to a generalizing statement. Is the latter generalization perhaps like the first generalization? Say: Not at all!" (Note in fact, ken "yinnaten," bo, and not as in v. 19, ken "ye'aseh" lo.) "Rather, when there is a generalization, followed by specifics, followed in turn by another generalization, you interpret the generalizing statements only in the light of the specifics. Now

[274] In actuality, there is nothing remarkable about this. Change and adaptation, as concepts of some theory to explain the nature of social realities, demand a critical awareness of process, demand a sophisticated interest in history;[15] and, like their contemporaries among pagan scholars, the Rabbis were innocent of this. As a number of scholars have repeatedly observed,[16] of real history, accurate information of the past, little was actually known by the majority of intellectuals, and anecdotes about the past told by pagan scholars and the Rabbis in the age of the Tannaim and Amoraim were intended principally either for the edification or amusement of audiences. *"Ces exem-*

the spelled-out specifics refer to the following conditions: the injuries are permanent ones, they affect the chief organs, the visible ones, and the injury is intentional—and in such a case one is subject only to payment of indemnity. Therefore whenever there is a case of permanent injury, affecting the chief organs, the visible ones, and the injury is intentional, one is subject only to payment of indemnity. And this is the meaning of the verse (Lev. 24:20), 'As he hath maimed a man,' that is, he intended to inflict the injury" (and is therefore subject only to payment of indemnity).

This text is certainly difficult, and its inconsistency with the laconic comment in the *baraita* quoted by the Talmud, B. Baba Qamma 84a, is also plainly manifest. One reason (it is not the only one!) I suspect the Mekilta text is so complicated and confusing is that it seems really to have been originally a comment on Lev. 24:20, and somehow got shifted to the Mekilta on Exod. 21:24 by association. Note above the question I have put in brackets.

I do not want to pretend that I am altogether satisfied with (much less confident about) my rendition of the Mekilta passage. Several other points deserve to be raised in connection with that text, but this note is already threatening to become interminable; and I hope to return to an analysis of the Mekilta text on some future occasion. However, by the way, see also the reaction of Shem Tob Falaqera on Maimonides, *Guide*, III, 41, and cf. the *Exodus Commentary* of Maimonides' son, Abraham, ed. Sassoon (London, 1959), p. 342.

J. Bonsirvon, *Le Judaïsme Palestinien* (Paris, 1935), II, 246, n. 3, raises the perfectly legitimate question, "Est-il bien sûr qu'à notre époque le talion n'était pas pratiqué?" (Cf. also the references he cites.) All the more impressive then is the tannaite "innocence"! Or are we to assume deliberate editorial erasure of recollection of the actual state of affairs? Why then should R. Eliezer's view have been preserved at all? Of course, note in fact that the Talmud cites R. Eliezer last, though he is earlier than the other Tannaim cited. But surely that is due to talmudic editing, since the redactors hope to demonstrate that in view of R. Ashi's explanation R. Eliezer is consistent with the generally accepted halakah after all. At all events, see the quotations from Wellhausen and Herdlitczka above in the note.

15. Cf. Scholem (see below n. 31): "Wenn wir das Problem der Tradition betrachten wollen, müssen wir natürlich zwischen der historischen Frage, wie es zur Bildung einer mit religiöser Dignität ausgestatteten Tradition überhaupt gekommen ist, und der anderen Frage, wie diese Tradition verstanden wurde, wenn sie als religiöses Phänomen einmal ergriffen wurde, unterscheiden. Wie stets bei der Verfestigung von religiösen Systemen wurde natürlich, als das Phänomen der Tradition einmal anerkannt war, von der Gläubigen die historische Fragestellung verworfen. Für den Historiker bleibt sie fundamental" (p. 21).

16. See E. J. Bickerman in *RB*, 59 (1952), p. 44. Cf. E. H. Carr, op. cit., p. 145: "Like the ancient civilizations of Asia, the classical civilization of Greece and Rome was basically unhistorical." R. G. Collingwood (*The Idea of History* [Oxford, 1961]) says of the Greeks: "They saw all nature as a spectacle of incessant change, and human life as changing more violently than anything else" (p. 22). But he, too, points out that "they could produce first-rate historical work without developing what in fact they never did develop, any lively curiosity concerning the remote past. . . . One might almost say that in ancient Greece there were no historians in the sense in which there were artists and philosophers; there were no people who devoted their lives to the study of history; the historian was only the autobiographer of his generation and autobiography is not a profession" (p. 26).

pla," writes Bickerman, *"leur servaient à émailler un discours ou à illustrer tel lieu commun de morale."* So that even that famous haggadic statement by Rabbi Nathan, added[17] in the regular editions to the end of the Mishnah Berakot, that when the laws are being broken, it is time to act in behalf of God, is not as such contemplating anything like *tempora mutantur* and we ought to adjust our institutions to them. What Rabbi Nathan—and Rabbi Meir who is cited in the Tosefta (6:24)—urges is that when you perceive that the Torah is being neglected, redouble your energies in its behalf: This is the time for all good men to renew their defenses of God's law.[18]

[275] An all-embracing formulation of a principle of change and adaptation is not, I believe, part of the midrashic-talmudic ambition or idiom. There are, to be sure, *taqqanot* and *gezerot*, enactments and decrees; these are ad hoc measures, and interestingly enough, once adopted, they tend to become permanent parts of the Law.[19] There are principles which motivate the adoption of certain policies—like *mipene darke shalom, mipene tiqqun ha'olam*,[20] legislation for the sake of general welfare, for the maintenance of good relations in society. If necessary, there is even the occasional daring to suspend a biblical order: when adultery grows rampant, Johanan ben Zakkai[21] orders a suspension of the biblical prescription in the case of the suspected wife[22]—here the text speaks of *hifsiqan*, "suspended." Apparently, it was even possible to go further. When the number of murders increases frightfully, בטלה עגלה ערופה, there comes an end to the ceremony of breaking the heifer's neck.[23] How melancholy (but also instructive!) is the note in the Tosefta (14:1) explanation: the ceremony is obligatory only when the identity of the murderer cannot be established, but now, ועכשיו הן בגלוי הן רוצחין, they murder in broad daylight! These, however, are all conceived of as something extraordinary, as a shocking interruption of the natural order of things; these enactments and suspensions

17. Cf. J. N. Epstein, *Mabo le-Nusah ha-Mishnah*, p. 975.

18. S. Lieberman's *Tosefta Commentary* makes this quite clear; see his "Long Commentary," p. 125. As regards the *prosbul* instituted by Hillel (cf. M. Shebi'it 10:3–4 and M. Gittin 4:3), it may be worth adding the following observations: (1) Note the problems with it and the frank surprise at its institution registered in B. Gittin 36a–b. (2) The very idiom of what motivated Hillel should be noted: "When he saw that folks refrained from extending loans to one another and *were thus transgressing the Scriptural ordinance* (Deut. 15:9), 'Beware that there be not a base thought in thy heart' etc." (M. Shebi'it 10:3). In other words, he too is impelled to adopt an *ad hoc* measure (note my following paragraph in the body of the paper) by the desire to protect the early, biblical, exhortation. On the *prosbul*, cf. E. Schürer, *Geschichte*, II⁴ (1907), pp. 427–28, and nn. 44–46 ad loc.; L. Blau, *Prosbol im Lichte der griechischen Papyri und der Rechtsgeschichte* (Budapest, 1927); and the references given by S. Lieberman in his *Tosefta Ki-Fshutah*, "Long Commentary" on T. Shebi'it 8, p. 589, n. 30.

19. Cf. Maimonides, Hilkot Mamrim 2:3 (note Kesef Mishneh and Radbaz ad loc.); see also B. Gittin 36b and J. H. Greenstone in *Jewish Encyclopaedia*, s.v. "Prosbul," X, p. 219, col b.

20. See, e.g., M. Gittin 5:3, 8–9.

21. Nevertheless, cf. J. N. Epstein, *Mebo'ot le Sifrut ha-Tannaim*, pp. 41, 400.

22. M. Sotah 9:9. See also T. Sotah 14:2.

23. M. Sotah, ibid., Deut. 21:1–9. See also M. Yoma 2:2 and T. Yoma 1:12, and Lieberman, *Tosefta Ki-Fshutah*, "Long Commentary," pp. 735–36.

are not necessarily (you will see later why I say "not necessarily") the outcome of a comprehensive conception of change and adaptation. And as passage after passage and prayer after prayer reaffirm: The time will come when much that could not be carried out, because pro tem Israel is compelled to live under *unnatural* conditions, will be restored[24]—for what God once revealed is permanently valid.[25] Little wonder then that even in the academy on high, one of the favorite pastimes of the Holy One, blessed be He, is to participate with the Sages who surround Him [276] in seminars on His Torah.[26] Here is a text that is never outdated. "O how familiar then was heaven!"

However, what is another way of saying "it is never outdated"? It is always relevant. But how are an ancient text and its contents kept relevant? To meet this assignment Judaism adopts not the neutral and descriptive terms of change and adaptation, but a view of revelation which is permanently at work through an activity called "Midrash." In change and adaptation we observe human society left either to its own resources or to the unaccountable whim of the gods and their representatives: the immediate is attended to almost entirely on its own terms, and the less said about precedent, the better. If there is only change and adaptation, discontinuity remains a permanent possibility—for the change may be so revolutionary that nothing less than a new beginning is required if there is to be either survival or revival. You may have to smash every vestige of Amun in order to instate Aton. In Midrash, on the other hand, though the pressure of the immediate is keenly appreciated (otherwise, why Midrash at all?), attention must *also* be directed to the original, classical patterns which have given the community its particular features. In Midrash, man is supplied with directions from the God of the Fathers. He is never on sabbatical,[27] and therefore no fatal rupture occurs between past and present, or present and future. Hence, regardless of what takes place, there is a continuity that triumphs over every threatening intermission. Moses received Torah from

24. Note the idiom of R. Yose's statement in M. Maʿaśer Sheni 5:2, "And it was contingent upon this, that when the Temple is rebuilt, the original practice will be restored." See also B. Shabbat 12b on Ishmael ben Elisha.

25. Cf. the idiom of Maimonides in his *Code*, Hilkot Yesode ha-Torah 9:1, beginning and end.

26. Cf. B. Baba Meṣia 86a and Pesahim 119a, and note also Elijah's reply to R. Nathan in B. Baba Meṣia 59b.

27. I have deliberately helped myself to this idiom suggested by the *Evangelium Veritatis*, ed. M. Malinine, H.-C. Puech, G. Quispel (Zürich, 1956), 32, 18ff., p. 104 (cf. notes ad loc., p. 57), on the Savior—"He labored, even on the Sabbath, for the lamb whom He found fallen into a pit. He saved the life of that lamb having caused it to be lifted out of the pit—in order that you may know, in [your] hearts, what is that Sabbath in the course of which [the work of] redemption must not remain inactive"—for this is typical Midrash the Gnostic is employing. As S. Spiegel puts it in another context (see below), "Even dissent and revolt are clothed in what is in name or shape but a commentary." On the halakic problem involved, cf. Zadokite Document (XI: 13–14, 16–17) in A. M. Habermann, *Megilloth Midbar Yehuda* (Israel, 1959), p. 85, and L. Ginzberg, *Eine unbekannte jüdische Sekte* (New York, 1922), pp. 97–98. See also B. Yoma 84b. Note how Justin, *Dialogue with Trypho*, XXIX, speaks of God not stopping to control movement of the universe on the Sabbath.

Sinai and handed it on to Joshua, who handed it on to the Elders, who handed it on to the Prophets, who handed it on to the Men of the Great Assembly, who handed it on to the *Zugot*, who handed it on to subsequent scholars, although in the interim the Temple had been destroyed[28]—and these in turn handed it on to their [277] disciples, and these to their disciples down to אפילו מה שתלמיד ותיק עתיד להורות לפני רבו.[29]

Midrash, however, is not mere reference to the past: it is the enlistment of the past in the service of the present. Even more specifically, it is a reinsertion into the present of the original divine Word, "memory / making past present,"[30] but a supernatural Word that is not simply the primitive hierogram: that Word is given definition and repeated application by men. Without man, without the scholar, there can be no Midrash. Theoretically, he is not free to invent meanings or implications independently of the Word. Therefore, from the first the divine Word consists of layers upon layers of intentions and instructions. And when the sage offers his interpretation he is making one more disclosure, he is laying bare one more implication, he is exposing to view still another radiance hitherto covered up.[31] Since the Word is the word of the Living God, it never ceases to make contact with the human world. The Word does not change, but it fulfills itself through disclosures and interpretations of the scholars. And if the world changes, the Word has been prepared for all contingencies from the outset. The permanent and the fluid, if I may say so, are not two opposed features, or even sharply distinguished from each [278] other. The Word is continuously directed to the world and the world is shaped by the Word through the instrumentality of the Sages.

28. Cf. Pirqe Abot, chaps. 1–2.
29. J. Peah 2:4 (R. Joshua ben Levi); and cf. R. Johanan in B. Megillah 19b who speaks of the obligation to read the Scroll of Esther on Purim as מה שהסופרים עתידין לחדש. See also the views expressed in Gen. R. 49:2, ed. Theodor-Albeck, p. 501. See also Duran on PA, 1:1.
30. I want to thank Miss Marianne Moore for permission to quote these wonderful words from her poem "An Expedient—Leonardo da Vinci's (and a Query)," *New Yorker*, April 16, 1964, p. 52, "quoted by me from the Note-books of Leonardo da Vinci. M.M."
31. After I had written out the first draft of the text of this paper I received from G. Scholem of Jerusalem an offprint of his splendid study, "Tradition und Kommentar als religiöse Kategorien im Judentum," *Eranos-Jahrbuch*, 31, (Zürich, 1963), pp. 19–48, in which I was delighted to find that he has anticipated me in a number of thoughts on the subject of Midrash and the scholar's role. In fact, he develops the aspect of the scholar's role even more fully than I do; and he retells (pp. 31–32) with excellent effect the narrative reported in B. Baba Meṣia 59b. I had decided not to draw again on this talmudic tale, for I had dealt with it, in an attempt to explore the meaning of "freedom," in a paper in the *Library Journal*, 72, (New York, 1952), pp. 1354–55. Incidentally, in his study Scholem (pp. 32 et seq.) proceeds to explore the kabbalistic treatment of the concept of the Word and its unfolding meanings.
One aspect of the rabbinic view of the scholar deserves more attention than, I believe, it generally receives; and perhaps on some future occasion I may return to it. I am referring to the notion of the scholar as priest in behalf of the congregation: Note well Abot de-Rabbi Natan, ed. Schechter, IV, p. 18: "The study of Torah is more beloved of God than burnt offerings. For if a man studies Torah he comes to know the will of God, as it is said (Prov. 2:5), 'Then shalt thou understand the fear of the Lord, and find the will of God.' Hence, when a sage sits and expounds to the congregation, Scripture accounts it to him as though he had offered up fat and blood on the altar." See also Schechter's n. 7, ad loc.

It is therefore not with change and adaptation as such that the Rabbis are preoccupied; this is not their fundamental orientation. It is with the preservation of that intimate relationship between the inexhaustible Word and human society that they are concerned. Since that relationship cannot be sustained without active human performances, commentary never ceases, and each generation's interpretations become, as it were, additional promptings to be reflected on in turn. And since, despite all their aspirations, human beings cannot escape being affected by what takes place in their own times, they keep interpreting the old in terms that grow directly from their own experiences.

By way of illustration allow me to appropriate a long section from a beautiful essay by Shalom Spiegel:

We can follow this afterlife of the Bible in scattered comments or orderly commentaries which mirror the temper and the trends of the Jewish Middle Ages. Moreover, the centrality of Scripture in the medieval scene accounts not only for the natural and unconscious metamorphosis of the biblical legacy in the course of time, but also for the frequency with which so much of the original creation of the Middle Ages was sunk into biblical exegesis. To gain foothold in medieval Israel, every spiritual endeavor had to be related to the chief concern of the people, Torah. Hence medieval expression is so often cast in the form of a commentary on Scripture. Even dissent and revolt are clothed in what is in name or shape but a commentary. The form succeeded in disguising and preserving a great deal of the independent achievement of the Middle Ages. Whatever their usefulness for the study of the Bible itself, the medieval Bible commentaries are invaluable and indispensable for the revelation of the internal life of the Jew in the Middle Ages.

An example from the Psalter will illustrate the vigor and variety of this invisible creativeness passing unchallenged as biblical interpretation.

Psalm 29 is probably a very old hymn, voicing the dread and the wonder of ancient man before the fury of the elements. A storm is gathering out at sea, "upon many waters," and breaks upon the land, tossing the cedars of Lebanon and rocking the snow-capped Hermon to its foundations. The massive mountains seem to shake helplessly like frightened animals. The storm and the winds, the peals of thunder and the "flames of fire" or the lightning flash herald the power of "the God of glory" as He sets out to strike at the insurgent foes. When the tempest dies away in the desert, all rebellion is quelled, and the conqueror can return to His celestial palace, built "upon the flood" or the upper waters above the firmament, there to receive the [279] tribute and honor due to a "king for ever." The heavenly ceremony is pictured after the fashion of earthly courts, or rather in images borrowed from prebiblical myths. We see the lesser divinities, the *bene elim*, or "the sons of the gods," assemble to pay homage to the victorious godhead. With such "praise on high" the Psalm opens, and it ends with a prayer for "peace on earth."

Already in the age of the Tannaim, the meaning of the Psalm was thoroughly overhauled:

"Rabbi Eleazer of Modaim said: When the Holy One, blessed be He, appeared to give the Torah to Israel, the earth shook and the mountains quaked, and all the sons of the mighty (*bene elim*) trembled in their palaces, as it is said: 'And in his palace every one says "Glory"' (Ps. 29:9). Whereupon the kings of the world assembled and came to Balaam, saying: What is the uproar that we heard? Is a flood to come to destroy the earth? Said he to them: 'The Lord sitteth upon the flood' (*ibid.*, 10). The Holy One, blessed be He, swore long ago that He would not bring a flood upon the world for ever. They then said to him: He will not bring a flood of water, but He may bring a flood of fire as it is said: 'For by fire will the Lord contend' (Isa. 66:16). But he said to them: He is going to bring neither a flood of water, nor a flood of fire. However, He possesses in His storehouse a priceless treasure, the Torah which He is to present to His sons, as it is said: 'The Lord will give strength unto His people' (Ps. 29:11). As soon as the kings heard that from him, they joined in the benediction: 'The Lord will bless His people with peace'" (*ibid*).

Rabbi Eleazar of Modaim died during the siege of Bethar (c. 135 c.e.) and taught in days when it became clear that the natural base of the Hebrew polity, the state and the sanctuary, were lost. However impoverished, Israel still possessed a priceless treasure from God's storehouse, the Torah. Hence the new stress on the gift of revelation, and on God's power in history rather than nature. Transposed, as it were, into a new key, the Psalm was employed in the liturgy of the Feast of Weeks, which commemorates the covenant at Sinai, when the Torah was given to Israel. . . .

Echoes of darker centuries survive in the *Midrash to the Psalms*, a collection of homilies from various times, some perhaps going back to days of Roman or Byzantine rule and oppression:

"*Bene elim*, 'the sons of the gods'—what does that mean? The sons of the dumb (*bene ilmim*) and the deaf (i.e., the sons of Israel) who could answer back the Holy One, blessed be He, but they refrain from answering back, and suffer the yoke of the nations for the sanctification of His name. This is what Isaiah said (42:19): 'Who is blind, but my servant, or deaf, as my messenger that I sent?'

"*Bene elim*—what else can that mean? The sons of those who are slain like rams (*elim*). Abraham said: I slay; Isaac says: I am (ready to be) slain."

Pained and puzzled by the triumph of the wicked, the religious conscience sought solace and support in the examples of patriarchal piety or the songs of the suffering servant. The ways of God were inscrutable. Abraham did not comprehend how a father could be commanded to [280] slay his only son, but he did not refuse or reproach God, he obeyed instead, to be rewarded and relieved in the end. Silently also the servant of the Lord must bear his martyrdom, a spoil and sport of all mankind, and yet it is with his stripes that the world will be healed. It was in the light of such memories or monition that Psalm 29 was reread in the early Middle Ages.

When the swift victories of Islam and the vast realm conquered by the new faith seemed to make the hopes of Jewish repatriation impracticable or illusory, the troubled heart turned again to the Psalter for courage and comfort. Psalm 29 was rendered as summoning the children of Israel to be *bene elim*, sons of might or men of valor, and to persevere in the faith as there was hope in their future. Verse 10 was understood to contain the solemn assurance that just as the Lord guards the universe against the flood, so He remains His people's king forever: "For as I have sworn that the waters of Noah should no more go over the earth, so have I sworn that I would not be wroth with thee, nor rebuke thee. For the mountains shall depart, and the hills be removed, but my kindness shall not depart from thee, neither shall the covenant of my peace be removed, saith the Lord that hath mercy on thee" (Isa. 54:9f.). The Psalm was so translated by Saadia, and his version is still current among Arabic-speaking Jews.

In the lands of medieval Christendom, the Psalms was construed as a prophecy about the days of Messianic deliverance, when "the cedars of Lebanon," the proud kingdoms of the earth will be humbled. The Lord will thunder "upon many waters"; these are the rich and rapacious that grab the goods of this world as greedily as waters cover the sea. But in the end, justice will be enthroned for ever, and in His temple all will say "Glory," as it is said: "Then will I turn to the peoples a pure language, that they may all call upon the Name of the Lord, to serve Him with one consent" (Zeph. 3:9).

After the banishment from Spain (1492), which uprooted the most populous and prosperous community of the Middle Ages, mystical tendencies gained the ascendancy. The Psalter was read fervently as an apocalypse in which every word is infused with references to the events of the imminently expected Messianic catastrophe or redemption. In fact, the Psalms themselves were discovered to be a book of war songs, an arsenal of mystic or magic weapons, "a sharp sword in Israel's hand" to strike at the root of evil and thus precipitate the end. When the crack of doom failed to come, and the Messianic fever wore away, there spread from Safed, a town in northern Gaililee, audacious new doctrines such as the cabbala of Isaac Luria (d. 1572), which gave a new answer to the basic and baffling facts of the historic experience of the Jew and a new meaning to his acts of worship.

The homelessness of the Jewish people was conceived to be but a detail in the general dislocation of the whole of existence due to a primordial flaw or fracture of all creation which the new cabbala called "the breaking of the vessels." Because of it, all realms of being were unhinged and deranged, thrown out of their proper and purposed station, everything in the order of creation was displaced, all were in exile, including God. Supernal lights fell in the abyss of darkness, and sparks of holiness [281] became imprisoned in shells of evil. The unity of the Divine Name was shattered (the new cabbala speaks of the letters YH being torn away from WH in the name YHWH). It was the mission of man and the purpose of religion to restore the broken name of God and so heal the original blemish of all the visible and invisible worlds. By observing the commandments of the Torah and the ordained discipline of worship, every Jew could become a partner in the work of redemption: he could help to lift the fallen lights of God and set free the holy sparks from the powers of evil.

With ardent precision every detail in form and language of the Psalms was instilled with mystic meaning and function. Concretely, in Psalm 29, three times it was said "Give unto the Lord," seven times "the voice of the Lord," eighteen times the Divine Name is spelled, making seventy-two letters or the numerical value of *hesed*, or mercy. The eleven verses of the Psalm equal WH in the tetragram, while the ninety-one words in the whole Psalm correspond to the sum total of YHWH and Adonai. By means of each of these mysteries of prayer, the worshiper who knew the secrets of the holy letters and was capable of utter inwardness (*kavvanah*) in his devotions, could work miracles of *tikkun* or restitution by which sparks scattered in the lower depths could be reassembled, and "the Holy One, praised by He, reunited with His exiled *Shekinah*." Acts of religion determine the fate of the world, and it is the essential distinction and dignity of man that without his free choice the breach of creation could not be mended. Feeble as man is, unlike the angels, he alone knows, in every breath of his, about the struggle of good and evil, and can influence it by his freedom of action. Hence only man, and not any of the celestial beings, can lead the banished glory of God back to the Master, and thus literally "give unto the Lord glory and strength," thereby completing His enthronement as "king for ever."

In this new myth, which burst forth in the heart of Judaism at so late a stage of the historic faith, mystic notions verge on magic, or perhaps revert to the origins of all worship in which prayer and spell commingle. As if the wheel had come full circle, and the new cabbala had recovered, on another plane, the prebiblical rudiments of magic, residual in the Psalms and perhaps irreducible from man's vocabulary of prayer.[32]

Here we have had occasion to observe what happens to a biblical text. But truth to say, this phenomenon of reinterpretation is not confined to the originally revealed and recorded words. Teachings of the Oral Law, too, flourish under such treatment, and thus make it possible for each generation to enact its own role with and within the "lines" it has inherited.[33] For example: Antigonus of Soko had said, "Be not like slaves (*ka-ʿabadim*) who [282] serve (*ha-meshamshin*) a master (*rab*) with an eye on their rations (*peras*); be rather like slaves who serve a master with no thought of their rations."[34] But already the earliest commentator[35] who reflected on this saying knew no way of expressing himself other than, "Shall a laborer (*poʿel*) work (*yaʿaseh melakah*) all day and not receive his reward ([wages] *sekaro*) in the evening?" Evidently by the commentator's time Antigonus' saying made sense only in the vocabulary of laborer and wages (even though the commentator knew of the institution of slavery!). And if there is a moral to be derived, it has to conform to the reality of the commentator's age.

Anachronism we call this, and for the historian it is the unpardonable sin; but anachronism is one of the firmest signs of the vitality of a tradition. To be able to recognize that and how we differ from those of other times and other places is no mean accomplishment of critical intelligence. But the equation of past with present is not failure of intellect. It may be innocent of historical discipline, but it is a pious act of imaginativeness. For to project our conduct into the practice of the Patriarchs is to reveal how profoundly we still crave their company and how close we feel to them. When Abraham, Isaac, and Jacob recite the morning, afternoon, and evening services which are second nature to the later generation,[36] we are certainly not observing history; but we

32. "On Medieval Hebrew Poetry" in Finkelstein, *The Jews* (New York, 1960), pp. 860–64.

33. On the use of the term "Midrash" in connection with interpretation of tannaite statements, cf. J. N. Epstein, *Meboʾot le-Sifrut ha-Tannaim*, p. 502.

34. PA, 1:3 and cf. E. J. Bickerman, "The Maxim of Antigonus of Socho" in *HTR*, 44 (1951), pp. 153ff.

35. ARN, V, 26.

36. On the Patriarchs and the *tefillot* see B. Berakot 26b (see Midrash Mishle 22:28, 47a), and cf. L. Ginzberg, *Legends*, VI, p. 449f. On the Patriarchs observing the Law, cf. Ginzberg, op. cit., V, p. 259, n. 275.

do witness the later generation identifying itself with its ancestors on whom it charitably confers the treasures it cherishes—because it cannot endure the loneliness which being only contemporary creates. Be of the *disciples* of Aaron, Hillel once said to priests who were content to be merely the *descendants* of Aaron.[37] What was it to be a *disciple* of Aaron? To love peace and pursue it, to love mankind and draw them to the Torah. But to love peace, to love mankind, to draw men to the Torah rather than alienate them from it, is surely a pursuit which even non-Aaronides would do well to cultivate. So by the second century, that saying of Hillel's is interpreted as a direction to all of society's members,[38] regardless of the original *mise en scène*.

[283] Simeon the Righteous had once declared that one of the pillars of the Age was *gemilut ḥasadim*.[39] As an old text reveals, *gemilut ḥasadim* was originally a term that included all kinds of pietistic acts, even prayer.[40] But by the time the Temple was destroyed a number of traditional concepts came to be reinterpreted, and thus *gemilut ḥasadim* became acts of love surpassing charity, and prayer moved over into the realm of *'abodah*, which had once been the institution of Temple worship. In Midrash the original is not so much displaced as enlarged, to embrace needs that suddenly become visible; thus the old and new live side by side.

I have deliberately chosen examples which reflect a determination to be literal even in the process of reinterpretation; that is to say, I am intentionally not enlisting illustrations of allegorical interpretation, although such appear in Midrash also; note, for instance, what the Mishnah[41] does with the biblical

37. PA, 1:12, and cf. J. Goldin in *Studies and Texts*, vol. 3, ed. A. Altmann [above, p. 222.—Ed.].

38. Cf. ARN, both versions, ed. Schechter, pp. 48–49.

39. PA, 1:2, and cf. *Proceedings, American Academy of Jewish Research* (henceforth *PAAJR*), 27 (1958), pp. 43–58 [above, p. 56.—Ed.]. In connection with the view expressed here on *'olam*, see also the Hebrew commentary on Ecclesiastes (1:10) by H. L. Ginsberg, *Koheleth* (Tel Aviv-Jerusalem, 1961), p. 62. And I might add the following: In Codex Kaufmann of M. Ta'anit 3:8 (and so too in the Mishnah, ed. Loewe!) the prayer attributed to Honi begins simply with רבוני and then someone corrected the *yod* to a *waw* and above the line *inserted* the words *shel 'olam*! Cf. the use of δέσποτα in Luke 2:29 and Acts 4:24. (Interestingly, in his excellent Hebrew translation of the New Testament Delitzsch renders δέσποτα by *'Adonai* and proceeds to use the same rendering for κύριε of Acts 4:29.) Cf. also, by the way, the commentary of K. Lake and H. J. Cadbury on Acts 13:46 (οὐκ ἀξίους . . . τῆς αἰωνίου ζωῆς) in *Beginnings of Christianity*, vol. 4 ed. F. Jackson and K. Lake, (London, 1933), p. 159. Unfortunately, I *am* familiar with the observations in *Journal of Jewish Studies*, 10 (1959), p. 169ff.: one morsel will serve as a specimen of their "scholarship"—"*Qoheleth* already seems to have used *'olam* in the new sense, as did *Ben Sira*." For Qoheleth the author supplies (n. 6) the reference of 3:11 and (n. 7) for Sirach 16:7. On *'olam* in Palestinian sources, cf. S. Lieberman, *Hayerushalmi Kiphshuto* (Jerusalem, 1934), p. 504. On the form *rbwny* of M. Ta'anit 3:8 cf. Mark 10:51 and John 20:16, and see the recent comment by N. Wieder in *Leshonénu*, 27–28, p. 214ff.

40. I do not understand how M. Smith, "The Dead Sea Sect" in *New Testament Studies*, 7, p. 356 (cf. n. 2 ibid.) explains ARN, p. 21; cf. *PAAJR*, 27, pp. 46–47, and notes ad loc. [above, p. 28.—Ed.].

41. M. Rosh ha-Shanah 3:8. For Philo's view see Legum Allegoria III, 186, and III, 45. Note too how Justin Martyr is fascinated by that biblical anecdote, *Dialogue with Trypho*, chaps. 90 and 97.

reports of the uplifted hands of Moses at the battle with Amalek, or of the effectiveness of the brazen serpent;[42] or, for that matter, observe what two tannaite schools of thought are capable of making out of the Song of Songs.[43] I refrain from referring to allegorizing exercises not because (as I said) they are absent from midrashic activity, but because, in my opinion, allegorical interpretation has [284] little to teach us about what we would call adaptation. Why is that? In allegorical exegesis the traces of the original Word tend to get erased. In allegory we create a dichotomy between the explicitly scriptural statement and its presumptive intent; we really do set up a kind of hierarchy of lower and higher meanings. Soon we discover—as one of the best-known practitioners of the art, Philo, himself informs us—that such exegesis tends to remove original practice from circulation, threatens to push the past into the expendable archaic, and the present becomes not an adaptation but an emancipation. Philo writes:

> There are some who, regarding laws in their literal sense in the light of symbols of matters belonging to the intellect, are overpunctilious about the latter, while treating the former with easy-going neglect. Such men I for my part should blame for handling the matter in too easy and offhand a manner: they ought to have given careful attention to both aims, to a more full and exact investigation of what is not seen and in what is seen to be stewards without reproach. As it is, as though they were living alone by themselves in a wilderness, or as though they had become disembodied souls, and knew neither city nor village nor household nor any company of human beings at all, overlooking all that the mass of men regard, they explore reality in its naked absoluteness. These men are taught by the sacred word to have thought for good repute, and to let go nothing that is part of the customs fixed by divinely empowered men greater than those of our time. It is quite true that the Seventh Day is meant to teach the power of the Unoriginate and the non-action of created beings. But let us not for this reason abrogate the laws laid down for its observance, and light fires or till the ground or carry loads or institute proceedings in court or act as jurors or demand the restoration of deposits or recover loans, or do all else that we are permitted to do as well on days that are not festival seasons. It is true that receiving circumcision does indeed portray the excision of pleasure and all passions, and the putting away of the impious conceit, under which the mind supposed that it was capable of begetting by its own power: but let us not on this account repeal the law laid down for circumcising. Why, we shall be ignoring the sanctity of the Temple and a thousand other things, if we are going to pay heed to nothing except what is shewn us by the inner meaning of things. Nay, we should look on all these outward observances as resembling the soul. It follows that, exactly as we have to take thought for the body, because it is the abode of the soul, so we must pay heed to the letter of the laws. If we keep and observe these, we shall gain a clearer conception of those things of which these are the symbols; and

42. M. Rosh ha-Shanah, ibid. For Philo's view see Legum Allegoria II, 79ff.: cf. De Agricultura, 95ff. Note Justin *First Apology*, chap. 60, *Dialogue with Trypho*, chap. 94.
43. See S. Lieberman in G. G. Scholem, *Jewish Gnosticism, Merkabah Mysticism, and Talmudic Tradition* (New York, 1960), pp. 118–26.

besides that we shall not incur the censure of the many and the charges they are sure to bring against us.[44]

Allegory in its passion to universalize and defend, rationalizes, [285] excuses; non-allegorizing Midrash—what I do not hesitate to call anachronism —absorbs and discloses, absorbs and discloses. Root, branch, and flower therefore remain united.

It is in this connection that I would like to comment briefly on a presumption which is frequently adopted by scholars in the study of classical Judaism, and while this presumption has something to recommend it on some occasions, on others it tends to mislead us and interfere indeed with *our* understanding of the development of the Jewish tradition. From Hoffmann to Epstein[45] it has been repeatedly underscored that when we encounter a view attributed, let us say, to a sage of the late second century (c.e.), that does not establish the origin of that view with that sage. The particular view may in fact be much older, and all our sources are preserving is merely one more, and perhaps late, transmitter of an old view. For example, it is the Tanna Rabbi Judah ben 'Il'ai who says that only compared to his wretched contemporaries was Noah a Ṣaddiq, as the verse says, "*in his generations* was Noah a Ṣaddiq." *Au royaume des aveugles les borgnes sont rois.* But that view, we know, is already expressed by Philo about two centuries earlier.[46] A number of halakic examples are cited by Epstein, who thereupon concludes,

And so we discover that midrashic views cited anonymously (*setam*) in the halakic midrashim, and even such views as are attributed to late Tannaim, may well be *very ancient* [his italics], and the Sages in whose name the particular midrash is handed on are no more than Tannaim who reported it and handed it on.[47]

There is no denying that on many occasions this is the case, for we know that whenever and where an oral tradition is vigorous, memory is actively cultivated and the remembrance of things past is truly impressive. All of us recall the fears expressed by the god Thamus to Theuth, "the father of letters," because Thamus did not want the "elixir" of memory to be replaced by devices for remembering.[48] But I should like to say that although we must not underestimate the contributions made to Judaism by good memories, we should not therewith underestimate the contributions made by forgetting. For not every-

44. *De Migratione Abrahami* 89–93, trans. Colson and Whitaker (Loeb Classics, IV, pp. 183–84.
45. D. Hoffmann, *Ha-Mishnah ha-Rishonah* (Berlin, 1913), pp. 42ff., 58–59; J. N. Epstein, *Mebo'ot le-Sifrut ha-Tannaim*, pp. 512ff. In all fairness it should be added that, of course, these scholars do not ignore the fact that some things were forgotten; see, e.g., Hoffmann, p. 54.
46. R. Judah's view in Gen. R. 30:9, ed. Theodor-Albeck, p. 275; Philo's view in De Abrahamo, 36. Cf. *Ventures* (Yale University), III (Winter, 1964), pp. 24ff.
47. Op. cit., p. 513.
48. Plato, Phaedrus, 247C–275A. See further below, pp. 231ff., and notes.

thing was remembered [286] and fortunately a good deal was forgotten. In addition to the examples cited earlier, a number of others might be presented. Thus, a warning against theurgic exploitation of the divine Name[49] becomes an admonition against deriving personal advantage from the words of the Torah;[50] an epicurean[51] is identified as the despiser of the Sages[52] or (with greater justice) as the violator of God's commandment[53]—although one midrashic passage does apparently recall accurately at least one correct view of such deniers of Providence;[54] a hedge about the Torah equals hedges the Sages made about their own words.[55]

Such exegesis clearly demonstrates that the original meaning and intention of a number of early teachings were indeed forgotten. Midrash, which gave the old statements "new" meaning and "new" direction—in other words, applicability in terms of the requirements or emphases of the later periods—could accomplish this because of what we may call "anachronism," the assumption by a later generation that ideas uppermost in its mind are necessarily the ideas uppermost in the mind of the earlier generation. Anachronism, naturally, is always at work in every society. But what makes it so congenial to and operative in classical Judaism is the combination we have been hinting at and now state explicitly—and this is what I meant when I said that, fortunately, a good deal was forgotten: on the one hand, great painstaking at conserving what has been handed down by the past, but on the other, firm conviction that the once-upon-a-time revealed Word and the subsequent words which are its outgrowth continue with unceasing life and liveliness to release successive truths which are not novel, [287] but only newly recognizable, permanent elements of the original content. Not "new written," as Thomas Fuller might have said, but newly scoured. Conserving saves the tradition from transiency; Midrash saves it from arteriosclerosis. And both conserving and commentary must be simultaneously at work; either without the other is empty of meaningfulness.

49. PA, 1:13 and see ARN, both versions, p. 56; cf. Scholem, *Jewish Gnosticism*, pp. 54 and 80f.

50. PA, 4:5. Note carefully the idiom of that Mishnah. Rabbi Ṣadoq warns against "misuse" of words of the Torah (apparently; on the text of *lo taʿaśem*, cf. C. Taylor, *Sayings of the Jewish Fathers* [Cambridge, 1900], II, 156). Presumably he thereupon quotes Hillel for support. Then follows הא למדת וכו׳, which is not necessarily R. Ṣadoq's statement, but someone else's derivation from R. Ṣadoq's statement and "prooftext." The matter is too complicated for a brief footnote. I would simply like to say that in many tannaite passages we come upon what I would like to call strata of interpretation brought together. On the nature of the structure of PA, 4:5, cf. PA, 1:5, and note ARN, pp. 33 and 35.

51. M. Sanhedrin 10:1.

52. B. Sanhedrin 99b.

53. Cf. Sifre Numbers 119, ed. Horovitz, p. 121 on Num. 15:31; cf. Targum Jonathan on the verse.

54. Midrash Psalms 1:22; cf. S. Lieberman, "How Much Greek in Jewish Palestine?" in A. Altmann (ed.), *Studies and Texts*, 1 (Cambridge, 1963), p. 130 and the note on *'epiqurus* in J. Goldin's Hebrew essay in the *Wolfson Jubilee Volume* (in press) [below, p. 233.—Ed.].

55. Cf. PA, 1:1, ARN, pp. 3 and 14, and J. Goldin's essay referred to above, n. 37. On forgetting see also B. Berakot 27b, ʿUla's report.

Here, it seems to me, we may begin to discover something of the implicit (and perhaps partly conscious) intent behind the resolute insistence on the cultivation of an Oral Torah. "That which is written thou mayest not recite by heart, that which is oral thou mayest not reduce to writing."[56] That certain teachings are not to be reduced to writing and are to be communicated only orally is a view not limited to Judaism, and possibly not even original to it.[57] Not all the doctrines of Pythagoras, a number of Pythagoreans used to say, were to be communicated to everyone;[58] according to Plutarch, Alexander received from Aristotle

> not only his doctrines of Morals and of Politics, but also something of those more abstruse and profound theories which these philosophers, [288] by the very names they gave them, professed to reserve for oral communication to the initiated, and did not allow many to become acquainted with.

Plutarch goes on to report that when Alexander

> was in Asia, and heard Aristotle had published some treatises of that kind, he wrote to him, using very plain language to him in behalf of philosophy . . . , "Alexander to Aristotle, greeting. You have not done well to publish your books of oral doctrine;

---

56. B. Gittin 60b and cf. de-be R. Ishmael, ibid.

57. I hope to elaborate on this point in a subsequent study. *Pro tem*, however, I would like to call attention to the misgivings toward the written word already encountered in the Phaedrus (see above) and Epistle VII (341C–E, 344 C–345A), and cf. W. Jaeger, *Paideia* (New York, 1960), III, 194ff. (see further below in this note). No significance, it seems to me, should be attached to the fact that the expression "Oral Torah" is not explicitly encountered in midrashic-talmudic sources before the first century C.E., perhaps even early in that century; cf. W. Bacher, '*Aggadot ha-Tannaim* (Hebrew) (Berlin, 5682), I, p. 56, n. 4. Emphasis on Oral Torah was already being made c. 250 B.C.E., as I have shown elsewhere (cf. n. 37, above).

In a sensitive analysis of the prayer at the end of the Phaedrus, T. G. Rosenmeyer (*Hermes*, 90 [1962], pp. 34–44) has explained that not writing *qua* writing is being objected to by Plato (see also his n. 1, p. 40, in regard to what Thamus is advocating!), "But care must be taken that the writing and mass communication remain in tune with and faithful to the knowledge and the convictions which are the original fruit of the philosophic discussion in the Academy" (p. 42, and see also Rosenmeyer's n. 2, ibid.). Very likely true enough; and note the quotation from Phaedrus 258D 1–5, Rosenmeyer brings in n. 3, p. 41. But as Rosenmeyer himself says (pp. 41–42), "For Plato, theoretically, the written can be as true as the spoken, but it can make that claim only to the extent that it is based on the spoken." The pre-eminence of the oral, then, remains a Platonic assumption. And I believe it is to the "Greek" world we are to look for the first signs of this attitude. (By the way, I owe the reference to Plutarch's *Life of Alexander*, below in the text of the paper, to Rosenmeyer's citation of it.) That the written continues to be regarded with some reserve, can be seen also in Philostratus (*Life of Appolonius* IV, 33 [ed. Loeb, I, 427]): "Palamedes discovered writing not only in order that people might write, but also in order that they might know what they must not write."

On "inner" and "outer" in Hebrew and Aramaic, see *Bulletin of Hebrew Language Studies*, II, of H. Yalon (Jerusalem, 1963), pp. 46–47.

When I recently discussed the subject of Oral Torah with Professor E. Bickerman, he put the matter rather neatly to me: In the oriental world the chief thing is the written word; in the Greek world it is the Word, the *logos*.

58. Diogenes Laertius 8:15 (Rosenmeyer also refers to this source).

for what is there now that we excel others in, if those things which we have been particularly instructed in be laid open to all?"[59]

A strong reluctance to put certain teachings in writing is therefore nothing strange. There is, certainly, something noteworthy about Judaism in this regard, namely, that the bulk of Oral Torah is not treated as though it were for a small elite of initiates;[60] The Sages, those shipwrights of the Oral Torah itself, never weary of pleading that (except for some truly esoteric teachings)[61] the contents of the Oral Torah ought to be accessible to *all* Israel. Even here, however, it seems to me that as historians we ought to beware of too sweeping a generalization. As I have already remarked parenthetically, there were certain themes of gnosis not to be publicly explored and disseminated. Even more: Lieberman has shown that on occasion the Sages would enact measures for [289] one reason but give out to the public another reason for the enactment.[62] This is certainly a kind of holding back, suggesting that not everything in the Oral Torah is fit for public consumption. And I am prepared to go further still: There are statements in our sources to support the contention that sometimes, even when non-esoteric substances were at issue, the general public is *not* invited.

"[Now these are the ordinances] which thou shalt set before them" (Exod. 21:1). It is not said here "before the children of Israel," but *before them*, their foremost ones

59. *Life of Alexander*, VII, Dryden-Clough translation (New York: Modern Library), p. 805.
60. Cf. A. Harnack, *Bible Reading in the Early Church* (New York, 1912), pp. 145–47: "The proof that the Bible in the Early Church was not a secret book but was accessible to all, and was also much read in private, involves a point of peculiar importance; it follows that the religion of the Early Church, however much of mystery and sacrament it gradually adopted, was, like Judaism, no mystery-religion. If the revelation of God—and according to Christian ideas the Bible included practically all instances of Divine revelation—was in its entirety accessible to all, if in regard to this revelation the priest was almost as much a 'layman' as the layman himself, if no ecclesiastical law, no clerical interference was allowed to come between God speaking in the Bible and the soul of him who listened and read, then the religion is in principle no mystery-religion, to whatever extent it may have become such in its accessories. . . . It was not yet a mystery-religion even about the year 300 . . . If it is asked how it happened that Christianity was able to preserve in principle its distinctive character and to defend its sacred writings from the encroachment of the priesthood amid a world of mystery-religion, we answer—it was because Christianity was the daughter of Judaism."
Note indeed the very emphasis made by the story of Shammai and Hillel and the Gentile who seeks to be converted—even to the proselyte one is eager to give over Torah *she-be'al peh* (ARN, p. 61, and parallels). As for exhortations that everyone ought to study Torah, they are legion and need not be quoted. I would like simply to call attention to the fact that already of the first Pair, Yose ben Joezer, in the first half of the second century B.C.E., is the author of the saying that one's house should be a meeting-place of the Sages and that one ought to drink their words thirstily (PA, 1:4). These Sages are Torah-sages, and on Wisdom-Torah, cf. Sirach, chap. 24.
61. See M. Ḥagigah 2:1 and also ARNB, p. 23, and cf. Sirach 3:21ff. Cf. Lieberman on T. Ḥagigah 2:1 et seq. in his "Long Commentary," pp. 1286 et. seq., as well as his observations in "How Much Greek in Jewish Palestine?" pp. 135ff.
62. *Hellenism in Jewish Palestine* (New York, 1962), pp. 139ff. Note also M. 'Abodah Zarah 2:5 and commentators ad loc.

(*le-panim she-lahem*). This teaches (*melammed*) that one does not teach (*shonin*) civil law[63] to an *'am ha-'areṣ*. Another interpretation: *Which thou shalt set before them*—even as a treasure[64] is not revealed to every person, so you have no right to immerse yourself in [?][65] words of Torah except in the presence of the right kind of people (*bene 'adam kesherin*).[66]

And perhaps the same notion lies buried under the following passage of the Tanḥuma:[67]

> *If ye walk in My statutes*, etc. In this connection the verse says (Prov. 1:20), *Wisdom crieth in the street, she uttereth her voice in the spacious places.* [Once] when Rabbi Jonathan ben Eleazar was standing in the market place, Rabbi Samuel bar Nahman asked him, saying, "Teach (*shanneh*) me a chapter." Said Rabbi Jonathan to him, "Go to the Talmud-house[68] and there I will teach you." Said Rabbi Samuel to him, "Master, did you not teach me (*limadetani*),[69] '*Wisdom crieth in the street*'?" Said Rabbi Jonathan to him, "You understand neither Scripture nor Mishnah. Do you know what [290] '*Wisdom crieth in the street*' means? In the street of Torah. Where are pearls sold? On the street reserved for the sale of pearls![70] So too the Torah is discussed in its own street. And what is the meaning of *in the spacious places*? In places where it is enlarged [extended].[71] And where is it enlarged? In the synagogues and study houses. That is the meaning of *she uttereth her voice in the spacious places*.'"

Despite such signals, however, it is a noteworthy feature of talmudic Judaism that Oral Torah is intended for all, for "everyone that thirsteth," and is not the reservoir of an exclusive fraternity. Unlike the crown of priesthood and

---

63. *Dine mamonot*. By the way, cf. Maimonides, *Guide*, III, 41, ed. Pines, p. 358.

64. *Penimah*, a play on the word *panim* (*lifnehem*). Cf. variants ad loc. See, however, *Bulletin* 2 of H. Yalon, p. 55.

65. Text, *'al* (rather than the prefix *be-*).

66. Mekilta Simeon, ed. Epstein-Melamed, p. 158. Perhaps with this view one ought to compare a sentiment fairly frequently expressed on not teaching the wicked; cf. ARN, p. 42, the second interpretation of "Do not associate with the wicked." It might not be amiss to point out that in Mekilta Simeon, op. cit., immediately after this passage, appears the story of Johanan ben Zakkai and Eleazar ben 'Arak on the latter's Merkabah discourse. Cf. further J. Goldin in *Wolfson Jubilee Volume* (cited above, n. 54). A thought occurs to me that seems worth mentioning: While the sources will discourage one from *teaching* the wicked, and occasionally, too, register a sentiment like—to the wicked God says, What have you to do with my Torah—there is no hesitation to encourage people to *study* Torah even if not out of the highest motives; for there is confidence that study of the Torah, begun even with low motives, will have the necessary elevating effect on the temporarily unworthy student. Cf. Lam. R., Petihta 2, ed. Buber, pp. 2–3.

67. Ed. Buber, III. 55a.

68. *Bet ha-Talmud*, the study house, the place where the Oral Law is studied.

69. Here the verb is *lammed*, a generalized term. I have purposely called attention in the text to the verb *shanneh* so that the character of study and teaching of Oral Law will be clear at a glance.

70. Literally, in its own street. A reflection by the way of the existence of shopping districts.

71. *Marḥivin*, playing on *reḥovot*.

unlike the crown of royalty, "the toil of Torah? Whoever wishes to take it on, let him come and take it on, as it is said, *Ho, everyone that thirsteth, come ye for water*."[72] And even in the more extreme language of Rabbi Meir:

> How do we know that even an idolator who studies Torah is like the high priest? The verse says, "*Which if a man do them, he shall live by them*. It is not said priests, levites, Israelites—but *man*. Hence you learn that even a gentile who studies Torah is like a high priest.[73]

One should teach (*yeshanneh*) everyone, said the School of Hillel, opposing the School of Shammai who felt that one is to teach (*yeshanneh*) only such as were talented, humble, of distinguished ancestry, and rich[74]—for many were the sinners in Israel who were drawn to the study of Torah and from them descended righteous, pious, and decent folk.[75] Significantly enough, even that comparison of the Mishnah, that is, the Oral Torah, to a "mystery," in Rabbi Judah be-rabbi Shalom's homily[76] is in thorough agreement with the sentiment expressed by the statements just cited. For what is it Rabbi Judah is underscoring? That when the nations of the world exhibit their Greek translations of Scripture as proof that *they* are [291] the true Israel, the Holy One, blessed be He, will affirm that only the elite in possession of His *mysterion* are the true Israel; in other words, the people (as a whole), the present Israel, is Israel—and it is their possession of the Oral Torah which distinguishes between Israel and the Gentiles, מה בין ישראל לאומות.[77] How like Alexander's words to Aristotle! "For what is there now that we excel others in, if those things which we have been particularly instructed in be laid open to all?"[78]

As far as Israel is concerned, then, devotion to Oral Torah is expected of everyone, and the content of Oral Torah is not to be reduced to writing. The existence of private *hypomnemata*[79] does not affect this resolution: When there is no official written text, you have no canonical scripture.[80] "Publish and

---

72. ARN, both versions, pp. 130–31 and parallels.

73. B. Sanhedrin 59a and parallels.

74. Cf. J. Goldin, *The Fathers According to Rabbi Nathan* (New Haven, Conn., 1955), p. 181, nn. 2–3.

75. ARN, both versions, pp. 14f. Cf. H. I. Marrou, *History of Education in Antiquity* (New York, 1956), pp. 38ff. In this connection I cannot resist quoting (though the context is different) Plato, Epistle VII, 337 B (Bury trans.): "Now those who have gained the mastery, whenever they become desirous of safety, ought always to choose out among themselves such men of Greek origin as they know by inquiry to be most excellent—men who are, in the first place, old, and who have wives and children at home" (cf. also M. Taʿanit 2:2), "and forefathers as numerous and good and famous as possible, and who are all in possession of ample property."

76. Pesiqta R. 14b; cf. Tanḥuma Va-Yera 5 and Ki Tissa 34.

77. In relation to the rest of the world, then, Israel is that small band of initiates: but it is *all* Israel, not a small group in it.

78. Cf. above, p. 232.

79. On the subject of such *hypomnemata*, cf. S. Lieberman, *Hellenism in Jewish Palestine*, pp. 87ff. and 205, and the literature he cites.

80. Cf. H. L. Strack, *Introduction to the Talmud and Midrash* (Philadelphia 1931), p. 17.

perish" would have been the attitude of the early Sages.[81] And the determination for almost a millennium[82] to preserve Oral Torah as oral is surely what made it possible for Midrash to sustain an elasticity which a written record makes more difficult.[83] The written word, as we have seen, does not prevent interpretation and reinterpretation—and therefore what in our language we call adaptation. But by limiting written-down revelation to work, and by reserving the role of exegesis to oral activity, a spaciousness, a resilience, a plasticity, a kind of responsible spiritual and intellectual flexibility was provided which made constant reinterpretation of the primary divine [292] Word not only possible but inevitable. Midrash thus became a genuine exercise at fulfilling the innumerable possibilities of the original Word through fresh explorations unrestricted by the strictly literal vocabulary of each generation's commentators: such a burden would have been unbearable and the sheer weight would have been crushing.[84] Witness what happens to certain speci-

---

Note, by the way, the reflection of R. Jonah Gerondi on PA, 3:13 *s.v. masoret*. And note also the Epistle of Sherira Gaon in A. Hyman, *Toldoth Tannaim Ve'Amoraim* (London, 1910), III, Igereth, pp. 28–29: . . .

וכן נמי לא הוו גרסי כולא
בפה אחד ולשון אחד ולא היו
להם דברים מתוקנים ומשנה
ידוע שהכל שונין אותה בפה
אחד ולשון אחד . . . כל אחד ואחד
מתני לתלמידיו באיזה חבור
שירצה ובאיזה דרך שירצה וכו'

81. See the statement attributed to R. Johanan in B. Temurah 14b and Tanḥuma references cited in n. 76 above. Cf. Lieberman, *HJP*, pp. 84ff.

82. "In the schools of the Amoraim, the discussion went on with no written copy in evidence to serve as a basis" (Strack, op. cit., and cf. the reference cited in his note 64, p. 246). Somewhere (unfortunately I am unable to locate where at the moment) Professor S. Rosenthal, of Jerusalem, has shown that even in the geonic yeshivot, and later too, the Talmud was studied orally. In the schools the talmudic substance was not so much read (לא נקרא) as presented orally (אלא הוצע). See also H. Z. Dimitrovsky in the *Sefunot* study (referred to below, n. 85), pp. 100ff.

83. Cf. Strack, loc. cit.

84. It seems to me that modern scholars have not paid sufficient attention to this aspect of the Oral Torah, though it is to some extent certainly appreciated by at least two comments in the Midrash; see Num. R. 14:10, 58d, the remark of R. Abba Sarungiya (cf. Rashash ad loc.) and also the first comment by R. Berechiah ha-kohen on Eccl. 12:11 (*maśmerot neṭuʿim*). It is frequently enough underscored, and doubtless in some measure rightly so, that ultimately Oral Torah had to be put in writing because the sheer quantity demanded it. However, this is certainly not the whole story. Note that when Maimonides in the introduction to his *Code* explains why Rabbi Judah the Prince compiled the Mishnah, he says that the Patriarch "observed that the number of students was continually diminishing, new disasters were increasing, the Roman empire was expanding more and more and growing stronger, and Israel was scattering to the ends of the world." Not a word, in short, about the vast quantity of the contents of the Oral Torah. Even for the composition of his own *Code* he does not quite speak of the impossibility of mastering the tradition because of its quantity, but because of calamitous times and the *difficulty of comprehension*!

Eventually, obviously, the Oral Torah was put into written form. But just as obviously for a long, long time there was powerful reluctance to do so (again, despite the fact that individuals kept private notes for their own use). And to a considerable degree this reluctance was due to a realization that there is something inflexible about the written word; cf. what R. Berechiah says on *neṭuʿim* versus *qebuʿim*, and note also the quotation from R. Sherira above, n. 80.

mens of late *pilpul* when it has lost the original spontaneity.[85] Any issue of *Ha-Pardes* will serve as an illustration. So long as Torah thrives *be-ʿal peh*, orally, the academicians can feel without any sense of incongruity that the words of them that forbid and the words of them that permit, the words of those who declare something unclean and the words of those who declare it clean, the words of them that declare something unfit and the words of them that declare it fit come into being because of one God, are transmitted by one leader, are the utterance of the Master over all things.[86]

[293] Doubtless, as homily this is praiseworthy; but how was it in practice? There certainly was tension between the ideal attitude and the practical demands, and if the society was not to disintegrate, some form of equilibrium had to be achieved. The clash between the Nasi Gamaliel II and his colleagues in the academy is perhaps one of the best known incidents of what must have been a recurring problem.[87] But note: the problem is not one of whether the Oral Torah was to be reduced to written form. Even to Gamaliel this never suggested itself. He would have loved to establish greater consistency and uniformity than seemed likely to prevail so long as everyone was at considerable liberty to intepret—just the kind of condition that an oral tradition encourages. But despite those lunar drawings on his walls to help determine the beginning of a new month,[88] he never contemplated putting the Mishnah into writing.

It is certainly not easy to lay down hard and fast lines in this matter, but I would like to put it this way: When Scripture is the only text, commentary reaches back directly and freely to it, even when interpretation is governed by tradition; when the Oral Torah gets *recorded*, direct access to the originally revealed Word is not cut off of course, but the commentator (particularly the advanced scholar) must first devote considerable energy and time to establish the correctness of the *text* of the tradition. Inevitably some of the original directness evaporates.

85. Cf. S. Asaf, *Meqorot le-Toledot ha-Ḥinuk be-Yisrael*, I (Tel Aviv, 1925), pp. xxiii–xxiv, 129ff. Of course, I am not implying that *pilpul* as such, before it has gone to artificiality and extremes, is alien to talmudic discourse (and even in the Talmud it can sometimes become fancy!). Cf. J. H. Greenstone, "The Pilpul System in the Talmud," in *Jewish Theological Seminary of American Students' Annual* (New York, 1914), pp. 152–62. For a splendid presentation of Spanish and the Safed School *pilpul*, see H. Z. Dimitrovsky in *Sefunot*, 7 (Jerusalem, 5723), pp. 77 et seq.

86. Cf. ARNA, pp. 67–68 and parallels. See also Scholem, "Tradition und Kommentar," pp. 30–31, 46. Therefore, not only in intellectual give-and-take but in legal decision, too, the overruled view is not to be dismissed as necessarily without substance: "Why, if the law follows majority opinion, is the view of the minority recorded along with that of the majority? So that if some (future) court favors the minority opinion, it may base its decision on that—but no court may reject the view of its (earlier) fellow-court unless the later one is greater than the earlier one in wisdom and in 'number'" (M. ʿEduyot 1:5, and on "number" see the commentators ad loc., and cf. J. Rosen, *Zaphnath Paneaḥ* [Jerusalem, 1961], pp. 91–92). "A dissent in a court of last resort," said Chief Justice Charles Evans Hughes, "is an appeal to the brooding spirit of the law, to the intelligence of a future day, when a later decision may possibly correct the error into which the dissenting judge believes the court to have been betrayed" (quoted by Anthony Lewis in the third of his series of articles, "Annuals of Law, the Gideon Case," *New Yorker*, May 9, 1964, p. 172). The two quotations are from two different worlds of thought, but the essential spirit of the two statements is the same. On authority, see below.

87. Cf. L. Finkelstein, *The Jews*, I, pp. 149ff. and references on pp. 207–8.

88. M. Rosh ha-Shanah 2:8. For notes on the wall, cf. J. Kila'im 1:1 (I owe this reference to

How then did the freedom to which an oral tradition can contribute escape anarchy? What finally contributed to restraint of centrifugal tendencies was a conception of authority. I should like to quote an important tannaite statement which will make clear how seriously the concept of authority was taken. At the same time, this very statement reveals how continuous interpretation could keep the Tradition in response to a variety of human needs. "According to the law which they shall teach thee," the verse in Deut. 17:11 reads, "and according to the judgment which they shall tell thee, thou shalt do; thou shalt not turn aside from the sentence which they shall declare unto thee, to the right hand, nor to the left." On which the Sifre[89] comments: "Even if in your eyes [294] they point to the right that it is left and to the left that it is right, obey them."[90] If I may put it this way: Authority protected exegesis from many possibilities of arbitrariness; but by the same token, so long as it remained sensitive to the requirements of the age, authority had the sanctions to extract from the Written and Oral Law such conclusions as would re-enforce the permanent relevance of Scripture and the legitimacy of the moment's needs for adequate and immediate attention, כדי לחזק הדת ולתקן העולם.[91] To paraphrase a remark of the Gaon Saadia:[92] No generation was left without the necessary resources for deriving from the Torah the guidance and the practices which were appropriate to the age.[93]

Lieberman, *Hellenism in Jewish Palestine*, p. 87). For business documents on walls, cf. Rostovtzeff, *Caravan Cities*, p. 116; see also pp. 207–8. See also his *Dura-Europos and Its Art* (Oxford, 1938), p. 31.

89. Deut. 154, ed. Finkelstein, p. 207.

90. On this passage, cf. L. Ginzberg, A. Marx, and S. Lieberman in *Hadoar* 39 (New York, 5706), pp. 904–05.

91. Maimonides, *Code*, Hilkot Mamrim 1:2; note how Midrash Tannaim, p. 103, has taken this over.

92. From *Sefer ha-Galuy*, chap 4. H. Malter (*Saadia Gaon*, [Philadelphia, 1921]) adopted this as the quotation at the head of his Saadia biography.

93. An incident of which I was myself a witness may illustrate what the *New Yorker* might perhaps call the Midrashic mind at work. Very late in the night of one Pentecost the telephone rang while a group of students were studying with a great halakic master in his apartment. "Pay no attention to it," he said, in reflex action as it were. No sooner had he said that however, since the telephone ringing persisted, than he turned to the students and said, "If one of you wishes to answer the phone, he may do so. People know that I do not answer the telephone on a holiday. It may therefore be for one of you: perhaps someone is sick." One of the students thereupon got up, answered the telephone, and it turned out indeed to be his wife calling him to take her to the hospital because she was about to give birth. When the student left, the master turned to one of the students who was an extremely pious chap, and said: "It was not that I permitted answering the telephone out of any desire to relax strict requirements of the law (of rest) on the festival; it is that I am stringent in the observance of the law of saving human life" (*Lo heqalti be-dine yom tov; maḥamir ani be-dine nefashot*). I have omitted all names for I am not sure this rabbinic authority would want to be identified. See also S. Y. Agnon, *Days of Awe* (New York, 1948), p. 199.

Reflections on Translation
and Midrash

[87] Although the verb *targem* occurs only once in Scripture, and in a rather late book at that, the word is apparently no parvenu in Semitic, as the lexicons and my smart friends instruct me. The Akkadian *targumanu* was an interpreter, and that is what the translator has always been. As Professor S. Lieberman underscored for a later period, ". . . [T]he first rudiment of the interpretation of a text is the ἑρμηνεία, the literal and exact equivalent of the Hebrew תרגום, which means both translation and interpretation." And the OED informs me that once upon a time the very English word "interpret" was used also for "translate." When we ask, What is the oldest Midrash that has been preserved, the scholars answer, The Septuagint.

No less than the word, the activity of translation is hardly a newcomer on the cultural scene. From the middle of the second millennium B.C.E. there have come down fragments of an Akkadian recension of the Gilgamesh epic current in the Hittite Empire, and, continues Speiser, "The same Boğazköy archives have yielded also important fragments of a Hittite translation, as well as a fragment of a Hurrian rendering of the epic." Tablet XII of that epic is, according to the experts, "a literal translation from the Sumerian." None of this should be surprising. The first translation in history probably occurred when the first reader began his first rereading of the first author's composition, and he, the reader, wanted to make sure that he understood what the text said. When Jacob said גלעד he was already behaving like many before him. And maybe in the mind of the author of the Genesis story, על כן קרא שמו גלעד reflects what happens repeatedly in cultural history, to wit, once a translation is proposed it tends to be adopted and is [88] treated as though it alone were the correct interpretation.

When the book of Jonah was read in a Christian church in Africa from Jerome's new Latin version, there was an uproar, because the miraculous plant (4:6), which in the older translation, based upon the Greek, had been rendered "gourd," was now identified with the "ivy."

When several years ago a "mist" ceased to rise from the earth, in the second Creation story, this omission caused a tumult for months on end.

If the Mishnah goes to the trouble to declare that when one translates וּמְזַרְעֲךָ לֹא תִתֵּן לְאַעְבָּרָא בְּאַרְמִיּוּתָא as וּמְזַרְעֲךָ, he is not only to be silenced but rebuked (מַשְׁתְּקִין אוֹתוֹ בִּנְזִיפָה), it is wittingly or unwittingly admitting that a translation and interpretation the Sages resent are popular in certain quarters: the translation and interpretation have taken hold (of some Karaites, too, centuries later), are passing for the real thing, and pretty soon everyone may begin to think that this is how the original reads.

Translation—because it really equals translation plus interpretation—is in truth effective. Because that is so, a kind of literary hybris tends to develop, and it may be demanded that the translation be treated no less solemnly than the original. When the Greek translation of the Pentateuch had been executed and read to τὸ πλῆθος τῶν Ἰουδαίων εἰς τὸν τόπον, there was a great ovation (a μεγάλη ἀποδοχή), and then the priests, the elders of the translators, some of the corporate body, and the leaders of the people rose and said,

> "Inasmuch as the translation has been well and piously made and is in every respect accurate (καὶ κατὰ πᾶν ἠκριβωμένως), it is right that it should remain in its present form and that no revision of any sort take place." When all had assented to what had been said, they bade that an imprecation be pronounced, according to their custom, upon any who should revise the text by adding or transposing anything whatever in what had been written down, or by making any excision; and in this they did well, so that the work might be preserved imperishable and unchanged always.

It may be that on hearing these words the author of [89] Deuteronomy would be taken aback, as perhaps also the Vizier Ptah-Hotep (though some have questioned the current rendition) and still another bureaucrat who spoke of how to deliver a message. It doesn't matter. Nor does it matter whether Aristeas is writing fiction or history. What does matter is the expression of an attitude, Don't underestimate translation.

Nor, to take one further step, do the talmudic Sages disagree with that view. I shall try to spend a little time with their views shortly. And we have already seen, they actively tried to silence a translator whose translation they disliked—evidently a sign of their not underestimating the damage a poor translation (from their point of view) can do. But it would be very far from the truth to present the talmudic Sages as unqualified opponents of translation. Again the Mishnah. It is describing the procedure of blessings and curses at Gerizim and Ebal; afterwards an altar to be built, and וְכָתַבְתָּ עָלָיו אֶת כָּל דִּבְרֵי הַתּוֹרָה בְּשִׁבְעִים לְשׁוֹן, שֶׁנֶּאֱמַר בַּאֵר הֵיטֵב. Targum Jonathan and Targum Yerushalmi and Neofiti are prepared to endorse this. Whether there should have been a holiday or fast day when the Torah was translated into Greek, for the author of the Mishnah statement it was certainly desirable to have the contents of the Torah translated and broadcast to the nations of the world in all the languages. What is באר היטב? To write out all the words of the Torah בשבעים לשון. When you want to make your work known, you translate (= translate and interpret) it into as many languages as you can. Even for domestic consumption you invent the role of the dragoman. Of course, you also lay down rules as to how he is to act his part: May he or may he not resort to a script? When may he speak up and when shut up? But apparently you need him and you use him.

Before proceeding with our principal discussion and examination of the attitudes of the talmudic Sages in some detail, there are three problems related to our subject which I am deliberately excluding because in my opinion they don't belong here.

First, the permissibility or prohibition of using a translation in public service. What must be recited in the original and what need not? Or what may or may not be the practice in the synagogues [90] of ללעוזות? And so forth. These reveal of course the presence of the possibilities of translation, but they are halakic-institutional problems. When you have a community, and especially an extensively spread out community, how much liberty in the use of languages can you afford to permit, or accept *faute de mieux*? The Roman Church is rediscovering today how complicated and dissolving this can be. I must say, I admire the Sages for liberating important expressions from their original cultic framework, I also admire them for their courage to allow the recitation of the *Shema*, the *Tefillah*, and the Grace after meals in any language. One of these days they'll visit Caesarea, and maybe then they will appreciate how sweet and risky are the uses of diversity. But that's their problem, not ours. It, therefore, is out of bounds for our reflections.

Another problem to be excluded is the relation of oral targums to written targums, or the apparent displeasure of any particular leading or run-of-the-mill sage with any particular targum text on the Temple-mount or anywhere else. Again, this may be partly halakic—what status should such written documents enjoy when there is a likely transgression of a biblical injunction? — and partly an individual's taste for a specific style. Anyway, that's out, as is a third and inherently interesting problem; but it requires brief digression.

Most of the time when our sources speak of translation they have the Scriptures in mind. Not always; witness the grandson of Sirach who in the second century B.C.E. translated a book, his grandfather's, not yet or ever to be part of the canon—Did he hope to create the feeling that possibly the book ought to be included, and therefore a Greek translation would suggest that like the canonical works, his grandfather's maxims also deserved publication and in more than the original version?

Or another example. A very good case has been made for the possibility that a little more than a century before Sirach's grandson produced his work, a

Jew who admired an Aramaic work undertook to translate it into Hebrew, with what results Professor H. L. Ginsberg has already demonstrated. It is not impossible that [91] the translator, too, thought that Solomon was the author of that cheerful treatise. No matter. While he was at work on his translation, it was still not part of the canon, though if it were already being attributed to Solomon, it would enjoy esteem in some circles. But it was then not yet catalogued in the library of כתבי הקדש. That is all I care to underline, my point being that the fingerprints of translation can be detected even on literary works that are not in the category of the sacred. Probably I'm belaboring the obvious. Be this as it may: It is understandable that translation of *sacred* scriptures might be undertaken, even though their custodians might be less than jubilant at the prospect of having to publicize, superficially at least, the esoteric messages in these writings; because if you want to circulate your truth among your neighbors and their neighbors, and among your own kindred whom you're determined to indoctrinate, how can you do it without translation and interpretation? But it is certainly interesting to recall that translation goes on even when writings are not sacred. And the problem which I wish to exclude from consideration is this: the relation of translation of the sacred to translation of the profane.

Hence we may revert to our principal discussion, which is translation-as-such, the activity of translating and interpreting; and it's not with the ancients only that I'm concerned, although I shall refer to them and help myself to examples from some of their texts; my concern is with the activity itself.

And the first thing to be said about it is that (except in one respect) it is a thoroughly frustrating and unrewarding occupation: I recommend it to anyone eager to develop an inferiority complex. Here is Sirach's grandson apologizing, entreating his readers "to be indulgent, if in any part of what we have labored to interpret we may seem to fail in some of the phrases." That's the Greek for הנני העני ממעש. He is obviously frightened that the savants in Alexandria will publish reviews in which they will point out that you cannot transfer the Hebrew to the Greek idiom. Hopeless, hopeless, for the simple fact is, the job can't be done: What's Greek is Greek and what's Hebrew is Hebrew, and if you try to say in one what is said in the other, you're misleading.

[92] And the translators of the King James Version have this to say: "It hath pleased God in his Divine Providence, here and there to scatter words and sentences of that difficulty and doubtfulness . . . that fearfulness would better beseem us than confidence . . . ."

And here is A. J. Arberry:

. . . The rhetoric and rhythm of the Arabic of the Koran are so characteristic, so powerful, so highly emotive, that any version whatsoever is bound in the nature of things to be but a poor copy of the glittering splendour of the original. Never was it more true than in this instance that *traduttore traditore*.

שבכל דור ודור עומדים עלינו. It's the same with every measure and every period of time. "All translations are reputed femalls, delivered at second hand," writes John Florio in his dedicatory epistle of his translation of Montaigne; and in his preface to the "courteous reader" he proceeds to list one apology and excuse after another: "Shall I apologize translation? Why but some hold (as for their free-hold) that such conversion is the subversion of Universities." So he tries to explain that the citadels of learning will not come down if works in one language are made accessible in another. After a number of other possible protests, he comes to this one: "Why but who ever did well in it?" He takes care of that and still other criticisms. He confesses ("and let confession make half amends") that every language has its own "Genius and inseparable form." He fears that he has made "of good French no good English." And of course he prays and entreats "you for your own sake to correct as you read; to amend as you list." In short, he knows he's in for it. You'll never get the footnote aficionados to approve because indeed they don't need the translation and they would rather not be annoyed by the static of a bad translation.

But this is not all. Even more resentful of the translation is none other than the author. He simply cannot be pleased, though he would like to be. He is both grateful and heartbroken, for he cannot help noting that his precious nuances have vanished, alas.

In the introduction to his wonderful translation of Cervantes' *Don Quixote*, Samuel Putnam quotes Cervantes on *his* attitude toward translation:

> But for all that, it appears to me that [93] translating from one language into another, unless it be from one of those two queenly tongues, Greek and Latin, is like gazing at a Flemish tapestry with the wrong side out: even though the figures are visible, they are full of threads that obscure the view and are not bright and smooth as when seen from the other side.

You'll never get the author happy (about the concrete translation, that is) because, naturally, he knows all the words he rejected before he decided on just that one, and the translator can't take his eyes off that one.

And if you think you'll fare any better with the public, you're living, beg pardon, in a fool's paradise. Nobody with any intelligence, particularly one who is engaged in translation, would deny that you can't go on interminably with the antiquated. The translator above all is no pillar of obscurity or devout unintelligibility, even if he happens to have a taste for that which has aged. The fact remains that the public, like the scholar and author, is unfriendly to translation. What it wants is jazz and prose that puts no strain on the mind: pop digest, which have their place in society, but these are not translation. "You look terrific!" is not a translation of "Shall I compare thee to a summer's day? /Thou art more lovely and more temperate." From the way a man translates you can tell whether he loves his source or his public. Ignore the exact meaning of words, start resorting to paraphrase, and you still can transmit more or less accurately the substance of the source, but you're not translating. You're after *tachlis*, quick returns, but not exegesis or science or art. והחסידות האמתי הנרצה .והנחמד רחוק מציור שכלנו. כי זה דבר פשוט, מילתא דלא רמיא עליה דאינש לאו אדעתיה The following translation is not misleading: "We find it difficult properly to conceive true saintliness, since we cannot grasp that to which we give no thought." For all their bad grammar, I miss that הנרצה והנחמד .'I miss כי זה דבר פשוט. And to me that translation says, Come on now, let's get this over with! "We find it difficult properly to conceive" is Report of the Dean's Committee; רחוק מציור שכלנו is style. I shall not quote Franz Rosenzweig — why, I don't know; or maybe I do. But I will quote from W. H. Auden, though you may think his problem is not ours. He writes (I'm not quoting in full): [94] "I don't know if it is any better with the Anglican Church in England, but the Episcopalian Church in America seems to have gone stark raving mad." He then gives several examples of a proposed reformed Holy Communion service, and the fourth is:

Worst of all, the Epistle and Gospel are read in some appalling "modern" translation. In one such, the Greek word which St. Paul uses in Romans VIII and which the Authorized Version translates as *flesh* turns into *our lower nature*, a concept which is not Christian, but Manichean.

Then Auden concludes:

And why? The poor Roman Catholics have had to start from scratch, and, as any of them with a feeling for language will admit, they have made a cacophonous horror of the Mass. We had the extraordinary good fortune in that our Book of Common Prayer was composed at exactly the right historical moment. The English language had already become more or less what it is today, so that the prayer Book is no more difficult to follow than Shakespeare, but the ecclesiastics of the sixteenth century still possessed a feeling for the ritual and ceremonious which today we have almost entirely lost. Why should we spit on our luck?

Nowhere is translation welcomed with open arms, and among the Jews (by whom I mean from hereon out the midrashic-talmudic rabbis and others), among the Jews it is no different. The attitude seems to be, With one hand keep at a distance, and pull towards you with the other. To say that the Jews are afraid of it is true; why shouldn't they be? How well they knew what havoc a translation can work! God be with you if you introduce a *parthenos* where it isn't too safe even for an *almah*. Centuries of polemics and worse-than-polemics may follow. Translation is certainly hazardous; but then what isn't? To say, or even to imply, however, that the Sages rejected translation is unwarranted when it isn't worse than that. Of Hillel's eighty disciples—thirty of whom could have done with the sun what Joshua did!—who was the greatest? Jonathan ben Uzziel! Wouldn't you know. And to recall what this signifies, all that is necessary to remember is that the least of that fellowship was Rabban Yoḥanan ben Zakkai. Hyperbole, obviously, and a lot more than translation is behind [95] and all over that statement. But if translator had meant traducer, גדול שבהם or גדול שבכולם could never have been Jonathan ben Uzziel; or better put it the other way around: had translator-interpreter meant traducer, Pseudo-Jonathan could never have acquired so fancy a name and reputation. The way some people avoid translation, you'd think birds were flying overhead.

But what of R. Judah's (or R. Eliezer's) statement that המתרגם פסוק כצורתו, בצורתו) הרי זה בדי, והמוסיף הרי זה מגדף (or מחרף ומגדף)? To begin with, the statement in the talmudic context is clearly being invoked for a halakic purpose, and that is not our problem, as we decided earlier. Second, the Sage is speaking of translation of sacred scriptures and that too, as we have detected, may bring on institutional shingles. However, we need not hesitate to consider the remark against the widest possible background. For what R. Judah or R. Eliezer is saying is absolutely true, and there isn't a translator in the business who would contradict him. At least the first half of that statement is verbatim what Walter Benjamin once said: "A translation that strove to be exactly similar to its original would not be a true translation." For this indeed is *the* fundamental challenge and frustration and hoped-for triumph beckoning the translator: When do you translate with strict literalness and when dare you not do so? When do you shrink or stretch the original and when dare you not do so? If I may use Onkelos as an example, in the same chapter, and in all reverence if you please: When do I content myself with three words exactly as in the original and say, לפורקנך סברית ה', and when do I seemingly go on and on? For example,

> Israel shall go round his city, the people shall build his temple, the righteous ones shall surround him and study [or carry out] the Torah in instruction with him, precious purple shall his garment be and his clothing wool, crimson-colored wool, yea, clothing splendid with color.

In the interior of that chapter the first translation, not the second, is astonishing.

Any way you translate you're sunk, whether you translate literally or expansively. But that's the assignment, to get it done properly (to the best of your ability); you're between the monster of lying and that female of blasphemy: go, navigate.

[96] For there is no formula you can formulate in advance, except of course the resolution, I may never be dishonest—let's be perfectly clear about that. And even that supposedly noble end, literal translation, that is, reproduce faithfully what the original wishes to say, how fugitive it is! ימצאהו בארץ מדבר, ובתהו ילל ישמן and so on, says the verse in Deuteronomy. One interpretation has ד"א ימצאהו בארץ מדבר, הכול מצוי ומסופק להם במדבר, באר עולה להם, מן יורד להם, שליו it,

וכו' וכו' מצוי להם, ענני כבוד מקיפות עליהם וכו'. In other words, ימצאהו is being interpreted as though it read ימציאהו. Homiletical exaggeration? I don't suppose that with some people the testimony of Onkelos, סופיק צורכיהון, will count for much; but here is the Septuagint translating αὐτάρκησεν αὐτόν. Somebody, evidently, thinks this is *peshat*.

Times change, styles of translation change, and this is as it should be if the voice of the classic is to be heard in our land. Changes there may be and will be; yet, I believe three things are constant in all translations:

(1) The way translation begins. It is a purely personal, unsocial, private act. Of course it can take on public and institutional interests, and there may even be at the outset a commission from a monarch or a society or publisher to undertake the job. But that is not the beginning of translation. Translation begins the moment I discover that I'm not sure I understand the text I'm reading; the moment I begin to suspect that all I'm getting out of my reading or study is general impressions, a kind of smog of comprehension. Nothing is precise, everything is only vaguely familiar, darkly intelligible, or mechanically hand-me-down. But if I ask myself, Just what exactly is the text saying, and why is it saying it this way and not another? and I cannot answer the question cleanly—no self-bluff or deception—then I know I have no alternative. I must clear the atmosphere. I must begin to translate. That will speedily disclose to me what I know and what I don't know: for what I *thought* I knew equals what I don't know. If the words *gemilut* — or even by chance *gemilot* — *hasadim* always mean acts of lovingkindness, who in his right mind would [97] ask, How could they be practised in Babylon where animal sacrifices were forbidden? or, Who would say in illustration of them that Daniel prayed three times a day? אין עזי אלא תוקפי, the Midrash enlightens me. Fine. What do I know now I did not know before? If again and again and again the reading crops up הוי שקוד ללמוד מה שתשיב לאפיקורוס, what does that mean, precisely?

Translation is for oneself, entirely, for me to gain correct understanding. That is all, and let no one tell you otherwise: especially that it is for the benefit of the world. A time may well come when the translator wishes to pass on his translation to the public. But that's no more than a biological reflex he shares with all who fill their bellies with learning or poetry or scientific theories or gossip: they can't keep it to themselves. The fear of one's own ignorance is the beginning of translation.

Shortly before the Second World War there lived in London a gentleman (שמריה מנשה הכהן אדלר) who seems to have been a *lamdan*. That he knew a respectable amount of Talmud and rabbinics is clear, but it is also clear that he was a formidable *nudnik*. Had his mouth been just a little cleaner, he might have deserved an A+ for his attacks on the Establishment, the Chief Rabbinate and boards of *beth-din* and so on. What a delight it is to see the way he writes out טשיף ראבי"י in Hebrew characters! Or to keep coming upon one of his favorite expressions, מסוה דקדושה מזויפת. Bravo. Now, when the Soncino translation of the Talmud began to appear, this valiant gent came out with an attack על גודל הפירצה כזו (הזו?) דבאמת פעולה כזו היא יסוד ושורש גדול לחורבן קיום האומה באמת... בגדר ע"ז גמורה נינהו כפי המוסכם בתורה who are ב"ד דפה לונדון and the אחב"י שבע"פ ובכל הפוסקים בלי שום חולק. Into the battle he even dragged the Gaon of Dvinsk and of course the opinions of still other *geonim addirim shelita*, all to the single effect that it is absolutely forbidden to translate תורה שבעל פה into a foreign language. Would indeed that even the written Torah had remained only in the original: ומי יתן והיתה תורה אתנו בני ישראל אמון מוצנע כאשר מלפנים אפילו אחאב לא רצה לתתה למלך ארם, כי כל הצרות נמשכו אחר זה. He can't forgive rabbis and reverends who study [98] foreign languages. In Jephthah's generation how impatient he would have been for Samuel's coming!

There are, needless to say, many fine points to establish—for example, whom are you translating for, us or them; what's the translation for; will you use a Hebrew alphabet or another; and other subjects too come in by association, like who is qualified to be a *dayyan*, or why Resh Lakish seems to have changed his mind regarding supporting or not supporting דייני בור, or whether he ever was a brigand, and so forth. I am not the person to discuss the halakic finesse or applicability of our friend's view, and I know that I am unable to read his hysterical prose and insults without wanting to laugh. That's my prejudice. But one complaint of his is surely justified. He reports — and I find no reason to disbelieve him, though in the heat of righteousness he may be exaggerating— that from the speeches at the gala celebration מפורש עיקר כוונתם דעי"ז יתקרבו ויתדבקון בקשר של קיימא חיבה וריעות ישראל לב"נ ובזה ישראל נושע תשועת עולמים, אוי לאזנים שככה שומעות. I agree fully. The motive for genuine translation is not to prove to the next person how pretty my text is—though that may come later. As we saw, the impulse if anything comes from an almost completely opposite direction.

(2) The basic unit of translation. What is it? It cannot be the single word. That seldom has a life of its own. A word I can look up, but I cannot translate it. That's why interlinears are trots but not translations. I don't doubt that Aquila pleased several important scholars; maybe subconsciously they hoped that after one hour with such Greek, a man would cry out, Give me Hebrew or give me death; or maybe those were still the early days of computer translation. With a single word, it's a little like what the Midrash says, ועדין הדבר תלי בדלא תלי ואין אנו יודעים. A word acquires its specific gravity from the context it's in.

What then? Shall I take the sentence as a whole? That is generally too long. It may give me the overall sense, but it tends to devaluate the individuality of many terms it contains. Consider this: [99]

וּכְנָטָף בַּיָּם כֵּן נֹאבֵדָה
עֲרִירִים בֵּין אַלְפֵי רְבָבָה–
מָה רַב, הוֹי, מָה רַב הַשָּׁמָּוֹן
בְּאֶרֶץ הָרֵיקָה, הָרְחָבָה

Now an English version:

> And like a drop of water in the sea
> We'll sink, and none will reckoning demand.
> Can loneliness more utter be
> Than in this wide, this empty land?

I get the idea, but I don't get the poem: instead of sipping, the translator gulps.

What then is the proper unit? Sometimes it is the phrase but most often and likely the clause. Here I see the word in its relation to its immediate neighbors and the unit is not too big for my embrace.

נשמת כל חי תברך את שמך, ה' אלהינו, ורוח כל בשר תפאר ותרומם זכרך מלכנו תמיד. מן העולם ועד העולם אתה אל, ומבלעדיך אין לנו מלך גואל ומושיע, פודה ומציל ומפרנס ומרחם בכל עת צרה וצוקה.

> The breath of all that lives shall bless Thy Name,
> O Lord our God; the spirit of all flesh
> Shall sing remembrance unto Thee, our King.
> From everlasting unto everlasting
> Thou wert and art the Lord; and but for Thee
> We have no King, and no deliverer,
> No savior, no redeemer, no provider,
> No fount of mercy in an evil day.

This translator is reading בכונה.

(3) The right *English* word and syntax. It is alas overlooked again and again by well-meaning people that the test of translation is met or missed—despite learning and despite virtue—in the choice of the right word, the exact word, the proper arrangements of the language one translates *into*, not the language one translates *from*. And beware of prepositions! They're merciless. Verbal equivalence by itself is not the way. A gift of flesh and blood [100] comes from a butcher shop. I cannot for the life of me believe that Joshua ben Perahya ever said, "And when thou judgest any man incline the balance in his favor," though he might have said, "tip the scale in his favor." "Incline the balance in his favor," forsooth. It's like the famous sermon once delivered (I'm told) in the Seminary synagogue on the text, "Israel is a nut." Or like that masterpeice rendering of שנים מי יודע, which ran, "Who knows the meaning of number two?" Unfortunately, I do. The language translated *into* is the test we must pass. And it is only a slight exaggeration (if that!) to say that a knowledge of that is more important than a knowledge of the original. For this is the question the translator must ask of himself every syllable along the way: If Akiba or Yohanan ben Zakkai or Joshua ben Levi or whoever had spoken American English the way (let us say) E.B. White or Auden writes it, how would he have

said what he wanted to say? Like a translation out of Jastrow? Like the trilingual posters in Meah Shearim admonishing women how to dress? Because he knows the English language superbly, though he does not know Swedish, Auden could translate Dag Hammarskjöld's *Markings* with the help of a Swede, Leif Sjöberg. The postscript to his foreword is a lesson to us all.

These are the three constants, and with industry they are attainable, it seems to me, by any student who loves his text. But there is one element which is not to be had by industry alone. That is why it cannot be a constant. It comes from an eardrum מן השמים: if one is lucky to be born with it, how fortunate for him; if one is not lucky, he may still be a competent journeyman—but don't expect miracles.

I would like to illustrate what I mean by a negative example, so to speak. In his delightful volume, *In Praise of Yiddish*, Mr. Maurice Samuel tries to explain why it is impossible to translate into English the monologues of Sholom Aleichem's Tevye. "To clarify the nature of Tevye's gnomic mutilations," he writes,

> we must imagine an American college graduate addressing an audience of his intellectual peers. We must further imagine that all of them once took a course in Latin, and have preserved in their memories [101] the familiar tags with which "cultivated" essays were peppered a century or two ago. The speaker throws them in from time to time accompanying them with English paraphrases and explications which are sometimes utterly nonsensical, sometimes ingeniously tangential, sometimes both, and always with a vague suggestion of authenticity and relevance.

Then come what Samuel calls some "imperfect examples":

> *Sic transit gloria mundi,* Here today and gone tomorrow.
> *Reductio ad absurdum,* A fool and his money are soon parted.
> *De mortuis nisi nil bonum,* Once you're dead it's for good.
> *Ars longa vita brevis,* That's the long and short of it.
> *Delenda est Cartago,* Neither a borrower nor a lender be.
> *Carpe diem,* Shoot the works.
> *Non compos mentis,* Look who's talking.

And so on. Sweat and possibly tears, too, lie behind this, but they did not create it.

Now, that midrashic texts should prove attractive, even irresistible, to translators is no surprise. There is, after all, a natural affinity between translation which is interpretation (as we saw from the outset) and Midrash which is commentary. Please allow me to italicize something immediately, lest we be swept away by some gothic nonsense, sentimental or pietistic. Regardless of what the case may have been in antiquity, for the modern student translation and the received interpretations of the Midrashim will coincide only to their mutual annihilation, except on rare, and possibly accidental, occasions—despite rightly-to-be-treasured felicities like אין פסיחה אלא חייס. There is a profound distinction between modern translation and the ancient Midrash, and to ignore it is to vulgarize or neo-hasidize our thinking and speech. What is it, therefore, that modern translation and the inherited Midrash share? The ambition to recapture the reverberations of the original. אם הוא בן גרים לא יאמר לו, זכור מעשה אבותיך, שנאמר, וגר לא תונה ולא תלחצנו. If a translation of Exodus 22:20 does not capture something of the moral tremor, it's diminished the charity of that verse. Beautiful as it is, I cannot be persuaded that Abba Saul's interpretation of ואנוהו is what Moses and the children of [102] Israel had in mind at the Red Sea. Contemporary fashion seems once again to prefer the suggestion of Yose son of the Damascene. In either event, both men are responding to the same wonder: What in the world are that peculiar verb and suffix doing here? Something of that wonder should survive. It may not distort, make either more or less of the original; but it must be within reach of the original. ואידך? If genuinely imaginative, the result is a sermon (no mean literary accomplishment!); otherwise, humbug.

But now our concern is not with midrashic interpretation of Scripture; it is with translating the Midrash, and that deserves, and requires, the same thoughtfulness as we bring to a biblical verse.

For the longest time I thought that the reason translators were drawn to Midrash—by which I mean specifically haggadic Midrash—was because it was easier than halakah. Tackle a halakic subject, *sugya*, and you know at once that it demands your whole tensed intellect; try as a refresher the *sugya* of יין נסך. There is a hardness to this material that is of an altogether different order from even a difficult midrashic passage. In the latter it may be a term we do not understand, or the connection of the prooftext with the statement or comment proposed; or the comment seems plain silly at first; or the mangled state of the text drives you to despair. Halakic material, on the other hand, may be inherently so complex, so involved and casuistical, it's uphill work even when every term is intelligible and the text impeccable.

Only an idiot would deny this. Yet I dare to propose that as regards translation, it is often easier to translate a straight halakic discussion of the Talmud than many, many Midrashim. I'm not saying this to be provocative. I actually made the experiment once, curious to see the outcome. What you need to do is saturate yourself for about three months (if you can stand it) with Bacon's *Essays* till some of his lapidary constructions affect your own speech, and then let yourself go. (Please excuse me for the mixed metaphor which may be present here.) Be sure to paragraph as you would if you were reproducing dialogue in English composition. Punctuate as though your life depended on it: commas, periods, question marks, quotation marks. Don't be frightened that in the [103] end the discussion is still unintelligible. Remember, so is the original. Were it not for Rashi, who would know where the Tanna *is* standing, what this is all about? In other words, halakic discussion or text is far from being untranslatable. It's unreadable, not incomprehensible. What it requires is the very thing the original too cannot do without: a running commentary—and nothing less than that. In this field much not only remains to be done, much can be done.

Perhaps the following is as close to the truth as I can get: If translation and Midrash find that there is a real kinship between them, it is no more than what was always true, that they were both engaged in interpretation. But there may be one aspect of Midrash that especially attracts the modern translator, and that is: Haggadic Midrash is the one branch of talmudic literature which *approaches* the character of belles-lettres. Midrash is not belles-lettres: It does not care to reflect on the beautiful for its own sake; it does not tell its stories for the sake and delight of the story itself (this may be an exaggeration); its poetry is not for the pleasure to be had from the poem itself. But in the reflections and parables and homilies of the Midrash, in the very daring to fly far beyond the literal as it creates hortatory exegesis, in the initiative it takes to explain the biblical past with the help of the present—beloved are anachronisms!—and the present as a prolongation of the biblical past, in the determination to prove appealing to scholar and non-scholar alike (though there were occasions when the Sage directed his remarks specifically to a non-scholarly audience), in the way it enjoys quoting biblical verses, one after the next and the next—thus stirring in the mind sounds and memories that would otherwise vanish, the surrealistic way it catches sight of signs of the future in biblical figures of speech: In all these ways it leads the modern man toward the discourse which has come to mean so much to him, the discourse of the humane and beautiful, the discourse that tries to satisfy a desperate *human* need: the need for flight from surrounding ugliness, the need to escape from the crushing commonplace. Who can resist, אם עשית רצונו כרצונך, לא עשית רצונו כרצונו. ואם עשית רצונו שלא כרצונך, עשית רצונו כרצונו. [104] רצונך שלא תמות, מות עד שלא תמות. רצונך שתחיה, אל תחיה, עד שתחיה. מוטב לך למות מיתה בעולם הזה, שעל כרחך אתה מת, מלמות מיתה לעתיד of כי אתה עשית. Or this, as commentary on לבא, שאם תרצה אי אתה מת Lamentations 1:21? ואל ואל תשיחי עם חברותיך, אל תה, משל למלך שנשא למטרונה; אמר לה, אל תשיחי עם חברותיך ואל תשאילי מהן ואל תשאילי להן. לימים כעס עליה המלך וטרדה חוץ לפלטין, וחזרה על כל שכנותיה ולא קבלו אותה; וחזרה לפלטין. אמר לה המלך, אקשית אפיך? אמרה המטרונה למלך, אדני, So Israel says to God, First לא הוון מקבלין לי? אלולי הייתי משאילה להן ושואלת מהן . . . you order me ולא תתחתן בם, בתך לא תתן לבנו ובתו לא תקח לבנך. You cut me off from the whole world fraternity, and now you decide to get rid of me? There is even a dear halakic irony embedded in this!

There are numerous other examples (as who should know better than an audience of the Academy?), some so incisive in honesty and unostentatiousness of diction, so graceful in their movements away from the strictly literal, and in total yet dignified submission to what God may decree, only the eloquence of prayer can equal it.

מי כמכה באלים ה׳
מי כמכה באילמים ה׳
מי כמוך
רואה בעלבון בניך ושותק

To respond to it is to want to understand as completely as possible, word for word and then the whole of it as a unity. Here translation begins, and lingers.

Saul Lieberman in memoriam
Kamah Gedolim Divrei Ḥakhamim

The Freedom and Restraint of Haggadah

[57] Again and again when the principal components of the Oral Law are listed or described in midrashic-talmudic literature, three terms are employed: *midrash, halakhot, aggadot*. This, then, is the formal curriculum of the academy. For example: "A man is duty bound to provide for himself [= to acquire] a master (*rav*) for his advanced learning (*le-ḥokhmah*), so that he might learn from him midrash, [the] halakhot, and [the] aggadot."[1] Although the following is apparently not unanimous,[2] it is nevertheless strongly urged that it is best to cover the whole curriculum with a single teacher, so that

> the interpretation (*ṭaʿam*) which the teacher neglected to tell him in the study of midrash, he will eventually tell him in the study of the halakhot; the interpretation which he neglected to tell him in study of the halakhot, he will eventually tell him in the study of aggadah. Thus that man remains in one place and is filled with good and blessing [i.e., has profited].[3]

Perhaps the passage is intended to emphasize how one becomes someone's disciple, not just an occasional or itinerant student.

1. Avot de Rabbi Natan A (ARNA), p. 39. Cf. statement on R. Akiva in Tractate Shekalim V, ed. A. Sofer (New York: Privately published, 1954), p. 56, and critical apparatus there. The terms *aggadah, aggadot, haggadah, haggadot* are interchangeable. Cf. W. Bacher, *Midrashic Terminology: Tannaim and Amoraim* (Hebrew), trans. E. Z. Rabinowitz (Tel Aviv, 1922; rpt. Jerusalem: Carmiel, 1970), pp. 24–25.

2. Cf. ARNA, p. 16, and S. Lieberman, *Siphre Zutta* (New York: JTS, 1968), pp. 89–90, n. 54 at bottom of page; and ARNB, p. 39. See also B. Avodah Zarah 19a–b; and *Sefer Dikduke Soferim* (Hebrew) (hereafter DS), ed. R. N. N. Rabinowitz (New York: M.P. Press, 1976), ad loc.

3. I have departed slightly from the reading adopted by S. Schechter (cf. his n. 3, p. 35), although Aknin, *Sepher Mussar*, ed. Bacher (Berlin: Mekitze Nirdamim, 1910), p. 11, seems to agree with ed. Schechter. Note L. Finkelstein's suggestion in *Baer Jubilee Volume* (n. 6, below), 30. On *ṭaʿam* cf. Lev. R. XXXVI 1, p. 833.

At all events, midrash, the halakhot, and the aggadot are the three parts of the Oral Law, or Mishnah, its overall name.[4] Sometimes we read of only halakhot and haggadot;[5] sometimes—but not at all frequently—the word *haggadah* seems to stand simply for interpretation of a verse not necessarily haggadic;[6] sometimes the reference may be haggadic but is a simple interpretation of a text.[7] But the standard formula, inventory, stereotype (call it what you will) is midrash, halakhot, and aggadot—midrash being what is legitimately derivative from study [58] and interpretation of the Scriptures, and also analysis and exposition of teachings; halakhot, those handed-down halakhic rulings formulated and assembled independently, very likely apodictically, unaccompanied by the biblical interpretation to which they may be related, or even hanging by a hair for lack of almost any biblical association; and, finally, haggadot, which is still best defined as non-halakhic discourse and instruction.

The fact that in these formulations haggadah (or haggadot) is mentioned last, after midrash and halakhot, is not necessarily an indication that haggadah is least important. When you have a number of items to list, one item is inevitably first and the others are not first. But there is much to justify the view that haggadah was truly not the major course in the *bet ha-midrash*. Regardless of what variation we meet, haggadah is never mentioned first in the academic curriculum. And, interestingly, in the midrash,[8] a second-generation Pales-

---

4. On God's program of studies, see Seder Eliyahu Rabbah, ed. Friedmann (Jerusalem: Bamberger and Wahrmann, 1960), p. 15. Cf. n. 79 below.

5. Cf., e.g., Canticles Rabbah (Vilna: Romm, 1938), II 5, 15b. Note also the combination of halakhot and haggadot (but midrash is referred to immediately preceding) in Sifre ad Deuteronomium, ed. L. Finkelstein (New York: JTS, 1969), sec. 48, p. 113; and in *Ginze Schechter*, (Hebrew) ed. L. Ginzberg (New York: JTS, 1929), vol. 2, p. 567, "midrash and tosafot and aggadot" (cf. below, n. 61).

6. Cf. L. Finkelstein in *Yitzhak F. Baer Jubilee Volume on the Occasion of His Seventieth Birthday* (Hebrew with English summaries), ed. S. W. Baron et al. (Jerusalem: Historical Society of Israel, 1960), pp. 31–32; and Bacher, *Midrashic Terminology*, p. 24. The statement in Mekilta VaYassa, ed. and trans. J. Z. Lauterbach (Philadelphia: Jewish Publication Society, 1933), vol. 2, p. 95, on Exod. 15:26, that "doing what is upright in His sight" is a reference to "the praiseworthy haggadot that appeal to all men," is homiletical exhortation pure and simple, and has nothing to do with academic program or planning, as the context plainly reveals. For haggadah as homily, cf. B. Sotah 7b, and Avot de Rabbi Natan (ARN), ed. S. Schechter (New York: Feldheim, 1945), p. 67.

7. Cf. Genesis Rabbah, ed. J. Theodor and Ch. Albeck (Jerusalem: Wahrmann, 1965), XLIV 8, p. 431: There are three to whom it was said, "Ask": Solomon, Aḥaz, and King Messiah. R. Berekhiah and R. Aḥi said in the name of R. Samuel bar Naḥman, "We can add two more from the aggadah, Abraham and Jacob," as can be proved from the idiom of Gen. 15:2 and 28:22b. On *shoneh be-haggadot*, see Midrash Psalms, ed. S. Buber (Vilna: Romm, 1892), LIX 3, p. 302 (but cf. Buber's n. 23): the "book" must refer to the expression "reading in the Torah."

8. Leviticus Rabbah, ed. M. Margulies (Jerusalem: Wahrmann, 1972), III 1, pp. 54–56 and Margulies' commentary. And observe how *bar aggadah* is referred to in anecdote, Genesis Rabbah LXXXI 2, p. 970! Note also, however, the praise of Israel, XL (XLI) 1, p. 388: "Some of them are masters of the Scripture, some of them masters of Mishnah, some of them masters of Talmud, some of them masters of aggadah." With the idiom here, cf. that of Leviticus Rabbah IX 3, p. 177. See also XIII 5, p. 282; XV 2, p. 322.

tinian Amora, R. Isaac,[9] speaks of men whose ambition it is to be known as *bar hilkhan* (expert of halakhot like those in the Mishnah and *baraitot*), as *bar mekhilta* (expert in the halakhic midrashim), as *bar ulpan* (talmudic expert), but makes no mention of *bar aggadeta*, of anyone with ambitions for the reputation as haggadah master. And yet there are sages in amoraic times famous as haggadic experts: R. Simeon bar Yehozadak (third-generation Amora) puts a question to R. Samuel bar Nahman, Because I've heard of you that you are a *ba῾ al haggadah*, a haggadic master;[10] R. Joshua ben Levi of the third century is known as *baki be-aggadah*, a know-it-all of haggadah,[11] although on his own he is unable to explain why, in the Exodus version of the Ten Commandments, in the commandment to honor father and mother it is not said "so that it will go well with thee," while in the Deuteronomy version it *is* said. And there are of course the *rabbanan de-aggadeta*!

The serious or, let us say, properly trained *talmid hakhamim* (student-scholar), or full-fledged *hakham* (teacher-authority), is one who is master of all three parts of the Oral Law. When you wish to compliment him (even allowing for bouquets of hyperbole, probably after his lifetime), you say (as was said of Yohanan ben Zakkai), "He did not neglect Scripture or mishnah, talmud [= midrash], halakhah, aggadah" (and go on: "Toseftot, the subtleties of Scripture or the subtleties of the Scribes, or any of the Sages' rules of interpretation—not a single thing in the Torah did he neglect to study").[12] Anyway, first and foremost talmud (i.e., midrash, as we have said), halakhot, and aggadot. The [59] tribute in the Talmud[13] is even more florid, but the tripod on which the Oral Law stands is not affected.

And so too, when you undertake to console a man for the loss of his son (as it happens, once again involving Yohanan ben Zakkai), if you're gifted you say, "So too, my Master, you had a son who studied Scripture—Pentateuch, Prophets, and the Writings—and studied the Oral Law (mishnah), midrash [so read!], halakhot, and aggadot."[14]

9. Cf. R. Halperin, *Atlas Etz Chayim* (Hebrew) (Tel Aviv: Ruah Yaakov, 1980), vol. 4: *Tannaim and Amoraim*, pt. 2, p. 238: R. Isaac bar Phineas.

10. Genesis Rabbah III 4, pp. 19–20.

11. B. Baba Kamma 55a. Said already of the Tanna R. Ishmael by R. Tarfon, in B. Moed Katan 28b. On *rabbanan de-aggadeta*, cf. J. Heineman, *Aggadah and Its Development* (Hebrew) (Jerusalem: Keter, 1974), p. 212, n. 4. On *baki* cf. H. Yalon, *Studies in Language* (Hebrew) (Jerusalem: Mossad Bialik, 1971), p. 315.

12. ARNA, p. 57. Schechter's edition reads "gemara" instead of "talmud": the censor's substitution (talmud = midrash, as we said: cf. J. N. Epstein, *Introductions to Tannaitic Literature* [Hebrew], ed. E. Z. Melamed [Jerusalem: Magnes; and Tel Aviv: Dvir, 1957], p. 501). On such praise as stereotype, cf. ARNB, p. 29.

13. B. Sukkah 28a—but see also ARNB, p. 58, where "targum" = midrash; cf. S. Lieberman, *Hellenism in Jewish Palestine: Studies in Literary Transmission, Beliefs and Manners of Palestine from the First Century* B.C.E. *to the Fourth Century* C.E. (New York: JTS, 1962), p. 48; but note *Small Tractates; Tractate Soferim* (Hebrew), ed. M. Higger (Jerusalem: Makor, 1970), p. 289. B. Baba Batra 134a. On toseftot see below, n. 61.

14. ARN, p. 59; note also the reading in Israel ben Joseph Al-Nakawa, *Sefer Menorat ha-Maor* (Hebrew), ed. H. G. Enelow (New York: Bloch, 1929–1932), pt. 3, pp. 522–23.

More remains to be said of our theme, but it will not be intelligible unless we first jet (so to speak) over almost five to eight hundred years.[15] In the tenth century we hear from Saadia Gaon of Sura (882–942), *ein somekhin al divrei aggadah*, one may not invoke haggadic sayings as support for certain views. And in the latter half of that century Sherira Gaon of Pumbedita (968–998) in his personal notes, similarly, with a brief addition:

> The derivations from verses of Scripture which are called midrash and aggadah are mere guesses (*umdana*) . . . hence *ein somekhin al aggadah*, one may not invoke haggadic sayings as support, *amru ein lemedin*[16] *min ha-aggadot*, and it's been said [literally, "they said"; who?], One may not derive (*lemedin*, precedents or rules) from the aggadot. . . . Those of them that can be rationally (*min ha-sekhel*) or biblically confirmed we shall accept, for there is no end or limit to the aggadot.

And in the eleventh century, his son Hai Gaon (998–1038), commenting on the treatise Ḥagigah (presumably on a passage on 14a), writes emphatically:

> Know ye [or know thou] that aggadic sayings are not like a received tradition (*ha-shemuʿah*); they are simply what an individual expresses [teaches, *doresh*] of what occurs to him personally—[such as] "it is like, it is possible, one may say"—it is not a clear-cut [decisive, *ḥatukh*] statement; and that is why they enjoy no authority [*ein somekhin aleihen*]. . . . These midrashic views are neither a received tradition nor a halakhic ruling; they are no more than perhapses.

Note that the formula *ein somekhin al ha-aggadah* has already become a refrain, repeated virtually verbatim, and this will continue down to the twentieth century when a most exacting scholar, the late Saul Lieberman, will legitimately summon the same words (of course citing the Geonim) to establish that in a disputation the saintly Naḥmanides, *peh kadosh*, was not speaking tongue in cheek when he protested that a haggadic teaching need be no more binding than *sermones* of a bishop: if you like them, fine; if you don't, no offense to the Faith; therefore the rabbi is under no compulsion to believe a particular talmudic statement about the Messiah.[17] By not *ein somekhin al*

15. I have obviously drawn on the material in B. M. Lewin, *Oẓar ha-Geonim: The Responsa of the Babylonian Geonim and Their Commentaries According to the Order of the Talmud* (Hebrew) (hereafter OhG), 13 vols. (vol. 1, Haifa: privately published, 1928; other vols. Jerusalem: various publishers, 1928–1943), especially the volumes on Berakhot and Ḥagigah. But no one familiar with that treasury will fail to recognize my indebtedness to S. Lieberman, both *Shkiin and Yemenite Midrashim* (Hebrew) (Jerusalem: Wahrmann, 1970).

16. An adaptation of the idiom in B. Sanhedrin 17b?

17. Lieberman, *Shkiin*, pp. 81–83. (Note also Lieberman in Leviticus Rabbah, p. 881.) This is in no way to be interpreted as Naḥmanides' indifference to haggadah. Note, for example, how on Lev. 18:24–25 (*Explications on the Torah by R. Moshe ben Naḥman [Ramban]*, ed. D. Chavel [Hebrew] [Jerusalem: Mossad Harav Kook, 1960], pp. 107ff.), he keeps weaving haggadic views with his own (and earlier) interpretations. And note especially A. Funkenstein, "Naḥmanides' Typological Reading of History" (Hebrew), Ẓion 45 (1980), pp. 35–59. See also Naḥmanides' poem at the head of his Torah commentary:

aggadah is itself become [60] a fixation, a kind of immovable tenet of about one-third of the classic Oral Law curriculum. This can even filter down to creators of massive haggadic compendia, R. Isaac Aboab[18] and the martyr R. Israel Al-Nakawa,[19] each of whom in his respective introduction apologizes— that is exactly the word I want—for his haggadic composition. It may not be halakhah but it can be useful!

Now, the geonic view of *ein somekhin* was not an arbitrary eruption of doctrinaire preference and idiosyncratic rejection, as we shall soon see. These scholars are living in an age and surroundings where Rationalism is the dominant intellectual persuasion. (There are already some mystics in the wings, but for the time being their voice is still not authoritative, at least in the higher echelons of the Babylonian yeshivot: Saadia's *Emunot ve-De'ot* has blazed the trail.) This Rationalism has certainly succeeded in removing the toxin from many dangerous, grossly anthropomorphic talmudic or para-talmudic sayings[20] on God's anatomy or laughter or tears or groaning and so on; or the specifics of Daniel's vision; or the experience of R. Ketina in the doorway of a necromancer.[21] So, too, the statement by R. Eleazar,[22] "when the Holy One, blessed be He, beheld the Flood generation," is not to be understood literally ... but is meant ... metaphorically.[23]

Obviously, purging was called for. In the twelfth century Maimonides reports[24] that he

> met a man who was a scholar, and as the Lord liveth, in his own opinion that man was expert since youth in the pugilism of Torah exercises (*milḥamtah shel Torah*);

nafshi ḥashkah ba-torah ...
lazet be-ikvei ha-rishonim ...
li-khtov ka-hem (ba-hem) peshatim bi-khtuvim u-midrashim be-mizvot ve-aggadah
arukhah va-kol u-shemurah
Va-asim li-meor panai ...
perushei rabenu shelomo ...
bi-devarav ehegeh ...
ve-imahem yihyeh lanu masa u-matan, derishah ve-ḥakirah
u-feshatav u-midrashav ve-kol aggadah bezurah, asher be-ferushav zekhura.

18. End of fourteenth century; see the introduction to Aboab's *Menorat ha-Maor* (Stettin: Schrentzel, 1866); no pagination but equals 4a and following (with the delightful observation that Talmud is like bread, haggadah is like water—and though one certainly needs bread to survive, water is all the more indispensable!).

19. Died Tammuz 1349 (cf. Enelow's introduction to Al-Nakawa *Menorat ha-Maor*, p. 15). How compare my work, writes Al-Nakawa (in *his* introduction, p. 12), to the works of the Sages? All [in my work] they knew on their own. But [the teachings here included] are scattered helter-skelter [Aboab also refers to this]. I'm not worthy to draw up such a work. Fortunately an angelic being (*ish ... ayom ve-nora'*) inspired the necessary trembling and resolution.

20. Cf. *OhG*, Ḥagigah, *Commentaries*, pp. 58–59.

21. B. Berakhot 59a; *OhG*, Berakhot, *Commentaries*, pp. 91ff., and *Responsa*, pp. 131–32.

22. B. Ḥagigah 12a.

23. *OhG* Ḥagigah. *Commentaries*, p. 54.

24. *Maamar Teḥiyyat ha-Metim*, ed. J. Finkel. *PAAJR* 9 (1939), p. 3, and J. M. Rabinowitz (Jerusalem, 1944), p. 345. As for Maimonides' views of *Shiur Komah*, see Lieberman apud Scholem, *Gnosticism* (New York: JTS, 1960), pp. 124–25.

yet that man was still uncertain whether the Lord was or was not corporeal, with eyes, hands and feet and intestines, as biblical verses put it.

Others from other countries whom Maimonides has met are not in doubt about it at all: He is a physical being, and anyone denying this they regard as a heretic! And they cite many *derashot* (or: *derashot* of the treatise Berakhot) as support of their views.

The demand to spiritualize and allegorize and to cultivate caution against unsophisticated literalism is not a prejudice of intellectual cranks who have been affected by some philosophical speculation. There is in addition a genuine need for defense against the charges of Karaite opponents (and sectarians and skeptics) who accuse talmudic teaching of blasphemy, no less. As early as the tenth century, the Karaite Salmon ben Yeruḥim (and very likely others before him too) rhymes in outrage,[25]

[The talmudic rabbis] also say that the Holy One, blessed be He, binds tefillin [around His head] / / and the name Israel is [61] inscribed on his turban / / and the name Jacob is inscribed on His canopy / / All such they say to infuriate Him. / / / / To the Garden of Eden [they say] the Holy One, blessed be He, will come and rejoice with His people / / and will drink and dance with His company / / and say, "I and you are alike, where you go I go," as it is said [Cant. 5:1], Eat, lovers, and drink: drink deep of love! / / Woe to them that speak such words—they, they are the ones who reduce Him to brute matter.

These are stock-in-trade charges,[26] "boisterous Objections," as Sir Thomas Browne would say.

When the Geonim reject aggadic literalism, they are nonetheless—or at least Rav Hai tries nonetheless[27]—to distinguish between aggadot incorporated in the Talmud and those preserved outside the talmudic canon. The latter are untrustworthy; and even those in the Talmud must be checked lest the text be corrupt or inexact. But whatever is included in the Talmud must be corrected if there is textual error, and if we don't know how to make the correction, the statement is to be treated like those sayings which are not halakhah. We don't have to go to such trouble with what is not included in the Talmud; but if the statement is proper and attractive, we interpret and teach it; otherwise we pay no attention to it.

Whatever the distinction, it is still fundamental (*ki kelal hu*) that *ein somekhin al aggadah*.[28] Or again, on the talmudic[29] exchange regarding

25. *Milḥamot ha-Shem*, ed. I. Davidson (New York: JTS, 1934), pp. 110–11.
26. As can be seen also in *Al-Qirqisani*—trans. L. Nemoy, *HUCA* 7 (1930), pp. 331, 350–51—who like Salmon ben Yeruḥim refers to works like *Shiur Komah, Hekhalot, Alphabet de Rabbi Akiva*. That one has to think hard about *Shiur Komah*: OhG, Berakhot, *Responsa*, p. 17; Ḥagigah, pp. 11–12.
27. *OhG*, Ḥagigah, *Commentaries*, p. 60.
28. Ibid., p. 29.
29. B. Berakhot 59a.

earthquakes (*zeva'ot*; the blessing to be recited[30] at such occurrences), Rav Hai:[31] "This discussion [subject, *milta*] is an aggadah, and of it and of everything like it our Sages (*rabbanan*) have said [where?] *ein somekhin al divrei aggadah*, haggadic statements are not to be employed as authoritative teaching"; he continues with a demonstration of a number of midrashic-talmudic expressions which must be interpreted metaphorically only and concludes, Although there are other views, the correct interpretation is as we have interpreted, and God forbid that there be a literal description [comparison, *dimui*] of our blessed and exalted Creator.

One thing is clear, namely, that there are obviously learned Jews, students of Talmud and Midrash, who are genuinely perplexed. To be sure, they pick up quite a number of notions from compositions and anthologies that circulate even among those who are Talmud devotees without reserve.[32] But these men are puzzled[33] not only by what they read in extra-talmudic haggadot; they are puzzled by what they find in the Talmud itself! That the gatherer of wood on the Sabbath (Num. [62] 15:32ff.) was Zelophehad (see Num. 27:1ff.) was R. Akiva's view;[34] and it is touché when Judah ben Batyra rebukes him, "Akiva, one way or another you will in the future [Future] have to answer for this. If what you say is right, you're revealing what Scripture saw fit to cover up; if you're not right, you're slandering that saint!" But surely Judah ben Batyra hardly improves on Akiva; all Judah can be credited with is that he will not invent a *gezerah shavah* on his own!

To describe Jews who are tempted to take talmudic haggadot literally as gullible is no more than name-calling.[35] Of course there were also stupid ones in their midst, as in every midst. My literal-mindedness is gullibility; very well, yours is comparative anthropology or literary criticism. So it goes in scholarship as in interdepartmental feuds. After all, the two Talmuds themselves include substantial haggadic material in the midst of their preponderant halakhic *sugyot*, their halakhic proceedings. Did the redactors intend the preserved haggadot as intermissions, relaxations of mental strain? On one occasion when R. Jeremiah asked R. Zera[36] to teach him, R. Zera replied, *halish libbai vela yakhelna*, I don't feel well and am unable to teach halakhah (*litnei*). Whereupon R. Jeremiah said, Then tell me (*lema*), Master, something aggadic.

---

30. Mishnah Berakhot 9:1: "Blessed is He Whose might and power fill the universe."
31. *OhG, Berakhot, Responsa,* pp. 131–32.
32. See Lieberman, all of *Shkiin and Yemenite Midrashim.*
33. Cf. *OhG,* Ḥagigah, *Commentaries,* p. 60, n. 4.
34. B. Shabbat 96b–97a. See also 97a on Aaron. Cf. Sifre Numbers, ed. H. S. Horovitz (Jerusalem: Wahrmann, 1966), sec. 113, p. 122; sec. 133, p. 177, but note also interlocutors in Siphre Zutta, pp. 287, 317.
35. See the important remarks by G. Scholem, *Elements of the Kabbalah and Its Symbolism* (Hebrew) (Jerusalem: Mossad Bialik, 1976), pp. 153, 155–156.
36. B. Taanit 7a and also R. Ḥanina bar Iddi. And see Rashi on Prov. 9:9, beginning. On R. Jeremiah and R. Zera unwittingly misled by each other, Cf. Genesis Rabbah LX 8, pp. 649–50. R. Jeremiah asks R. Zera a halakhic question in presence of a scholar's bier (but R. Zera replies): XCVI, p. 1238. See also Midrash Psalms XIX 14, p. 171 (R. Jeremiah?).

Said R. Zera to him, This is what R. Yoḥanan said: Why is it written [Deut. 20:19], "For man is as a tree of the field?" Observe, immediately preceding [ibid.] it is written, "For of it [masculine, him] you eat and it [him] you shall not cut down." This is to tell you, If a scholar is a decent person (*hagun*), then eat from him and don't cut him down; otherwise destroy him utterly.

What is this? *Aggadeta* is only for the weak-minded (*ḥalish libbai*)? Or an illustration of the extreme modesty of R. Zera? Or a left-handed rebuke of R. Jeremiah, that *he* may not measure up to the right kind of tree of the field? Poor R. Zera, his studies apparently used to wear him out.[37] But if we are going to build on such anecdotes, then we might as well subscribe to R. Ḥanina bar Iddi's myth that Torah has been compared to water to teach that even as water flows from top to bottom, "so the words of Torah leave him who is of haughty disposition and descend to him who is of humble disposition." Even as moralizing it lacks magnetism.

It is not in the least surprising that those loyal to talmudic authority should be tempted to accept all of it—its halakhah of course, but its haggadah, too, at first; since its haggadah is also the creation of the Tannaim and Amoraim, the initial impulse is to treat these "mighty hammers" seriously, reverently, whenever they speak up. These Jews [63] can't forget how R. Yoḥanan reduced a skeptical student to a mound of bones[38]—doubtless a byword, but a potent repudiation. There *is* a difference between halakhah and haggadah which the men who turn for guidance to the Geonim are surely aware of—namely, that in halakhah you are essentially engaged with traditions that have come down from and been accepted by the ancients; *amar Rabbi Yoḥanan, mi-pi shemuʿah amarah, mi-pi Ḥaggai, Zekhariah u-Malakhi,*[39] [R. Yose's] view is not his own, but a tradition from as far back as the post-exilic prophets, hence incontestable. Of course disagreements (*maḥlokot*) can exist. What is the Talmud if not a storage of scholarly debates within the academy? The very controversies testify to the determination of the Rabbis and their constituencies to be faithful to the traditions they have inherited (Akavyah ben Mahalalel in M. Eduyot 5:6–7 is sufficient example) and to the exegesis which will demonstrate their continuing vitality; acceptance of reports of visions too. Controversy, however, is not the fabric of haggadah even though some of the preeminent Tannaim and Amoraim were masters of both halakhah *and* haggadah, and there may be disagreements in haggadah too. Yet, haggadah is literally

---

37. B. Berakhot 28a. On R. Zera turning sarcastically on R. Jeremiah cf. S. Spiegel in *Harry Austryn Wolfson Jubilee Volume on the Occasion of His Seventy-Fifth Birthday* (English and Hebrew) 3 vols. (Jerusalem: American Academy for Jewish Research, 1965) (Hebrew), vol. 3, p. 252.

38. B. Sanhedrin 100a and parallels. See also Isi ben Akiva in Midrash Psalms XXIII 5, p. 201.

39. B. Ḥullin 137b, top. (Note: *shemuʿah*, not *masoret*; cf. Bacher, *Midrashic Terminology*, pp. 74–75, 227. On *masoret haggadah*, cf. Leviticus Rabbah XVIII 2, p. 402, n. to l.6).

free of all restraints, *ein sof ve-lo tikhlah le-aggadot*, and rejoices especially when the other side, be that other side what it may in your time and place, agrees,[40] even if reluctantly.[41] There may even be overlapping. The chief thing is that haggadah is not restricted by ancient legacy of practice—public or private, theoretical or applicable. In haggadah one is at liberty to draw cheerfully on his own intellect or imagination, on popular narratives and folk sayings, on anything congenial to his own spirit, to interpret a biblical verse or create a homily or amplify a scriptural anecdote or solicit parables or invoke a national or universal bon mot and so on. The key word here is *free*, be it explanation or musing. None of that *im halakhah nekabel, ve-im le-din yesh teshuvah*, if it's a tradition, very well; if your reasoning or logic, I can refute (Sifre Deut. 253, p. 279). Wit does not wait for precedent.

We must not misinterpret this sensation and phenomenon of freedom to create the impression that when the Sages indulge in haggadic speculation or teaching, all thought of tradition is expelled. "The old distinction between tradition and originality," writes T. G. Rosenmeyer in his *Art of Aeschylus*,[42] "crumbles before our increasing awareness of the subtle crosscurrents between the fluidity of the tradition, the autonomy of the creative forces latent in it, the limitations upon authorial freedom." The Sages are not interested in escaping tradition, [64] even as they give free rein to associating verses from one end of Scripture with the other end; in other words, even in their constantly surprising and original *petiḥot*, the proems or overtures to their immediate commentaries when the meaning of a verse in Genesis, let us say, can be produced by explanation of a verse in Job. The key word, we said, is *free*; the accompanying key word is *original*. In haggadah a man could display his originality.

Needless to say, approval may be hard to win. To return to early sources: when R. Akiva explains (Exod. 8:2) "And the frog [*ha-ẓefardeaʿ* singular] came up and covered the land of Egypt," as "There was only one frog and it filled the whole land of Egypt,"[43] R. Eleazar ben Azariah protests vehemently: "Akiva,

---

40. For example, see R. Judah in Genesis Rabbah XLIX 9, p. 511, and cf. H. de Lubac, "La Belle Captive," in *Exégèse médiévale: Les quatres sens de l'écriture* (Paris: Aubier, 1959), I, i, pp. 290–304.

41. Cf. St. Augustine, *City of God*, ed. T. E. Page et al., trans. Philip Levine (London: William Heinemann, Cambridge: Harvard University Press, 1966), 13:16, Loeb Classics, vol. 4, p. 191, ". . . who plume themselves on being called or being Platonists and whose pride in this name makes them ashamed to be Christians. They fear that, if they share one designation with the common mass (cum vulgo), it will detract for the wearers of the Greek cloak from the prestige of their fewness, for they are puffed up in inverse proportion to their numbers."

42. Berkeley: University of California Press, 1982, p. 315; and see also the frequently cited essay by T. S. Eliot, "Tradition and the Individual Talent," in his *Selected Essays*, new ed. (New York: Harcourt, Brace, 1950), pp. 3–11. On the latter, see S. E. Hyman, *The Armed Vision: A Study in the Methods of Modern Literary Criticism* (New York: A. A. Knopf, 1952), pp. 79–83.

43. B. Sanhedrin 67b; cf. Seder Eliyahu Rabbah, p. 41. See also Midrash Psalms I 8, p. 9. If for the benefit of the Age to Come one behemoth can squat over one thousand mountains (amoraic, Leviticus Rabbah XXII 10, pp. 524–25; see also Tannaim, pp. 525–26), why not one

what business have you with haggadah? Cut out (*kaleh* or *kelakh*) such talk and go back to the subjects of plagues and tenting uncleannesses!" I appreciate the disapproval—though I must say, since we're talking of miracles, why not Akiva's emphasis on the singular *ha-ẓefardea'* and the following *va-tekhas* [and *it* covered] of the verse? And that outrageous reprimand, Go back to the laws of plagues and defilements—granted, not the lightest reading of the Talmud, and demanding profoundest expertise, hence an undeniable compliment—why should that unnerve a pious talmudist? Is Eleazar ben Azariah's explanation easier to digest? He says, "There was only one frog, but it croaked [literally, hissed] to all [the other frogs] and they came [and covered Egypt]." Then what of the singular *va-tekhas*? Is it to be understood as the frog caused the other frogs to cover (*piel* as *hifil*)?

R. Eleazar ben Azariah seems to have relished his own style of rebuttal.[44] This may therefore be no more than a topos, and not too much is revealed by it, although it remains baffling that anyone would presume to minimize Akiva's haggadic prowess—for to Akiva we are indebted for some of the finest theological instruction.[45] Is Eleazar ben Azariah nursing a grudge of some sort?

Rejection of some haggadic views, in other words, exists, and anyone studying Talmud would be familiar with it, because it is not altogether rare. When R. Levi[46] interpreted the passive "was circumcised" (*nimol*) in connection with Abraham as, Abraham "inspected himself and found himself circumcised," R. Abba bar Kahana (who was really a good friend of Levi's[47]) let him have it: Liar, faker, Abraham was suffering pain so that the Holy One, blessed be He, might double his [65] reward! Oriental rhetoric of course, but rejection no less (although Levi's interpretation is after all far from extreme as haggadah can go!).

For men who study Talmud or what they regard as talmudical, there could certainly be nothing extraordinary about rejecting a haggadic statement. And when in the midst of a halakhic give-and-take[48] there is an exclamation, "Are midrashot a matter of faith?[49] *derosh ve-kabel sakhar*, Go ahead and interpret midrashically and be rewarded"; in other words, don't take it too seriously, no one need be put off, for *derosh ve-kabel sakhar* is a cliché if ever there was one, especially in discussion[50] of halakhot now become theoretical. Note inciden-

---

frog teem at miracles in Egypt? One man's fantasy is the next man's ridiculousness. Haggadah is full of this.

44. B. Sanhedrin 38b; Midrash Psalms CIV 9, p. 442. See also B. Yoma 75b, Ishmael to Akiva.

45. "Toward a Profile of . . . Aqiba ben Joseph," in *JAOS* 96 (1976), pp. 38–56. See also L. Ginzberg in *Jewish Encyclopaedia*, vol. 1 (1901 ed.), pp. 304–10.

46. Genesis Rabbah XLVII 9, p. 476.

47. Cf. Theodor's note to line 5, ibid.

48. P. Nazir 7:2.

49. Cf. Lieberman, *Shkiin*, p. 82.

50. To be revived in messianic times, B. Sanhedrin 51b; or regarding the rebellious son or

tally, not, Drop these subjects or pay them no mind or don't study them till you're forty years old, but, There's some reward even in study of these subjects albeit nothing practical will come of it.

Once upon a time, said R. Levi,[51] when money was abundant a man yearned to listen to mishnah and halakhah and talmud discussions; but now when money is scarce, and above all a result of being worn out by subjection to the nations, people want to listen only to words of blessing and of comfort.[52] The most natural thing in the world! When you're in need of consolation, law reviews are not much help. And if people are listening to haggadah,[53] they are paying close attention to it, as they have been taught to do when studying the sources. And when they hear sensational things—like the varieties of the names of God[54] or the significance of dreams,[55]—or receive rumors and reports of mind-boggling stunts and experiences,[56] what more natural than to turn to the leading talmudic authorities and expect an explanation? Indeed, how *rational* is their inquiry; *u-mah hefresh bein ma'aseh nevi'ut le-ma'aseh khashfanut u-mah hi aḥizat einayim,* By what criterion is one to distinguish between accounts of prophetic acts and acts of witchcraft; and what is this pulling the wool over one's eyes, this business of delusion?[57]

These are serious men (in another decade, who will believe the account of the Entebbe rescue?), neither strangers to the intellectual demands of Talmud study nor simpletons. The Geonim do not reply to them contemptuously. But what do they say? *ein somekhin ve-ein mevi'in re'ayah mi-kol divrei aggadah ve-ein makshin mi-divrei aggadah,* You base nothing on and bring no proof from any aggadic statements and you don't raise questions because of

the condemned town or the house leprously afflicted, 71a; or haggadic, Prov. 24:27, B. Sotah 44a.

51. Canticles Rabbah II 5, 15a.

52. Says the *Yefeh Kol,* "Therefore they do not listen even to words of aggadah!" But note also *Agadath Shir Hashirim,* ed. S. Schechter (Cambridge: Deighton Bell, 1896), p. 30, lines 844–45. Pesikta de Rav Kahana, ed. Mandelbaum (New York: JTS, 1962), p. 205, and critical apparatus there.

53. Cf. also the touching story about R. Abbahu and R. Ḥiyya bar Abba in B. Sotah 40a. See also the quotation in n. 6, above.

54. *OhG,* Ḥagigah, *Responsa,* pp. 22–23. On Stoic speculation on varieties of deity's name, cf. *Diogenes Laertius,* trans. R. D. Hicks, ed. T. E. Page et al. (London: William Heinemann, 1959), VII, 147, Loeb Classics, vol. 2, pp. 251–52.

55. *OhG,* Ḥagigah, *Responsa,* p. 25. See also R. J. White, *The Oneirocritica by Artemidorus* (Park Ridge, N.J.: Noyes, 1975), pp. 7–10.

56. *OhG,* Ḥagigah, *Responsa,* pp. 16ff.

57. Ibid., p. 18. See, by the way, the exchange between Yoḥanan ben Zakkai, a heathen, and Yoḥanan's disciples in Pesikta de Rav Kahana, p. 74 and parallels (cf. Midrash Psalms L 1, pp. 278–79, in connection with R. Simlai; anti-Christian?). See also Maimonides, *Introduction to Mishnah Avot* (Hebrew), ed. J. Kafih (Jerusalem: Mossad Harav Kook, 1964), VI, p. 259a. On *aḥizat einayim* cf. M. Kosovsky, *Concordance to the Palestinian Talmud* (Hebrew), 3 vols. (Jerusalem: Ministry of Education and Culture of the Israeli Government and the Jewish Theological Seminary of America), vol. 1 (1979), p. 190, col. b. G. H. Dalman, *Aramaisch-Neuhebräisches Handwörterbuch zu Targum, Talmud, und Midrasch* (Hildesheim: Olms, 1967), 13a, s.v. *aḥiza.*

264 : *Thematic Studies*

them.[58] An attempt will be made to distinguish between haggadot to be found in the Talmud and haggadot in other [66] apparently popular compositions (as we said), but the pronouncement is summary, *ein somekhin, ein lemedin*.

I cannot find this rule in the Talmud itself.[59] How did it become an oft-repeated formula? The statement by R. Zeira in the name of Samuel in the Palestinian Talmud[60]—*ein lemedin min ha-halakhot ve-lo min ha-haggadot ve-lo min ha-tosafot ella min ha-Talmud*, or, as P. Ḥagigah 1:8 reads, *ein morin*, that is, No decision is to be made from the compilations of the halakhot (mishnah) or from the haggadot or from the tosafot (Mishnaic supplements)[61] but only from the Talmud—is not talking about our subject. J. N. Epstein[62] has even put parentheses around the words "or from the haggadot," quite rightly, for what is being discussed in that passage is on what basis may you arrive at a practical, halakhic decision; and even if you adopt the reading of the regular printed editions, that is still the intent; and it is reminiscent of the *baraita* in the Babylonian Talmud:[63] *ein melamdin*, one is not to teach (= to decide) a halakhah either on the basis of academic study (*talmud*) or even on the basis of what was an actual case, but one must be taught the halakhah specifically on the basis of a halakhah now to be applicable (*halakhah le-maʿ aseh*).[64] The nature of haggadah is not here the issue. For rendering decision it is useless, as are the halakhot or tosafot. True.

Ein somekhin al ha-aggadah is pretty strong, sweeping language. However, while nothing so categorical is known to me from the Talmud and Midrash themselves, no careful reading of the classical sources can obscure what I would like to call "early traces" of the idea, and by early I do mean tannaite. To begin with, there is the report of those legal scholars[65] (intellectual

---

58. *OhG*, Ḥagigah, Supplement, p. 65.

59. "In the Talmuds and midrashim, particular haggadic interpretations may be dismissed for one reason or another; but it is never said there in summary fashion that haggadah can't be invoked as authoritative doctrine. . . . Quite naturally, for that is still the creative and self-understood period. A principle like *ein somekhin* . . . becomes articulate only after a traditional text has been sanctified in the course of time, and people come uncritically to treat every statement in it as the equivalent in value of every other statement in it. Rationalistic Geonim and subsequent rabbis thereupon attempt to restore balance or proper perspective. Their principle is not intended as disdain of lessons that may be learned from haggadah; it is a denial of the obligatory, doctrinaire character of the haggadah" (J. Goldin, "Midrash and Haggadah," in the forthcoming *Cambridge History of Judaism*, written 1974–75).

60. P. Peah 2:4.

61. See J. N. Epstein, *Introductions to Tannaitic Literature* (Jerusalem: Magnes, and Tel Aviv: Dvir, 1957), pp. 241ff. (on the Tosefta).

62. Ibid., p. 241.

63. B. Baba Batra 130b; on the word *talmud*, cf. *DS*, ad loc. See also Genesis Rabbah LVI 6, pp. 601–02. See Ch. Albeck, *Introduction to the Talmud* (Hebrew) (Tel Aviv: Dvir, 1969), p. 548, n. 44.

64. Cf. B. Niddah 7b, bottom. Pirkoi ben Baboi will make much of it. Cf. Ginzberg, *Ginze Schechter*, vol. 2, pp. 556–59 (with reference to R. Yehudai Gaon), pp. 562, 571–72. And on Pirkoi, see the important study by S. Spiegel, *Harry Wolfson Jubilee Volume*, pp. 243ff. See also Genesis Rabbah C 7, p. 1291.

65. Sifre Deuteronomy, 48, p. 113.

snobs? halakhah practitioners impatient with the stiff requirements of analysis and probing?) who say, I study halakhot, that's enough for me. Then the Midrash admonishes, "Study midrash, halakhot, and haggadot," and then proceeds to quote and interpret the biblical verse (Deut. 8:3), "man does not live on bread alone": "that refers to midrash"; "but [man lives] by everything which comes forth from the mouth of the Lord," "that refers to the halakhot and the haggadot." So there are halakhic scholars who apparently feel superior to haggadah or feel that haggadah is superfluous, just as there are those who like to say, I will study the difficult sections (parashah) and pass up the easy ones. Both types (or are they one?) are to be rebuked (Deut. 32:47), "for this is no trifling thing for you"; what you call trifling "is your very own life." This association of "I will study only what's difficult, enough for me are the halakhot" registers clearly a disparagement [67] of haggadah study though the normal curriculum calls for it too. And maybe it is in such scholars that the first signs of condescension toward haggadah rise to the surface. Did they feel that way towards haggadah because they thought it was easy, because it was *infra dig*?[66]

A superior attitude of this sort will not escape criticism, as the deuteronomic verses cited and interpreted above already testify. But there is even bolder rebuke, and that too in the Sifre. First a thoroughly innocent and we might say well-nigh literal comment.[67] "Take to heart these words with which I charge you this day" (Deut. 6:6), says the Sifre, "Take to heart these words, for thus you will come to recognize[68] Him who Spake and the World Came to Be and cleave to His ways." However you wish to understand "these words," halakhically or haggadically, we are manifestly being exhorted to cleave to His ways. You can do that by taking His words to heart.

But then on Deut. 11:22, on the expression "cleave to Him,"[69] when astonishment is recorded—How can a human being ascend on high and cleave

66. There are presumably easy halakhic discussions: Leviticus Rabbah XXXIV 4, p. 779.
67. Sifre Deuteronomy, 33, p. 59.
68. le-hakir; see also Mekhilta Shirta 3, vol. 2, p. 26, makirin atem oto.
69. Sifre Deuteronomy, 49, pp. 114–15. See also Pitron Torah (Hebrew) ed. Urbach (Jerusalem: Magnes, 1978), p. 251. Cf. Leviticus Rabbah XXV 3, pp. 572f. Note in addition B. Ketubot 111b.
The very question "How can a human being ascend on high and *cleave to the Fire?*" may suggest a touch of mystical feeling. I'm not convinced that in the present instance it is so—despite what may lie *behind* the expression (on "Fire," cf. H. Lewy, *Chaldaean Oracles and Theurgy: Mysticism, Magic and Platonism in the Later Roman Empire* [Paris: Michel Tardieu, 1978], pp. 25, 83f, 201, 241–45; and alah may well reflect anagoge, see ibid., pp. 487–89). But not every metaphor, even a bold one, is necessarily an expression of mysticism; and while our Sifre passage is echoing sounds of the Moses legend (see L. Ginzberg, *Legends of the Jews* [Philadelphia: Jewish Publication Society, 1910], vol. 3, pp. 109–14; vol. 6, pp. 47–48], it is speaking of "man" (efshar lo le-adam), not of Moses, and especially of "as though" (ke-ilu alitah), not of actual ascension. There is nothing in our Sifre passage of "ecstatic mysticism" or a mystical exercise or an elitist gnosis or secret password. See the excellent remarks of D. J. Halperin, *The Merkabah in Rabbinic Literature* (New Haven: American Oriental Society, 1980), p. 139, on ma'aseh merkavah mysticism.

to the Fire?—first comes a rationalizing answer: This means "cleave to scholars and their disciples, and I shall account it to thee as though thou hast ascended on high" and taken the Torah captive—that seems to be the object of the concluding phrases: to overcome the angels who tried to prevent the giving of the Torah to Israel.[70]

Immediately after this we read:[71] "*doreshei haggadot*, the expositors of haggadot say, If you wish to recognize (*le-hakir*, know, get a notion of, make known, acknowledge?) Him Who Spake and the World Came to Be, study haggadah, for thus you will recognize Him Who Spake and the World Came to Be and cleave to His ways." Is this hyperbole triumphant? On the contrary! There is a finesse, a chastity of speech here it would be poor taste to bypass. First, it is to be noticed that there are obviously students or even masters known as *doreshei haggadot*, men who make haggadah study an important part of their intellectual pursuits. Second, since the biblical verse speaks of cleaving (*u-le-davkah*), these expositors adopt this very strong verb[72]—they do not paraphrase or modify or resort to synonym. Third, it is not the *doreshei haggadot*, who speak of cleaving to the Fire; in their saying no reference is made to the Fire on high: only to "study haggadah." Fourth, note the refinement of observation: Scripture does not hesitate to say *u-le-davkah vo*, and cleave to Him— but the haggadists say, "and cleave to His ways!" Talk of avoiding possible offensive language about the Creator, in the haggadah! And if you're curious about what God's ways are, the [68] beginning of that very section of the Sifre[73] is ready to tell you in terms even stronger than those of Epictetus's *Discourses* as reported by Arrian:[74] no ifs, no maybes, no *if* faithful, *if* free, *if* beneficent, *if* high-minded, no *ei piston, ei elevtheron, ei energetikon, ei megalofron*. The Holy One, blessed be He, surely *is*, as Scripture teaches, *rahum ve-hanun, zaddik, hasid*; these are His ways, and so be yours if you seek intimate fellowship with Him.[75]

If you wish to cleave to His ways, study haggadah. On the importance of study of the halakhah, which is compared to the staff of life,[76] there is ready assent among the Rabbis. And as grandiose promise for such preoccupation there is, "He who studies (reviews, *shoneh*) the halakhot may be certain that he

70. ARN, p. 10; B. Shabbat 88b–89a. On the angels opposed to the *creation* of Adam, see ARNB, p. 23 (but cf. also Ginzberg, *Legends*, vol. 5, p. 84, n. 33).

71. Note Finkelstein's critical apparatus. To this day, and despite Lauterbach, I'm still not sure I understand (*doreshei) reshumot*; but cf. Bacher, *Midrashic Terminology*, p. 125.

72. I have already commented on this verb in the *Harry Wolfson Jubilee Volume*, pp. 82–83 and nn. 44–47, 50.

73. Sifre Deuteronomy, 49, p. 114.

74. II, 14:13 (Loeb Classics, vol. I, pp. 308–09).

75. Cf. Mekhilta Shirta 3, vol. 2, p. 25, "Abba Saul."

76. Cf. B. Hagigah 14a, "'Every prop of food' (Isa. 3:1, literally, bread) is a reference to the masters of talmud (cf. Rashi ad loc., s.v. *lehem*), as it is said (Prov. 9:5), 'Come, eat my food (*lahmi*)' . . ." Note by the way Isaiah da Trani on the Proverbs verse, III. p. 19, top. And see Aboab, *Menorat ha-Maor* (4d; cf. n. 19 above) quoting B. Baba Batra 145b.

will be included in the World to Come."[77] But no one promises that if you study halakhot you will come to recognize the Holy One, blessed be He, and achieve *imitatio dei* although it is affirmed by the Babylonian Rav Ḥisda[78] that

> the Lord loves the gates of academe devoted to halakhic studies more than the synagogues and academies (*batei midrashot*): as the following was transmitted in the name of Ulla [second-third generation Palestinian Amora?], "Since the destruction of the Temple, with His whole world [to choose from] God confines Himself to the four ells of the halakhah."[79]

Or are these value judgments, as I now want to suggest, polemical remarks? These are not now, however, uppermost in my mind. I can get into the World to Come by taking a stroll of four ells in the Land of Israel[80]—which demonstrates how instructive such counsels are!

Now, these praises of halakhah are amoraic statements, but my contention is that they are a *continuation* of moods encouraged even in tannaite times in Palestine, as the midrash of the *doreshei haggadot* and as the self-satisfaction of "I've studied halakhot, enough" reveal. No anachronism is intended.

Those who study and teach haggadot are not talking to themselves or fantasizing or promising farfetched, fairy-tale rewards. They are *engagé*, they are involved in argument with those who have a good word only for halakhah, who feel that the highest level of achievement is that of the *nomikos*, the man who will deal with midrash, with halakhot, and never mind the aggadot though they are the third required era of concentration of the *bet ha-midrash*. The *doreshei haggadot* declare, It is through the haggadot (does this mean only the haggadot?—I think [69] it does) that you will come to cleave to His ways properly. The statement is a magisterial counterpolemic.

In short, already in the tannaite centuries there is a discernible tension between the two parts of the accepted curriculum, between midrash and halakhot on the one hand and haggadah on the other. And the Geonim, even if they hesitate to admit this explicitly (or maybe they do somewhere—Saadia

---

77. Twice in the Babylonian Talmud, Megillah 28b, bottom, and end of Niddah (where see also the last Tosafot), both quoting Tanna de-bei Eliyahu. See Seder Eliyahu Zuta, p. 173, and cf. Friedmann, introduction, ibid., p. 45. D. Halivni, *Sources and Traditions* (Hebrew), *Seder Moed Shabbat* (New York: JTS, 1982), p. 23, n. 67.

78. B. Berakhot 8a. For identity of Ulla, cf. A. Hyman, *Histories of Tannaim and Amoraim* (Hebrew) (London: Express, 1910), III, 973a. And note DS ad loc. For haggadic praise of halakhah, see also Midrash Psalms XLIX 1, p. 278.

79. But note DS. Genesis Rabbah XLIX 2, p. 501: In the name of R. Judah (bar Ezekiel), "Not a day passes without the Holy One, blessed be He, offering fresh halakhot in the Court on high." See also n. 4 above.

80. B. Ketubot 11a. And on the passage at the end of Shekalim III, ed. Sofer, p. 37, see Y. Sussmann in *Researches in Talmudic Literature* (Hebrew) (Jerusalem: Israel Academy of Sciences and Humanities, 1983), pp. 50, 69. On this formula (promise) in mystical speculation, in *Merkavah Shelemah* (Hebrew) (Jerusalem: Mosaiev, 5681 [1921]), 39b, so! See S. Lieberman apud G. Scholem, *Gnosticism*, p. 123.

does not hesitate to oppose a haggadic view),[81] are nevertheless sensitive to it. Not completely on their own do they invoke *ein somekhin*. And since they are principally students of the law, heads of academies where the law is constantly explored, their minds are inevitably upon it; and since they feel themselves above all responsible for the cohesiveness of the Jewish community, they opt for the most part in behalf of the Establishment, for what will stabilize it, and not for what is free association, the individual mind taking off on its own flight of fancy or the literalism dangerously close to a fundamentalism of vocabulary and understanding.

There are three parts of the Oral Law, midrash, halakhot, and aggadot, and I wish to submit that already in the early talmudic centuries there had developed a tension between the first two parts and the third. Keep to the four ells of the halakhah means bluntly, Haggadah is not important. Study haggadah if you wish to recognize the Creator and cleave to His ways means bluntly, It's not from halakhot that you'll learn this momentous lesson. We are in the presence of the permanent human agon between restraint and freedom. Generally we speak of halakhah and haggadah as though they were the literary remains of antiquity and refraction also of the social history of their times, which indeed they are. Or they are presented as the highway to proper conduct and exhortation.[82] But they were always much more than that. They are an articulation of the fundamental, universal, interminable combat of obedience and individual conceit.

To resolve the tension or to transform the conflict into a creative collaboration takes genius. Yet even here the Talmud furnishes a charming anecdote, making good use at the same time of an Aesop fable.[83] Two scholars once visited R. Isaac Nappaha (second-third generation Palestinian Amora). Said one to him, Sir, tell us something halakhic; the other said, Sir, tell us something aggadic; when R. Isaac began to speak of an aggadah, the one visitor would not let him go on; when he began to speak of a halakhah, the other visitor would not [70] let him go on. R. Isaac said to them: You know what this is like? To a

81. Cf. *Saadia's Polemic against Hivi Al-Balkhi*, ed. I. Davidson (New York: JTS, 1915), p. 58, n. 177. On the vigor of the Geonim to establish Babylonian, rather than Palestinian, teaching everywhere, cf. Spiegel, *Harry Wolfson Jubilee Volume*, pp. 246ff., 262ff.

82. On the inadequacy of the halakhah strictly applied, cf. Genesis Rabbah XXXIII 3, pp. 304ff. Note also the anecdote about R. Yose the Galilean, XVII 3, pp. 152–55. Cf. R. Joshua in B. Baba Kamma 55b (bottom). See also J. T. Noonan, Jr., on Cardozo, in *Persons and Masks of the Law* (New York: Farrar, Straus and Giroux, 1976), pp. 111ff. But either way, halakhah without haggadah or vice versa is reduction of a rich, complex construction to efficiency row housing.

83. B. Baba Kamma 60b, and see *Babrius and Phaedrus*, ed. and trans. B. Perry (London: W. Heinemann, 1965), pp. 33–34, Babrius, fable 22 and Phaedrus, pp. 235–36.

It takes a John M. Woolsey of the United States District Court of the Southern District of New York, attentive to "all questions of law and fact involved," to decide in 1933 on *legal grounds* that *Ulysses* "may . . . be admitted into the United States" for it must also "always be remembered that" the author's "locale was Celtic and his season Spring" (James Joyce, *Ulysses* [New York: Random House, 1934], pp. ix–xiv).

man who has two wives, one young and one old. The young one keeps pulling out his white hairs and the old one keeps pulling out his black hairs. As a result he ends up completely bald! So he said to them, I will tell you something that should appeal to both of you. It is said (in Exod. 22:5), "When a fire is started and spreads to thorns," that is, the fire started of its own, "he who started the fire must make restitution": The Holy One, blessed be He, said, I have to make restitution for the fire I started—it was I who set fire to Zion, as it is said (Lam. 4:11), "He kindled a fire in Zion which consumed its foundations"; therefore in the future I will rebuild it in fire, as it is said (Zach. 2:9), "And I Myself will be a wall of fire all around it, and I will be a glory inside it."

Now to the halakhic lesson. The Exodus verse began by speaking of damages caused by what a person owns (*mamono*; the reference is to that which is his property, not to him personally) and concluded by speaking of damages he personally was responsible for. This is to teach you that the fire one starts is like the arrow he shoots (in both cases the person is held responsible regardless of the distance travelled by the arrow or fire).

Maybe R. Isaac Nappaha was a genius. Anyway, I'm glad he began with the aggadic lesson.[84] It's not immaterial to the halakhah just taught. Or alternatively, possibly, the halakhah may have provoked the haggadah.

---

84. Cf. Rabbah's pedagogic practice in B. Shabbat 30b.

From Text to Interpretation and From Experience to the Interpreted Text°

[157] I shall begin with a statement which appears in several midrashim and also in the Talmud: Isi ben Judah said (Isi ben Judah is presumably a Tanna of the latter half of the second century of our era): Isi said, There are five verses in the Pentateuch still undetermined (syntactically, *she'ein lahem hekhrea'*). The five verses are Gen. 4:7, Gen. 49:7, Exod. 17:9, Exod. 25:34, Deut. 31:16. Actually one more problematic verse can be added, to wit, Gen. 34:7.[1] For our immediate discussion, the identification of the mobile term or vocable in the verses is not of primary importance, although I hasten to add parenthetically that what Isi reports is reflected in ancient versions and translations,[2] hence not to be dismissed as midrashic flourish or exaggeration: oh, you know, midrash.

Isi has here preserved a reminder of what we innocently do not recall often enough. What is a biblical verse?[3] There must have been schools or biblical scholars once upon a time who decided, Here one verse begins, there another. A look at the Dead Sea Isaiah Scroll is enough to underscore that (1) without vowel points and without punctuation (provided, for example, by something like our cantillating signs, the *ṭe'amim*; or orally transmitted), it is often uncertain how to read; but (2) already in this manuscript there is evidence of the adoption of spacings between so-to-speak sections or units that largely coincide with what our accepted Hebrew texts display. There must have been a long tradition of the way to read even before the Tannaim, and not everything

---

° This paper was presented at a conference on "Midrash and the Text" held at Yale University in February 1982.

1. See Gen. R. 80:6, 957f. and commentary ad loc. plus parallels in midrashim and Talmud.
2. Cf. the commentary in Gen. R. ibid.
3. Cf., for example, H. L. Ginsberg, *Koheleth* (Jerusalem, 1961), 105f. on Eccl. 8:2–3 and 109 on 8:10–11.

was settled once and for all. Thanks to Isi we have been reminded of this fact: that the very readings of the Hebrew Scriptures had once to be established and some of these are not yet decided.

[158] Isi's testimony is reenforced by still other observations. For example, we are taught that in the Pentateuch there are ten dotted passages. Each of these is even furnished with a midrashic explanation. Dots (*stigmai*) as editorial marks are what scribes used to indicate suspected or uncertain reading. And indeed, our passage states: Ezra the Scribe said, If when Elijah comes, he protests to me, Why did you adopt the doubtful readings, I'll say to him, Notice I put dots over them; and if he says to me, You've copied well, I'll then remove the dots.[4] In other words, what we have inherited from the past is a text, some of whose readings remain uncertain. By the same token, however, these and still other examples of variants imply that the texts we have inherited are not haphazard or capriciously compiled, but the workmanship of serious editors.

For myself, I call such editorial activity, plus a number of rhetorical features in the Bible itself—to which Seeligmann called attention about thirty years ago and described as *Bibelerklarung innerhalb der Bibel*[5]—such activity I call "proto-midrashic." First, because when we encounter the elaborated midrashic exercises from the tannaite period onward, we see clearly that they have not erupted out of a background of zero. Dead Sea *pesharim* alone would be sufficient to bear this out. Second, I call them *proto*-midrash, because although they exemplify serious preoccupation with the text (which midrash is after all), they do not yet reflect that readiness, better still that eagerness for sweeping association, for welcome of multiplicity of interpretations, of what might almost be ̣ ̣rded as infinite variety, seven times seven faces of the Torah,[6] for frequent exposition by means of parable, for referring by name, when they can, to sages whose views they quote, that our midrashic texts preserve. And this variety and far-flung attestation and verbal equation and association of verse whenever possible with the theme of Torah, I regard as a product of the institution known as *bet midrash*, where scholars agree, disagree, argue, and stimulate each other. This atmosphere the redactors of our midrashic texts retained for us.

Some of this is inevitably hypothetical—for how much do we know concretely of the exegetical activity before the last century B.C.E.? And, after all, to refer to one feature, there are parables in the Bible itself.[7] But something like

4. Cf. Abot deRabbi Natan, Version A, pp. 100–101 and Version B, 97f. and parallels. On a long list of variants in the Torah copy from Jerusalem in the Rome synagogue, see R. Moshe haDarshan, Bereshit Rabbati, ed. Albeck, pp. 209–12.

5. *Supplement to VT* 1 (1953), 150–81 (the quotation is on p. 171) and recently (on Chronicles) in *Tarbiz* 49 (1979–80): 14ff.

6. For example, Tanḥuma Bemidbar 24, Ḥukkat 9.

7. But note that neither in Judg. 8:7 nor in 2 Sam. 12:1 is the "parable" introduced either by verbal or nominal *mashal*. In Scripture, of course, *mashal* has quite a semantic range, including "parable" as in Ezek. 17:1ff. (but note the translation in the RSV and New JPS!). The frequency of parables in midrash is therefore particularly impressive. See further, D. Stern,

the distinction made, I suspect, must be true if the activity of the Sages from tannaite times and beyond is to make sense. They do not hesitate to take over biblical manners of glossing and etymology and exploitation of neighboring sounds, but as schoolmen they developed the art of interpretation professionally, as academic, curricular activity, and a methodology became a literary genre.

Now, it is the response to awareness of indeterminacy on the one hand, and on the other, of reception of what has been handed down, that I think the phenomenon of *al tikre* may go back to—for example, the [159] famous one, *vekhol banayikh limudei hashem,* "'When all your sons are instructed by the Lord, through your sons peace will increase' (Isa. 54:13), read not *banayikh,* your sons, but *bonayikh,* your teachers, those who make you to understand"[8]— may go back to a frame of mind ultimately and not necessarily subconsciously derived from appreciation of the rich potential of a text. "One thing God has spoken; two things have I heard." That is to say, since the text we have has been organized so carefully, though some unfixity still remains, don't amend, don't alter; leave the text as it stands, but illuminate as you discern possibilities of meaning in the terms. (Here the point is "Scholars increase peace in the world." Hence, if "All thy children shall be taught of the Lord," then "Great shall be the peace of those who love thy Torah" [Ps. 119:165].)[9] This never stops. Of Rachel, weeping for her sons (Jer. 31:14), says a late midrash, "Read not *raḥel* (Rachel) but *ruaḥ el* (spirit of God).[10]

To summarize my first point, I would put it this way: A lively consciousness exists, even as late as the tannaite period, of the seriousness or solemnity which accompanied the editing of the Hebrew Scriptures in earlier centuries, and of the presence still of undetermined elements; and this consciousness acted as impulse to attempt to explain the Scripture both atomistically and thematically, all of it, in every way of interpretation available in their world in their times.

On the ways of exegesis in their time and in their world, I need not enlarge, since these ways are described at length by Lieberman and Marrou; so too by Yitzhak Heinemann.[11] The late Elias Bickerman was no less a master of such historical exposition and commentary.

Let me instead select a few aspects of midrash which may serve as representative, not of all the varieties of midrashic exercises—I can't count them:

"Interpreting in Parables" (Ph.D. diss., Harvard University, 1980), and pro tem idem, "Rhetoric and Midrash: The Case of the Mashal," in *Prooftexts* 1 (1981): 261–91.

8. B. Berakot, end. Compare also H. Yalon, *Pirkei lashon* (Jerusalem, 1971), 123ff.

9. See also Tanḥuma Exodus, ed. Buber, 38b no. 13, end.

10. Tanna debe Eliyahu, ed. Friedmann, 148.

11. S. Lieberman, *Hellenism in Jewish Palestine* (New York, 1962); H. I. Marrou, *A History of Education in Antiquity* (New York, 1956); Y. Heinemann, *Darkhei ha'aggadah* (Jerusalem, 1970). E. Bickerman, e.g., *Studies in Jewish and Christian History*, vols. 1 and 2 (Leiden, 1976, 1980), passim.

Let me select several passages which exhibit the way midrash treats problems, or creates them in order to bring Scripture up to date.

Consider the following (Deut. 32:10): *Yimtsa'ehu be'erets midbar / uvetohu yelel yeshimon // Yesovevenhu yevonenehu / yitsrenhu ke'ishon 'eino.* The latest English translation goes: He found him in a desert region, in an empty howling waste. He engirded him, watched over him, guarded him as the pupil of his eye.

For this verse, the Sifre[12] provides four interpretations. This is not extra-ordinary. A verse (as we've already said) may have a number of interpre-tations, for in the revealed words are impacted many intentions. Nor is this to be overlooked: We are dealing with a text which is nonhalakhic, not involved with formulation of public or private practice. In short, we are exploring a text of the realm of human speculation and imaginativeness, where the intellect or imagination is *free* to suggest what strikes it as appropriate—for this is the realm of haggadah, and in this realm the possibilities are as endless as they are (to cite one example) in literary criticism. So, again, a verse may legitimately release a number [160] of applications: on *ya'arof kamatar likhi,* May my discourse come down as the rain (Deut. 32:2), ten—possibly eleven—interpre-tations are offered.[13] Four explanations for Deut. 32:10, therefore, are hardly remarkable. What are they?

The first applies the verse to God's discovering of Abraham; verses are then enlisted to support this view.

The second interpretation applies the verse to Israel when God protected them at Sinai in the dangerous wilderness. Like the first, the second interpre-tation is not farfetched. And the same may be said of the fourth comment, that God's discovery of Israel in the wilderness refers to the Age to Come, when He will protect them from all dangers even as He did in the first wilderness period—again and again for the midrash the past is symptomatic of the future (cf. Ezek. 20:33ff.).

But the third comment, which we have skipped in our paraphrase, puts us into perplexity: *Yimtsa'ehu be'erets midbar* translated literally says, He found him in a desert land. But the third interpretation of our midrash ignores the grammatically straightforward meaning, and says instead, (The verse means,) Everything was made accessible to them in the wilderness, they were provided with everything—a well of water surged up for them, manna came down for them, quail was made available to them, the clouds of glory protected them on all sides. But how do we get to this meaning?

Bewilderment is created, certainly not because midrash is confined to the literal; and not because the midrash does not indulge in metathesis, or does not pun, or does not engage in *al tikres*, or does not recommend surprising identi-fications, or does not convert tenses, or does not split words and transpose letters

12. Deut. 313, ed. L. Finkelstein, 354–56.
13. Sifre Deut. 306, pp. 335–40.

(e.g., *karmel* = *rakh mal*, soft but brittle), or does not invert parts of a verse. Indeed, the midrash does all these things and more, and such literary conduct is congenial to it. Moreover, when for some reason elaborated midrashic exegesis is called for, the midrash will not hesitate to amplify and supplement. See, for example, the Targum on Jacob's blessing in Gen. 49, where what is surprising in that section is not the haggadic elaborations but the literal rendering of one tiny verse, *lefurkanakh sabarit Adonai* for *liyshuᶜatkha kiviti Adonai*, Lord, I await your salvation (triumph).

And yet it is not unfair to ask *why* the midrash moves away from "He found him in the desert land" to "Everything was made available to them." In Hebrew we can see the grammatical change easily and immediately; the midrash is reading *yimtsa'ehu* (ימצאהו) as though it were vocalized *yamtsi'ehu*. Why, however, is the midrash doing it?

Before attempting to answer this question, I must make explicit a principle that governs my reading of midrashic literature. Actually it is a simple principle, one so elementary, even self-evident, for students of classical and general literature, that I'm in danger of sounding [161] pretentious, let alone naïve. The principle is this: There is always a reason for a midrashic comment. I don't say that I always find the reason; indeed often I don't. But I still insist that a midrashic comment, even when so-to-speak playful, is the result of some provocation. If we were discussing Talmud, there would be no need to invoke the principle, first of all, because in the Talmud there are by and large sufficient signs of editorial arrangement, and of course there is always Rashi; but second, in halakhic studies the students and the scholars have been instructed and trained to search and search yet again. However, as regards haggadic midrash, the widespread attitude is, In haggadah it does not matter. There has certainly been a change in the last half century. And there certainly are excellent commentators of haggadah. But the earlier attitude, general assumption, is still current. I think I know why, but do not care to quarrel with halakhic critics of haggadic freedom from restraint, any more than I care to quarrel with haggadic critics of halakhic demands for unwavering conformity. I simply state what I always assume, that midrashic expression is the result of something specific pressing on the *baᶜal midrash*, the midrashic spokesman, and if I can't find that specific cause, it's my tough luck. But there *is* a cause.

At times the provocation is lexical, growing directly out of the biblical text; at times the lexical is not the immediate provocation, but some idea or mood or speculation or resentment, for which the midrash accommodatingly provides the biblical idiom—a phrase, a clause, even a singular term if need be—to confirm, as it were, *dekula ba*, that everything is either in the Scriptures or under their surface. At times both provocations may be present and interact. Let's begin with an example of lexical provocation, in other words, go back to our question. Why substitute for the perfectly plausible *yimtsa'ehu*, an interpretation that is based on *yamtsi'ehu*?

We consult Targum Onkelos, and what do we find? *Sapik tsorkheihon*, He provided for their needs. Rashi, by the way, had already noted the Targum's view, though he seemingly prefers the more common alternative. What of the Septuagint? *Autarkēsen auton en tē erēmō*, He maintained him in the wilderness. In short, the third interpretation of our midrash is not something piquant but an expression of awareness, that there is a reading or understanding of our biblical text as *yamtsi'ehu*. Therefore that too calls for comment.

And for a partial roundup of this reading or understanding of that provoking verb plus object-suffix, let me quote Yosef Bekor Shor, one of the finest of plainspoken medieval commentators—he of course is not recommending emendation of text; he is a devotee of *peshat*, the direct and unembroidered explanation of the biblical statement. *Yimtsa'ehu*, he says, is to be understood as *yamtsi'ehu*, for He provided for all their needs in the wilderness, manna, quail, the well, their garments did not wear [162] out, their feet did not swell.[14] And this he offers as his *only* explanation of the verse! Obviously he's gotten it from the Sifre. But it is noteworthy that he pays no attention to the three other Sifre interpretations which appeared so natural.

Let's examine another passage, perhaps not as spectacular as the first, nevertheless also instructive. *Hasket ushemaʿ yisra'el* (Deut. 27:9), Moses and the levitical priests commanded all Israel, "Silence! Hear O Israel," as some of the latest English Pentateuch translations read. The exclamation "Silence," הסכת, is apparently related to an Akkadian word *sakātu* (which the Rabbis could not know) and also the Arabic *sakkatta*. So our modern lexicographers.[15] How do the Rabbis handle this word *hasket*? The midrash[16]—which varies slightly from the version in the Talmud (B. Berakot 63b)—offers the following: *hasket = has vekattet*, i.e., the word is to be split in two to convey, first keep quiet, then grind away; that is, the procedure in learning should be, first absorb what is being taught, only afterward ask and reason and explore and analyze— in other words, only after you've learned what the text says are you to try to master it in depth and in its complexities: *has*, first learn without questioning and then *kattet*, only later advance to intricate analysis. Perhaps this means *pilpul*.

All this is charming and even commendable scholastic pedagogy, in the spirit of much midrashic exercise, like *karmel = rakh umal*, which we have already met. Yet it is fair to ask, Does the midrash offer any other suggestions? Not really. Still playing on the syllable *kat*, it suggests that Moses advises us to form *kittot kittot* for study, that is, not to study by oneself but in compan-

14. Bekor Shor, commentary on Deut. (Jerusalem, ca. 1976), on the verse, p. 73. Note also the reading *y'mtshw* (= *ye'amtsehu*? related to *'ammits*, strong, mighty?) in the Samaritan Torah.

This clause is interpreted ca. eleventh century by Abu-l-ḥasan haTsuri (ed. A. S. Halkin in *Leshonenu*, 32 [1967–68]: 228, and cf. ibid., 213, n. 85) as, "This refers to the feeling of confidence stirred up in his [i.e., Jacob's] heart, instead of the fear he felt on going down to Egypt, lest he die [there] and not be buried with his fathers."

15. BDB, p. 698; Koehler-Baumgartner, p. 658.

16. Tanḥuma Ki-Tavo 2; Tanḥuma Deut., ed. Buber, 23b–24a.

ionship with others (a preference of many orientals and in sophisticated give-and-take among Hellenic scholars as well—it grows out of a school image of master and disciples' relationship with each other).[17] Or again, *kat* is an exhortation to give up one's life if necessary and not give up studying Torah. For this emphasis it even tells part of the story of the martyrdom of Rabbi Akiva. He studied Torah till the crushing point.

Now, what is happening here? Not one so-called literal, manifest meaning is offered. Targum אצית and ציית, which means "hearken, give ear," are an intelligent guess on the basis of the following word שמע. Septuagint gives us *siōpa*, the Vulgate, *attende*. Why is there not in our midrash at least a reference to such a possibility?

The answer is—and it was already perceived by Ibn Ezra—that the word *hasket* is a hapax; it occurs only in Deut. 27:9, and the midrashic-talmudic Sages don't know what it means. As Ibn Ezra says, the word *'ein lo rea'* does not occur again, hence *perusho lefi mekomo*, the meaning has to be derived from the context, and Ibn Ezra does what the Targum had done; but the midrash did not do it. Not knowing what the word might or did mean, it did the next best thing: It adopted a meaning the way that is done in interpreting dreams: a single word is broken into two, a [163] common practice in oneiro-critica,[18] dream interpretation, dream speech. An idiosyncratic word has thus released several meanings. Here at all events is another principle. When a midrash adopts only forced, baroque explanations of a word, it reveals that it is having difficulties with that word. But that itself can become encouragement to seek a useful or valuable homiletical lesson.

There are many more examples of this feature of midrash, but let us move on to midrash where the original impulse is not a lexical detail, but where midrash equips an independent idea or mood and so on with a biblical verse as justification, or as ancient anticipation of what the present reveals. It is in such midrashim, especially, that an outlet for protest is provided. Here a pious folk gives expression to what is bitterly on its mind.

"Judah has gone into exile because of misery and harsh oppression," and so forth, the verse in Lamentations (1:3) reads. And the midrash,[19] proceeding atomistically, pauses at the two opening words, *galetah yehudah*, Judah has gone into exile, and remarks or muses, "Judah has gone into exile; and are not the Nations of the World also exiled?" In other words, why this loud lamenting and self-pity of Israel? It is hardly a misfortune unique to Israel. The retort has an almost contemporary sociological ring.

The midrash replies: The exile of the other nations is not really exile, for wherever they're exiled to, they still can eat of the bread of their captors and drink of their beverages—that's hardly exile. But in the case of Israel who

17. Cf. Eccl. Rabba 4:9:1.
18. Cf. Lieberman, 70ff., 75f.
19. Lam. Rabba, ed. Buber, 31b.

cannot share their captors' food or drink—that's real exile. Exile for Israel is not just a geographical shift, a migration; it is total uprooting. Even our sufferings are unique.

In two words arrested from what follows, the midrash has made audible the calamity and fate of Israel. We have here a reflection on Galut which must have occurred every time the Book of Lamentations was read, as well as at other times, when one contemplated where he was forced to live or was overcome by an indoctrinated nostalgia. The theme is profoundly felt in midrashic-talmudic times, no less, let us say, than it was felt by Yitzhak Fritz Baer in our times, when he reflected on the meaning of Exile. But in particular we note on this occasion that the midrash has tied such thinking and feeling to the vocabulary of the Bible. It is even possible that the evidence of such thinking survived only because it was attached to a biblical verse.

Our midrash is not a lexical by-product. We may even say that the midrash is a biblicization of independent, Jewish, human speculation and protest. In my disturbances the appropriate verse will be found. The verse creates a permanent record.

This indeed is the midrashic assumption, and that assumption is often adopted by the medieval commentators also—of course not all to the same degree. I shall not refer to Rashi, who is easily and universally [164] recognized as the preeminent master of combining *peshat* and *derush*; nor to Naḥmanides for whom a verse is frequently an opportunity for profound theological and historical speculation. I deliberately choose Ibn Ezra, who so concentrates on matters of philology and grammar and comparative linguistics and particularities of text, you'd think he had almost no ear or eye for anything beyond these: although he doesn't hesitate to admit when need be, *ummaḥshevot hashem ʿamukot*, Inscrutable are God's thoughts.[20] Well, commenting on Exod. 14:13, and Moses said to the people who panicked when they saw Pharaoh's armies overtaking them, Have no fears, stand firm and behold the victory which the Lord will achieve for you today, first Ibn Ezra explains—the meaning is, you won't have to engage in battle, for today you will witness *God's* victory. But Ibn Ezra does not stop with this; he continues,

> Here is something astonishing: Why should a huge army of 600,000 adult males be frightened of those pursuing them? And why won't they fight for their lives and children? The answer is that the Egyptians had been Israel's masters, and this generation of the exodus had learned from early years on to bear the Egyptian yoke, and were timid in spirit. How could they now battle with their masters? For Israel were slack, inexperienced in war. And only the Lord—who performs miracles and by Whom all is set aright—brought it about that all the males of the people who left Egypt should die because they did not have the strength to battle the Canaanites.

20. For example, on Exod. 14:1.

> Then rose a generation after the Wilderness generation who never experienced Exile (Galut) and they were of high spirits.[21]

What a telling anachronism, "who never experienced Exile"!

Here we have realism, or what Ibn Ezra regards as realism, put to the service of exegesis. This, by the way, recurs in his interpretations. For instance, his second explanation of Exod. 2:3, why it was necessary for Moses to be raised in the Egyptian royal house, is this: "For had he grown up among his brethren, and had they been familiar with him from his early years on, they would not have been in awe of him and would have regarded him [only] as their equal."

Commentary, in short, has not grown out of an irregularity of syntax or vocabulary of the verse. Rather, a verse has been revealed as anticipating the thinking and feeling of a later age.

There are many examples of this, as one might well suspect even without having read midrash. It is practised by all communicants of book religions. Let me, however, offer one last example which may be regarded as a parallel view to the passage we looked at before quoting Ibn Ezra, and yet, I believe, in what follows the mood is in some respects much sadder and more self-critical. It may well be historical reality with a vengeance.[22] Here mood and attention to a particular word combine—not that the word is odd or difficult; on the contrary, it recurs, it is that very recurrence which helps make the observation striking.

[165] In the name of Resh Lakish, R. Judah ben Naḥman presents the following comment on Gen. 8:8–9, "Then [Noah] sent out the dove to see whether the waters had decreased from the surface of the ground. But the dove could not find a resting place (*manoaḥ*) for its foot, and returned to him to the ark."[23] So the verses; and the commentary is,

> Had it found a resting place, it would not have returned. Similarly, when she [Israel] settled among the nations, she found no rest (*manoaḥ*; Lam 1:3)—had they found it, they would not have returned. Similarly again (Deut. 28:65), Yet even among the nations you shall find no peace, nor shall your foot find a place to rest (*manoaḥ*)—were they to find it, they would not return.

The repetition of *manoaḥ*, the iconography of the dove as Israel (or, if iconography is too strong a term for our discussions, then the figure of Israel as

21. יש לתמוה, איך יירא מחנה גדול של שש מאות אלף איש, מהרודפים אחריהם. ולמה לא ילחמו על נפשם ועל בניהם. התשובה, כי המצרים היו אדונים לישראל, וזה הדור היוצא ממצרים למד מנעוריו לסבול עול מצרים, ונפשו שפלה. ואיך יוכל עתה להלחם על אדוניו. והיו ישראל נרפים ואינם מלומדים למלחמה. והשם לבדו שהוא עושה גדולות ולו נתכנו עלילות. סבב שמתו כל העם היוצא ממצרים הזכרים. כי אין בהם כח להלחם בכנענים, עד שקם דור אחר דור המדבר, שלא ראו גלות, והיתה להם נפש גבוהה.

22. Note also the view in Deut. Rabba, ed. Lieberman, 71 (bottom and top 72), when Israel obey.

23. Gen. Rabba 33:6, 310. Note also Lam. Rabba 1:29, 14a, in the paragraph following "Judah . . . exile."

dove), and who knows, perhaps also the pun of *manoaḥ* on the name Noah (note also Isa. 54:9, *mei noaḥ*), have stirred up thoughts not only of the primeval flood but of the experience of Israel for generations and centuries over land and sea. An event from the remote past, from even before the days of Abraham, has been personalized, has been detected as a prefiguration of the behavior and destiny of *Israel*. For the masters of midrash, Jewish history can be in the end a disclosure of the earliest designs for the universe, and vice versa.

Now, without the word *manoaḥ*, this would not be explicit. (Naturally with other words and other verses, the rhetoric can be repeated; but we are here discussing the verses of Noah's dove.) We need the term *manoaḥ*. But the thought, the reflection, the mood, the self-criticism are the result of what might be called autonomous experience. Locate the brooding in the vocabulary of a verse, and Scripture becomes contemporary and permanently relevant. Which the Rabbis never wearied of trying to achieve. And why? Because they felt and were brought up to feel its immediacy. Midrash is not just a device. It is pedagogy. Pedagogy makes use of devices; devices do not make pedagogy.

I have deliberately avoided speaking of the so-called opposition between those siblings eisegesis and exegesis, for two reasons: first, the midrash itself treats both identically, that is, when it cites supporting prooftexts, it treats the one exactly as it treats the other, and its midrashic outlook, not ours, is what I wish to describe; but second, and more important, what we prefer to call eisegesis is as complex an act as is exegesis, that is, even as in severest objective analysis, it is impossible to avoid subjective presumptions entirely, so in subjective synthesis there is always at least a hard, indissoluble, objective factor. That factor in midrash is the nature of the Sages' upbringing. Their minds are filled with biblical language, narratives, themes, figures of speech, exhortations, formulae, lists, and these have shaped the speech and contents of their thinking. They do not come empty-headed to their texts. They [166] approach a verse and recall parallels and semi-parallels and quasi-parallels, and, once again, who knows with what earlier interpretations they received, and read both into and out, line by line and between the lines; and it is one of the hardest things in the world to diagnose accurately in all ancient texts where the objective begins and the subjective ends, particularly when the ambition is didactic. The psychological divide is unstable and unpredictable. One example should be enough. *Beito zo 'ishto*, says R. Judah in the Mishna (Yoma 1:1), His house means his wife. This may be Freudian, but long before modern times R. Yose had already announced that "I never called my wife 'Wife' or my ox 'Ox'. Instead, my wife I called 'My house,' my ox I called 'My field'" (B. Shabbat 118b). The metaphor is already ancient, and it is not we or even the Rabbis, perhaps, who have introduced it.

Let us conclude. A commentary by its nature is attached to a text (a picture can also be a text; a musical score can also be a text), and midrash likewise is attached to its text, the Hebrew Scriptures. The varieties of thoroughness displayed by midrash—from instances of forthright and undistracted literalness (which we have not discussed) or midrash in the New Testament (also not referred to), or midrashic treatment of nonbiblical texts, or (a very important need) midrash as polemic and counterpolemic, or association of far-flung verses to create confirmations in each biblical book of any other biblical book, or resort to stereotypes, to the discoveries of relevance to a later age—if artificial, are artificial only in our sight (for we bring other expectations and desires to the sinaitic words). That is to say, the Sages also recognize that there are interpretations that are forced, but the fundamental conviction that biblical verses yield more than meets the eye is unanimously approved, willingly accepted. In all interpretation there is an element of the arbitrary. And here, it seems to me, lies the miracle of this whole performance, that the Sages, like heirs or curators of a rare collection, charged to preserve a sacred text, are not dumbfounded by it into silent adoration. Instead, with a combination of reverence and spontaneity, they so open up and arrange and illuminate the individual volumes of the entrusted collection that they and their contemporaries will discover the reflection of their own features in it, and the response to their own needs and even fantasies.

Or as Elias Bickerman once put it:[24]

> The sacred books of all other religions, from the Avesta to the *commentarii* of the Roman pontifices, were ritual texts to be used or recited by priests. In the Mithra temple at Dura it is a Magian in his sacred dress who keeps the sacred roll closed in his hand. In the synagogue of Dura a layman, without any sign of office, is represented reading the open scroll.

Indeed, this is how the Scriptures survived, not as antiquated message or esoteric password, but as an address intended to be [167] perennially timely. There is no lack of midrashic statements to insist on this.

24. *Studies in Jewish and Christian History* (Leiden, 1976), 1: 199.

On the Account of the Banning of R. Eliezer ben Hyrqanus: An Analysis and Proposal[1]

It seems best after all to accept as historical that the colleagues of R. Eliezer ben Hyrqanus imposed a ban on him, although the talmudic reports certainly are a combination of fact and fantasy that reveals more of the storyteller's mentality, or redactor's, than of what actually took place (hardly unique in the world of narrative). In the Talmud the account appears twice, in B. Baba Meṣiʿa 59b and P. Moʿed Qaṭan 3:1, 81c-d. Why the story should have been included in the latter source is obvious. The mishnah ad locum, in listing those who are permitted to cut their hair on the intermediate days of a festival, includes "him who had been under a ban and was now released by the sages." It therefore makes sense to explain and illustrate in the talmudic give-and-take incidents of *nidduy* (banning). Indeed, in the *sugya* of the Palestinian Talmud not only is the story about R. Eliezer told but a number of examples of contemplated bans are assembled and arranged one after another.[2] However, in the Babylonian Talmud, where the story is narrated in better-wrought

---

1. I am indebted to Professor Martin Ostwald of Swarthmore and Professor Yakov Sussmann of Jerusalem for counsel and helpful criticism.

In the following pages there is no intention to obscure or minimize the importance of *yaḥid we-rabbim* as an operating principle, especially in the ʿAknay-oven case. What *is* suggested is that *yaḥid we-rabbim* is not a mere arithmetical strategy, and that the concept of *shemuʿah* is related to it, as can be discerned clearly is M. ʿEduyot 5:7 quoted below; and in the question put to R. Eliezer in B. Sukkah 28a, "Is everything you say only by way of *shemuʿah*?" The storyteller's phrase in Baba Meṣiʿa, *kol teshubot she-ba-ʿolam*, is pure rhetorical exaggeration; it does not appear in the parallel versions.

2. The expression in the Palestinian Talmud "they sought to ban" = "they banned"; see S. Abramson in *Hebrew Language Studies* presented to Prof. Zeev Ben-Hayyim, (Heb.; Jerusalem: Magnes, 1983), 1–3. Note continuation of PT account. The expression may have been adopted to correspond to the idiom of the preceding report about R. Meʾir as well as to that of the stories that follow.

composition and continued with presumable further consequences of that remarkable academic session (so also P. Moʿed Qaṭan), the issue of *nidduy* is not at all primary. The relevant mishnah (Baba Meṣiʿa 4:10) states that even as in buying and selling there is such a thing as wronging (ʾonaʾah) and that it is forbidden, "so is there such a thing as wronging by mere speech." Now, since Rabban Gamaliel had apparently approved of the ban and thus brought grief to R. Eliezer, R. Eliezer's wife (Gamaliel's sister) was convinced that her brother's death was the result of her husband's supplications to God—for all the gates to heaven may (on occasion) be closed to one who offers up prayer, but never to one who has been wronged in speech: his prayer will always be answered (see also B. Baba Meṣiʿa 58b, R. Yoḥanan in name of R. Simeon ben Yoḥai).

In other words, in the Babylonian Talmud the theme is ʾonaʾah. The banning of R. Eliezer is reported not for its own sake but almost as a prolegomenon to dramatic exemplification of what happens when there is ʾonaʾah of speech. Not of *nidduy* (banning) but of ʾonaʾah (wronging) is the discussion in Baba Meṣiʿa.

The story as it is finally drafted in both versions cannot be earlier than the third/fourth century, and maybe even a bit later, since it cites R. Jeremiah (Baba Meṣiʿa) or R. Ḥaninah (Moʿed Qaṭan),[3] both *amoraim*. In both versions the debate of the scholars is accompanied by sensational (and incomprehensible!) signs—an uprooted carob tree (in the Palestinian Talmud, once again amazingly replanted) thrown a distance of one hundred ells (some say four hundred ells!); the current of a stream turned in reverse;[4] walls about to tumble down but don't completely, out of consideration for the dignity of the chief protagonists in the debate. R. Eliezer had invoked such supernatural support because his colleagues had refused to accept any of his arguments in behalf of his views, says the Babylonian Talmud; and they refused to be impressed by celestial performances—uprooted carob trees, streams going berserk, walls tumbling *prove* nothing. And that is just as true of the last appeal of R. Eliezer: "'If the halakah agrees with me, let heaven be the proof!' A *bat qol*[5] thereupon proclaimed, 'How dare you oppose Rabbi Eliezer, whose views are everywhere [correct] halakah!'" At that point R. Joshua rose to his feet and declared: "[The right answer,] it is not in heaven" (Deut. 30:12). This is now explained by R. Jeremiah (or R. Ḥaninah) to mean that ever since Torah was given at Mount Sinai, "we pay no attention to a *bat qol*, for Thou hast already written in the Torah at Mount Sinai (Exod. 23:2), 'You must follow the majority [opinion].'"

3. Ḥaninah bar Ḥama (?), first generation Palestinian *amora*; Jeremiah, fourth generation (?). On R. Ḥaninah (!), see B. Baba Batra 23b.

4. This miracle is not referred to in the Palestinian Talmud ad loc., and the next is only lightly mentioned and in slightly different words. On "four hundred," cf. *PAAJR* 46–47: 63–65 [above, pp. 106ff.—Ed.].

5. Cf. S. Lieberman, *Hellenism in Jewish Palestine* (New York, 1962), 194ff.

When scholars are engaged in debate, the supernatural is out of order (P. Moʿed Qaṭan)!

This is perhaps the most emphatic and triumphant defense of intellectual "freedom" (better, independence) preserved by the Talmud and is rightly cherished by students of Jewish literature and thought.[6] The Palestinian Talmud in fact exclaims, After all those supernatural endorsements, is the law not to be in accordance with R. Eliezer's view? Inevitably, however, another question must be asked: What is the specific meaning of R. Eliezer's fantastic (but successful!) appeals itemized by the storyteller:[7] uprooted and far-flung carob tree, stream flowing backward, walls beginning to tumble down ("and still sloping in that position")?

The latter question (to my knowledge) has yet to be answered satisfactorily by either the traditional commentators or by modern students (as for the *bat qol*, see below). But one thing, it seems to me, may be said confidently, namely, that the storyteller—either by inventing or by drawing upon current folkloristic motifs—is doing all he can to make us appreciate that the controversy between R. Eliezer and his colleagues over the oven of ʿAknay[8] is not just another customary halakic controversy between sages (characteristic of talmudic literature as a whole) or R. Eliezer and his colleagues, but of fundamental and permanent consequence. Though he had heaven as his ally, Eliezer could not prevail:[9] that earthenware oven—with sandfill between the horizontal earthenware segments into which the oven was divided, then plastered over—which Eliezer said was not susceptible to uncleanness, the sages said was susceptible. And no arguments or reasonings which may have been brought up by R. Eliezer availed. Even a heavenly *bat qol* in his support was rejected; as R. Joshua declared at that point of the exchange, Not heaven but the scholars decided what is halakah; and as the cited *amoraim* spell it out, that means the halakah is in accordance with the view of the majority. Thereupon "they burned in the fire all the *toharot*[10] which R. Eliezer had ruled as clean." And

---

6. See, for example, G. Scholem in *Eranos-Jahrbuch* 31 (Zürich, 1963), 31ff.

7. See, for example, *Shiṭṭah Mequbbeṣet Baba Meṣiʿa* ad loc. (New York, 1972) (and *Ḥiddushe Geonim* in ʿEyn Yaʿaqob, Baba Meṣiʿa, ad loc. [New York, 1955]), quoting R. Ḥananel and R. Nissim Gaon (on the latter cf. the fragment in S. Abramson, *R. Nissim Gaon* [Jerusalem, 1965], 164f.), and cf. Maharsha and ʿAnaf Yosef in ʿEyn Yaʿacob.

8. So the vocalization of Yalon in M. Kelim 5:10; in the Palestinian Talmud, *ḥkynyy* (cf. the Tosafot in Baba Meṣiʿa, s.v., *zeh tannur*). (See also the text published by J. N. Epstein in *Alexander Marx Jubilee Volume* [Heb., New York, 1950], p. 29.) It is interesting that already in the time of the *amora* Samuel the word ʿAknay calls for explanation (Baba Meṣiʿa 59b, top). On the name ʿ*kyn'y* see B. Shabbat 49a.

9. Note how P. Moʿed Qaṭan undertakes to defend Eliezer's resistance and resentment of the decision and action of the sages "to his face"!

10. Rashi: ". . . When into the hollow space of this oven there had fallen an unclean object and then on that oven clean foods (*toharot*) were prepared, R. Eliezer rules that they were clean. Now (the sages) brought these and burned them up in his presence."

If not for Rashi, with whom it is almost preposterous to disagree, I would be tempted to interpret "On that day they brought all the *toharot* which R. Eliezer had ruled as clean and burned them in the fire" as reference to some kind of records or archive in which R. Eliezer's

they imposed the ban on him. Or, as R. Aqiba put it delicately, "Master, it seems to me that the scholar-colleagues are staying away from you."[11]

That there can be sharp disagreements in talmudic debates is in no way extraordinary.[12] But in the case of the ʿAknay oven the intransigence on both sides is so extreme and absolute, and the aftereffects so devastating,[13] it is not unjust to propose that for the storyteller, and in fact, a fundamental issue was at stake. That issue was *shemuʿah* versus *rabbim* (*merubbim*), that is, received tradition by an individual versus majority opinion.

Let me explain. Even though the term *shemuʿah* and its Aramaic equivalent seem to be of amoraic currency,[14] what it represents ("received tradition") was not unknown in tannaite centuries.[15] Not the word, then, are we focusing

rulings were preserved. The word *ṭoharot* is of course used for foods (e.g., B. Sukkah 42a, bot., etc.; T. Demai 2:20, euphemistically, *unclean* foods), but it is also a title of a whole order of the Mishnah, of a treatise in that order as well. Further, "burning" is used in connection with what is written down (I'm not thinking of Apostomos' burning the Torah; what else could you expect? B. Taʿanit 28b; cf. also Josephus, *War*, II, 229), e.g., Ḥullin 60b, in the translation of S. Lieberman (*Hellenism*, 110 plus note), "There are many [single] verses which [one might think] may be burnt like the books of Homer." Or again the imagery in the B. Shabbat 115b saying, "Those who write down benedictions are like them that burn the Torah" (cf. Rashi ad loc.). See also Temurah 14b on those who write down halakot, and cf. the two explanations in Rashi. On the image see also Version B of ARN, 123, toward bot.

All I'm trying to point out is that the verb "burn" or the expression "burn in the fire" is indeed applicable to what is in writing. And J. N. Epstein (*Mebo'ot le-Sifrut ha-Tannaim*, [Jerusalem–Tel Aviv, 1957], 70) speaks of "apparently (*knr'h*), R. Eliezer recorded (*ršm*) his mishnahs [traditions; views?], but of course as was customary at that time and later, recorded them for himself only, personal-private notes, and handed on [his teachings] orally."

But Professor Yakov Sussmann reminds me rightly that in talmudic sources when they wish to refer to writings being put out of circulation, the verb used is *ganaz* and not *śaraf*. A telling criticism. Yet these two verbs, as alternative treatments, can be thought of in connection with a Torah scroll (prepared by a *min* or a heathen), in other words, something written down, B. Giṭṭin 45b; and "burning" would be even harsher treatment than "suppressing." Note, by the way, the view attributed to R. Eliezer, ibid. (Yet the force of Sussmann's remark is not diminished, for "like them who burn the Torah" is topos.)

My problem is that I can't picture all those baked or cooked foodstuffs left lying around as though waiting to be burned or not; particularly if any credence is to be given to the Tosefta (ʿEduyot 2:1), that "over the ʿAknay oven there were many (= for a long time?) controversies in Israel." (Or does this mean that even after the Eliezer ben Hyrqanus affair, the halakah was occasionally still debated because Eliezer's view was not entirely dismissed? On an unaccepted view of R. Eliezer's adopted [by R. Joshua!] after Eliezer's death, see T. Niddah 1:5.)

The expression "on that day" in the story is a stereotype employed for dramatic effect. As for the oven, cf., Y. Brand, *Klei ha-Ḥeres* (Jerusalem, 1953), 565f.

11. This is not reported in the Palestinian Talmud, Moʿed Qaṭan, ibid.

12. This hardly requires elaborate documentation; let these few references to lively and even sharp disagreements suffice: M. Yadayim 4:3; M. Makshirin 6:8; M. Negaʿim 5:3 (the retort to R. Aqiba); T. Shabbat 1:16–17; B. Ḥullin 6b–7a; Sifre Num. 118, ed. Horovitz, 141 (cf. Midrash Tannaim, 88), and so on and on.

On Eliezer opposed to a number of sages, cf. also B. Baba Qamma 84a.

13. See both Talmuds on R. Eliezer's fatal stare. Cf. B. Shabbat 33b on Simeon ben Yoḥai. See L. Blau, *Altjüdische Zauberwesen* (Graz, 1974), 152–56. A folklore cliché.

14. See Bacher, *Erke Midrash*, s.v. *shemuʿah*, 306. But see T. ʿEduyot 1:3. See next note. In Scripture *shemuʿah* = report, news.

15. As Bacher himself notes, 131. And I think the word involves this, too, in M. ʿEduyot 5:7; and see Sifra 6b (R. Ṭarfon), in ed. Finkelstein (New York, 1983), 37f., where note in

on but on an intellectual attitude for which a noun will prove useful before long—a presumption, a confident assumption that the correct teaching or doctrine is the inherited one, what one has learned from his master and the latter from his master, and so on. Typical of this attitude are well-known statements like the following: "Nahum the *librarius* said, I received it from R. Miasha, who received it from Father [or, Abba], who received it from the *Zugot*, who received it from the Prophets, a halakah [transmitted] to Moses from Sinai" (M. Peah 2:6). "R. Joshua [!] said, I have received from Rabban Yohanan ben Zakkai who learned it [*shama'* !] from his teacher and his teacher from *his* teacher, a halakah [transmitted] to Moses from Sinai" (M. 'Eduyot 8:7). "I have received it from Rabban Yohanan ben Zakkai who learned it (*shama'*) from his teacher and his teacher from his teacher as far back as halakah [transmitted] to Moses from Sinai" (R. Eliezer, in M. Yadayim 4:3). Doubtless stereotypical, but let's go on.[16] When in connection with a give-and-take of Shammaites and Hillelites, it is proposed that R. Yose (father of Ishmael ben Yose) is offering a compromise view, R. Yohanan the *amora* declares, [Not so! R. Yose's view is not an original personal one] but a tradition (*shemu'ah*) received from Haggai, Zechariah, and Malachi (Hullin 137a-b). In his prolonged argument with the Batyrites, Hillel fails to convince them, though he resorts to one exegetical device after another, until he finally invokes the authority of his teachers, "so I learned (*shama'ti*) from Shemaiah and Abtalyon."[17] Or R. Aqiba to R. Joshua, "If it's a halakic tradition [halakah], I'll accept; if it's [independent] reasoning (*din*), counterargument is possible."[18]

In other words, at no time do either *tannaim* or *amoraim* disparage *shemu'ah* or take it lightly. One scholar might report that he had heard (*shama'ti*) a halakah and therefore debate is superfluous, and a second scholar (R. Joshua!) might reply, "I can't contradict you, but you heard the general statement while I heard the explicit one (*be-perush*)."[19] (See further below, p. 293.) But no one says anything like, Never mind the *shemu'ah*, or, It's only a *shemu'ah*! The attitude is in some ways akin to what H. I. Marrou says of classical humanism:

> For in the last resort classical humanism was based on tradition, something imparted by one's teachers and handed on unquestioningly. This, incidentally, . . . meant that all the minds of one generation, and indeed of a whole historical period,

---

particular Aqiba's brillance, and then ARN, p. 29. On the word *masoret*, cf. Bacher, 74f. and 227.

16. Note also the idiom quoted by S. Lieberman in *Tosefta Ki-Fshutah*, Berakot (New York 1955), 33, lines 8–9.

17. P. Pesahim 6:1; cf. T. Pesahim 4:1–2, ed. Lieberman, p. 165.

18. Sifra, ed. Weiss, 16c; cf. Sifre Deut. 253, ed. Finkelstein, 279, the sages to R. Simeon and his reply [!] with which cf. M. Yebamot 8:3.

19. Sifre Zuta, ed. Horovitz, 313, and on the halakah cf. S. Lieberman, *Siphre Zutta* (New York, 1968), 59f.

had a fundamental homogeneity which made communication and genuine communion easier.[20]

Received tradition is always taken seriously. And in the earlier centuries, at least up to the Hillelites and Shammaites, it was almost the exclusive principle governing the methods to arrive at a conclusion or resolution of disagreement, in the rabbinic academies. Naturally there were controversies: the one over *semikah* seemed interminable.[21] And surely the account in T. Ḥagigah 2:8–9[22] is idealization or romanticization of sorts—but the notion that when a difficulty could not be resolved, one turned for help to superiors or the more expert should not be dismissed as fanciful. This, however, is not our immediate problem.

All that is being underscored at the moment is that in the pharisaic-early tannaite academies (before the Yabneh reorganization), though there were disagreements, they were probably not prolonged indefinitely despite *semikah* (and that is one reason the sources preserve so few[23] and *semikah is* recalled). To arrive at agreement there must have been resort to some pragmatic arrangement; perhaps occasionally they did take a count, or men acted in accordance with the view they preferred without a special passion for uniformity.[24]

In the early period *shemuʿah* is the governing principle in the academy (and court related to it) and, as we noted above, was always highly regarded, even after the disastrous Revolt of 66–73 (and even after 132–35). No scholars denied its significance. But apparently its most articulate champion was Eliezer ben Hyrqanus of whom it was said, שלא אמר דבר שלא שמע מימיו, who never in all his days said anything he had not received as a *shemuʿah*.[25] Of his teacher too (Yoḥanan ben Zakkai, but for whose program there might never have been a Yabneh and its glorious developments), it was said among other praises that "he never said anything he had not received as a *shemuʿah* from

20. H.I. Marrou, *A History of Education in Antiquity* (New York, 1956), 224. Note also a haggadic *qabbalah* cited by Resh Laqish in B. Shabbat 119b.

21. See M. Ḥagigah 2:2 and cf. L. Ginzberg in *On Jewish Law and Lore* (Philadelphia, 1955), 89ff.; Lieberman, *Tosefta Ki-Fshuṭah*, Moʿed (1962), 1300.

22. Cf. *Tosefta Ki-Fshuṭah*, Moʿed, 1296–99. See also T. Sanhedrin 7:1. Note also the (tannaite) anachronism in Temurah 15b, toward bot.

23. See P. Ḥagigah 2:2, beginning.

24. See, for example. T. Berakot 1:4 or M. Yebamot 1:4. Incidentally, even in late first-early second century there were scholars who acted in accordance with Shammaite teaching. And see the remarkable statement (M. Demai 6:6) on the conduct of the especially fastidious among the Hillelites! S. Lieberman in appendices to I. Gruenwald, *Apocalyptic and Merkavah Mysticism* (Leiden, 1980), 241ff., especially 244, deserves more than brief attention.

25. T. Yebamot 3 (ed. Lieberman, p. 9, end; and cf. ibid. for references to parallels). Apparently the same (in Aramaic) was said of the *amora* R. Ḥanina—*Tosefta Ki-Fshuṭah*, Yebamot (1967), 24 ("Ḥaninah *ha-gadol*, the elder?" in contrast to Ḥaninah *qara*'; cf. B. Taʿanit 27b. Note also below, n. 58.)

And when does Eliezer compliment a sage? When the latter can confirm the view of earlier sages; cf. M. Negaʿim 9:3 (and 11:7).

his master."[26] This is no reason to deprive R. Eliezer of this particular tribute, for it is certainly meant as such, so long as we do not misinterpret it. No one ever intended by that statement that Eliezer never had an idea of his own! In his very legendary biography it is said that when he finally submitted to Yoḥanan ben Zakkai's prodding to deliver the lecture (and this at the beginning of Eliezer's recognition as a scholar), Eliezer "arose and delivered a discourse (*pataḥ we-darash*) upon things which no ear had ever before heard."[27] Obviously hyperbole, and more revealing of the storyteller's gifts at panegyric than of his subject. But such language is testimony that at least even the ancients did not hesitate to credit Eliezer with originality. The way you interpret the definite article (we-*ha*-beged in Lev. 13:47), R. Ishmael once protested to R. Eliezer, it's as though you were ordering the verse, Hush, I've still to *interpret* (*'edrosh*). You're no more than a mountain palm (incapable of producing good fruit [Rabbenu Hillel ad loc.]), Eliezer retorted.[28] Eliezer does not say that he learned this midrash from anyone.

Modern scholarship is even more instructive. It was already Zacharia Frankel[29] (and perhaps he is not the first) who undertook to show that there was genuine analytic exercise (e.g., in use of *qal wa-ḥomer*, p. 82; striving for consistency in ruling on sundry subjects, p. 83) on the part of Eliezer in exchanges with his colleagues. And in recent years Y. D. Gilat[30] in his dissertation admirably described and systematically brought together teachings on all halakic subjects where R. Eliezer is referred to or quoted and argues analytically. R. Eliezer clearly emerges as essentially conservative, but just as clearly not uniformly so, and not as though he were deprived of independent judgment.

Statements like "he never said anything he had not received as a *shemuʿah*" are like the midrashic formula, "This term everywhere (*be-kol maqom*) means nothing other than" this or that[31]—it has about as much value as "I never met a man I didn't like" (Will Rogers)—inflated generalization which collapses into nonsense when put to the test. What it seems to mean is, when he could, Eliezer's first impulse was to draw upon *shemuʿot* available to

26. B. Sukkah 28a.
27. *Abot de-Rabbi Natan*, ed. S. Schechter, Version A, p. 31; Version, p. 32, "Rabbi Eliezer sat [like a master?] discoursing [*doresh*] on things even more [profounder?] than what was told to Moses at Sinai").
28. Sifra 68b.
29. *Darke ha-Mishna* (Warsaw, 1923), 78ff. — though I don't quite follow him in his interpretation (p. 86) that "he never said a thing," etc., means that when something was not completely clear to him, he did not try by forced counterargument to justify his own view, but admitted without embarrassment that he had no *shemuʿah*. See also Ch. Albeck, *Mabo la-Talmudim* (Tel Aviv, 1969), 156.
30. *Mishnato shel R. Eliezer ben Hyrqanus* (Tel-Aviv, 1968). See for example 56ff., 70ff., 123ff., 165, 197, 205f.; 295f. (disagreeing with Shammaites).
31. For example, Mekilta, Be-Shallaḥ 1 (ed. Lauterbach, I, 169, 170 [on which cf. A. Mirsky in *Lešonénu*, 30:302]); 3 (ed. Lauterbach I, 210). Cf. Lieberman, *Hellenism*, 51.

him even as and when others had their *shemuʿot*[32] or wished to debate by means of purely logical argument.

With *shemuʿah* and a small number of rules of interpretation of Scripture and early commentary, intellectual activity could thrive in the academies for a long time, from whenever it began until after the Revolt of 66–73 (obviously I'm speaking in approximate dates). And the consequences of that uprising and defeat were not only political and economic and social (and religious—the destruction of the Temple and its cult) but also, inevitably, juristic, intellectual, and academic. No one has more carefully described the immediate and long-range results of that revolt than Gedaliahu Allon,[33] despite his approach, dominated by an intense nationalist emotion. Through his Mommsen-like dissection and interpretation of talmudic and extratalmudic primary sources, he made vivid the devastation after 70—not only of the Temple and all it represented but of Jerusalem as a whole, and of other parts of the country too—and the gradual rehabilitation of institutional and spiritual life. He should be read without attempted intermediating paraphrase on my part. All I wish to underline in the present discussion is that the move from Jerusalem to Yabneh involved not just a change of location or a migration of scholars from one center to another, or reinterpretation of biblical verses to boost morale, or promulgation of necessary *taqqanot* but a gradual (albeit not slow!) realization that past methods of study and requirements of interpretation had to be supplemented—because in the course of upheavals, despite insistence on continuity of uninterrupted tradition, as reflected by the first chapter and part of the second of Pirqe 'Abot, much may have been lost, or authorities of one sort or another may have been slain or disappeared or withdrew from the Yabneh group; or, because adjustments to daily life were radically transformed, or, what rabbis felt, there was serious threat to adherence to proper Jewish conduct. And naturally there was also forgetting.[34] The past curriculum by itself would not be sufficient; *shemuʿah* and the few rules of exegesis available could not any longer by themselves be enough for intellectual and religious

---

32. This is well illustrated by the exchange between R. Eliezer and R. Joshua in T. Niddah 1:5 (cf. M. Niddah 1:3) where R. Eliezer says that the rule *dayyan shaʿatan* (the moment is sufficient for them: that is, only from the time they discover their flow, not assuming that it had begun earlier) applies to four classes of women: virgins, pregnant women, nursing ones, and old women.

R. Joshua said, I have received a *shemuʿah* only concerning virgins. R. Eliezer said to him: A person who has not seen the new moon is not told to come and testify [whether he's seen it], only one who has seen it. You did not receive [the full] *shemuʿah*, but we did; you received the *shemuʿah* of only one class, but we received it concerning all four.
Note, Joshua also bases his view on a *shemuʿah*, but Eliezer insists that it was an incomplete one. See in this connection the report also in B. Sukkah 28a.

33. In the first volume of his *Toledot ha-Yehudim be-'Ereṣ Yiśra'el bi-Tequfat ha-Mishnah we-ha-Talmud* (Israel, 1952), especially pp. 25–192. "Mommsen-like" was said already by Y. F. Baer in the obituary preface to that volume. I think it is not amiss to call attention to Yehoshafat Harkabi, *Be-Toqef ha-Meṣi'ut* (Jerusalem, 1981) even for historical study.

34. See for example T. Parah 4:7. Cf. J. Goldin in *History of Religions*, 4 (Chicago, 1965), 285–87 [above, p. 159.—Ed.].

instruction and reaching a decision. When the sages came to Yabneh and were worried about what would happen in the future to the words of Torah and the words of the *soferim*, they then adopted the principle of "the rule is according to the majority."[35] Some time then (though I cannot say exactly when) the new principle was introduced—maybe not long before or in the course of the debate over the ʿAknay oven.

There seems to be something so reasonable about the principle "majority rules" that at first it is hard to understand R. Eliezer's defiance of it. The Palestinian Talmud registers almost the same bewilderment: "And did not R. Eliezer know that one must adopt the majority opinion?"—assuming that what was adopted (formally) as a result of the present controversy was unanimously subscribed to even before. And its answer is that Eliezer (did not challenge the principle but) was offended by his colleagues "burning his *toharot* in his presence" out of disrespect for him (Qorban ha-ʿEdah ad loc.). Although "burning in his presence" is said in B. Berakot 19a, hence Rashi in Baba Meṣiʿa also, this is not said in the Baba Meṣiʿa version, where R. Eliezer is portrayed as simply unyielding to his colleagues. But why should he have been opposed to so sensible a method for arriving at what is generally accepted as right (or at least as most dependable) when there is disagreement among authorities?

That "majority rules" should override a *shemuʿah*, however, is not as self-evident as may appear at first thought, at least in talmudic literature. For there was a dramatic occasion when a vote was taken on a number of laws, and Shammaites outnumbered the Hillelites; eighteen issues were decided according to Shammaite views; "and that day was as grievous for Israel as the day the [golden] calf was made."[36] Majority rule as such is no cause for celebration.

Needless to say, this report—even if it, as well as the event it refers to, be dated to the years before the destruction of the Temple—is of triumph over the Hillelites and apparently included use of force (*koah ha-zeroaʿ*, as Lieberman puts it). Hillelite storytellers—and most midrashic-talmudic storytellers are Hillelite sympathizers—would be grieved by a vote favoring Shammaites. But the report does refract an awareness that a vote as such does not automatically lead to the ideal conclusion.

This is certainly Eliezer's point of view, even after he had been subjected to the ban. (Eliezer is not inclined to give up his opinions, even in his last hours (see Abot de-Rabbi Natan, pp. 70, 80, 81). When Yose son of the Damascene visited him in Lydda, he found him in a bakery shop; and Yose brought him news of the vote taken in the academy. Whereupon Eliezer burst into tears and

---

35. I am obviously trying to appropriate the idiom of T. ʿEduyot 1:1, beginning, and am *not* reproducing what the Tosefta says (q.v.). (See also B. Shabbat 138b and *Diqduqe Soferim* ad loc.) But I do not feel that I'm misrepresenting what was on the mind of the sages, as M. ʿEduyot 1:3–6, in my opinion, almost certainly reflects (as well as 5:6–7, on which see below).

36. T. Shabbat 1:16–17. See especially *Tosefta Ki-Fshuṭah*, Moʿed, 13–16 and S. Lieberman, *Hayerushalmi Kiphshuṭo* (Jerusalem, 1934), 37–39, to which Lieberman himself refers.

said, "Go tell them, Don't worry about your voting! I received [the identical teaching] from Rabban Yoḥanan ben Zakkai who received that *shemuʿah* from his teacher who in turn received it from his teacher, a halakah [transmitted] to Moses from Sinai."[37] No vote outweighs the significance of a received tradition, R. Eliezer says. (Contrast on the other hand R. Meir in M. Kilʾaim 2:11 and Albeck ad loc.) Though Eliezer does not elaborate, have we not the right to ask (in his defense), Does a majority never make a mistake?[38]

It's not as though talmudic tradition is insensitive to this. The halakah, says the Tosefta,[39] is always established in accordance with the majority. Nevertheless (when studying the halakah: Albeck) the minority (literally, the individual's, *yaḥid*) dissension is also recalled. Why? (1) To teach a lesson to be learned from the Fathers of the universe, Shammai and Hillel, who were prepared to adopt views in conflict with theirs, that one should not stubbornly insist on his own view; (2) that if under certain conditions the original minority view comes to be preferred by a later and proper majority, the preserved minority view will be available to serve as support; (3) that if a person protests that his teaching is a received tradition, he can be told: Your *shemuʿah* is only So-and-so's view.

Whatever the historical reality behind this speculative reasoning, it exhibits commitment to the principle of *halakah ki-merubbim*, but simultaneously resolution to remember *dibre ha-yaḥid*. By the time the Mishnah and Tosefta texts are formulated, Shammai and Hillel have become role models, and the way R. Judah expresses himself in the Tosefta—if one were to say, "Such and such a thing is unclean," he is told, "You have received a *shemuʿah* in accordance with R. Eliezer's view"—is reminiscent of the debate of the ʿAknay oven.[40] The halakah follows majority opinion but minority opinion is not to be forgotten; it has its uses! (Note also, by the way, B. Yoma 36b!)

Halakah ki-merubbim may very well have been resorted to occasionally, pragmatically, *faute de mieux*, even before the destruction of the Temple and Jerusalem academic institutions. But it was not till after 66–73 that a concerted effort was made to get this rule adopted in academic debate (as it is in court trials,) for *shemuʿah* by itself could not be depended on; it might not be sufficiently specific. For example, whether a grave area[41] can make (the area

37. M. Yadayim 4:3 and T. Yadayim 2:16, and note the stylization of the links in the chain of transmission in the Tosefta. Is the Tosefta reference to "sitting in the bakery shop" intended to suggest that at that time Eliezer had no scholars as companions? Note above, p. 286, how Aqiba expresses himself.

38. And perhaps it is not unjust to add that the clause from Exod. 23:2 which R. Ḥaninah or R. Jeremiah interprets as "You must follow the majority opinon" (see also Maimonides, *Code*, Sanhedrin 9:3, and note how Midrash ha-Gadol, Exodus, ed. M. Margulies, 532, reads) is not free of syntactical ambiguity; cf. LXX and Rashi and Ibn Ezra on the verse, let alone modern translations. Of course this is not to deny that midrashically clauses from a verse are very often treated as independent units.

39. T. ʿEduyot 1:4 and cf. M. ʿEduyot 1:4–6. Note also Soferim 16, ed. Higger, 287f.

40. Although in that case Eliezer is the one who is *meṭaher*.

41. *Bet ha-peras*. I'm indebted to Danby for this translation. On the halakah being debated,

beyond it) into another grave area is argued by R. Eliezer (yes) and by R. Joshua (sometimes yes and sometimes no). Now in the Sifre Zuta[42] it is reported that R. Simeon, brother of Azariah, broke into the argument with, Why are you arguing? I have a *shemuᶜah* that a grave area does make such another area. To this R. Joshua replies: I can't contradict you but (lit., for) you heard the rule in general terms (*setam*) while I heard it with its proper (specified) interpretation. And he proceeds to spell that out.[43]

In the turbulence of the period, as well as in the increasing sophistication of legalistic instruction, *shemuᶜah* had to be supplemented by practical procedure at what seemed conducive to reliable conclusion. This supplementary academic principle was not greeted by all scholars at once, and collisions occurred particularly since there was constant debate in the academies. Dilemma was inevitable, and it is excellently represented by at least part of the Aqabya ben Mahalalel story, also having to do with *nidduy*, as recorded in the Mishnah: My son, said Aqabya when he was close to death, draw back from the four rulings that I had upheld; whereupon the son said, "What about you, why did you not draw back?"[44] And Aqabya replies,

I received my *shemuᶜah* from *merubbim*, and they [my colleagues] received their *shemuᶜah* from *merubbim*; I stood fast by my *shemuᶜah* and they stood fast by their *shemuᶜah*. But you received your *shemuᶜah* from an individual and from the many. It is best to leave the opinion of the *yaḥid* and to hold onto that of the *merubbim*.[45]

see M. 'Ohalot ('Ahilot) 17:1–2, A. Goldberg in his edition (Jerusalem, 1955), 124. See further the references in the next note.

42. Cf. Lieberman in *Siphre Zutta*, 59f. and Sifre Zuta, ed. Horovitz, p. 313.

43. Cf. B. Sukkah, 28a, top.

44. So Kaufmann Codex at 5:9. For references see next note.

45. M. ᶜEduyot 5:6–7. On 5:6 see also Sifre Num. 7, ed. Horovitz, p. 11 and Horovitz's references to parallel sources. Neither Sifre nor B. Berakot 19a quotes the father and son exchange. Note how A. Saldarini treats the M. ᶜEduyot section in *Journal of Jewish Studies*, 33 (1982), 548f.

It is impossible to say when the Aqabya incident presumably took place, though from the storyteller's language, "and we will make you 'Ab bet din le-Yiśra'el," I infer that the storyteller realizes that the sages could not have said, We will make you *nasi—nasi* is already reserved for the Hillelite dynasty and, besides, appointing a *nasi* is not up to the sages exclusively. Hyperbole or fancy though there may be, if therefore the storyteller speaks of 'Ab bet din as though that's the very high reward, this must be (despite M. Ḥagigah 2:2) a time when the office of 'Ab bet din as secundus is *familiar*. That would be at best late first–early second century. (On improper mourning for an 'Ab bet din who died, cf. B. Sukkah 29a; but the statement is unclear.) The very expression 'Ab bet din le-Yiśra'el is ambiguous, as L. Ginzberg observed long ago. I have tried to discuss this more fully in the supplementary note to my chapter on "The Teachers" (written 1974–75) for the forthcoming *Cambridge History of Judaism*, ed. W. D. Davies and L. Finkelstein.

Two points ought to be added or perspective is lost: (1) That so much and sharp controversy should be reported about issues of cleanliness-uncleanliness (and of course other themes too) reveals how seriously the sages regarded this matter, which would hardly surprise anthropologists. A whole order of the Mishnah, Ṭoharot, is occupied and preoccupied with the subject. Two of the three cases of *nidduy* in the Talmud (Eliezer, Aqabya, Eliezer ben Ḥanoch)

It is difficult to give up *shemuʿah*, but the times call for additional methods, and therefore the principle of *merubbim* must be adopted if there is to be discipline in the academy and its decisions. And R. Aqiba will not hesitate to say as much forthrightly even to the patriarch (Gamaliel!): "You yourself taught us so![46] For controversies flourished in the course of time, and when disciples of Shammai and Hillel did not attend upon their masters sufficiently, controversies increased in Israel and the one Torah became like two Torahs.[47] That controversies multiplied is evident on virtually every page of the Talmud, and the talmudic explanation thereof may have this much to justify it: By *lo shimshu kol ṣorkan* is meant among other things, possibly, that sufficient care was not taken with *shemuʿot* they had received. At all events there is increasing uncertainty with regard to received traditions, and "majority rules" is being encouraged as both a principle and method for the academy—to overcome doubts as well as disagreements.

Let us return to the ʿAknay oven. Why this particular problem should have been the cause for drastic action is not clear, though it is ridiculous to assume that for the sages it was a trivial matter, any more than questions like: In burial how should one orient the corpse eastward, head first or feet first? Should wine for the Mass be white or red? May or may not one stand on a rug in whose design is incorporated (holy) Arabic script? When you're committed to a system, none of its details is likely to be trivial in your sight. And perhaps the more petty the more finicky. That ʿAknay oven is referred to in several contexts,[48] and always with seriousness. Was this suddenly to be a test case? R. Eliezer, we are told by one source, tried "all the arguments in the world" but the scholars remained unmoved. Then came all those astonishing manifest signs, but the scholars refused to be impressed. Even a heavenly *bat qol* proved ineffective—although (according to the *amora* Samuel)[49] after Shammaites and Hillelites had been debating for three years, a *bat qol* exclaimed that the

---

were cleanliness-uncleanliness ones, and that was also part of the Aqabya four teachings. In condemning the behavior of some officiating priests which led to a horrible incident, the Talmud (B. Yoma 23a,b) says that for these priests the purity of vessels was more important than bloodshed! This of course is said of priests and is a furious reprimand with, perhaps, exaggeration too. But the frame of mind, that ritual punctilio is supreme obligation, is not confined to priests, though it may (if sanity survives) escape the extremes of the incident reported by the Talmud. On the Yoma story, cf. Lieberman, *Tosefta Ki-Fshuṭah*, Yoma, 735f.

(2) The idiom of ʿEduyot 5:7 (*'ani shamaʿati, hem shameʿu*) dramatizes for us the delicate task of the sages: The rule will be in accordance with the many but there may well be *shemuʿah* vs. *shemuʿah*, of the *yaḥid* and *merubbim*. Therefore, how act? And the storyteller reports how Aqabya advised his son and thus others too: after all, Aqabya had received his *shemuʿah* also from *merubbim*!

46. B. Berakot 37a, bottom.
47. B. Sanhedrin 88b.
48. In addition to B. Baba Meṣiʿa and P. Moʿed Qaṭan, see M. Kelim 5:10, T. ʿEduyot 2:1, B. Berakot 19a.
49. B. ʿErubin 13b. But also note ibid. 7a (top) that R. Joshua always disregards *bat qol*, and cf. Tosafot in B. Berakot 52a, s.v., *we-rabbi yehoshuaʿ* and in B. Pesaḥim 114a, s.v., *de-'amar*.

views of both were the words of the living God, nevertheless the halakah is as the Hillelites have it. In other words, a *bat qol* in support of the Hillelites is received favorably but snubbed when it tries to support R. Eliezer, in part surely because he favors many Shammaite views.[50] And this, too, may be reflected by the ʿAknay oven storyteller. The storyteller has his reasons for going to extremes, for he wishes to make it unforgettable that woe betide anyone who refuses to accept the new principle, *halakah ki-merubbim*, even if he can summon the supernatural to his aid. And since R. Eliezer did refuse, the scholars imposed *nidduy*. God Himself was all smiles when they did!

So the storyteller or tellers. And it is to him or them that we owe the knowledge that Eliezer was banned. That is most probably not fantasy but fact. For other incidents reported about Eliezer would seem to bear this out. As we have already noted, Eliezer had to ask Yose son of the Damascene what was new in the academy[51] and thus learned that in his absence they had taken a vote about a matter that he had already known by received tradition. In his last illness,[52] when the scholars called on him, they sat before him "at a distance of four ells."

Now, in his note (p. 80, n. 25, ad loc.) S. Schechter reports that the phrase "at a distance of four ells" does not occur in the Abot de-Rabbi Natan manuscripts. Nor does it occur in the version of the story in M. Gaster's *Exempla of the Rabbis*, p. 86. It does not occur in the abbreviated version of P. Shabbat 2:6. But it does occur in B. Sanhedrin 68a, ʿEyn Yaʿaqob, and also in Haggadoth Hatalmud 106d. It is repeated in Midrash ha-Gadol, Deuteronomy (ed. Fisch, 421). Granted, these latter sources reiterate B. Sanhedrin and thus are not independent testimony. But it is significant that their respective compilers felt no need to edit (and see also B. Baba Meṣiʿa 59b when Aqiba informs Eliezer of the ban).

It will not do to say that there has been deliberate doctoring of some sources to create consistency between various details and the principal account, for if doctoring had been decided on (not impossible of course) it is difficult to understand why a story of the banning of a leading *tanna* like R. Eliezer should have been preserved at all. The rabbis are not unskilled in protecting reputations (note R. Judah in M. ʿEduyot 5:6 or in B. Rosh ha-Shanah 22a).

On objective grounds it seems to me impossible to decide which is the correct reading; indeed it may well be that we have here survival of two literary traditions. And that which does not speak of "a distance of four ells" may be due to a desire to spare Eliezer's feelings, as it were, especially at the end of his life. For he had been a very distinguished scholar—according to one

---

50. Cf. Gilat, 309ff. But not always! See Gilat, 227, 295f., 313ff. And see also the citation from the Palestinian Talmud in Gilat, 283, on a *bat qol* interpreted as tribute to Eliezer.

51. For the idiom "what new interpretations in the academy," cf. Abot de-Rabbi Natan, p. 67 (R. Joshua!).

52. ARN, pp. 80–81. For the expression "at a distance of four ells," see also B. Shabbat 127b (R. Joshua).

view,[53] the most distinguished of Yoḥanan ben Zakkai's disciples; a man with a memory that forgot nothing;[54] an expert in *ṭoharot, ṭum'ot* and *miqwa'ot*;[55] from the verse (Exod. 22:17) "Thou shalt not suffer a sorceress to live," he could derive (! but the verb is *shoneh*) three hundred—maybe three thousand—halakot.[56] And after this death reverence for his memory increased, especially on the part of R. Joshua, of all people![57] R. Eliezer remains one of the most frequently cited teachers in the Mishnah. And legend will later say that even God quotes him![58]

Such and several additional statements after his death about his eminence have all the traces of a mixture of fact and eulogy, to the permanent frustration of the historian.[59] And we never escape that. But the conclusion of the story of that last visit, told after Eliezer's death in the language of high praise, as is to be expected, includes a necessary detail. We are told that the scholars put questions to R. Eliezer (on problems of cleanness and uncleanness!) and Eliezer's last reply-and-word was "pure." Forthwith R. Eleazar ben Azariah rent his clothes, and came out weeping to the sages and said to them, "Masters, come behold Rabbi Eliezer, for he is in a state of purity for the world to come, for his soul has gone forth pure."[60] *Ṭahor* is figurative of course and a reference to his last answer, but its meaning here is indubitable. The ban he had been under is now lifted.[61]

---

53. Abot 2:8, ARN, p. 58.

54. Ibid.; cf. Diogenes Laertius, *Lives of Eminent Philosophers*, 7:37. We might say, I suppose, a man with a "photographic" memory; and maybe this accounts for his clinging to *shemu'ah*.

55. ARN, p. 80.

56. ARN, p. 81. Or: all these halakot he had learned (by way of *shemu'ah*).

57. Cf. B. Giṭṭin 83b.

58. Pesiqta R., ed. Friedmann, 64b. See the story (of more or less similar flavor) about R. Aqiba in Menaḥot 29b. There may well have been in antiquity a cycle of Moses stories in encounter on high with leading sages.

On R. Eliezer called "R. Eliezer ha-gadol," cf. ARN, pp. 62, 63. See also *Batei Midrashot* I, ed. Wertheimer (Jerusalem, 1950), 112. (*Gadol=rich?* Cf. Lieberman in E. S. Rosenthal, *Yerushalmi Neziqin* [Jerusalem, 1983], 153, n.1.)

59. For example, Cant. R. 1:3:1 (end), 6c, on R. Joshua kissing the stone which was reserved for R. Eliezer to sit on in his arena-like *bet midrash* (once again R. Joshua!). And yet this may be a subdued midrash on Ps. 118:22, the stone which the *scholars* (see H. Yalon, *Pirqe Lashon* [Jerusalem, 1971], 123ff., *bonim*) rejected! (On amoraic *'eben* [stone, scholar] cf. B. Ta'anit 4a, and Rashi s.v. *barzel*.)

60. ARN, p. 81. "Come" = "approach."

61. In B. Sanhedrin 68a the exclamation is simply "Released is the vow (*neder*), and the exclaimer is R. Joshua. The vow refers to the *nidduy* that he had been put under (cf. Rashi and Haggadoth Hatalmud 106d) and perhaps there is a play on *nidduy-neder*. In Sanhedrin it is not said "in a state of purity *for the world to come*." But this hardly affects the point of the story, that R. Eliezer had been under a ban and was now released from it. (For the idiom "gone forth [=terminate] pure," cf. M. Kelim, end.) The conclusion in both ARN and Sanhedrin may also be an attempt to explain why no stone was laid on Eliezer's coffin (cf. M. 'Eduyot 5:5). Note that we have not been told that in the end he accepted the *'aḥare rabbim* ruling, only that his last word was *ṭahor*. (Is there a muffled echo of the 'Aknay debate?)

I feel no difficulty in *niknesu le-baqer* (a standard expression; see the concordances). The sages could call on him and yet keep the proper distance.

To put it all in a few closing sentences: Because R. Eliezer refused to accept the rule *halakah ki-merubbim* but insisted on the exclusive legitimacy of *shemu'ah* (the past is pattern!)—even though, says the storyteller, he had miraculous support—even so prominent a sage as Eliezer was put under a ban. From now on, as a result of the out-of-joint times, majority opinion determines the rule. The scholars of the academy are to be guided by *shemu'ah*, but governed by *'aḥare rabbim*.[62] But that *'aḥare rabbim* should have had to be defended so vigorously down into amoraic centuries, as reflected by the account of the banning of R. Eliezer in both Talmuds, is itself commentary on the continuing appeal and hold of *shemu'ah* within the rabbinic academy.

62. *Nidduy* is obviously a disciplinary measure to establish obedience and conformity. And apparently the authorities of the *bet ha-midrash* are prepared to resort to it, or contemplate resorting to it, in a number of situations, as the examples drawn up in P. Mo'ed Qatan 3:1 illustrate. It will be invoked therefore against great scholars also. But *nidduy* will be applied or contemplated only against those who still submit to rabbinic authority. There is no *nidduy* pronounced against Elisha ben Abuyah.

Toward a Profile of the Tanna, Aqiba ben Joseph*

[38] Every time a student attempts a study of talmudic sages, he is threatened by pitfalls. For despite the impressive quantities of midrashic and talmudic material, there is not one sage of the approximately 420 Tannaim and 3,400 Amoraim[1] who are quoted or referred to—even the most famous among them, like Hillel or Yohanan ben Zakkai or Eliezer ben Hyrqanos or Joshua ben Hananiah or the Gamaliels and their sons, or Aqiba, or Meir or Judah bar Ilai or Simeon ben Yohai or Judah the Prince and so on and on with (among the Amoraim) Rabbi Yohanan and Resh Laqish or Joshua ben Levi or Abbahu, or (in Babylonia) Rab and Samuel, or Rabbah and Rab Joseph, or Abbaye and Raba—of not one of these 3,820 men is it possible to write a biography in the serious sense of the word. Strictly speaking, little biographical information is furnished. Very often attributions are contradictory and [39] uncertain;[2] very

---

* A brief preliminary summary of the analysis of the Mishnah Gittin was presented at the 19 April 1974 meeting of the American Philosophical Society in Philadelphia.
On background for the present study, see J. Goldin, *The Song at the Sea* (New Haven, 1971), 59, note 1, second paragraph.
My colleague Professor Robert E. A. Palmer calls to my attention that the name Aqiba (Achiba, Aciba, Acibas) is not uncommon and occurs on gravestones and in documents; the name can be found in the index ("except to Vol. VI, Rome") to the volumes of the *Corpus Inscriptionum Latinarum*.

1. For these figures I am indebted to A. Hyman, *Toldoth Tannaim Ve-Amoraim* (London, 1910), III, last page of the biographical entries.
2. Cf. the conclusion of M. Yoma and J. Goldin in *Quest* 2 (London, 1967), 44–48 [above, pp. 141–149.—Ed.]. At present I shall not even contemplate the difficulties that can be created by the errors of scribes and copyists. ". . . Scribes are capable of anything. . . . The result is greatly to complicate the task of the textual critic, making the true restoration of a corrupt passage at once more difficult, . . ." etc. (F. G. Kenyon, *Books and Readers in Ancient Greece and Rome* [Oxford, 1932], 70).

often views or sayings are recorded with no adequate context to speak of, so that even though every single term may be lexically intelligible, the sum total is not.[3] Again, stories about the lives, or incidents in the lives, of sages are not primarily told as reports per se but as exempla of some ideal, as an exhibition of a virtue in action. Where is the boundary between the fact and the idealization?[4] Not biography is the aim of the storyteller, but hagiographa; and sometimes not even that, but simply partial commentary by illustration. And although there is a good deal that may be learned from such narratives,[5] legend and presumable actuality interpenetrate one another so thoroughly, there is no escaping the feeling of uncertainty that remains even after every caution has been taken in the course of study; for even if it may sometimes turn out that the literal may be detected behind what at first appeared as utterly fanciful and homiletical,[6] it still remains true that in the majority of cases our sources let us down in one respect: they present the teachings and opinions of the talmudic teachers without any signals of earlier and later, in other words, they deprive us of any clues of *development*, just what the historian must know if his account is to have some correspondence with recognizable reality.[7]

None of these difficulties, of course, is the stumbling block laid in the way of the student of midrashic-talmudic literature only. Every student of ancient literature, every classicist and medievalist (and modernist too) is familiar with the pervasiveness of the problematic. I have taken the liberty, however, of referring to the difficulties briefly because that most conveniently will explain why at best I want to attempt no more than a profile, rather than a rounded portrait, of Aqiba. In fact, it is with one fundamental view of his that I want to

---

3. Cf. *PA* 1:11.

4. Note the stories about Rabbi Aqiba and Rabbi Eliezer ben Hyrqanos in *ARNA* and *ARNB*, pp. 28–33, which are intended to illustrate that either poor or rich to begin with, if one is determined he can become a master of the Torah, even though at first he was an illiterate well on in years.

5. For example, that certain rhetorical forms are commonplace. It would take me too far afield at present to discuss properly various problems in methodology, which is unquestionably very important. For the time being I would like to say only that the recognition of a Greco-Roman rhetorical topos or literary stereotype in a midrashic-talmudic source is certainly significant but of itself no proof that we are dealing with non-history. By itself all that presence demonstrates is that there are current convenient and attractive manners of speaking to which everyone helps himself. (Such borrowings may actually be the tribute one culture pays to another: as if to say, "*That's* the best way to put it.") All stories are always told in the manner of storytelling of the storyteller's age, from the author(s) of Gilgamesh down to the latest imitators of Kafka; and the same is true of biographers. Loan forms and loan expressions—not to speak of loan words—tend to appear when a minority is surrounded by and is in the sphere of influence of a strong majority. (Sometimes, apparently, you can't even be sure, despite striking congruence; see the remark in *TK* ad *T. Berakot*, 120, last paragraph.) And while the Jews of first- and early-second-century Judea were not surrounded by a single, unified majority, in one respect the dominant surrounding cultures did represent a concerted challenge, in that they were a conjunction of varieties of paganism in all its power and riches and temptation.

6. Cf., for example, S. Lieberman on the torments of Hell in the *Louis Ginzberg Jubilee Volume* (New York, 1946; Hebrew volume), 249ff.

7. Cf. C. J. Adams (ed.), *A Reader's Guide to the Great Religions* (New York and London, 1965), 223.

deal. The discussion may in the end enable us to appreciate why it is fundamental.

We read in the *Mekilta de-Rabbi Ishmael*, among the comments on the word *w' nwhw* (Exod. 15:2):[8]

> Rabbi Aqiba says: Before all the Nations of the World I shall hold forth on the beauties and splendors of Him Who Spake and the World Came to Be! For, lo, the Nations of the World keep asking Israel, "How is your Beloved better than another, that you adjure us so" (Cant. 5:9),[9] that for His sake you die, for His [40] sake you let yourselves be slain . . . ?[10] Look you! You're attractive, look you! you're brave. Come, merge with us!
>
> But Israel reply to the Nations of the World: Have you any notion of Him? Let us tell you a little bit about His Glory: "My beloved is clear-skinned and ruddy" etc. (Cant. 5:10ff.).[11]
>
> And when the Nations of the World hear but a little bit of the Glory of Him Who Spake and the World Came to Be, they say to Israel, Let us go along with you, as it is said, "Whither is thy Beloved gone, O thou fairest among women? Whither hath thy Beloved turned Him, that we may seek Him with thee" (Cant. 6:1)?
>
> But Israel reply to the Nations of the World: You have no part of Him; on the contrary, "My Beloved is mine, and I am His" (Cant. 2:16), "I am my Beloved's and my Beloved is mine" etc. (Cant. 6:3).[12]

This passage is not without several serious difficulties, which we shall note shortly. First, however, a methodological bias, to wit, that what a text says is to be taken seriously, unless not to be taken so makes better sense. As Harry A. Wolfson apparently used to teach, "There is no reason for rejecting a statement which is not inherently impossible nor contradicted by a more reliable source."[13]

If our Midrash, then, reports in the name of Aqiba that Gentiles are baffled by Israel's stubborn clinging to their faith,[14] that Gentiles try to win over Jews to the Gentile way of life; if in the dialogue or exchange between Israel and the Nations we are informed that the Jews so describe their God as to make the Gentiles eager to adopt His worship but the Jews now say, nothing doing, only *I am His and He is mine alone*—if this is what the Midrash reports, then it is best

---

8. Three words in the Greek, *kai doxaso auton*, and I shall glorify him. Cf. *Mekilta, Shirta* 3 (II, 26f.); *MRS*, p. 79; *The Song at the Sea* 115–17.

9. Translation of the verses based on *The Five Megilloth and Jonah*, introductions by H. L. Ginsberg (Philadelphia, 1969).

10. Cf. Romans 8:35–39. And see below, p. 55 and note 37.

11. Cf. also E. Z. Melamed in *Tarbiz* 40 (1970–71), 213–215. On Cant. 5:10, see now M. H. Pope and J. H. Tigay, "A Description of Baal," in *Ugarit-Forschungen* 3 (Neukirchen-Vluyn, 1971), 127.

12. Cf. *Sifre Deut.* 343, p. 399, and L. Finkelstein's note for parallel passages. Now see also *MhG, Deut.* ed. S. Fisch (Jerusalem, 1972), 753.

13. See H. Mantel, *Studies in the History of the Sanhedrin* (Cambridge, Mass., 1965), 19, note 12.

14. Cf. I. H. Weiss, *Dor Dor we-Dorshaw* (Wilna, 1895), II, 119.

to assume that something like this encounter and dialogue must have occurred at least occasionally. Otherwise, Aqiba's interpretation of the verse and his homily would be completely incomprehensible to his audience, who would certainly retort, "When did the Gentiles ever say to us, *hry ʾtm gbwrym, hry ʾtm nʾym*, Look you! You're attractive, look you! you're brave, why for His sake do you let yourselves be slain?" Come now, join our country clubs! Or, when did the Gentiles ever offer to join us?

Of Gentiles being attracted by Judaism we know,[15] just as we know of Jews attracted by the non-Jewish world. Thus far, therefore, the Midrash is plausible. But when we get down to particulars credibility falters.

To begin with the give-and-take: It is transparently stylized. The Nations start out with a quotation of verse 9 from the fifth chapter of Song of Songs, and Israel replies with the immediately following verses. To which in turn the Nations respond with the words of the very verse (6:1) which comes after Israel's response. And Israel's last word on the subject is again made up of Song of Songs verses (2:16[16] and 6:3).

[41] We have been given, then, not a transcript of what Jews and Gentiles are saying to each other in natural speech, but a Midrash, that is, the substance of the dialogue has been transposed into biblical verses understood in a particular light. Even when they are not quoting the Bible verbatim, the Nations are made to appropriate biblical expressions like "merge with us," which is an adaptation of Psalm 106:35, *wytʿrbw bgwym*, or, "Let us go along with you," which echoes Zechariah 8:23, *nlkh ʿmkm*.

The initial response of Israel to the invitation of the Nations to merge with them is unfortunately obscure. The verses beginning with "My Beloved is clear-skinned and ruddy," etc., manifestly were explained in some mystic or perhaps even secret, gnostic manner as a glorious but bold description of the person of God. These verses served indeed as an account of "a little bit about His Glory." And from the way the dialogue between Israel and the Nations continues, we are justified in assuming that at least the Jews assumed that the

---

15. ". . . [T]he writings of Moses have moved many even of those alien to Jewish culture to believe, as the writings claim, that the God who first made these laws and gave them to Moses was the Creator of the world. For it was fitting that the Creator of the whole world should have appointed laws for the whole world and given a power to the words that was able to overcome men everywhere." (Origen, *Contra Celsum* I, 18, ed. Chadwick, 19f.) See also Augustine, *City of God* VI:11, quoting Seneca.

See further: E. Schürer, *Geschichte des jüdischen Volkes*[4] (Leipzig, 1909), III, 150ff.; J. Juster, *Les Juifs dans lʾ Empire romain* (Paris, 1914), I, 253–337; B. J. Bamberger, *Proselytism in the Talmudic Period* (Cincinnati, 1939), 13ff., 214ff.

On Jews attracted by the non-Jewish world there is ample evidence from before Maccabean times on. It will be enough for our purposes to refer to the later views of R. Yudan and R. Hunya in *Gen. R.* 80:11, p. 966 (depite R. Huna ad loc.!): for social commentary, one hardly needs more. Or for an early record, cf. I Mac. 1:12ff. And see *Sifre Deut.* 87, p. 152 (Yose the Galilean), and Jer. 2:11 (already noted by the Neṣib).

16. Note that this verse is wanting in *MRS*, and that reading may indeed be the original one. Cant. 2:16 may have been *added* by association. Note that Luther translates both verses the same way: "Mein Freund ist mein, und ich bin sein."

Nations found that description irresistible: "And when the Nations . . . hear but a little bit about the Glory of [God] . . . , they say to Israel, let us go along with you . . . ." But specifically what was so extraordinary about the description is nowhere preserved. Perhaps the interpretation of those Song of Songs verses bordered on the esoteric, which should not be allowed to become public knowledge, though oddly enough it was not improper to communicate to the Nations![17]

Even more astonishing is Israel's rebuff of the Nations after the latter have entreated, "Let us go along with you." Surely this echo of Zechariah 8:23 deserved a favorable response if the biblical verse itself is to be taken at face value. In the original context the words *nlkh 'mkm* are part of a promise to look forward to!

> Thus says the Lord of Hosts: In those days ten men from the nations of every tongue shall take hold of the robe of a Jew, saying, *nlkh 'mkm*, Let us go with you: for we have heard that God is with you.

There is not even an intonation of rejection in the prophet's words. Yet in the Aqiba Midrash the verse has been turned upside down; those who say, Let us go with you, are rejected, as though their request was impertinent.[18]

Above all, however, not only in its details, but taken as a whole, the Midrash is bewildering. "Before all the Nations of the World," Israel declares according to Rabbi Aqiba, "I shall hold forth on the beauties and splendors of Him Who Spake and the World Came to Be." The majority (if not all) of the manuscripts definitely give this reading: "before all the Nations of the World."[19] In other words, Israel proclaims to the world the special splendor of her God. That itself would suggest that Israel is engaged in propagandizing, in winning over adherents to her God. At first the Nations are perplexed: Why such uncompromising, persisting loyalty to this God? There are plenty of gods and splendid ones at that.[20] But Israel says, Let me tell you a little bit about this God of

17. Was the description of the "physical" parts intended also to say, He is more splendid than your most splendid, lifeless, idolatrous images?

18. Tg Jonathan still takes the verse at face value. Of course this is not to imply that otherwise the Midrash never upsets the biblical syntax. Cf., for example, R. Levi in *Gen. R.* 49:9, p. 511, or the comments on "as a widow" (Lam. 1:1) in *Lam. R.* 1:3, 10d.

19. This is to be seen in the critical apparatus of both the Horovitz-Rabin and Lauterbach editions. I have personally confirmed this as regards the Munich MS. The same reading occurs in Vatican Heb. MS 299 (A microfilm of which was made available to me by Professor M. Schmelzer, the Librarian of the Jewish Theological Seminary of America). The phrase does not appear here either in the Constantinople (1515) or Venice (1545) edition; but as the passage continues, *šhry 'mwt h'wlm* etc., it is plain that even in the printed editions an exchange between Gentiles and Jews is being presented, MS Casanata 2736 (referred to by L. Finkelstein in *PAAJR* 5 [1934], 6, note 4) I have been unable to locate.

The phrase "before all the Nations of the World" in Rabbi Yose's statement before Aqiba's, appears in the MSS and the printed editions. On the statements by Yose and Aqiba, cf. below, note 129.

20. Cf. Origen, *Contra Celsum* IV, 48 (ed. Chadwick, p. 223) and V, 57 (p. 308). See also III, 36 (p. 152, and note 1 ad loc.).

304 : *Thematic Studies*

mine; then you'll appreciate why I cling to Him only. Apparently the description is effective, for after it is supplied the Nations ask to come along—and just at this point Israel rejects them?! Then why all the fuss about proclaiming and describing this God to the Nations? Naturally, one might say that Aqiba is enjoying leading on the enemy only to mock him in the end. But nothing in the text suggests mockery; that could hardly lead to '*nwhw*, the glorification of God before the Nations of the World. What is more, nothing in Aqiba's views otherwise known would [42] lead one to expect so cynical an attitude. How precious is *man*, for he was created in accordance with the image; and all the more precious is he in that it was made known to him that he was created in the image.[21] There are, it is true, differences of opinion among the commentators regarding the exact meaning of *bṣlm*, "in the image," in this saying,[22] but not one controverts the value judgment *ḥbyb 'dm*, precious is man. Israel in Aqiba's view is especially precious (as that Mishnah further records) because to her was given the Torah by means of which the world was created. But under no circumstance is man, man as such, scorned or disdained.

And even more forcefully is this brought out in the following:[23] "Rabbi Aqiba says: He who sheds innocent blood destroys the *dmwt*, the likeness of God, as it is said (Gen. 9:6), 'Whoso sheddeth man's blood, by man shall his blood be shed,'" and as the verse goes on, "'for in the image of God made He man.'" Here almost definitely the image must be the image of God,[24] as the parable in the Mekilta[25] illustrates:

> This is to be compared to a king of flesh and blood who came to a province. Icons were set up in his honor, images were made in his honor, coins were minted in his honor. After a time they upset the icons and smashed the images and discredited the coins, and thus diminished [the number of copies] of the *dmwt* of the king.[26]

As the Mishnah manuscripts record anonymously and correctly and in another connection,[27] Whoever destroys one human soul is accounted by Scripture as

21. I'm quoting the text according to Codex Kaufmann, *PA* 3:14. See also *ARNA*, p. 118, in the name of R. Meir.

22. Cf. *Machsor Vitry*, ed. S. Hurwitz (Nuremberg, 1923), 514. See also H. A. Wolfson, *Philo* (Cambridge, Mass., 1947), I, 238–39.

23. *T. Yebamot* 8:7; cf. *Gen. R.* 34:14, p. 326; *Mekilta, Yitro* 8 (II, 262); *B. Yebamot* 63b.

24. *T. Yebamot* 8:7, and see *TK* ad loc., p. 74. There is no need to refer to Aqiba's favorable views of the Medes (*B. Berakot* 8b). That is mere politesse.

25. II, 262.

26. Note also what is attributed to Aqiba, *B. Yebamot* 63b (observe marginal reading of the name). Cf. I. Ziegler, *Die Königsgleichnisse des Midrasch* (Breslau, 1903) 23–27, and L. Friedländer, *Roman Life and Manners Under the Early Empire* (London, 1965), II, 278–80. On image and likeness see also Origen, *Contra Celsum* IV, 30 (p. 205).

27. *M. Sanhedrin* 4:5 in Codex Kaufmann; so, too, MS Parma, ed. Naples, ed. Lowe, Seder Eliyahu R., ed. Friedmann, p. 53 (and see Friedmann's note ad loc.), Albeck in his edition of the Mishnah, p. 445 (but he strikes me as wavering [I see now, however, that in his second edition, 1953, p. 511, he adopts the reading definitely]), and cf. *Legends* V, 67. Accordingly,

though he had destroyed a whole world; but whoever saves one human soul is accounted by Scripture as though he had saved a whole world. This may be exhortation, but if it were no more than that, it could hardly put fear into the hearts of witnesses at a capital trial. To be sure, questions of homicide are everywhere regarded with extraordinary gravity even if there are antagonisms within a society. But at least these latter statements about human life demonstrate that the dialogue presented by Aqiba is far from being self-evidently hostile toward human beings because they don't happen to be Israel: you can't start out by broadcasting your God's excellences, and then when your audience is persuaded and wishes to join you, say churlishly, We'll have nothing of you.

There have been discussions of our text by modern scholars, but it is puzzling that almost none have cared to stress the audible dissonance between the beginning and the end of Aqiba's Midrash.

Gedaliahu Allon[28] rightly observes that the passage reflects the deep love Aqiba always expressed for Israel. He points out that it makes no sense to date the passage in the period after the Bar Kokba war (132–135), and says that it should be assigned to the period which the Mishnah calls the war (*polemos*) of Quietus.[29] But about our problem, not a word.

Yitzhaq Fritz Baer[30] is convinced that what is reflected by the Aqiba Midrash is "the ecstatic visions experienced by the Jewish martyrs as they were being tortured and martyred." For [43] him this is further proof that the talmudic sages were mystics.[31] As for the beginning and end of Aqiba's Midrash, he says nothing about them.

The ambiguity of our passage did not escape Louis Finkelstein (the only one who faces up to it), but if I'm not misunderstanding him, he says that Rabbi Aqiba is here teaching the following:[32]

> In what sense . . . could God be described as being in a singularly intimate relation with Israel? . . . Israel must expect neither power, nor riches, nor prestige, as the select of God; it has been given nothing but the opportunity to serve Him. It is Israel's mission to glorify Him before the Nations, but even in the end when all will accept God, Israel will continue to understand Him more completely than the others.

therefore, correct the reading in *Exod. R.* 30:16 (for additional references, R. David Luria, ibid.). (However, even if we should say that the *Exod. R.* reading should not be emended, we would be compelled to maintain that that source probably no longer understood the force of the original statement. I regret that I do not have available any *Exod. R.* MSS or early editions.)

28. *History of the Jews in the Land of Israel in the Period of the Mishnah and Talmud* (Heb., Tel Aviv, 1952), I, 327.

29. *M. Sotah* 9:14 in the reading of Codex Kaufmann. Quietus was governor of Judea in 117 c.e.. See recently M. Avi-Yonah in *IEJ* 23 (1973), 209–13.

30. In *Zion* 21 (1956), 3.

31. Cf. note 7, ibid. On Aqiba as mystic cf. *T. Hagigah* 2:4 and *TK* ad loc., 1290.

32. *Akiba* (New York, 1936), 212f.

That Aqiba believed Israel is to glorify God before the Nations is explicitly stated (and that in the end he personally bore witness to this is also a matter of record); but there is not one word in our passage about the end, the *eschaton*. Indeed, the dialogue has vitality and relevance only if we recognize it as a give-and-take between Jews and Gentiles referring to what is right here on earth in this age and not a trans-historical epoch or setting: note, in fact, the categorical dismissal, "You have no part of Him!"

Although Abraham Heschel does not discuss the contradiction, or at least tension, between the beginning and end of the Midrash, he also could not help noticing the blunt rejoinder at its end; he is offended by it; he offered, there-fore, still another interpretation.[33] This is not Rabbi Aqiba at his best, he tells us, this Midrash of his was uttered only by an Aqiba whose spirits had finally been crushed and who was embittered by and disillusioned with the Gentiles. You can't hold a man responsible for what he says in his grief, Heschel says. Needless to say, this interpretation is *possible*. But there is not the slightest indication in our text or in the parallel references that this Midrash was taught by Aqiba either in old age or young, ecstatic or depressed. (Heschel seems to imply that Aqiba authored this Midrash in the course of or after [?] the Bar Kokba war.) There is absolutely no reference to time or mood. And the implication of Heschel's interpretation—that Rabbi Aqiba spoke in this fashion when he was out of character—is untrue.[34] Our Midrash here, as I hope to show, is in keeping with other statements and teachings of Aqiba.[35]

Let us recall what Aqiba is doing. In order to explain the verb and its object-suffix, *w' nwhw*, he draws upon an exchange between the Gentiles and Jews of his time, not verbatim, as we have already observed, but in a stylized fashion, by representing the interlocutors directing at each other verses from the Song of Songs in a sequential order, from Canticles 5:9 through 6:3.[36] The Gentiles begin with one verse, Israel responds with several that follow, to which the Gentiles reply with a verse, and Israel rebuffs them with "I belong to my Beloved and my Beloved belongs to *me*." The dialogue, then, is composed principally of Song of Songs verses,[37] presented as a unit. Now this cannot be without significance. For, as we all know, it was Aqiba who insisted on the

---

33. *Torah min ha-Shamayim* (London and New York, 5722), I, 162.

34. Moreover, Heschel's adding here the view of Aqiba on the Generation of the Wilderness and on the Ten Tribes is of no help except homiletically.

35. In G. F. Moore, *Judaism* (Cambridge, Mass., 1927–40), our Midrash is not discussed at all. J. Bonsirven, *Le Judaïsme palestinien* (Paris, 1934), I, 100, merely "quotes": "Je suis le Dieu de tous ceux qui viennent au monde, mais à vous seuls j'ai uni mon nom; je ne suis pas appelé le Dieu des idolâtres, mais le Dieu d'Israël." "Il aime Israël à l'exclusion des autres peuples; les israélites le disent 'leur bien-aimé', aux autres ils refusent toute part avec lui." Cf. also II, 42 and 47. In his *Ḥazal* (Jerusalem, 1969), E. E. Urbach of course discusses teachings of Aqiba, but he does not take up the problem of our Midrash; he refers to the passage on 34, note 20, also on p. 131.

36. Note the reading in the *Mekilta*.

37. Note too the interpolation, *'l kn 'lmwt 'hbwk*. Cf. below, note 55, and above, note 10.

preeminent sanctity of the Song of Songs:[38] If the [44] other books of Scripture are holy, then the Song of Songs is sanctum sanctorum, the holiest of the holy. There isn't an age[39] as worthy as the one in which the Song of Songs was given to Israel. For Aqiba, verses of the Song of Songs refer to the occasion of the Revelation at Sinai. And Aqiba declares that whoever treats the Song of Songs as though it were a song for a cocktail lounge, has no share in the world to come.[40] Marvin Pope has even suggested (orally) that there may here be a reference to orgies. He may have something there, though I have not yet been persuaded: for any verses from any biblical book sung inappropriately would be the ruin of the world,[41] not just Song of Songs. At all events, the superlative sanctity and significance of the Song of Songs are an Aqiba fixation. And if he adopts Song of Songs verses to represent the dialogue between the Nations and Israel, he is not only taking the dialogue seriously, but communicating something special.

For the Song of Songs is the allegory of the love affair between God and Israel[42] (and later the Church Fathers will adopt this view, except that for them the allegory represents the love between the Christ and the Church[43]). It is love

38. *M. Yadayim* 3:5. For an eloquent defense of Aqiba's point of view of the Song of Songs, see G. D. Cohen, "The Song of Songs and the Jewish Religious Mentality," in *The Samuel Friedland Lectures* (New York, 1966), 1–21. Note especially his point, p. 6: "The very same commandment that forbids the worship of other gods or the making of graven images concludes with a thundering warning: 'For I the Lord, your God, am an impassioned God.' The idential root *qana*, impassioned or jealous, is used elsewhere in the Pentateuch, Num. 15:14, in the technical sense of a husband who is jealous of his wife. In other words, the earliest documents of Israelite religion had already expressed the requirement of religious fidelity in the terms employed for the demands of marital fidelity."

For the suggestion of a sacred origin of Song of Songs, see S. N. Kramer, *The Sacred Marriage Rite* (Bloomington, 1969), 85ff. and notes ad loc. (but note, too, 99).

Our concern here is not with the original or imposed-upon meaning of the Song of Songs; our task is to get *Aqiba* in focus. See further below, note 45.

39. Cf. A. S. Halkin in *Alexander Marx Jubilee Volume* (New York, 1950), 393, note 21, and S. Lieberman apud G. Scholem, *Jewish Gnosticism, Merkabah Mysticism, and Talmudic Tradition* (New York, 1960), 118, note 3a. Cf. also Urbach, op. cit., on Revelation and Canticles verses.

40. *T. Sanhedrin* 12:10, but there is no mention of "drinking house" in *ARN*, 108ff. or in *Kallah* (ed. Higger), 127 (but cf. critical apparatus), 177. In (a *baraita, tnw rbnn*) *B. Sanhedrin* 101a, "He who recites a verse from the Song of Songs treating it like an ordinary song, and he who recites [any] verse in a feasting (=drinking) place out of season, brings disaster into the world." Cf. *Zohar* II, 144a.

41. *B. Sanhedrin* 101a; *Kallah* 4, ed. Higger, p. 127; *Kallah R.* 6, p. 177.

42. This is not Aqiba's invention. Note Yohanan ben Zakkai in *ARNA*, chap. 17, p. 65 (and Schechter ad loc. for additional references). While from the reading of *ARNA*, p. 72, top line, one might at first get the impression (cf. E. E. Urbach in *Tarbiz* 30 [1961], 1f. and again in *Scripta Hierosolymitana* 22 [1971], 248) that R. Hananiah, prefect of the priests, is the author of the comment on Song of Songs 1:6, note Schechter's correction on p. 145; indeed, note his note 8 on p. 72. In *Seder Eliyahu R.*, ed. Friedmann, p. 143, there is no mention of Hananiah.

43. Something once struck me while reading the *Life of St. Teresa*. In it, I believe, she never quotes the Song of Songs (if she does it is extremely rare; imagery and idiom, however, may well be present); yet at one point (chap. 27) she writes: "If two people, in this life, love one another and are of good intelligence, they seem to understand one another without signs,

the Song [45] of Songs celebrates, holy allegory if you wish, or if not allegory, then literally love poems;[44] either way, however, the theme is love. Love is the subject of those poetic lines from "Let him kiss me with the kisses of his mouth" to "the mountains of spices."[45]

A brief general comment at this point may prove useful, for it will make a number of texts which follow comprehensible without undue explanation or digressions.

All the categories that we humans employ must inevitably rise out of human experience. (I do not know if this is true in mathematics.) This does not mean that therefore all our categories must remain confined to their human base. The reverse is true: Very many categories, though they originate in human experience, gradually transcend that experience, get transfigured—I have no objection to saying even get purified and spiritualized. But their debut is grounded in the human. In this sense I would say anthropology precedes theology.

Second, love never was nor is restricted to sexual activity exclusively. Yet an element of sexual responsiveness seems to be present, though sublimated, in varieties of socially ratified loving relationships.[46] It would be outrageous to

merely by the exchange of a glance; and this must be the case too in the experience I have been speaking of. For without seeing one another, we look on one another face to face, as two lovers do. It is as the Bridegroom says to the Bride in the Song of Songs, I believe; at least I have been told that it is said there" (trans. J. M. Cohen, Penguin Classics, 1958, p. 191). Does this mean that Teresa was forbidden to read the Song of Songs? Yet she apparently wrote on the book; cf. P. P. Parente, "The Canticle of Canticles," in *CBQ* 6 (1944), 150–52. (I am indebted to Professor Marvin Pope for the Parente reference.)

On forbidden reading of the Song of Songs, cf. Origen, *The Song of Songs Commentary and Homilies*, trans. by R. P. Lawson (London, 1957), Prologue to commentary, p. 23: ". . . I advise and counsel everyone who is not yet rid of the vexations of flesh and blood and has not ceased to feel the passion of his bodily nature, to refrain completely from reading this little book *and the things that will be said about it*" (my italics). "For they say that with the Hebrews also care is taken to allow no one even to hold this book in his hands, who has not reached a full and ripe age. And there is another practice too that we have received from them—namely, that all the Scriptures should be delivered to boys by teachers and wise men, while at the same time the four that they call *deuteroseis*—that is to say, the beginning of Genesis, in which the creation of the world is described; the first chapters of Ezekiel, which tell about the cherubim; the end of that same, which contains the building of the Temple; and this book of the Song of Songs—should be reserved for study till the last." Note Parente himself, "A carnal man should not read this book" (p. 150).

See further S. Lieberman, *Yemenite Midrashim* (Heb., Jerusalem, 1940), 16f. and the reference ibid. to A. Marmorstein in *REJ* 71 (1920), 195ff. But cf. especially G. G. Scholem, *Jewish Gnosticism, Merkabah Mysticism, and Talmudic Tradition*, 36–42.

44. For there were those who at one time did not regard Song of Songs as sacred, as can be seen in *ARNA*, p. 2.

45. It is a nice observation of Urbach's in his *Ḥazal*, p. 367, that the concept of love begins to take on an added intensity with the teaching of Rabbi Aqiba; that intensity, however, Urbach immediately associates with martyrological and mystical features. See also the essay referred to above, note 38. That martyrdom and mystical speculation are very much part, and prominent part, of the Aqiba story, is in no way to be minimized. But my point is that Aqiba's preoccupation with "love" is not confined to martyrological and mystical contexts, as the various texts analyzed and cited in this study amply demonstrate.

46. The theme of pastoral love is irrelevant here. Cf. below, note 89.

suggest that loving God includes what is carnal, and of course I shall not say anything of the sort.[47] But what I do say is that the notion of loving God could not have arisen if there had not been an experience of human love, and the experience of human love (in other words, a very strong emotional force) can point the way to an understanding of a preoccupation with a love which no longer has in mind what we call sexual love: and it is still love!

Finally, everywhere in antiquity the purpose of marriage was the begetting of children,[48] and that marriage had to do with love was not necessarily recognized or acknowledged, though Isaac loved Rebecca and Jacob loved Rachel and Elkanah loved Hannah. But that marriage had to do with sex was clear, and that sex and love were in many ways inseparable did not go unnoticed.[49]

Enough of generalizations and back to Aqiba. It is no accident that this man saw a dialogue of love in the Song of Songs, for the truth is, the vocabulary of the book is full of it; this is its content and its atmosphere, and the theme seems to have been uppermost in his mind—and I am thinking of much, much more than the romantic legend about him and his wife,[50] though it is interesting indeed that he should be the only sage about whom such a story[51] should have grown up. Let us examine some texts.[52]

> Rabbi Aqiba says: If one weds a woman that is unfit for him, he transgresses five negative commandments: "Thou shalt not take vengeance" (Lev. 19:19), "Nor bear any grudge" (ibid.), "Thou shalt not hate thy brother in thy heart" (Lev. 19:17), "But thou shalt love thy neighbor as thyself" (Lev. 19:18), "That [46] thy brother may live with thee" (Lev. 25:36). [Moreover] since he hates her, he desires her death and thus neglects the commandment to be fruitful and to multiply in the world.

The wife you cannot love and should not marry[53]—for this is what '*ynh*

47. We are not discussing fertility cults or anything like a *hieros gamos*; they are irrelevant here, as are varieties of Carpocratianism.

48. Cf. B. Cohen, *Jewish and Roman Law* (New York, 1966), I, 389ff. and the rich references ad loc.; II, 782.

49. Cf. Plato, *Symposium* 206c–207b. For classical times, see the study, "Classical Greek Attitudes to Sexual Behaviour," by K. J. Dover, in *Arethusa* 6 (Spring, 1973), 59–73.

50. Cf. *ARNA* and *ARNB*, pp. 29–30, and the references to parallels ad loc.

51. Note the embarrassment of the students: ordinarily, people do not act that way! *ARNA* and *ARNB* (in the latter, "his sons"!), p. 30. Possibly one might also note what is said of Ben Azzai in *B. Ketubot* 63a (cf., however, *Tosafot*, ibid., s.v., *brtyh dr' 'qyb'* and see *TK*, Hagigah, 1290).

52. *ARNA*, p. 83, and cf. *T. Sotah* 5:11 (ed. Zuckermandel, p. 302) in name of R. Meir (Aqiba's disciple); and on the use of these verses, cf. L. Finkelstein's note in *Sifre Deut.* 186–187, p. 226. On "negative commandments," cf. J. Goldin, *The Fathers According to Rabbi Nathan* (New Haven, 1955), 200, notes 19–20, and *Mid. Tan.*, p. 158, lines 4–3 from bottom.

53. Aqiba does not entertain naively romantic or sentimental notions about women; see, e.g., *M. Ketubot* 9:2; *M. Toharot* 7:9 and cf. Albeck, ad loc., s.v., *wky mpny*, and additional note, p. 573.

In *T. Terumot*, end (and cf. *TK*, ad loc., p. 480) the expression "a woman who is not *hwgnt lw*," appears to mean simply, a woman whom he (the priest) is forbidden to marry by

mhwgnt lw (or, *'ynh hwgnt lw*) has to include if those Leviticus verses are to make sense—a wife you cannot love is the ruin of a marriage, the cause of serious moral transgressions, and the negation of the very purpose for which marriage was instituted.

We are now in a position to understand a controversy in the Mishnah which has been commented on by others as well, but perhaps deserves another look. What are reasonable grounds for divorce? The last Mishnah of the treatise Gittin[54] reads as follows:

> The School of Shammai says: A man may divorce his wife only if he has found her guilty of unchaste conduct, as it is said (Deut. 24:1), "because he hath found some *unseemly* (*'rwt, 'rwh*) thing in her." But the School of Hillel says: [Not only for that, but] even if she ruined his supper, as it is said, "because he hath found *anything (dbr)*[55] unseemly in her." Rabbi Aqiba says: [He may divorce her] even if it's only that he found another woman more attractive than she, as it is said (ibid.), "and if it cometh to pass that she found no favor in his eyes."[56]

It has been suggested[57] that the Mishnah ascribes to the school of Hillel a "happy-go-lucky" outlook toward divorce and "even more cynicism" to Aqiba.[58]

Regardless of how one wishes to interpret this legal controversy,[59] there is, as far as I can see, not the slightest trace of happy-go-luckiness or cynicism about it. The late Louis Ginzberg—in a study[60] that had a profound influence on students of Pharisaism and Rabbinism for more than three decades—once

law (Lev. 21:7). But perhaps a psychological hortatory note is part of an undertone here too, that he will eventually cease to love her.

54. Mishnah Codex Kaufmann; *Sifre Deut.* 269, p. 288; *Mid. Tan.*, p. 154; *MhG. Deut.* 24:1, p. 537.

55. On *'rwt dbr* see M. Weinfeld, *Deuternomy and the Deuternomic School* (Oxford, 1972), 269, note 4. Cf. LXX on Deut. 24:1 (3). See also Tg Onqelos and Tg Jonathan; cf. M. A. Friedman in *PAAJR* 27 (1969), 51, and note 94 ibid. On the other hand, cf. Neofiti and Peshitta. Cf. Albeck's comment on the Mishnah. On the basis of the reading of the Palestinian Talmud, David Weiss ha-Livni (*Sources and Traditions* [Heb., Tel Aviv, 1968], 612) makes the astute suggestion that the Mishnah text of the Palestinian Talmud did not include the Aqiba statement (the fact that the Mishnah ed. Lowe does contain that statement or that the Leiden MS of the Palestinian Talmud also has it; or that M. Schachter, *The Babylonian and Jerusalem Mishnah* [Jerusalem, 1959], registers no difference between the Babylonian and Palestinian Mishnah texts here—of course, does not disprove Weiss' contention). This however does not establish that Aqiba did not actually say what the Babylonian Mishnah and Talmud (cf. also *Sifre Deut.* 269, p. 288) attribute to him. The view and the statement are authentic Aqiba.

56. For another possible reason for divorce, cf. S. Lieberman in *TK* ad *T. Demai* 3, p. 226, line 32. On the Shammaite view and the Karaites, idem, *Shkiin* (Jerusalem, 1970), 21f.

57. By G. Vermes in the *Cambridge History of the Bible* (1970), 206f. Cf. the review of this volume by M. Smith in *The American Historical Review* 77 (Feb. 1972), 94–100.

58. In actuality this is along the lines of Schürer, op. cit., II, 576f. (and others too).

59. Heschel (op. cit., I, 34f.) only adds to the confusion.

60. *Meqomah shel ha-Halakah* (Jerusalem, 5691), 41f. (note 24). I do not find this discussion in the English version (prepared by A. Hertzberg) in *On Jewish Law and Lore* (Phila., 1955). Did Professor Ginzberg himself change his mind about the validity of this explanation?

suggested that views recorded in the Mishnah and other sources often reflect a fact of social history: The conservative upper classes, he said, had to treat their womenfolk with consideration and their women enjoyed more rights than other women; the women of the lower economic and social classes had fewer rights, as a result the power of their husbands over them was considerable. Hence, Ginzberg continued, the Shammaites who represented the upper conservative class insisted that only for something unforgivable like *dbr 'rwh* could a woman be divorced. On the other hand, such stringency was not demanded by the representatives of the more popular class, the Hillelites.

There may be something to this explanation though I now think it is sociologically schematic [47] for the most part. There surely were differences of view about divorce among the talmudic sages, and great care and casuistry were devoted to the subject in order to make sure that though the husband unmistakably has the upper hand, for both economic and moral reasons (as Louis Epstein put it) it was best to make it hard for a man to divorce his wife, *hy' qšh b' ynyw lgršh*. If anything, it seems to me that the talmudic teachers (conservative, liberal, *mhmyrym, mqylym*) tried their utmost to prevent divorce when they could.[61]

Since Geonic times we have been instructed that Haggadah may not be invoked as authority for halakic purposes;[62] but Haggadah is surely a valuable source for recovery of moods and attitudes in a society. A brief anecdote therefore can provide circumstantial evidence.

[If a man lives with his wife for ten years and she bears no children, he should divorce her.]

In Sidon, once, a man married a woman and lived with her for ten years; but she did not give birth to any children.[63] So they came to Rabbi Simeon ben Yohai to get divorced. The husband then said to his wife, Take whatever precious object you find in my house and go back to your father's house. Rabbi Simeon ben Yohai said to them, You got married amid festivities, hence you shall not part from each other save in festivity. What did that woman do? She prepared a lavish feast and got her man deeply drunk; she signalled to her maidservants and said to them, Take him to my father's house. In the middle of the night he woke up from his sleep and said to them, Where am I? His wife said to him, Didn't you tell me, Take whatever precious object you find in my house and go back to your father's house? Well now, I have nothing more precious than you. When Rabbi Simeon ben Yohai heard about this, he offered up prayer in their behalf, and they were delivered from barrenness.[64]

61. L. M. Epstein, *The Jewish Marriage Contract* (New York, 1927), 22ff. See *P. Ketubot* 8:11. See also the references below, note 77.

62. *Otzar ha-Geonim*, Hagigah, ed. B. M. Lewin (Jerusalem, 1931), 59f.

63. Cf. B. Cohen, op. cit., I, 391–92, on "the first instance of divorce at Rome on record."

64. *Pesiqta Kahana*, ed. Mandelbaum, p. 327. Cf. *Cant. R.* 1:4, 8a–b. See also B. Cohen, op. cit. I, 393; *Kallah R.* p. 217, and cf. *ARNB*, p. 50, on Aaron who reconciled husbands and wives. See also *BhM* III, 128.

The story is not without wit,[65] but it is certainly not taking divorce light-heartedly.[66]

Let us return to our Mishnah; what is going on there? A debate on what constitutes grounds for divorce. Those who are familiar with John Milton's tract on divorce know that such a debate can be very serious indeed. The Shammaites who were, or tended to be, strict literalists—what we might call, strict constructionists—interpret the verse in Deuteronomy (24:1) quite liter-ally, "because he hath found ʿ*rwt dbr* in her," because he has found in her *dbr* ʿ*rwh*. Now from our point of view, it is at first surprising that the Hillelites, who already in early talmudic sources have the reputation of being gentle, and patient, and more [48] tolerant and generous toward others, should maintain that a wife might be divorced "even if she no more than ruined his supper." Although it is possible to regard this expression as a euphemism,[67] it is really best to asume that the Hillelites mean just what they say, simply. The Talmuds, both the Babylonian and the Palestinian, explain that while for the Shammaites the word in the verse to be emphasized is ʿ*rwt*, the first word in that idiom, for the Hillelites the word to be emphasized is *dbr*, hence, anything, any reason.

That such technical exegetical exercises can produce the respective views need not be denied. Scholars and jurists don't take words or documents lightly.[68] But something more seems to be here, what may be called, in the

---

65. Cf. B. Cohen, op. cit., I, 393.—I feel no particular strain in assuming that in its essentials this anecdote is literally true. In connection with a much more sensational story, E. R. Dodds (*The Greeks and the Irrational* [Berkeley and Los Angeles, 1951], 72) is prepared to say, "There is no reason to doubt the substantial truth of this story which has parallels in other countries." Even if not literally true, however, whoever told this story certainly tried to show how a *sage* frustrated plans for divorce when he found that despite the legal ruling there was affection on the part of husband and wife toward each other. Rabbi Simeon is the disciple of Rabbi Aqiba! On ignoring the demands of the law because of compassion for a former (!) wife, see the (amoraic) anecdote in *Gen. R.* 33:3, pp. 304f., and cf. H. Yalon, *Pirqe Lashon* (Jerusalem, 1971), 294–96.

66. On discouraging divorce, cf. *M. Nedarim* 9:9. See indeed *B.* and *P. Gittin*, end, on divorcing the first wife; cf. *DS*, ad loc.; cf. B. M. Lewin, *Otzar ha-Geonim* on Gittin (Jerusalem, 1941), 211f. and also 251.

I do not wish to suggest anything like a one-sided (much less idealized!) view as though there were no more to be said of the matter. There is no denying that for some forms of what the rabbis regarded as brazen (and worse) behavior, they did not hesitate to express themselves strongly in favor of divorce; see in fact the end of *B. Gittin* (and cf. *TK Ketubot*, 291, top and Plutarch, *Moralia*, 142D, 31). And there are expressions characteristic of all male-dominant societies. But nowhere, it seems to me, is divorce taken by them lightheartedly. In the idiom of that Mishnah, Nedarim 9:9, at least, one easily overhears what gossip could be like (and the rabbis tried to make impossible): Do you want your daughters talked about this way? Is there any woman who can live with a man like that? And the Midrash, *Lam. R.*, ed. Buber, 39b (on Lam. 1:14) certainly reveals how it might be with a man who could *not* get rid of his wife!

67. Cf. Z. W. Rabinowitz, *Shaʿare Torath Babel* (Jerusalem, 1961), 127f. See, by the way, *TK* ad *T. Berakot* 6:18, p. 121, line 88. See *Sifre Deut.* 235, p. 267, line 10.

68. "On the whole, it should be remembered that the rabbis, like most jurists, do not ordinarily disclose their inner motivations but mostly give technical reasons for their interpretations. Consequently we are frequently left to our resources to conjecture the inner processes of their minds" (B. Cohen, op. cit., I, 53). See also S. Lieberman, *Hellenism in Jewish Palestine* (New York, 1962), 139.

words of Whitehead,[69] one of the Talmuds' "unconscious assumptions." We must not forget that we are dealing with an essentially patriarchal society; and if in the law about divorce the Bible speaks in terms of the man doing the divorcing,[70] clearly the Hillelites, in keeping with their customary policy of striving to make the law more lenient,[71] use the word *dbr* as their instrument to liberalize the law and make it possible for the man to divorce his wife even if something less that *'rwh* were involved.[72] Milton would certainly have applauded their approach.[73] That in other societies in other times a different view of the matter might be taken—for example, thinking about divorce in terms appealing to contemporary Western society—hardly affects what the law in first-century Judea corresponded to.[74]

This finally brings us to Aqiba's view which demonstrates not only what the logic of liberalizing can lead to but what Aqiba expects from the institution of marriage. For on the surface of it his statement is preposterous. If I have found, he says, someone more attractive than my wife, I may divorce her. But why need I divorce her at all? Why don't I simply marry the other woman—for polygamy, though rare, is still not forbidden![75] To my surprise, among the early commentators, the only one (I think) to observe this is Maimonides (1135–1204), in his commentary on our Mishnah.[76] This is in fact, he says, why [49] the law is not in accordance with Rabbi Aqiba's view!

69. A. N. Whitehead, *Science in the Modern World* (New York, Mentor, 1948), 25. On the tendency to think in masculine terms, cf. *TK* ad *T. Berakot* 2:12, p. 20, line 33.

70. Deut. 24:1 Cf. B. Cohen, op. cit. I, 402f., II, 782. On the situation in Elephantine cf. R. Yaron, *Introduction to the Law of the Aramaic Papyri* (Oxford, 1961), 53ff. and B. Porten, *Archives from Elephantine* (Berkeley and Los Angeles, 1968), 209 and note 37, 261f. and note 55 ibid. See M. A. Friedman, op. cit., 31ff. On the statement in P. Qiddushin 1:1, "either one may divorce the other," cf. B. Cohen, *Law and Tradition in Judaism* (New York, 1959), 104, and as to the rabbinical attitude, 106.

71. To suggest that the Hillelites were happy-go-lucky in their attitude toward divorce is to ignore completely their attitude toward brides; cf. *Kallah*, ed. Higger, 323–35.

72. Cf. R. Hananel in *Otzar ha-Geonim* on Gittin, p. 56!

73. ". . . [I]n the Hebrew it sounds 'nakedness of aught, or any real nakedness:' which by all the learned interpreters is referred to the mind as well as to the body. And what greater nakedness or unfitness of mind than that which hinders ever the solace and peaceful society of the married couple? And what hinders that more than the unfitness and defectiveness of an unconjugal mind?" ("Doctrine and Discipline of Divorce," in F. A. Patterson, *The Student's Milton* [New York, 1934], 581). See also the quotation from James Bryce on divorce law in B. Cohen, *Law and Tradition in Judaism*, 100.

74. "Papinian quoted in *Digest* I 5, 9: *In multis juris nostri articulis deterior est condicio feminarum quam masculorum*: in many parts of our law, the condition of women is worse than that of men" (B. Cohen, *Jewish and Roman Law*, I, 130). On sensitivity to the law's being unfair to women, see *Sifre Num.* 133, p. 176. On the presence of inconsistency and paradox in law, cf. *Tanhuma Num.*, 23, ed. Buber, 58b–59a, and note 232, ibid.

75. On permission to marry more than one wife, see Justin Martyr, *Dialogue with Trypho* (ed. A. L. Williams, London, 1930), CXXXIV:1 (p. 276 and cf. ibid. p. 288) and William's note 1 ad loc. Note the halakic problem brought to R. Eliezer by an *epitropos* of King Agrippa (II), B. *Sukkah* 27a.

76. Perhaps it is relevant to recall here that Maimonides is a Sefardi. Cf. also Z. W. Falk, *Jewish Matrimonial Law in the Middle Ages* (Oxford, 1966), 11ff. (According to S. D. Goitein [*Conservative Judaism* 29, 1974, p. 25], Maimonides was born in 1138.)

Of course, one might argue that it is expensive for a man to maintain two wives. But it is not inexpensive to divorce a wife,[77] for her rights and compensation are no small matter in Jewish law. Again, one might wish to say that even if Aqiba's view is impractical, students of the law will often deal with theoretical conditions because the science of law in all traditions pushes on to extremes of logic and consequence. And if the query is, What are legitimate grounds for divorce? then the disciple of thinking through will lead one even to as farfetched a view as Aqiba's. On the other hand, law, wrote a distinguished comparativist of Jewish and Roman law, Boaz Cohen,[78] cannot

> afford the luxury of logic at the expense of human living which is not explainable solely in terms of logic .... [It cannot] make presumptions that have little basis in the realities of human thinking and behavior ....

It seems best to me, therefore, to take Aqiba at his word. If I find a woman more attractive than my wife, this is enough to justify divorce proceedings, according to Aqiba—unlike the earlier sages who insisted more or less on what the Gospel of Matthew (5:32) insists:

> ... I say unto you, That whosoever shall put away his wife, saving for the cause of fornication, causeth her to commit adultery: and whosoever shall marry her that is divorced committeth adultery.[79]

Following the direction already indicated by the Hillelites,[80] Aqiba does insist that a man may divorce his wife if she no longer finds favor in his eyes.

And Aqiba holds this view and ignores the stratagem of marrying an additional wife because he insists, I submit, that in a marriage, first, the relationship must be based on love, and, second, that love is an exclusive relationship, a one-to-one relationship (as we might say nowadays) where three is already a crowd. The relationship between a man and his wife is a relationship between lover and beloved, and a relationship between lover and beloved leaves no room for outsiders to come along for the ride.[81]

---

77. Cf. *B. Yebamot* 63b (here the spokesmen are Amoraim) and *B. Ketubot* 82b, *P. Ketubot* 8:11 especially; *M. Nedarim* 9:5 (Aqiba!). For an example of divorce being expensive in Elephantine, cf. Porten, op. cit., 224.

78. Op. cit., I, 80f.

79. Cf. Mark 10:1–12, Luke 16:18. See also the long discussion in *Strack-Billerbeck*, I, 312, *et seq.*

80. Cf. Talmud ad loc., and the view of R. Elhanan in Tosafot (90a) s.v., *Byt Šm'y* (contra Ri). But see Z. W. Rabinowitz, *Sha'are Torath Eretz Israel* (Jerusalem, 5700), 427.

81. See already (though tentatively) Z. Frankel, *Darke ha-Mishnah* (Warsaw, 1923), 126. Cf. B. Cohen, *Law and Tradition in Judaism*, 105. To marry an additional wife and ignore the needs of the first one would be brutal behavior; cf., for example, *T. Ketubot* 5:6.

I see now that Falk, op. cit. 114, note 2 makes the same suggestion as in our discussion (except that I don't know that I would agree on "*prerequisite* of marriage").

It seems to me that Aqiba's attitude toward the relationship of husband and wife can

Expressed in these words, the sentence moves dangerously close to some twentieth-century Hollywood banality, so that one is almost embarrassed to spell it out, particularly since, as we noted earlier, marriage for the ancients is not thought of in terms of a love affair. Well, my point is that it *is* in terms of a relationship of love[82] that Aqiba does think of marriage.[83] Hence we are [50] now in a better position to appreciate why Aqiba felt that one who marries a woman unsuitable to himself transgresses a number of commands: for the man will quickly come to resent her, and then may well appear that frame of mind which is a psychological nightmare to at least some rabbis. It is of one of Aqiba's teachers, Rabbi Eliezer, that we are told[84] that he was in terror when he made love to his wife, for fear that another woman would come to his mind at such a time! The offspring of such cohabitation, he feared, might almost be regarded as illegitimate. Or here is Aqiba himself on a psychologically related possibility:[85] The pot in which your fellow did his cooking is not for you to cook in. And when ad locum the question is raised, What does that mean? the Talmud correctly explains, Marrying a divorcée while her former husband is still alive. For the Master said,[86] When a divorced man marries a divorcée,

---

explain why (in addition to the exegetical basis given by the Talmud—cf. above, note 68) he felt that when a wife was suspected of infidelity the ritual of sotah had to be (*ḥwbh*) followed: B. *Sotah* 3a. If doubts remained in the husband's mind, how could a genuine relationship survive?

Cf. Aristotle, *Ethics*, Book VIII, vi, 1158a: "To be a friend to many people, in the way of the perfect friendship, is not possible; just as you cannot be in love with many at once: it is, so to speak, a state of excess which naturally has but one object; and besides, it is not an easy thing for one man to be very much pleased with many people at the same time, nor perhaps to find many really good. Again, a man needs experience, and to be in habits of close intimacy, which is very difficult."

On the disaster of two wives in the house, cf. *Mid. Tan.*, p. 131.

82. Ephesians 5:25, "Husbands, love your wives." Cf. the tannaite statement (*tnw rbnn*) on *loving* one's wife as oneself, and so forth in B. Yebamot 62b (see also Ephesians 5:38 and 33 and Colossians 3:18ff.). On what is a fortunate lot in life, cf. Eccl. 9:9; and see also *Ecclus.* 26:1–4 and the relevant following verses. But note that Ben Sira does not speak of the husband loving his (good and modest and respectful) wife. The closest we seem to get to that is 25:2 (in Segal's edition, p. 151). Should the anonymous statement in *Sifre Deut.* 271, end, p. 292, be attributed to Aqiba (or his school)?

83. What Hollywood has devoted itself to is not so much love as "love story," of course, and with the latter Aqiba has absolutely nothing in common. It would be closer to the truth to say that for Aqiba "love is not love where it alteration finds." The preposterousness of the Hollywood fantasy is nowhere more lucidly exposed than in E. B. White's essay "Movies," in his *One Man's Meat* (New York, 1944), 63–67.

What (seemingly) Aqiba thinks of the husband who looks forward to his wife's death so that he might marry her sister (or so that he might inherit her possessions) is stated in *ARNA*, p. 15 (cf. *T. Sotah* 5:10, anonymously); note also the reading in the name of Joshua ben Qorha in *ARNB*, p. 16. And on Joshua ben Qorha, cf. Z. Frankel, op. cit., 187 and A. Hyman, *Toldoth*, II, 648! However, cf. *TK, Ketubot*, 244.

84. Cf. B. *Nedarim* 20b, *Kallah*, ed. Higger, pp. 138, 185. Cf. *Legends* IV, 82; VI, 246, note 11. On tenderness toward one's wife accompanying love, cf. *Kallah*, pp. 160 and 206.

85. B. *Pesaḥim* 112a. See also the beginning of the midrash by Resh Laqish in B. *Berakot* 32b.

86. Cf. E. Z. Melamed, *Eshnab ha-Talmud* (Jerusalem, 5714), 13, bottom.

there are four persons in the bed; and if you wish, say, the same is true when it's a widow. And the rest of it.[87]

When Aqiba talks about love in passages like this, there is nothing ambiguous about his emphasis, any more than there is, for example, about the emphasis in Matthew 5:27–28:

> Ye have heard that it was said by them of old time, Thou shalt not commit adultery: But I say unto you, That whosoever looketh on a woman to lust after her hath committed adultery with her already in his heart.[88]

For Aqiba an emphasis on love in the relationship of husband and wife is not romantic speech or pastoral rhetoric.[89] He has realistic, natural, concrete considerations in mind. Talmudic sources preserve a significant record. Since during her menstrual period husband and wife must keep apart from each other,[90] the earlier sages maintained that it would be best for the wife to make herself as unattractive as possible during the forbidden days to discourage the husband's advances.[91] In an old text, indeed, this is the only view which is cited and cited plainly with approval.[92]

> Hence it was said: She that neglects herself in the days of her impurity, with her the sages are pleased; but she that adorns herself in the days of her impurity, with her the sages are displeased.

Note, by the way, that from this text one would not necessarily guess that this was an *early*[93] view, or that there might be any other view of the matter.

87. On rather strong expressions, literal or euphemistic (which may indeed have been specimens of common talk), cf. *Kallah*, ed. Higger, p. 136. On what is ideal speech of the sages cf. *M. Sanhedrin* 8:1 (*M. Niddah* 6:11). See further Lieberman, *Hellenism in Jewish Palestine*, 34, note 39. On unrestrained coarseness of exclamation (which is universal of course) see, for example, Plutarch's quotation (of Sotades to Ptolemy Philadelphus) in his essay on *Education of Children*, 14. [Note also the anecdote in *Num. R.* 9:34, 31d (bot.) – 32a (top).]

88. *Kallah* 1 in the regular Talmud editions (and cf. ed. Higger, p. 132, critical apparatus to line 44), *kl hmstkl b' šh bkwwnh k'lw b' 'lyh*, and see *Strack-Billerbeck*, loc. cit. (note 79 above). Incidentally, this seems to lie behind the reason why Job would not lay his eyes even on a virgin (let alone someone else's wife), *ARNA*, pp. 12f., *ARNB*, p. 8. Cf. also *B. Abodah Zarah* 20a–b.

89. On love in pastoral, cf. T. G. Rosenmeyer, *The Green Cabinet* (Berkeley and Los Angeles, 1969), 77–85.

To obviate misunderstanding, let me state that I am not attempting anything like a Freudian interpretation of Aqiba: All I am undertaking is to show how a number of views ascribed to Aqiba help make intelligible his homily on *w' nwhw*, and thereby also reveal what is a dominating thought of his mind, as is to be seen also in his forceful statement in *B. Sotah* 17a: "fire" is more than a *jeu de mots* here! Cf. the Amora Raba in *B. Sotah*, ibid. on love and fire.

90. Lev. 18:17.

91. *ARNA*, p. 8; *ARNB*, p. 12.

92. As we can tell from the Elijah story too, ibid.

93. Note the reading *mk' n 'mrw ḥkmym* in *ARNB*, p. 12.

[51] But then we read elsewhere in the Midrash and Talmud,[94]

> As to the verse (Lev. 15:33), "And she that is sick in her impurity," the early sages ruled: That means that she must not rouge nor paint nor adorn herself in colorful garments[95]—until Rabbi Aqiba came along and taught: If so, you make her repulsive to her husband, with the result that he will divorce her! What then is intended by that Leviticus verse [above]? She shall remain in her impurity until she has had a ritual bath.

In other words, here is a relaxation of a severe ruling in a religious sphere—purity and impurity of women[96]—where there was a tendency to be strict,[97] and it is Aqiba who is responsible for that relaxation. And his motive? So that the husband be not repelled by his wife! Nor is this the only time we hear Aqiba expressing himself this way. Scripture teaches (Num. 30:9, 13) that a husband has the authority to nullify his wife's vow; but there are conditions when the husband may *not* do so.[98] However, in what is called *tglḥt ḥṭwm'h*[99]—that is, in the case where she would have to do a complete recount of her nazirate days in a state of purity—Rabbi Aqiba maintains that her husband may certainly nullify her vow, because he may declare, *'y 'pšy b'šh mnwwlt*, I can't stand a squalid wife.[100]

---

94. *Sifre*, ed. Weiss, 79c, B. *Shabbat* 64b.

95. That such would be women's attire, see *Sifre Deut.* 226, p. 258; B. *Abodah Zarah* 20b. (They may also have been easier to clean than white garments; see the quotation from the Palestinian Talmud in *TK* ad T. Shabbat, p. 22, line 54.) A wife is not to vow that she won't wear such garments, T. *Ketubot* 7:8. Cf. however the note struck in the anonymous moralistic treatise, *The Ways of the Righteous* (Heb., ed. S. J. Cohen, Jerusalem–New York, 1969), 30. On the date and country of origin of this treatise, see now H. Z. Dimitrovsky in *S. W. Baron Jubilee Volume* (Jerusalem, 1975), III, 174ff. On a wife's duty to be attractive to her husband, see the strong expression in T. *Qiddushin* 1:11.

96. Note for example the view of Hillel (!) in *M. Niddah* 1:1 (*M. Eduyot* 1:1); see also Rabbi Joshua at the beginning of *M. Zabim* 4:1. A *Sadducean* woman takes such strictness seriously: T. *Niddah* 5:3, B. *Niddah* 33b, bottom. See also beginning of T. *Shabbat* 1:14 and *TK* ad loc. That Aqiba is not inclined to take matters of this sort lightly can be seen, e.g., in *M. Niddah* 2:3, and cf. Albeck in his edition, p. 585. And yet note well what is reported in *M. Niddah* 8:3 (Aqiba and his surprised students). There may really be a tendency on the part of Aqiba to reduce the rigours connected with laws of purity and impurity; cf. Aqiba's strong retort to colleagues in *M. Zabin* 2:2! Is there an overtone or undertone of, Who asked you to be holier than thou? This, however, requires further study.

97. This can be seen, for example, in the reaction of Vitry and others to the reading (e.g., MS Parma) *b'štw nydh* of PA 1:5; cf. *ARN*, pp. 174f.; Taylor, *Sayings of the Jewish Fathers* (Cambridge, 1900), "Notes on the Text," 136. This reading is most likely *not* to be adopted, and the commentators are prompt to endorse the thought of the generally current text, Even with your own wife keep conversation down to a minimum; all the more *b'štw nydh*.

See also Maimonides ad *M. Niddah*, end of chap. 2, and the reference furnished by Kapah. Of course this is not meant to imply that the sages are uniformly severe for the sake of severity; note, for example, the first half of *M. Niddah* 2:4.

98. See *M. Nazir* 4:5 and Albeck's additional note, p. 374.

99. Cf. also *M. Nazir* 6:6.

100. One who denies herself the delights (pleasures, wine) of this world; but see *TK*, *Nazir*, 532f. Note also Rabbi ad loc.: *'p btglḥt hṭhrh ypr, šhw' ykwl lwmr, 'y 'pšy b'šh mglḥt.* (Cf.

[52] All this from the man who ruled that if the husband found another woman who pleased him more, he might divorce his wife! But there is not paradox or inconsistency here, for Aqiba sensed that once a man ceased to *love* his wife, to desire her, it was no longer a marriage of true minds. Hence his strong objections to what is corrosive of love.

It seems to me that we are led by such an outlook to the *brink* of a monogamous conception—not because the texts use the vocabulary of husband and wife in the singular; that is, after all, the standard and convenient economy of the language of formulas. More to the point is the fact that one does encounter in these times articulate support of monogamy. Some sectarians insist on it.[101] But they are not the only ones. It meets with approval even in some rabbinic quarters.

Rabbi Judah ben Bathyra [a contemporary of Aqiba!] says, Job kept pondering the words of the verse, "What portion did God on high allot us, what lot did the Almighty on high set aside for us?"[102] If it had been proper for Adam to have ten wives, God would have given them to him! Well, for me too, my own wife is enough for me.[103]

Be this as it may, a recognition of the emphasis by Aqiba on the seriousness of love—on what I would like to call the *literalness* of love—between husband and wife helps restore for us the force and freshness of his well-known sayings about transcendent love. The word is still *'hb, 'hbh*,[104] but it has risen to a

---

TK, loc. cit.) Cf. also Rabbi Aqiba in *Kallah*, 8, ed. Higger, p. 133, critical apparatus to line 51. (By the way, note also how Aqiba supports his view of discouraging the taking of a "captive woman," in *Sifre Deut.* 212, pp. 245–46.) On Aqiba's sensitivity to physical attractiveness, see his interpretation of Lam. 3:17 in *Pirqe Derek Ereṣ* 1 (in *Seder Eliyahu*, ed. Friedmann, Jerusalem, 5720, p. 3). See also the delightful anecdote *about* R. Aqiba in *B. Abodah Zarah* 20a. And possibly this is why according to Aqiba (?) Moses did not *on his own* tell husbands to keep away from their wives before the Revelation at Sinai; cf. *Exod. R.* 46:3 (see also 19:3)—but in *ARNA*, p. 10, the view is given in the name of R. Judah ben Bathyra, Aqiba's contemporary.

Although there is no question that halakically divorce is a unilateral act on the husband's part, there is a possibility where the wife may say about her husband, "He disgusts me" (*B. Ketubot* 63b, and Rashi and Tosafot, s.v., *'bl*, ad loc.). Cf. M. A. Friedman, op. cit., 34, 55. (Note, by the way, what the sages say a widow might say to her levir who is a tanner, even though her husband had been one: Him I could tolerate, not you! *M. Ketubot* 7:10, end.) When all is said, however, the view of the rabbis, which they share with the ancients, is that expressed in *Seder Eliyahu R.*, p. 51, Only she who does what her husband wants her to do is a fine and upstanding women (*'šh kšrh*: my translation is not literal but is intended to convey the real meaning; on the meaning of *'šh kšrh* in some contexts, cf. further S. Lieberman, *Tosefeth Rishonim* [Jerusalem, 1937–39], II, 148 and now also *TK Ketubot*, 192). See also the conversation between Aqiba and his son about the latter's wife, in *Midrash Ps.* 59:3, ed. Buber, 151b and cf. Sidonius Apollinaris, *Epistles*, II, 10:5 (Loeb Classics, I, 467); and on Aqiba's son and his wife, see also *T. Ketubot* 4:7.

101. Cf. *Zadokite Documents*, ed. C. Rabin (Oxford, 1958), 16f. (iv. lines 20ff.); L. Ginzberg, *Eine unbekannte jüdische Sekte* (New York, 1922), 24ff.

102. Job 31:2.

103. *ARNB*, p. 9, and see Schechter's note 6, ibid.!

104. Cf. St. Augustine's exploration of the terms *amor, dilectio, caritas*, in *City of God* XIV:7.

plane where it is completely transfigured, spiritualized, where only heart and soul are embraced;[105] where the direction is from desire to zeal, from receiving to surrendering to the other's needs, the other's demands. What is the *kll gdwl šbtwrh*, the fundamental principle of the Torah?[106] It is,[107] Aqiba says, *w'hbt lr'k kmwk*, Thou shalt *love* thy neighbor as thyself (Lev. 19:18).[108] And when he was being martyred and was asked how he could endure the frightful tortures, he replied—according to the legend[109]—that all his life he had been waiting for an opportunity to express his *love* of God with all his mind (*holes tes dianoias*)[110] and all his soul, *w'hbt 't H' 'lhyk bkl lbbk wbkl npšk* (Deut. 6:5).[111] Very likely, every word counts: *Love* the Lord who is *thy* God—"thy," second person singular: the discourse is direct and to the individual—"with *all* thy heart" (= mind), and "with *all* thy soul" (= life): no reservations, no holding back. But even if the story should not here be underlining the second person singular of the verse, the intent is plain: In relating to God the love must be total; if my Beloved is to be mine, then I must be His entirely. And perhaps this is in actuality the meaning Aqiba sought to proclaim with his last recitation on earth: Hear, O Israel, the Lord is [53] our God, the Lord *alone*. Him and only Him one must love, not Him also.[112]

It has been suggested[113] and may well be that in the Hellenistic centuries the theme of love had become a popular one in many quarters, and Aqiba may have been influenced by that, or possibly, more plausibly, have been reflecting a widespread interest. Whether or not so, however, love is clearly uppermost in

105. If Rashi (*B. Sotah* 27b, bottom) is right, that Joshua ben Hyrqanos was the disciple of Aqiba, then it seems to me that the discussion of Job's piety in *M. Sotah* 5:5, that it was motivated by *love* of God, should also be taken into account. For, as the idiom of that whole Mishnah reflects, the Job theme was on the mind of the leading rabbis for at least several generations, and it took a disciple of Aqiba's to "settle" the matter once for all that out of love Job spoke and acted as he did.

106. *P. Nedarim* 9:4, *Gen. R.* 24, end, pp. 236f.

107. *Sifra*, ed. Weiss, 89b.

108. This may explain the attribution to Aqiba in the anecdote of *ARNB*, p. 53. See further the supplementary note at the end of this paper.

109. See L. Ginzberg in *The Jewish Encyclopaedia* (New York and London, 1901), I, 308b. And if so, how chaste! "When Rabbi Akiba, perhaps the most revered figure in the whole rabbinic tradition, was executed by the Romans a century after Jesus' time, none of his disciples saw him risen or ascending into the heavens." (M. Smith, *The Secret Gospel* [New York, 1973], 111.)

110. On the meaning, see further below, and with this cf. Aqiba's *literal* interpretation of (Gen. 22:1) *nsh* in *Gen. R.* 55:6, pp. 588–89, and note ad loc. Cf. A. Marmorstein in *HUCA* 6 (1929), 150ff.

111. Cf. Matthew 22:37–40.

112. See also Deut. 6:4 in the new version of the JPS translation. And if this *is* the literal meaning, Aqiba may well be emphasizing, not innovating. However, even if we were to say that *'hd* here = One, the Aqiba message is still unmistakable. See S. Lieberman in *Annuaire de l'Institut de Philologie ed d'Histoire Orientales et Slaves* 7 (1939–44), 425 and notes 78–79 ibid., 421.

113. Cf. G. D. Cohen, op. cit., 16 and note 15 ibid.; with this, however, cf. M. Smith, "The Common Theology of the Ancient Near East," in *JBL*, 71 (1952), 142, note 37, and E. R. Dodds, op. cit., p. 35 and p. 54, note 38.

his mind. In his imagination he does not hesitate to credit "the righteous women [wives]" of Israel of "that generation" in the distant past, with the merit that brought redemption from Egypt, a merit that grew directly out of the act of love.[114]

It is time to return to the Midrash of the dialogue of the Nations of the World and Israel by means of the Song of Songs verses. What is there about your Beloved more than other beloved ones, the Nations ask Israel, that you are prepared to be slain for His sake? Why don't you merge with us and learn our ways?[115] In short, that Israel is prepared to die for His sake does not impress them favorably; indeed, such extreme devotion strikes the Nations as bigoted and stupid.[116] Come over to us, they say invitingly.

But Israel replies: If only you had some idea of how splendid my Beloved is! For all its grace, our text, alas, does not spell out the meaning of the imagery,[117] but obviously, according to Israel, that did convey something glorious to the Nations, even though it was only a partial account. And therefore the Nations now respond, Let us go along with you. Plainly this is a deity worth being attached to. But Israel protests, That's impossible, *I* am my Beloved's and my Beloved is mine, '*ny ldwdy wdwdy ly*.

Why this rejection, we asked, particularly after Aqiba's urging that Israel should proclaim God's *doxa* before the Nations of the World? Because apparently the Nations do not begin to understand what is meant by *love* of God. In the first place, they fail to understand that love is an exclusive relationship. You cannot simply add on the God of Israel to all the other gods you worship and pay Him respects too. He does not share love. He is not one more object of affection. This the Nations can't quite grasp. As Elias Bickerman put it in his study "Altars of the [54] Gentiles":[118]

A "god-fearing" gentile remained *theosebes* and did not embrace the faith of Abraham, Isaac, and Jacob, precisely for the reason that the contradiction between

---

114. *Exod. R.* 1:12. In *B. Sotah* 11b the reading is Rab ʿAwwira (but not the marginal comment ibid.). *Yalqut Shemot* 163 and *Be-Shallah* 245 reads "Aqiba."

115. Cf. the idiom in Ps. 106:35.

116. Cf. *Contra Celsum* II, 17 (ed. Chadwick, p. 83) and also VIII, 65 (p. 501) where Origen quotes Celsus on those who die for God's sake: ". . . mad . . . deliberately rush forward to arouse the wrath of an emperor or governor which brings . . . blows and tortures and even death."

117. How is your beloved better than another, / O fairest of women? / How is your beloved better than another, / That you adjure us so? / My beloved is clear-skinned and ruddy. / Pre-eminent among ten thousand. / His head is finest gold, / His locks are curled / And black as a raven. / His eyes are like doves / By watercourses, / Bathed in milk, / Set by a brimming pool. / His cheeks are like beds of spices, / Banks of perfume / His lips are like lilies; / They drip flowing myrrh. / His hands are rods of gold. / Studded with beryl; / His belly a tablet of ivory, / Adorned with sapphires. / His legs are like marble pillars / Set in sockets of fine gold. / He is majestic as Lebanon, / Stately as the cedars. / His mouth is delicious / And all of him is delightful. / Such is my beloved, / Such is my darling . . . (Translation from *The Five Megilloth and Jonah*; cf. above, note 9)

118. *Revue Internationale des Droits de l'Antiquité* 5 (1958), 156.

Jewish monotheism and his polytheistic ideas was not evident to him. He just wanted to add the Eternal God, or let us say another Eternal Deity, to his pantheon.

A very reflective man might well entertain profoundest thoughts about the nature of deity,[119] reject the crude things said about the gods by the poets, and still acknowledge his debt to Asclepius:[120] quite right, for him reflection and religion are two separate spheres.

In the second place, the Nations fail to grasp that love of God, like genuine human love, is not simply a fair-weather affair. Martyrdom struck them as silly at best. Why don't you give up such conduct and join us? Only when they heard that ornate description of all the parts of His person (the ivory and the sapphires and the gold and the cedars and the marble and the lilies and the magnificent scents and sweets) did they request to have Him, too, as their deity. To Rabbi Aqiba this is no relationship worth its name.[121] For this is how he put it on another occasion:[122] What is the meaning of the verse coming right after the Ten Commandments (Exod. 20:20), "With Me, therefore, you shall not make any gods of silver, nor shall you make for yourselves any gods of gold"? "You shall not behave toward Me," God says, "the way the others [= the Gentiles] behave toward their deities. That is, when good comes upon them, they honor their gods . . . but when calamity overtakes them, they curse their gods. . . . Not you, however: if I bring good upon you, give thanks; if I bring sufferings upon you, give thanks." Or again, and this time in connection with the very verse which is recalled in the story of his martyrdom: Rabbi Aqiba says,[123] If the verse has already spoken of the duty to love God with all of one's life, what's the point of adding *bkl m' dk*, with all thy means?[124] But the verse

119. Justin, *Dialogue with Trypho* I:3 (ed. A. L. Williams [London, 1930] 2): "And is not this the business of philosophy, to make enquiries into the nature of divinity?" Cf. H. A. Wolfson, *Studies in the History of Philosophy and Religion*, I, ed. I. Twersky and G. H. Williams (Cambridge, Mass., 1973), 71.

120. "Though Celsus will not agree, the Jews do possess *some deeper wisdom*, not only more than the multitude, but also than those who seem to be philosophers, because the philosophers in spite of their impressive philosophical teachings fall down to idols and daemons, while even the lowest Jew looks only to the supreme God." (Origen, *Contra Celsum* V, 43, p. 298.) And see especially VI, 4, p. 318.

On Asclepius see E. J. and L. Edelstein, *Asclepius* (Baltimore, 1945), II, 108ff., and cf. M. P. Nilsson, *Greek Piety* (Oxford, 1948), 71f.

121. Cf. Plato, *Symposium* 179.

Aqiba apparently does not reject proselytes; one of his disciples seems to have been of Egyptian origins. Cf. *Sifre Deut.* 253, p. 279, and L. Finkelstein's notes to lines 15 and 17. But I am unsure of this detail, for there is ambiguity of readings (cf. *MhG Deut.* 520, line 3) and of Aqiba's halakic view in the parallel sources, which I am unable to resolve.

122. *Mekilta, Ba-Hodesh*, 10 (II, 277). Cf. also Aqiba's disciple, Rabbi Meir, in *T. Berakot* 6:1 (and see *TK* ad loc., pp. 102f.) and 6:7. On others = Gentiles, cf. *The Song at the Sea* 194.

123. *Sifre Deut.* 32, pp. 55f., and see L. Finkelstein's note ad loc. for further references.

124. See *Sifre Deut.*, loc. cit.; cf. *M. Berakot* 9:5. (See also the anecdote in *Deut. R.*, ed. Lieberman, 70). Note indeed that the expression does not recur in Deut. 11:13; cf. 10:12, 13:14; also 26:16; 30:6, 10. (On the other hand, cf. II Kings 23:25).

teaches that be the measure—the portion—He measures out to thee[125] what it may—be it auspicious or calamitous—(thou must love him). So, too, David says, "I will lift up the cup of salvation, and call upon the name of the Lord" (Ps. 116:13) and also "I found trouble and sorrow, but I called upon the name of the Lord" (Ps. 116:3f.). So, too, Job says, "The Lord gave, and the Lord hath taken away; blessed be the name of the Lord" (Job 1:21).

Love of God, says Aqiba, is for keeps. You can depend on it that He is just and that we get what is coming to us.[126] But what we get is not always as we expect. Yet we cannot love God only when it's to our liking. That is not love. [55] And since in this connection there is no possibility of divorce—for there is none more comely, as those Song of Songs verses demonstrate—only one alternative remains: love. Therefore we have to be prepared to say, Blessed be the name of the Lord, even when He takes away.

And, according to Rabbi Aqiba, the Gentiles fail to understand this. They simply don't get the point. They cannot understand why Israel is so fanatically loyal to Him even when He leads her to death. They cannot understand why if they seek to become His beloved, like Israel, they have to give up all their other gods who, after all, also have claims on them: the whole cultured world recognizes this![127] They cannot understand that this one-to-one relationship is for Aqiba the only true definition of love and that therefore one must be ready to put up with sufferings and punishments if this is what the Lover sees fit to bestow. Failing to understand this definition or interpretation of love, they cannot be admitted into the interior and intimacy of 'ny ldwdy wdwdy ly, I belong to my Beloved and my Beloved is mine. They cannot appreciate that the verse deliberately reads w' nwhw, for it is a cipher of 'ny whw':[128] I and He.

This is Aqiba's Midrash. Before all the world Israel is to proclaim what *love* of God is. 'l kn 'lmwt 'hbwk, that is, 'd mwt 'hbwk: not even death will us part.[129] This is the position adopted by monotheism. Face to face with the

125. There is a play on the words m'd and mdh (in pronunciation the 'aleph of m'd would not be discerned; note also, for example, *Gen. R.* 56:7, p. 603). Cf. S. Spiegel, "On the Language of the Early Paytanim," *Hadoar*, New York, 5 April 1963, 21f.

126. See the dialogue with Pappias in *Mekilta, Be-Shallah,* 7 (I, 248); *MRS* p. 68. Cf. also *PA* 3:16 (Aqiba): "and the judgment is a just one."

127. Cf. *Contra Celsum* I, 52 (ed. Chadwick, p. 48). Note Festugière (below, note 129), 117.

128. See *The Song at the Sea,* 117. See also p. 114 on the view of Abba Saul.

It would not surprise me (though I would hesitate to press it) if the vocabulary of the text, in keeping with its stylization, were deliberately made to hint that the Gentiles adopt a double standard as it were; when they invite Israel to join them, they say ht'rbw (merge) with us; however, when they propose to come along with Israel, they say only, nlkh (let us go) with you.

129. Cf. Leqaḥ Tob on Canticles, ed. A. W. Greenup (London, 1909), p. 16, bottom. See also *T. Berakot* 6:7. The Vatican MS of the Mekilta reads 'hbnwk, we have loved Thee.

And *perhaps* the difference between R. Yose and R. Aqiba (cf. above, note 19, second paragraph) lies in this: R. Yose speaks simply of proclaiming God's *doxa* to the Nations of the World (in the hope of winning them over); while R. Aqiba insists that the proclamation must be accompanied by a clear statement and exemplification of what is meant by love of God: nothing less will do.

Nations of the World Aqiba teaches Israel what he knows about love, and insists that to be united with the God of Israel, the Nations must love Him as Israel loves Him, Him only.[130]

Even if the sentence in the Mekilta be regarded as an interpolation, it is a correct interpretation of Aqiba's view.

And yet in this connection it is not inappropriate to call attention to A. J. Festugière, *Personal Religion among the Greeks* (Berkeley and Los Angeles, 1960), 80, that the kind of demand made by Aqiba need not necessarily and always have been incomprehensible: "There is, however, at least one feature (in Apuleius, *The Golden Ass*) which is new. Lucius is not merely called to initiation; he is called to consecrate his entire life to Isis: 'Be sure to remember and keep graven in thy inmost heart that all the remaining course of thy life, even to thy last breath, is pledged to me.' It is precisely because the obligation will last as long as life that Lucius hesitates to commit himself; who can be sure of what he will be tomorrow? That is an original touch, practically unknown among the ancients, which can only be compared with religious vocation among Christians."

It seems to me that in Lucius the transformation is the result of an instant, miraculous, personal deliverance, and exclusive devotion to the goddess. In Aqiba, apparently, the devotion grows out of reflection on human behavior in recurrent experiences and responses.

130. More than seventy years ago L. Ginzberg wrote as the last sentence of his encyclopedia article on the biography of Aqiba (*Jewish Encyclopaedia*, I, 308b), "Pure monotheism was for Akiba the essence of Judaism: he lived, worked, and died for it."

Supplementary Note: "'Thou shalt love thy neighbor as thyself': Rabbi Aqiba says, This is a fundamental principle (*kll gdwl*) of the Torah. Ben Azzai says, (The verse, Gen. 5:1), 'This is the record of Adam's line' (etc.), is even more fundamental."

In what way is Ben Azzai's verse more fundamental?

Rabad ad loc. offers the following explanation: According to Rabbi Aqiba the verse "Thou shalt love thy neighbor as thyself" is fundamental because "What is hateful to thee thou art not to do to thy fellow." And for most of the commandments this is indeed fundamental. According to Ben Azzai, however, the verse "This is the record of Adam's line.—When God created man, He made him in the likeness of God," is the more fundamental, for from Aqiba's verse we learn only that the neighbor is to be loved "as thyself." But if I've been disgraced or cursed or attacked, shall my fellow be similarly treated by me? Hence the importance of the verse, "He made him in the likeness of God." Do you realize whom you would be disgracing, whom you would be cursing if you treated your fellow as shamefully as you were treated? The very image of God! Hence this verse is a more fundamental principle than the verse cited by Aqiba.

Put in other terms, what Rabad says is that Aqiba's principle can serve only if a person has self-love, self-esteem. [Indeed, on self-esteem, cf. M. Sanhedrin 4:5, toward end.] It then makes sense to say, Love thy neighbor as thyself. But self-esteem, as is well known, is not always present. If there is no self-esteem (hence no "as thyself"), where is the whole deductive process to begin? Only with the verse that says that every man was created in God's image. One must esteem himself for one is in His image. In Rabad's words: Do you realize whom you would be disgracing? The very image of God! From the verse about man in God's image self-love is learned; then follows Aqiba's command about love of fellowman. The former is the more fundamental principle, for it includes Aqiba's, while Aqiba's does not necessarily include it. (This interpretation was offered in 1963 by Joel Greenberg, then age 7.)

A Short Note
on the Archangel Gabriel

[1] Even the ancients knew that the authors of Holy Writ occasionally had difficulty reporting phenomena for which human vocabulary was inadequate. They said, therefore, that the expressions used in such instances were only approximate, figurative, or metaphorical.[1] This was indeed "the hedge the Prophets made about their words."[2] For example,

> Scripture says: "The lion has roared; who will not fear? (Amos 3:8). Perhaps His voice is only like the voice of a lion. Say then: Who gave a voice to the lion? Is it not He? But this is the way He is described metaphorically to His creatures so that the ear be unoffended and be able to hear.[3]

Or as the companion text puts it, "But the eye is shown what it can see and the ear is permitted to hear what it can hear."[4]

Another example of such resort to metaphor is to be seen, according to the *Mekilta*,[5] in Exod. 19:18.[6] Still another example is Isa. 42:13, where we must understand that the Lord goes forth not just as one "mighty man," but as more mighty than all the mighty men in the world.[7]

---

1. On euphemism, cf. *Mekilta, Shirta* 6, ed. J. Z. Lauterbach (Philadelphia, 1933–35), 2:43–44.

2. *Abot de-Rabbi Natan*, ed. S. Schechter (Vienna, 1887), p. 7a.

3. ARN, Version B, trans. A. J. Saldarini (Leiden, 1975), p. 46, and n. 9.

4. Version A of ARN, ed. Schechter, p. 7a.

5. *Mekilta, Ba-Hodesh* 4.2.221; *Mekilta R. Simeon*, eds, J. N. Epstein and E. Z. Melamed (Jerusalem, 1955), p. 144, plus additional examples; *Midrash ha-Gadol, Gen.* ed. M. Margulies (Jerusalem, 1947), Intro., p. 30. Cf. Rashi on the verses as well.

6. With reference to Deut. 4:11, see also ARN, trans. Saldarini, p. 46, n. 11.

7. Cf. Version A of ARN, ed. Schechter, p. 7a, n. 71.

And still another:

So too, Scripture says: "And behold the glory of the God of Israel came from the east; and the sound of His [coming] was like the sound of many waters"[8] (Ezek. 43:2). Say then: Who gave a voice to the waters:[9] was it not He? But this is the way He is described metaphorically to His creatures so that the ear be unoffended and be able to hear.[10]

Such is the way Version B of *Abot de-Rabbi Natan* puts it. Version A,[11] on the other hand, is more expository and very likely making an additional emphasis of its own.

"And His voice was like the sound of many waters; and the earth did shine with His glory" (Ezek. 43:2). — The[12] *sound of many waters* refers to the angel Gabriel. *And the earth did shine with His glory* refers to the presence of the Shekinah. —Now, is there not an inference to be drawn here? If Gabriel, who is but one of thousands upon thousands and myriads upon myriads that stand before Him, has a voice which travels from one end of the world to the other, how much more so the King of kings over kings . . . who created the whole universe, who created the beings on high and the beings below! But the eye is shown what it can see [etc.].[13]

To avoid dangerous literalness in description of the divine, one might well be led to explain "the sound of many waters" as a reference to the angel [2] Gabriel. The Septuagint, for instance, possibly its *Vorlage* too, does not speak of *His* voice as the voice (sound) of many waters in Ezek. 43:2 (*kai phonē tēs parembolēs, hôs phonē diplasiazontôn pollôn*)[14] while in 1:24 the sound of the wings "like the sound of many waters, like the sound of the Almighty [Shaddai],"[15] (as the Vulgate also: *quasi sonum sublimis Dei*) is reduced and

8. Version B of ARN does not quote the rest of the verse (see further below) and therefore does not comment on it. On the voice of one like unto the son of man as the sound of many waters, cf. Rev. 1:15. On the "rush of many waters" following God, see the hymn in J. A. Sanders, *The Psalms Scroll of Qumran. Cave 11* (Oxford, 1965), p. 89, col. 26, 1. 10, and note (p. 90). In J. Licht, *Thanksgiving Scroll* (Jerusalem, 1957), p. 68, 1. 16b, and p. 71, 1. 27, the reference is not to God and the imagery is meant to suggest overpowering sound and strength.

9. Cf. *Zohar Ḥadash* 18d, in I. Tishby, *Mishnat ha-Zohar* (Jerusalem, 5709), 1: 441, and on "the sound of the waters like the voice of Shaddai" (Ezek. 1:24), see further below.

10. Version B of ARN, ed. Schechter, p. 7a, and ARN, trans. Saldarini, p. 46. Cf. *Yalqut Shimeoni* (Salonica, 1521) on the verse.

11. ARN, ed. Schechter, p. 46.

12. Cf. n. 8, above.

13. Note how appendix B in ARN, ed. Schechter, p. 77a (towards bottom), reads. And note how Maimonides, *Guide of the Perplexed*, 3. 9, trans. S. Pines (Chicago, 1963), pp. 436–37, makes use of the Ezek. verse, and how Albo does, *Ikkarim* 2.29, ed. I. Husik (Philadelphia, 1946), 2: 188.

14. On this reading, cf. Jerome's emphasis in F. Field, *Origenis Hexaplorum* (Oxford, 1875), 2: 885, n. 2.

15. And on the reading *hôs phônēn hikanou* (!), cf. Field, ibid., p. 771, and n. 64: *šdy* equated with *dy*. Cf. *B. Ḥagigah* 12a (Resh Laqish).

adapted to the sound of their wings *en to poreuesthai auta hōs phōnēn hudatos pollou.*

The Targum similarly, on 43:2, creates a buffer expression: "And behold, the glory [*yqr*] of the God of Israel was revealed [*'tgly*] from the way [direction] of the east and *the sound of those who praise His name* [*mbrky šmyh*] [was] like the sound of many waters"; no less in 1:24: "I heard the sound of their wings like the sound of many waters, like the sound *from before Shaddai*,[16] as they walk about, the sound of *what they utter as they*" *praise God* is like the sound of the camp of the angels on high, and so forth.

God's voice, of course, travels from one end of the world to the other. It did so, for example, at the Revelation.[17] But other sounds or voices do the same— for example, the sun in its revolution, the tumult of the city (of Rome), the sound of the soul when it leaves the body; some say also (the cry) at childbirth, and still others say the sound of Ridya.[18] Nor is it only sounds that may be said to travel "from one end of the world to the other." When Adam was created, "his soulless lump was laid out from one end of the world to the other."[19] One of the ways in which demons resemble the ministering angels is that they travel from one end of the world to the other.[20] Not only Moses but the righteous can see from one end of the world to the other.[21] And many other examples are to be found in a variety of contexts. In other words, "from one end of the world to the other" is a cliché adopted to express the superlative, the extreme, the uttermost. Legend cheerfully appropriates it because legend is thereby spared the trouble of inventing fresh figures of speech each time a wonder is to be recorded. The hyperbole is so natural indeed that the pedantry of documentation is almost superfluous. There is nothing extraordinary, then, in a statement that Gabriel's voice carried from one end of the world to the other.

But what in the Ezek. 43:2 verse suggests that the voice or sound[22] of many waters is a reference to *Gabriel*? There is a tradition that Gabriel brings astonishing and good tidings.[23] Muslims may say that Gabriel brought on the choking in the Prophet as the beginning of Revelation.[24] The mystics will

16. Cf. David Qimhi on Ezek. 43:2, *Miqraot Gedolot* (Warsaw, 1865), and see also Zohar (Wilna, 1930), 1: 71b, on "'like the voice of Shaddai,' which never grows silent."

17. *Sifre Deuteronomy* 343, ed. L. Finkelstein (Berlin, 1939), p. 399.

18. *B. Yoma* 20b–21a. On Ridya, cf. Rashi on this passage, and M. Jastrow, *Dictionary* (New York-Berlin, 1926), s.v. "Ridya," On A. Kohut, *Aruch completum* (New York, 1955), 7: 257–58, cf. 9: 38 1b, s.v. *"radayya."*

19. Version B of ARN, ed. Schechter, p. 11b; Saldarini, ARN, p. 76, n. 10.

20. Version A of ARN, ed. Schechter, p. 55a.

21. *Sifre Numbers* 136, ed. S. Horovitz (Jerusalem, 1966), p. 182.

22. "*Qwl*," the same word for both. On the name Gabriel, cf. H. L. Ginsberg, *Studies in Daniel* (New York, 1948), p. 81, n. 22. Note in ARN not just "Gabriel" but "the angel Gabriel."

23. Luke 1:18ff. For the gnostic notion in Pistis-Sophia, cf. J. Doresse, *Secret Books of the Egyptian Gnostics* (London, 1960), p. 113, n. 116.

24. Ibn Khaldŭn, *The Muqaddimah*, trans. F. Rosenthal (Princeton, 1967), 1: 201f., p. 261, n. 34.

associate gold with Gabriel, and he is appointed messenger for this world.[25] Gabriel's outcry, as he is struck under his wings, can set cocks crowing at midnight.[26] Some men will say that a seventeenth-century messiah, to escape being taken prisoner, ascended to heaven and that Gabriel had assumed his form.[27] Much more is included from earliest times in the lore about Gabriel,[28] but still no word about Gabriel and "the sound of many waters" (whose sound God's voice surpasses), at least not in earlier sources. Where does this association come from?

It seems to me that Version A of *Abot de-Rabbi Natan* has preserved for us a [3] midrash in the form of numerical equation, *gematria*; for the Hebrew consonants of "many waters," *m-y-m* (40-10-40) *r-b-y-m* (200-2-10-40) add up to the sum as "the angel Gabriel," *g-b-r-y-'-l* (3-2-200-10-1-30) *h-m-l-'-k* (5-40-30-1-20), to wit, 342. (In Scripture the order of the words is, first *we-ha-ish*, then "Gabriel.") "Many waters" in the verse, therefore, equals "the angel Gabriel."

Interpretation by means of *gematria* may sometimes be playful[29] but not necessarily so; nor need it be late, nor is it limited to rabbinic exegesis.[30] Nor is it likely to come from unmotivated reading of the biblical text. By this last sentence I mean the following: It seems to me that in connection with Ezek. 43:2 there was a (mystical? Merkabah?) tradition that "the sound of many waters" referred to Gabriel and that the *gematria* substantiated it, not the other way around, that *gematria* exercises per se put the angel Gabriel into the verse arbitrarily or by chance.[31] Of course it is impossible to say definitely which came first (verse interpreted by *gematria* leading to discovery of Gabriel, or thoughts about Gabriel leading to discovery of him in the verse by means of *gematria*), or if there is such a thing as first and second with a Bible reader, particularly with a reader of Ezekiel's visions.[32] There was the text and there

---

25. *Zohar* 2: 147a–b; 2: 23 1a.

26. G. Scholem, *On the Kabbalah and Its Symbolism* (New York, 1965), p. 147.

27. G. Scholem, *Sabbatai Sevi* (Princeton, 1973), p. 605. Long before that there was the notion that Gabriel could assume different guises; cf. L. Ginzberg, *Legends of the Jews* (Philadelphia, 1909–38), vol. 5, p. 423, n. 146, vol. 6, p. 34, n. 195. See also E. Rohde's reference to the Boccaccio story, in *Psyche* (New York, 1966), 1: 155, n. 134. For Gabriel on the right hand of a scholar with unchaste intentions, cf. *Seder Eliyahu Rabba*, ed. M. Friedmann (Jerusalem, 1960), Additions, p. 39.

28. See, for example, B. Cohen's *Index* to Ginzberg's *Legends*, vol. 7, pp. 172–74, or the material assembled by Billerbeck in his *Kommentar zum Neun Testament* (Munich, 1924), 2: 89–97. Cf. Rashi on Gen. 37:15. Doresse, *Secret Books*, pp. 233–34, refers to an unpublished ninth-century text, "The Investiture of the Archangel Gabriel," in which Gabriel is first in a series of angels. Gabriel is an extraordinary polyglot and even Aramaic is not beyond him: B. *Sotah* 33a and 36b (bottom).

29. "Enter wine [*y-y-n* = 70], exit secret [*s-w-d* = 70]," B. *Sanhedrin* 38a.

30. Cf. S. Lieberman, *Hellenism in Jewish Palestine* (New York, 1962), pp. 69, 72f. See also C. B. Welles on a first-century Gen. codex fragment in *Yale University Library Gazette*, 39 (1964), p. 8.

31. In other words, it does not seem to me that the mention of Gabriel is accidental and that all the statement means is "any angel."

32. The expression "many waters" occurs more frequently in Ezekiel (about 11 times) than in any other biblical book. The next in frequency is Psalms (6 times).

were traditions of interpretation,[33] and one found elements in the text that supported a particular interpretation which was part of a much larger frame of speculations and references already favored.

And having recognized how "the sound of many waters" refers to Gabriel, perhaps the following speculation may be allowed. Until Rabbi Isaac had publicly preached that the light which illuminated the world on the first day of Creation (*fiat lux*) came from the robe (*stolē*)[34] with which the Holy One, blessed be He, covered Himself, Rabbi Berekiah (fourth century c.e.)[35] taught (in the name of Rabbi Isaac)[36] that Ezekiel's words, "and the earth did shine with His Glory," referred to the site of the Temple, that is, that the light came from there (*kabod*, glory = Temple).[37] Doubtless because of views to the contrary, Rabbi Berekiah was surely *underscoring* that from Ezekiel's words one could learn at least that the Temple site was still charged with divine sanctity. The statement is not pointless.

Similarly, the second part of our brief midrash may be emphasizing more than is at first self-evident. "'And the earth did shine with His glory' refers to the presence of the Shekinah," or, to render with a literalness indifferent to the requirements of literary translation, "'And the earth lit up from His glory [*doxa*]' refers to the presence [the face] of the Shekinah [*pne Ha-Shekinah*]." The expression "*pne* Shekinah" is not uncommon and appears in a number of hortatory statements.[38] The *Mekilta* declares that whoever welcomes "the face of the sages is as though he welcomes '*pne* Shekinah.'"[39] In the age to come, Rabbi Simeon ben Yohai says, the righteous will welcome (greet) "*pne* Shekinah."[40] According to Rabbi Meir, one who carries out the *ṣiṣit* commandment (Num. 15:37–41) is accounted, regarded, as though he had welcomed "*pne* Shekinah."[41] This is not to imply that the expression "*pne* Shekinah" is to be taken lightly because of its relative frequency; [4] however, it is to imply that there was apparently no excessive hesistancy about using it for purposes of exhortation and promise of reward.

For the remainder let us confine our discussion when possible to *Abot de-Rabbi Natan*. Version A is prepared to speak of "the splendor of *the* Shekinah

33. Cf. above, nn. 14–16.

34. With the reading of *Pesiqta Kahana*, ed. B. Mandelbaum (New York, 1962), p. 323, cf. *M. Gittin* 7.5.

35. Cf. H. L. Strack, *Introduction to the Talmud and Midrash* (Philadelphia, 1931), pp. 131 and 324, n. 5.

36. So too *Gen. R.*, Vatican, Hebrew MS 60. Cf. next note.

37. See *Gen. R.* 3.4, ed. J. Theodor and Ch. Albeck (Berlin, 1912–27), p. 20; *Lev. R.* 31.7, ed. M. Margulies (Jerusalem, 1953–60), p. 726; *Pesiqta Kahana*, ed. Mandelbaum, p. 324. On the conception of the presence of Shekinah in the first Temple only ("only in the tents of Shem"), cf. *Gen. R.* 36.8, p. 342, and Ginzberg, *Legends*, 5: 193 (top); L. Ginzberg, *Commentary on the Palestinian Talmud* (New York, 1941), 3: 396–97.

38. For a number of references in the Babylonian Talmud, cf. Ch. J. and B. Kasowski's *Talmud Concordance* (Jerusalem, 1972), 31: 247, s.v., "*pny škynh.*"

39. *Mekilta, Amalek* 3, 2: 178 (for the reading "sages," cf. S. Lieberman, *Hayerushalmi Kipshuto* [Jerusalem, 1934], p. 291; S. Lieberman in *Kirjath Sepher* 12 [1935–36], 62).

40. *Sifre Deut.* 47, p. 105.

41. *Sifre Num.* 115, p. 126.

[*zyw Hškynh*],"[42] which the righteous will enjoy in the future, of "the wings of *the* Shekinah [*knpy Hškynh*]"[43] that shelter proselytes; otherwise, "Shekinah" without the definite article.[44] Version B talks of *the* Shekinah (but immediately thereafter, of the Holy One, blessed be He) making the rounds,[45] of *the* Shekinah being revealed.[46] But "the face of *the* Shekinah" seems to be if not unique, extremely rare. It is most likely a very bold expression, and it too is almost certainly not pointless.

God's voice was more powerful than Gabriel's, and God's *doxa*, we are told, refers to the *face* of *the* Shekinah. Does this mean no more than that while the first clause (sound) refers to Gabriel, the second (light) refers to God Himself? Or does this mean that the light which Ezekiel beheld in his vision as lighting up the earth was stronger, brighter, than that of the prince of fire?[47] Were there those who thought that the light which Ezekiel beheld did not come from the Shekinah but came from a lesser source?

---

42. Italics mine. There is also "the light [*ma'or*] of the Shekinah" in *Sifre Num.* 41, p. 44; cf. *Sifre Zuta*, ed. Horovitz, in the same volume, pp. 247, 248, and note also *Midrash ha-Gadol, Num.*, ed. S. Fisch (London, 1957–63), 1: 156 and 154, and n. 180 ibid. In *Pesiqta Kahana*, ed. Mandelbaum, p. 4, we read that not even the chamber behind the Holy of Holies (cf. Lieberman, *Hellenism in Jewish Palestine*, p. 172), "no place is void of the Shekinah." [Note ibid., lines 12 and 13, *zyw hškynh*.]

43. Version A of ARN, ed. Schechter, p. 27a; italics mine. For the reading *gpy hškynh* in Version B, p. 26a (bottom), cf. S. Lieberman, *Tosefta Ki-Fshutah, Sotah* (New York, 1973), pp. 651f. For "under the wings of heaven [*knpy šmym*]," see, for example, Version B of ARN, ed. Schechter, p. 27a-b (according to Schechter, p. 85b, the reading of Parma MS for 27b, line 11, is *knpy hmqwm*).

44. For example, greeting *pne Shekinah* in the Temple during the pilgrimage festivals (ibid., Version A, p. 28a); the equal of Shekinah (43a); ten descents and ascents of Shekinah (51b); etc. Once (Rabbi Tarfon, 23a), "His Shekinah." Ditto, anonymously, 53a.

45. Ibid., p. 28a; note also p. 20b.

46. Ibid., p. 37b. On the "great sight [vision = revelation of Shekinah]," cf. *Passover Haggadah*, ed. E. D. Goldschmidt (Jerusalem, 1960), p. 46. All these examples are representative, not complete.

47. Cf. *B. Yoma* 21b (and Rashi, s.v., "*dgbry'l*," as well as the "early commentary" in B. M. Lewin, *Otzar ha-Gaonim* (Jerusalem, 1934), 6: 84, bottom, and Ginzberg, *Legends*, 6: 202, n. 105; see also how Albo, *Ikkarim* 4:16 (4: 147), discusses this. On Gabriel as "herald of light," *Legends*, 5: 70. Was it Gabriel who came to the rescue of Tamar (*B. Sotah* 10b) because she was about to be cast into fire (Gen. 38:24)? (But in the *Targums Jonathan and Yerushalmi* and *Neofiti*, Michael.) Shekinah is "fire that consumes fire": *B. Yoma* 21b.

On Honi the Circle-Maker:
A Demanding Prayer

[233] One spring in the latter half of the month Adar,[1] some time after the death[2] of Salome Alexandra (76–67 B.C.E.), "there was a certain Onias, who, being a righteous man and dear to God, . . . in a rainless period prayed to God ($\eta \check{v}\xi \alpha \tau o\ \tau \hat{\omega}\ \Theta \epsilon \hat{\omega}$) to end the drought, and God . . . heard his prayer and sent rain . . . ."[3] The story of Honi (Onias), so plainly told by Josephus, is reported much more dramatically in the talmudic sources.[4] According to one source,[5] the drought had lasted three years. As the story is reported in the Mishnah (Taanit 3:8) and in the Baraita cited by the Talmud (23a),[6] after Honi prayed and no rains came, he "drew a circle, stood inside it, and said before Him: 'Master of the universe, Thy children look upon me as though I were a member of Thy household.[7] I swear by Thy great Name that I shall not stir from here until Thou hast compassion on Thy children.'" The rains came, at first not quite as they should, but eventually in the right amounts, just as Honi asked for them.

---

1. See B. Taanit 23a.

2. Ibid., and cf. J. Derenbourg, *Essai sur l'histoire et la géographie de la Palestine* (Paris, 1867), pp. 112f.

3. Josephus, Antiquities, XIV, 22 (Loeb, VII, 459f., R. Marcus's trans.).

4. See the references in B. Taanit 19a in the edition of H. Malter (N.Y., 1930), p. 73, col. b, and cf. the variants and comments in his notes ibid., and 23a, pp. 96–98. In addition to the references supplied by Malter, cf. Tanhuma Ki Tabo 4 and Gaster, *Exempla* (London-Leipzig, 1924), p. 164, no. 422.

5. Megillat Taanit, ed. Lichtenstein, p. 92, HUCA, VIII–IX (1931–32), p. 348.

6. See also the Palestinian Talmud, J. Taanit III, 66d.

7. On the expression "member of household," *ben bayyit*, see A. Büchler, *Types of Jewish-Palestinian Piety* (London, 1922), p. 203, n. 1; E. Z. Melammed in *Leshonenu*, XX (5716 [1956]), pp. 110–11; recently W. F. Albright in BASOR, no. 163 (Oct. 1961), p. 47, and notes 54–56; but above all H. L. Ginsberg, *Koheleth* (Tel Aviv-Jerusalem, 1961), p. 68, commentary to v. 7.

The performance was notably an impressive one, as the talmudic sources underscore. Indeed, a leading Sage even resented Honi's imperious tone of voice and conduct: had it been anyone other than Honi, excommunication would have been in order.

It has been customary to explain the strange act of Honi's circle-drawing as a magical act by means of which the magician cut out for himself, as it were, a precinct over which demonic spirits could have no influence;[8] and in 1955 I, too, adopted this explanation. But it no [234] longer seems to me correct.[9] If we approach the story as it is told in the talmudic sources without any preconceptions, what is it that it states? That Honi drew a circle, stood inside it, and spoke in imperious language to his God: I swear that I shan't stir from here until you grant me what I ask for! When the rainfall was unsatisfactory, Honi continued in the same demanding tone of voice until he got what he wanted. And the Sage, Simeon ben Shetah, who rebuked him, similarly, did not accuse Honi of resorting to magical stunts, but of behaving like a favorite child, father's pet, who can wheedle out of his father whatever he wants.[10] Honi's behavior is in fact regarded by the Talmud in another connection[11] as an example of arrogance towards Heaven (megis daato kelappe maalah).

The drawing of the circle seems to me best explained in terms of an account of a historical incident; this explanation, I now find, was already suggested by

8. Thus, for instance, J. Trachtenberg, *Jewish Magic and Superstition* (N.Y., 1939), p. 121: "The circle is another ancient and universal magical symbol. The invocation of demons is a dangerous business, and the magician must take steps to protect himself in the event that his spirit adjutants get out of hand. What simpler or more obvious device than to exclude them from his immediate environment? 'Those who invoke demons draw circles around themselves because the spirits have not the power to trespass from the public to a private area,' explained Menahem Ziyuni. By this magic act the ground and atmosphere surrounding the magician become a private, forbidden precinct. One of the most picturesque of ancient Jewish miracleworkers was Honi *Ha-Meagel* (first century B.C.E.), whose penchant for standing within a circle while he called down rain from heaven won him his title, 'the circle-drawer.'" See also the note ibid.

9. J. Goldin, *The Fathers According to Rabbi Nathan* (New Haven, 1955), p. 187, n. 25. Note also S. Daiches, *Babylonian Oil Magic in the Talmud and in the Later Jewish Literature* (London, 1913), p. 33: "That the 'circle' was an important element in the [magical] ceremony we also see from the fact that the miracle-worker Honi mentioned in Talmud Babli, Taanit 19a and 23aff., was called *meaggel*, 'the circle maker,' after the circle which he used to make and in the midst of which he used to stand when he adjured God to grant his request and to cause rain to fall. Honi's actions showed a curious blend of pure monotheistic belief and faith in the efficacy of magic (see also Blau, *Das altjüdische Zauberwesen*, p. 33)." Frazer's discussion of the magical control of rain has nothing relevant to our story; see further below, n. 12, for Büchler's comment. On rain-making see also recently J. A. Bellamy, *Kitāb ar-Rumūz*, in JAOS, LXXXI (1961), pp. 230ff., and notes ad loc.

10. Cf. the idiom in M. Taanit and Talmud ad loc., and the commentators on *mithate*. The view that Honi was an Essene, pressed by K. Kohler and others, is utterly gratuitous, as is amply demonstrated by Büchler, op. cit., pp. 199ff., 246ff.

11. B. Berakot 19a. Moreover, see Büchler, op. cit., p. 201, n. 2 for a tradition that *meaggel* may reflect a place name and not refer to circle-drawing—this tradition is not to be dismissed cavalierly: whatever else one may say, ʿwg and ʿgl are not the same root.

Büchler[12] in 1922, and I had overlooked it. In [235] the summer of 168 B.C.E.,[13] Antiochus IV undertook a second expedition against Egypt; he had every expectation of success, but this time the Romans had apparently decided to interfere: they dispatched a senatorial decree ordering him to abandon his schemes against Egypt. Polybius (XXIX, 27)[14] writes:

> But when the king, after reading it, said he would like to communicate with his friends about this intelligence, Popilius acted in a manner which was thought to be offensive and exceedingly arrogant ($\tau\epsilon\lambda\dot\epsilon\omega\varsigma\;\dot\upsilon\pi\epsilon\rho\dot\eta\phi\alpha\nu\omicron\nu$). He was carrying a stick cut from a vine, and with this he drew a circle around Antiochus and told him he must remain inside this circle until he gave his decision about the contents of the letter. The king was astonished at this authoritative proceeding ($\tau\dot\eta\nu\;\dot\upsilon\pi\epsilon\rho\omicron\chi\dot\eta\nu$), but after a few moments' hesitation, said he would do all that the Romans demanded.

This story seems to have made a profound impression on a number of writers, for it is frequently retold.[15] This was a dramatic, perhaps sensational, example of peremptoriness. Of course Honi cannot draw a circle around his God and say to Him $\dot\epsilon\nu\tau\alpha\hat\upsilon\theta\alpha\;\beta\omicron\upsilon\lambda\epsilon\dot\upsilon\omicron\upsilon$ (Appian). Honi draws the circle round himself and then makes his demand.[16]

---

12. In a footnote, op. cit., p. 247 (end of n. 2, p. 246): "A comparison of Honi's method with the various magical and other practices all over the world for obtaining rains, in Frazer, *Golden Bough*[3], I, I, 247–311, and Hastings, *Encyclopaedia of Religion and Ethics*, X (1918), 562–5, shows that Honi applied none of them, nor any magic at all; for even the circle which he drew and which reminds us of the circle drawn by Popilius Laenas round Antiochus IV Epiphanes in Egypt (Livy, XLV, 12; Schürer, *Geschichte*, I[3], 197), has nothing in common with the magical circle drawn by the conjurer for his own protection from the ghost (Hastings, *Encyclopaedia of Religion*, VIII, 321ff.)." But Büchler's subsequent statement (p. 254) that "The apparent presumption of Honi . . . is not in agreement with general Jewish principles, and reminds one of the methods of a magician or a heathen priest in praying for rain," is virtually a retreat from his earlier observation, and the sources do not support the statement that what Honi did is not in agreement with Jewish principles. See further n. 16 below. Other points discussed in the body of the present paper are not referred to at all by Büchler.

13. Cf. E. Bickermann, *Der Gott der Makkabäer* (Berlin, 1937), pp. 13 and 162.

14. Loeb VI, 90f., W. R. Paton's trans.

15. See the references cited by Schürer, *Geschichte*, I[4], 197, n. 33 and add Plutarch, *Moralia*, 202 F; cf. F. W. Walbank, *A Historical Commentary on Polybius* (Oxford, 1957), p. 217: "In fact, the ultimatum delivered by C. Popilius Laenas to Antiochus Epiphanes in 168 . . . was both sensational in itself and catastrophic in its result."

16. Examples of "demanding prayer" are not wanting in midrashic literature. First, note Midrash Psalms 77:1 (ed. Buber, 172a), where it is said of the prophet Habakkuk that he "drew the figure (of a circle)" — *ṣr ṣwrh*, a play on the word *mṣwr* of Hab. 2:I — "and standing inside it said before the Holy One, blessed be He: 'I shall not stir from here until Thou hast told me how long Thou wilt be long-suffering with the wicked in this world'"; cf. also op. cit., 7:17, 36a, for the same idiom. Second, the Midrash also speaks of a special talent enjoyed by some in prayer: they know how to present their petitions cleverly, and so are not refused whatever they ask for; cf. Leviticus Rabbah 5:8, ed. Margulies, pp. 122ff. and references ad loc. In B. Berakot 34b Rabban Yohanan ben Zakkai is reported as acknowledging that he would not have been able to prevail in prayer (during his child's illness), whereas his disciple Hanina ben Dosa could: "for the latter is like the king's servant" (Rashi: enjoying entree to the king at all times), "whereas I am like the king's officer" (and hence can be admitted only by appointment, and therefore am not on such intimate terms with the monarch).

334 : Thematic Studies

[236] To students of classical Hebrew the clause "drew a circle and stood inside it" (another very like it)[17] is a familiar one, though it is far from common in talmudic-midrashic sources. Now, it is an interesting thing that in these sources the peremptory note involved in drawing a circle and ordering God to do something occurs only when the speaker, like Honi, is not making some request for himself,[18] but is demanding *in behalf of someone else who is in straits*. Thus, in addition to the Honi story, we have a description of how Moses interceded in behalf of Miriam:[19] Aaron pleads with Moses, Shall we let our sister perish? "Thereupon Moses drew a small [!] circle and stood within it, and beseeched mercy in her behalf, saying, 'I shall not stir from here until Miriam my sister is healed.' As it is said, 'Heal her *now*, O God, I beseech Thee'" (Num. 12:13).[20]

And, therefore, in Deuteronomy Rabbah 11:10, where Moses is pleading for his own sake, pleading to be admitted into the Promised Land, the reading "and he drew a small circle and stood within it" is definitely wrong: the fact is that the clause does not occur in the Midrash Petirat Mosheh (Midrash on the Death of Moses),[21] to which the whole text of that midrash in Deuteronomy Rabbah is closely related.[22]

In turn we can now understand the expression, "I shall not stir from here." It means simply: *immediately*; that is, I demand to be answered, or, I demand that my request be granted at once, on the spot. Naturally, it is a very apt expression in a scene of drawing a circle and speaking while standing inside it. But the expression can occur even in contexts where no circles or circle drawings are spoken of. Thus, for example, we read:[23] "If a man transgressed a positive commandment and repented, he is forgiven on the spot, before he has so much as stirred from his place."[24] Or again: "Rabbi Eliezer son of Rabbi Yose says: [237] If one sins and repents and continues [!] uprightly, he is forgiven before he stirs from the spot."[25]

Regardless, therefore, of what the act of circle-drawing came to mean to

17. Cf. the Midrash Psalms reference in the preceding note.

18. And perhaps Popilius, too, dared to act so arrogantly because he was representing not merely himself. See indeed Polybius's own reflection on Popilius's neglecting the conventional sign of friendship.

19. Abot de-Rabbi Natan, ed. Schechter, p. 41; see p. 156, where the clause "and beseeched mercy in her behalf" is omitted (!, as understandable) and Schechter's note 28, p. 41.

20. Goldin, op. cit., pp. 55f. On the conception of prayer in behalf of another, see also Midrash Psalms 2:2, 13a.

21. Bet Hamidrash, ed. Jellinek, I, 120, which reads: "and stood up (= began) to pray, and said, I shall not stir," etc.

22. And therefore L. Ginzberg, *Legends*, III, 418 is to be corrected accordingly.

23. Abot de-Rabbi Natan, XXIX, p. 88 (my trans., p. 122, top).

24. Lit., "he does not (= shall not) stir from there until they forgive him at once." The identical idiom in Mekilta Bahodesh, VII, ed. Lauterbach, II, 250, except for the last word, "at once," *miyyad* (which does not occur in ed. Horovitz-Rabin, p. 228, either), and in all essentials in *all* the parallel passages (see Lauterbach's references).

25. Abot de-Rabbi Natan, XL, p. 120 (my trans., p. 164). See also Leviticus Rabbah 19:6, p. 439, and cf. B. Sanhedrin 14a on the death of Judah ben Baba.

post-talmudic writers in mediaeval times,[26] in the story of Honi there is no trace of thaumaturgy. Josephus described him accurately, as he was thought of by the earliest generations, δίκαιος ἀνὴρ καὶ θεοφιλής — and therefore worthy of having a miracle performed for his sake, as were the three youths, "the relatives of Daniel," who were δικαίους καὶ θεοφιλεῖς.[27]

26. Cf. Trachtenberg, loc. cit., and G. Scholem, *Gnosticism*, p. 109, line 1.
27. Josephus, Antiquities, X, 215.

The Magic of Magic and Superstition

[115] By the magic of magic and superstition I mean their astonishing persistence, and universal diffusion, and success.[1] A thirteenth floor between the twelfth and fourteenth in fashionable twentieth-century American high-rise apartment houses would be a refreshing discovery. That magic is everywhere, the anthropologists and scholars of comparative cultures and civilizations have documented. That it succeeds does not mean that every time a spell is whispered the wished-for result is obtained, despite the promise by the magus. But then, neither is the outcome of every surgical operation successful. By the success of magic is meant simply that very many insist on believing in it,[2] and that even those who may have some doubts about it wonder periodically: "Maybe, maybe." There are so many examples, it is impossible to do justice to the subject; let us take two that are fairly well known.

The younger Pliny is in many ways a sensible person and a cultivated one. He writes a letter (VII, xvii, Loeb Classics 2.67–77) to his friend Sura for advice about spectres, "whether you believe they actually exist and have their own proper shapes and a measure of divinity, or are only the false impressions of a terrified imagination."

---

1. For the purposes of this paper, I think little is to be gained by distinguishing and classifying the different forms of magic and superstition, such as oaths, divination, astrology charms, amulets, etc. They all share a belief in the efficacy of the object or act or the recital in compelling supernatural forces to perform in some desired way if the act or recitation is carried out properly.

2. Philostratus, *Life of Apollonius* 7.39 (LC, II, 259): "Nor does any amount of failure in their [i.e., the athletes', the simple-minded people's] enterprises shake their faith in it, they merely say such things as this: 'If I had only offered this sacrifice or that, if I had only burnt that perfume in place of another, I should not have failed to win.' And they really believe what they say." But see also M. Nilsson, *Greek Piety* (Oxford: Clarendon Press, 1948), pp. 169f.

The letter, Pliny goes on to say, is prompted by three circumstances: (1) by the story he heard of what overtook [116] one Curtius Rufus as the figure of a woman had foretold; (2) by what was related to him about Athenodorous the philosopher in an ill-reputed house in Athens; and (3) finally, by what he can himself affirm of one of his own freed-men and slave boys who had their hair cut off by apparitions.

Nothing in the letter is hysterical or panicky. Pliny simply wants to know. "And though," Pliny ends his letter, "you should after your manner, argue on both sides"—this by the way is itself instructive: it's possible to argue on both sides of the question—"yet," Pliny says, "I hope you will throw your weightiest reasons into one scale, lest you should dismiss me in suspense and uncertainty, whereas I consult you on purpose to determine my doubts."

Remove my doubts, says Pliny, for he is ready to believe, one way or the other, but does not dismiss the possibility that there are spectres. That's the whole point of the letter.

Let us look at another example, a different kind of puzzled belief: After Pentecost of 164 B.C.E. (so it seems), Judah Maccabee's forces engaged Gorgias, the governor of Jamnia, in battle and ran into difficulties: "and it came to pass that a few of the Jews fell" (2 Macc. 12:34). When subsequently the Jews rested and went to recover the corpses of the slain to bury them properly, "they discovered under the shirts of every one of the dead men amulets of the idols of Jamnia—a practice," adds the author of 2 Maccabees (12:39; or is he quoting Jason of Cyrene?), "forbidden Jews by law. All saw at once that this was why they had perished," and so forth. Who were these Jews wearing amulets of the idols of Jamnia? The Hellenizers, as fifth columnists? The author of 2 Maccabees would not have suppressed this fact. On the contrary, these were loyal Partisans of Judah's army, Zealots of the Law, risking their lives for the Torah and Temple of the God of Israel! Yet under their shirts are idolatrous amulets.[3] They, too, very likely belong to the Maybe Maybe tribe, a numerous tribe historically.

[117] Belief, or wonder about the plausibility of belief as in magic, is pervasive because fear and desire, and fantasy which is the product of these, are permanent: fear of sickness, of an enemy, possibly of a business competitor,[4] of bureaucracy, of the dangers of childbirth, of the day of death, or death in battle, of uncertainties of the harvest, of removal of your crops by neighbors,[5] of wild beasts and floods, of the effects of the evil eye;[6] desire to win

---

3. Cf. W.O.E. Oesterley in R. H. Charles, *Apocrypha and Pseudepigrapha*, I (Oxford: Clarendon Press, 1913), 1 Macc. 5:67 and J. Moffatt in 2 Macc. ad loc. Did they wear amulets of the idols of Jamnia because such would prevail over the hosts of the governor of Jamnia? Or were there hucksters in the neighborhood selling Jamnia amulets? On the conjunction, by the way, of Temple and Torah, cf. the charge against Stephen in Acts 6:13.

4. Cf. Razim, 93, n. 16, and this may well be the intent behind "capsize a ship," 69.

5. A. D. Nock, *Essays on Religion and the Ancient World*, ed. Z. Stewart (Oxford: Clarendon, 1972), I, 316.

6. See Fragment 17, verso, *Fragmenta Hebraica Cairensia Talmudica*, II, Westminster

at the horse races, to know the future, to win the favor of officials or the favor of a woman (prominent, rich or beautiful), to gain admission to kings and judges, to consult the stars or ghosts (as did Saul) or spirits, or to know the meaning of your dreams, to disturb your enemy's sleep, to heat up a stove in the cold, to overcome magical spells against you, to assist your friend, to put down fire in the bath-house, to behold Helios "who informs you whether the man lying sick will live or die."[7] And there are "initiatives" (*katarchai*) like, Will a son about to be born have a big nose?[8]

This list of fears and desires can be multiplied and diversified,[9] and for all of them there are concrete prescriptions. These prescriptions, in fact, add to the sense of mystery which surrounds the whole business of magic. Far from making the belief grotesque, the mystery encourages it. And no one is altogether unaffected by it.

For self-protection, and to reduce the amounts of confusion and disorderly conduct within society, the authorities do well to draw up lists of the forbidden and the not-forbidden. In talmudic literature there is a list like that. Items: *mi-darke ha-Emori*, of the Ways of the Amorites; items: not *mi-darke ha-Emori*, not regarded as superstitious Amorite acts. Already the author of Jubilees (29:11) speaks of Amorites as "wicked and sinful, and there is no people today which has wrought to the full all their sins."[10] Why one should speak of the ways of the Amorites rather than of the ways of the Canaanites, for example, I still do not understand, despite Jubilees. Or is *Emori* (Amorite) a deliberate "metathesis" for *Romai* (Roman)? At all events, in the Tosefta an (incomplete) list of [118] forbidden superstitions and magical practices called "Of the Ways of the Amorites" is conveniently drawn up.[11]

To begin with, these are not really Jewish magic at all, that is to say, there is hardly anything ethnic about the practices (though ethnic touches may be added) any more than you could attach their invention to any particular

College (Cambridge): "To overcome fear of the evil eye, take the eye of a wolf, let it dry, put it in a garment or inside a skin [pouch] and wear it around your [neck?]. Then so long as you wear it, you'll have no fear of the evil eye or sorcery. In whatever you turn to you'll succeed. Your enemies also will fall under [=be defeated by] you. You'll fear neither demons nor plague and you'll find favor in the sight of all." Cf. H. L. Strack and P. Billerbeck, *Kommentar zum Neuen Testament aus Talmud und Midrasch* (Munich: Beck, 1922–28) on Acts 13:9b, pp. 713–715; R. Yose be-R. Haninah in Gen. Rabba 56:11, p. 611, on Abraham and Isaac, and Theodor's citations ad loc.

7. Unless otherwise noted, all examples are from Razim.

8. F. Cumont, *Oriental Religions in Roman Paganism* (New York: Dover Publications, 1956), 165.

9. Note also Nock, *Essays on Religion*, I, 191.

10. On views of the Amorites cf. the statements by R. Yose and Rabban Simeon ben Gamaliel in T. Shabbat 7:23, 25. On the association of Amorites with fornication, cf. Testament of Judah, 12:2. Note, too, the combination of fornication, stealing, magic, etc., in Didache 2:2. My suggestion of "metathesis" is of course conjectural only. See J. H. Levy, *Olamot Nifgashim* (Jerusalem, 1960), 67.

11. T. Shabbat, ed. S. Lieberman, chaps. 6–7, pp. 22–29.

nationality.[12] They are practices, however, current among Jews; and if you will consult Heinrich Lewy's translation and comments in the *Zeitschrift des Vereins für Volkskunde* for 1893, Ludwig Blau's *Das altjüdische Zauberwesen* (Strassburg, 1898), Saul Lieberman's *Greek in Jewish Palestine* (New York, 1942), pages 97 and following, and above all his commentary on the Tosefta (*Tosefta Ki-Fshutah, Shabbat* [New York, 1962], where he supplies our first two and still other references), you will immediately be brought into contact with identical and virtually identical data from the Hellenistic and Roman worlds and even the world of the Middle Ages. To exclaim "Gesundheit" when someone sneezes is apparently dangerous in several cultures.[13] A cock crowing in the evening or at the wrong time is a bad sign for Trimalchio no less than for superstitious Jews.[14] And so it goes, and there is nothing unexpected or striking about this.

What does call attention to itself and may create perplexity is the seemingly utter arbitrariness of the *reaction* to the practices. For example:

Tie a red string around your finger—that's Amorite behavior. (Lewy has already shown that this was widespread in the ancient world.) But later authorities, on the sensible principle that one is not to add to the original list of the *Darke ha-Emori* practices, do not forbid a red string around any other part of the body.[15] It is forbidden to say, "Leave a light on the ground to the discomfiture of the dead," but some post-talmudic teachers apparently have no objection to leaving a light on the floor at the entrance of the house so that the soul of the dead person might find its way back.[16] To throw an iron object into [119] the cemetery and call "Hada" (possibly like the "hic, hoc" pagan spell to which the elder Pliny refers)[17] is the way of the Amorites; on the other hand, to throw it there in order to nullify the actions of sorcerers is permitted—because you may defeat sorcery by sorcery (Satan cast out Satan?). Sympathetic magic is everywhere appealing. If a bone gets stuck in your throat, the Babylonian Talmud[18] tells us, put on top of your head a bone of similar kind and recite (with the bone in your throat?), "One [to?] one, down, swallow; swallow, down, one [to?] one." And this is *not* classified as Amorite practice. Fortunately, both Talmuds, the Palestinian and the Babylonian,[19] declare that whatever heals is not to be regarded as of *Darke ha-Emori*. But what heals, and how can you ever be sure? Professor Lieberman quotes a wise and beautiful observation by one of

---

12. They are encountered in a variety of and even antagonistic cultures.
13. TK, 94 and also n. 20. Note by the way, the "Tale of the Fuller's Wife" in Apuleius, *The Golden Ass*, IX.
14. TK, 85.
15. TK, 82.
16. TK, 83.
17. TK, 88.
18. Shabbat 67a; cf. T. Shabbat 7:21, TK, 102; P. Shabbat 6:9. On Aristides' dream of a bone stuck in his throat, and the cure for that, cf. A. J. Festugière, *Personal Religion among the Greeks* (Berkeley: University of California Press, 1960), p. 101f.
19. Loc. cit., in the names of different sages.

my favorite talmudic commentators, the Meiri of Perpignan[20] (thirteenth century, died 1315), that since in those times people had confidence in such practices (e.g., spells, incantations, popular remedies), they really would get better by resorting to these nostrums, and because they were accustomed to them, they truly helped them. Hence, allowable. The law permits you to wear outdoors on the Sabbath a tried and tested amulet—whose healing powers have been demonstrated once, twice, and thrice—even if you do not fear to be overtaken by serious illness.[21]

That we have difficulty arriving at the principle that divides the magical from the non-magical, the forbidden from the permitted or at least tolerated, is to be expected because frankly there are such wide gaps between the pieces of our knowledge of antiquity, and the vagaries of the human spirit are unpredictable. We must attempt at least a temporary suspension of disbelief and the ancients must be allowed their tastes. My point is, however, that many types of ambiguity are inherent in the response to magic, be the response cautious, or negative, or, for that matter, positive, and these ambiguities are in the minds of the ancients themselves. It is this I wish to underline.

[120] For even in pieties insulated (possibly) from magic and superstition, ambiguities may persist, and the most austere halakists can put up with the contradictory and the puzzling and the irrational ceremony with humble affirmation. Life itself being filled with ambiguities, how can pieties or impieties escape them?

Magic, however, pretends that it is more clear-minded and efficient; hence its demands for absolute precision of operations and accuracy in recitation, even if what is recited is unintelligible, and confident promises of fulfillment. Do this and that *will* follow, say the following and the outcome *will* be—so the magician declares with authority.[22]

Many obviously believe him—the rhetoric of confidence produces persuasion. Nevertheless, in response to magic shades and traces of ambiguity continue to hang on. For example:

According to the Palestinian Talmud,[23] Rabbi Yohanan is the authority for the rule that whatever (*kol she-hu*) heals does not fall under the heading of an "Amorite Way." Yet in the Mishnah it is stated that one who whispers charms over a wound and recites the verse (Exod. 15:26), "I will not bring upon you any of the diseases that I brought upon the Egyptians, for I the Lord am your healer," will have no share in the World to Come.[24] That's meant to convey

20. TK, 103f. and n. 63.
21. T. Shabbat 4:9, and cf. TK ad loc.
22. The language of piety is literal, but may be allowed to be metaphorical; the magician's vocabulary is expected to be strictly literal and precise. Yet the Establishment boasts that what it says is strictly true, but what the magician says is deliberately obscure and full of deceitful double entendres.
23. Shabbat 6:9; note the names in the Babylonian Talmud.
24. Sanhedrin 10:1. People may have preferred spells out of lack of confidence in the ordinary physicians; note even Philo *Special Laws* 1.25f. (LC, VII, 245f.)

quite a stiff penalty, as is obvious from the context of that whole Mishnah; and if Rabbi Aqiba, to whom the statement is attributed, is prepared to go to such lengths, it seems to me fair to say that (1) despite the great risk involved, this practice is noticeably widespread and perhaps out of control, and (2) that he must feel that such recitation is downright sacrilegious and blasphemous. I hasten to add that this particular bit of sorcery is *not* included in the list of *Darke ha-Emori*, maybe because the Amorites don't know Scripture![25] But apparently a current Jewish superstitious practice is reported and condemned strongly, though there must have been those who wondered why. In the Talmud[26] we are informed that you lose your share in the World to Come only if you spit as [121] you recite the verse, for[27] the offensive part is in the spitting. This must refer to imitation of the practice of heathen magi.[28] Other sages add indeed that the objection extends to the recitation of thoroughly innocuous verses. Not bibliomancy disturbs them therefore, but the act of spitting which accompanies it. But the distinction and prohibition do not put a halt to the practice, and rabbinic ingenuity is compelled to continue in latter centuries to find some ways of coming to terms with the practice.[29] People don't want to lose their share in the Future World, but they want to get well in this one.

Nowhere, it seems to me, is the internal perplexity over the phenomenon of magic more candidly—and hence movingly—displayed than in the following midrash,[30] which is reproduced in several midrashic compilations. Here we are not dealing at all with *Darke ha-Emori* but with the ritual of an explicit biblical command.

> A heathen once asked Rabban Yohanan ben Zakkai: These things you do [cf. Num. 19] appear like acts of witchcraft. You bring a [red] heifer, slaughter it, burn it, beat it down to a powder, then take the ashes; and if one of you is defiled by a dead body, you sprinkle two or three drops and say to him, You've been cleansed.
>
> Said Yohanan to the heathen, Has a demonic spirit[31] ever taken possession of you?

---

25. The rabbis don't hesitate, when it suits their purpose, to put biblical verses in the mouths of Gentiles; see, for example, J. Goldin, *The Song at the Sea* (New Haven: Yale, 1971), 116f. This is of course haggadic. Now note the anecdote in M. Abodah Zarah 3:4 (see also W. A. L. Elmslie in his edition [Cambridge: University Press, 1911], 47ff.) where a halakic problem is involved.

26. 101a in the name of R. Yohanan; in the Palestinian Talmud in the name of Rab. But see already Tosefta 12:10 (ed. Zuckermandel, p. 443). See the delightful anecdote about R. Meir in P. Sotah 1:4.

27. B. Shebuot 15b also.

28. Cf. Rashi in Sanhedrin 101a, s.v. *wbrwqq*; cf. the reference to Galen in J. Trachtenberg, *Jewish Magic and Superstition* (Cleveland: World Publishing Co., 1961), 120ff. and 293, n. 7. On the use of spittle see S. Eitrem, *Some Notes on the Demonology in the New Testament* (Oslo, 1966), 56ff.

29. See briefly Trachtenberg, p. 107 and Yoreh Deah 179:8.

30. PK, 74f. and cf. ibid. for references to parallels.

31. See I. Löw, *Flora der Juden* (Hildesheim: Ohlms, 1967), I, 92, n., *Wutanfall*, fit of rage. Cf. Preuss, *Biblisch-talmudische Medizin* (Berlin, 1911), 367, who speaks of "der Geist

The heathen replied, No.[32]

Yohanan said to him, Have you ever seen anyone possessed by a demonic spirit? Indeed, the heathen replied.

What do you do in such a case? Yohanan asked him.

The heathen said: We bring [certain] roots, [kindle them,] let the smoke rise under him; then we spray water on the [demonic] spirit and it flees.

Said Rabban Yohanan to him: Why don't your ears listen to what your own mouth is saying? That [demonic] spirit is a *spirit of uncleanness*, as it is written (Zech. 13:2), "And also I will remove from the land the prophets and the *unclean spirit*," etc. [Sprinkle water of lustration on the unclean person and the unclean spirit runs away.][33]

[122] When the heathen took off, Yohanan's disciples said to him: Master, him you could put off with a straw argument;[34] what have you to say to us, however?

Yohanan said to them: By your life![35] It is not the corpse that makes unclean, and it is not the waters that make clean. But this all is a decree of the Holy One, blessed be He. The Holy One, blessed be He, declared, I have proclaimed a statute,[36] I have decreed a decree, and you are not permitted to transgress what I have decreed. "This is the ritual law that the Lord has commanded" (Num. 19:1).

What honesty and pathos in this story. The heathen is of course right: the goings-on do resemble witchcraft, and when Yohanan compares the rite of cleansing one defiled by a corpse to the practice of expelling a demonic spirit familiar to the heathen, he, Yohanan, has only confirmed what the heathen said. If one is magic, why is the other not? Yohanan's disciples are right to be puzzled: Is this how one is to interpret a biblical ritual? Yohanan has given an answer in the end which does not make the ceremony intelligible. But it is an honest answer: what is the meaning of what we do, I do not know; but it's what God commanded.

Put in less awesome terms, what is magic and what is not, the authorities determine,[37] and what they declare as legitimate is what has come down as

thezazith." In MhG, Numbers (ed. Z.M. Rabinowitz, Jerusalem, 1967), 325, the editor explains it as spirit of madness, *shetuth*.

32. I think this is intended to suggest: here is a well-balanced man, not one with a sick mind. However, the meaning may also be: Have you ever had experience in these matters or are you simply being cantankerous and mocking with questions?

33. So the addition in *Numbers Rabba* 19:8. On the connection of the number seven with the "red heifer", cf. PK, 59. On the order "burn," "beat down" (*ktš*, but in Exod. 32:20 *thn*; note, however, Deut. 9:21, *ktt* and *thn*).

34. Literally, with a reed, but other sources read literally "with straw."

35. This is an oath, by the way; cf. S. Lieberman, *Greek in Jewish Palestine* (New York: Jewish Theological Seminary of America, 1942), 115f. and n. 2. See also M. Greenberg in *Journal of Biblical Literature* 76 (1957), 37, n. 18.

36. *Huqqah*, a commandment to be obeyed though no explanation for it is available. Though we do not have it, note that Philo apparently did have an allegorical explanation in mind. Cf. *Special Laws* 1.269 (LC, VII, 255, and note c).

37. The magician also calls what he does magic (of course not referring to himself as quack; cf. A. D. Nock, *Essays on Religion*, I, 309, 313); perhaps even prefers that his work be regarded as nonconformist or irregular, so that he may continue to fascinate clients. Cf. A. D. Nock, *St. Paul* (London: Oxford University Press, 1960), 99. But it's what the authorities declare which

commanded or approved from the past and has thus been purged of possibly compromising ingredients. And if now something newfangled appears, or something that was disapproved of (or resembles something that was disapproved of) in the past, the Establishment is likely to regard it with suspicion. But ambiguousness does not disappear. One is simply to obey and trust the authorities.

It is as A. D. Nock observed, that for the ancients there was not, "as with us, a sphere of magic in contrast to the sphere of religion,"[38] and we may go on with Pfister whom Nock quotes with approval, "dass kein prinzipieller Unterschied zwischen Zauberspruch und Gebet so wenig [123] wie zwischen Zauberei und Religion besteht." All the more reason, I would say, why the Establishment resents the magician. He is fundamentally a threat, because he boasts that he has recourse to powers and influences superior to and independent of the order and limitations which regulate society. He says he can produce desired results promptly.[39] Like respectable healers, he demonstrates that he too can unite high and low. And not only the simple folk but the Establishment believes him, it believes he can do what he says he can. It believes because there are practices and beliefs it endorses which are indistinguishable, sometimes even to the opponents of the magician, from the magician's actions. Because of its own belief, therefore, the Establishment declares the magician's exercises illegitimate. It sees in him both competition and caricature of itself. Sometimes perhaps it may believe him more even than he believes himself.

The rabbis, too, forbid, but apparently when they find that they are helpless to destroy the whole complex of magic, they try to outwit it.[40] Needless to say, there were practices and notions they themselves accepted as legitimate, as did their contemporaries in the Greco-Roman and Babylonian worlds, for these were the science of the day.[41] Some embarrassing practices they left alone, doubtless out of prudence, despite their affinity to pagan practices, because there was something like precedence for them in ancient Jewish custom.[42] And I can't resist guessing that there must have been practices which surely irritated them, but they simply shut their eyes to them and must have muttered under

---

brings magic into conflict with the *law*. For the reaction of satirists, see Lucian, "Alexander the False Prophet."

38. *Essays on Religion*, I, 314f.

39. See further M. Smith. *Clement of Alexandria and a Secret Gospel of Mark* (Cambridge, Mass.: Harvard University Press, 1973), 231ff. The magician's task may be more difficult than piety's, for the latter's promises are frequently granted an extension (if the reward or punishment is delayed, there's the future when it will take place); the magician is expected to produce immediate results (or within the time limits he set) if his credibility is not to suffer.

40. See S. Lieberman, *Greek in Jewish Palestine*, 92.

41. Ibid., 110f., 114.

42. TK, 94, 95.

their breath the equivalent of, Oh, to hell with it. Or they cleverly converted what may have been magical spells to begin with into religious prayers and thus removed the sting of superstition from them.[43] Or it might be that they would sanction a superstition which they themselves accepted, by endowing it with a religious value.[44]

A case in point is a form of bibliomancy, which is of course universal: among Jews, Christians, Muslims, anyone [124] with sacred scriptures. There are at least 180 Old Testament verses that have been used for omens and spells at one time or another.[45] Some of this so-called misuse may have annoyed the rabbis; on the other hand, this also gave them an opportunity to drive home a lesson they were delighted to inculcate. For instance:

For an inflammatory fever take an all-iron knife [that is, whose handle is also of iron] and go where there is a thorn-bush and tie to it a white twisted string. On the first day make a small notch and recite (Exod. 3:2), "An angel of the Lord appeared to him in a blazing fire out of a bush." On the morrow make [another] notch and recite (Exod. 3:3), "Moses said, I must turn aside to look at this marvellous sight; why is the bush not burnt?" On the following day make [still another] small notch and recite (Exod. 3:4), "When the Lord saw that he has turned aside to look, God called to him out of the bush: Moses, Moses! He answered, Here I am." ...

And when cutting [the bush] down, bend down low and recite as follows: "Thorn-bush, O thorn-bush, not because you are the tallest of trees did the Holy One, blessed be He, cause His Shekinah to rest upon you; rather because you were the smallest of all trees did the Holy One, blessed be He, cause His Shekinah to rest upon you. And even as the fire beheld Hananiah, Mishael, and Azariah and fled from them, so may the fire [of fever] behold So-and-so son of that woman[46] and flee from him."[47]

The ingenious manipulation of the biblical verses associates the burning bush that would not be consumed at God's self-revelation with a high fever. But note how an actual midrash and moral lesson have unexpectedly been incorporated in the mumbo jumbo. The midrash is none other than Rabbi Eliezer's, who is *not* discussing fevers:

43. TK, 102.

44. Lieberman, *Greek in Jewish Palestine*, 104–106.

45. Cf. *Jewish Encyclopedia* (New York, 1901–1905), s.v. "Bibliomancy" for the listing of the verses. See L. Ginzberg, *Legends of the Jews* (Philadelphia: Jewish Publication Society of America, 1913–1938), VI, 468.

46. In spells and charms you refer to a person's mother rather than to the father. You're always sure of the identity of the mother, and in magical formulae you have to be sure. See also E. R. Goodenough, *Jewish Symbols in the Greco-Roman Period*, (New York: Pantheon Books, 1953), II, 196, n. 180. On the triad of Hananiah, Mishrael, and Azariah and the evil eye, cf. *Genesis Rabba* 56, end (611f.) and Ginzberg, *Legends*, VI, 419.

47. B. Shabbat 67a, J. Preuss, *Biblisch-talmudische Medizin*, p. 185. Cf. B. Lewin, *Otzar ha-Gaonim, Shabbat* (Haifa, 1930), 66 (of Responsa) and 28 (explanation, by R. Hai Gaon).

Rabbi Eliezer says:[48] Why did the Holy One, blessed be He, reveal Himself from the high heavens and speak to him [i.e., Moses] out of the midst of the bush? Only because the bush is the lowliest of all the trees in the world. So Israel descended to the very lowest level and the Holy One, [125] blessed be He, came down to be with them and redeemed them, as it is said (Exod. 3:8), "And I came down to save them from the power of Egypt."

That is the midrash. And who knows? Maybe it was not the spell that drew upon a midrash but Rabbi Eliezer who drew upon an old incantation for his own midrashic purposes. Rabbi Eliezer was not entirely a stranger to magic. He was able to teach three hundred—perhaps three thousand—halakot in connection with the verse (Exod. 22:17), "thou shalt not suffer a sorceress to live."[49]

In post-talmudic times we come upon a ceremony whose background and subsequent course have been described in detail by J. Z. Lauterbach.[50] The ceremony is called *Tashlik*. On the afternoon of the first day of Rosh ha-Shanah, the Jewish new year, if it does not come on the Sabbath Day (otherwise the ceremony takes place on the second day of Rosh ha-Shanah), you go to a seashore or a river or some body of water, empty into the water what crumbs you may have brought along, and recite a number of biblical verses and passages. They are beautiful verses, and from one of them, Micah 7:19, comes the Hebrew word *tashlik* (which may be rendered in this context as "the casting off," or "away with you!"), from which the ceremony gets it name: "He will again have compassion upon us; He will subdue [or, suppress][51] our iniquities: And Thou wilt cast (*we-tashlik*) all their [=our] sins in the depths of the sea." The elements which seem to have united behind the practice, sometimes far behind, sometimes close, include the feeling that the deity prefers an abode by water, that other supernatural beings also favor such a location, that it was a favorite spot for synagogues (Tertullian also mentions "the prayers at the seashore")[52] and so on, along with ideas about angels and evil spirits. Compounded with these is naturally the expectation of good riddance to one's sins, the notion of atonement by means of a surrogate (a ceremonial development once part of the *Tashlik* conceptions), and of course the warding off of those powers who block forgiveness from arriving.

[126] Down through the ages there has been considerable opposition to the

48. MRS, p. 1 and also p. 2, in the name of Eleazar ben Arak. But see also MRS, ed. D. Hoffmann (Frankfurt a. M., 1905), p. 2. See further Lieberman in *Tarbiz*, 27 (1958), 186f.

49. *Abot de-Rabbi Natan*, ed. S. Schechter (Vienna, 1887), 41a.

50. Lauterbach in *Hebrew Union College Annual* 11 (1936), 207–340; and cf. S. Spiegel, *The Last Trial* (New York: Pantheon Books, 1967), p. 65f, and nn. 19–22. See also R. Dalven, "The Yearly Cycle of the Ioannine Jews," in *Conservative Judaism* (Winter 1974), 50, for a charming *Tashlik* custom when it rains.

51. M. L. Margolis, *Micah: The Holy Scriptures with Commentary* (Philadelphia: Jewish Publication Society of America, 1908), 79.

52. Lauterbach, 239.

ceremony itself or to parts of it. Some protests are strong and some are mild.[53] But clearly the folk won't give it up. The rabbis who let it go on offer reinterpretation and this in turn is seized upon as justification. Again, therefore, what we have is an aspect of the relationship between magical or superstitious behavior and the rabbinic authorities. It's a sort of "If you can't beat them, join them"—that is, the practice can't be eliminated, hence it is diverted to the approved avenues of piety. In the end you may even discern several sophisticated symbolic lessons in the people's conduct.[54]

It is certainly correct to see in such a development the successful deliverance of a folk from the dangers of superstition. On the other hand, it is not incorrect to see here another instance of the magic of magic, that is, it simply refuses to disappear, and because it has few scruples it is even prepared to adopt the alibis and masks of piety in order to survive. A small price to pay.

Ambiguity in magic, which is partly created by the offensive of the authorities, persists despite the simultaneous insistence on precision in recitation of the formulas and in the actions demanded by the prescriptions; and that is not fatal to it any more than it is to the legally prescribed forms of piety. This may be an additional reason why the Establishment is uncomfortable with the magus: for the ambiguity makes it impossible for him to adapt to all requirements, and that which remains inexplicable may fascinate even more than what is intelligible. Haggadic midrash is no stranger to this. Let me illustrate:

One of the Amorite practices, the *Tosefta* tells us,[55] is to cast stones, pebbles, into the sea and count as one does so. The counting is the objectionable feature and the reference is to a form of hydromancy. Nevertheless, counting pebbles or not counting, the depths of waters as such are not an innocuous

---

53. Ibid., 287ff.
54. See for example, the quotation from R. Moses Isserles (1520–1572) in Lauterbach, n. 115:

Even a mere custom (*minhag*) of Israel is Torah. Consider this going to a body of water and reciting, 'Cast all our sins into the depths of the sea.' For from contemplation of the deeps (of the sea) one learns the truth of the creation of the universe—for the deep of the sea is the abyss (*tehom*) and it is the very deepest part of the sea. Now it is of the fundamental nature of the elements that the waters cover the earth, and the earth is the center, and it is the lowest point of the whole universe. Now then, the earth was intended to serve mankind, all its inhabitants, and this is not independent of the purpose of the Creator, for it is He who brought the universe into being according to His will and with the aim of having the earth inhabited. That is why we go to a body of water to behold how here (at the shore), He set a boundary to the creation of the sea, declaring, Thus far you come, no further (cf. Jer. 5:22 and Job 38:11). Now when we go to the sea, we behold there the omnipotence of the Creator. This is why we go to some body of water on Rosh ha-Shanah, for it is the Day of Judgment when everyone ought to put his mind on the theme of the creation of the universe, and that the Lord, may He be exalted, is King over the earth. There is recited 'Thou shalt cast our sins into the depths of the sea,' for indeed he who puts his mind to the theme of the depth of the sea and recognizes that the world is created, thereby comes to know of the existence of the Lord, may He be exalted, and thereby regrets all his iniquities; and his sins are forgiven. And thus the sins are cast into the depths of the sea.
55. T. Shabbat 6:1, TK, ad loc., and n. 25.

region;[56] demons may lurk or abide there.[57] Strange scenes may be seen at the sea.[58] What, therefore, are we to make of the following?

[127] When the children of Israel left Egypt, the Mekilta reports,[59] Moses recalled Joseph's adjuration that his bones were to be taken out of Egypt along with the redeemed Israelites. Where, however, was Joseph buried? According to one view, actually presented as the first by our source, Serah, the daughter of Asher, informed Moses that Joseph was in a metal casket which the Egyptians had sunk in the Nile.[60] Thereupon Moses went to the shore of the Nile and—I now quote the reading of the Munich manuscript which Lauterbach (not Horovitz-Rabin)[61] adopted in his edition—

> took a gold tablet, engraved on it the Ineffable Name, cast it into the Nile and cried out: Joseph ben Jacob, the time has come for the oath to be fulfilled which the Holy One, blessed be He, promised to Father Abraham, that He would redeem his children. If you rise to the surface, fine; otherwise we're scot-free of the oath you placed us under! Forthwith Joseph's coffin rose to the surface,

and so forth. And the Mekilta reassures us that the iron casket rising to the surface is no more astonishing than what is reported in 2 Kings 6:1–6. Moses was more than a match for Elisha.

This is embarrassing, to say the least. Moses engraving the Ineffable Name of God on a golden tablet[62] and casting it into the Nile (itself, by the way, something of a deity), then calling on Joseph—and only thereafter does the casket rise. Clearly we have here a remarkable survival of a belief—if not more—once regarded by Judaism as inoffensive. Once, but not for long. For if you consult the parallel passages you will look in vain for the golden tablet. *Mekilta de-Rabbi Simeon* (ed. Epstein-Melamed, 46) supplies only, "Moses went and stood at the shore of the Nile and called, Joseph, Joseph," and so forth: thoroughly impeccable behavior. No tablet, no Ineffable Name, no casting.[63]

56. Cf. Lauterbach, 251.

57. Ginzberg, *Legends*, V, 87, n. 40.

58. See for example, the lovely apparition of Isis in Apuleius, *The Golden Ass*, XI.

59. *Mekilta*, Be-Shallah 1, (I, 176). Cf. E. E. Urbach, *Ḥazal* (Jerusalem, 1969), pp. 104f.

60. Ginzberg, *Legends*, II, 181 and notes ad loc. See also *Memar Marqah* 1:10 (ed. MacDonald, II, pp. 40ff.).

61. Rabbi M. M. Kasher, *Torah Shelemah*, XIV, 16, does reproduce this reading.

62. On a beautiful gold tablet, about 2 inches long and 1 3/4 inches wide, referring to the city of Apqu of the Assyrian Empire, which I had the privilege of seeing and handling thanks to the late Albrecht Goetze and first called to my attention by S. D. Walters, see F. J. Stephens in vol. VII (1953), 73f., of the *Journal of Cuneiform Studies*. Reference to a gold tablet on which a biblical text is inscribed—M. Yoma 3:10. See also Suetonius on Nero, 10 (LC, II, 103). On a gold sheet with instructions for the dead, cf. D. C. Kurtz and J. Boardman, *Greek Burial Customs* (Ithaca, N.Y.: Cornell University Press, 1971), 210; see also 217. See further Goodenough, *Jewish Symbols*, II, 194 (top of page) and 204; PGM, IV, 1215 (I, 114). On the Mekilta passage cf. also Goodenough, II, 283.

63. See also *Yalqut Shimeoni* (Salonica, 1526–27) or Exod. 13:19 and MhG, Exodus, ed. Margulies, on the verse.

No sign of these either in the Tosefta (Sotah 4:7). The Babylonian Talmud (Sotah 13a) is like the Tosefta. The Midrash, *Exodus Rabba* (20:19) in the regular editions, refers to magical golden dogs[64] guarding the royal burial place where Joseph's tomb had been deposited. But this [128] belongs to an alternative view of where Joseph was buried and has nothing to do with our passage, in connection with which *Exodus Rabba* says, "What did Moses do, etc.[!][65] . . . He began to cry, Joseph, Joseph, the time has come. . . . Forthwith the coffin bestirred itself and Moses took it. . . ."

The reading in *Pesikta de-Rav Kahana* (ed. Mandelbaum, 187) is illuminating on two counts. First, as in the other sources above, not a word is said about tablets, engravings, Divine Name, casting into the Nile. But once that comment is done with, we read: "And some say, Moses took a *shard* and wrote the Ineffable Name on it, and cast it into the Nile:[66] forthwith the coffin rose to the surface." Everything Moses did in the *Mekilta de-Rabbi Ishmael* he did in the *Pesikta*—with the one exception that he used a shard, a fragment of cheap everyday pottery, rather than a gold tablet. As though this could eliminate the toxic ingredient from the story.

The Midrash *Tanhuma*[67] also deserves to be looked at. "Moses stood by the Nile, took a small stone [a pebble], engraved on it 'Rise, O Ox,'[68] and cried out,

---

64. On the dogs, cf. PK, 187f. and Ginzberg, *Legends*, VI, 1, n. 3. Of course there is some significance to the fact that here, too, "gold" is spoken of. On gold, see also Razim, 66, 102, 105.

65. "Etc.": so the printed text.

66. *Midrash Aggadah*, Exod., ed. Buber, p. 143, says, "And Moses wrote out the Ineffable Name and cast it into the Nile." Not a word of what he wrote on.

67. Be-Shallah 2; Eqeb 6 is of no help here; nor is *Deut. Rabba* 11:7, nor *Yalqut* on Deut. 34:6.

68. On "Ox" (or "Bull") cf. Deut. 33:17. See also BhM, II, 11. As for the reading in the latter *'ly šwr* (rather than *'lh šwr*), Professor Saul Lieberman writes me that it is associated with the reading of Gen. 49:22, *'ale shur*!

In *Sekel Tob*, Exodus, 170, the reading is, "he took a pebble and threw it into (the Nile) and cried out, 'Rise, O ox, Rise, O ox. . . .'"

Particularly interesting is the reading of the *Midrash Shir ha-Shirim* (ed. L. Grünhut), 13a–b:

When Moses came to raise (Joseph's) casket, he inscribed and engraved on four silver tablets (plates; cf. below) the image of (the) four living creatures (cf. Ezek. 1)–(on one) the image of a lion, (on one) the image of a human being, (on one) the image of an eagle, (and on one) the image of an ox (bull). (See also the exorcism in Goodenough, *Jewish Symbols*, II, 182.) He threw the one with the image of the lion (into the Nile) and that place grew turbulent. He threw in the one with the image of the human being, and Joseph's bones assembled. He threw in the one with the image of the eagle, and the casket rose to the surface. In his hand remained only the plate (=tablet) with the image of the ox. And while Moses was occupied with Joseph's casket, he gave that plate to a woman and forgot about it. When (later Israel) gathered the gold to make the (golden) calf, the woman gave the tablet to them and they threw it in the fire and out came that calf (cf. Exod. 32:24). . . .

Cf. Ginzberg, *Legends*, III, 122 and VI, 51f. See also TK ad Megillah, 1218f. And my colleague Professor Jeffrey Tigay calls my attention to the paper by S. E. Loewenstamm in *Biblica* 48 (1967), 481–490, "The Making and Destruction of the Golden Calf."

A *silver* plate for the *golden* calf: is there some textual fusion here?

The engraving of the Ineffable Name does not appear here, but engraving does, and it is picturesquely associated with the vision of Ezekiel, in turn related to the story of the golden

Joseph, Joseph, the time has come" and the rest of it. The tablet has now become a valueless pebble thrown in the sea which serves no purpose.[69] The inscription "Rise, O Ox," which may indeed be a spell anyway, takes the place of the Ineffable Name. (Our text probably has a lacuna and should include the clause, "Moses cast the pebble into the Nile," after the words "Rise, O Ox.") Finally, for our purpose, *Lekah Tob*, Exodus, 40b, has cleaned it all up with the reading, "Moses came and stood by the Nile, took a pebble and threw it into [the Nile],[70] and said, Joseph . . ." and the rest.

This brief excursion into variations on a textual reading need not suggest that *all* versions other than that of the Munich manuscript of the *Mekilta* have been doctored and been made respectable: In any event, some still retain traces of attempts at modification. It may be that there were once different traditions about the way Moses recovered [129] Joseph's remains, some, so-called rationalistic, explaining that Moses simply summoned Joseph to rise, others frankly magical in outlook. The *Mekilta* belongs to the latter and unblushingly describes Moses as engaged in a rite which at the least excites surprise. In time, later texts apparently prefer to present the story in more restrained terms. And displacement of the golden tablet by shard and pebble reflects in my opinion just that ambiguity and bewilderment of the Establishment to which we referred.

There may be one more aspect to this bewilderment which deserves consideration—and by bewilderment I do not mean that the talmudic sages are reluctant to take a stand. They certainly condemn, for example,[71] a cult in which there were libations of wine and offerings of myrrh and frankincense and sacrifice of whole white cocks to angels, spirits, constellations. But what is condemned does not for that reason go out of existence; the condemnation, in fact, may add impetus. This requires neither underscoring nor documentation.

Nor is it at all necessary to assume that the populace in general, by responding to the whispered invitations and performances of magi, intended rebellion against rabbinic authority, though some very likely did. Some forms of magic fascinate by their very strangeness,[72] as we have already suggested. But there is also such a thing as the very appetite for piety which sometimes seems to know no bounds. It craves to do more and more, more than what the by-now habitual orthodoxy provides, and therefore it reaches out to, and takes hold of suggestions, prescriptions, acts beyond the pale. Here, you might say, superstition outwits the rabbis. The *Tashlik* ceremony we mentioned earlier

calf. At all events, magic has not disappeared from the legend. Nor from the version of the story in MhG, Gen. 887, where Moses writes (=draws images) on pieces of Joseph's cup.

69. Cf. M. Shebuot 3:5.

70. Cf. n. 69 above.

71. See in this connection S. Lieberman in *Jewish Quarterly Review* 37 (1946), 46, and on the white cock, 50f.

72. Cf. A. D. Nock, *Essays on Religion*, I, 315: "What then do the ancients mean by *magia?* . . . *the religions belong to aliens* or on any general ground disapproved." (The italics are mine.)

becomes an example of this in the course of time. There are other examples. In getting dressed, put on your right shoe first, but lace the left one first.[73] I see a young Jewish girl going off to a party, and as she leaves her house she lifts her right hand to the mezuzah on the doorpost and kisses it.[74] By what right may I tell her that I saw the identical behavior on the part of a Greek girl with [130] an icon in a Christian chapel? And who knows, perhaps these gestures and acts reminded both of them at their respective parties of how not to behave as the evening grew merry? Call such, if you wish, the mnemonic aids of piety.

On the other hand, there is also the browbeating which may be called strong-arm piety, which is of course interdenominational and pan-sectarian and is not far removed from the lesser forms of brainwashing so appealing to religious no less than to political bigots. The element of superstition in these should never be minimized, for the fears of omission of the apotropaic act can assume a lunatic fixation in the mind of the believer, whose self-righteousness is perhaps less susceptible to doubts and hesitations than is the self-confidence of any other kind of magician or legal authority.

One should not underestimate the margin of elasticity, patchwork, downright inconsistency and contrariness admitted resignedly, sometimes even gladly, by prescribed religious practice and doctrine whose approved forms may themselves have been, to begin with, reconciliations between conflicting interests inside a pattern of indoctrination. And there is never a loss for a prooftext to validate what desire can't resist.

In a religion like Judaism this inconsistency is especially likely to happen, I think, for the religion is so severely and imperatively monotheistic, and monotheism[75] is the hardest system on earth to live by *day by day*, crisis after crisis. Even intellectuals stumble. Summarizing the talmudic views regarding idolatry, Maimonides writes:

.In the days of Enosh, the people fell into gross error, and the counsel of the wise men of the generation became foolish. Enosh himself was among those who erred. Their error was as follows: "Since God," they said, "created these stars and spheres to guide the world, set them on high and allotted unto them honour, and since they are ministers who minister before Him, they deserve to be praised and glorified, and honour should be rendered them; and it is the will of God, blessed be He, [131] that men should aggrandise and honour those whom He aggrandised and honoured— just as a king desires that respect should be shown to the officers who stand before him, and thus honour is shown to the king." When this idea arose in their minds, they began to erect temples to the stars, offered up sacrifices to them, praised and glorified them in speech, and prostrated themselves before them—their purpose,

---

73. Cf. S. Ganzfried, *Kitsur Shulhan Aruk*, 3:4. On notions of right and left, cf. the references in Goldin, 149. See also G. Scholem, *Sabbatai Sevi* (Princeton, 1973), 91.

74. Cf. S. H. Kook, *Iyyunim u-Mehqarim*, II (Jerusalem, 1963), pp. 67f.

75. For Islam cf. Ibn Khaldûn, *The Muqaddimah*, trans. F. Rosenthal (Princeton: Princeton University Press, 1967), I, lxxii; III, 159ff.

according to their perverse notions, being to obtain the Creator's favour. This was the root of idolatry. . . .[76]

The intellectuals arrive by analogy at the realization that though there is one God, He must have many ministers who are to be treated with religious courtesy. The simple man, driven by his impulses and instructed by his authoritative Scriptures and by the tradition that angels exist—after all, they too were created by God—need not speculate interminably. He turns to these angels and spirits for assistance. He has been reassured many times that the Lord is nigh; but angels and ministers of grace, and demons, are nigher. Soon the universe gets congested with beings, some of whom the rabbis themselves believe in (why not?) and address. It has been observed[77] that one of the reasons for the influence of Jewish magicians in the Hellenistic-Roman world of magic was Judaism's angelology. How many angels that Jewess in Juvenal (*Satires* VI, 542–547), who predicted the future and interpreted dreams for elegant Roman matrons, was familiar with, the satirist fails to tell us, doubtless because he was too outraged to investigate. But if she had needed any, there was no lack of them. To give an idea of what this could be like, let me say that in the *Sefer ha-Razim* (a word about this book in a moment), discovered several years ago, the index lists 704 angels, and while a few names may be doublets, the reality of a number in the several hundreds in that small treatise remains unaffected. The empty space between God and man is filled, the world grows a little cozier, but at the same time a little less private, and therefore calls for more precaution and secretiveness. But then again there's [132] someone close by to talk to, and is there anyone who doesn't need a confidant?

Now that someone is near, what do you say and what do you do? Inevitably you draw on the forms and vocabulary from the worship you're familiar with in the established institution,[78] or on an imitation of what's familiar (like everyone else, the magician is seldom original). Familiar are some of the names of deity[79] and angels, slogans that are repeated in prayers and psalms, verses that are used as refrains and that read nicely also as they are read backwards. There are also, however, varieties or a new prescription that has been recommended as having been successful elsewhere. This last named is at first a departure from the familiar, but in an emergency one must hazard because

76. Hilkot Abodah Zarah 1:1 (M. Hyamson's translation). Cf. Festugière, *Personal Religion*, p. 117.

77. See, e.g., A. D. Nock, *Essays on Religion*, I, 188f. On Jews famous as magicians, see also E. Braver, *Sefer Magnes* (Jerusalem, 1938), 61.

78. All this can be seen in the vocabulary of Razim.

79. On Judaism's awesome attitude toward the Name (and Names) of God, see, for example, M. Sanhedrin 10:1, *Abot de-Rabbi Natan*, 28b (cf. TK ad Yoma 2:1, 755, n. 14; G. Scholem, *Jewish Gnosticism, Merkabah Mysticism, and Talmudic Tradition* (New York: Jewish Theological Seminary of America, 1960), 46, 54, n. 36; M. Yoma 6:2 (and cf. Albeck in his edition, 470). See also Razim, 99.

there seems to be no alternative. Besides, if some words and names sound odd, that's all the more mysterious and thrilling. Above all, one has professional assistance and guidance.[80] He is our magus.

A Jewish magician of either the third or fourth century C.E.[81] has left us a beautifully written booklet in Hebrew, *Sefer ha-Razim*, the *Book of Secrets* (or *Mysteries*), which was discovered and pieced together by the late Mordecai Margalioth. It contains a description of the seven heavens and the names of their guardian (officer) angels under whom serve troops or "camps"[82] of angels, as well as of the services they perform if they are approached the right way. A number of the angelic names are intelligible; some can be deciphered as Greek terms or names in a kind of Jewish disguise;[83] many remain incomprehensible. Following the names, the author furnishes the prescriptions: If you want this or that, do and recite the following. There is no need to go into detail for the requests and recipes are similar to what we find in Greek (and other) magical papyri and in amulets, and Professor Margalioth has already called attention to quite a number of similarities, often of phraseology and of objects employed. One example should be enough to convey the flavor; it is connected with the fifth camp of the first heaven:

Now if you wish to consult a ghost ['*ob!* cf. Deut. 18:9–14], stand over against a grave and name the angels of the fifth camp while in your hand is a new glass phial in which is a mixture of oil and honey, and recite the following: "I adjure you, spirit of Kriophoros [=Hermes] who dwells in cemeteries by the bones of the dead, that you receive this offering from my hand and do my will, and bring back to me So-and-so son of So-and-so[84] who is dead. Set him up so that he may speak with me without fear; and let him tell me the truth, [speak to me] without deception; and let me not be afraid of him; and let him answer me as I require of him." [The dead person] will then rise at once. But if he doesn't, adjure still another time, up to three times. And when [the dead person] has come forth, place the phial before him and then say what you have to say. A myrtle-rod should be in your hand. And if you wish to release [dismiss] him, strike him three times with the myrtle [=rod] and pour out the oil and the honey, and break the glass, and throw away the myrtle [=rod] and go home another way.[85]

80. On what papyri reveal of *professional* nature, cf. A.D. Nock, *Essays on Religion*, I, 179.
81. See on this and the following, Razim, Introduction and Text.
82. Cf. Gen. 32:2f.
83. Note especially the brilliant decipherment by Professor Morton Smith in *Sefer ha-Razim*, 12, and similarly brilliant decipherment and interpretation of names and places in *Hekalot Rabbati*, by J. H. Levy in *Studies in Jewish Hellenism* (Hebrew, Jerusalem, 1960), 259–265.
84. Probably the name of the mother; cf. note 46 above.
85. Razim, 76f. and notes. I might add that the text on the first heaven is the longest in this work and contains more "excitement" than the other heavens. To me this suggests that the heaven closest to man is the most easily reached, and it is therefore natural to turn to that region.

The work is plainly a textbook or book of magical recipes whose purpose is utilitarian, but it is a genuine literary composition with an introduction,[86] peroration, and the principal substance in well-organized order.

Who is the author? Of course he won't tell us. Doubtless he is as vain as the most modest of us, and if in his time there had been such a thing as royalties, he would not have scorned them. But what he wants above all is to be read in all seriousness. He knows that no one will take the trouble to consult a book of *his*. Who or what is he, after all? But a book given to Noah, or possibly to Adam, and handed down very carefully from one generation to another until it finally got to that master of wizards and the wise, Solomon, and which the magus has a copy of—that may command acceptance.[87]

There is a possibility that work in our hands is not by one author but by several, and only the modern editor has made of it a single unified treatise. But nothing I can [134] see in it reveals breaks or inconsistency between parts or forced cohesion of disparate, mutually antagonistic views or teachings. Doubtless the possibility remains that several hands, not one, are responsible for the work. But nothing compels us to adopt such a view. That the magus drew on various sources, compiled and organized them into a unitary composition, does not deprive him of the right to be called author.[88]

For whom did he prepare the work? I suspect for apprentices, coming to learn his trade. Perhaps they studied it with him so he could teach them how to do what the book prescribed, and especially the lore about the numerous angels. However, one ought not to rule out the possibility that it is also meant as a do-it-yourself manual; though this is not decisive, note that the idiom throughout (as in kindred compositions) is, "If thou seekest" this or that or the other, recite the following and do as follows—second person singular, addressed directly. Yet I don't think he meant to be only an author and to give up practice. Further, I don't think that the book was intended for women—not because the second person singular is in the masculine (that is simply conventional style), but because there is a level of culture to the writing which probably was not common among women with or without an appetite for sorcery, although we do know of some women in talmudic times with noteworthy culture. Even if women could handle the work on their own, men were certainly the chief audience. *Razim* will tell you several times how a man will win a woman, but never how a woman can make a man want to win her.[89]

The modern editor, who was a devout talmudist as well as a fine scholar,

86. Note, however, S. Spiegel in *Harry A. Wolfson Jubilee Volume* (Hebrew, Jerusalem, 1965), 261 (top of page).

87. Cf. E. J. Bickerman, "Faux Littéraires dans l'Antiquité Classique," in *Rivista de Filologia* 101 (1973), 27ff., and especially 31ff. On the great power of Solomon's wizardry "among us to this day" (first cent.), cf. Josephus, *Antiquities*, 8.45–49 (LC, V, 595f.). Cf. the quotation from Zeller in Scholem, *Major Trends in Jewish Mysticism*, pp. 189, 190f.

88. For additional discussion of the authorship, cf. Razim, 26ff.

89. This is not surprising. Note also the several injunctions to avoid impurity—81, 91, 103— which would be directed only to a man.

confesses in his preface that the composition shocked him profoundly. Prayers to Helios, offerings to angels, making stone images, appeals to Aphrodite,[90] consulting ghosts explicitly forbidden by the Scriptures, petitions to win at horse races: What place, he asked, have such within talmudic Judaism? Maybe halakists can answer his question.

[135] But one may turn the question around in a discussion like this and ask, What place has Judaism in magic like this? This, I think, has some significance for historians of culture no less than religion.

As among all peoples, all along there have been practitioners of magic among the Jews, as biblical and talmudic and post-talmudic protest reflects, and in the pagan world too there are references to Jews as expert magicians.[91] Along with their magic, by the way, these practitioners, when they moved in gentile circles, may even have been purveyors of certain Jewish ideas and tabus. *Sefer ha-Razim*, as we shall see in a moment, expresses not only (what we might call) the crude but some fairly fundamental Jewish emphases about God. Maybe those Roman fathers who abstained from pork (Juvenal, *Satires*, XIV, 96–106) did so because some mendicant Jewish magician advised the abstinence,[92] even as he urged not working one day in seven, to the exasperation of Seneca.

Wherever magic has been practiced, as the footnotes by Margalioth themselves demonstrate, it's been more or less along the lines described by the author of *Sefer ha-Razim*. (We are not discussing black magic.) It is questionable whether he introduced anything new into the world—neither his prescriptions for healing, nor the way to capture a woman's heart,[93] nor the methods for destroying an enemy, nor even for winning at the races and praying in behalf of the jockey.[94] Margalioth, however, points to something which may be significant, namely, that though the suppliant prays to the angels and spirits and demons and the moon, and even brings offerings to them, he does not regard them as autonomous or as deities. For him they are all not divinities but angels, in other words, ministers and emissaries of the Supreme God. The magician is very careful not to slip. Even Helios, as Margalioth points out, is not the Greek sun god for the magus but only the "angel Helios."[95]

90. Cf. Goodenough, *Jewish Symbols*, II, 199.

91. See also Razim, 15. ". . . the proportion of charms containing no Jewish elements at all is so surprisingly small that it is quite apparent that the pagans hold Jewish magic in high honor" (Goodenough, *Jewish Symbols*, II, 206). See also M. Simon, *Verus Israel* (Paris: De Boccard, 1948), 395ff. Cf. M. Smith, *Clement*, 233, n. 10, on the frequency of *Iao*.

92. Cf. PGM, IV, 3079 (I, 172) and Eitrem, *Some Notes on Demonology*, p. 22. Cf. A. Deissmann, *Light from the Ancient East* (London, 1911), pp. 259–260. Seneca: In St. Augustine, *City of God*, VI, 11.

93. Cf. Philostratus, loc. cit. (above, note 2). See also PGM, IV, 400–405 (I, 84f.).

94. Razim, pp. x and 94. On horse racing passion, cf. Philostratus, *Life of Apollonius* 5.26 (LC, I, 521); and cf. A. A. Barb, "The Survival of Magic Arts," in A. Momigliano, ed., *The Conflict Between Paganism and Christianity in the Fourth Century* (Oxford: Clarendon Press, 1964), 119f.

95. Contrast Goodenough, *Jewish Symbols*, II, 194, 200.

Margalioth's observation of the fact is fair enough, but I would like to press this just a bit further, because while an [136] individual is busy with his strenuous magical operations, how much room remains in his mind to remember the God who alone is God? Yet, as we noted earlier, it is from his tradition that a person inherits his vocabulary for religious discourse and even for the formulae of many of his spells. This is not to deny that he also learns new words and new ideas, some, like "Abraxas" for example,[96] apparently being irresistible. But if he does not completely abandon (does one ever?) association with his basic vocabulary, though he may fill those words with different meanings, the original momentum of those words continues. Even as he behaves in less than monotheistic ways, the solemnity of his monotheism weighs upon him. The monotheistic vocabulary of the magician affects him too, the magician.

We have here, I think, once again ambiguity, that is, the ambiguity of a monotheist. The author of the *Sefer ha-Razim* is a magician; he teaches and practices his craft with all the reverence due it. But the language he uses he borrows heavily from the language of his religion. This is true all along and may even be of some comfort to his clients who recognize the words from other contexts familiar to them. Finally, we might say, he is overcome: when he pauses to contemplate not the heavenly crowd with whom he must maintain contact, but the heavenly sovereign, his reverence shifts, as it were, from the pragmatic practitioner to the awe-struck visionary. Toward his angels and spheres he is most respectful; but when he finally gets to his description of the seventh heaven with its sevenfold light, he is spectacularly uplifted. Our author writes a beautiful, lucid Hebrew: his clichés are no more numerous than in other texts of his time. He knows the Scriptures and helps himself freely to the biblical expressions, and not necessarily in a stereotyped or mechanical way. The regions he describes, and the roles he reports, he conveys with vivid directness; I do not know whom specifically he has in mind when he says that those on the sixth station of the second heaven are "awe-inspiring like the sages of the [137] academy [?]," or perhaps, "like the sages in session,"[97] but the whole description there would do no injustice to certain traditional statements about the talmudic savants, the *hakamim*. Like others, our author is fully conscious of the effects of rhetoric:[98] "I adjure you angels cloaked in fire by Him who is wholly fire and whose seat is on a throne of fire and whose ministers are a flaming fire, and camps of fire minister before Him. . . ."[99] He uses postbiblical Hebrew expressions in a natural way: "by Him who Spake and the World

96. Cf. Razim, 8.

97. P. 86, line 93 (of second heaven). Perhaps, however, the term *yeshivah* should be understood as high-court/chief-academy as the term in the Genizah documents in later centuries is explained by S. D. Goitein in *Zion* 26 (1961), 177; see also S. Spiegel, *Wolfson Jubilee Volume*, 250, n. 4.

98. Of course, in this he is not unique; cf. an eloquent adjuration in Goodenough, *Jewish Symbols*, II, 198, or 182 (for reference to fire).

99. Razim, 95.

Came to Be";[100] on one occasion he falls into the standard way of introducing a prooftext, *she-neemar* ("as it is said.")[101] Margalioth has also called attention to forms hitherto familiar to us only in *piyyut*.

Our magus is a cultivated man who unquestionably drew on magicians' handbooks for the necessary *materia magica*. But he knew his Bible, too, and drew on it as well. And when he reaches the seventh heaven where the Throne of Glory is, all hocus pocus is ended. Here is description of Glory, and the One in His holy habitation seeks justice and righteousness and none can see Him, not even His entourage, and there is enormous luminosity, and heavenly hosts proclaim the trisagion[102] out loud but with humility too—all is splendor and doxology. The whole is a kind of Merkabah and Hekalot exaltation, and the Jewishness runs through not only the words and imagery,[103] and fourteen-fold repetition of *Baruk shemo . . . u-mevorak* ("Blessed be His Name . . . and be it blessed") in the different parts of the universe,[104] but through the thorough monotheistic commitment. Now there is no client to help out, no petition to present or formula to follow. Like the traditional Jew (= the Jew submitting to talmudic authority) our magus declares that only God is the King over kings of kings and besides Him there is no El and other than He is no Elohim. But the tension between serving Him alone and serving His agents, too, remains. After all, in addition to the seventh heaven there are the other six. For these, likewise, biblical language is apt. Ambiguity is still [138] with us, therefore. As in other respects, the holy and profane accompany each other uneasily, but, in all fairness let it be added, they reenforce each other as well.

100. Razim, 102.

101. Razim, 108. And note an "echo" of PA, beginning, on 66, line 25. He is likewise familiar with a commonplace Aramaic legal formula, 75 (top.). On *piyyut* forms, 27, n. 11.

102. Cf. Goodenough, *Jewish Symbols*, II, 176.

103. Note the lovely image on 108, "suspends the world like a cluster [of grapes]." Professor Shalom Spiegel calls to my attention (the fact as well as the following references) that the figure of speech and image occur already in Ras Shamra—W. F. Albright, *Journal of the Palestine Oriental Society* 14 (1934), 133f.—and appear also in medieval Hebrew poetry, as noted by L. Zunz, *Synagogale Poesie des Mittelalters* (Frankfurt: O. J. Kauffmann, 1920), 510f., and referred to also by G. Scholem, *Einige kabbalistische Handschriften in British Museum* (Berlin: Schocken, 1932), 26f.

104. P. 109. Once (109, line 31) *kebodo* rather than *shemo*; but *kabod* here equals *shem*. For the combination *baruk u-mevorak*, cf. H. Yalon, *Introduction to the Vocalization of the Mishna* (Hebrew, Jerusalem, 1964), 96.

Of Midrash and
the Messianic Theme[*]

Prefatory Statement

To the messianic theme, the Midrash reacts as it does to all themes, that is, it discloses the theme's presence inside the ancient biblical verse, which by interpretation—either more or less literally, or ingeniously, fancifully—can be demonstrated to contain allusions to the immediate theme, in our case, to the messianic age and the elements of ultimate redemption. For example, commenting on the verse (Exod. 12:2), "This month shall mark for you the beginning of the months; it shall be the first of the months of the year for you," one rabbi says, "The Holy One, blessed be He, said to Israel, 'Children, in the Age to Come you will experience renewal by virtue of redemption'; and a second rabbi says, "The renewal [designed] for the Age to Come you will experience right here [at the redemption from Egyptian bondage]":

> Even as in the Age to Come, "Then the eyes of the blind shall be opened" (Isa. 35:5), so now, "All the people witnessed the thunder and lightning" (Exod. 20:19);
> Even as in the Age to Come, "And the ears of the deaf shall be unstopped" (Isa. 35:5), so now, "All that the Lord has spoken we will do and listen to" (Exod. 24:7);
> Even as in the Age to Come, "Then the lame shall be strong-legged as a leaping deer" (Isa. 35:6), so now, "Moses led the people out of the camp toward [God, and they stood upright]" etc. (Exod. 19:17);
> Even as in the Age to Come, "And the tongue of the dumb shall shout aloud" (Isa. 35:6), so now, "All the people answered as one, saying . . ." (Exod. 19:8).[1]

* Originally presented at a conference on Jewish messianism, Columbia University, April 13, 1981.
1. Pesiqta Kahana, ed. Mandelbaum, 105; cf. also ibid., 99, note to line 11 and ibid., 218.

The language of Isaiah makes the meaning of Exodus clear, and in turn, what will happen at the messianic redemption is already foreshadowed by Scripture of the first redemption. Every age is thus itself and also may be paradigmatic of another, for, according to the Rabbis, the biblical vocabulary addressed past generations, but present and future ones no less, each according to its requirements, since the absence of a verb or every tense of a verb can serve, if need be, our age and the Age to Come.[2]

At the supplementary conclusion of the Mishnah Sotah,[3] just before Phineas ben Yair's curriculum for perfection which leads to resurrection initiated by the prophet Elijah, of blessed memory,[4] two Tannaim[5] are quoted on the frightful deterioration of the times since the Temple was destroyed, משחרב בית המקדש, מיום שחרב בית המקדש. The statements are not a verbatim duplication, but the substance is identical, except that the second spells out in slightly more detail what the first had already communicated, namely, How terrible are these days! And quoting from the latter half of Ezek. 34:6, both conclude with a moan, "On whom can we now lean for support? On our Father who is in heaven, על מי לנו להשען? על אבינו שבשמים." Nothing or no one else can any longer be of help.

A third statement follows, spelling out the demoralization in still additional detail—it might even serve as a summary of university life in the sixties and seventies of our century—and it also concludes with what is by now a refrain, "On whom can we now lean for support? On our Father who is in heaven."

In other words, like the first two statements, the third also describes a collapse of the social and other conditions of the course of life. But it relates these not to the immediate consequences of the destruction of the Temple, but to the עקבות משיחא (cf. Ps. 89:52), to the time following upon the heels of the Messiah.

There is really no irreconcilable difference between מיום שחרב בית המקדש and בעקבות משיחא for expectation of the Messiah was widespread (or, as the Midrash—Tanhuma Wa-Yeṣe 9—might say, "they hungered for redemption"), and thinking of him might well lead Sages and others to date the breakdown of national fortune and conduct to the tragedy of the Destruction. That's when it all began, and it won't improve till *after* the appearance of the Messiah and his takeover, if even then!

Support for this view may be provided by the reading of Babylonian

2. Cf. L. Ginzberg, *An Unknown Jewish Sect* (New York, 1976), 234f. See also R. Abun in Pesiqta Kahana, 410, on the character of the *Hallel*.

3. M. Sotah 9:15; J. N. Epstein, *Mabo le-Nusaḥ ha-Mishnah* (Jerusalem, 5708), 976.

4. Cf. L. Ginzberg, *Legends of the Jews*, vol. VI (Philadelphia, 1939), 316, n. 1 and 325, n. 45; S. Lieberman, *Greek in Jewish Palestine* (New York, 1942), 70, n. 23; A. Bendavid in *Leshonenu la-'Am*, vol. 23 (5723), 247.

5. R. Phineas ben Yair and R. Eliezer ha-Gadol (= ben Hyrqanos); note the reading in ed. Lowe, and the readings in B. Sanhedrin 97a. In ed. Naples, end of Nashim, there is no paragraph בעקבות משיחא. (I am indebted to Professor Morton Smith for correction in understanding of this expression.)

Talmud, Sanhedrin 97a. Here the familiar Sotah passages are introduced by several Tannaim and an Amora, with the introductory formula דור שבן דוד בא בו, "In the generation when the scion of David (= the Messiah) arrives":[6] no one feels called upon to refer to "Since the Temple was destroyed," as though that were needless to say, as though one did wish to imply, The disasters which followed the destruction of the Temple will not disappear even when the Messiah for whom we long has arrived.

The grim descriptions in the Mishnah Sotah and the Talmud Sanhedrin are most likely intended to discourage messianic preoccupations by drawing on a number of contemporary social features of decline, as scholars have observed.[7] There are still other statements to the same effect. At first this is puzzling. Even when the Messiah arrives there will be no relief? Yet the view is almost a commonplace and even has psychological appeal. "And Joseph burst into loud sobs" (Gen. 45:2), Scripture says; "Even as Joseph was not reconciled to his brothers except through weeping," the Midrash explains, "so the Holy One, blessed be He, will not redeem Israel except through weeping, as it is said (Jer. 31:8), 'They shall come with weeping, and with compassion will I guide them. I will lead them to streams of water' etc."[8] Redemption is always more dramatic when it succeeds the lowest depths of despair. The sea splits just as the Israelites are about to be overtaken there by the pursuing Egyptians. Similarly: The scion of David "will arrive only when the last penny is gone from our pockets," or, "when all hope of redemption has been given up."[9] There is also fear of a false alarm: best not to be precipitous.

Some thought (not messianic) of what can or will happen at a time beyond the present life, occurs, for example, in the reflection of Aqabya ben Mahalalel in Pirqe Abot 3:1: "And [know] before whom thou art destined to give an account and reckoning." The statement in 2:7, "If one acquires for himself knowledge of the Torah he acquires for himself life in the World to Come," may not be Hillel the Elder's;[10] besides, though it refers to life in the World to

---

6. Apparently no variants; cf. *Diqduqe Soferim*, ad loc.

7. See for example J. Klausner, *The Messianic Idea in Israel* (Heb., Jerusalem, 5687) 283ff.; G. Scholem, *The Messianic Idea in Judaism* (New York, 1971), 12f. On rebellion against God in messianic days, see Midrash Tannaim, 194 (cf. Sifre Deut. 318, 362).

8. Gen. R. 93:12, 1171. Cf. Pesiqta Kahana, ed. Mandelbaum, 97, line 10. Gen. R. may even be hinting at Messiah ben Joseph; note Jer. 31:8, end, cited in full in Tanhuma Wa-Yiggash 5, end.

9. B. Sanhedrin 97a. "From utmost agony to utmost bliss" (G. Goldin). I am not referring to such statements as, If only Israel would observe one Sabbath properly (Lev. R. 3:1, 57f., parallels quoted by Margulies), etc., because those are typical oriental rhetoric to observe commandments. Other statements are not so self-evident, but they reveal a preoccupation with themes whose speculative character (e.g., B. Yebamot 62a, bottom) or critical purpose (e.g., B. Sanhedrin 38a, toward top) acquires a rhetorical amplitude by being associated with messianic expectation. "The scion of David will not come until . . ." thus becomes stereotypical.

10. Cf. Epstein, op. cit., 1182f., though he does not refer to 2:7. For additional references to 'olam ha-ba' in Pirqe Abot, see 2:16; 3:11; 4:1, 16f., 22; 5:19, and in chap. 6:4, 9. E. E. Urbach (*Hazal*, [Jerusalem, 1969], 587f.) assumes reasonably that even before Yohanan ben Zakkai, belief in notions of redemption and messianic age had already crystallized.

Come, and though at times *'olam haba'* and *teḥiyyat ha-metim* and *yemot ha-mashiaḥ* may overlap,[11] the saying teaches us nothing about the messianic age.

Specific reference to the Messiah we meet in prudential exhortation by Yohanan ben Zakkai in early tannaite times. To him the following is attributed:[12] "If there was a seedling in your hand and you were informed, 'King[13] Messiah has arrived,' first go plant the seedling, afterwards go forth to greet him." The statement is neither cynical nor erratic. Recall how Yohanan pleaded with the men of Jerusalem in the War of 66–73 to make peace with and submit to Rome.[14] One does find in him a tendency toward restraint from extremist action. Note the following also attributed to him:

> If youngsters say to you, "Let's go and build the Temple," don't listen to them; if elders say to you, "Come, let's tear down the Temple," listen to them. For the building up of youngsters is a tearing down, and the tearing down of elders is a building up. Proof of the matter? Rehoboam, Solomon's son.[15]

Still another saying, in the same spirit: "Don't tear down their altars,[16] lest with your own hands you will have to rebuild them. Don't tear down their brick [structures], lest they tell you, 'come now and make them of stone.'"[17]

11. "The ambiguity exists in the use of the World to Come, which . . . is sometimes the messianic age, sometimes the new order of things after the resurrection, and . . . occasionally the state of the soul between death and the resurrection. It is probable that these stages of the future were not so sharply distinguished in thought as we should like to have them" (G. F. Moore, *Judaism* [Cambridge, Mass., 1927,] vol. II, 391). See further L. Finkelstein, *Mabo le-Massektot Abot ve-Abot d'Rabbi Natan* (New York, 1950), 213ff.

12. Abot de-Rabbi Natan, Version B (ed. S. Schechter, Vienna, 1887), 66f.; cf. A. J. Saldarini, *The Fathers According to Rabbi Nathan*, Version B (Leiden, 1975), 181f. and full notes ad loc.

13. Instead of the text *lk*, reading *mlk* (= melek) in accordance with L. Ginzberg in JBL, vol. 41 (1922), 134, n. 46.

14. Cf. Version A of ARN, 22: ". . . Rabban Yohanan ben Zakkai . . . sent for the men of Jerusalem and said to them: 'children (*banai*), why do you destroy this city and why do you seek to burn the Temple? For what is it that he asks of you? Verily he asks naught of you save one bow or one arrow, and he will go off from you'"; see also Version B, 19 (and cf. S. Lieberman, *Tosefta ki-Fshuṭah,*, Nashim, 989ff.). Cf. Midrash Prov. 15, 40a-b (note the fragment in Z. M. Rabinovitz, *Ginzé Midrash* (Tel-Aviv, 1976), 226f. and note 57).

15. ARNB, 67. Cf. T. Abodah Zarah 1:19, B. Megillah 31b, B. Nedarim 40a (which read "Simeon ben Eleazar"). Conflicting attributions are always a problem, and in our classical midrashic-talmudic sources especially so, as scholars have observed even before modern critical-textual investigations. Note, for example, R. David Luria on Lev. R. 1:5, n. 13, Lam. R. 2:4, n. 13; R. Mattityahu Straschun, *Mattat-Yah* (Vilna, 1892), on Gen. R. 11:1 (p. 6), 13:2 (p. 8), 19:3 (p. 11), 48:2 (p. 28), Lam. R. 2:1 (p. 144), etc. However, even if one wished to decide that Simeon ben Eleazar was *not* quoting Yohanan ben Zakkai but was the more likely author of that saying (because Simeon is the less famous personality)—neither attribution of course can be established beyond doubt—it is significant that a redactor felt that the saying was in keeping with other sayings by Yohanan, and hence credited it to him. Note also Midrash Tannaim, 58.

16. Lit., their high places. Contrast, e.g., Deut. 6:5, 12:2f. Cf. Josephus, *Contra Apionem*, I, 192f. Or should one read *bymwsyhm* = Greek *bōmos*, altar? Cf. W.A.L. Elmslie, *The Mishna on Idolatry* (Cambridge, 1911), 109 (ad "p. 54").

17. ARNB, ibid.; cf. Midrash Tannaim, 58, but note also how the text continues ibid.; see S. Lieberman in JQR, vol. 36 (1946), 365f.

It is surely, therefore, not unjust to say of Yohanan ben Zakkai that he cautions against messianic impetuousness. But we are not yet through with him. It is reported that on his deathbed he exclaimed, "Clear the house of uncleanness and prepare a throne for Hezekiah king of Judah."[18] In other words, Yohanan ben Zakkai is not like that later Amora Rabbi Hillel who had to be rebuked because he denied that Israel still had a messiah to look forward to, for the benefits of that messiah (in the days of Hezekiah!) had already been enjoyed.[19] For Yohanan ben Zakkai, Hezekiah, as messianic figure or scholar greeting him, Yohanan, on his entrance into a better life,[20] is a welcome reality.

I would like to consider Yohanan's exclamation for a moment. On his deathbed a man may well recant earlier convictions, and Yohanan may be said to exemplify such behavior. But this would be the easiest, misleading explanation of our text, particularly since the sources say nothing of a retraction. What is more, twice in the Palestinian Talmud[21] we can see that Yohanan's exclamation is one of a repeated formulation, and no change of heart is involved. So some scholars speak at the end of their lives. Of course, they may have been imitating Yohanan.

In the regular editions of the Babylonian Talmud, treatise Berakot 28b, Yohanan is quoted as saying, "and prepare a throne for Hezekiah, King of Judah, who is [or, has] come, שבא."[22] This reading is apparently unwarranted.[23] But whoever added it surely wished to emphasize Yohanan's certainty of Hezekiah's arrival.

How then are we to regard Yohanan's attitude? He is prepared for the Messiah's coming, but he is apprehensive as well. Why this ambivalence, and already *before* Hadrianic and post-Hadrianic years? Because among other things, pursuit after the Messiah (a) is a radical break with the productive occupations and routines of daily life, hence an invitation to chaos, and (b) along with that, a likely rebellion against rabbinic authority.[24] The first is self-

---

18. ARNA, 80. On a Menahem ben Hezekiah as Messiah, cf. J. Eben Shmuel, *Midreshe Geulah* (Jerusalem, 5714), 302. See Lam. R., ed Buber, p. 45a.

19. B. Sanhedrin 98b and 99a. What our R. Hillel has in mind is possibly the extraordinary deliverance reported in II Kings 18:13–19:36 (Isa. 36–37): nothing that extraordinary will happen again? But note also DS ad 98b, *'en mashiah*. Or is it possible that he means, After that event only God will be the redeemer? Cf. below n. 64 and Professor E. J. Bickerman's communication. On Jews who maintain that biblical "redemption" promises and consolations refer to Second Temple times, cf. Saadia, *Emunot we-Deot* VIII:7, trans. S. Rosenblatt, 312ff.

20. Cf. Moore, op. cit., II, 347f. and n. 4, and III, 201f. (L. Ginzberg). On the reading *hu' hayah 'omer* = "he said," cf. PAAJR, XXVII (1958), 56, n. 51 [above, p. 19.—Ed.]. Note also that in Abot 4:19, although the saying of the sage is a biblical quotation, hence presumably could be frequently on his lips, the text says simply *Shemuel . . . 'omer*, not *hayah 'omer*. So, too, cf. the citation in *Meleket Shelomo* ad loc. On Yohanan ben Zakkai's last hours, cf. ARNA, 79.

21. P. Sotah towards end; P. Abodah Zarah 3:1, toward end.

22. So, too, in one ARN manuscript; cf. 80, n. 16, toward end.

23. Cf. DS ad loc.

24. Cf. Scholem, op. cit., 56 and further below, 22f. Interestingly, that it might be dangerous to speak publicly and openly of expecting King Messiah, one has to learn from

evident: if you drop what you're supposed to be doing when rumors of the Messiah's arrival reach you, you run the risk of being doubly disappointed, with your crop and by an absent or false messiah. As for the second, there is a significant tannaite passage, which may be post-Hadrianic, but it is impossible to say, since it is anonymous; at all events it is tannaite.[25]

Thus: Commenting on Deut. 11:13, "[If, then, you obey the commandments] which I enjoin upon you this day," the Sifre Deuteronomy elaborates:[26]

How do you know that if a person has heard a [proper] interpretation [lit., a word, something, דבר] from even the least[27] in Israel, it ought to be regarded by him as though he had heard it from a scholar? The verse says, "Which I enjoin upon you."[28] And not only as though he had heard it from one scholar, but as though he had heard it from many scholars; for it is said (Eccl. 12:11), "The sayings of the scholars are like goads": even as a goad directs the beast along the furrows, to bring what is life-giving to its master, so the words of Torah direct a man's will (דעת) to the will of God.

And not only as though [the person] had heard it from many scholars, but as though he had heard it from the Sanhedrin [itself], for it is said (Eccl. 12:11), "Those gathered together"; and "those gathered together" is a reference to the Sanhedrin, as it is said (Num. 11:16), "Gather for Me seventy of Israel's elders."

And not only as though He had heard it from the Sanhedrin but as though he had heard it from the mouth of Moses, for it is said (Eccl. 12:11), "They were given by the singular shepherd,"[29] and it says (Isa. 63:11), "Then He remembered the ancient days, His people . . . [along with the shepherd of His flock]."

And not only as though He had heard it from the mouth of Moses, but as though he had heard it from the mouth of the Almighty, for it is said (Eccl. 12:11), "They were given by the Shepherd who is One,"[29] and it says (Ps. 80:2), "Give ear, O Shepherd of Israel who leads Joseph like a flock, appear, You who are enthroned on the cherubim," and it says (Deut. 6:4), "Hear, O Israel! The Lord is our God, the Lord is One."

The midrash goes on without any transition (although the editor quite rightly begins a new paragraph here):

sources other than Midrash (see, for example, Acts 17:7)—Abot 3:2a may be obliquely referring to it. But see also Tanhuma Debarim 4 (ed. Buber 1 b), *shello yegallu et ha-qeṣ.*

25. Though first impression of P. Sanhedrin 10:1, toward end, might make one think that this is a statement by Resh Laqish. I am unable to shake off the impression that the passage in ARNA, 72, top, is indeed a reference to first century reactions (cf. Josephus, *War*, II, 118 and Antiq., XVIII, 23?), despite G. Allon's analysis (*Meḥqarim*, I [Tel Aviv, 1957], 316–18). Attribution to Hananiah, prefect of the priests, is also to be rejected; cf. JAOS, vol. 96 (1976), 44, n. 42.

26. Sifre Deuteronomy 41, ed. L. Finkelstein, 86f.

27. *Qaṭan*: it may even mean a "minor," but I don't think this is what is principally intended here; emphasis is on one who is not a distinguished scholar. Note that Venice edition does not read "in Israel." Cf. also Vitry (p. 521), Bertinoro, Albeck on Abot 4:1. "Even as one is not ashamed to say to his inferior, 'Let me have a drink of water,' so ought he not to be ashamed to say to his inferior (*qaṭan*), 'Teach me Torah. . . .'" (Tanhuma Wa-Yaqhel 8).

28. This prooftext is not clear. Cf. L. Finkelstein's note to line 5, ibid.

29. On the ambiguity of this verse and other readings, cf. Finkelstein's note to line 11, ibid. But see also Midrash Tannaim, 34.

The verse in Canticles (7:5) says, "Your eyes are like pools in Heshbon, by the gate of Bath-rabbim."

"Your eyes" is a reference to the elders [זקנים, scholars authorized to act as judges];[30] who are appointed over the community. [Note also R. Aqiba and other sages in Lev. R. 11:8, 237f.] And so, too, it says (Isa. 29:10), "For the Lord has spread over you [the prophets and leaders] a spirit of deep sleep, and has shut your eyes."

"Pools" [teaches] that just as no man can make out what is deep down in a pool, so no man can fully comprehend the words of the Sages.

"In Heshbon" [refers] to deliberations,[31] to conclusions arrived at by mutual counsel and thought. Where are such conclusions arrived at? In the academies, "by the gate of Bath-rabbim," of the house of Rabbis.[32]

How does the Canticles verse continue? "Your face[33] is like the Lebanon tower that looks towards Damascus." If you have carried out the Torah,[34] look forward to Elijah, to whom I said (I Kings 19:15), "Go back by the way you came, on to the wilderness of Damascus." Moreover it says (Mal. 3:23–24), "Be mindful of the Teaching [Torah] of My servant Moses," etc., "Lo, I will send the prophet [Elijah]," etc.; "he shall reconcile [fathers]" etc.

Our passage is evidently in two parts, not logically combined but, as often in midrash, combined by association of thoughts—the Sanhedrin, incidentally, has already been referred to in part one: First, we are to listen very attentively to the proper teaching of even the least in Israel (as though we were listening to the Almighty Himself—who, according to the statement attributed to Resh Laqish,[35] will personally teach Israel Torah in the World to Come); second, If you are looking forward to Elijah's coming, then obey the instruction of the properly constituted authorities, the *zeqenim*, the Rabbis—even when you don't understand the reasons for their instruction.[36] Not rebellion against the Sages but obedience of, adherence to them[37] leads to legitimate expectations of the messianic herald.

That this should be stressed at all is indicative of the wide currency of

30. Cf. Lev. R. 2:4, 42; see also Sifre Num. 92, 92, and Sefer Pitron Torah, ed. E. E. Urbach, 259.

31. Obviously a play on *heshbon*, not in strictly arithmetical, reckoning sense (cf. Abot 4:22) but in deliberation and summing up when dealing with a problem. See also Pesiqta Kahana, 82, line 2, note.

32. Again a play on words, as though "Bath" = *beth* and *rabbim* were the plural of *rabbi*. A somewhat similar play on *rabbim* in Pesiqta Kahana, 16.

33. On 'p = "face," cf. dual form 'pym and BDB, 60.

34. Cf. S. Abramson in *Leshonenu* (5714), 61ff. Is the statement anti-Pauline? anti–Dead Sea sectarians? I take the statement to mean: If you carry out the Torah as the *hakamim* instruct, then you will merit the appearance of Elijah as herald of the Messiah. Cf. Ginzberg, *Sect*, 226f. and n. 84 ibid. See now further the supplementary note at the end of this paper.

35. Gen. R. 95:3, 1190 and note the citation in note to line 4 ibid. Cf. Deut. R., ed. Lieberman, 121, top, and n. 1 ad loc., and Tanhuma Ki Tabo 4, R. Jonah in R. Levi's name etc.; also Tanhuma Balak 14.

36. Note this *mood* in connection with *God's* decrees in Midrash ha-Gadol, Deut., ed. Fisch, 698, lines 18–21.

37. See also Sifre Deut. 49, 114 bottom, 115 top.

responsiveness to messianic propaganda and of the Rabbis' attempt to prevent such responsiveness from breaking down the structure of rabbinic doctrine and practice.[38] Are you eager to behold Elijah? Don't reject the instruction of Bathrabbim, even if you don't understand it entirely. (What is now obscure will become clear in the future: Tanhuma Ḥuqqat 8.) And as we move further along into the amoraic centuries, the precautionary, qualifying, hesitating note of Rabbis becomes more and more distinct. Let me mention just two texts which I find especially revealing. Rabbi Hanin said,[39]

> Israel will not require the teaching (*talmud*) of King Messiah in the Age to Come, for it is said (Isa. 11:10), 'Gentiles shall seek his instruction,' [Gentiles,] not Israel. If so, why is King Messiah coming, to what purpose? To assemble Israel's exiled ones and to give them thirty commandments. . . .

Leaving aside at present those highly problematic "thirty commandments,"[40] this much is clear: According to Rabbi Hanin, in the messianic age the scattered ones of Israel will be gathered together by the Messiah, which is as we would naturally expect in the light of interpretations of prophetic promises and daily prayers;[41] but the Messiah is to have no teaching role in Israel—hardly a compliment in the Jewish system of values; and that of course means that we can expect no new Torah from him (despite what some maintain).[42] For instruction, the Jews have their recognized Sages,[43] or, in the Age to Come, the Holy One, blessed be He.[44]

Now a second and perhaps more striking passage.[45] It was thanks to the patriarch Jacob that Samson could be buried in the grave of his father Manoah (= resting place?). For Jacob was looking ahead prophetically and beheld Samson in his mighty last act (Judg. 16:23–31). Jacob "then thought that Samson was King Messiah. But when Jacob saw that Samson died, Jacob exclaimed: 'So this one too has died! "I wait for *Your* deliverance, O Lord"' (Gen. 49:18)." In my opinion, not only is this a flashback to the failure of the Bar Kokba uprising (Samson an echo of the great luminary, or son of the star?

38. Cf. Scholem, op. cit., 54–57. Is this also reflected in part by Pesiqta Rabbati (ed. Friedmann) 42a (middle)? On crescendo of disobedience when the teachings of the Sages are ignored: Sifra 111b–c.

39. Gen. R. 98:9, 1260. Just before R. Hanin's statement, the "Rabbis" (רבנן) say that the Messiah will correct (but note comment to line 2) "their mistakes."

40. See the comments to lines 2 and 8 in Gen. R. 1260. But note also Ginzberg, *Sect*, 213 and note 18 ibid.

41. For example, Isa. 11:11–12, I Chron. 16:35, etc.; benediction 10 of the *Amidah* (and cf. L. Finkelstein, *Pharisaism in the Making* [New York, 1972], pp. 316f.; see further below, p. 375): actions performed by the Lord, but related to messianic events.

42. See below, n. 88.

43. Cf. Urbach, op. cit., 595. Note Tanhuma Naso 29.

44. Cf. the reference in n. 35, above, on God's daily creative teaching, Gen. R. 49:2. 501.

45. Gen. R. 98:14, 1265; cf. 99:11, 1282. On Samson as Redeemer, cf. Sifre Deut. 357, p. 425. For differing amoraic views of Manoah, cf. B. Berakot 61a.

See also Ginzberg, *Legends*, vol. VI, 206), but a criticism (or perhaps apology) by a play on the names *Aqiba* and *Ya'aqob*. Be that as it may, I have here learned that one who might have been regarded as a messiah died (and he's not Messiah, scion of Joseph); that at first *Ya'aqob* (no less! = Israel?) thought that Samson was the Messiah; that Jacob was wrong; and what is there left to say? [46]לישועתך קויתי ה' the biblical equivalent of על אבינו שבשמים על מי לנו להשען?. If salvation (triumph, deliverance) or redemption comes, it will come only from the Holy One, blessed be He. Even a mighty Samson, who brought down the temple on the jubilant Philistines and their god (note also Judg. 16:30), is not the genuine Messiah, and mistakes are possible. And if mistakes are possible the wise will be temperate. If you have to say such things, it's a sign that they are intemperate.

Thus far, the texts—both tannaite and amoraic—have represented the Sages as essentially guarded in their response to the messianic theme. To be so, I submit, required an extraordinary sense of realism; in a believing society which has been indoctrinated and persuaded by recurring biblical recitation and interpretation (of Pentateuch, prophetic writings, and an allegorized Canticles) that there is indeed such a thing as an Appointed Time when triumph and vindication are to be achieved, that a sorely defeated nation will finally be acknowledged as truly exalted, that reward is surely forthcoming to those loyal to divine imperatives and ideals, that God will be exalted in the world (and recognized universally) when like a chief justice He sentences the nations (Tanhuma Qedoshim 1)—in such a believing society to be able to discriminate between the shared belief and the unlikely translation of many of its components into immediate realization is, let me say it plainly, part of the rabbinic genius. I do not deny that Rabbis tried to check the messianic impatience of their contemporaries. Even the few passages we have cited are sufficient to demonstrate the rabbinic exercise of restraint in matters messianic. But that restraint was not merely an adopted device—a purely instrumental policy, a tactical reaching outward to keep the masses in their place—though it may have included that too. What the Rabbis were saying, from Yohanan ben Zakkai on, was what messianic speculation and doctrine had come to mean to *them*, to their own understanding, to their own intellectual grasp as a result of experience and reflection. The cautions they proclaimed at large were cautions perceived by themselves as built-in limitations or impossibilities of the vocabulary of messianic promises. Therefore they felt dutybound to communicate these cautions to the folk and to resort to strong rhetoric.

There were shrewd Rabbis—I'm not saying the Rabbis were shrewd; if we are to speak of *the* Rabbis we will have to assert, I believe, that they range over the whole spectrum, from naive to disillusioned: let's not forget that Elisha ben

---

46. Note how in 99:11, 1282, the reference moves over to Elijah of the tribe of Gad. On Jacob and the Messiah, see also R. Moshe ha-Darshan, *Bereshit Rabbati*, ed. Albeck, 249, n. 11.

368 : *Thematic Studies*

Abuyah was once one of them, and he was probably not the only one.[47] Furthermore, most if not all the rabbis were jurists (*nomikoi*), gifted at interpreting and reinterpreting a document. To repeat, a number of rabbis were shrewd and knew when necessary how to put off inquisitive questioners or critics, with a reed or comparison or protest of strict piety;[48] but their passion for the cohesion purposed by the Law (cf. Sifre Deut. 354, 416) and their fear of profaning the Name, it seems to me, saved them from joining the fraternity that holds, Let the people believe whatever they like, so long as they don't do anything about it.[49] Except for purposes of fiction or legend, the Rabbis should not be idealized, but neither should they be diminished to no more than ecclesiastical opportunists.[50] (Tanhuma Wa-Yeḥi 6 is pathetic, dispirited, defeatist, not contradictory of what is said here.)

It is of course undeniable that in their caution the Sages were influenced by historical events and circumstances, of the periods even before the tragic wars of the first and second centuries and the accompanying devastations. One's insight into his inherited texts, written and oral, is always affected by his experiences.[51] Like all other ideas, ideas of messianism are not immobile. They advance and retreat in the changing climate of history. In this sphere also, in visions as well, time and place are coefficient.

In the minds of many (perhaps most) rabbis, then, there has thus been created a dialectical strain between certainty of expectation and an intuition of the unlikelihood of its prompt realization and its overwrought pictorialization—for when one contemplates the features of the messianic age, one does not reflect on it to the exclusion of other themes and values and their survival; the whole long range of Torah and the authority of the Sages and the importance of correct practice and the nature of reward for steadfast loyalty and interruption and continuity and restitution must also be contemplated, as they

47. Note R. Simeon ben Yohai in M. Hagigah 1:7—observe the reading *talmid ḥakam* (= *ḥakamim*) in Codex Kaufmann—and see also Sifra be-Ḥuqqotai 110c, bot. line.

48. See Pesiqta Kahana, 74f. and parallels; cf. J. Goldin in E. S. Fiorenza, ed., *Aspects of Religious Propaganda in Judaism and Early Christianity* (Notre Dame, 1976), 141, nn. 33–35 [above, p. 365.—Ed.]. ARNB, 23f. (Saldarini, 79ff.); ARNA, 63.

49. Note only Pirqe Abot 1:11 (see also Seder Eliyahu R., ed. Friedmann, 12), 4:4, 5:9, but also, e.g., M. Shebout 6:7, end, and Tosafot Yom Tob ad loc. after quoting the Tosafists 43a, bottom, and citing Al-fasi. See also B. Berakot 19b, toward top.

What is running through my mind is Gibbon's well-known and brilliant observation in *Decline and Fall*, I, ii, right after the opening paragraph: "The various modes of worship which prevailed in the Roman world were all considered by the people as equally true; by the philosopher as equally false; and by the magistrate as equally useful." You can't fit the Rabbis into this scheme, and this applies to beliefs as well as to ritual; though when the Rabbis find that people cling to certain practices which border on the objectionable, they try to modify and make innocuous. Cf. S. Lieberman, *Greek in Jewish Palestine*, 92, 144.

50. This is in no way negated by the fact that "in order to make the people accept a new *ordinance* the Rabbis occasionally substituted some formal legalistic grounds for the real motive" (S. Lieberman, *Hellenism in Jewish Palestine*, 139ff.; my italics). To persuade people to adopt a regulation is not propagation of false doctrine, of what you don't believe.

51. The Midrash is full of this. Note indeed what might be called a *historical* awareness in Gen. R. 63:6, 684! Cf. also Yohanan ben Zakkai to his disciples on Cant. 1:8 in ARNA, 65.

are understood in the present and as they are meant to thrive in the future. This strain does not disappear.

Aqiba apparently was the only prominently known Sage (I do not mean to slight Eleazar ha-Moda'i) who prepared to translate the ideal into immediate action, and what Yohanan ben Torta said to him is well known.[52] The remark may be offensive, but alas it was true.

The characteristic caution and realism of the midrashic-talmudic Rabbis should not however blind us to the apocalyptic and utopian descriptions they have also created, or appropriated, or both—as homiletical promise of post-poned reward for the righteous. The beginning of the Sifra Be-Ḥuqqotai (ed. Weiss 110d–111b) contains a nice collection of them: That in the time to come there will be abundant and unfailing rains, which will never fall at inopportune hours. Fertility and wealth will be of supernatural proportions. The very bark of trees will be edible (like the *etrog* tree? cf. Pesiqta Kahana, 314), not to speak of once-barren trees now bearing fruit. To be satisfied, even small amounts of food will suffice. Gone will be all fears, and wild beasts will no longer be dangerous (note also Isa. 35:9 and Philo, *Rewards and Punishments*, 85–91). It will be a reign of peace, which outweighs everything else. So the sayings continue, attended by the relevant biblical verses, and the statements would not be out of place even in some of the post-talmudic pseudepigrapha collected by Judah Eben Shmuel. One particularly daring passage in the Sifra deserves more than paraphrase; it is the comment on "I will be ever present (*we-hithalakti*) in your midst" of Lev. 26:12[53] (and see also Deut. R. 1:12 and 5:8, 110c)—

It is to be expressed by means of parable; to what may this be likened? To a king who went out to stroll in his orchard (*pardes*[!]) with his tenant farmer, and [out of

52. Lam. R. 2:4, 21a; P. Taanit 4:5, 68d. Cf. G. Allon, *Toledot ha-Yehudim* (Israel, 1955), II, 33–38, and 41–43 (with part of which I disagree).

I do not find in any of the sources that *large* numbers of Rabbis joined Aqiba in the Bar Kokba revolt; the *shemad* reported of his numerous disciples is not only late (Sherira Gaon) but is almost certainly an elaboration of the tradition (ARNB, p. 29) of the extraordinary number of disciples he attracted. Indeed, to judge from the accounts of scholars visiting the imprisoned Aqiba, one would be led to conclude that at least these men, moving about cautiously but freely, did not participate in the militant activities. Even as he is martyred, the haggadah pictures disciples as standing by and engaging Aqiba in "conversation."

It is possible of course to propose that the sources have been deliberately edited, after the defeat, to remove all traces of a large rabbinic following. In that event, however, how come that the statement of Aqiba about Bar Kokba has been allowed to survive? This is particularly embarrassing. On Aqiba's confidence, see Lam. R. on 5:18, 31a–b.

Naturally I do not deny that there may have been scholars who followed Aqiba's example. We do come upon the expression, "R. Aqiba and his *ḥaberim*" (c.f., e.g., R. Yohanan in B. Rosh ha-Shanah 23a, bottom). But I'm speaking of "prominently known sages"; that is the emphasis (again without intention to detract from the stature of Eleazar ha-Moda'i).

53. For the reading cf. Midrash ha-Gadol, Lev. (ed. Rabinowitz), 664 (ed. Steinsalz, 738) and Masoret ha-Talmud in Sifra, ed. Weiss, ad loc. Cf. S. Lieberman, *Shkiin* (Jerusalem, 1970), 14, 99. See I. Ziegler, *Die Königsgleichnisse des Midrasch* (Breslau, 1903), 226. And cf. Philo, *Rewards and Punishments*, 123 (Loeb Classics, VIII, 387).

respect] that tenant kept hiding himself from the presence of the king. So the king said to that tenant, "Why do you hide from me? Behold, I, you—we're alike!" Similarly[54] in the Age to Come the Holy One, blessed be He, will stroll with the righteous in the Garden of Eden, but when the righteous see Him they will tremble before Him; and the Holy One, blessed be He, will say to them, "Why is it that you tremble before Me? Behold, I, you—we're alike!"

Here is a dizzying prospect, God describing Himself as הריני כיוצא בכם, I, you—we're alike! (This may mean: You and I have the same interests, or, the same terms of praise are applied to God and to the righteous,)[55] No wonder the Sifra adds immediately, "Is this to say that you will no longer have fear/ reverence of Me? The verse [ibid.] reads, 'I will [still] be your God, and you shall be My *people*.'"

One additional aspect of rabbinic thought should be noted, to wit, that study of the Law—all of it, whether capable of being put to practice or theoretical for the time being—continued to be a reminder of what was to take place "when the Temple will be rebuilt." Such thinking was probably more conscious in rabbinic than in popular circles; but it encouraged nostalgia for the messianic era and very likely reinforced or was reinforced by the more readily comprehended forecasts to the people at large.

As in all literature, therefore, thoughts of the Hereafter for those to be rewarded lead to hyperbole.[56] Such thoughts are even more sensational in connection with those to be punished.[57] Early or late, heterodox or orthodox, cautious and reckless, scholarly and non-scholarly, the flamboyant promises are irresistible. Hence all the more reason for attempting to curb the imagination given to excessive anticipation. Enough to be reassured that in the End the nation will be redeemed and all the exiled will be brought back together to a supernaturally enlarged Holy City and Land;[58] and a descendant of the Davidic dynasty—perhaps miraculously David himself[59]—will be their king or prince. This restoration is permanent.[60] And if you feel a flourish is still needed, there's Leviticus Rabba announcing, "For in this world it is that the Shekinah is revealed to [choice] individuals; but of the World to Come what is written?

54. Reading with Midrash ha-Gadol, ibid. On "Stroll" cf. A. Mirsky in *Sinai*, 87 (5740), 221ff., s.v. *ṭyyl*.

55. Cf. Seder Eliyahu R., ed. Friedmann, 35; reproduced in Lev. R. 2:10, 51. See also R. Yannai in Pesiqta Kahana, 87, last line; Pesiqta Rabbati, 70b.

56. See J. Klausner, op. cit., chapters on the Pseudepigrapha. On King Messiah as judge in Jerusalem in the Age to Come, Pesiqta Kahana, 300.

57. Cf. S. Lieberman in *Louis Ginzberg Jubilee Volume* (Heb., New York, 1945), 249ff. Here what is being discussed is not national calamity, but the sentencing of wicked individuals. On visions of hell more vivid than those of heaven, cf. M. W. Bloomfield, *The Seven Deadly Sins* (Michigan, 1967), 93 and n. 254, ibid.

58. Cf. Lev. R. 10:9, 218 and ARNA, p. 106; see also Tanhuma Exod., ed. Buber, 39a.

59. Cf. B. Sanhedrin 98b, toward bottom. See also Abarbanel on Ezek. 37:24.

60. Cf. Sefer Pitron Torah, 244; cf. Deut. R. 3:11, end, and on verb "plant" see J. Goldin, *The Song at the Sea* (New Haven, 1971), 40f.

'The *Presence* of the Lord shall be revealed, and all flesh, as one, shall behold [it]'" (Isa. 40:5).[61]

The midrashic-talmudic Rabbis were certainly an Establishment or, perhaps better put, did everything in their power to become the Establishment and to be acknowledged as such. We're speaking of course of a religious-intellectual Establishment. Truth is, however, that "religious," "intellectual" too, here includes so many aspects of social life and individual deportment that it is more enlightening to expect rabbinic appetite for influence and authority in a wider rather than narrower extent. The Rabbis do not hesitate to express their respective points of view on any subject that has come to their attention, certainly on so contagious a theme as messianism. And on such a theme, what interests them, and how they treat it, can be detected beyond rabbinic circles too. One midrashic anecdote reflects this admirably.[62]

An *'am ha-'areṣ*, חד עם דאראעא, said to R. Hoshaya: "If I tell you an attractive interpretation,[63] will you repeat it in public [probably = use it in a sermon] in my name?" "What is it?" R. Hoshaya said to him. The man replied: "[I can prove that] all the gifts which Father Jacob gave to Esau (Gen. 33:10–11), will be returned to King Messiah by the nations of the world in the Age to Come. Proof: The verse (Ps. 72:10) reads, 'The kings of Tarshish and of the isles of gifts will'—note, it doesn't say 'will bring' (יביא), but 'will bring back'" (ישיבו). Said R. Hoshaya to him, "By your life! That's an excellent interpretation you've presented. I shall certainly repeat it in your name."

R. Hoshaya can't resist his admiration: "By your life!" (euphemism for "by my life").

Such is the midrash of an *'am ha-'areṣ*, and I don't think a rabbi could do better.

In other words, there is a good deal of common discourse—and even manner of expression—between the men who present themselves as the élite and the rest of society; and by fairly or relatively close contact between them, two things are achieved (I confine myself here to the subject of messianism—the whole question of the relations of the Rabbis to the folk is too big to be dealt with in one paper): (1) the Establishment doesn't withdraw too far away from the folk *lore*: (2) by sharing it, the Establishment hopes that it may direct the folk to moderation when abandonment of reasonableness threatens.

Consider, for example, the calculators of the messianic due date, the מחשבי קצין, from Daniel to Maimonides (and his family tradition)[64] to Sir Isaac

---

61. Lev. R. 1:14, p. 32; see also Tanhuma Miqqeṣ 2, end, ed. Buber, 96b.

62. Gen. R. 78:12, 932f. (note the reading in Tanhuma, ed. Buber, referred to in the Gen. R. commentary ad loc.!). Sages being taught by those not learned can be seen also in Gen. R. 32:10, 296f.

63. חדא מילא מבא. In Tanhuma, ed. Buber (Gen. 85a) טיבו של מדרש (a kind of midrash?).

64. Maimonides, *Epistle to Yemen* (ed. A. S. Halkin, New York, 1952), 80ff. See R. Yose in Derek Ereṣ, ed. Higger, p. 313.

Newton and beyond.[65] If a messiah or redemption is to come, particularly if subjection to aliens drags on interminably, the temptation to discover hints of the redeemer's hour of arrival is overpowering—imagine, if you can, a wedding invitation with the date left out. The Sages themselves can't help indulging in the exercise. And when Rab declares כלו כל הקיצין, all the calculations have failed,[66] he sounds to me like one who has experimented with many computations but found that none of them worked. Apparently therefore אין הדבר תלוי אלא בתשובה ומעשים טובים, redemption now depends only on repentance and good works. That repentance is necessary, the Tanna R. Eliezer maintained, in any event until he was silenced. At least in one version of a *baraita*, the Tanna Rabbi Joshua could conceive of redemption taking place even in the absence of *teshubah*: there is a fixed time for redemption, repentance or no repentance[67]—but we don't know what time it is. If I understand him correctly, Rabbi Joshua is saying: There is unquestionably a קץ, as promised by that man clothed in linen (Dan. 12:7), but it is a mystery (Dan. 12:8-9). And a mystery is not what one understands, it's what one comes to terms with.

We will return shortly to the End-time calculations. First, however, a word or two about Samuel's famous saying,[68] which proved so appealing almost a millennium later to Maimonides, that אין בין העולם הזה לימות המשיח אלא שעבוד מלכויות (גלויות) בלבד, only subjection to foreign powers distinguishes the present age from the days of the Messiah;[69] for instance, there will be poor then also as there are now. And the Talmud[70] has justice on its side when in one version of a *baraita* it finds a correspondence between the view of the Tanna R. Eliezer and Samuel the Amora's view, for R. Eliezer believes that in the messianic age military hardware will still be needed. The persistence of the poor and the persistence of war as the two illustrations—you might almost make a Marxist *derashah* out of that. Clearly for Samuel, extravagant messianic promises—highly charged visionary exaggerations—are uncalled for. But let us not minimize what he, too, does anticipate, the disappearance of שעבוד מלכויות—no

65. See R. Popkin, "Jewish Messianism and Christian Millenarianism," in P. Zagorin, ed., *Culture and Politics from Puritanism to the Enlightenment* (Los Angeles, 1980), 67–90. On the expression *dohaqin 'et ha-qeṣ* cf. Lev. R. 19:5, 429, Margulies' note to line 1. In Mekilta, Be-Shallaḥ 1 (ed. Lauterbach I, 120), *'al she-'abru 'al ha-qeṣ*; in Pesiqta Kahana, 186, *'al she-ṭa'u 'et ha-qeṣ*. . . . On *qeṣ* = God's right hand = redemption, ibid., 286. In Cant. R. 2:7, 16c, *shelo' yidḥaqu 'al ha-qeṣ*.

66. B. Sanhedrin 97b.

67. B. Sanhedrin 97b–98a. Note also the interlocutors in Tanhuma Be-Ḥuqqotai 3, end, but cf. ed. Buber, 56a.

68. B. Berakhot 34b and parallels. (In B. Shabbat 63a and Sanhedrin 91b the reading is *galuyyot* rather than *malkiyyot*, and the statement in Sanhedrin 99a is wanting in MSS, according to DS.) Note Tosafot ad Shabbat 63a. Is Samuel's statement in the spirit of the Hillelites regarding *yeṣirat ha-welad* in the Age to Come, Lev. R. 14:9, 315f.?

69. On why Maimonides "codified" Samuel's view, see now I. Twersky, *Introduction to the Code of Maimonides* (New Haven, 1980), 66ff., 476f., and 451 plus its notes 231–233.

70. B. Shabbat 63a.

little matter in the third and subsequent centuries. A free and independent Israel would surely be something of a messianic, miraculous happening to generations of Jews, especially those for whom the language of the Prophets transcended metaphor.

Let me repeat: I do not deny that Samuel's statement is meant also to check utopian extravagance, and maybe it did to some degree. All I'm trying to emphasize is that his own statement also incorporates big, ambitious, spectacular hopefulness. Anyway, although Samuel may be discouraging apocalyptic expectations, for him no less than for others, messianic times are a by no means minor departure from the present. As to how the Messiah will come, maybe what is reported of Samuel's mocking retort to the provocative mockery of King Sapur[71] is enough to suggest that here, too, supernatural intervention will be required. For regardless of the sober or inflammatory or utopian view of a Sage, all recognized in the arrival of the Messiah or messianic kingdom a supernatural event, something that could not come to pass without the Superterrestrial in command.

George Foot Moore (*Judaism* II, 371) has said it well:

> The expectation of a golden age of the Jewish nation attached itself to the prophecies of liberation from foreign dominion, and restoration of independence under the rule of a wise and good king of the old line of kings of Judah, an age crowded with all the blessings of God. About the fate of other nations in that time there were diverse predictions; they should be subjugated, or destroyed, or converted. Whatever became of them they would no longer be an affliction or a menace or a temptation to God's people.

One may even add that in the Age to Come–messianic days, the nations will use their expertise to serve Israel.[72]

So long as the promise of redemption is not denied, whether in milder or in fantasy terms, new attempts are made after each failure to arrive at the correct messianic date. From a *baraita* citing R. Nathan[73] we learn that a number of "our Rabbis" (*rabbotenu*) engaged in calculating the End, that so did Rabbi Simlai, and so did Rabbi Aqiba. That the practice was even more common, and that it continued into amoraic times (and beyond), we learn from an outburst by R. Jonathan (ben Eleazar) as he was quoted by R. Samuel bar Nahman: "Blast the very existence of the *qeṣ* calculators." Why the rabbi resorts to such explosive denunciation is fortunately made explicit by what he adds—in short, no conjectures are necessary in this instance. Damn these *qeṣ* calculators,

71. B. Sanhedrin 98a.

72. Deut. R., ed. Lieberman, 73, and notes ad loc.

73. B. Sanhedrin 97b. (Is this really a *baraita*? Note inclusion of R. Simlai; so, too, in Yalqut Shimeoni [photo offset, Salonica, 1521] on the Hab. verse; was this interpolated in the *baraita*?) For a homily on what makes Israel capable of waiting, cf. Pesiqta Kahana, 305f. (Pesiqta Rabbati, 106a–b): God is Himself surprised by their fidelity.

"because when a *qeṣ* arrived and there was still no sign of the Messiah, they would say, 'He'll never come.'" Instead, the rabbi urges,

> "Wait for him, as it is said (Hab. 2:3), 'Even if he tarries, wait for him still.' And if you protest, 'We *are* waiting, it's he who is [no longer] waiting,' the verse (Isa. 30:18) declares, 'Truly, the Lord is waiting to show you grace, truly He will arise to show you compassion [for the Lord is a God of justice]!'"
>
> "Since we're waiting and He's waiting, what's holding Him back?"
>
> "The demands of justice are holding Him back," that is, the time for redemption has not yet come because we are still sin-laden, or the nations have not yet filled their quota of sins.
>
> "Well then, if it's the demands of justice holding Him back, what point is there to our waiting?"
>
> "To be rewarded [for the act of waiting], for it is said (Isa., 30:18), 'Happy are all who wait for Him.'"[74]

And Maimonides, that exemplar of sober and humane messianism, much later pleads eloquently in his Epistle to Yemen (60–61), "The longer the delay, the more fervently shall you hope."[75]

The pathos of waiting and waiting (note also the blending of God and Messiah in the interpretation of the verses) with hardly lively expectation of speedy or early fulfillment is seldom so poignantly formulated. (Yohanan ben Torta certainly did not expect the Messiah in the near future.) And I hasten to add: This must not be treated as a mere literary tour de force. We are led here to a level of theology which repeatedly must serve as a station in contemplating the abyss between divine promise and human disappointment, between the edicts of Revelation and the sordid demands of human survival. One must wait because human enterprise, or craving, or appeal, or exertion, by itself, is not the only course of action. "They also serve who only stand and wait,"[76] albeit "also" sounds more like resignation than affirmation. The dialectic we referred to earlier is still with us.

Much in medieval rabbinic teaching and expectation is a continuation of the teaching and expectations of midrashic-talmudic centuries, as is to be anticipated. But there is a fundamental difference that must not be obscured.

---

74. Cf. Tanhuma Exodus, ed. Buber, 30a–b.

75. Maimonides, *Epistle to Yemen* (60–61). Trans. Boaz Cohen in A. Halkin and B. Cohen, *Epistle to Yemen* (New York, 1952), xii.

76. God keeps to His own purpose while we are otherwise engaged. Cf. Gen. R. 85:1, 1030: While the tribes were busy getting Joseph sold, and Jacob was busy with his mourning sackcloth and fasting, and Judah was busy getting a wife, the Holy One, blessed be He, was shaping the loaf of the King Messiah (reading *bode'*, lit. "setting aside," instead of *bore'* and *se'oro*—lit., "fermenting dough"—rather than *'oro*, according to S. Lieberman, *Shkiin*, 74). On the reading *se'or* rather than *ma'or*, cf. Lam. R., ed. Buber, Petiḥta 2, p. 3.

"There are two cardinal sins from which all the others spring: impatience and laziness. Because of impatience we were driven out of Paradise, because of laziness we cannot return" (Franz Kafka, "Reflections" no. 3, in *The Great Wall of China* [Shocken: New York, 1946], 278).

What had been for the authors of early apocalypses, for the Tannaim, and for the Amoraim, repeated exhortation, emphasis, accepted expression of promise, unobstructed vista, something of almost final doctrine, too,[77] had grown into dogma, *yesod* (given that eminence particularly by Maimonides),[78] into fixed assumption, axiomatical theory and doctrinal orthodoxy first in the succeeding geonic period and then in the medieval one (though in the latter period it was especially subjected also to radical allegorization). This is not to say that in the tannaite-amoraic centuries the messianic idea had not taken hold of learned and popular audiences; but it is to say that the idea as a basic unquestioned principle, in other words, as a universally accepted dogmatic affirmation, was still in a formative stage of sorts. This can serve to explain the legitimacy of assorted views regarding the conditions in which the Messiah would come, the duration of the messianic period, the different names for the Messiah as compliment and dubious compliment.[79] This still formative (though important and attractive although hazardous as well) messianism helps explain why a Rabbi Hillel can be rebuked, but no one's stare reduces him to a heap of bones nor is he warned that he may lose his share in the World to Come: the sources at least don't report that. How different if he had dared to deny Resurrection (B. Sanhedrin 90a)!

Indeed, except for the strong belief shared apparently by all the Sages and those accepting their authority (and others, too), that in the End Israel would finally be redeemed and vindicated (and that this was not likely to happen before the Wicked Empire fell, or happen peacefully), it is not so much *a* view of the messianic future which midrashic sources provide, as it is many views and many guesses of different Rabbis, with more or less unrestrained imaginativeness and an exhibition of exegetical dexterity.

It may help explain one other feature of what was to become the authoritative source for Judaism, namely, the Talmud. On the doctrine or rule of belief in a forthcoming Messiah or messianic age, the Mishnah says nothing—as it says nothing about angels. Interestingly, the discussion of the messianic theme is introduced in the Babylonian Talmud (Sanhedrin 96b, bottom, through 99a) not because the Mishnah (10:1, Talmud 11:1) contains a ruling on the subject. The Mishnah speaks of those who deny the teaching of Resur-

---

77. Note texts of benedictions 1 and 15 of *Amidah* in L. Finkelstein, *Pharisaism in the Making* (New York, 1972), 304, 322; God as Redeemer, benediction 7, 147ff.

78. Introduction to M. Sandehrin X, ed. Kafiḥ, 139–140a, 144b.

79. B. Sanhedrin 96b, 98b. In a letter (3/22/81), Professor Elias Bickerman writes: "The doctrine (i.e., messianism), by the way, is quite late and has been advanced, I imagine, by anti-Hasmonean and anti-Herodian elements. Before, say, 150 B.C.E. the Jews, rather, had believed that the Lord Himself would come (or would send an angel, etc.) to destroy the nations and to establish His kingdom forever."

Perhaps, therefore, what has been observed above, pp. 363, 370, and 372–373 end, can be explained as a faint persistence of this older view even in centuries when a messiah is spoken of. Cf. conclusion of Tanhuma Aḥare Mot, and ed. Buber 36a. The Messiah is after all an agent of God. On names of the Messiah cf. Midrash Prov. 19, 44a, and Buber's n. 22.

376 : *Thematic Studies*

rection. Hence, first the Talmud discusses this at length (beginning with 90a) and then moves on to closely related subjects (from 92b on, on ancient worthies saved from death miraculously, etc.), and finally takes up the messianic motif. This is reasonable, intelligible and intelligent redaction.

But in the Palestinian Talmud, on the same Mishnah ruling, not a word of the messianic teachings. There are of course messianic statements in the Palestinian as in the Babylonian Talmud. But the redaction of what might be called *sugya*, that is, a collection or review of messianic sayings by *ḥakamim* on our Mishnah Sanhedrin, is wanting.

To my mind, *tentatively* (for many are the discussions in the Palestinian Talmud which, compared to the Babylonian, are considerably shorter); that itself may be a sign of the teaching still in a formative state. Were the editors of the Palestinian Talmud less interested in the Messiah than their Babylonian counterparts? Of course not. (Note indeed the Palestinian Sages quoted in B. Sanhedrin 98a–b.) But the Palestinian redactors had yet to put together their messianic materials, if ever.[80]

One final observation. There is no denying, as we have said, that already in midrashic-talmudic centuries, more so even later, the Rabbis tried to check thought and conduct that would give unrestricted sway to messianic ideas and imagery taken literally. The Amora R. Yohanan of the third century could teach on the one hand that the world was created for the sake of the Messiah, and on the other hand exclaim, May I not live to see him arrive![81] He is not the only Sage preferring to forego the catastrophic privilege, preliminary to the messianic dénouement.[82] Remarks like these were an attempt to impede messianic enthusiasts in their activity. Gradually the messianic visions and cravings were therefore transposed into routinized piety, rehearsed yearnings becoming part of a vocabulary liturgized, a sentiment of normative recitative, and wistful remembrance with some ceremonialism, too, occasionally

80. The Palestinian Talmud is shorter than the Babylonian, and I am not suggesting that this is due only to editorial failure to be fuller in discussions. Other factors may also be responsible. For example, although its Mishnah also lists in Sanhedrin 10:1 "the one who says, Torah is not from Heaven" (but note extremely brief exchange in Talmud ad loc.) "and the one who denies Resurrection," the Palestinian Talmud ad loc. (cf. T. Sanhedrin 12:9) does not take these up but proceeds along lines other than those of the Babylonian. Moreover, the Babylonian Talmud had at least another century of give-and-take plus the attention of the *Saboraim*. It is impossible to say definitely why the Palestinian brevity.

81. B. Sanhedrin 98b. Note also ibid. his concern for those who are to suffer and cf. B. Megillah 10b; cf. P. Baba Qamma 8:4, end. Note, too, J. Heinemann in *Bar Ilan Annual*, VII–VIII (5729–30), 80ff.

82. B. Sanhedrin, ibid. The contrast between the classical messianic conception and the Lurianic one is vividly and vigorously drawn by Scholem (see the first essay in his *Messianic Idea* and the first chapter of his *Sabbatai Ṣevi*), that while in the latter, messianic redemption is regarded as an outgrowth, a logical process, "natural" development out of the recovery and perfection gradually attained by man, the former (midrashic-talmudic) envisages the arrival of the messianic age as a catastrophic event, a discontinuous stage at history's end. This very conception, therefore, must have contributed to the feelings of anxiety and caution of the Tannaim and Amoraim.

attached.[83] In other words, something like what happened in connection with the whole sacrificial cult has happened here: a manifold activity has been reduced to study and recitation; which is another way of saying, without the collaboration of propitious historical circumstances, literal realization is inevitably postponed to eschatology. So was lost the sense of any immediately compelling summons to the messianic idea. And very likely the Rabbis, because of their influence, are the ones chiefly responsible for that,[84] though disappointment must also have contributed to incredulity and disillusionment. Rationalistic philosophers probably also had some effect.

Now, we know that the Rabbis did not always succeed, that messianic movements of one kind or another continued to erupt, that sects and sectarianism of various shades continued to divide Jewish society throughout the Jewish Middle Ages.[85] "The sons of Korah did not die." Rabbinic authorities, when themselves unpersuaded—for of course there were Rabbis as vulnerable as their flock or their communities—resolved to suppress them and were anything but gentle in their offensive.[86] We are not called upon to approve of or imitate their tactics. But we do have the advantage of hindsight; there are, therefore, no grounds for assuming that our partisanship is the product of wisdom or clairvoyance on our part. Knowing what we do about the dynamics and outcome of the messianic movements in Israel familiar to us,[87] and without attributing to midrashic-talmudic Sages the possibly more thoroughly organized polemic and strategies of the post-talmudic rabbis, it seems to me fair to say that the Tannaim and Amoraim were responding to a presentiment. They foresaw a real danger in a doctrine they shared with their people and therefore tried to draw the limits of a promise which yet preserved a profound hope and

---

83. Cf. Scholem, op. cit., 56f. But note also Philo, *On the Virtues*, 119–20. On "Ani Ma'amin" as martyrs' hymn during the Nazi Holocaust, cf. *Encyclopaedia Judaica* (1972), 3:5.

84. Cf. Cant. R. 2:7, 16c, and R. David Luria ad loc. The medieval radical allegorization— sometimes one may even say, evaporation—of the messianic concept has recently been described by M. Saperstein, *Decoding the Rabbis* (Cambridge, Mass., 1980), 102ff., 116ff.; note above all 250, n. 153!

85. Cf. A. Z. Aescoly, *Jewish Messianic Movements* (Heb., Jerusalem, 1956), chaps. 3 (end)–5 (on the list of sects, cf. ibid., 102, n. 30). Note especially Z. Ankori, *Karaites in Byzantium* (New York-Jerusalem, 1959), 10f., 16. See also G. D. Cohen, "Messianic Postures of Ashkenazim and Sephardim" in *Studies of the Leo Baeck Institute*, ed. M. Kreutzberger (New York, 1967), 117ff.

86. Cf., e.g., Aescoly, 158, 163. A summary of post-talmudic literary-philosophical opposition to messianic calculation, in A. H. Silver, *A History of Messianic Speculation in Israel* (New York, 1927), 207ff.

87. Made vivid by Scholem; see especially his "Redemption Through Sin" in *Messianic Idea in Judaism*, 78–141; *Sabbatai Ṣevi* (Princeton, 1973); and also the relevant discussions (by use of Index) in *Major Trends in Jewish Mysticism* (New York, 1961).

"David Biale: 'Is the Gush Emunim a modern-day version of the Sabbatian movement?'

"Gershom Scholem: 'Yes they are like the Sabbatians, their messianic program can only lead to disaster. In the seventeenth century, of course, the failure of Sabbatianism had only spiritual consequences; it led to a breakdown of Jewish belief. Today, the consequences of such messianism are also political and that is the great danger.'" ("The Threat of Messianism: an Interview with Gershom Scholem," in *The New York Review*, 14 August 1980, p. 22.)

consolation; thus they surrendered to a severe (should I say, permanent?) tension in their faith, but prevented Israel from splitting into a post-Lutheran multitude of denominations after each devastating disappointment. This is not the least of their endowments.[88]

88. On new Torah cf. Scholem, *Messianic Idea*, 55f. and the references in his notes, 344. The statements about a new Torah or new Torah-teachings חדושי תורה remain difficult. For example, the authenticity of the statement in Alpha Beta de-Rabbi Aqiba (*Bet ha-Midrasch*, ed. Jellinek, III, 27), that in the future God will sit with the righteous in the Garden of Eden and will teach them "the [secret?] meanings of the new Torah (טעמי תורה חדשה) which the Holy One, blessed be He, will give to them by the hand of Messiah," Albeck in Gen. R. (1260, note to line 2) suspects. But see also Ginzberg, *Sect*, 213f. and nn. 20–22. And see also Eccl. R. 11:8, 29c.

I think that Margulies is right (not just rationalizing) in his commentary on Lev. R. 9:7, 185f., that since in the Age to Come there will be neither sins nor unsatisfied needs, only thanksgiving offerings and thanksgiving prayers are meaningful.

As for *ḥiddushe Torah* (Lev. R. 13:3, 278), note that this appears in context of forbidden and permitted edibles. Now, Lev. 11:44f. states clearly that the food laws of that chapter were given so that Israel would sanctify themselves, and in 20:26 separation from the nations is spoken of. See also Sifra (ed. Weiss) 57b and 93d. On separation of Israel, cf. Midrash ha-Gadol, Lev. (ed. Rabinowitz), 516 (ed. Steinsalz, 583f.). But in messianic triumph such isolation will no longer be necessary. Of themselves, therefore, such foods could theoretically be desirable: note the statement by R. Eleazar ben Azariah at the end of Sifra Qedoshim (93d), and note Rashi's reading on Lev. 20:26. Cf. Sifre Deut. 72, p. 136 and Midrash Tannaim 51 (and 92?). To this it seems to me *ḥiddushe Torah* may be related.

From the reading of Midrash Ps. 146, p. 535 (here more than forbidden foods are spoken of)—and note also Buber's note 4 ibid.—Scholem (p. 344, n. 10) quotes the statement on cohabitation as evidence of fantasy and the purely speculative taking over. But the statement might well be in the spirit of what Rab was fond of saying, מרגלא בפומיה (B. Berakot 17a; in Kallah, ed. Higger, 194f. it is introduced as a *baraita, tanya*), that in the World to Come there will be no eating or drinking or פריה ורביה, etc. The vocabulary in Midrash Ps., however, is more sweeping (תשמיש המטה). But is this frame of mind radically different from Maimonides'? Cf. I. Twersky, op. cit., 465 ff. Note also the attitude in Lev. R. 14:15, 308; Deut. R. 11, toward end. As to extraordinary conception in Alphabet of Ben Sira (ed. Habermann, *Ḥadashim Gam Jeshanim* [Jerusalem, 1975], p. 125), cf. L. Ginzberg, in *Jewish Encyclopedia* (1902), II, 680a and *Legends*, VI, 401f. See also what is reported of the Besht in S. Dubnow, *History of Hasidism* (Heb., Tel-Aviv, 1931), 415, top—whether authentic or invented is immaterial. (Cf. *In Praise of the Baal Shem Tov*, trans. D. Ben-Amos and J. R. Mintz [Bloomington, 1970], p. 258, no. 249, and note ad loc.) My point is, fantasy though this be, apparently it continues to attract various types of thinkers and pneumatics in all ages. Similar views may not be commonplace, but are still capable of being favored even in the twentieth century; cf. *New York Times*, 12 October 1980, page 12 of the first section.

Apropos resurrection and the married state, see Saadia's remark in op. cit., VII:7 (trans. 282).

In connection with the subject of shrouds for a corpse, whether these too must be free of diverse kinds of material (see Lev. 19:19), that is, if some mixture were present but was invisible, might the shroud still be used, R. Yohanan is cited (in Niddah 61b; note anonymous quotation in Deut. R., ed. Lieberman, 38), "Once a man dies the commandments are no longer binding on him" (note the midrashic play on Ps. 88:6). Cf. Romans 7:1–6. Rab Joseph apparently (Niddah, ibid.) understood that to mean "The commandments are not binding in the Age to Come" (by the way, see Tosafot ibid., s.v., "*'amar rab Yosef*"). The Meiri ad loc. (ed. A. Sofer, New York, 1949, p. 257) adds simply that the living are not bound to provide the dead with shrouds of unmixed materials. Cf. Maimonides, *Code*, Seeds, Kilayim 10:25, beginning, and *Pne Mosheh* at P. Kilayim 9:3, beginning.

Such is the context of R. Yohanan's-Rab Joseph's remark. In short, I wonder whether Age to Come here refers only (?) to Resurrection. See also S. Lieberman, *Shkiin*, 81, 102. (P.s. In B. Abodah Zarah 65b the reading is "shrouds for a *met miṣwah*," a corpse found with no one to attend to it. The same reading in ed. S. Abramson, except that someone has crossed out the word *miṣwah*, still clearly visible. On *met miṣwah*, cf. Lev. R. 26:8, 611. Note also S. Lieberman, *Tosefta ki-Fshuṭah*, Moed, 325, n. 31)

For reflections on the Christian messiah and midrashic-talmudic views of the *aqedah*, see S. Spiegel, *The Last Trial* (New York, 1967), IX, 77–120.

Supplementary Note (see above, n. 34) On 1 September 1981 I received my copy of the March (!) 1981 issue of the JBL (vol. 100, no. 1), which contains a stimulating paper by M. M. Faierstein (pp. 75–86), in which the author points out that in midrashic-talmudic literature, with the exception of B. Erubin 43b (and Tg. Jonathan), Elijah is not spoken of as forerunner of Messiah. I do not accept his conclusion for our Sifre passage because then at best what the Sifre promises would be pointless, at worst meaningless.

If we carry out the Torah (= if we carry out the injunctions of the Torah as the Sages define them), then and only then are we to look forward to Elijah's coming. What will Elijah's arrival accomplish? And end to academic controversies and stabilization of families? But our whole passage, "Your eyes are like pools in Heshbon," is hardly an exhortation to academes, to the *ḥakamim*—they know quite well without being told that there are views deep as pools that can't be made clear to the folk, they are the ones who know that the authoritative views are adopted in the precincts of the *rabbim*, the Rabbis; they always insist that the eyes of the community are the *zeqenim*. It is the community, the folk, that have to be encouraged to obey the *ḥakamim*, whether the folk understand why the teachers rule as they do or don't understand. If, therefore, the folk are exhorted and promised that obedience will bring Elijah, for what purpose is Elijah to come? This I take to be, he is coming as the herald of the Messiah. (To settle academic disputes and demonstrate whom to bring near and whom to keep at a distance would appeal if not exclusively, then principally, only to scholars.)

And this in turn, I believe, makes clear the audience intended by the first half on "which I enjoin upon you," that is indeed a homily to *ḥakamim*—listen attentively to even the least in your midst, as though his view were held not just by one scholar but by many, as though the view were the expression of Moses, of the Almighty who is (also?) One (one?). Thus the two paragraphs complement each other, the first an exhortation to scholars, the second an exhortation to the folk.

Of the Midrash and Talmud Teachers*

In order to avoid extravagant generalization, let's get our bearings at once and specify *whom* we're talking about, the *time* we're talking about, and the *place* we're talking about. First, therefore, *whom* are we talking about? They are the men whom we generally refer to as "the Rabbis." The word "rabbi" means "my master." For example, a slave has a *rab*, a master, to whom he submits and must always obey. One may even speak of a *rab*, chief, of weavers. When I was chief of brigands, says a third century Palestinian sage, I was addressed as Rabbi and now I'm a scholar, they still call me Rabbi. Not everyone called Rabbi is a rabbi, any more than anyone I address as Sir has been knighted. It is a term of courtesy. "Rabbouni," says a blind man to Jesus. By the way, the Hebrew alphabet has only consonants, and quite often it is hard to decide how a word is pronounced; it is from the New Testament, which is written in Greek, that we learn that the Hebrew consonants *r*, *b*, *y* should be pronounced "rabbi." Oriental Jews and others in fact prefer the pronunciation *ribbi, ribboni*. And there is still another pronunciation favored by some, and preserved in the vocalization of a famous manuscript, *rebbi* (nothing to do with hasidic leaders).

The men we're talking about, the Rabbis, are masters; but why? Because they are *teachers*. Let's get specific, maybe even a little pedantic: Do rabbis constitute a restricted class of people, like the priests or the prophets, the two prominent groups familiar to us from the literature of the Hebrew Bible? The answer is clear, but it cannot be a one-word answer. The Rabbis *are* a group and some of them even sport a special form of dress. But the Rabbis are not priests. In Judaism one is born a priest, and only one whose father was a priest

* The Miriam and William Horowitz Inaugural Public Lecture, Yale University, 22 April 1985.

and was properly married can serve as a priest. The chief responsibility of a priest is service in the Jerusalem Temple. In short, one is a priest only by descent, and his chief duties are ritualistic.

What about a prophet? Here descent is irrelevant. A prophet is anyone to whom God revealed Himself and directly communicated a message to be addressed to the folk: Go and say to Israel, and so on. A man can't choose to be a prophet, just as a man can't choose to be a priest. Indeed, some prophets would have preferred not to be chosen for their role. The prophet is chosen by God: Leave your flock and sycamores and go north and tell those people what I plan to do with them. If a person has not received a direct supernatural summons, he is not a prophet. If a person says "Thus saith the Lord" and in truth has not received a supernatural message, he is a false prophet.

Now what is a rabbi? He is a scholar and teacher, a *ḥakam*, a man with learning. A rabbi is not a prophet and receives no supernatural messages, although he might occasionally wish for supernatural vindication or support. But that is wishful and useless. When Rabbi Eliezer exclaimed in debate, If I am right, let the nearby stream reverse its current, and the stream did as ordered, Rabbi Joshua protested, Pay no attention to these celestial stunts; the Torah was given to human beings to study and interpret, and no heavenly interference is allowed in the academy. *We* will determine the law! and Rabbi Eliezer was out-voted.

A rabbi is something you *become*, you achieve, you accomplish. A rabbi is chosen by human decision; his ancestry has nothing to do with the case. It is possible for a priest to become a rabbi, but not because he is a descendant of priests. I suppose if there had been rabbis in biblical days and a prophet had wanted to become one of them, he could have done so. Maybe. But there were no rabbis in those days. *Anyone* can become a rabbi regardless of ancestry, regardless of talent or lack of it for intimacy with the supernatural. "Anyone" means literally any male, aristocrat or plebeian, rich or poor, countryman or urbanite, for a rabbi is one who studies and teaches. These are his two responsibilities and functions, study and teaching; therefore, he can issue decisions when his mastery is recognized or solicited.

A rabbi, then, is a scholar and teacher. What does he study, what teach? The answer is, Torah, and this word "Torah" calls for explanation. "Torah" is a Hebrew word, and literally means "instruction," "teaching." But this hardly scratches the surface. From the way the word is used in all the sources, it is clear that the word serves a number of purposes. In many places Torah stands for the Five Books of Moses. Then again Torah is equated with all the books of the Hebrew Bible. When Torah refers to any or all parts of the biblical books, it is characterized as the Written Torah—for the biblical books come to us in written form on scrolls, on papyrus, on parchment, on leather also; in short, they are literally books, works written down.

But, "Torah" stands not only for the ancient written-down works; it is the standard term for the whole oral content, the sum total of the entire unwritten-down tradition of interpretation of the sacred Scriptures and the legitimate derivations thereof. This enormous heritage of commentary and scholarly give-and-take never ceases—or as the Talmud puts it, Whatsoever a diligent student adds to the inherited mass of interpretation—that is the Oral Torah. Originally it was not intended to be recorded in writing; it was to be forever in vital flux, by ear and word of mouth, received and communicated from masters to disciples in all generations, early and recent—first, to make the Bible intelligible, and, second, relevant to the needs of every age. Between scholars and Torah there is a permanent connection—if there were no rabbis, the entire dimension of intellectual activity would vanish; if there were no Torah, there would be no need for rabbis. The occupation of the rabbi is to study Torah, the Written and the Oral Torah, and rule accordingly if required.

We will return to the theme of scholars and Oral Torah, for this is our major concern. But before doing so, let us fix the time framework *when* these Rabbis, these Teachers, were active.

Speaking very roughly, the period is from about 250 B.C.E. down to approximately 500 C.E., but I shall concentrate on the first two or two and a half centuries C.E.. Why? Because in these two centuries the basic themes and the ways to treat them took shape; in the centuries thereafter, these themes and ways served as examples for further development. Moreover, it was the Teachers of these centuries that the ones of succeeding centuries looked up to as authoritative. By now "Rabbi" has become a title.

What was the dominant, overall culture of the eastern Mediterranean world during these centuries, that is, in Syria and Palestine and Egypt? (Just listing these geographical names gives to our discussion an almost contemporary complexion!) The dominant culture of that world in these centuries was what we call Hellenistic or Hellenistic-Roman. That is to say, the specific native cultures of these important centers were affected, sometimes even saturated, by the use of the Greek language, Greek institutions and fashions and styles of living. Permit me to mention two elementary details. In what language have we inherited the books of the New Testament? In Greek. What is the oldest translation of the Old Testament? Greek, begun already about 250 B.C.E. This is the period when we meet Jews—I have in mind completely loyal Jews, not those who forsake their historic affiliation—well, we meet Jews with names like Alexander, Antigonus, Hyrkanus, Abtalyon, Symmakos; we come upon Greek words that have been appropriated by Hebrew so thoroughly as to have remained permanent increments of Hebrew vocabulary—for example, *Sanhedrin, sanegor, kategor, exedron, epitropos, hegemon, icon, pinax* (*pinkas*), *epikuros*, and so on and on. The way vocabulary travels is a superb index of the influence of a major culture. Note the Americanization of the world in our own times—jazz, rock, jeans, T-shirts, pipeline (prounounced by the French, *peepleen*), *le smash* (in tennis), *une loftette*, mixer, snack bar,

384 : *Thematic Studies*

cocktails, *le car*. In France this phenomenon became known as *franglais*, and it used to drive de Gaulle wild with rage. A paperback was actually published with the title, *Parlez-vous Franglais*. The invasion of such speech was even described as a "U.S. Plot to Ruin Language" (*New York Times*, 5 April 1964).

It is often said that such mobility of language is due to people's needing a knowledge of the language of the dominant Power, because they have to communicate with various officials of that Power. And there is much truth to that. How is one to plead with a tax collector, or argue in court, or draw up a petition, or ask directions from total strangers? How can you possibly partic- ipate in the activities at the gymnasium (one of the indispensable institutions in the Greek city) without a knowledge of Greek? To repeat, need is certainly a powerful factor in the taking up of foreign terms; how without a major language can you engage in international trade? But it's not necessity alone which brings on the adoption of terms from another language. There is also such a thing as desire to appear up-to-date and sophisticated. Languages travel, get mixed up, bump into each other and get bruised, then adopted, particularly when one language enjoys a richness and circulation and prestige in contrast to that of the so-called minority which is governed by a great Power. Little wonder, therefore, that in the first two centuries c.e. Jews were trilingual: they used Hebrew for religious and especially intellectual purposes, Aramaic for daily and constant use, and Greek in order to be able to relate to the universe around them.

However, in all this discussion of the first two centuries c.e., and before and after that too, there is a qualification that must be introduced.

For we have oversimplified the language phenomenon much too much. From the discussion thus far you might wish to conclude that because Greek was the language of the dominant eastern Mediterranean environment, when- ever and wherever it appeared it swept out of earshot the native languages in Syria, Galilee, Samaria, Judea, Idumea, Egypt. Suddenly we are tempted to say, the "whole world" is talking Greek. That however is false, nothing of the sort happened, any more than in the Mexican countryside everyone is talking English. Who in all these regions adopted Greek as a second and even first language? Only the rich and so-called aristocratic classes, and perhaps the merchants of the big shops in the big cities. But the permanent majority in history, the poor, the ones who could not yet afford to become social climbers, or those provincials content to stay put where they lived and not travel, these people might only know some of what we may call "street Greek," or current lingo, a minimum of necessary Greek words and expressions for practical purposes. For, as Rostovtzeff, of Yale if you please, pointed out long ago, Greek in the Near Eastern world was essentially an upper class veneer. This does not mean that the cultured classes were really unaffected by Hellenistic civiliza- tion. They certainly were affected, as we can tell by the architecture of the region, its pottery, its fashions in clothing, its pleasure in Greek expression (for example, inscriptions on tombstones or public structures). Nevertheless, they constituted a minority, often a powerful minority to be sure, but a minority nonetheless, yet powerful enough very often to determine the political and economic fate of the respective populations whom they may even have despised. The waves of Hellenism certainly washed over the speech and tastes of the East Mediterranean peoples, especially in the urban centers, but they did not uproot the native languages or dialects. With the help of assistants, for example, Josephus wrote his history of the great revolt in the first century (which culminated in the destruction of the Jerusalem Temple in 70 c.e.). Josephus wrote that history in Greek; but he himself tells us that he first composed it in Aramaic, "my vernacular tongue," as he puts it, and sent it off to the barbarians, that is, non-Greek-speaking readers.

In a study like ours appearances can be especially deceptive. We know today, thanks to Saul Lieberman's investigations, that a number of Jewish sayings and views are in origin Greek or modeled after Hellenistic sayings and views; Jewish teachers simply formulated these in Hebrew. Let me present just one example. Before a Jew begins the core of his morning prayers, there are a number of blessings he may recite in gratitude for God's mercies to him. One of these blessings reads: Blessed art Thou (that is, Thank You), Lord, our God, King of the universe, for not making me a woman. (A woman says, Thank you, Lord, for making me as You wish.) I don't think it is necessary to linger on the outburst this thanksgiving prayer produces in an age of high-pitched and advancing feminism. So that's the attitude of Judaism, is it? Thanking God for not making me a woman, forsooth.

Now let me quote what is attributed to the astronomer Thales or Socrates,

> that he used to say there were three blessings for which he was grateful to Fortune (the goddess Tyche, Fortuna): "first that I was born a human being and not one of the brutes; next, that I was born a man and not a woman; thirdly, a Greek and not a barbarian."

The parallelism is surely striking.

Does this mean that the Jews took it from the Greeks? Possibly, of course (and sometimes I still think so), but not necessarily. The view is a commonplace and in a certain region and period is shared by many, and apparently, though challenged today, strikes everyone as sensible. But here we learn an important lesson in method of study, that is, it is not true that whenever you find a parallel, you have proof of dependence, of borrowing from one culture by another. Possible, yes, but not certain. Some ideas are universal even at the outset (even if one is not a Jungian), they arise independently in several societies, perhaps even simultaneously as part of a zeitgeist; sometimes so-called borrowing is quite passive and innocent, and even what is borrowed may be radically transformed. In brief, in the period from about 250 B.C.E. to 250

C.E., hellenization was certainly going on throughout the eastern Mediterranean world, but it did not destroy the native languages and cultures of that world; it enriched them, maybe even confirmed them in many ways, but they did not abolish or suspend natural, native, autonomous development, and this was especially true of Judaism and self-conscious Jewish society, as those who did not like Jews often and particularly broadcast.

So much, therefore, for the time factor and a little bit of what it reflects, and now the geographical location. Since we agreed to concentrate on the first two centuries of our era, we need not take up Babylonia, though there the Babylonian Talmud was created. But we will confine ourselves to the country which the big Powers referred to under several names. Sometimes they regarded it as only an extension of Syria. Or they called it Palestine, because much of the coastal area had been occupied long ago by the Philistines, and it was descendants of Philistines you would have encountered on first arrival from the west. The country was also known as Judea: When the Romans minted coins after their victory in the war of 66–70, they had inscribed on them *Judaea capta*, Judea conquered, meaning "the land of the Judeans, the Jews, had been captured." In the Bible, earlier, this is the land promised already to Abraham, and when named, it is the land of Canaan, the land of the seven nations to be conquered by Joshua and his forces. The Jews, certainly from before the first century, called it Eretz Yisrael, and they held on to this identification throughout all subsequent centuries. The country might be conquered, the country might be reduced to no more than a backwater province of imperial Powers. The land has been promised to Abraham and all his descendants; hence, call it what you will, for the Jews it remained Eretz Yisrael, the Land of Israel, regardless of who ruled it.

Not only Jews lived there. In cities like Caesarea (on the Mediterranean coast) the majority population most of the time seems to have been pagan settlers from many parts of the Hellenistic world: these might be Syrians, Greeks from Asia Minor or even the mainland, Idumeans who had converted or not converted, as the case may be, Roman troops and veterans. In Jerusalem the majority was likely to be Jews so long as the Temple stood, though foreign troops would be stationed there, especially during Passover. Among pagans in particular the main features of Hellenistic-Roman civilization flourished: public baths, hippodromes, gymnasiums, sport clubs, races, theatres, circuses, sites of monumental sculpture, and, naturally, schools for their own children. But Jews did not shun the popular rendezvous of comfort and amusement. Even in the best days, I suspect, tensions between the monotheistic and aniconic Jews and their polytheistic and idolatrous neighbors did not disappear entirely, though it would be untrue to say that good relations could not exist. The Jewish law recorded in the first postbiblical code-textbook lays down that in the interests of peace and community welfare, the poor among the gentiles are not to be held back from sharing in the charities of harvest gleanings, the forgotten sheaf, the corner of the field which the owner must leave for the indigent. The poor among the gentiles are to be supported along with Israel's poor—so speaks an early law in the supplementary source; the dead of the gentiles are to be eulogized and buried, and gentile mourners are to be comforted for the sake of peace. Public relations statements? Every bit as sincere as institutional protestations down to our own days. Don't underestimate such injunctions—proper funeral arrangements and burial are of fundamental importance not only for the Jews, but for the Greeks, the Egyptians, the Romans, the inhabitants of ancient Mesopotamia, for all pagans, actually for all nations. But strain there was, particularly during wars and instigated riots, or when imperial procurators were insensitive and corrupt. The country enjoyed political independence for only eighty years.

In the long run, however, neither chronology nor geography is most revealing of the significance of this land, indispensable as such subjects are for the study of history. What proved of *lasting* influence was the activity of the Rabbis—especially the result of the program of the Rabbis of succeeding generations, to whom we now return. They were recruited from all segments of society and constituted the country's Jewish intellectuals, resolved to make both intelligible and relevant the contents of the Written Torah, and especially the multitude of unwritten traditions and interpretations transmitted through the ages, so that divine law would not become antiquated or an esoteric doctrine reserved only for privileged members of a secret fraternity. It was these Teachers who declared, Study is the obligation of every single man in society: rich, poor, priest, non-priest, prince and pauper—no one was to say, I'm not able to be an intellectual, let the scholars study; no one was to say, I have no time, I'll study when I retire; no one was to say, I can't afford the luxury of study. No alibis or excuses are acceptable. Apparently, it was conceivable that even a gentile might study Torah, for according to one view at least, a gentile who studies Torah takes precedence even over the High Priest. Even as hyperbole, it is quite revealing. When you come down to it, the Teachers declared, study is one of the highest forms of worship, if not the highest.

It is interesting to note: In the Bible you meet a variety of types: priest, prophet, judge and military leader, king, royal officer. You meet what are known as "wise men" (like the authors of Wisdom literature, Proverbs, Kohelet, Job, and so on). These characters also issue commands, tell stories, make heated speeches, formulate proverbs, maybe indulge in allegories also, and what have you. But you won't find one intellectual in that whole cast of characters. Even Moses, the greatest of the prophets, God's agent for delivery of the laws, who was told to put into writing certain communications—of not one law in the Bible is he the originator. There is one institution in the Bible that is not of divine origin: the administration of justice, the structure of courts and judges. Even of that Moses is not the inventor, but his father-in-law, the *Midianite* priest, Jethro! Absolutely nothing (except pleading in behalf of his people) is originated by Moses; Moses is the intermediary through whom God communicates commands and wishes. Moses can argue, but never on intellectual grounds, never by means of erudition or independent human reasoning. Moses can appeal, but not like a trained lawyer or philosopher. I hope you don't misinterpret what I say to mean that I regard Moses as stupid. But in the Bible he is not an intellectual. It is the Rabbis who portrayed him as one, as though to imply, Surely he could not have been inferior to us!

We have arrived at the heart of the matter. What is an intellectual? What is the intellectual calling? It is study, just that, study to achieve mastery of the whole tradition. It is not (to use the talmudic idiom) so that one might be addressed as "Rabbi"; not so that people might say, How smart or expert he is. It is not so that I may become rich; not so that I may be given one of the best seats in the academy; not so that I may be rewarded in the World to Come; not so that I may live long. Why study? For the love of it, by which the Rabbis meant, for the love of God, or as they put it in that wonderful phrase of theirs, *torah li-shemah*, Torah for no ulterior purpose. Nothing like this extreme valuation is to be found in Scripture, Old or New. In Scripture you're told to study and review the laws, etc., in order to know how to put them into practice. But that's typical of every piety. My mother also wants me to be pious. And of course like everybody else the Rabbis are very sensitive to the demands of piety. They resent strongly study indifferent to or divorced from practice; their ideal is, as that beautiful prayer reads, ". . . put it into our hearts to understand and discern, to attend to, to study and teach, to observe, carry out and fix firmly all the contents of the teaching of Thy Torah—all with love." But above all what they seek is *an intellectualization of the pious life.* They urge: Study in the daytime, study at night, study and then review and review; don't say, What I learned from my teacher is enough for me; come now, some originality! And if the material is hard, don't give up.

Obviously statements and ideals of this sort are hyperbole, the kind of exaggeration that can easily lead to frustration and caricature. Truth to say, a number of rabbis themselves criticize such unrestrained exhortation. Says one prominent rabbi, Splendid is the study of Torah when it is combined with a worldly occupation; without a worldly occupation, it will come to nothing. An even earlier teacher protests, If you study all the time, when will you be able to make a living? This, as you can guess, provokes a rejoinder: If you're busy plowing in plowing season and sowing in sowing season and reaping in reaping season, when will you have time for study?

All kinds of views are represented and there is, in fact, some justice to them all, depending on your mood. When the extreme demands for study are made, it's not that the Teachers are unrealistic—they are talking like all masters and artists passionately devoted to their vocation. A distinguished violinist I know, with plenty of problems of livelihood to boot, once told me that ideally and literally she should practice eight hours a day every day. A former dancer once told me that properly to be in shape for performance requires hours and hours of body exercise every single day; you must not miss a day. This is the rhetoric

Teachers of Torah employ, because they know what discipline ideally must accompany devotion to Torah.

But why the Torah? you may ask; what is there about the Torah, especially as Oral Tradition and commentary, that inspires them to set up such superlative standards? It is true that for them, both the Written Torah and the Oral Torah are divinely ordained, and a divine revelation is overwhelming for its recipients and witnesses. But what persuaded them that their Oral Torah in particular belongs to that continuous transmission since Moses received it at Mount Sinai? After all, there were Jews, and high up in Temple circles at that, let alone gentiles, who refused to acknowledge the authority and value judgments of the rabbinic Oral Torah!

The answer is—and I deliberately answer in exclusively humanist, not theological terms—the Rabbis were persuaded that their Torah deserved uninterrupted study and reflection because they were convinced that everything, literally everything, was in it.

What does this mean? There wasn't a subject in their time and place which they were unable to connect with the Torah. It goes without saying that their Torah interpreted the Scriptures. But how little does an answer like this convey! Their Torah demanded that they study agricultural law; their Torah demanded that they have a solid foundation in mathematics and astronomy, animal and human anatomy and diseases; all questions of civil and criminal law; laws of bethrothal, marriage, divorce, and inheritance; the maintenance of communal and private charities; and once more it goes without saying that they would tackle all the fine intricacies in the observance of the Sabbath and holy days, for these fundamental institutuions had been ordained already in the Written Torah, the Bible. They take real pleasure in splitting a hair or two, and more, in discovering kinship between distant particles. Then there were all the moral and imaginative and folkloristic and free interpretations of biblical and extrabiblical themes which tried to guess what God did before He created the world, the role of the angels, why must Israel (the people) not give up their individuality, the varied experiences of the biblical personalities, the exercises in trying to comfort the men and women of their time, the promises and predictions of reward and punishment and redemption, the debates with God. Even the mere attempt at listing the contents of their interests seems hopeless. In one way or another they strove to relate all these subjects and more to the Written and Oral Torah, and my experimental paraphrase or summary inevitably falls short. They did not classify the different sciences the way medieval scholars were to do later, but they certainly practiced systematic organization of subject matter. Contrast the Mishnah with the biblical law collections!

Given their perspective, it is no surprise that they felt that everything is in the Torah and demanded a lifetime of studying. And by way of footnote let me add: After the Jerusalem Temple was destroyed, very many laws having to do with such subjects as sacrifices, routine of the Temple cult, purity and impurity regulations, ceased to be operative; yet the scholars continued to study these now theoretical subjects intensively. The immediately practical was not the only criterion of importance. Of course this is not meant to ignore their confidence in the ultimate messianic restoration of all that had been temporarily suspended.

In the five centuries between 250 B.C.E. and 250 C.E., we said, aspects of Hellenism or of Hellenistic-Roman culture came to influence the life and thought patterns of the peoples in the Near East. Palestine, or Judea, was similarly affected, not only by the gentile population within the country, but by the Jewish as well, and definite traces of this Hellenistic influence appear in the teaching and speech of the Rabbis, the men who were the intellectual élite. Indeed, it would have been unnatural if men with strong intellectual interests had been completely sound-proofed against a vigorous and aggressive civilization. Or let me put it this way: There is always some ambivalence, some sense of insecurity, toward cultural values that are not one's own to begin with; after a while, once become familiar, they may well be welcomed, even admired. Note how in the second half of the nineteenth century French impressionist painting at first met with derision from the art critics no less than from the public, and later was praised with enthusiasm. Ask Sotheby's. Change and reversal of attitudes toward the new are universal. And Judaism is no exception.

Naturally, the Rabbis rejected those elements of hellenization which threatened to compromise the absolute monotheism and ethical imperatives and strict ritualistic demands of Judaism. But they were not indifferent to the foreign cultures which they felt could only add to the better understanding and appreciation of Torah. It is true that in times of bitterness against the mighty Powers and heathen neighbors—for their cruelty, and for their suppressions, and for their inexcusable mockeries and slanders of the Jewish religion and people—the rabbinic attitude would itself grow less hospitable, even hostile, toward alien influences, and the Rabbis themselves, like sundry Church Fathers, would recommend withdrawal from relaxed contact with the gentile world. And of course there always were the more tolerant and less tolerant among them—we're talking of men, not plaster-cast models. But fundamentally, as students, scholars, teachers, their eyes were open to all that went on around them, and the eyes are the channels of the environment. Certainly idolatrous practices are forbidden, but you may study them in order to know what they are like, so that you may teach what is permissible and what is not. Like scholars everywhere, they were a cautious group, for they did not want the Jews to be paganized, and they feared heresies, anything disparaging the Torah. But the commitment to study—that study of the tradition, Written and Oral—was the ideal they never abandoned. It was, they felt, the surest course to the discovery of the will of God, or the purpose for the creation of the universe. "If thou hast been much occupied in thy study of Torah, take no credit for thyself, for to this end wast thou created, for human beings were created only on condition that they study Torah."

To understand the Rabbis, one must always return to the term and concept of Torah, which since Sinai, they declared, guided the Jewish people. The anachronism was virtually irresistible. It is through Torah in its far-reaching implications that Judaism, which began as a prophetic religion, was transformed into an intellectual discipline and illumination. To be a prophet, you have to be the beneficiary of charisma, an unaccountable divine grace. But you and I, all of us, can be students, and teachers also.

About Shalom Spiegel°

[5] Long before it had become a cliché, זכין לאדם שלא בפניו, ואין חבין לו אלא בפניו had already gained currency as a principle which the law invoked in a variety of halakic contexts—manumission of slaves, *erub* of courtyards, the baptism of a fatherless minor proselyte, and so on. Since the principle seems never to be questioned (though whether something is *zechut* or *hovah* may of course be argued), and since it is obviously summoned whenever it is regarded as applicable, it is legitimate to refer to in the midst of these festivities: not as a *melitzah*—Professor Spiegel despises *melitzot*—but in its forthright sense: If you're going to do a man a good turn, you may do it behind his back, you don't need his consent; if what you're going to do to a man may bring injury to him, you need his agreement. Well, this is our dilemma—I would be delighted to do Professor Spiegel a good turn (why not?), and the law after all does not forbid it in the person's presence. Nevertheless, such things are in better taste when the recipient isn't around to be publicly embarrassed. As for the reverse, doing something which might turn out to be injurious, חוס לשלום, this alas remains a terrifying possibility in life. We often wound unwittingly, or with stupid miscalculation. There are no infallible safeguards. It's just as well, then, that he is present. But I shall take shelter, perhaps comfort, in something Professor Spiegel once taught me (and it has served me now for over two decades). What is a friend? he asked me one evening in the midst of a socratic conversation about this and that. I tried several definitions and he demolished each one, rightly so. Finally I asked him in irritation, Very well, smart one, you tell me, What is a friend? He answered calmly, A friend is someone who does not want to hurt you.

° Tribute to Professor Shalom Spiegel, delivered at the Sixth Annual Conference of the Association for Jewish Studies, 27 October 1974.

Not logically, but by association, the mind recalls at this point what surely should not go unmentioned, namely, that one of the best friends of חכמת ישראל in this century has been our guest of honor. With an unsurpassed devotion, for more years than I can count, to the publication committee of *Mekize Nirdamim* and especially the Kohut Foundation, and privately, he has been responsible for major publications in the fields of Halakah, of exegesis, of medieval and modern letters—texts, commentaries, monographs. Who would have known this if it had not been for some prefaces? And always on the side of encouragement and generosity.

Does this perhaps suggest an eagerness to relax carefully-considered judgment occasionally? Some day—I'm sure Spiegel would prefer that I made no mention of this—see a review he did for *Speculum* of a potboiler on Judah ha-Levi, or (more seriously) some observations of his on Moshe Chaim Luzzato in his *Hebrew Reborn*, or some introductory comments in connection with the poetry of Eleazar berabbi Abun:

אך משתפוג קדחת המציאה משנה חובה הוא שנחזור בנו ונשנן לנו כי סמיכות מקום בכ"י הגניזה אינה מעידה ולא כלום בשאלת בעלים בספרות, ויש שמחברים רחוקים בזמן ובמקום שכנים ובני־ מצר הם בפתק ישן ... לא ראי קונטרס פיוטים, שריד מספרי תפלות בבית כנסת ישן בפסטאט של מצרים, כראי אנתולוגיא לתולדות הספרות בטעם ארצות המערב בימינו.

Did you catch that lesson in methodology, by the way?

Truth is, however, he does not care particularly for criticism. He likes to say—I think, echoing Nietzsche—Don't argue, sing!

No, the matter is simple and ought to be made part of the record. We are enjoying an enormous amount of Hebrew and Jewish studies because this retiring man, who has remained aristocratically aloof from all the contrivances of publicity and put-on humility, has put himself out extravagantly in behalf of genuine Jewish learning and scholarship.

A scholarship to which he handed over his enviable gifts. But why synegorize? Let the defendant speak or write for himself, and maybe we can then add some ordinary glosses. We are discussing the themes and structure of the book of Job—really this is paramount, though you can be sure that Spiegel will not tell until he has drawn on Canaanite relics, Ugaritic texts, Jewish and Muslim legends, and anything anyone first-rate ever said about that trio, Noah, Danel, and Job. Here is Spiegel:

It is the glory of the poem, and of the faith of which it is a flowering, that this challenge of the prevailing doctrine neither issues, nor results in unbelief. Quite the contrary, it stems from the passionate conviction that although condemned by men, the innocent sufferer does not incur the displeasure of God, nor is he barred from His grace. However afflicted, his is still the nearness and fellowship of a loving God. . . .

The friends in the dialogue uphold the traditional dogma. They fear that its denial would imperil religion (15:4), and hence should never be allowed. They must therefore seek of necessity for some secret sin which will prove to their satisfaction that what failed is not virtue, for virtue cannot fail. The course of the dialogue discloses how a false principle will debase character. For if doctrine cannot be abandoned, and being false, it must clash with the facts, a zealous adherent will sooner or later do away with the unwelcome facts. He will learn before long to find or invent the facts which invariably favor his theory, and wittingly or unwittingly he will end in mendacity. Admirable is the art, and the restraint of the author who vehemently disagreed with the spokesmen of the orthodoxy of his day, and yet did not suffer ire or irony to creep into his pen and caricature the views of his opponents.

[6] To be dropped from a helicopter onto a mountain top is not the same as climbing the mountain to its top. Only the latter gives a sense of ascent. What Spiegel offers in the quoted passage—so revealing of the biblical poem, so provocative even when we have laid the book aside and begun to brood over the meaning of honesty—is a summit, but a summit to which one has had to climb with many views along the way up. He is an addict of detail, and this is what makes his generalizations and eloquence so firm and so persuasive. To know Job is to learn first of the particles that combine in the whole rugged myth of man's possible innocence and deliverance. It is to learn that Ezekiel is referring to Danel and not to Daniel, that in the end Aqhat is very likely delivered and returned to life, that there are deliberate layers of an older tale and a later legend, that unselfish prayer is not in vain. And even then, positive, but the opposite of opinionated:

אך כאמור השערות הן אלה ותו לא, וכבר הזהירו חז״ל הוי אוהב את השמא

Or again:

שמא מרובה וברי מועט יש כאן

Or still again:

סוף דבר, לקח וגם עידות אצורים וצרורים בפרקי הפולמוס לרב פירקוי, שניצלו באורח־ פלא משכחת דורות. המפורש בהם טרם נתברר, והמרומז עדיין תעלומה. אך דומה, כבר עתה יש ללמוד מהם פורתא על מוקדם ומאוחר בתקופת הגאונים.

However, let us consider another aspect of Spiegel's thinking and writing quite apart from detail and quite apart from eloquence (though these are never absent); I shall pay no attention to chronology or objective, for this aspect, too, has been constant. The first is from an essay on Jewish legends.

With the sacred writings of the Jews there traveled to the nations of East and West who had adopted them traditions and tales current among the Jews. Along with the Bible, legends of the Bible spread far and wide, leaving their imprint in many a celebrated center of art and literature, gaining at times a surprising hold upon popular imagination.

For example: the Saint-Chapelle in Paris has been rightly called the most wonderful of pictured Bibles. Eleven huge windows (out of a total of fifteen) are devoted to the Hebrew Scriptures, illustrating in countless medallions of stained glass the history and heroes of ancient Israel. The Genesis window (mostly a modern restoration, but following the thirteenth-century pattern) unrolls the stages of creation and the story of the patriarchs in eighty-four medallions. They follow a set sequence of themes, familiar to any reader of the Bible and easily recognizable, from Adam's disobedience to the death of Abel. But what comes next (in medallion 21) records the story, unknown to the Bible but current as a legend of the Bible, of how the blind Lamech, in an untoward hunting accident, killed his ancestor Cain, unwittingly avenging the slaying of Abel.

One can study the details of the tale in two panels of a stained-glass window at Tours, or in related illustrations such as the Manchester Bible, or the Munich Psalter of Queen Isabella, or in two frescoes by Italian masters, one by Pietro di Puccio in the Composanto at Pisa, the other in the Green Cloister at Florence, attributed to Paolo Ucello or to Dello Delli. The legend is also vividly carved in many famous cathedrals of France, England, Spain, and Italy. It was known to the Eastern Church as well, and survives in Greek Bible miniatures and superb Byzantine mosaics. The printing press and the mystery plays made the tale even more widely known. It was still capable of imaginative retelling in the sixteenth century, both in the East and West. The Greek poem by Georgios Chumnos, a native of Crete, displays no mean power of narration and feeling, and must have warmed many a pious soul by its chaste restatement of medieval faith. On the other hand, the engraving by the Dutch artist Lucas van Leyden, dated 1524, revels in candid corporeality as exhibited in the nude bodies of the huge Lamech and his chubby boy. It bespeaks the spirit and temper of the new age, impatient and wearied with the austerity and otherworldliness of the Middle Ages.

Let us postpone comment until we have listened to Spiegel a little longer; he is after all the bridegroom of this festival. This time he is getting ready to discuss an eighteenth century "soul"—"soul" is the right word—whose name has already been mentioned this evening. :פתח רבי שלום ואמר

From the unlovely Corso Cavour in Rome a steep staircase leads up to a secluded square where the forsaken church of San Pietro in Vincoli is situated. Though it is an early Christian basilica, the Doric columns in its nave suggest that it may be a Roman temple appropriated early in the fifth Christian century, when the pagan divinity of the southland had to make way for the less pictorial Asiatic cult.

Art lovers come on pilgrimages to this church in whose dusky interior is enshrined Michelangelo's magnificent statue of Moses. This "Moses," like the "Slaves" in the Louvre, is merely a fragment of the gigantic sepulcher planned by the powerful Pope Julian II. Though it is wedged between two female figures usually taken for Rachel and Leah, and imprisoned within a frame which dwarfs and constricts the form of the Jewish Prophet—or, rather, of the giant Italian condottiere—one can understand how not only the art-loving compatriots of Michelangelo, but even the image-less and image-hating Jews swarmed out of their

Ghetto like cranes to see it (so Vasari relates) and wore away the great toe of its outstretched foot with devout kisses.

[7] The rudiments of the sepulcher planned by Julian II are, of course, included in the obligatory rounds one makes to famed works of art in Rome. In the same church, following the advice of Baedeker and Burckhart's guide book, one observes the badly faded paintings of the enigmatical Massaccio, and tells himself that many of these things, when judged from photographs and descriptions, promise much more: a feeling that every museum visitor knows. I had viewed all these things and was about to leave the church when I happened to overhear the assiduous Italian mendicant monk lauding the art of a tomb that I had found merely conventional, but my attention was caught by his remark that it harbored the remains of Nicholas Cusanus. In the dimness of that *composite* sanctuary, devoted first to the antique Roman divinity and then to the Christian god, and which was now become a shrine for art lovers through the genius of Michelangelo, there rests the remarkable, richly contradictory, *composite* personality which, Janus-headed, faced both the Middle Ages and modern times. A profound man, whose mind was still shadowed, like this church wherein he is buried, by the mystic half-light of scholasticism, though he burned with the desire for light and knowledge. Rigidly pious and orthodox—for he was a high dignitary of the church—and yet drawn to pantheism; modern in his criticism of the modes of cognition and in his anticipation of Copernicus' revolutionary ideas, but rooted deep in the Middle Ages by his speculations concerning the attributes of the angels, his prophecies of the end of the world, and his call to crusades against the infidels. Giordano Bruno thought it was the cardinal's robe which impeded Cusanus' free stride; in truth, however, it was not outward considerations, but an inner bond with the things of old which restrained the forerunner of the free spirits of modern times—of Bacon and Descartes.

A last example where background is no longer ancillary but has been fully assimilated to the theme at hand.

הד קדומים מממנהגי פולחן עתיק מבצבץ ועולה מבין השיטין של מדרש זה. ואמנם אפשר לסייע לו
לר' בנייה מסדרי קרבנות שנשתמרו בכתובות כנעניות. נתגלו בצפונה של אפריקא באלג'יר
בקרבת מקום אל נגאוס (Ngaus) הוא Nicivibus של הרומאים), בין החרבות של מקדש ישן
לסטורנוס או שבתאי, שלש מצבות מסוף המאה השניה או תחילת המאה השלישית אחר ספה"נ,
היינו מזמנו של ר' בנייה חרותה. בהן דמות דיוקנו של האל, כשהוא אוחז מאכלת בימינו ולפניו ירבץ
אייל כבספור העקדה. מתחת לציור כתובות בלשון רומי, המספרות על פלוני ופלונית, איש ואשתו,
המבקשים להזכר ולהכתב להם לטובה, כי עשו כאשר צוו במראה מחזיונות לילה או כפי נדרם אשר
נדרו והעלו שה לעולה תחת (בכור?) ילדיהם. אף על פי שחדלה שפת כנען מלשמש לשון הדבור
בפרובינציא רומית זו, נשמרו בחיי הדת מלות ואמונות כנעניות. ובכתובות הלטיניות האלו נקרא
קרבן זה בשם ששרד מן השפה הפונית והמצוי בכתובות פוניות: Molchomor או Morchomor,
שהוא מלך אמר או קרבן שה. להלכה לא נשכחה תביעת הדת העתיקה: פטר כל רחם קדש לאלים,
וגם מבכורות אדם מן הדין שינתן להם. אלא שלמעשה הסכימו עליונים להיות מתרצים בחילופו של
בן אדם, בזבח שה. כנראה מן הכתובות היה המקריב מלך אמר עונה ואומר לפני האל: נפש תחת
נפש, דם תחת דם, חיים תחת חיים הרי השה תמורה. מכאן למדנו, מטבע זה של לשון היכן נולד.
מוצאו ויסודתו בחיי הדת הקדמונית, מקומו הראשון בהלכות זבח, ולא בדיני נפשות או ממונות.
מלות לואי הן. שנאמרו אגב קרבן החליפין.

Of course I'm overpowered by this cornucopia of learning and allusion and perceptiveness, by our author's complete at-homeness in the primary sources and no less by his sure footing in the tropical forest of secondary literature. But on the footnote terrain, Spiegel has his equals. Not too many, I hasten to add, but without question there are others similarly thoroughgoing and encyclopedic in their expeditions. To repeat, however: It's not the rare but not unique talent at assembling treasuries of information, including the even rarer flourishes from the institutes of the art historians—though if you think that's *tour de force* or merely cosmetic, try it on your own some time—it's not these which draw one back frequently to Spiegel's writings, though undeniably they're a source of delight. It is something else entirely, which the three passages quoted at length were meant to display. Whatever Spiegel has written about—and he has been writing on Hebrew and Jewish expression almost exclusively—he has consistently related to the humanistic and humane tradition as a whole. He has never contracted his subject. Sainte-Chapelle, Nicholas of Cusa, a Punic inscription, Jerome, a Nestorian Catholicos (some of these details first observed also by a few others), a medieval or Renaissance work of art, Marbury versus Madison (long before Watergate)—these are all brought within earshot of the poem or prophet or speculation Spiegel is studying. And suddenly the true reach and sweep of the Jewish expression are shockingly recognized. It's as though he were saying, if I may paraphrase a midrash, True, the Torah was revealed at Sinai to our ancestors, but from the outset it was consulted for the creation of a world, היה הקב״ה מביט בתורה ובורא העולם. No modern scholar I know has so [8] conscientiously helped us to see, as has Spiegel from the days he was advising what texts should be prepared for the Bet Sefer Reali and earlier, that Jewish longing, imagination, grief, and defiance are not just a shtetl idosyncrasy, but a tumult and response in all the continents of the mind. There *are* islands, where else is one to live; but there is passage too, and it is on a number of occasions two-way. Even in heartbreak days. "בהר, ה' יראה, *in angustia, Deus videbit;* מי שרחם את אברהם בהר המוריה, הוא ירחם גם אותנו—*In monte Dominus videbitur: hoc est, sicut Abrahae misertus est, miserebitur et nostri.*"

Finally a remark about what I would like to call לשון שפיגל. It's been occasionally compared with Agnon's Hebrew. What the comparison has meant is that both men deliberately adopt a classical, or perhaps better, a historical manner in their writings. I suppose that thus far the comparison is true, partly. But how different are their points of the compass! Agnon utilized classical Hebrew, and also old-fashioned expression, in order to turn the eyes of the contemporary *back* to a world he had dismissed or rejected, to make him recall a world gone by. Come, Agnon seems to say to us, I'll show you something of the complexity and charm and confusions and sanctity of a world you think you've surpassed with one thousand words, and your modern westernization and your so-called enlightenment. By using a past mannerism of speaking,

Agnon has tried to attach the present to the past. I'll even show you, he says, sweet twentieth-century marital infidelity with the chaste vocabulary of sacred folios. So Agnon.

That's not Spiegel, יבדל לחיים טובים. His Hebrew has not been a solicitation to yesterday. On the contrary, if his eyes have been anywhere, they've been on the present, on the right now. Like all of us, of course, he too has his affectations. But what he has done is Auden-like, let us say, called back into today's diction and into the breakdown of its syntactical grace, a speech and radiation from the accents of earlier generations which were lost by inattention, or Haskalah biblicisms, or rabbinic indifference, or, later, journalism, but which the present needs for its own uses. His attachment to the medieval poets is the result of *his* hearing the tremors of live idiom in their lines—not just artifice.

אמר בלב ימים ללב רגז
חרד מאד כי נשאו דכים
אם תאמן באל אשר עשה
הים ועד נצח שמו קים
אל יחרידך ים בשוא גליו
כי עמך השם גבול לים.

Artifice? So be it. Then so is a תפלת גשם from outside the מחזור which Spiegel, the lifelong student of Jeremiah, also loves.

Thou art indeed just, Lord, if I contend
With thee; but, sir, so what I plead is just.
Why do sinners' ways prosper? and why must
Disappointment all I endeavor end?
     Wert thou my enemy, O thou my friend,
How wouldst thou worse, I wonder, than thou dost
Defeat, thwart me? . . .
Mine, O thou lord of life, send my roots rain.

Without artifice this could not have come into being, but artifice never brought it into being.

Spiegel draws on the resources of Scripture, Midrash, Talmud, medieval hymns and dirges and chronicles in order to increase the precision, to recover cadence and style (if you please) in the language of the present. His look is forward; and if he, too, draws heavily on the past, it is a memorandum: To whom it may concern, from Shalom Spiegel—The true deserves the beautiful and is not sentenced by the clock. In civilized culture, the ancient monuments address the descendants also, and instigate the present mind to fresh action and innovation.

ראשי הישיבות המחוקקים
בני הלל, אשר הם ידיך נושקים
גזעיהם בצדקם מתחזקים
בזכותם יהי צור בכסלך
מלכד בעוז ישמור רגלך.
היתפאר בייחוס רב ממך
משרה גם מלוכה על שכמך
קום וצלח, רכב, כי אל עמך
יהי שלום ושלוה בחילך
כי על יד ימינך הוא צלך.

Bibliography of the Scholarly Publications of Judah Goldin

BOOKS

1955   *The Fathers According to Rabbi Nathan.* Yale Judaica Series 10. New Haven: Yale University Press. Reprint. New York: Schocken, 1974.

1955   *The Living Talmud. The Wisdom of the Fathers and its Classical Commentaries.* Chicago: University of Chicago Press. Paperback edition. New York: New American Library. Edition with Hebrew text and drawings by Ben-Zion. New York: Limited Editions, 1960. Reprint of the latter edition. New York: Heritage Press, 1962.

1967   *The Last Trial* (translation, with introduction, of Shalom Spiegel, *Me-Aggadot ha-Akedah*). New York: Pantheon, 1967. Repr. Philadelphia: Jewish Publication Society of America, 1968; New York: Behrman House, 1979.

1970   *The Jewish Expression* (ed.). New York: Bantam. Repr. New Haven: Yale University Press, 1976.

1971   *The Song at the Sea.* New Haven: Yale University Press.

1980   *The Munich Mekilta* (ed.). Copenhagen: Rosenkilde and Bagger.

ARTICLES

1946   "The Two Versions of Abot de-Rabbi Natan." *Hebrew Union College Annual* 19:97–120.

1946   "Hillel the Elder." *Journal of Religion* 26:263–77.

1949   "The Period of the Talmud (135 B.C.E.–1035 C.E.)." Pp. 115–215 in *The Jews. Their History, Culture, and Religion*, vol. 1. Ed. Louis Finkelstein. New York: Harper & Brothers, and Philadelphia: Jewish Publication Society. 3d. ed. Philadelphia: Jewish Publication Society, 1960. Paperback ed. *The Jews: Their History.* New York: Schocken, 1971.

1953   "The First Chapter of Abot de-Rabbi Natan." Pp. 263–80 in *Mordecai M. Kaplan Jubilee Volume*. Ed. Moshe Davis. New York: Jewish Theological Seminary of America.

1958   "The Three Pillars of Simeon the Righteous." *Proceedings of the American Academy for Jewish Research* 27:43–58.

1963   "On Honi the Circle-Maker: A Demanding Prayer." *Harvard Theological Review* 56:233–237.

1963   "The Relevance of Pirke Abot. . .The Wisdom of the Fathers." *The Jewish Exponent*. Philadelphia, April 12, p. 21, 22.

1964-65   ?קטע של שטר – עם חתימתו של הרמב׳׳ם ("Fragment of a Legal Deed Containing Maimonides' Signature?"). *Tarbiz* 34:65–71.

1965   "A Philosophical Session in a Tannaite Academy." *Traditio* 21:1–21. Repr. Pp. 357–77 in *Exploring the Talmud*. Ed. H.Z. Dimitrovsky. New York: KTAV, 1976. Hebrew version, משהו על בית מדרשו של רבן בן יוחנן בן זכאי. Pp. 69–92 in *Harry A. Wolfson Jubilee Volume*. Ed. Saul Lieberman et al. Jerusalem: American Academy for Jewish Research, 1965.

1965   "On a Selective Bibliography in English for the Study of Judaism." Pp. 191–228 in *A Readers' Guide to the Great Religions*. Ed. Charles J. Adams. New York: Free Press; London: Collier-Macmillan. Repr. as "Early and Classical Judaism." Pp. 283–320 in the second edition of the same work, 1977.

1965   "Of Change and Adaptation in Judaism." *History of Religions* 4:269–94.

1965   "The Third Chapter of 'Abot de-Rabbi Natan." *Harvard Theological Review* 58:365–86.

1965   "Introduction" to S.Y. Agnon, *Days of Awe*. New York: Schocken, pp. vii–xxx.

1966   "The End of Ecclesiastes: Literal Exegesis and its Transformation." Pp. 135–58 in *Biblical Motifs*. Ed. Alexander Altmann. Cambridge, Mass.: Harvard University Press.

1967   "Reflections on a Mishnah." *Quest*. London: New London Synagogue, 2:44–48.

1967   "Japhet in Shem's Tents." Pp. 111–21 in *The Education of American Jewish Teachers*. Ed. Oscar I. Janowski. Boston: Beacon Press.

1968   "'Not by Means of an Angel and Not by Means of a Messenger.'" Pp. 412–24 in *Religions in Antiquity. Essays in Memory of Erwin Ramsdell Goodenough*. Studies in the History of Religions (Supplements to *Numen*), 14. Leiden: Brill.

1968   "Some Minor Supplementary Notes on the Murphy Haggadah." *Yale University Library Gazette* 43/1 (July): 39–43.

1969   "Prolegomenon. On Charles Taylor's *Sayings of the Jewish Fathers*." Pp. v–xv in Charles Taylor, *Sayings of the Jewish Fathers*. The Library of Jewish Classics. New York: KTAV.

1972   Articles in *Encyclopaedia Britannica*. Chicago: William Benton:
        "Hillel." Vol. 11: 496.
        "Johanan ben Zakkai." Vol. 13:15.
        "Shammai." Vol. 20: 344.

1972   Articles in *Encyclopaedia Judaica*. Jerusalem: Keter, and New York: Macmillan:
        "Avot." Vol. 3: 983–84.
        "Avot de Rabbi Nathan." Vol. 3: 984–86.

1972   "Several Sidelights of a Torah Education in Tannaite and Early Amoraic Times." Pp. 176–91 in *Ex Orbe Religionum. Studia Geo Widengren Oblata*, vol. 1. Leiden: Brill (1972): Repr. Pp. 3–18 in *Exploring the Talmud*. Ed. H.Z. Dimitrovsky. New York: KTAV, 1976.

1975   "About Shalom Spiegel." *Association for Jewish Studies Newsletter*, no. 13 (February): 5–8.

1975   "'This Song.'" Pp. 539–54 in *Salo Wittmayer Baron Jubilee Volume*, English section, vol. 1. Ed. S. Lieberman and A. Hyman. Jerusalem: American Academy for Jewish Research.

1975   "Reflections on Translation and Midrash." *Proceedings of the American Academy for Jewish Research* 41–42: 87–104.

1976   "The Magic of Magic and Superstition." Pp. 115–47 in *Aspects of Religious Propaganda in Judaism and Early Christianity*. Ed. E.S. Fiorenza. Notre Dame, Indiana: University of Notre Dame Press.

1976   "Toward a Profile of the Tanna, Aqiba ben Joseph." *Journal of the American Oriental Society* 96:38–56.

1976   "Foreword." Pp. 1–19 in *Hebrew Ethical Wills*. Ed. I. Abrahams. Philadelphia: Jewish Publication Society of America.

1977   "The Youngest Son or Where Does Genesis 38 Belong." *Journal of Biblical Literature* 96:27–44.

1977   "A Short Note on the Archangel Gabriel." Pp. 1–6 in *Law, Church and Society. Essays in Honor of Stephan Kuttner*. Ed. K. Pennington and R. Somerville. Philadelphia: University of Pennsylvania Press.

1980   תוך כדי עיונים במסכת אבות דר' נתן ("Glosses on the Abot de-Rabbi Natan"). Pp. 59–65 in *American Academy for Jewish Research Jubilee Volume*. *PAAJR* 46–47. New York: American Academy for Jewish Research.

1980   "The First Pair (Yose ben Yoezer and Yose ben Yohanan) or the Home of a Pharisee." *Association for Jewish Studies Review* 5:41–62.

1983   "From Text to Interpretation and from Experience to the Interpreted Text." *Prooftexts* 3:157–68.

1986   "The Freedom and Restraint of Haggadah." Pp. 57–86 in *Midrash and Literature*. Ed. Geoffrey H. Hartman and Sanford Budick. New Haven: Yale University Press.

1987   "The Death of Moses: An Exercise in Midrashic Transposition." In *Love and Death in the Ancient Near East. Studies Presented to Marvin H. Pope on the Occasion of His Sixty-fifth Birthday*. Ed. John Marks and Robert Good. Guilford, Conn.: Four Quarters, 1987.

In Press "On the Account of the Banning of R. Eliezer B. Hyrqanus: An Analysis and Proposal." In *Ancient Studies in Memory of Elias Bickerman*. Ed. S. J. D. Cohen, E. Greenstein, and D. Marcus. *Journal of the Ancient Near Eastern Society*, vols. 16–17, in press.

REVIEWS AND REVIEW ARTICLES

1955   "Midrash Shemuel" (on Maurice Samuel, *Certain People of the Book*). *Jewish Frontier*, 22/9(no.244) (September): 35–41.

1956   "The Thinking of the Rabbis" (on Max Kadushin, *The Theology of Seder Eliahu, Organic Thinking*, and *The Rabbinic Mind*). *Judaism* 5(1956): 3–12.

1977   "Bickerman's Collected Studies." *History of Religions* 17:73–85.

1980   "On the Sleuth of Slobodka and the Cortez of Kabbalah" (on Leo W. Schwarz, *Wolfson of Harvard*). *The American Scholar* 49 (Summer, 1980): 391–404.

1982   "Bickerman's *Studies in History II.*" *Jewish Quarterly Review* 72:206–12.

Index of Texts Discussed

Page references to textual discussions in this volume are listed to the right of the specific text.

Subject Index